THE HAWKER
TYPHOON AND TEMPEST

Francis K. Mason

With Foreword by
Wg. Cdr. R.P. Beamont
C.B.E., D.S.O. & Bar, D.F.C. & Bar

ASTON PUBLICATIONS

Published in 1988 by Aston Publications Limited,
Bourne End House, Harvest Hill,
Bourne End, Bucks., SL8 5JJ

Reprinted 1989

ISBN 0 946627 19 3

Designed by Francis K. Mason

Photoset and printed in England by
Redwood Burn Limited,
Trowbridge, Wiltshire

Sole distributors to the
U.K. book trade,
Springfield Books Ltd.,
Norman Road, Denby Dale,
Huddersfield,
West Yorkshire, HD8 8TH

Sole distributors in the
United States,
Motorbooks International,
729 Prospect Avenue,
Osceola,
Wisconsin 54020

Contents

Acknowledgements

Of all those many kind people who gave so much of their time to assist me in preparing this book Wing Commander Bee Beamont has not only done me the signal honour of contributing the Foreword but went so much further in reading the entire text and checking facts. 'Bee' must unquestionably rank among the highest echelons of British aviation, alongside the greatest Service pilots and Captains of Industry. In a lifetime of Service and test flying his career embraces the Battle of France and Battle of Britain in 1940, the Channel sweeps of 1941, the Dieppe landing in 1942, the Normandy landings and the invasion of Europe in 1944; he test flew the Hurricane, Typhoon, Tempest, Canberra, Lightning and TSR-2, and was Director of Flight Operations on the Panavia Tornado for a dozen years. He commanded one of the first Typhoon squadrons and the first Tempest Wing and, but for the ending of the Pacific War, would have led the first Tempest Wing in the Far East. Not surprisingly he has always been "Mister Typhoon" to me, and I cannot imagine any book on these aeroplanes worth its salt being published without Bee's name sharing the title page. And when I was in danger of spinning into some of the Typhoon's "mythology", Bee was there to apply opposite rudder.

Many other Typhoon and Tempest pilots contributed records and recollections without which no aeroplane can "live". I am indebted to Group Captain Sammy Wroath, CBE, AFC and Bar, for his recollections of his Typhoon work at Boscombe Down, to Flight Lieutenant Ralph Stockburn, DFC, of Nos 174, 274 and 501 Squadrons, and the Flight Lieutenant C. F. Hackett of No. 164 Squadron (and his son Philip); to Pam Gollen, and her fellow pilots of the Air Transport Auxiliary who delivered Typhoons to the operational squadrons; and to members of the Typhoon and Tempest Association who kindly gave me so many useful notes on their own experiences.

I am indebted to my old friend Bruce Quarrie who undertook to edit my text and did so with so much care and thoroughness, to Anna McIlwaine at the Royal Air Force Museum who contributed a most useful map at short notice, and to staff members at the Public Records Office who steered me through vast quantities of references with such understanding of my quests.

Chris Ashworth came up with a fine selection of photographs, as did Richard Ward (of Modeldecal, Farnborough), Dick Ward (of Whitstable), and Ray Sturtivant; other individual acknowledgements for photographs accompany their respective captions, and are most gratefully given.

Much appreciated research assistance was provided by F. B. Edge-Hardy, Esq., ex-SAAF; Neil Robinson, Esq., Rotherham; Jerry Scutts, Esq., Blackheath; Ivan Venour, Esq., Melbourne, Australia; Graham Winstanley, Esq., ex-RNZAF; and Douglas Young, Esq., ex-RCAF/RAF.

In conclusion I must record my gratitude to three very great gentlemen whose contribution will be obvious to the reader of this book. The late Sir Sydney Camm, CBE, shortly before his death passed to me all his surviving correspondence, photographs and records covering forty years with Hawker Aircraft Limited. The late Philip Lucas, GM, also spent many hours going through the old Hawker Flight Test Records with me, records which spanned the years 1931 to 1951—from Hawker Fury biplane to Hawker Hunter jet fighter. Finally I include the name of the late Wing Commander Bob Stanford-Tuck, DSO DFC and two Bars, who sadly died earlier in 1987. Bob was at Duxford when the first Typhoons arrived and, although he scarcely had time to settle into the aeroplane before being posted away, he entertained me for several memorable hours with a wealth of anecdote (in his inimitable style) that was more valuable to a writer than many days among lifeless records. To him the Typhoon had a "presence".

Foreword

by Wing Commander R. P. Beamont,
C.B.E., D.S.O. and BAR, D.F.C. and BAR, D.L., F.R.AE.S.

In the summer of 1940 the Royal Air Force defeated Hitler's *Luftwaffe* over the Channel and the South of England with two of the world's finest types of fighter aircraft, the Hurricane and Spitfire.

Their performance was roughly comparable to that of the main adversary, the Messerschmitt Bf 109E, but in the hands of a group of fighter pilots who have since become legendary, these famous aeroplanes, with their superior combat manoeuvrability, altered the course of history by preventing the first invasion of these islands for a thousand years. But their supremacy was soon to be challenged.

In 1941 the advent of the improved Messerschmitt Bf 109F immediately rendered the slower Hurricane obsolete in the European theatre in the air combat rôle; and then the appearance over the Channel of the excellent Focke-Wulf Fw 190 caused consternation when it showed clear superiority even over the new Spitfire Mark V.

The design teams of Sydney Camm at Hawkers and Reginald Mitchell at Supermarines had, in the late 1930's, anticipated the need for even more performance, and major aircraft historian Frank Mason, in this latest volume in his impressive series of aircraft type-histories, has with dedicated research described the evolution, development and operational service of Camm's solution, the Hawker 'heavy fighters', the Typhoon, Tornado and Tempest.

With the great increase in power becoming available from the new Napier Sabre, Rolls-Royce Vulture and Bristol Centaurus engines, at least 100 miles per hour more than the Hurricane was expected and achieved. Yet, following their first flights in 1939–40, the Tornado and Typhoon both encountered severe engine and airframe problems during development, and by 1941 were still in no position to take over the air combat rôle from the Spitfire and Hurricane. There was also a new requirement emerging for a powerful ground attack 'tactical' fighter as the RAF started to go over to the offensive on all fronts.

The testing, early service and consequent rejection of the Typhoon as a Spitfire replacement is fully described in this book, as is its proving in a new and vital rôle which led to its ultimate success in providing a most powerful impact in the final battles for Europe. Frank Mason has presented a well-balanced account of this important aircraft with much fascinating and authentic technical and operational detail.

He goes on to describe the successful development of the Typhoon II—ultimately named Tempest—which, though not produced in sufficient numbers to achieve world fame before the end of the War in Europe, played a vital part in the defence of London against the V–1 flying bombs in 1944; it then went on to widely acclaimed success in 2nd Tactical Air Force from Normandy to the Baltic as arguably the best tactical fighter of 1944–45.

In describing the engineering and operating characteristics of these aircraft, the Author's technical knowledge and experience—as a fighter pilot himself—comes through loud and clear, and contributes greatly to the quality of this comprehensive and valuable history of two important British fighter aircraft.

R.P.B., November 1987

Introduction

With the exception of the post-War BAC TSR-2 there was possibly never a British military aeroplane that suffered such constant sniping by its critics as the Hawker Typhoon, as committee after committee fulminated and conference after conference raged—often discussing setbacks, frequently complaining of delays, occasionally demanding outright cancellation and, eventually, seeking acceleration of delivery rates. The fundamental difference between the TSR-2's lengthy obstacle course and that of the wartime Typhoon was that the former suffered ultimate defeat at the hands of a rapacious government while the latter, having circumvented a nightmarish chapter of problems and confounded the most vociferous of critics, survived to become one of the mightiest of RAF tactical support aircraft when British and American forces were ready to undertake the liberation of Europe in 1944.

No one could argue that the Typhoon, originally intended to supersede the classic Hawker Hurricane in RAF service, represented brilliance of design or a major advance in technology, although it *did* take the famous Hawker family of fighters out of the age of wood and fabric into that of monocoque. Its advance, and therein the source of main trouble, lay in the engine—that immensely powerful yet complex Napier Sabre—an engine which was recognized at an early stage as being fundamentally sound but one that demanded, and was never allowed a long period of development. At a time when Hurricanes and Spitfires were entering service with Merlin engines developing one thousand horsepower the Sabre was already giving twice that amount. And the aeroplane designer was being asked to conjure an airframe—roughly the same size as that of the Hurricane—capable of accommodating this hefty chunk of machinery as well as an armament with twice the weight of fire as that of the famous Battle of Britain fighters.

Yet without recourse to new technology Sydney Camm achieved just that aeroplane, not without considerable difficulty, but with success. When one considers that this was achieved with the benefit of an absurdly small number of prototypes and that, "warts and all", the Typhoon joined the Royal Air Force in the very month demanded by the Air Ministry three years earlier when it existed only as a "paper aeroplane", the achievement is all the more astonishing.

It was the very "workhorse" nature of the Typhoon—albeit the first 400 mph workhorse to join the Royal Air Force—that placed it at the forefront of ground support fighters, capable of fending for itself in the presence of enemy fighters at low level yet able eventually to deliver a pair of 1,000-lb bombs or a salvo of rockets equivalent to a couple of 6-inch gun-armed cruisers' broadsides. That the Typhoon failed in its originally intended rôle as a conventional dogfighter, that is one that could meet and match enemy fighters at any altitude, cannot be denied; Camm's over-riding design philosophies before the War had not allowed for thin and, for him by implication, delicate wings, but when combat above 20,000 feet came to be regarded as the norm for the modern fighter the burly Typhoon with its thick wing simply couldn't cope. When, however, the Germans sent over their tip-and-run Focke-Wulfs at "nought feet" above the Channel it was the Typhoon that coped where all others failed.

One is often asked how Camm rated his Typhoon. A straightforward answer is almost impossible to provide, for Camm could be very reserved in his opinion about "his own" creations. Certainly he always considered the Hurricane as his most important design, and he regarded the Tempest as the perfection of the wartime fighter. In all likelihood the Typhoon represented for him a natural development of the Hurricane. After all, its design passed through his offices relatively quickly during that twilight period immediately before the outbreak of war, a time when all and sundry were demanding more and better Hurricanes. Once the Typhoon had passed into production—at a factory remote from Kingston—he was impatient to produce what eventually emerged as the Tempest. He *knew* that when he could apply the "thin wing" to the Typhoon he would have a winner, a fighter that would outclass any contemporary. And so it transpired. It is often forgotten that the Tempest could easily be flown at a speed of Mach 0.75 and remain perfectly steady and entirely controllable, capable at that speed of aiming and firing its guns without the wings coming off; the same could not be said for the early jet fighters—British or German, let alone such other excellent aircraft as the P-47, P-51 or Spitfire—and what the Typhoon could carry, whether bombs or rockets, the Tempest carried more than 50 mph faster! Little wonder that just three Tempest squadrons destroyed more flying bombs than all other Allied fighters combined, and that more Tempest pilots destroyed German jet aircraft than those of any other Allied fighter.

And what did the pilots of these Hawker fighters think of them? That the Typhoon was a handful goes almost without saying; it was certainly unforgiving of carelessness. Yet most pilots who flew the aeroplane for any length of time—and there were hundreds of them—espoused considerable affection for the "Tiffy", aware that it was an immensely powerful machine (so long as the engine continued to do its duty) and, if flown "by the book" capable of doing everything demanded of it. Most pilots walked away from some sort of involuntary landing during their stint on Typhoons—but their very survival imparted tremendous confidence in the strength of the aeroplane. As far as is known the facts surrounding the circumstances of tail failure have not previously been published and it is to be hoped that what is said in this book will help to place the facts in their true perspective. Yet for all their affection for the Typhoon, the pilots simply couldn't wait to get their hands on the Tempest.

Of course preoccupation with the Tempest imposed one significant penalty upon the Hawker design team: it was not able to participate in the first generation of jet fighters although, in all likelihood, this did not worry Camm overmuch. He was never renowned for radical advance—save perhaps in his last great achievement, the Harrier— nor did he express enthusiasm for the early jet fighter designs, whether British, German or American; "groping in the dark" he described them. He was indeed content to wring the last ounce of potential from his successful Tempest formula just so long as the Royal Air Force and Royal Navy demanded it. And when he was ready to embark on the inevitable jet fighter it was the Tempest/Fury that was his jumping-off point. "Put a Rolls-Royce jet in the middle of a Fury with the pilot where he can see out; round off the sharp edges and you have the basis of a good jet fighter." And so started the successful Sea Hawk, Hunter and Harrier formula. But that is another story.

The late P. G. Lucas, GM. One of the truly great test pilots of the wartime period, Philip Gadesden Lucas had held a Short Service Commission in the Royal Air Force from 1926 until 1931 when he joined the H. G. Hawker Engineering Co. Ltd. as a test pilot, working under "George" Bulman. Being awarded the George Medal for saving the prototype Typhoon from destruction in 1940, he was appointed Chief Test Pilot that year and remained in this post until 1946.

WAR ON THE HORIZON—1936

"Arm! Arm! it is—it is—the cannon's opening roar!"
Byron, *Childe Harold*

On a late autumn day in 1935 a new shape appeared in the skies over Surrey, a small silver monoplane so radical that anyone who bothered to seek the source of noise cannot have failed to wonder at its portent. Its grace indeed betrayed the secret of its power for this, the Hawker Hurricane figher, was to become—two years hence—the first interceptor to reach the Royal Air Force capable of a speed of 300 miles an hour. Gone were the struts and wires so familiar in the age-old biplane fighters, the Furies, Bulldogs, Demons and the others that had thrilled the crowds at the annual RAF displays; gone even were the landing wheels, now tucked neatly inside the sleek lines of wings and fuselage. None but very few were privvy to the secret that this little monoplane would soon be armed with no fewer than eight machine guns, a source of incredible destruction in the hands of a single pilot.

This, and the graceful Spitfire—to follow half a year later—were the creations of gifted designers who had answered a call by the nation's air force for fighters that could break the mould of biplane tradition and move with accelerating technology into the future, a future fraught with hazard already clouding the international horizon of politics.

These were the years of British military expansion—no one could yet say "preparation", for that would imply a definition of the threat. Nevertheless the aura of unease that permeated the portals of government had espoused realization that Britain's armed forces were living in a past age; the Royal Navy, charged with safeguarding the sea lanes of Empire, sailed battleships whose guns had fired at Jutland; the Army sat in tanks whose biggest gun was smaller than those carried by the monsters over the old Western Front; and the Royal Air Force still flew fighters and bombers scarcely better than those that had led the world more than a dozen years before.

That Germany would somehow constitute a future threat to European peace few now doubted, and it had been the words of warning uttered in Parliament following the resurgence of German militarism under Hitler's assumption of dictatorial powers in 1933 that sparked the fuse of Britain's military expansion one year later.

★　　★　　★

The years 1935 and 1936 were a period of unaccustomed effort and activity by Britain's Air Ministry and aircraft industry alike. True, the Hurricane and Spitfire were the manifestations of advance by the most spectacular of all aeroplanes—the nimble fighter—yet in most other facets of aircraft design there had been similar radical progress. Two years of hard work, commercial speculation, design and construction brought forth an entirely new generation of monoplanes that took wing in the spring and summer of 1936 to follow in the slipstream of the Hurricane—the Spitfire on 5 March, the Fairey Battle light bomber on 10 March, the Armstrong Whitworth Whitley heavy bomber on 17 March, the Wellington heavy bomber and Westland Lysander army co-operation aircraft on 15 June, the Handley Page Hampden medium bomber on 21 June and the Bristol Blenheim light bomber on 25 June. Led by Sydney Camm's immortal Hurricane, these were the aeroplanes that constituted the arsenal with which the Royal Air Force faced the spectre of world war just three short years hence.

When the prototypes of these new aircraft were displayed before the public for the first time in the New Types Park at the 1936 Royal Air Force Display at Hendon the British people could be forgiven for its euphoria and belief that the RAF's newly created Fighter and Bomber Command led the world with their futuristic arsenal of monoplanes. Yet behind the scenes in Whitehall and the aircraft industry, as preparations were made for Service evaluation and development for production, a nagging suspicion persisted that, radical though the "first generation" of aeroplanes might outwardly appear, its superiority—if indeed superiority there was—might be at best shortlived, at worst illusory. Answers were beginning to be sought by the devil's advocates to the questions "Have we examined all aspects of the advance in aircraft design?" and "How may these aeroplanes fail to perform their traditional tasks in the event of war in the foreseeable future?"

For instance, if Germany were to become the active enemy of Britain once more, would the heavy bombers have adequate range to reach that country from British bases, carrying a sufficiency of bombs to render their journey worthwhile, and could they defend themselves from enemy interceptors? And even if Germany herself possessed bombers capable of reaching Britain, would the RAF's fighters possess adequate armament to penetrate armour plate—if carried in those bombers?

After all, fresh in the minds of those at the Directorate of Technical Development in the Air Ministry was the fiasco that had surrounded a recent attempt to break the pattern of the biplane fighter with radial engine and two machine guns that had persisted since 1918. A radical Specification had been issued in 1930 calling for a 25 per cent speed increase and the doubling of gun armament. In the belief that the new in-line engines then being introduced would enable the aircraft industry to come up with a "world beater", the Air Ministry looked forward to the introduction of such a fighter at relatively low cost. In the event the engine favoured—the steam-cooled Rolls-Royce Goshawk—failed to match up to expectations; much effort, ingenuity and money was largely wasted, and the result was that the successful contender emerged as a two-gun, radial engine biplane, the Gloster Gauntlet! From this was developed the four-gun Gladiator which at least met the armament and speed requirements of the original Specification but, by the time it reached the RAF in 1937 was, by international standards, not the hoped-for world beater but unequivocally obsolete. Farsighted though the 1930 Specification undoubtedly was, it could not be imaginative enough—for who, in the throes of the great Depression, could predict that Germany would emerge as a major military power within half a decade?

Even if the generation of new British aeroplanes that appeared in 1935 and 1936 matched the contemporary efforts by Germany in technology—which from all accounts they appeared to do—there remained the need for substantial resources to sustain the momentum to match the increasing strength of the new German *Luftwaffe*. Such a philosophy, while constituting the normal process of future defence planning, nevertheless implied a huge increase in spending on research, which in the past had been almost entirely borne by the aircraft industry's own resources.

To illustrate just what this burden could entail, it is worthwhile here to examine the situation facing the British aircraft engine manufacturers, of which four major companies dominated the military market, namely Rolls-Royce Ltd., D. Napier & Sons Ltd., the Bristol Engine Company Ltd., and Armstrong-Siddeley Motors Ltd. The eight new aeroplanes mentioned above employed engines from three of these manufacturers (the Bristol Pegasus radial in the Wellington and Hampden, the Bristol Mercury radial in the Blenheim and Lysander, the Rolls-Royce Merlin in-line in the Battle, Hurricane and Spitfire, and the Armstrong-Siddeley Tiger radial in the Whitley). Napier was also required to provide Dagger air-cooled in-line engines for the Hawker Hector—an interim army co-operation biplane—and for one hundred Handley Page Herefords, a variant of the Hampden bomber.

The cost of developing these engines had already been very high, particularly so in the instance of the Merlin; and in 1936, with the new production aircraft at least a year away, Rolls-Royce was indeed fortunate in being able to underwrite these costs with the revenue from enormous orders for Kestrel engines which were used in the hundreds of Hawker Hart variants which were on order to provide the major elements of the early Expansion programme.

The Rolls-Royce Merlin, itself in effect a refinement of the excellent Kestrel twelve-cylinder liquid-cooled in-line engine, produced around 1,000 horse power in its earliest form, but had only achieved its preliminary 50-hour certification early in 1936, and still showed signs of problems ahead. If past experience was a reliable criterion, the normal development process could be expected to increase the power output of the Merlin by up to about 50–60 per cent during the next half-dozen years, and this might be adequate to meet the increasing demands of the Hurricane and Spitfire as they themselves underwent improvement in due course. But superiority on the battlefield is never gained by simply matching the strength of the enemy. Moreover an age-old tenet holds that an aggressor nation invariably ensures that it possesses overwhelming strength to achieve its aims. Just how strong would Herr Hitler's forces be by the time the Royal Air Force's new aeroplanes were ready to participate in a world war?

Preparing for a Second Generation

At the time of the Hawker Hurricane's first flight on 6 November 1935 the Air Member for Research and Development on the Air Council was Air Marshal Sir Hugh Dowding, KCB, CMG, unquestionably the one man who fully understood the urgency to advance the capabilities of Britain's air defences and who, since 1930 had devoted his special genius, influence and energies towards that aim. He had moreover gained the appointment of some of the most gifted and imaginative officers of middle rank to key posts in departments of the Air Ministry concerned with future RAF equipment. His right-hand man was Air Commodore Henry Cave-Browne-Cave, Director of Technical Development at the Air Ministry, along with Air Commodore John Bradley, OBE, Director of Equipment, and Group Captain Ronald Graham, DSO, DSC, DFC, in the armament section of the DTD, as well as officers and civilians whose experience in aircraft engine development during the early 'thirties had provided an especially close working relationship between the industry, the Royal Aircraft Establishment at Farnborough, and the Aeroplane and Armament Experimental Establishment at Martlesham Heath; prominent among these was Major George Purvis Bulman, OBE, who since 1929 had been Deputy Director of Engine Development at the Air Ministry. Henry Tizard (later Sir Henry, KCB, AFC, FRS) was Chairman of the Aeronautical Research Committee and continued to provide a rare diplomacy that allowed Dowding unfettered access to such respected engineers as Arthur Hall, CBE, the Chief Superintendent at the RAE. And it was this freedom of interchange of ideas and requirements that existed between the captains of industry, the research bodies and establishments, and the Air Council, that achieved so much during 1935–36.

Apart from the urgent need to expand the metal-working fitter trades in the Royal Air Force—seen as of the utmost priority by the Directorates of Training and Equipment—two main areas of essential research were identified if the progress in military aircraft development was to be maintained. These were in aircraft armament and engines, in many respects interrelated.

So far as armament was concerned, it was seen that not only were the bombs carried by RAF bombers far too small to be of any real value in a strategic bombing campaign of the future (still held to be the ultimate purpose of the Service), but also that the rifle-calibre machine gun would be wholly inadequate for air combat in the event of war.

As a first step to overcome the first of these shortcomings—for the RAF's heaviest bomb (for which the Wellington and Whitley had been designed) was the one-thousand-pounder, while the most-widely-used weapons were of no more than 250-lb and 500-lb—development was started of a 2,000-lb bomb, to carry which a number of new heavy bomber specifications was issued in 1936 and 1937—aircraft that would materialize four years hence as the Stirling, Halifax and Manchester. In the realm of fighter armament, the Armament Group at Eastchurch (whose Air Officer Commanding was Air Commodore Lawrence Pattinson, CB, DSO, MC, DFC) supported a case for the introduction of the Oerlikon 20-mm cannon, but as yet it was generally considered that no aircraft with even a semblance of fighter-like performance existed that might carry more than one such gun. And it was Dowding himself who characteristically lent support to the policy of "demanding the impossible so that you may get the improbable". Accordingly Specification F.37/35 was evolved, effectively calling for a single-seat fighter to be armed with *four* 20-mm cannon. The point of interest about this Specification was that its terms almost exactly mirrored those of a German requirement—whose existence was totally unsuspected at the Air Ministry, yet was formulated at exactly the same time. The resulting aircraft were both twin-engine fighters, the British essay to become the Westland Whirlwind, the German the two-seat Messerschmitt Bf 110; both came initially to be used as escort fighters for day bombers, the former with a top speed in service configuration of around 355 mph at 15,000 feet, and the latter about 325 mph at 18,000 feet.

While the Air Ministry remained sceptical as to whether a single-engine interceptor could accommodate the 20-mm cannon at all, Sydney Camm demonstrated that it was geometrically feasible to fit four such guns inside the wings of the Hurricane—and, indeed, submitted a formal tender to Specification F.37/35 of such a design in 1936—but it was acknowledged that the Hurricane as it was then being pursued, with 1,000-hp Merlin and fabric-covered wings, would retain no more than a pedestrian performance. Nevertheless it did sow the seeds of interest in the DTD, and these would germinate as the form of a new fighter requirement took shape in the minds of the Joint Directorate of Research and Development at the Air Ministry, where Group Captain (later Air Vice-Marshal, CB, CBE, MC) George Brindley Aufrere Baker was Director of Armament Development.

Before passing on to the evolution of the new fighter requirement mentioned above, it is necessary to take a closer look at the investigation of future engine projects being undertaken by the major engine manufacturers. Rolls-Royce at Derby was heavily preoccupied with extensive trials of the early Merlin development engines, while the design department had been exploring the possibility of producing a de-rated and much lightened version of that engine which might be suitable for twin-engine aircraft installation, being initially intended as a possible alternative for the radial Pegasus engines in the Blenheim; this was never seriously considered by Bristol despite the fact that the proposed Rolls-Royce engine, the Peregrine, with much lower drag and installed weight and increased power output, would have almost certainly bestowed a much better performance on the Blenheim—its structural weight being little different from that of the Whirlwind, which eventually received the Peregrine.

At the same time as the Peregrine itself was being developed, it was also the subject of an imaginative project in which two such engines were combined, one as an upright-Vee above another inverted, using a common crankcase enclosing two crankshafts geared to drive a single propeller; it was argued that the single crankcase and common camshaft drive off-take would result in considerable weight economy while achieving twice the overall power of a single Peregrine engine. This engine, of which the first example was completed in 1937, was to become the Rolls-Royce Vulture 24-cylinder liquid-cooled X-type in-line engine.

The Bristol Aeroplane Company's Engine Division had been producing air-cooled radial engines for the RAF for many years and since 1932 had embarked on a successful family of sleeve-valve radials, commencing with the nine-cylinder single-row Perseus; this was followed by the 14-cylinder two-row Hercules in 1936, and two years later by the much smaller Taurus, also with 14 cylinders. One of the many advantages of the sleeve-valve radial lay in the reduction in overall diameter due to the elimination of the push-rod operated overhead valves on top of each cylinder. It was the Hercules that formed the basis of an 18-cylinder sleeve-valve radial engine project that underwent initial type-testing in 1938 and came—illogically—to be named the Centaurus; in-service power expectations were to be "more than 2,000 horse power".

Third manufacturer to undertake an advanced, high-performance engine project was D. Napier & Son Ltd of Acton and Luton. This company had been producing a family of air-cooled upright-H, double-crank in-line engines, beginning with the 395-hp Rapier 16-cylinder design, this being followed by the 24-cylinder 1,000-hp Dagger upright-H engine. Design of an entirely new engine of 24 cylinders started in 1935, the engine eventually being named the Sabre. Yet despite the perpetuation of the "weapon family" names, the

Sabre entered what were for Napier entirely new realms of technology. The H-form was retained but laid on its side, so that one crankshaft was above the other; the customary poppet valve gear was discarded in favour of reciprocating sleeve valves and, unlike Napier's recent engines, the Sabre was liquid-cooled. Compared to the Centaurus' 18 cylinders which had a total capacity of 53.6 litres, the 24-cylinder capacity of Napier's new engine was a mere 36.65 litres—giving a cylinder size only two-thirds that of the Rolls-Royce Merlin. The target power for certification (which, as will be told in due course, was not achieved until 1940) was to be 2,200 hp at 3,700 rpm—roughly twice that of the early Merlins. The power/weight ratios of the early production Vulture, Centaurus and Sabre engines would be 0.79 hp/lb, 0.95 hp/lb and 1.12 hp/lb respectively, illustrating the great attraction promised by the new Napier project.

From the outset it was acknowledged that both the Centaurus and Sabre engines would probably demand rather longer development processes, so that the second generation of RAF heavy bombers, conceived in 1935–36, were to abstain from use of the more radical engines, the first to be subject of a Specification in July 1936—the B.12/36 Stirling—employing four of the new but conventional Bristol Hercules radials. The other two, euphemistically termed "high-speed bombers", the Manchester and Halifax, were designed to P.13/36, issued in September that year, and were originally intended to have a pair of Vultures, but in anticipation of delays in the engine's development the design of the Halifax was changed to accommodate four Merlins.

All three of the powerful new engines were considered in the context of the new fighter Requirement whose evolution started in the late summer of 1936, shortly after the 54-year-old Dowding had left the Air Ministry to take up his appointment as the first Air Officer Commanding-in-Chief of the new Fighter Command. His successor as Air Council Member for Research and Development was to be Air Vice-Marshal Wilfrid Freeman, CB, DSO, MC, fresh from the post of the Commandant of the RAF Staff College.

One can only speculate on the early processes of reasoning adopted in producing the initial draft requirements for the new fighter. To begin with, no one yet knew how the Hurricane and Spitfire would match up to foreign "competition"; nor could one judge with any certainty how the new high performance fighters would fit into the defence structure now being supervised under the direction of Dowding himself. One must therefore assume that the new performance demands were to be arbitrary, yet representing a substantial increase over that of the Hurricane and Spitfire in the foreseeable future, even allowing for increasing power available from the Merlin engine.

What is known is that Hawker Aircraft Ltd was initially excluded from the early discussions when various aircraft designers were approached late in 1936 to contribute their ideas. The reason for this, according to Sydney Camm's records, was that Hawker's preoccupation with the fabric-covered Hurricane (with the Air Ministry's wholehearted approval) tended to disqualify the company from production of an all-metal monocoque fighter in the short term, not being staffed with personnel experienced to undertake it.

When the Board of Directors of the Hawker Siddeley Group learned of this (particularly when it was clear that some other companies, even less equipped to produce the new fighter, were privy to the early discussions) Sir Thomas Sopwith let it be known with some vigour that the Kingston company, with its long-standing expertise in fighter design, would certainly expect to be given the opportunity to tender designs, even if production of the aircraft were to be undertaken elsewhere in the Group. In any case it was pointed out that Hawker Aircraft Ltd was engaged in the early negotiations to secure land for the site of a new factory (at Langley, Buckinghamshire) which would be perfectly adequate to undertake production of both the Hurricane and the new fighter.

The first meeting with Hawker to discuss the new Requirement, which included Sydney Camm, was held at Canbury Park Road, Kingston-upon-Thames, in March 1937, with Major George Bulman, OBE,[1] and Squadron Leader John Buchanan,

[1] Not of course to be confused with Hawker's Chief Test Pilot, Flight Lieutenant P. W. S. ("George") Bulman MC, AFC, whose sobriquet remained with him all his life, owing to an inability to recall the names of acquaintances whom he invariably referred to as "George".

CBE visiting from the Air Ministry. No records appear to have survived of this meeting, although Camm's records henceforth refer to the Specification's designation—F.18/37—and to two alternative aircraft, the N-type fighter (with Napier engine) and the R-type (with Rolls-Royce engine); it appears that a third alternative, with the Bristol Centaurus, was mentioned as being considered at the DTD, although Camm felt that this "was probably a rearguard action to appease the old radial engine fraternity".

Three fundamental demands were evidently being put forward: a target speed of 400 mph at 20,000 feet, a weight of fire from its gun armament at least 50 per cent greater than the Hurricane and Spitfire, and—particularly significant for Hawker, as it transpired—the ability of the aircraft to operate from "soft", that is grass, airfields.

Bearing in mind that, from the outset, it was obvious that the Sabre engine enjoyed the Air Ministry's preference among the alternatives (a preference by no means unreservedly shared by Camm at the time), and that all three engines had installed weights at least 60 per cent greater than that of the Merlin, Camm realized that the new fighter would be a "very hefty aeroplane" indeed, and one detects that this was anathema to a man who for more than a dozen years had revelled in the challenge to produce nimble aeroplanes of outstanding aestheticism, of which the little Fury biplane had been his favourite. With installed weights of the Sabre and Vulture engines being forecast by their manufacturers in 1937 at 2,250 and 2,050 lb respectively, it is worth recording the characteristics of Camm's fighters to illustrate just how the proposed fighters compared:

Date	Aircraft	Normal All-up Weight (lb)	Wing Span (ft)	Wing Area (sq. ft)	Power Loading (bhp/lb)	Wing Loading (lb/sq. ft)	Maximum Speed (mph)	Engine
1925	Danecock	3,045	32.58	340	0.13	8.995	145	385-hp Armstrong-Siddeley Jaguar
1925	Heron	3,126	31.83	291	0.15	10.74	156	455-hp Bristol Jupiter
1926	Hornbill	3,769	31.00	317	0.19	11.84	187	698-hp Rolls-Royce Condor
1929	Fury I	3,490	30.00	252	0.15	13.85	207	525-hp Rolls-Royce Kestrel IIS
1933	P.V.3	4,670	34.00	290.5	0.15	16.08	224	695-hp Rolls-Royce Goshawk
1935	Fury II	3,609	30.00	252	0.18	14.32	223	640-hp Rolls-Royce Kestrel VI
1936	Hurricane I	6,600	40.00	257.5	0.16	25.93	318	1,030-hp Rolls-Royce Merlin I
1937	F.18/37 (R)	8,900 (estimated)	40.00 (proposed)	260 (proposed)	0.20	34.23	400 (estimated)	1,800-hp Rolls Royce Vulture (estimated)
1937	F.18/37 (N)	9,250 (estimated)	40.00 (proposed)	260 (proposed)	0.22	35.58	405 (estimated)	2,000-hp Napier Sabre (estimated)
1939	Tornado I	9,450	41.58	279	0.19	33.87	396	1,760-hp Rolls-Royce Vulture I
1940	Typhoon IB	9,800	41.58	279	0.22	35.13	412	2,150-hp Napier Sabre IIA

From this it is interesting to note that the 'radical' Hurricane possessed a top speed some 95 mph greater than the Fury Mark II (which entered RAF service in 1937), compared with a margin between the top speeds of the Hurricane and the Typhoon of 94 mph. Perhaps even more significant is the overall speed margin between the 1937 Fury II and the Typhoon which joined the RAF in 1941; the difference of 189 mph represented a speed increase of almost 85 per cent in four years! Yet the young men who were 20-year-old Pilot Officers in 1937 were 24-year-old Squadron Leaders in 1941 . . .

★   ★   ★

Armed thus with information about the Air Ministry's ideas for the new fighter, Camm's small team of project designers set about scheming up rough designs for aircraft with the Napier and Rolls-Royce engines in May 1937. Not unnaturally the "starting point" was an airframe envelope approximating to that of the Hurricane, and in overall configuration the main structural features were retained, including an inward retracting, wide-track undercarriage, ventral radiator and gun armament in the outer wings. However, owing to the increased consumptions of the big engines (although specific fuel consumption remained little changed), larger fuel and oil tanks had to be accommodated, while the much greater weight of the engines resulted in shorter nose, and with larger propellers anticipated the landing gear would be longer. To limit the increase in landing gear oleos a very slightly "cranked" wing form was adopted, the centre section possessing slight (effective) anhedral. By increasing the width of this centre section over that of the Hurricane it proved possible to further increase the undercarriage track and at the same time move the wheel bays apart, thereby permitting the large ventral radiator fairing to be mounted directly below the centre of gravity. Indeed, compared with the Hurricane, the main longitudinal load moments about the cg were somewhat shorter.

Generous landing flap and aileron areas were provided, and these could have been accommodated in a wing of the same span and area as those of the Hurricane had there been any firm indication of what armament would finally be demanded by the Air Ministry; as it was, Hawker opted to design for the "worst eventuality", that of a cannon armament. And it was the bulky Oerlikons, then being studied by the Armament Branch, that largely dictated the relatively thick wing which was to compromise the Typhoon's high altitude performance. (It was to be further compromised when it was found necessary to reduce the Sabre's fully-supercharged (FS) rated altitude by some 3,000 feet.)

It is perhaps a little-known fact that the F.18/37 designs made provision to accommodate *six* 20-mm cannon from the start, though with slightly smaller ammunition drums. When it became obvious that a reliable cannon armament would not be available until after the Typhoon was due in RAF service (expected to be sometime in 1941 if all went smoothly with engine development) the decision was taken to cater for an initial armament of 12 0.303-inch Browning guns with generous ammunition capacity. When eventually the cannons became available for production aircraft at the end of 1941 the Air Ministry evinced only lukewarm interest in the six-gun scheme and, although Hawker hand-tooled a set of six-cannon wings, it was never flown.

By March 1938 when 90 per cent of the prototype manufacturing drawings had been completed, and the Air Ministry had been acquainted with preliminary performance estimates, Hawker received a Contract, No. 815124/38, dated 3 March, 1938, to produce four prototypes—two with Rolls-Royce Vulture and two with Napier Sabre engines. By that date, however, orders had been received, or were being finalized for a total of no fewer than 2,500 Hurricanes—for delivery by the end of 1941—and with completion of the Langley factory still a year away it was clear to all that plans must be laid to decentralize Hurricane and F.18/37 production. The Hawker Siddeley Group therefore started making arrangements to reorganize work on the Kingston-originating aircraft:

A. Completion of outstanding Hawker Hinds (17 for Afghanistan, 35 for Persia, three for Latvia and 55 for the RAF) to run out at Brooklands. Conversion of Harts and Hinds to trainers to be completed by General Aircraft Ltd., Hanworth.

B. All outstanding flight development work on the Hawker Henley to be transferred to Gloster Aircraft Company Ltd., Brockworth, Gloucester (production having been transferred there in 1937).

C. Production of the Hurricane to be divided between Hawker (1,400 aircraft) and Gloster (1,100).

D. Manufacture of prototype F.18/37 aircraft and a small production batch to be completed by Hawker, and all production of Sabre-powered aircraft thereafter to be undertaken by Gloster Aircraft Company Ltd.

E. All production of Vulture-powered F.18/37 aircraft to be undertaken by "another" Group company—in the event A. V. Roe & Co Ltd was selected.

F. Design authority and all experimental flight development of the F.18/37 to be centred upon Hawker Aircraft Ltd at Kingston and Langley.

2

THE TORNADO

It was ironic that of all the F.18/37 designs produced by Camm's team the Vulture-powered Tornado was to be the one to suffer eventual cancellation—and that the aircraft which, in 1939, was expected to be the least likely to find favour, the Centaurus-powered project, would enjoy the longest service in the Royal Air Force, albeit in a rather different guise. To add to the irony was the fact that the reason for the Vulture's cancellation lay in its general unreliability in, and unsuitability for the Avro Manchester "high speed" heavy bomber, while Hawker was to encounter somewhat fewer problems with the big engine in the Tornado than with the Sabre in the Typhoon.

The truth was that all three engines represented long strides forward in complexity and power output, as already explained, the Vulture in effect constituting paired Peregrines and the Sabre a pair of "flat-twelves". By gearing together the crankshafts it had been assumed that mechanical synchronization would overcome any significant vibration, but this was not to be. Nor had such critical engine demands as cooling and lubrication been adequately satisfied in the foreshortened development period anticipated.

Rolls-Royce possessed some advantage over Napier in that the 12-cylinder Peregrine was flying (in the Whirlwind), and was in effect a lightened and de-rated development of the Kestrel/Merlin "family" and, incidentally, gave reliable though limited service in the RAF. The Sabre, by far the most problematical and speculative step into the unknown, was of liquid-cooled, sleeve-valve configuration, while its manufacturer's recent experience lay almost exclusively in the relatively low-powered air-cooled Rapier and Dagger engines. And while British engine technology was far ahead of the rest of the world in sleeve-valve design and metallurgy, most of this experience and know-how lay with Bristol in its air-cooled radials (such as the Hercules and Taurus), and would become evident in the 18-cylinder Centaurus.

Thus it was that when Vulture (Mark II) engine number 12 was delivered for installation in the first Tornado prototype, *P5219*, at the beginning of that fateful month, September 1939, it possessed only very limited flight history (the first twin-Vulture Manchester prototype having flown at Ringway on 25 July). Other flight work was carried out on the Hawker Henley prototype, *K5115*, that aeroplane having long since been relegated from its intended dive bombing rôle to that of the humble target tug. The 1,030-hp Merlin II had been replaced by a 1,750-hp Vulture whose greatly increased weight necessitated loading 200 lb of lead ballast in the aeroplane's tail for centre of gravity compensation! Not surprisingly the Vulture-Henley touched down on landing at 120 mph. Although the Vulture installation in the Henley was to some extent intended to duplicate that in the Manchester, with large four-banked exhaust manifolds and carburettor air intake on top of the engine (severely limiting the pilot's field of view in the Henley), the redundancy of the Hawker dive bomber's ventral bomb bay permitted the inclusion of a huge radiator "bath" in much the same position as in the Hurricane.

Indeed for many months the design of the Tornado had progressed (as had that of the Typhoon), perpetuating the Hurricane-style ventral radiator, now incorporating the oil cooler and carburettor air intake as well. By the time that doubts were being expressed by Rolls-Royce as to the efficiency of the ventral position, particularly when the engine was running on the ground or at low flying speeds, it was too late to alter the design of *P5219* without severely delaying the flight programme—already the subject of Air Ministry impatience.

15

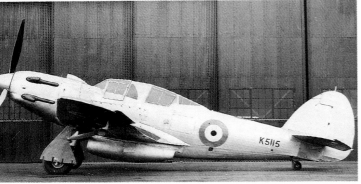

The Vulture Henley prototype K5115 whose generous ventral radiator suggests that Rolls-Royce was not unaware of the big engine's cooling requirements. (Photos: Rolls-Royce Ltd., Neg Nos HDM64 and HDM65)

It is worth reflecting briefly on the whole matter of the cooling problems with liquid-cooled engines in aircraft, perhaps if only to illustrate that although such problems may in the course of this narrative seem to have dominated the development of the F.18/37 prototypes, they were probably not in fact much more serious than with any other aircraft at the time. The design problem itself lay in striking the most efficient balance between the cooling system's efficiency at low and high speeds. In the days already long past aircraft, such as the Hawker Hart, employed fairly small retractable radiators which could be extended into the airstream during taxying and take-off, and at least partly retracted to produce less drag (but adequate cooling) during cruising flight. The new, high performance monoplane fighters with their powerful engines demanded much more efficient cooling systems for coolant and oil. Steam (evaporative) systems had been tried but long since discarded in fighters, mainly on account of weight and vulnerability, so that there appeared to be no alternative to the large, fixed radiator—itself sometimes incorporating a semi-integral oil cooler. To regulate the cooling airflow to meet the range of cooling demands by the engine a controllable shutter was added over the exit from the radiator duct. In theory such an arrangement should have worked well, but each aircraft possessed design features which tended to reduce the efficiency of the radiator. For instance the early Spitfires featured a small radiator under one wing root and the oil cooler under the other; both suffered airflow instability around the faces of these fairings, and when the more powerful versions of the Merlin were introduced a second radiator was provided, and both had eventually to be enlarged; and even so Spitfire pilots will recall that "hanging about at the end of the runway" usually gave rise to anxieties about overheating engines. The same could be said for the wonderful Mosquito which, with its radiators forming the leading edge of the wing centre-section, was always prone to overheating on the ground owing to the engine nacelles or fuselage masking the radiator faces. Scarcely any aircraft with liquid-cooled engines was entirely free from cooling problems in some operating regime. These had, after all, been the basis of arguments put forward long ago by the protagonists of the air-cooled radial engine when a rearguard action had to be fought by radial engine manufacturers in their attempts to withstand the introduction of the smoothly-cowled in-line engines. Yet history showed that in the mid-1930s the radial-engined Gloster Gladiator had out-performed all the Kestrel- and Goshawk-powered competitors. Moreover, as will be ultimately shown, it would be the air-cooled radial engine that would take the single-engine fighter to the end of the "piston" era.

★   ★   ★

P5219's airframe was "hand-built" in the experimental shop at Canbury Park Road in Kingston, but final assembly of the aeroplane was completed at Langley in Hawker's new factory. Undercarriage functioning and system checks were all performed in the new experimental flight department, the Tornado prototype being the first to pass through its hands at the end of September. From surviving records it appears that these checks passed off without serious problems, although from the outset Philip Lucas, Hawker's Chief Experimental Test Pilot, expressed concern at the speed with which the engine cylinder head temperatures increased during ground running and, on advice from Rolls-Royce, each engine run against the chocks was limited to no more than five minutes before shutting down. Moreover it was clear that much remained to be done to improve piston ring tolerances if the unabating clouds of oil smoke from the exhausts was any criterion; such was the oil consumption of Vulture No. 12 that almost half the oil in the system was "consumed" after 30 minutes' engine running.

On 1 October Lucas embarked on the preliminary taxying trials on the grass airfield at Langley, confining these to fairly short runs during the first two days to check wheel braking and to record the rate of engine temperature increase. On the 3rd he carried out a number of high speed runs on the grass to acclimatize himself with the directional control characteristics.

On the 6th Lucas took *P5219* aloft for its maiden flight, advised by the Rolls-Royce engineers to keep a very careful watch on the coolant temperatures and oil pressures. Thermocouples had been provided on six engine cylinders, distributed among all four banks to give indications of cooling efficiencies throughout the engine, with a row of gauges lining the windscreen coaming. As expected the temperatures quickly increased to the maximum permitted limit but, after becoming airborne, they dropped slightly, though remaining fairly high until landing when they increased once more.

Further flights were made, during which Lucas flew *P5219* up to a true airspeed of 370 mph at 15,000 feet. Examination of the oil filter after each flight disclosed traces of metal particles which analysis suggested were from engine bearing races—probably on the big ends.

Close-up of the original radiator on the Tornado P5219 showing the circular oil cooler matrix and the twin carburettor intakes above the radiator itself. (Photo: Hawker Aircraft Ltd., Neg No 73P, dated 18 July 1939.)

1/2–10–39	Preliminary taxying trials	Vulture II No 12	Rotol 3-blade DB 330/A/1	8,785 lb
3–10–39	3rd taxying trials	..	..	8,749 lb
6/7–10–39	1st and 2nd flights	..	..	9,127 lb
12–10–39	3rd flight. Handling	..	..	9,127 lb
18/10–39	Handling (2)	..	..	9,127 lb
27–10–39	Handling (3)	..	..	9,127 lb
9/10–11–39	Handling (4 and 5)	..	..	9,127 lb
19–11–39	Level speeds and intake pressures	..	Rotol 14-ft Magnesium No 665	9,251 lb
28–11–39	Handling and level speeds	..	..	9,251 lb

Meanwhile the design and manufacture of a new radiator fairing, relocated under the nose of the aircraft, had been completed so that when *P5219* was scheduled to be grounded for a limited strip examination of the Vulture, the first major modification was carried out, all necessary airframe changes being effected inside a week and without delaying the flight programme.

An interesting feature of the take-off procedure adopted by Lucas during those early flights (some-

what reminiscent of that by the old Schneider Trophy seaplanes) was imposed by the considerable engine torque as much as a lack of directional control. He would run up the engine to take-off power to clear the plugs and check for mag drop at an angle to, and some distance from the end of the grass runway and, without throttling back, release the wheelbrakes, accelerating into a sweeping arc until, by the time he was pointing into wind, he had almost reached unstick speed. Even when airborne full rudder trim was incapable of holding the aircraft straight until a speed of at least 150 mph had been reached.

Such a technique, demanding exceptionally fine judgement, might be pursued by a pilot of Lucas' experience and ability (and was adopted by pilots flying the Tornado-Henley at Hucknall), but would not, of course, be appropriate in service, and would in any case be impossible when met-

The first Tornado prototype, P5219, with the ventral radiator originally fitted. (Photo: Sydney Camm Collection)

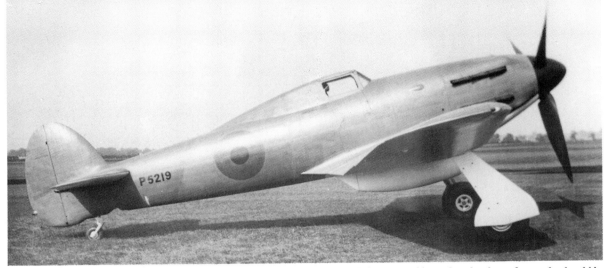

Tornado P5219 in its original guise; note the small fin and rudder, "restricted view" cockpit canopy, white starboard under surfaces and red-and-blue fuselage roundel. (Photo: Author's Collection, from Sydney Camm Collection)

alled runways came to be laid on all operational airfields.

The strip examination of the Vulture disclosed no significant wear or damage and it was decided, on account of a shortage of flight-cleared engines, to retain engine No. 12 for the foreseeable future while gradually relaxing the various limitations as improvements in the ancillary systems were adopted.

On 6 December Lucas was airborne once more in *P5219* which now featured what was to become the characteristic "chin" radiator. Gone were the elegantly-cowled, slim nose lines, changed irrevocably to a bulky, inherently aggressive-looking profile; indeed its cross-section must have been little different from that of current radial engines! However, it was at once evident that the cooling situation had been eased, although much still remained to be done to obtain the best results from the oil cooler which now formed the core of the coolant radiator matrix. Nor was Lucas happy with

the directional stability which, if anything, had further deteriorated following relocation of the radiator.

Wind tunnel tests on a model with nose radiator had disclosed fairly severe airflow instability aft of the radiator exit, and this was aggravated by the segment of the landing gear mainwheels which remained uncovered in their bays when retracted. This became apparent in flight by a low frequency rumbling which suggested that the airflow instability was extending as far aft as the base of the rudder. The next flights by *P5219* on 10, 16 and 20 January 1940, were with D-doors hinged to the lower edge of the fairings attached to the undercarriage oleos which automatically enclosed the wheels on retraction. (Such doors had been fitted on the Hurricane and Henley prototypes but had been quickly discarded as being vulnerable to clogging or damage from surface debris.) Wool-tufting under the fuselage suggested that the Tornado's D-doors improved the local airflow, but they were later to run into trouble as airspeeds increased.

General handling flights with *P5219* continued throughout February and, as told in the following Chapter, the first Typhoon prototype, *P5212* with Sabre engine, was flown on the 24th. In March Lucas began a systematic exploration of the Tornado's flight envelope, including recording the

Early views of the Tornado P5224 at Langley in March 1941. Those on the left show the aircraft without D-door wheel flaps, the photos being taken on "modified-ortho" film (so that the aircraft's undersurface, which was yellow, appeared as black. The circled "P" prototype marking had not been applied. (Photos: Sydney Camm Collection)

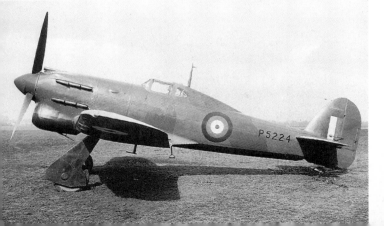

maximum performance at rated altitude (20,500 feet) in fully-supercharged gear. This disclosed a maximum speed of 384 mph, albeit with considerable control instability. This was to be alleviated to some extent by extending the radiator fairing aft by some three inches, thereby smoothing the airflow around the wing root leading edge.

On 9 May the prototype Typhoon suffered a near-catastrophic accident, causing it to be grounded until July, so that *P5219* was once more the only F.18/37 prototype available for flight. It was at this point that the vertical tail surfaces (on both *P5212* and *P5219*) were enlarged to provide improved directional stability, the larger rudder also improving control on take-off. At last Lucas was able to take off in a straight line! The first flight with the enlarged tail was made on 16 May, and on 12 June *P5219* flew with tailwheel doors added as yet another step to improve airflow stability under the rear fuselage.

At this point it became clear that little more could be done to perfect the airframe until the Vulture was cleared for higher performance, and it was decided that more would be gained by sending the aircraft up to Hucknall where Rolls-Royce could carry out flight trials on an improved oil system by progressively modifying engine No. 12.

In mid-July the aircraft returned to Langley having been fitted in the meantime with a Rotol propeller of 13 ft 2½ in diameter. It was now that Dick Reynell joined Lucas in flying the Typhoon and Tornado prototypes. On the 27th *P5219* was flown for the first time at its design all-up weight of 10,225 lb, with guns (12 wing-mounted Browning machine guns), full fuel and ballast for full ammunition, returning a maximum true airspeed of 396.5 mph at 20,800 feet, and a time to 20,000 feet of 6.6 minutes—the highest figures yet achieved by

Cockpit of the Tornado P5224. Just discernible on the left is the open port "car door" showing its position in relation to the throttle quadrant. (Photo: Sydney Camm Collection)

any known fighter at its operational weight. Unfortunately, during a flight by Reynell on 31 July, the Vulture suffered failure in the air (thought to have been caused by the simultaneous fatigue fracture of several connecting rods), and *P5219* also suffered some damage in the subsequent forced landing. Reynell, alas, was never to fly the Tornado again for, during the period of its repair, he applied to visit an operational RAF fighter squadron to obtain combat experience.[1] He joined No. 43 Squadron, flying Hurricanes from Tangmere at the beginning of September, and was involved in

[1] Richard Carew Reynell held the rank of Flight Lieutenant in the General Duties Branch of the Reserve of Royal Air Force Officers.

The second Tornado P5224 during a visit to Boscombe Down in October 1941. By this date the prototype "P" marking had been added on the fuselage and the aircraft features a cut-back carburettor air intake above the nose. (Photo: Sydney Camm Collection)

the famous air battle over the Thames Estuary in the evening of the 7th. The Squadron ran into a large number of Messerschmitt Bf 109Es over the Isle of Sheppey and both Reynell and his commanding officer, the popular South African Squadron Leader Caesar Hull, were shot down and killed.

At Langley Reynell's place was taken by Kenneth Gordon Seth-Smith (a Flying Officer in the Reserve of Royal Air Force Officers) who, with Reynell, had previously been doing much of the experimental Hurricane flying at Brooklands.

On 5 December 1940, the second prototype Tornado, *P5224*, started its first taxying tests, and was flown by Lucas for the first time two days later at an all-up weight of 9,600 lb and with a production Vulture II, No. 132.

★　　★　　★

In the meantime the Vulture-powered Avro Manchester had entered service when on 5 August the first production aircraft, *L7276*, had been delivered to the RAF. The first deliveries to a bomber squadron were made to No. 207 Squadron at Waddington at the beginning of November. Despite early euphoria expressed by the crews, who found the aircraft pleasant to fly and capable of lifting a considerable bomb load by current standards, the Manchester was soon in trouble when it was discovered that rotating the Botha-type dorsal turret created such severe turbulence that the central tail fin suffered failure of its structure. Moreover it was already suspected that all was still far from well with the Vulture engine, pilots reporting very high engine and oil temperatures. When a spate of engine failures occurred following prolonged heavy-load climbs at take-off power, limitations were imposed (both in fuel and bomb load) and

these were accepted by the RAF as a temporary expedient.

While the airframe problems were ironed out (by removal of the central tail fin and eventually enlarging the twin "Zulu-shield" endplate fins and rudders), Rolls-Royce could read the writing on the wall so far as the Vulture in the Manchester was concerned. By the beginning of 1941 the engine was producing 1,845 hp for take-off in moderately supercharged gear, provided that maximum boost was not maintained for more than 90 seconds. Yet it would be an exceptionally brave or foolhardy pilot—with 8,000-lb of bombs on board a twin-engine aircraft—who throttled back even a fraction before attaining safety speed at night!

Nor could Rolls-Royce find sufficient resources to pursue the necessary all-out development programme to remedy the engine faults now known to be almost entirely confined to failure of the connecting rod bolts, possibly due to unbalanced crankshafts. With production and development of the Merlin in full swing for Hurricanes, Spitfires, Halifaxes, Whitleys, Wellingtons, Defiants and Beaufighters—and planned for the Mosquito—the manufacturers were already working at full stretch.

1940 had also seen ratification of a draft Ministry of Aircraft Production Contract with A. V. Roe & Co Ltd to build one Tornado prototype and 200 production examples (the choice of that company being made so as to concentrate delivery of all Vultures to a single destination to simplify their installation and flight test). And it was Avro itself that determined on a course to seek an alternative powerplant to the still-recalcitrant Vulture even before No. 207 Squadron had flown its first Manchesters! The Manchester Mark II was proposed as being powered by either a pair of Napier Sabres or

Below and opposite, **flying views of Tornado P5224, probably taken during a visit to Boscombe Down. Although probably taken on the same flight, the photograph below shows the aircraft with the prototype "P" marking whereas the picture opposite has been doctored by the wartime censor to omit the marking. (Photos: via R. C. B. Ashworth and R. C. Sturtivant)**

of Bristol Centaurus radials,[2] while the Manchester Mark III was to employ a locally modified wing with four underslung Merlin X engines. The latter prototype was flown at Woodford on 9 January 1941, and from the outset gave every indication of constituting the basis of a truly magnificent heavy bomber. Thus was born the Lancaster.

When, in January 1941, a draft Contract was raised with A. V. Roe & Co foreshadowing plans to terminate production of the Manchester (even before it carried out its first bombing raid) by completing the final one hundred aircraft on order as Lancasters, it was but a short step towards cancellation of the entire Vulture development programme, and with it all production plans for the Tornado. As will be told in the following Chapter, opinions were already being expressed that the Typhoon should also be discontinued, though as yet for no fault of the aircraft or engine.

★   ★   ★

Although rumours reached Hawker that the Tornado programme was under threat of abandonment in January 1941, Rolls-Royce was still under a firm obligation to pursue a programme to develop the Vulture as an acceptable operational engine. After all, production of the Manchester was continuing and at least half a dozen squadrons were scheduled to be equipped with the bomber. (As it transpired, Manchesters did not fly their last bombing raid until June 1942—18 months hence—by which time their Vulture engines, though somewhat tired, were at least functioning to the RAF's satisfaction.)

When *P5224* made its maiden flight in December 1940 it was felt that the Vulture II had overcome the most serious problems associated with its oil system so far as the engine design itself was concerned. Crankshaft balancing and connecting rod design was of much more fundamental concern for Rolls-Royce. Lucas, however, reported that

engine vibration was still "rather disconcerting"—though not as bad as in the Sabre—and that oil and coolant temperatures were still on the high side, suggesting that more work needed to be done on the Tornado's radiator and its fairing.

Yet despite suggestions that the future of the Tornado was being questioned A. V. Roe & Co was still under contract to make preparations for the production programme and, so long as those preparations were in hand, Hawker was determined to press ahead with development of the Tornado airframe, come what may. After all, there were so many design features common to Tornado and Typhoon and so few available prototypes that work done on one aircraft would likely benefit the other. For example both the Typhoon and Tornado were scheduled to enter service with an initial armament of 12 machine guns, so that a gun-heating system would be common to both, and flight trials were therefore undertaken to check that the heating system functioned efficiently in the Tornado. This proved a fortunate decision as it was discovered early on that carbon monoxide tended to seep from the hot air trunk leading through the cockpit from the engine to the gun bays so that, by the time gun heating trials were carried out on the Typhoon, the problem was not only fully understood but a remedy was in hand. (Although carbon monoxide contamination was to occur later as the result of a manufacturing difficulty unconnected with gun heating, the early Tornado tests certainly saved much effort during the Service clearance of the Typhoon.)

By the time Hawker was officially notified that "in all probability" production of the Tornado would not go ahead in mid-March 1941, both *P5219* and *P5224* were flying (the former once more at Hucknall, now fitted with a fully-modified Vulture V, No. 164), but still only one Typhoon prototype was under test. It is perhaps astonishing that the first flight by a *production* Typhoon was only two months away at the Brockworth factory, and with fewer than 50 flying hours completed on the one Typhoon prototype the importance of the

<hr />

[2] Indeed Centaurus radials were installed in a Manchester, but not flown owing to the immediate promise shown by the Manchester Mark III

The sole production Tornado I, P7936, spent almost all its life as an engine and propeller test bed. The upper picture shows the aircraft at Hucknall where Rolls-Royce employed it for Vulture development. In the lower photograph the aircraft is seen at Staverton, Gloucester, where Rotol Ltd flew the aircraft with a variety of early contra-rotating propellers. (Photos, Rolls-Royce Ltd., Neg No 108/127A, and Rotol Ltd., Neg No Min 7/32451 dated 7 May 1945)

Tornado prototype test programme may be appreciated. Fortunately the new Vulture gave scarcely any trouble, so that *P5219* could embark on airframe development with little need to waste time on engine problems. *P5224* had suffered a slight mishap resulting in a forced landing on 21 March, but resumed flying to "use up" the remaining engine hours; it was then grounded while a Vulture V (No. 126) was installed, resuming flight test on 11 June, flown by Seth-Smith.

A. V. Roe & Co was formally instructed to halt production preparations for the Tornado, probably in June (though the exact date is not known), and was instructed to complete the planned prototype *R7936* and despatch completed components of two other airframes to the Langley factory. *R7936* was first flown by Lucas at Langley on 31 August powered by a production Vulture V (No. 4252) driving a standard three-blade Rotol RS6/1 constant-speed propeller. Already a full schedule of "production testing" had been drawn up by Avro for the Tornado, and the Avro-built aeroplane met all the criteria when flown to this sched-

ule by Seth-Smith. Indeed those Service pilots, who flew the aircraft during September and October, expressed complete satisfaction with its performance and handling, remarking in one instance on the lack of vibration in the engine; on the other hand almost all the pilots criticized *R7936* on account of its very poor rearward field of view—but this was to be a widely-expressed criticism of all the F.18/37 aircraft, and will be covered more fully in the following Chapter. The only performance measurements that have been traced, which refer to *R7936* at full military load at an all-up weight of 10,550 lb (and therefore representative of the "production" Tornado), record a maximum speed in fully-supercharged (FS) gear of 402 mph at 21,800 feet, and a time to 20,000 feet of 6.9 minutes. The highest recorded altitude reached by the aircraft before it left Langley on its travels was no more than 29,600 feet.

Because production Typhoons started arriving at Langley from Gloster in June 1941 it was felt that *R7936* could contribute little more to the flight programme after it had been checked out and so

this aeroplane embarked on a long career of general test flying with Rolls-Royce, the Aeroplane and Armament Experimental Establishment (A&AEE) at Boscombe Down, the Royal Aircraft Establishment (RAE) at Farnborough, and with the propeller manufacturers, Rotol and de Havilland. It spent some time at the Rotol factory at Staverton, near Cheltenham, as a test bed for early contra-rotating propellers, and paid occasional visits to Langley fitted with de Havilland three- and four-blade propellers to provide vibration comparisons with production Typhoons.

Radial engines once more

The story of British interceptor fighter design throughout the 1930s demonstrated that it was the single-minded perseverance by Rolls-Royce that gained for its liquid-cooled in-line family of engines an ascendancy over the traditional air-cooled radials produced by Bristol and Armstrong-Siddeley. The Bristol Jupiter and Mercury, and Armstrong-Siddeley Jaguar and Panther radials of the 1920s had been largely superseded by the Rolls-Royce Kestrel, an excellent engine that was to evolve into the classic Merlin, although the Jupiter-powered Bristol Bulldog biplane survived in service—for reasons of relatively low cost—until 1936; moreover the radial Mercury-powered Gloster Gauntlet and Gladiator enjoyed a surprisingly long period of renaissance, originally intended as "stop-gap" fighters pending the arrival in service of the Merlin-powered Hurricane and Spitfire interceptors.

Inevitably the Merlin itself underwent considerable development and, apart from a proliferation of improvements of the basic 27-litre design, was also enlarged to become the 36.7-litre Griffon—perpetuating the configuration and general overall dimensions of the Rolls-Royce 'R' racing engine of the old Schneider Trophy seaplanes of the early 1930s.

Meanwhile, as already recounted, the three major engine manufacturers had during 1935–36 put forward proposals for powerplants of much increased power, engines that were to become the Rolls-Royce Vulture, Napier Sabre and Bristol Centaurus. Of these the radial, air-cooled 18-cylinder sleeve-valve Centaurus of no less than 53.6 litres capacity promised the greatest power output—yet with an installed weight roughly similar to that of the Sabre.

The Centaurus had been type-tested as early as 1938 and, as an academic exercise only, was suggested by Camm as one of the alternative engines for his F.18/37 design tenders during that year. However, in the absence of detailed design records, one senses that Camm tended to remain reluctant to take seriously the feasibility of the big, bulky radial, particularly as the other two in-line

engines seemed capable of being accommodated in slim, low-drag cowlings—as demonstrated on the original Tornado.

In 1940 however, as both Vulture and Sabre installations adopted the prominent "chin" radiators, and the engines themselves started to run into fairly serious trouble, the Centaurus installation became the focus of increased interest and a wooden mock-up of a "typical" installation in an F.18/37 airframe was erected in the experimental shop in Canbury Park Road, Kingston. This convincingly demonstrated that in the absence of push rod-operated overhead valvegear the Centaurus

Above, the original Centaurus installation mock-up at Kingston in 1940. *Below*, Centaurus CE4S No 19, as delivered to Hawker with nine exhaust manifolds grouped forward for the radial collector ring. (Photos: Hawker Aircraft Ltd.)

engine could be accommodated in a fairly respectable cowling whose cross-section was only seven per cent greater than that of the Sabre with chin radiator; moreover the absence of radiator and coolant system resulted in a marginally lower installed weight for the Centaurus.

Thus encouraged, Camm increased the number of design personnel from three to 18 working on the Centaurus installation by March 1941 in the experimental design offices at Claremont, near Esher. When the Vulture-Tornado programme was formally terminated work went ahead to produce a new Tornado airframe using components from the two "spare" unfinished aircraft produced by A. V. Roe and Co, and this was completed at Langley as *HG641*.

When *HG641* was first rolled out in October 1941, fitted with Centaurus IV (CE4S No. 19) driving a three-blade Rotol HX6/3 constant-speed propeller with small spinner, the otherwise tidy cowling lines were marred by a single large-diameter exhaust manifold extending from the collector ring in front of the cowling to below the port wing root, thereby passing the hot exhaust gases over the undercarriage fairing when retracted, a feature that stemmed directly from traditional practice adopted on twin-engine medium bombers! Situated between the landing wheel wells was a big intake fairing for the oil cooler and it was to be this excrescence that was to give most trouble. Engine cooling air, having passed between the cylinders discharged on either side of the fuselage, the flow being regulated by four controllable gills each side. The gun armament was omitted, although light ballast was necessary to contain the cg within design limits, and mainwheel D-doors were retained as having been included in the Avro-built components, and regarded as necessary owing to the hot exhaust passing over the landing gear. It is of interest to observe that the main landing gear oleo fairing on the port side did suffer buckling from the first flight on, but this was not considered to be of any consequence and the fairing remained distorted throughout the entire life of *HG641*— there was simply no Tornado replacement available.

Philip Lucas first flew the Centaurus Tornado on 23 October 1941 (and again four days later) at an

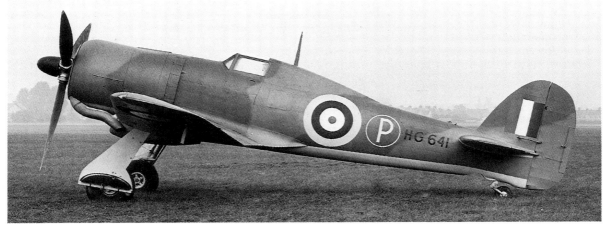

Employing redundant production components the Tornado HG641 was completed as a development aircraft for the Centaurus radial engine. These views show the aircraft in its initial form at Langley in October 1941 with the large external exhaust pipe and separately faired oil cooler air intake. (Photos: Author's Collection)

Instrument panel of the Centaurus Tornado HG641 showing the row of four cylinder head temperature gauges (cylinder numbers 1, 4, 7 and 11) arranged above the blind flying panel; oil and air temperature gauges are on the right. (Photo: Author's Collection)

all-up weight of 9,658 lb, contenting himself with brief handling tests. Flight Test Report No. L311 records that although the engine ran smoothly and that a speed of 345 mph TAS was recorded, the oil and engine temperatures remained continuously at their maximum permitted limit. This had been foreshadowed during engine trials at Filton, and Bristol had given a 25-hour clearance for flight and ground running in *HG641*, so that further flights were made on the 29th and 31st, during which Lucas flew the aircraft up to 378 mph TAS at 20,000 feet. As a result of these flights it became clear that the very high engine temperatures were affecting the engine bulkhead sealing and that carbon monoxide contamination of the cockpit was quite unacceptable—even with the side canopy panels wound fully down.

The aircraft was then grounded for a month while tunnel test results were examined to try to discover why the oil cooler was proving inadequate, and to instrument the cockpit to measure the CO contamination. It was discovered that the air pressure at the face of the cooler was less than 70 per cent of that achieved during the Bristol tests, suggesting that airflow instability under the engine cowling was reducing the ram effect on the oil cooler. Bearing in mind the short running clearance given to this engine, it was decided to do no more than cut back the cooler fairing lip for the time being, and two further flights (on 7 and 11 December) were made to record the airflow instability (using wooltufting) and pressures on the cooler face. The engine was then removed for return to Bristol, and *HG641* remained grounded awaiting a replacement engine.

★ ★ ★

It was at this time that reports started filtering

through from RAF Fighter Command of a new German radial engine fighter that was making its presence felt over Northern France. That the arrival in service of the Focke-Wulf Fw 190A came as a thoroughly unpleasant surprise cannot be denied. After all, the Spitfire VB had been introduced as Fighter Command's "standard" dogfighter during 1941, and had proved capable of holding its own against the Messerschmitt Bf 109F in most tactical situations. Moreover, with Typhoons only now just beginning to arrive on the first RAF squadrons and still some weeks away from achieving operational status, no answer could quickly be found to cope adequately with the new German fighters whose pilots were beginning to take a fast mounting toll of Spitfires. More will be told of this depressing situation in due course. Suffice to say at this point that it was not until 23 June 1942 that the RAF was presented with an intact example of the Fw 190,[3] and the secrets of its exceptionally efficient radial engine installation were laid bare. In all three critical regimes of difficulties being experienced by Hawker and Bristol— engine cooling, exhaust collection and discharge, and bulkhead design—the German fighter appeared to have achieved successful remedies. (Nor, for that matter, did the excellent all-round field of view afforded the German pilot go unremarked in Fighter Command circles.)

Broadly speaking the German BMW 801 installation incorporated an annular oil cooler situated round the inside of the engine cowling leading edge, and employed an engine-driven 12-blade fan immediately forward of the engine itself. Efficient airflow entry to this fan was assisted by a large spinner. Exhaust gases from each of the 14 cylinders were led *aft* through individual pipes to discharge from the sides of the fuselage forward of the cooling air exit louvres. An exceptionally clean cowling was thus achieved without recourse to external oil cooler and exhaust manifold.

To adopt such features in the Centaurus would clearly demand considerable modification both to engine and airframe, and such work was indeed put in hand forthwith where practical; however it was decided as an interim expedient to gain flight experience in the Tornado *HG641* employing no more than a modified engine cowling with a relocated oil cooler.

Thus modified *HG641* was airborne once more in the hands of Lucas on 23 December 1942, powered now by Centaurus IV (No. CE 27) driving a Rotol four-blade propeller, and at an all-up weight of 10,094 lb. Despite a most unsightly cowling shape with huge intake faired into the bottom of the nose, the flight reports indicated that a con-

---

[3] On that evening a Focke-Wulf Fw 190A–3, flown by Oberleutnant Arnim Faber, adjutant of *Jagdgeschwader 2 "Udet"*, landed at Pembrey in South Wales after combat with Spitfires, apparently in mistake for its base in Northern France.

siderable improvement in cooling efficiency had been achieved, although the increased drag cancelled out the benefit of slightly increased engine power. A total of 20 flights was all that was necessary for *HG641* to be checked out prior to delivery to Filton for a further extensive flying programme:

The Tornado HG641 at Langley in November 1942 with the Centaurus IV driving a Rotol four-blade propeller and with the oil cooler intake moved forward and faired into the engine cowling. Already however the examination of a Focke-Wulf Fw 190 had rendered this installation obsolete. Use of ortho film in the photo below highlights the skin distortion on the port undercarriage fairing. (Photos: Sydney Camm Collection)

Date	Trial	Engine		Propeller		AUW
23/24–12–42	First handling trials	Centaurus IV No 27		Rotol EH.263		10,094 lb
29–12–42	Cylinder temperatures	..	..	..	..	10,094 lb
29–12–42	Fuel consumption measurements	..	..	..	..	10,094 lb
30–12–42	CO contamination measurements	..	..	..	..	10,094 lb
2–1–43	Further CO measurements	..	..	..	..	10,094 lb
8/9–1–43	Performance, cylinder temperatures and fuel consumption (6 flights)	..	..	..	..	
9–1–43	Further CO measurements	..	..	..	..	10,094 lb
17–1–43	Propeller evaluation (2 flights)	..	..	..	..	10,094 lb
2–2–43	Final CO measurements with modified lower engine panel	..	..	..	..	10,100 lb
3–2–43	Full performance measurements; engine bay recordings; final check before delivery.	..	..	..	..	10,094 lb
	(Maximum level speed attained, 403 mph TAS at 22,000 feet)					

As far as is known *HG641* did not return to Langley other than for routine airframe inspection, but continued to provide important flight data on the Centaurus installation at Filton, information that continued to flow back to Hawker. Just three months later a new Hawker fighter, powered by a Centaurus, would take the air with an engine installation no less efficient than that of the redoubtable Focke-Wulf Fw 190.

3

THE SABRE
THAT RATTLED

It is necessary now to return to the beginning of the War to follow the early fortunes of Camm's second F.18/37 essay, the Napier Sabre-powered Typhoon, for the first prototype airframe had followed some three months behind that of the first Tornado. While this airframe remained in the experimental assembly shop in Canbury Park Road, Kingston, the second structure was moved to Claremont, near Esher, where it was set up on trestles in the entrance hall of the fine mansion whither the experimental design staff had repaired to escape possible German bombing attacks on Kingston.

Camm described the period between September and December 1939 as being one of "suck it and see" concerning the Typhoon. He confessed that, while the installation of the Vulture in the Tornado had posed few structural problems, the Sabre taxed the ingenuity of his design team to the utmost, not least when it became clear that, in addition to the much greater weight of the Sabre, the entire radiator and oil cooler would have to be moved forward to the nose. It was, however, by having a convenient space-frame structure on the premises that Camm's staff were able to "trot downstairs" to scheme up the necessary changes that resulted in the chin radiator design, drawings of which were passed to Canbury Park Road and Langley for modification of the first Tornado and completion of the first Typhoon. In the case of the Typhoon the change was complicated by the necessity to move the entire engine aft by nearly seven inches to keep the aircraft's cg within acceptable limits, this involving changing all engine bearer structures, secondary structural components and upper nose panels. It did, however,

The first Typhoon prototype, P5212, during manufacture in the small experimental assembly shop in Canbury Park Road. Recognisable by the triple exhaust manifolds, the aircraft is shown at the time the radiator was being relocated under the nose, indicated by the unpainted panels. (Photo: Hawker Aircraft Ltd, Neg No 93P dated 28 December 1939)

The enormous gun bay and generous access panels provided in the F.18/37 fighters. Shown here is the starboard wing of one of the prototypes with six Browning guns; as explained in the text, the gun bay was designed to accommodate three 20-mm cannon in each wing. (Photo: Author's Collection, dated February 1940)

simplify one aspect of the engine mounting: the Sabre's rear engine mounting pick-ups, which had previously been located forward of the main wing spar and therefore demanded a complex and weighty N-structure to cope with torsional stresses on the spar, could now engage directly with the spar attachments to the fuselage. This weight-saving of about 120 lb, and the general shortening of the nose structure, probably offset the added

forward moment about the cg of the newly-located radiator.

It has, however, been said that the mounting of the engine directly "on" the main spar attachment points may have accentuated the effects of un-damped engine vibration—for which the Sabre was to become notorious—and contributed a sec-ondary harmonic, via the inboard wing structure and rear spar, to the centre and rear fuselage. More of this in due course.

Thus, although final manufacturing drawings were delivered to the experimental shops for com-pletion of the first Typhoon prototype, *P5212*, as late as the last week in December 1939, the aircraft (whose Sabre had been delivered in November) was ready for flight on 23 February 1940. On that day Philip Lucas carried out taxying runs on the airfield at Langley as well as a single take-off "dummy run", confirming that with the small-chord fin and rudder the directional control was, like that of the Tornado, barely acceptable. Indeed he stated in his "flight" report that at an indicated speed of 70 mph—on the ground—he was applying full rudder and the aircraft was still turning steadily to port. Nevertheless, with about a dozen flights in the Tornado behind him, he ex-pressed himself happy to take the aircraft up, and on the following day he flew *P5212* for the first time. Contenting himself with a flight of no more than 20 minutes he climbed to 8,000 feet to carry out a number of stalls with wheels and flaps up and down. Engine temperatures, though high, remained just within the limits set by the Napier engineers. On the landing approach he found it necessary to maintain a fairly high throttle setting, as much to retain some rudder "feel" as to counter

These "roll-out" pictures of the first Typhoon P5212 depict a superbly finished aeroplane. Note the small vertical tail surfaces and the three long exhaust stacks on the side of the nose (these soon giving rise to cockpit contamination by exhaust seepage under the car doors). Wheel D-doors, radio and guns were not fitted at this stage. During its life this aircraft suffered no fewer than seventeen engine failures: (Photo: Sydney Camm Collection)

Views (*above* and *below*) which emphasise the very wide track undercarriage of the Typhoon as well as the early aircraft's extremely poor rearward field of vision from the cockpit. (Photos: Sydney Camm Collection, dated March 1940)

the very fast sink with full flap.

Overshadowing all other aspects of Lucas' flight report were his remarks on engine noise and vibration on which, despite prognostications by the Napier engineers, he vituperated with considerable asperity—something that was completely out of character with that superb pilot. The noise level in the cockpit, he reported, was at least 50 per cent higher than in the Tornado, and twice as high as in the Hurricane, while the vibration throughout at least the top 400 rpm of engine speed was such as to make it quite impossible to read any instruments on account of a severe low-frequency buzz throughout the cockpit.

In attempts to reduce these effects the mountings of the blind flying instrument panel were tightened slightly, thick bungee gromets were added to the pilot's seat mounting and the landing wheel spigots were shortened by $^3/_{16}$-inch (as it was thought that the retracted wheels were transmitting vibration from the front spar up through the cockpit structure).

As far as the noise level in the cockpit was concerned the Napier engineers expressed the opinion that this was probably as much due to the design of

the engine exhaust pipes (admitted as being unsuitable for the Typhoon) as to the numerous reciprocating movements inside the engine itself. On the important matters of engine and oil cooling Lucas stated that the flight had been too short and limited in scope to do more than note the maximum temperatures, but he suspected that prolonged and energetic manoeuvres might well be accompanied by dangerously high temperatures.

A week later Lucas went aloft in *P5212* for the second time, but this flight was cut short when a large panel on the side of the nose broke adrift from its fastenings and was carried away, prompting an immediate landing. Subsequent inspection failed to establish whether the fastenings had failed or whether one or more had not fully engaged when being closed before flight; however it was decided to change most of the nose panel fasteners to the positive "push-twist" type.

In March *P5212* flew a total of eight times and Lucas was able to report that the general vibration—at least such as was experienced by the pilot—had been reduced to a barely tolerable level, though still far too high. During the course of these flights he flew the Typhoon up to 376 mph

TAS and 20,400 feet, carried out low-g manoeuvres and took copious readings of engine temperatures. By the end of the last flight it was noted that the engine was throwing large quantities of oil, so much so that Lucas had to shut down the engine immediately after touchdown as the two oil temperature gauges had gone "off the clock"; as the engine was stopped the coolant header tank relief valve blew off violently. Moreover detailed examination of the throttle setting records during these flights indicated that considerable fuel flow fluctuations were occurring at constant engine speeds; indeed the overall fuel consumption was regarded as unacceptably high, something that had not been foreshadowed during bench running.

A new fuel pump with lower-geared drive and with simplified piping was introduced for a flight on 4 April and this gave some improvement. However, the Sabre (No. 95005) had now reached a total of 25 hours' running (including ten hours' flying time) and was due for strip examination. A new flight engine was then delivered with a set of modified mountings incorporating thick rubber composition pads in the front and ball-and-socket trunnions at the rear; this form of mounting had undergone tests at the Royal Aircraft Establishment whose engineers asked that a Vibrograph be flown in the Typhoon during the next series of flights.

Lucas was airborne once more in *P5212* on 7 May and reported that both engine and airframe vibration had been slightly reduced. On the next flight however, two days later, with the Vibrograph operating to record airframe vibration frequencies and while Lucas was flying at an indicated airspeed of 270 mph at 10,500 feet he experienced a "sudden lurch, followed by violent twitching of the controls"; the aircraft yawed sharply to the left and, on attempting to straighten up, the pilot became aware of a loud roar from just aft of his seat. Diagnosing some failure of the fuselage structure, he throttled back and started a careful letdown towards Langley. Without the benefit of radio (this had been removed to make space for the Vibrograph) he was unable to contact the ground and started a long, powered approach, using partial flap and only dropping the landing gear when he was certain of touching down on the airfield.

On examination of the Typhoon it was found that two members of the primary structure (the vertical tube at the rear of the left cockpit longeron, and the diagonal compression strut between the joint of this longeron and the top of the main fuselage frame aft of the cockpit) had failed, causing a buckling of the monocoque and progressive failure of the stressed skin down the left side of the fuselage aft of the cockpit as far as the wing trailing edge fillet. Fortunately distortion of the fuselage had been confined to the upper half of the structure, so that the tail controls in the lower section were not damaged. Nevertheless the damage disclosed signs of progressive further disintegration of the monocoque, and Lucas would have been entirely justified in abandoning the aircraft. Instead, by bringing the aircraft safely down with the Vibrograph records intact, he ensured that a minute examination could be carried out of the likely path of the destructive stresses.

No trace of the ensuing reports has been found, and it is only possible to read fairly brief references to the remedial actions taken in Camm's own records. Indeed it seems that the Typhoon's main structure was judged to be blameless, and that the failure had not occurred as the result of continuing fatigue in the structure. It was evidently concluded that vibration had caused stresses in the rear longeron joint (possibly by an interaction of severe vibration transmitted along the longeron and the vertical member) causing a crack to start, so that when eventual failure of the joint occurred the vertical member failed in compression and the diagonal member failed in tension; together these two failures caused a torsional failure of the monocoque on the starboard side of the cockpit. The answer clearly lay in identifying the nature of the vibrations (assumed all to emanate from the engine) and progressively reducing them, or at least damping them so that their effect could be dissipated without causing undue stress in the primary structure.

It was moreover concluded that the initial damage to the longeron joint had probably started during the first flights when Sabre No. 95009 was fitted with rigid mountings and had already come close to eventual failure when the improved mountings with the second engine were introduced. On this assumption it was also assumed, correctly as it transpired, that only local reinforcement of the longeron joint was necessary and, after repair of the fuselage, *P5212* was ready once more—with the second engine still fitted—for flight on 7 July. And on that day, as Lucas continued the programme to check fuel consumption, this engine itself failed, apparently as a result of an ignition fault, and once more *P5212* had to force land at Langley.

By August a third Sabre had been fitted, together with the enlarged fin and rudder (already flown on the Tornado) and Lucas began a series of flights to assess the various efforts being made to improve the Typhoon's directional control. (The Boscombe Down test pilot, Flight Lieutenant "Sammy" Wroath, who visited Claremont to "look over" the second Typhoon prototype on its trestles, recalls remarking on the thickness of the fin, within earshot of Camm. The great man turned slowly round and quietly asked "And how many aeroplanes have *you* designed?" Some months later, after increased fin chord and larger rudder had effectively transformed the Typhoon's direc-

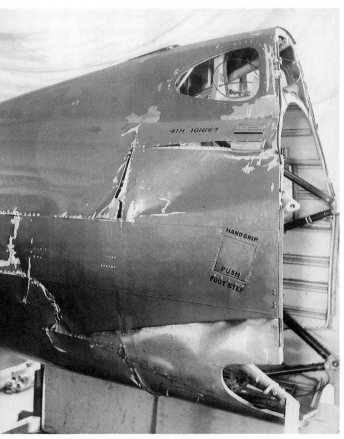

The prototype Typhoon's fuselage after structural failure on 9th May 1940. (Photo: Author's Collection)

tional control, Camm encountered Wroath once more and had the grace to remark "Ah yes, the pilot who spotted the thick fin!")

After confirming that the larger fin did indeed improve directional stability, Lucas continued to press for better directional control at low speed, the rudder being ineffective owing to the break-away of airflow behind the "thick fin", with the result that cords (of ever-increasing thickness) were taped to the trailing edge of the rudder to induce some measure of control sensitivity; in the end the rudder itself was also enlarged, as was the trim tab. However the Typhoon's powerful deter-mination to swing on take-off was not, and never could be overcome owing to the enormous torque, large diameter propeller and high engine speed; yet at least the very wide track undercarriage and much improved tail design enabled any average pilot, warned beforehand, to counter the incipient swing and to take off in a straight line.

The third Sabre engine ran out of flying hours without mishap at the end of August and a new engine, No. 95018, was introduced which incor-porated new exhaust stubs, six ejector stubs being employed on each side in place of the three long tapered pipes which Napier had considered "unsuitable".

The Battle of Britain

For two months the Battle of Britain had been raging over Southern England and, although there had been little disruption of the flying programme at Langley, the final outcome of the great battle had still to be decided and Fighter Command's ability to survive hung in the balance, its losses in pilots and aircraft being particularly heavy at the end of August; indeed for something like a fort-night those losses amounted to the equivalent of two entire squadrons every day.

In the face of such losses the Air Ministry was pressing all manner of expedients to maintain the flow of new pilots into Fighter Command, while the Ministry of Aircraft Production was at pains to ensure that nothing stood in the way of a smooth flow of Hurricanes and Spitfires from the aircraft factories, not to mention the vital Merlin engines from Rolls-Royce. Without victory in the Battle of Britain the Royal Air Force would never need the Typhoon . . .

Thus it was that Hawker was instructed to pro-ceed slowly with development of the new fighter, virtually all the manufacturing capacity at Langley being confined to Hurricane IIs, the first of which joined Fighter Command early in September. In the Royal Air Force it was already known that the Typhoon was beset with problems, and was still apparently dogged by trouble with the Sabre. The decision was therefore taken to submit the aircraft for an initial evaluation by the Aeroplane and Armament Experimental Establishment without further delay so that a decision might be reached on the future of the fighter. There is no doubt that scepticism existed at Air Staff level as to the need to introduce the Typhoon at all, much—and per-haps much too much—faith being placed in the abilities of the Hurricane II and Spitfire V, the latter still some months away from service.

However, due to the fact that only one Typhoon prototype existed and that that aeroplane seemed to display a voracious appetite for new engines, it was arranged for the evaluation to be undertaken at Langley, where full maintenance could be car-ried out by the manufacturers, rather than at Bos-combe Down—itself an operational fighter station involved in the Battle of Britain. Thus it was that during the autumn of 1940 Flight Lieutenant Sammy Wroath and Dr. George Hislop, the Minis-try's technical representative in charge of the Ty-phoon project, were detached from Boscombe Down to Langley for the evaluation. All things considered, these trials proceeded surprisingly well and this must speak volumes for the skills of Wroath (himself a superb pilot with considerable flying experience in the prototype and other early Hurricanes as well as the Spitfire) and the obvious rapport that must have existed with Lucas in whose

31

home he stayed during the Langley trials.[1] Sabre No. 95022 continued to run without serious mishap throughout the trials, and although Wroath confirmed that the engine vibration was still too severe and that the Typhoon's limited field of view for its pilot (like that in the Tornado) was probably unacceptable to the Service, he reported very favourably on the performance and handling of the aircraft in the air. Moreover, the high speeds achieved by the Typhoon, and the manoeuvrability of the aeroplane at these high speeds, obviously carried much weight with Fighter Command where, following the end of the Battle of Britain, Air Marshal Sir William Sholto Douglas had succeeded Air Chief Marshal Sir Hugh Dowding as Commander-in-Chief.

With victory gained in the great daylight battle the emphasis in RAF fighter operations began a profound shift from the traditional interception of hostile bombers in which a rapid rate of climb was demanded together with manoeuvrability at high altitude, towards high performance at low and medium altitude with heavy armament. This shift in fighter demands came about as a consequence of Fighter Command's gradual assumption of the offensive with the start of daylight cross-Channel sweeps whose ultimate aim would be to draw the *Luftwaffe* into the air over France where it could be brought to battle. On the face of it the Typhoon seemed ideally suited for such operations—if only the Sabre could be "smoothed out".

It must therefore stand largely to the credit of Wroath and Dr. Hislop that the Typhoon was reprieved and that as a result instructions were passed for the preparations to go ahead for its quantity production.

Be that as it may the whole pattern of operations undertaken by Fighter Command evolved only gradually, these operations being necessarily flown by the pilots in aircraft already available in service. At the beginning of 1941 these were the

---

[1] At the beginning of September it was announced that Philip Lucas had been awarded the George Medal—one of the first such awards to be made—for his action in saving the Typhoon prototype on 9th May. Lucas held the rank of Flight Lieutenant in the RAF's Reserve of Air Force Officers.

The second Typhoon prototype, P5216, during completion at Langley in December 1940, shortly after its move from Claremont, Esher. In this view the cockpit is open for normal access with starboard car door and overhead panel open. The photo gives an excellent impression of the compactness and complexity of the Sabre engine (whose front exhaust manifold has not been attached). (Photo: Hawker Aircraft Ltd., Neg No PRC8, dated 30 December 1940)

The second Typhoon prototype, P5216, at Langley. With its definitive gun armament of four 20-mm Hispano cannon the aircraft was in effect the prototype Typhoon Mark IB. (Photo: Author's Collection)

Hurricane I and II, and the Spitfire I, II and V, of which all but the early Hurricanes were capable of matching the German Messerschmitt Bf 109E. With the appearance in service of the Bf 109F early in 1941, only the Spitfire VB could be regarded as adequate and it was therefore this version on which Fighter Command opted to standardize. It came to be generally regarded as the most pleasant to fly of all Spitfires, with a good turn of speed and manoeuvrability at heights of around 20,000 feet; it possessed an armament of two 20-mm cannon and four machine guns and, provided that combat could be confined to that altitude or above, the average Fighter Command squadron pilot held his own with the German fighters. When, however, the Spitfires were sent out as close escort for bombing raids by Blenheims and other RAF light and medium bombers—the very operations which tended to attract the *Luftwaffe* into the air—the Spitfires were often at a considerable disadvantage, frequently being attacked from above and having to stay close to the bombers which were limited to operating between 10,000 and 15,000 feet. Thus was introduced the "top cover", comprising one or two squadrons of Spitfires whose pilots were briefed to fly well above the bombers to guard against attack from above. This in turn led to the creation of the famous "Spitfire Wings" which, often flying as many as 60 or more aircraft, achieved considerable success during the first nine months of 1941, in the event that German fighters came up to intercept. Indeed it has been said that in such combats the nimble Spitfire VBs and Bf 109Fs were the last true "dogfighters" cast in the traditional mould.

More will be said about the development of these cross-Channel operations in the following chapters. Suffice it to say here that the gradual change in air fighting tactics that came about in 1941 imposed some difficulty in deciding exactly how the Typhoon would fit into Fighter Command operations, while a growing suspicion among Spitfire pilots that the Typhoon was to be developed as the principal "cross-Channel" dogfighter at the expense of the Spitfire sowed the seeds of opposition to the Hawker fighter that was to threaten its continuation one year hence.

★   ★   ★

Although production of the Hurricane was still in full swing at Gloster Aircraft Company's Brockworth factory early in 1941, the floor space formerly occupied by the Hawker Henley production line was now set aside for preliminary component manufacture of the Typhoon as part of the production dispersal of Hawker aircraft elsewhere in the Hawker Siddeley Group factories (Gloster having no aircraft of its own approaching the production stage). In January that year the first production jigs were assembled and a start was made to sub-contract major component manufacture.

On the other hand Napier had produced no more than about 26 Sabre engines by that month, of which about half had been cleared for flight—and none of these could be regarded as "production" engines.

Thus far *P5212* had remained the only Typhoon to have flown, and in February was fitted with its sixth engine (No. 95022) with "fully-flexible" mountings and dynamically-balanced crankshafts, modifications that produced a marked reduction in airframe vibration—and, incidentally, a considerable improvement in engine reliability. Attention turned to investigating whether a Rotol propeller produced a further reduction in vibration compared with the de Havilland Hydromatic airscrew, but without significant improvement.

On 3 May, however, the second Typhoon prototype, *P5216* (which had stood in Claremont's entrance hall for so long), was flown, the first of the F.18/37 prototypes with an armament of four 20-mm Hispano Mark I cannon. Compared with *P5212* with armament ballast at an all-up weight of 10,600 lb, the new prototype weighed 10,735 lb, and was fitted with Sabre No. 95023, the first of the flight engines representative of the proposed production version. Fewer than half a dozen flights were made in *P5216* before the next milestone was

Two views of the first Typhoon, P5212, after the commencement of the "tidying-up" development; rear quarterlight panels have been added and, in the picture on the right (taken at Boscombe Down) the aircraft features tailwheel doors—not adopted until the arrival of the Tempest. (Photos: Author's Collection)

reached when, on 27 May, Michael Daunt at Brockworth made the first flight of the first production Typhoon *R7576*, an astonishing feat of organization by those at Glosters.

It should, however, be emphasized that the first 30 or so Typhoons produced at Brockworth, armed with twelve 0.303-in Browning machine guns and thereafter termed Mark IA Typhoons, were little more than replicas of the first prototype *P5212*; the first two production aircraft were moreover powered by Sabre engines with the "semi-flexible" mountings and statically-balanced crankshafts, designated Sabre Is (Nos. S45 and S49 respectively). These two Typhoons, *R7576* and *R7577*, therefore effectively constituted prototypes and accordingly joined *P5212* and *P5216* at Langley in the flight development programme; they would in due course be joined by many others.

At this point Lucas was joined by Kenneth Seth-Smith and Hubert Broad in flying the Typhoon at Langley, and Bill Humble shortly afterwards. All three had been engaged in the Hurricane's flight development, but as RAF pilots were now being attached to Hawker to participate in this work, it was felt that the experienced test pilots should assume some of the tremendous burden that had hitherto fallen on Lucas; Seth-Smith had in any case been flying the Tornado, in addition to Hurricanes, for some months.

Tidying up the Typhoon

Now that an increasing number of Typhoons was becoming available for development work at Langley a host of modifications could be pursued to counter the wide-ranging criticisms levelled at the aircraft, of which the most pressing was unquestionably improvement of the pilot's view from the cockpit. It is probably logical here to describe briefly the Typhoon's structure in the vicinity of the cockpit, as the form of fuselage structure selected for this part of the fuselage dictated the entire design of the cockpit, its canopy and the aft hood fairing. Because of this any significant

change in the canopy and aft fairing to provide better field of vision for the pilot would involve fundamental structural changes.

The Typhoon's fuselage may be likened superficially to the body of an open sports car in which all fore and aft load stresses are carried by the lower body structure, chassis or frame, there being no permanent upper door frames, windscreen pillars and hood structure through which to acquire body stiffness. In the Typhoon all fore and aft loads were transmitted through the four fore-and-aft longerons from the engine and structure forward of the cockpit to the main fuselage frame immediately aft of the cockpit, to which the rear fuselage monocoque was attached. The upper longerons, instead of running at about cockpit sill level, passed from front to rear about 18 inches below sill level to allow for provision of "car doors" on each side of the fuselage; this commonly-used description of the doors was entirely apt in that they were hinged on their forward edge, incorporated a window frame as well as wind-down transparent panels and were opened and closed by a levered handle on the outside of the fuselage; moreover the doors were "floating" structures in that, when closed, they contributed no significant strength to the fuselage. For this reason the windscreen and quarterlight frames had to constitute an integrally stiff—indeed very strong—structure without any fore-and-aft support by a load-bearing canopy. An overhead trans-

The first Typhoon four-cannon installation destined for the prototype P5216. (Photo: Hawker, Neg No 297 dated 6 April 1941)

The trial installation of the Scheme B cockpit canopy was carried out on a damaged Typhoon R7646, shown above during repair at Langley. *Below*, the completed aircraft on the airfield during the spring of 1942 before the appearance of the Typhoon's characteristic recognition stripes under the wings. (Photos: Author's Collection)

parent panel was hinged along the upper line of the port car door, so that normal entry to and exit from the cockpit was invariably through the starboard door, with the overhead panel hinged up. General canopy stiffness was achieved when both doors and the overhead panel were secured shut, but it must be emphasized that no structural loads were carried by these components. The provision of two doors, both of which were jettisonable, when only one was normally used, was to assist in abandoning the aircraft in an emergency either in the air or in the event of overturning on the ground.

Aft of the pilot's seat and back armour the entire rear fuselage and tail structure loads were carried by a substantial fuselage frame to whose circumference were attached a number of load-bearing members bolted to the rear ends of the four longerons already mentioned. Because these members did not form the exterior contours of the fairing behind the cockpit canopy, peripheral rigidity of this fairing was provided by semi-monocoque skin-

ning which had not allowed for any transparent panels aft of the car-door frame. Thus the pilot was unable to see rearwards from the "3-o'clock" to "9-o'clock" hemisphere without leaning forward and peering over his shoulder. As such one could hardly refer to it as "rearward vision" for the fighter pilot, particularly in an energetic dogfight.[2]

The most urgent need therefore was to introduce a local modification that could be incorporated in the Typhoon airframes already nearing

---

[2] One is inclined to suggest that, in an exceptionally long line of excellent fighters, almost all of which came to be regarded by those who flew them as being "pilots' aeroplanes"—for Camm forever regarded the human occupant of his aircraft as a paramount consideration—the Typhoon's cockpit was his most notorious design lapse. It came about in all likelihood following early criticism of the Hurricane's canopy (particularly by his own Chief Test Pilot, George Bulman—who disliked enclosed canopies in any case), a canopy that was not necessarily unsatisfactory by the standards of 1935, and one that Camm was never permitted the time in which to improve, such was the urgency to produce Hurricanes.

completion at Brockworth without in any way altering their primary structure, and it was to an earlier expedient that the designers turned. After the second flight by *P5212* in February 1940 a pair of rear quarterlights had been cut in the monocoque immediately aft of the cabin doors, with perspex panels secured by locally-applied internal stiffening strips riveted to the inside of the skin. These afforded some degree of rearward vision but, following the structural failure which almost resulted in the loss of *P5212*, it had been decided to discard the quarterlights in case these had contributed to the progressive tearing of the skin. Now, however, it was concluded that the provision of properly stiffened quarterlights could in no way endanger the monocoque, and modification drawings were prepared and a trial installation "checked out" in *P5212* on 26th June. It was acknowledged that this could only be a temporary expedient, but would at least enable the first few aircraft to be delivered to the RAF when otherwise cleared for service. In the meantime a more elaborate modification, involving entirely new contours in the rear fuselage, was put in hand. The new canopy would not appear in production aircraft for a further nine months.

In June 1941 the first few Sabre II engines were completed, these being delivered direct to Brockworth where it was found that a new crop of problems with the oil system had arisen. Two of the prototype engines, Nos. 95018 and 95026, were therefore modified and fitted in *P5212* and *P5216* to develop an improved oil cooling system, using various cone fairings in the nose intake to give improved ram effect on the face of the cooler.

By the end of July the production Typhoon IA *R7577* had been brought up to the latest modification standard, with rear quarterlights, Sabre II No 177, new-pattern car doors (produced by Fox & Nicholls), pressurized oil system with large intake cone and enlarged rudder trim tab with thick trailing edge cord. The engine itself had been cleared to 50 hours between major inspections and was giving rather better vibration results on the Vibrograph. A series of "performance flights" was made during August by Lucas and Seth-Smith and, confirmed by Boscombe Down pilots, these returned the following figures: time to 20,000 feet, 7.1 minutes; maximum level speeds of 402 mph TAS at 20,400 feet in FS gear, and 396 mph TAS at 17,400 feet in MS gear; rate of roll (50-pound stick force) at 10,000 feet at 310 mph TAS, 50 degrees per second. Gun firing was carried out at 10,000, 20,000 and 25,000 feet, but at the latter height stoppages due to gun bay icing were experienced in all but four guns.

On the basis of these figures the Typhoon IA was given an initial Service clearance and the first eight production aircraft were delivered to No. 13 Maintenance Unit at the beginning of September

for installation of Service radio and IFF equipment; they were then returned to Brockworth for examination of the gun-bay heating trunk.

A naval Typhoon?

As long ago as 1939 the Air Ministry had begun attending to the matter of replacements for the Fleet Air Arm's Blackburn Skua, Gloster Sea Gladiator and Fairey Fulmar shipborne fighters, an extraordinarily belated recognition of the obsolescence of these aircraft whose performance was such that they would have been hard-pressed to match the latest German bombers. Not yet fully aware of the penalties to be paid in performance by demanding accommodation for the second crew member in single-engine fighters, the Air Ministry circulated two Specifications to the aircraft industry, N.8/39 and N.9/39, calling for two two-seat naval interceptors, the former with a wing-mounted armament of four 20-mm cannon and the latter with a four-gun dorsal turret mounting machine-guns.

When first examined by Camm's small project team it was realized that no suitable powerplant yet existed capable of dragging an aeroplane such as those envisaged from a carrier deck—with all the naval accoutrements demanded—and producing a fighter-like performance, and Camm expressed no interest. A very half-hearted attempt was made to investigate a development of the Hotspur turret fighter with Sabre engine and folding wings, but Camm quickly ordered this work to be discontinued.

The two Specifications met with similar response elsewhere, but the Royal Navy persisted in its demand for a second crew member in one of the Requirements, and N.9/39 was re-issued to become N.5/40, for which the Fairey Firefly two-seater with four-cannon wing became the successful contender; though this aeroplane persisted in service, in its later versions, until the 1950s it did little more than perpetuate the age-old formula of the Fairey Fulmar—itself generally regarded as a 'white-knuckle' Battle.

N.8/39 was however re-written as N.11/40 by eliminating the second crew member, a step that re-awakened interest by Camm's designers who were instructed to look at the possibility of developing a folding-wing version of the Typhoon, retaining the Sabre, adding arrester gear and extending the wings to permit inclusion of much larger landing flaps and additional fuel to meet the naval range requirements. Considerable design work was done on this project, designated the Hawker P.1009, and various mock-ups of the wing arrangement were completed to arrive at a suitable flap design which, because of the wing-fold, would have to extend to six separate sections. A reduced-width wing centre-section was incorporated with

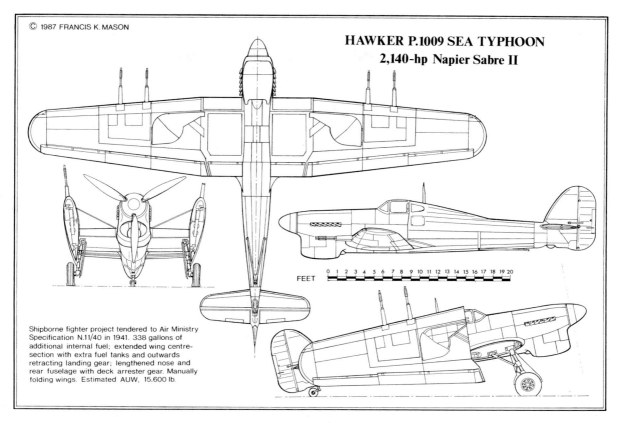

© 1987 FRANCIS K. MASON

HAWKER P.1009 SEA TYPHOON
2,140-hp Napier Sabre II

Shipborne fighter project tendered to Air Ministry
Specification N.11/40 in 1941. 338 gallons of
additional internal fuel; extended wing centre-
section with extra fuel tanks and outwards
retracting landing gear; lengthened nose and
rear fuselage with deck arrester gear. Manually
folding wings. Estimated AUW, 15,600 lb.

FEET 0 1 2 3 4 5 6 7 8 9 10 11 12 13 14 15 16 17 18 19 20

the necessary long-stroke landing gear units retracting outwards so as to leave the deep-section
wing roots available for fuel tanks. By employing
standard Typhoon outer wings the existing cannon
bays for up to six cannon (as in Camm's F.18/37
designs) were retained, the greater armament op-
tion being offered, and the overall wing span of 49
ft 7 in remained within the maximum permitted in
the Specification of 50 feet (dictated by carrier lift
size). Powered by the second-stage Sabre OD.45
project (later to become the 2,300-hp Sabre III),
the P.1009 was calculated to have a maximum
speed of 378 mph at 15,000 feet and a normal range
of 900 miles at 260 mph at 12,500 feet.

Although Camm insisted that a full design tender be submitted in February 1941, he was aware
that the Admiralty was already vacillating over the
requirements, particularly when it seemed that the
Hurricane might well suffice for naval fighter
needs for the foreseeable future—at a fraction of
the cost and timescale—and would be capable of
operation from the much smaller carriers being
favoured by the Admiralty after the loss of several
fleet carriers early in the War.

In the event a design from Blackburn (a traditional naval aircraft contractor) was ordered,
and this became the Firebrand. The Sea Hurricane
indeed remained in service until the end of the
War, being joined by the Seafire in 1943, with the
result that, following allocation of all Sabre engine
production to the Hawker Typhoon and Tempest,

the Firebrand did not join the Royal Navy in full
squadron service until September 1945—and then
as a Centaurus-powered single-seat torpedo-carry-
ing "fighter".

The P.1109 project intruded on the Typhoon
programme in an isolated instance. When sub-
mitting the N.11/40 design tender early in 1941
Camm had suggested flying as a trial installation in
P5212 wings extended to about 44 feet span to
investigate the effect on take-off and landing in the
light of the naval requirements. The extended
wing tips and ailerons were constructed but had to
await an opportunity to fly them. That chance
arose in October when *P5216* was grounded while
enlarged rear-view quarterlights were being incorporated, and it was felt that the extended wing tips
could be flown simultaneously; the first flight in
this configuration was made on 9 November. The
original purpose of the trial had, however, lapsed
and it was decided to investigate any significant
improvement in the high altitude performance resulting from the extended wings. Unfortunately,
although the wings continued to be flown until
February 1942, the engine (No. 95018, still fitted)
was beginning to give considerable power fluctuations above 20,000 feet and any accurate performance measurements were impossible. Several
pilots who flew *P5216* during this period considered the larger ailerons to give much improved
control and roll performance, but such opinions
remained academic and the trial was discontinued.

⋆   ⋆   ⋆

As told in the following Chapter the Typhoon started delivery to the first Royal Air Force Squadron, No. 56 at Duxford, in September 1941. However, bearing in mind that, despite the preliminary Service clearance just given to the fighter, the Typhoon was still subject of some "tidying up"—just how much remained to be seen—and Fighter Command's estimate of no more than three months for the Squadron to become fully operational on the aircraft was optimistic to say the least.

The gun bay heating problem was fairly simply overcome, or so it was thought, by increasing the hot gas mass flow from the engine bay by use of a larger diameter gas trunk. This involved enlarging the holes in the bulkhead between engine and cockpit, something that could be carried out on the airframes while standing in their jigs at Brockworth, and was followed by similar remedial action on the test Typhoons at Langley.

The first indication that all was not well was manifest in November when Duxford returned an aircraft, *R7591*, to Langley with a report that pilots had complained of severe nausea caused it was thought by inhaling "engine fumes". Lucas accordingly flew the aircraft with a CO analyser and confirmed that the level of contamination was far above the level regarded as acceptable.

Although it was immediately suspected that the enlarged gun heating trunk was probably responsible, an immediate check of all aircraft failed to disclose any leaks; however Seth-Smith, in one of his flight reports, suggested that while the trunk itself might remain intact, repeated flights at high intensity—as would be expected on an RAF squadron—might, because of prolonged engine vibration, be causing the sealant in the bulkhead to distort, thereby allowing engine gases to seep into the cockpit. Such a leak might not be detectable if checked when the engine was cold.

At about the same time Napier reported high levels of CO contamination in one of its early Typhoons—an aircraft not fitted with guns nor a gun-bay heating trunk! The engineers had reached the conclusion that the short engine exhaust stubs were responsible and that exhaust gases were seeping into the cockpit, probably at the base of the starboard door. To overcome this a set of exhaust stubs, extended laterally inboard of the junction branch by four inches, had been bench tested and another set would be delivered to Langley for flight test in a standard production aircraft. In the meantime the RAF was warned to check to ensure that the starboard door (the one in constant use) fitted snugly, to inspect the sealant on the front bulkhead when the engine was hot to ensure the heating trunk remained tight, and suggested that the port car door window be left partially open.

Duxford itself issued an order for all pilots to breathe oxygen throughout all flights.

One other modification was being introduced in Typhoons leaving Brockworth from mid-November onwards with the re-design of the pilot's seat mounting. This had hitherto been attached (semi-rigidly with bungee gromets) to a pair of cantilever arms mounted on a cross-member between the longerons on either side of the cockpit—a very long-established method of mounting pilots' seats in British fighters, though without the bungee gromets. It had been this attachment via the longerons on the Typhoon prototype that had caused Lucas so much discomfort in the early days, and more than a dozen different seat mountings had been tried at Langley in continuing efforts to alleviate the pilots' discomfort. This proved rather more complicated than it appeared at first glance owing to the different vibration frequencies being transmitted through the structure—and it was even established that pilots of different weights would experience different vibration frequencies. The modification that appeared to provide the least discomfort—certainly among the pilots of lesser physical stature—employed the mounting of a pair of twin vertical struts capable of parallel movement, damped by a number of softer bungee gromets than previously used. (A fully-sprung seat mounting had been evaluated, but this had caused neck injury to an RAF test pilot when the seat "bottomed" during a heavy landing; the mounting would re-appear in a modified form some months later.)

One more event occurred before the end of 1941 worth recording. This was the completion of the first Langley-built production Typhoon, again a Mark IA, *R8198*. It was the first of a batch of just 15 aircraft that had been laid down in the previous year with the intention of employing them in the development programme at Langley, leaving Brockworth free to concentrate wholly on standard production exclusively for the RAF. The speed with which Gloster had completed its production line and produced the first Typhoons had naturally resulted in early aircraft being employed at Langley for development purposes, and this resulted in a slow-down in the completion of the Langley-built Typhoons owing to the introduction of modifications which were more relevant to the main production line.

As will be shown in the following Chapter, the arrival over France of the new German Focke-Wulf Fw 190A fighter caused some anxiety in Fighter Command such that Gloster was instructed to be ready to increase its rate of delivery of Typhoons at short notice. This instruction acted as a spur to Hawker to complete the programme of "tidying up"—not so much by addressing itself to minor, uncured ailments but to the process of standardizing the 60-odd aircraft distributed between three Maintenance Units, Duxford and Brockworth—scarcely any two of which could be regarded as of common modification standard.

The first step taken was to create what came to be known as Purgatory Stores, the first being logically situated at Duxford, through which the aircraft at the most advanced modification standard would be passed so that the smaller number of modifications necessary could be completed quickly and with the least disruption to Service operations. Next, all completed Typhoons at Brockworth were to be quickly flown to the Maintenance Units and advanced as far as modification kits allowed and, finally, the production line at Brockworth was to be halted until all new aircraft could be completed to the latest modification standard. In the meantime the experimental flight department at Langley, using the locally manufactured production Typhoons, evolved a programme of "special production tests"—in effect a series of carefully programmed flights to check all aspects of the Typhoon, its structural integrity, performance, use of armament and, above all, freedom from cockpit contamination by carbon monoxide. These checks were what one would consider as constituting the normal function of the routine production flying by the manufacturers' test pilots on the completion of each aircraft; however, such had been the proliferation of modifications that a more elaborate check programme had to be evolved, particularly as many of the Typhoons had completed a surprisingly large number of flying hours—with and without some of the more important modifications incorporated. In the event Gloster was able to revert to the standard production flight test programme once its assembly line restarted.

What had happened of course was that the speed and efficiency with which Gloster had managed to build the first 60 Typhoons had in fact resulted in aircraft finding their way to all manner of "customers" (including Boscombe Down, Farnborough and Napier, as well as various destinations within the RAF) without being subject of a conventional, centralized modification authority. Henceforth that authority would be centred on Brockworth through the MUs and eventually to a Typhoon Pool at Duxford, it being intended that this RAF station would become the location at which all new Typhoon squadrons would receive their conversion training or re-equipment for the foreseeable future.

Such was the efficiency with which these various measures took effect that not more than three days passed before the Brockworth production line was re-started, while pilots of the Air Transport Auxiliary cleared the park of completed aircraft at the Gloster factory in just two days.

It is not proposed to dwell further on the wide range of relatively minor improvements (one per-

Four views of the Hawker-built Typhoon IB, R8224; the aircraft, photographed in November 1942, retains the white nose (one of the experimental recognition schemes investigated in the previous summer) and features the four-inch extended exhaust stubs. (Photos: Sydney Camm Collection)

haps should say "perfection of improvements" already commenced) that continued to occupy the manufacturers of the Typhoon during the next two years. By March the aircraft was performing at least up to design expectations, serviceability rates were good and improving (within the between-overhaul limit—as yet only 50 hours—on the Sabre, imposed by the manufacturer), and the first four-cannon Typhoon IBs had already passed through the MUs on their way to the squadrons.

One remaining major crisis now occurred. This broke early in 1942 with reports, which first arrived via Brockworth at Langley from two Maintenance Units, that two (or possibly three) Typhoons had suffered fatal flying accidents in circumstances which suggested that sudden and catastrophic structural failure had occurred, allowing the pilot no time either to transmit an emergency message or to abandon the aircraft. From a superficial examination of the remains of the aircraft it was suspected that in each case the aircraft's rear fuselage structure had failed, causing the entire tail unit to become detached in flight. In such an event the main part of the aircraft would, with the engine running, immediately become transformed into a violently spinning body, pitching and rolling and gradually disintegrating as it fell to earth; in each instance fire had consumed this wreckage on hitting the ground. Only the fact that the empennage, in each case found to have fallen about half a mile away, was unburned gave the clue to the cause of the accidents.

When, shortly afterwards, two of Duxford's Typhoons appeared to have suffered almost identical catastrophe, Camm himself at once ordered new calculations to be undertaken by his Stress Office to discover whether indeed any conceivable flight loads experienced by a Typhoon performing normal manoeuvres (including recovery from a full-throttle dive from maximum permitted altitude) could possibly have caused failure of the rear fuselage structure. On being assured that this was not so, he obtained permission for a member of the experimental department to examine all wreckage—and particularly the points of failure in the unburned tail units.

The process of investigation which lasted from the end of April 1942 until about October 1943 of these most disturbing accidents was to be one that was dogged at the outset by misunderstanding and a lack of lucid communication between Service and manufacturer. Yet, after being pursued with the utmost care and painstaking research and test by Hawker and RAE pilots—frequently in conditions of utmost personal hazard—the Typhoon emerged as a superb aircraft whose operating flight envelope embraced parameters far in advance of current service ground attack aircraft, and unquestionably contributed in no small measure to the emergence of the Tempest as the best Allied single-seat fighter of the War.

To begin with, about the only known factor common in all instances of the recent spate of accidents (other than those following engine failure) was that structural failure had occurred at the

The late Philip Edward Gerald Sayer.

rear fuselage transport joint. This failure was initially diagnosed as having occurred as the result of fatigue and not, as suggested by the Service, from an inherent structural weakness of the fuselage, although it was accepted that the transport joint *was* the "least strong" area of the structure while being perfectly capable of accommodating any conceivable flight load imposed during normal flight manoeuvres.

It was "Gerry" Sayer, Gloster's Chief Test Pilot, who first suggested that engine-induced vibration might be the cause of fatigue failure, for it was well known that "1P" oscillations (that is, of propeller-speed frequency) was present in the top pair of longerons; this had to some extent been reduced by modified engine mountings, while improved seat mounting had reduced pilot discomfort. Sayer believed that it was possible that the residual vibration could well be causing progressive deterioration of the rear transport joint. As a result of this hypothesis an interim measure, that of riveting a single continuous steel strip round the transport joint, was adopted as being the simplest expedient.

This explanation did not however fully satisfy some members of the staff of Hawker's experimental department, among them Philip Lucas. For one thing it was known that the Typhoon tail controls were not yet entirely satisfactory, and the rudder control in particular was under investigation (early Typhoons had possessed external horn balancing, and this was superseded by internal mass balancing in July 1942). It was known that vibration had been caused by inadequate rudder balancing and the suspicion lurked that this could have contributed to some form of fatigue failure of the transport joint. Such suspicions were expressed in a number of flight reports raised in July.

When, however, a fatal accident occurred in August to a Hawker-flown Typhoon (killing K. G. Seth-Smith, see page 43), which incorporated the improved rudder mass balance, further investigation led to the discovery that the aircraft had suffered a fatigue failure of the *elevator* mass balance mounting bracket. The question was now posed: How had such fatigue in a "detached" component been induced? Engine vibration was considered unlikely. Certainly if it could be established that vibration, however caused, had resulted in the failure of the bracket, this would certainly account for the catastrophic tail breakage; an unbalanced control surface would cause uncontrollable flutter, in turn imposing enormous loads on the entire tail unit which would almost certainly break off at the weakest point—the transport joint.

Investigation now centred upon the elevators, their mounting and their control circuits. As an immediate make-shift remedy a modification was introduced to strengthen considerably the elevator mass balance bracket, though it was accepted that this could only be an interim measure.

In a lengthy programme aimed at all-round improvement in longitudinal control and stability, the first step taken was to re-tension the elevator control circuit by adopting needle bearings in the elevator countershaft; this enabled the circuit tension to be increased, thereby eliminating control backlash (present in virtually all fighter aircraft up to that time) without increasing control friction.

Flight report No. L 773 contains the significant remark by Lucas "that the controls will never be completely satisfactory until fitted throughout with needle or ball bearings".

An inter-relation was soon confirmed between the elevator mass balance moment and the aircraft's tendency to tighten up in a turn (a characteristic which the Typhoon displayed at about $4\frac{1}{2}$g), and it was therefore decided to perform a detailed analysis of flight results using different elevator mass balance weights and varying inertia weights applied to the control column. By July 1943 tests on Typhoon *EK229* showed that, with nose-balanced elevators and an 8-lb inertia weight on the control column, turns up to 5 g could be carried out, while strain gauge measurements on the elevator countershaft and transport joint indicated "oscillatory stresses that were in no way excessive".

The ultimate solution, arrived at in October 1943 in concert with the RAE at Farnborough, was to employ a 16-lb control column inertia weight, 8-lb elevator mass balance—retaining the reinforced mounting bracket—changing the geared balance tab to an ordinary adjustable trimming tab and removing the damping cords on the trailing edge of the rudder. The needle bearings had of course been introduced throughout the elevator control circuit.

In performance and handling tests—including diving trials, with dives at well over 500 mph by Squadron Leader R. P. Beamont, while with Hawker, "to see if the tail came off"—it was found that up to $6\frac{1}{2}$ g turns could be pulled at 5,000 feet without any tendency to tighten up, while strain gauge measurements recorded in harsh dive recov-

A "tidied-up" Typhoon IB, EK122, at Langley in the late summer of 1942. It features the small perspex fairing over a rear view mirror on the Scheme B canopy as well as faired cannon barrels; the latter modification was undertaken simultaneously by Hawker and the Service which had suggested employing the same fairings as used on the Spitfire VB, although in production an improved design was developed. (Photo: Hawker Aircraft Ltd., Neg No TYG4)

ery at the highest attainable speeds showed no excessive loads in the elevator mountings or transport joint. These modifications came to be included in all "MN" and later Typhoon batches, and were retrospectively incorporated in earlier aircraft. (According to Service Department records no Typhoon incorporating the modifications ever suffered tail breakage; even following the reinforcement of the elevator balance brackets in the autumn of 1942 diagnosis of the cause of five known instances of tail breakages showed the presence of unrelated factors such as undetected battle damage, incorrectly rigged control circuits and, in one case, a sheared elevator countershaft.)

That the Typhoon was the victim of this design weakness—for it cannot conceivably be described otherwise, however small the offending component may have been—was unfortunate indeed. It must, nevertheless, be seen in the context of what the aeroplane represented, the first "400-mph" fighter in the RAF, and one that was expected to do what a 300-mph aircraft could do, and more. The very nature of the Typhoon, with its big engine, thick wings, high power-loading and high performance represented an unprecedented advance in operational potential, while demands for increasing loads and, by implication in-flight loading, broke new ground in fighter design. It was the nature of these increasing demands—in particular those associated with the punishing ground attack rôle, itself a relatively new function of fighters—that demanded the prolonged programme to perfect the Typhoon's structural integrity.

Ground attack duties

If this chapter has hitherto appeared to the reader as a mournful commentary of unremitting setback and tragedy, suggesting that the Typhoon and its Sabre engine were fundamentally unsound, this view was not now shared by those in Fighter Command headquarters who were intent on acquiring the Typhoon in large numbers, and quickly. In wartime little energy is spared for retrospective analysis of mistakes and apportioning of blame for them, but simply to rectify any difficult situation as quickly as possible with the resources available. Of course it can now be seen that the entire F.18/37 fighter project had been accelerated to such an extent that development of the powerplant could not possibly keep pace with that of the airframe and that, if indeed the Sabre had emerged as a conventional, quietly performing yet immensely powerful engine, the Typhoon would have in all likelihood progressed through its development phases and passed into RAF service with little comment. It was no doubt the urgency to acquire the Typhoon, which began to be expressed towards the end of 1941, that focussed attention on the apparently never-ending run of difficulties with

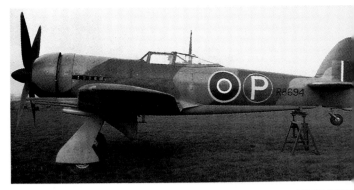

In an attempt to achieve improved engine cooling efficiency in the Sabre engine, Napier modified the early Typhoon, R8694, to incorporate an annular radiator with front fan. Aerodynamic drag was not much greater than that of the standard Typhoon and the company persisted with their efforts for almost three years. (Photos: D. Napier & Sons)

the aircraft.

Mistakes had certainly been made, of which the most serious was unquestionably the original reluctance to order more than a pair of Typhoon prototypes, of which only one had been pursued with any real sense of urgency. The contract calling for 15 Langley "production" aircraft was, in particular, badly administered by the Air Ministry and perhaps unimaginatively interpreted by the manufacturers themselves. Those aeroplanes were correctly intended to be what would normally be regarded as "pre-production" Typhoons, and should have started appearing on the flight line at Langley before the end of 1940, and could probably have done so if the "Hurricanes and Spitfires at any cost" policy been rescinded by Fighter Command as soon as the immediate threat of invasion passed in September that year. (It may be asked, if Gloster managed to erect an entire Typhoon production line in four months, could not Hawker have contrived to produce just 15 aircraft in three?) As it was, the second Typhoon prototype flew about a year after the first, and when *P5212* was so frequently rendered earthbound in 1940, not one Typhoon had been available for flight, a situation that remained virtually unchanged up to the moment when the Gloster-built "production" aircraft started streaming from the factory. When the Focke-Wulf Fw 190 started its depredations over the Channel—while so many "400-mph Typhoons" stood around awaiting clearance for active service—who can blame those at Fighter Command for their impatience to get their hands on the aircraft?

If the Typhoon constituted something of an answer to the low-flying Fw 190A fighter-bombers, which started their low-level attacks on Southern England in 1942, the presence of the new British fighters in No. 11 Group encouraged an investigation by RAF pilots—notably by Squadron Leader R. P. Beamont—into an offensive rôle by the Typhoon at low level, both by day and night. And it was largely thanks to these early operations by No. 609 Squadron, for which the Typhoon was found to be particularly suitable, that a shift of emphasis in its primary rôle gradually came about. This had started with instructions to Langley to begin investigations as to the fighter's ability to carry offensive armament in addition to the now-standard Mark IB's four cannon.

The flight programme, begun in June 1942, embraced certain clearly defined stages of investigation:

1. Diving trials, involving steep dives from high altitude and shallow dives from about 10,000 feet.
2. Aircraft stability and general combat suitability when flying at high speed at low level.
3. Carriage of external stores and the effect of such stores on the aircraft's handling in diving and low-level flight.

Much of the flying in (1) and (2) above was carried out at Langley while, not unnaturally, the majority of the weapon trials was undertaken at Boscombe Down. Those that were performed by the Hawker pilots are set out in some detail in Appendix B, and it is perhaps only necessary here to pass comment on one specific experiment undertaken, that of "clipping" the Typhoon's wings. On 27 July a DTD aircraft (the second Gloster-built Mark IA, *R7577*) was flown by Bill Humble with wings reduced in span to 38 ft 10 in by replacing the rounded tip sections by chordwise straight tip fair-

ings. These wings continued to be flown for three months, but their effect on low altitude performance was disappointing, returning an increase in roll-rate of only about two degrees per second, and an increase in speed of no more than four miles per hour; on the other hand, at the stall, the starboard wing dropped suddenly without any buffet warning, and the experiment was dropped.

Shortly after carrying out a performance check flight on this aircraft at the end of July, Ken Seth-Smith crashed at Thorpe, near Windsor, in Typhoon IB *R7692* and was killed. He had been investigating the effects on flying the aircraft with the overhead canopy panel removed. When a thorough search of the area failed to locate the starboard car door it was generally considered at first that, with the canopy panel removed, the door had broken loose and struck the tailplane, causing the tail unit to break off. However when a much closer examination of the tail unit—which had indeed failed at the transport joint, but which was otherwise little damaged—was carried out, it was discovered that fatigue failure had occurred in the bracket attaching the elevator mass balance. This was probably the earliest first-hand evidence gained by the Hawker design office as to the true cause of tail breakages among Typhoons (see page 41). While a prolonged investigation into the cause of the bracket fatigue and failure now commenced, an immediate modification was ordered to be made to the mass balance brackets in every Typhoon so far completed. It may thus be said that this fine test pilot had not died in vain.

By this time a major alteration had been made to the cockpit canopy, involving reduction of the fuselage cross section aft of the cockpit. The trial installation had been carried out when repairing a damaged Typhoon (*R7646*) and resulted in mounting a fully transparent rear hood fairing on top of the fuselage while retaining the car doors and overhead hinged panel. This improvement (known as the Stage B hood) was welcomed by the Service, although it soon came to be regarded with some reservations when the Typhoon started intensive low-level operations over the French coast as the pilots found that constant searching for enemy aircraft above and behind still demanded uncomfortable leaning and twisting to look over the shoulder past the crash pylon, while the curved perspex fairing severely distorted their field of view. Recourse to the conventional rear-view mirror above the windscreen, covered by a perspex fairing, had been one answer until it was found that this small excrescence imposed a surprisingly severe penalty on the Typhoon's maximum speed.

While on the subject of the maximum speed of the Typhoons then entering service it is worth mentioning that the extended exhaust stubs, introduced to eliminate CO seepage into the cockpit

R8762 was one of the store trials aircraft flown at Boscombe Down in 1942–43, seen here with 44-gallon underwing drop tanks in January 1943. Note the absence of recognition stripes. (Photo: Sydney Camm Collection)

(possibly under the car door), were found to reduce the aircraft's maximum speed by as much as 12 mph in full-supercharger gear, and 14 mph in moderate gear. By reverting to the original short stubs and adopting extractor louvres (as developed in the Sabre-powered Firebrand prototypes) the maximum speed of the Typhoon IB returned to 408.5 mph at 20,650 feet.

Meanwhile Boscombe Down had cleared the Typhoon to carry a pair of 250-lb bombs under the wings, but before proceeding further Hawker was asked to carry out preliminary handling with 500-lb bombs, and these were flown by Lucas on 8 September in R7646 at an all-up weight of 12,176 lb. Later that month Lucas dived the aircraft at 30 degrees from 20,000 feet, reaching a true airspeed of 520 mph before recovering at 4,000 feet without trouble. The following month Humble flew R8762 with a pair of Hurricane-type cylindrical 44-gallon drop tanks. Before the end of the year Boscombe Down cleared the Typhoon to operate with 500-lb bombs.

By the end of the summer Hawker had embarked on the last stage of its programme to alleviate vibration from the Sabre. Use was being made of a different type of recorder, the Askania, in place of the original RAE Vibrograph, and by more accurately analysing the various vibration amplitudes throughout the fuselage structure a new source of possible trouble had been identified, namely the radiator mountings, and when these were modified a further marked reduction in vibration was noted. Finally in an attempt to reduce the low-frequency vibration—the so-called 1P amplitude, or that associated with the propeller rotation—four-blade de Havilland propellers were flown on a number of Typhoons at Langley. While this change certainly alleviated the most aggravating cockpit vibration, it was also found that despite a slight increase in aircraft weight the time to height was significantly reduced, while the maximum speed at about 18,000 feet was increased by about 12 mph. The ultimate stage of virtually vibration-free conditions in the cockpit was reached in November with R7617 flying with 30,000 lb/in Dynaflex mountings at the rear of the engine, a Rotol four-blade propeller and a modified, fully-sprung seat (which effectively prevented "bottoming") and—with the exception that the DH four-blade propeller was retained—this became the standard of preparation for the Typhoon in production for the next few months.

Although the Stage B canopy was to remain present in production Typhoons for several months (and indeed came to be retrospectively incorporated in aircraft requiring extensive repair after accidents) a new canopy came to be introduced early in 1943 at Langley. Attempts had been made to improve the rear view in the Stage B canopy by removing the crash pylon and substituting a piece of armoured glass, but this did not improve the distortion of view through the rear perspex. Instead an entirely new, single piece blown-perspex sliding hood was designed, which moved forward on rails to engage flush against the front windscreen and quarterlight frame; in so doing it necessitated eliminating the car doors and

Close-up view of the Typhoon's standard 44-gallon drop tank. (Photo: Hawker Aircraft Ltd., Neg No TYC/111.)

thereby remove any danger of CO seepage through the side of the cockpit. The sliding hood was first fitted on the DTD Typhoon *R8809* and flown by Lucas on 17 January 1943; it proved an immediate success, yet on account of the extensive alterations necessary to the fuselage structure it was to be more than eight months before production aircraft appeared with this feature.

It is worth pausing once more to summarize the performance of the standard Typhoon IB as it was reaching Fighter Command in March 1943. By then a further small refinement had been added—fairings which fully enclosed the cannon barrels—and this resulted in a 6–8 mph speed increase, giving the aircraft a 417 mph TAS maximum level speed at 20,400 feet in FS gear with three-blade propeller (or 427 mph with four-blade propeller). Climb to 20,000 feet occupied 7.4 minutes with three-blade or 6.9 minutes with four-blade propeller. Maximum true airspeed permitted in a dive while carrying two 500-lb bombs was 500 mph at 5,000 feet (although Lucas had demonstrated the

Above, trial installation of the first single-piece sliding hood on Typhoon R8809 at Langley; note the "scars" left after eliminating the car doors. *Below*, JP752 was representative of Typhoon IBs being produced by Glosters during the autumn of 1943. (Photos: Hawker Aircraft Ltd.)

Another view of JP752. Although representative of the latest standard Typhoons being produced by Glosters at the end of the autumn of 1943 not all aircraft were being completed with the four-blade propeller, and this feature was not present in aircraft delivered to the Service until 1944. (Photo: Hawker Aircraft Ltd., Neg No TYG/13)

ease of recovery from a 530-mph dive in this configuration). Engine reliability was still giving cause for concern, although the Sabre II was by now cleared to 100 hours between major overhauls. The Langley Typhoons were in fact suffering an average of one engine failure in about every 80 hours' running, amounting to about three failures per month, although most of the failures occurred during ground running; and it should be emphasized that the nature of the test flying imposed far greater strains upon the engines than would be anticipated in service other than actual combat.

The Desert Typhoons

One of the relatively little known episodes in the Typhoon's history was an outcome of the plan, tentatively put forward by the Air Staff, to introduce the aircraft into service in the Mediterranean. It will be recalled that in August 1942 both the result of a major battle in front of Cairo (at El Alamein) and of the future "Torch" landings were entirely speculative, despite the air of optimism professed by the Chiefs of Staff.

On the assumption that the Axis forces would be able to continue resisting the growing strength of the Allies in the Mediterranean for many months to come, an instruction was issued to Hawker, Napier and Gloster in September 1942 to upgrade their preliminary investigation into the Typhoon's suitability for tropical service. A DTD aircraft, *R8925*, with a prototype tropical air cleaner had been prepared, but unfortunately this was crash landed by Bill Humble on its second flight following engine failure on 18 November, and was extensively damaged. A second aircraft, *R8889*, with modified air cleaner control was flown within a week—and, incidentally dived to 525 mph IAS without trouble.

An initial batch of six aircraft was then prepared for trials with experimental Vokes dry filter air intake cleaners (generally referred to as the "interim" filter). Three of these aircraft, *R8891*, *DN323* and *EJ906*—all Gloster-built—were to be shipped to North Africa while the other three (to be joined by 12 more in 1943) were to undergo development in the United Kingdom, it being intended either to ship them with an RAF squadron to North Africa or to re-equip a Middle East squadron with Typhoons.

Meanwhile events had moved swiftly in North Africa following the Battle of Alamein and the "Torch" landings, while the Typhoon's future in Western Europe as a ground attack fighter had become assured. Nevertheless the trials were ordered to go ahead—largely on account of the Spitfire V's inability to counter the Focke-Wulf Fw 190, which was beginning to arrive in the Mediterranean in increasing numbers.

On 26 April 1943, Philip Lucas and John Gale (representing Hawker) and Mr Richardson of Napier landed at Algiers, having flown via Lisbon and Gibraltar, and, on reporting to Air Vice-Marshal G. G. Dawson—the energetic Senior Maintenance and Supply Officer in North Africa—were told that the three Typhoons had just been disembarked at Casablanca; they had been packed with engines installed, but with wings, tailplanes, rudders, propellers and cowlings detached.

The Typhoons were transported to nearby No. 145 Maintenance Unit as the civilian engineers flew there to meet the RAF contingent, consisting of Flying Officer Myall (a very experienced ex-No. 56 Squadron Typhoon pilot), a Sergeant, who had no Typhoon experience whatsoever, and two very capable fitters. Fortunately the MU itself possessed an NCO with Typhoon experience and he was co-opted. Although tools and spares were slow arriving at Casablanca from the United Kingdom the first aircraft, *DN323*, was uncrated on 28 April and was ready for Lucas to take it aloft on 7 May; the last aircraft was completed and passed its check flight on the 18th, the day on which the first assembly equipment arrived by sea!

On 22nd May Lucas was informed that all three aircraft were to be flown to the Middle East (Canal Zone) where development flying and servicing facilities were much better—and harsh desert conditions more realistic. In due course two of the Typhoons arrived at Cairo on 3 June (*EJ906* having suffered a forced landing following a supercharger clutch failure on take-off; fortunately three spare Sabres had just arrived at Algiers).

At Cairo arrangements were made for the Typhoons to be taken over by No. 103 MU at Aboukir where they underwent inspection and modification updating, as Myall returned to Casablanca to collect *EJ906*. Realizing that the "interim" cleaner was highly susceptible to fire (becoming saturated in fuel draining down from the carbuettor butterflies), Lucas signalled Hawker to have modified wet-type filters sent out, and these arrived within 48 hours.

In the meantime it had been decided that No.

Two views of one of the Typhoons destined for tropical trials in North Africa, DN323, just visible is the long ventral fairing over the air cleaner below the cockpit, a feature of all the tropical Typhoons. The colour scheme applied to these aircraft comprised sand and mid-stone camouflage on the upper surfaces and light blue undersurfaces. (Photos: Hawker Aircraft Ltd., Neg Nos DT36 and 1127)

Typhoons in North Africa. *Right*, EJ906—much stained by the Sabre's exhaust efflux—photographed at Idku; note that, unlike the other two Typhoons, this aircraft featured faired gun barrels. *Left*, a tropical Typhoon, also probably at Idku, flies past the Hurricanes of No 451 Squadron. (Photos: via Richard Ward, Farnborough)

451 Squadron, Royal Australian Air Force—then at Idku nearby, kicking its heels in frustrating defensive patrols over the Suez Canal—would undertake limited operational trials with the Typhoons and, if successful, would in due course complete re-equipment with the aircraft. Moreover, in view of the possibility of the Typhoon entering service in the theatre, stocks of spares began flooding into the Canal Zone, only to become "lost" in the maze of stores administration—so that they became distributed between three Maintenance Units (Nos. 103, 107 and 111), and were either entered in three stores' manifests, or not at all. Thus when a wheel door fell off a Typhoon into a lake and was lost, it was quickly replaced by a spare located at No. 107 MU, but when a Dowty live-line pump failed at Idku, no spare could be found in any manifest; Gale therefore flew to the airfield himself to collect the pump and delivered it to Aboukir for repair.

(On another occasion, following failure of one of the Vokes air cleaners, Gale and Richardson prepared some rough sketches to attempt the installation of an unfamiliar American cleaner; they were entrusted to an anonymous Egyptian artisan who not only completed the job successfully within a day, but with such care and skill that that particular cleaner remained troublefree for the entire course of the trials.) Another problem that had not been anticipated was that the Typhoon possessed almost the only 24-volt electrical system in the whole of Middle East Command so that scarcely any electrical component listed in the spares manifests was suitable for the Typhoons!

No. 451 Squadron, commanded by Squadron Leader J. Paine, started handling flights on the Typhoon on 13 June while Lucas was still available to provide the necessary briefing on the aeroplane's fundamentals, and when he left to return to

Considering that all but a handful of Typhoons were built by Gloster, it is perhaps extraordinary that many more pictures of the Brockworth factory and airfield do not include the aircraft. DN411, shown here at the Gloster factory in 1943, was one of the tropical Typhoons set aside for development of a desert radiator; as far as is known, it was later converted to standard and served with the RAF in Britain. (Photo: Author's Collection)

the United Kingdom on the 22nd his place was taken by Myall. Two days later *R8891* went unserviceable with a useless air cleaner and while it was being replaced by the American type, a detachment of pilots from No. 451 Squadron moved to L.G.106 (about 100 miles to the west of Alexandria) with *DN323* and *EJ906* under the command of Flight Lieutenant R. T. Hudson and with seven other pilots, including Myall.

The object of the trials was to complete an average of 100 hours' flying by each aircraft and to report on the ease and manner with which various problems were overcome. Despite frequent instances of unserviceability—almost entirely due to the lack of spares or the difficulty in locating them—and a couple of forced landings in the desert (on one occasion the big Sabre engine being removed using shear legs with block and tackle and taken 56 miles by truck over trackless desert), the Typhoons completed a total of 312 hours' desert flying, of which 238 were at L.G.106. On 26 September both Nos. 206 and 219 Groups expressed the opinion that the trials had indeed been successful and that the aircraft could embark on operational flying with No. 451 Squadron. Gale flew home on 12 October and returned to Langley 12 days later.

However, although the other twelve "desert" Typhoons were all finally completed and fully prepared for shipment to the Middle East in October 1943, such had been the success of Allied land operations in Italy by then that the decision to fully equip No. 451 Squadron was rescinded. It is believed, however, that all three of the trials aircraft continued to fly for several months until finally

grounded for lack of spares in February 1944 when, in any case, the Squadron moved to El Gamil with Spitfire IXs.

Moreover, owing to the increasing demand for Typhoons by the RAF in Britain for the fighter-bomber squadrons, the 12 "desert" aircraft were converted to standard "temperate" condition. One further DTD Typhoon, *R7646* (which had been used in the canopy development flying) was converted to tropical standard and provided much of the test experience which ultimately led to the adoption of the Tempest Mark VI by the RAF in the Middle East after the War.

Bombs and rockets galore

The last year of the Typhoon's development was devoted almost exclusively to extending its operational capabilities, principally in the ground attack rôle, although it worth mentioning two other areas of investigation that occupied Hawker briefly.

No doubt encouraged by Squadron Leader R. P. Beamont's early report on the suitability of the Typhoon as a "fair weather" night fighter, the Air Ministry ordered the preparation of a single aircraft equipped with AI Mark IV with pilot-interpreted cockpit display. Although Fighter Command had in 1940 started to acquire the purpose-designed twin-engine Beaufighter as its standard radar-equipped night fighter, and this by mid-1941 had indeed become an exceptionally efficient aircraft by the then-current standards, there lingered a dogged belief that the single-seat, single-engine fighter would still be the most effi-

The single example of the Typhoon NF Mark IB night fighter, R7881, at Langley before commencement of flight trials. At this stage the radar equipment had not been fitted, other than the external aerials. The blade aerial beneath the fuselage (just visible below the cockpit) was associated with the AI radar and was not the IFF aerial, adopted later; the aircraft retains the early IFF wire aerial extending from fuselage to tailplane. For performance measurement purposes the aircraft carried standard 44-gallon drop tanks, and the port tank was replaced by a similar store containing the radar. (Photo: Hawker Aircraft Ltd., Neg No 4263)

cient destroyer of enemy raiders at night—even if some other sort of aircraft had the means to locate the target. Thus was born the Turbinlite "experiment" in which a twin-engine aircraft, usually the otherwise worthless American Havoc, equipped with airborne radar and a powerful nose-mounted searchlight, would roam the night sky under control by ground radar stations, in company with a Hurricane. In the event that the radar-equipped Havoc located a target and successfully illuminated it, the theory was that the Hurricane pilot would then close in to destroy the raider. Despite perseverance for about 18 months, and the employment of numerous fighter squadrons, only one German bomber was in fact destroyed. The Hurricanes were the four-cannon Mark IIC, but the general opinion expressed by the pilots was that while it certainly possessed a suitable armament for the destruction of German bombers it was probably too slow to catch them. To meet this hypothetical situation it was perhaps natural to

adopt the Typhoon IB. The trial of a standard Typhoon day fighter by No. 534 Squadron in the autumn of 1942 was however shortlived as it was now found that the Typhoon was "too fast for the Havoc", so that the two pilots spent much of their time looking for each other having become separated; in any case Fighter Command felt that too much effort would be required to train night flying Typhoon pilots.

Notwithstanding the latter reasoning the special AI-equipped Typhoon NF Mark IB, *R7881*, went ahead and was first flown at Langley by Lucas on 23 March 1943 at an all-up weight of 11,900 lb. Among the requirements were that the radar equipment should be capable of fitting within a container of the same shape and size as that of the standard cylindrical 44-gallon underwing fuel tank; the aircraft was therefore ballasted with two such standard tanks and for inclusion of the cockpit equipment—as well as being fitted with the full array of wing aerials. It was then delivered to the

Comparative views of the Typhoon night fighter, R7881, seen, *above*, immediately after manufacture and, *below*, in 1944 when the aircraft was undergoing trials at Farnborough in 1944. In the latter picture the aircraft is shown with four-blade propeller (Sabre IIA engine), radar containers under the wings and recognition stripes. (Photos: Hawker Aircraft Ltd., Neg No 4264, and Author's Collection)

TRE for installation of the radar and subsequently underwent prolonged evaluation, ending up at the RAE in 1944, by which time it had acquired a late-series Sabre IIB driving a four-blade propeller. The underwing stores were not jettisonable and the maximum speed (as recorded in Hawker's Flight Report No. L853) was 368 mph TAS at MPA in FS gear with the three-blade propeller.

One other experiment involving the non-standard application of electronic equipment to the Typhoon was the use of "Abdullah", a radar homer developed by Dr Robert Cockburn to pinpoint the exact location of German *Würzburg* gun-director radars known to be located on the French coast and which were scheduled for destruction by the RAF prior to the Normandy landings. Following an instruction to Hawker to determine the maximum safe speed at which a Typhoon might be flown while carrying a pair of small smoke bombs in addition to the "Abdullah" equipment (established at 522 mph TAS at about 7,000 feet), a Typhoon, *MN254*, was fitted with the homer early in 1944 and, flown by Squadron Leader C. H. Hartley (later Air Vice-Marshal Sir Christopher, KCB, CBE, DFC, AFC), commanding officer of the Fighter Interception Unit, gave promising results when used "against" the captured *Würzburg* set up at Tantallon Castle. The tactics to be employed operationally involved a single Abdullah-equipped Typhoon with a No. 2 as escort flying directly towards a transmitting *Würzburg* whose signals would be received by the homer and converted into a series of dots and dashes in the pilot's headphones to direct him on to the radar on which he would dive to release his smoke markers. Simultaneously a formation of low-flying Typhoons, approaching from the landward direction, would saturate the area indicated with salvoes of rockets.

In the event the Fighter Interception Unit converted six "Abdullah" Typhoons which were then detached to the airfield at Holmesley South in Hampshire, the base of a number of Typhoon squadrons. In April, when the order was given to commence the systematic destruction of the German radars, the first "Abdullah" operation was attempted. Unfortunately the German radar operators were not inclined to co-operate and as soon as their equipment picked up the fast approaching Typhoons they promptly switched off the radar, leaving the "Abdullah" pilot—not to mention a couple of Typhoon squadrons over France—without any idea of the target's location.[3]

---

[3] Fortunately an adequate system for locating the radars, using triangulation backed up by photographic reconnaissance, was available and this proved adequate to enable setpiece attacks to be carried out. It is perhaps interesting to note that as late at 1982, during the Falkland Islands campaign, anti-radar missiles—combining the function of "Abdullah" *and* the strike Typhoons in a single weapon—were used to good effect by the RAF, although "switching off" still caused difficulties and some embarrassment.

Much of the early development of rocket-firing Typhoons was carried out on EK497, seen here at Boscombe Down early in 1943. (Photo: A&AEE, Neg No 1238)

★　　★　　★

As already remarked, clearance had been gained to operate the Typhoon with 500-lb bombs by the end of 1942, yet even before these came into general use in February 1943 Hawker was checking the stresses involved in loading a pair of 1,000-pounders. Thus equipped, *DN340* was flown by Humble on 17 March at an all-up weight of 13,248 lb (the greatest weight thus far flown by a Typhoon), the bombs being flown without fins for jettison tests. Unfortunately, owing to a fault in the bomb gear, the starboard bomb hung up, and Bill Humble was faced with an extremely tricky landing with his big bomb still in place. It was successfully carried out without use of flap while maintaining the minimum flying speed at which the wing could be held up, touching down at something over 130 mph! In a later check flight *DN340* was dived at 548 mph TAS dropping the bombs immediately before recovery. *DN340* then went to Boscombe Down to take part in the clearance trials which were successfully concluded less than three months later.

The next major trial was to develop and clear the Typhoon to mount the standard three-inch rocket projectile, a weapon that was to feature prominently in the RAF's armoury for the remainder of the War—and long after. The projectile itself was solid fuel-propelled, the propellant being packed into a fairly crude three-inch iron pipe and ignited electrically on closure of a firing circuit in the aircraft; burning time was fractionally under four seconds. Various warheads, screwed on to the front of this body, were employed, the normal six-inch calibre head being nominally of 60-lb weight, either of armour-piercing, semi-armour piercing, or high explosive "shot". Four cruciform plain square fins were welded on to the rear of the three-inch pipe and provided a reasonable degree of stability, if not accuracy. The rockets were suspended from a groove between two parallel rails attached under the wing of the aircraft, two spring "callipers" gripping the rocket body immediately aft of the warhead and forward of the fins. On

firing, the rocket moved forward, the callipers sliding in the groove and springing free on disengagement.

The three-inch RP was not a particularly accurate weapon, being difficult to aim owing to the considerable gravity drop, which increased sharply after burn-out. However, it was found that the steeper the dive the more accurate the rocket became, and a compromise of about 35 degrees diving attack was usually adopted when tactically possible. The rockets could be fired in pairs, fours, or in a "ripple" salvo—the latter normally being employed against a single large target, such as a ship, bridge, building or concentration of enemy vehicles, when perhaps only a single pass was possible.

All flight trials to clear the rocket-firing Typhoon were carried out at the A&AEE, or RAF Establishments and units; Hawker was only required to check out the effects on handling of the

Top, in-flight view of the rocket trials Typhoon IB, EK497. *Above*, the Typhoon's ultimate hitting power: MN861 fitted with "double-stacked" 60-pound rockets—a total of sixteen missiles being carried. (Photo: via Sqn Ldr R. C. B. Ashworth). *Below*, preparation of the first armoured Typhoon by Hawker; sheets of 4-mm armour extended from the rear of the cockpit forward to the front of the engine but imposed little penalty on the aircraft's performance.

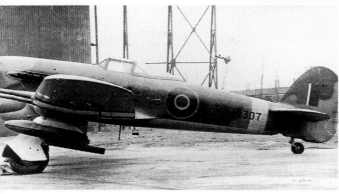

Top, early smoke curtain installation, as used operationally early in 1944. *Above*, M.10 smoke tanks, as developed in 1944, fitted on Typhoons JR307 (Stage B canopy) and MN519 (sliding hood). (Photos, PRO AIR 37/798 and RAE Neg No 55747)

rails and rockets and to provide local strongpoints for attachment of the rails, a modification that became standard among all Service Typhoons. *EK497* was the first aircraft employed for live firing, operating out of Boscombe Down, and the first provisional clearance was given in May 1943, although it was to be several months before RAF Squadrons underwent full rocket-firing training for operations. Boscombe Down later went further and cleared the Typhoon to mount the rockets in double tiers, that is to say suspending a pair of rockets from each rail. The noise and destruction by 16 such weapons, each with a 60-lb warhead, must have been awesome indeed!

In normal set piece attacks, where a specific target was briefed for attack, the Typhoon was customarily loaded with a full complement of eight rockets but, with clearance already achieved for the use of 44-gallon drop tanks, it was deemed convenient to carry a drop tank under one wing and four rockets under the other. After clearance of the aircraft to operate at higher all-up weights, it was found possible to mount both drop tanks symmetrically with a pair of rockets outboard of each; such an arrangement made for simpler aiming and less discomfort when flying home with a drop tank (if retained) under each wing. The use of mixed tank and rocket load was particularly valuable during armed reconnaissance patrols and the "cab-rank" standing patrols when increased range or endurance, together with a few rockets for targets of opportunity, were valuable assets.

Once the maximum performance, load and handling parameters of the Typhoon had been established, it was relatively straightforward to clear almost any type of store for carriage by the aircraft. Boscombe Down's job was usually confined to investigation of the best method of dropping or using the store, checking to ensure it did not foul the aircraft when released, and preparing operating recommendations and flying procedures for the benefit of the line squadrons. These stores ranged from cluster bombs and supply containers to various type of smoke generating tanks and smoke bombs.

By mid-1944 all that could be done to ensure that the Typhoon could perform the tasks now likely to be demanded of it as dawn broke over the coast of Normandy on that June day, had been done by the manufacturers and by the pilots whose job it had been to produce a fighting weapon for the Royal Air Force. It is now time to describe the fortunes of the Typhoon in the hands of that Service.

The Hawker test pilots outside the pilots' Mess, "Old Timbers", at Langley in 1943. *Left to right*, Philip Lucas, Hubert Broad, Bill Humble, Frank Silk, unidentified, Merryck Hymans, unidentified, Sqn Ldr R. P. Beamont, unidentified, Frank Fox, unidentified. (Photo: Wg Cdr R. P. Beamont, CBE, DSO, DFC)

4

THE TYPHOON JOINS THE R.A.F.

Early in the morning of 11 September 1941, the first two Typhoons landed at Duxford, south of Cambridge. Both aircraft were 12-Browning gun-armed Mark IAs, and both were allocated to No. 56 Squadron, then commanded by the Battle of France veteran, Squadron Leader Peter Prosser Hanks (later Group Captain DSO, DFC, AFC). Within a couple of hours one of the new fighters, *R7853*, was being flown by Flight Lieutenant Drake, attached as training officer, followed by

Flight Lieutenant Wicks, Squadron Leader Hanks, Pilot Officer M. R. Ingle-Finch and, on the 13th, by the Wing Leader, Wing Commander R. R. Stanford Tuck.[1] By the end of the month three

[1] Wing Commander Stanford Tuck (later DSO, DFC and two Bars) was to be posted away from Duxford before the end of September. Some years before his death in 1987 he told the Author that although he only flew the Typhoon about a dozen times his opinion of the aircraft was that it "seemed to be a sort of souped-up Hurricane and one that took a big stride past the Spitfire".

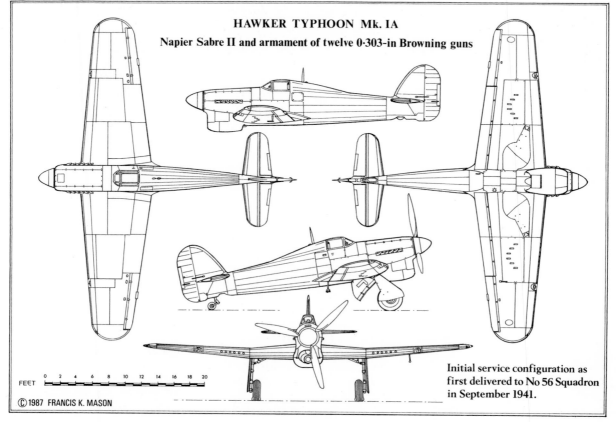

HAWKER TYPHOON Mk. IA

Napier Sabre II and armament of twelve 0·303-in Browning guns

FEET 0 2 4 6 8 10 12 14 16 18 20

© 1987 FRANCIS K. MASON

Initial service configuration as first delivered to No 56 Squadron in September 1941.

further aircraft had arrived at Duxford, followed by eight in October.

★   ★   ★

Following the Battle of Britain, Royal Air Force Fighter Command had undergone a number of significant changes among its top appointments. Air Chief Marshal Sir Hugh Dowding, the Commander-in-Chief and supreme architect of Britain's survival in the great daylight battle, was succeeded by Air Marshal William Sholto Douglas, while Air Marshal Keith Park, brilliant commander of the vital No. 11 Group, was replaced by No. 12 Group's former Air Officer Commanding, Air Marshal Trafford Leigh-Mallory.

Leigh-Mallory, whose defence responsibility in the Battle of Britain had been less sharply defined than that of Park, had favoured the use in combat of assembled squadrons (or Wings), whereas Park—with much shorter warning of approaching raids—was more sparing in the use of his resources, preferring to "feed" individual squadrons into the battle. Leigh-Mallory's theory was simple: to bring the largest number of fighters to bear upon an approaching raid so as to overwhelm the German fighter escorts. In practice however these tactics almost invariably failed, and many a raid by the *Luftwaffe* over Leigh-Mallory's Group area either escaped interception or had already bombed and turned for home before the Wing of fighters had assembled.

Nevertheless Leigh-Mallory's theory attracted considerable sympathy among the Air Staff, despite justifiable complaints by Park that, at moments when his own hard-pressed squadrons were in need of reinforcements, the No. 12 Group squadrons were slow in arriving on the scene of battle, their leaders under orders to assemble as a Wing—no simple task with Hurricanes and Spitfires of somewhat differing performance and often being scrambled from more than one airfield (Duxford and Fowlmere).

Sholto Douglas, previously Deputy Chief of the Air Staff, had had no recent experience of a flying command, having been at the Imperial Defence College or at the Air Ministry for eight years—during that crucial period when fighters and their tactics had undergone unprecedented change and advance. Yet the doctrines propounded at the IDC, which Leigh-Mallory had attended in the 1930s, were largely based on the traditional Principles of War, and so the concentration of strength in battle was seen as synonymous with security of defence, and any failure by Leigh-Mallory's tactics during the Battle of Britain were seen by Sholto Douglas as the outcome of technical difficulties as distinct from a weakness in his defensive philosophy. Such, of course, was to gainsay Park's instinctive capacity to improvise a steadfast defence at times of extreme pressure.

The departure of Dowding and Park in their hour of victory—Dowding himself had been closely involved with the creation of Britain's air defence system throughout the 1930s and was already overdue for normal retirement in 1940, while Park was euphemistically "rested" after the great battle—was generally regarded by the Air Staff as essential if Fighter Command was to shake itself free from its necessary but pervasive attitude of home defence at all costs.

Like Bomber Command, which had abandoned daylight bombing in the early months of the War following catastrophic losses from German fighters, the *Luftwaffe* went over to a prolonged night bombing offensive (the Blitz) against Britain after its failure to destroy Fighter Command in 1940. Unfortunately Fighter Command could do little in the early months to counter the night bombing threat, possessing only a small number of effective night fighters but a fast-growing number of day interceptor fighter squadrons. True, an increasing number of Defiant and Hurricane squadrons became operational at night and took a steadily increasing toll of the night bombers, but it was not until the purpose-designed Beaufighter arrived in numbers and its crews mastered its airborne radar equipment that an efficient night fighter defence came into being, itself a legacy of Dowding's farsighted development of the radar defence network.

Thus it was that Sholto Douglas and Leigh-Mallory arrived at the helm of Fighter Command, theoretically and ironically the two men best suited to take the Command over to the offensive. No one can have failed to be impressed by the use made by the *Luftwaffe* of its excellent Messerschmitt Bf 109Es (the classic "Emils") during the Battle of Britain, particularly in their '*frei Jagd*' or free chase tactics whereby groups of single-seat fighters were sent over to carry out offensive sweeps in attempts to catch the weary British fighter pilots low on fuel and ammunition, or to encourage RAF fighter controllers to order Hurricanes and Spitfires into the air where they could be caught and shot down in the act of taking off.

To emulate these and other German tactics Leigh-Mallory introduced fighter (and later fighter-bomber) sweeps over Northern France, Belgium and Holland—"leaning forward into Europe" as Sholto Douglas called it. These were carried out by the growing number of Hurricane and Spitfire squadrons in the Command and came to be categorized, being generically identified according to the number and nature of aircraft taking part.

Largest form of fighter sweep was the *Ranger*, consisting of a Wing (and later of two or three Wings) and sent out to trail its coat along the German-held coast of France. Ordered at Command or Group level, the *Ranger* was a fairly elab-

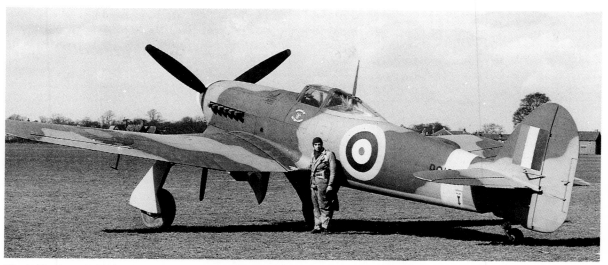

Like the Hurricane the Typhoon was subject of some bogus application of "presentation attribution" inscriptions on the side of the aircraft ostensibly purchased by public subscription. The aircraft shown here, in fact the first Hawker-built development aircraft, *R8198*, carries the Borough Arms of Sutton and Cheam—but later carried inscriptions of at least 30 other subscribing bodies. The gentleman posing by the Typhoon, dressed as a "pilot", appeared in countless pictures of subscription aircraft. (Photo: Author's Collection)

orate operation, with one squadron flying at relatively low level and with a covering squadron flying slightly higher and to one side, and a third as top cover. As one wag put it at the time, "Leigh-Mallory now has two or three days to assemble his squadrons". The *Ranger*'s route was usually intended to pass close to German airfields in an attempt to lure the Messerschmitt fighters into the air where they might be brought to combat. However, by and large the Germans tended to avoid being drawn by *Rangers* unless they were already reacting to an attack by RAF bombers in the vicinity (see below).

Sweeps by single squadrons of RAF fighters were categorized as *Rodeos*, usually set in motion at Station level (but with Group's authority) at less than 24 hours' notice. Although briefed to fly a predetermined course, the pilots were often encouraged to attack worthwhile targets of opportunity, such as German aircraft on the ground, enemy coastal shipping and road and rail traffic. It should be noted that in 1941 the Germans disposed relatively little mobile flak, preferring to concentrate the light gun defences around their ports and airfields.

Smallest of the fighter attacks was the *Rhubarb*, often undertaken by up to four pilots (but usually only two). It was generally flown almost "on the spur of the moment" with sanction from Flight or Squadron Commander during periods of general inactivity. The pilots would simply fly out to launch a nuisance attack on any likely target—having of course been briefed on any other operations in the selected area. Literally thousands of these small freelance sorties were flown by Fighter Command pilots during the War, and it is not surprising that their tally of targets destroyed—road and rail vehicles, aircraft on the ground, river and coastal

craft, airfield and port installations, bridges and so on—far exceeded those accounted for during the more formal or setpiece attacks. Such was the individualistic character of the fighter pilot.

Often the RAF fighters operated over the Continent in support of bomber operations—usually in 1941 by Blenheim light bombers. The *Circus* involved a sweep by bombers, sometimes not even carrying bombs but sent to provide enemy fighters with a worthwhile target. Fighters would fly close escort and top cover, ready to take on any German fighters that might threaten. Generally speaking the *Circuses* were least effective; they were not sufficient of a threat to attract enemy reaction, and if bombs *were* carried they were inadequate to cause significant damage, while the fighter pilots were usually ordered not to go looking for trouble unless attacked. The *Ramrod*, often flown by several squadrons of bombers with at least a Wing (and later up to four Wings) of fighters, was a different story. Sent against specific targets—Abbeville and Amiens were favourites—*Ramrods* resulted in some of the biggest daylight air battles over France in 1942 and 1943.

Not unnaturally enemy shipping in the English Channel, as well as the Scheldt estuary and off the Dutch coast, was increasingly attacked by the RAF, although little effective damage could be done in 1941 by the fighters available to Leigh-Mallory, armed as they were with only two cannon (as in the Spitfire VB). Gradually, as the four-cannon Hurricane and Typhoon became available together with 250-lb and 500-lb bombs (and later still with rockets), the anti-shipping strikes, known as *Roadsteads*, became deadly in their effect. Later on, as determined efforts were made to deny the enemy use of the Channel by shipping—particularly after the embarrassing escape by the *Scharn-*

57

horst, Gneisenau and *Prinz Eugen* from Brest early in 1942—*Channel Stop* operations were flown by all manner of aircraft, including fighters and fighter-bombers, the most common targets being blockade runners, German destroyers and E-boats. Such shipping attacks demanded carefully rehearsed tactics owing to the increasing presence of enemy flak ships whose guns took a heavy toll of attacking aircraft.

By the summer of 1941 the fighters most widely flown by Fighter Command were the Hurricane IIA and IIB, now frequently carrying a pair of 250-lb bombs, and the Spitfire VB. Against them were ranged a slowly dwindling number of German *Jagdgeschwader* (fighter Wings), equipped with the Messerschmitt Bf 109E and F. The "Emil" had proved highly effective during the Battle of Britain but in most circumstances could be matched by both the Hurricane I and Spitfire I and II. The arrival in service of the Spitfire VB with higher performance and two 20-mm cannon and four machine guns gave Fighter Command a distinct edge over the "Emil", but then, early in 1941, the improved 109F appeared and the balance was restored, although the Hurricane now tended to be outclassed in most combat circumstances.

Gradually however the Germans started to redeploy most of the *Jagdgeschwader* to other war theatres, first to the Mediterranean and Balkans, and, in June, to the Eastern Front when Hitler opened his massive campaign against the Soviet Union. Inexorably Fighter Command gained a considerable numerical fighter superiority in the West, a circumstance that was seen as ample justification for Leigh-Mallory's "coat trailing" tactics over the Channel coast. By the same token, with fewer than 250 German fighters airworthy at any particular time, it encouraged reluctance by the German fighter pilots to be drawn needlessly into what could easily become a massacre.

This then was the background of operational tactics being employed when the Typhoon was first delivered to No. 56 Squadron at Duxford in September 1941. In the first instance its arrival in service was the result of an apparently normal, though painful, process of development; there was no premeditated policy to introduce the aircraft into service to recover any sort of tactical inferiority being suffered by Fighter Command.

★　　★　　★

At the time of the Typhoon's delivery to Duxford on 11 September, production was well underway at Gloster, with about 50 aircraft having been completed and undergoing the various routines necessary for release to operational units. Such, however, was the nature of the Typhoon, its engine and, not least, its performance (for it was to be the RAF's first fighter capable of a level speed of over 400 mph—compared with the Spitfire VB's

375 mph), that it was anticipated that No. 56 Squadron, which had been flying Hurricane IIBs in any case, would take about three months to become fully operational with its new aircraft.

Having said this, one must emphasize that the Typhoon, with its radical Sabre engine, had been flying for only 18 months, of which more than six had been spent in relatively little development activity (owing to other priorities during the Battle of Britain and uncertainty as to its future). Moreover, much of the development work had been carried out on a single prototype with unrepresentative engines, while production had been undertaken at a factory remote from the main design and flight testing authority.

As suggested in the previous Chapter, it can now be appreciated that the Typhoon—by accepted criteria—probably entered production at Gloster at least three months prematurely, almost certainly as the gradual run down of Hurricane production by Gloster would otherwise have resulted in unused manufacturing capacity, before all the Typhoon's teething problems were fully understood and rectified in a conventional flight development programme. Of course the cancellation of the Tornado brought its complications, and the situation would have been alleviated if those 15 pre-production Typhoons had been completed by Hawker before the end of 1940.

Bearing in mind the apparent lack of urgency to introduce the Typhoon, and the problems being examined by Hawker, Gloster and at Boscombe Down, it is difficult to understand exactly what lay behind the decision to do so, and in the absence of any traceable Staff document one is only able to speculate. After all, when fairly serious trouble occurred—the matter of carbon monoxide contamination, already referred to—a great number of modifications, for this and other remedies, had to be incorporated in Typhoons which had already started fairly widespread distribution. That the decision to start Typhoon deliveries lay with the Air Staff—and presumably with Fighter Command's C-in-C—goes without saying. The most likely motive may well have been for the very reason that the aircraft *was* still giving trouble during trials, and that Leigh-Mallory felt that a line squadron was best suited to pinpoint operating defects, and the absence of urgency to commit the Typhoon to combat may have encouraged its early delivery so that No. 56 Squadron could pursue an unhurried working-up period.

Nevertheless it is conceivable that a more sinister reason lay behind the Typhoon's Service debut. Since June 1941 early examples of the new German Focke-Wulf Fw 190A radial-engine fighter had been undergoing operational trials at Le Bourget, and the following month Oberstleutnant Adolf Galland's *Jagdgeschwader 26 "Schlageter"*, recently arrived in the Abbeville/St

Omer area in Northern France, received its first Fw 190A-1s and A-2s. Although RAF fighter pilots did not first encounter these formidable enemy fighters (at least surviving to tell the tale) until 27 September—more than a fortnight *after* Duxford's first Typhoon deliveries—it is inconceivable that intelligence sources had not learned of the Fw 190's imminent debut; such intelligence may have been gleaned through the Enigma signal interpretation[1], photographic reconnaissance of the French airfields, or information received from agents in France. However if such advance warning of the Fw 190's existence in France had been gained, it was carefully prevented from reaching the ears of Fighter Command's line pilots who persisted for some weeks in reporting the enemy fighters as "captured Curtiss Hawks" or other familiar radial engine fighters. The ease with which the Fw 190 dealt with Fighter Command's Spitfire VBs and Hurricanes belied such fantasies! What is certain, however, is that Duxford's Typhoons were not delivered with any thought that they might be employed against the Focke-Wulf Fw 190 in the near future—as has been so frequently suggested ever since 1941.

Meanwhile, as operational sorties continued to be flown in Hurricanes by No. 56 Squadron, conversion training on the Typhoon went ahead simultaneously for the remainder of the year. Although there was great enthusiasm among the pilots to convert on to the powerful new fighter, their first impressions of the aircraft, despite impassioned lectures beforehand, were that the Sabre engine, one started, was bent on shaking the aeroplane to pieces. Yet once airborne the Typhoon proved to be a remarkably agile and apparently viceless fighter despite those thick wings. The view from the cockpits of those early aircraft was still strongly

criticized, but it was explained that the forward curved windscreen quarterlights were already being replaced on aircraft being completed by Gloster, and that rear quarterlights were being provided aft of the side doors. There was apparently no criticism of the car doors, and the ability to jettison both these and the overhead panel in an emergency was reassuring, and gave promise of quick and unrestricted departure from the aircraft.

On 1 November the Squadron suffered its first fatal accident when Pilot Officer Dack was seen to enter a dive at 3,000 feet and hit the ground under full power. The subsequent investigation indicated that the pilot had been overcome by carbon monoxide poisoning and had lost consciousness. All the Squadron's Typhoons were forthwith grounded while a working party visited Duxford to carry out bulkhead re-sealing and, when the aircraft were eventually cleared once more, orders were given for the pilots to use oxygen throughout all flying—just in case. On 1 December the Gloster test pilot John Crosby-Warren paid a visit to No. 56 Squadron to start a series of flight trials on all aircraft to check for traces of CO contamination and confirmed what was already suspected by the manufacturers—that some seepage was also occurring aft of the exhaust manifolds from *outside* the fuselage. The first four-inch exhaust stubs were fitted in mid-December and on 1 January, 1942, Michael Daunt, also visiting from Brockworth, made a personal check of all aircraft to ensure that, provided the starboard car door was properly secured, the Typhoon was entirely safe to fly with regard to the carbon monoxide contamination problem.

From this point on No. 56 Squadron's operation training got underway in earnest, and Hurricane operations tailed off rapidly (the last such aircraft being flown away on 3 March). On 14 February the Under-Secretary of State for Air, Captain Harold Balfour (later Baron Balfour of Inchyre) paid a visit to the Squadron and flew a Typhoon—pos-

---

[1] Sholto Douglas would certainly have been privvy to this type of intelligence if indeed it had been in any way the subject of Enigma signals traffic.

R7625, a Typhoon IA, suffered engine failure on its landing approach to Duxford on its delivery flight in December 1942. It was little damaged and joined No 266 Squadron about three months later. (Photo: Author's Collection)

An early Typhoon survived collision with a barrage balloon cable. The aircraft was struck on the port landing light, the cable slicing through the front wingspar before being severed on reaching the rear spar; the aircraft made a safe wheels-down landing. (Photo: Hawker Aircraft Ltd., Neg No TYC/37)

sibly the only senior Parliamentarian ever to fly a high performance fighter without full training instruction![2]

The real reason for Balfour's visit to Duxford at this time is not known; it was, however, established that early in 1942 a new surge of opposition to the Typhoon had occurred within the RAF, sparked by the "Spitfire lobby", and that, fuelled by the accidents at Maintenance Units and elsewhere (referred to in the previous Chapter), the opinions of one or two prominent Wing Leaders—fearful that they might be required to give up their Spitfires in favour of Typhoons—had reached the ears of Parliament. The parting words of Balfour, recalled by several who served at Duxford at the time, may be coincidental; "If an old buffer like me can fly the Typhoon and walk away, anyone can".

---

[2] This may be an appropriate point to repeat an anecdote, widely quoted, which I am assured is not apocryphal. Some surprise was occasioned throughout the War among operational pilots that the delivery of Typhoons to the squadrons was most frequently undertaken by women pilots of the Air Transport Auxiliary. It was firmly believed by the male pilots of that splendid organization that the exceptionally severe vibration experienced in the Typhoon adversely affected their virility, while the ladies—who professed complete indifference to any discomfort—were perfectly happy to deliver *any* aeroplane that was placed in their line of duty!

Early in the New Year some of the 12-gun Typhoon IAs were flown away to training units, their place being taken by four-cannon Mark IBs, and the latter gradually came to provide the main equipment of the Squadron. Prosser Hanks' place as the Squadron's commanding officer had been taken by Squadron Leader Hugh 'Cocky' Dundas (later Group Captain, DSO and Bar, DFC), a distinguished Battle of Britain veteran who was to remain with No. 56 for a year before being posted overseas.

Meanwhile, with the solution found to the cockpit contamination problem, a second Typhoon squadron, No. 266, started receiving the fighters at King's Cliffe in Northamptonshire on 1 January 1942, and completed a move to Duxford at the end of the month where it joined No. 56 in operational conversion. One of the new Squadron's pilots had a lucky escape on 11 February when he found he could lower only one undercarriage leg for landing; after "banging the aircraft down" on the one extended leg, the pilot over-shot when the red light indicator for the other leg came on, showing that it had unlocked and was coming down; he was then able to complete a normal landing. It was considered a fine piece of flying as it required considerable skill to touch down on one wheel without sinking on to the propeller—especially in a Typhoon, with its very wide-track undercarriage.

No. 56 Squadron was the first to declare one Flight fully operation on 29 May, although No. 266 did scramble a single aircraft (*R7631*, flown by Pilot Officer G. Elcombe) to investigate an X-raid on the previous day, which turned out to be a Spitfire. On the 29th No. 56 Squadron sent detachments south, four Typhoons flying to Westhampnett near Tangmere, and four to Manston, under orders to bolster No. 11 Group's defence against the fleeting "tip and run" raids by Focke-Wulf Fw 190A fighter-bombers that were proving too fast for its Spitfire VBs.

The detachments began in tragedy when, two days after arrival in the south, the Manston-based Typhoons were attacked by Spitfires of No. 401 Squadron, RCAF, while on patrol; the aircraft flown by Sergeant Stuart-Turner (*R8199*) and Pilot Officer P. H. Deugo (*R7678*) were shot down, the former pilot being killed. The Canadian pilots had mistaken the Typhoons for Focke-Wulf raiders. Two months later, on 30 July, a Norwegian pilot on No. 56 Squadron, Flying Office E. Haabjoern, was shot down in *R7853* by Spitfires while returning from an offensive sweep over Cap Gris Nez; fortunately the pilot was able to bale out over the Channel and was rescued unhurt.

The superficial similarity between the Typhoon and the Fw 190 had certainly caused confusion among the defences in Southern England, and the widespread "trigger happinesss" was clearly engendered by the Fw 190s' tactics. Little or no warning of their approach was possible as they swept in from the sea at very low altitude beneath radar cover, dropping their bombs on coastal towns and making good their escape in attacks that often occupied less than a couple of minutes. These attacks were carried out by a tiny force of fighter-bombers based in Northern France and were but a foretaste of much more serious attacks to come. Yet they created widespread confusion, quite out of proportion to the number of aircraft employed, as well as causing the loss of more RAF aircraft shot down by the defences than of German raiders.

After the loss of the No. 56 Squadron Typhoons to "friendly" Spitfires the immediate remedy adopted was to paint a prominent yellow bar on the upper surface of the Typhoon's starboard wing, but this was no aid to recognition for Bofors gunners on the ground who continued to blaze away whenever they caught sight of a low flying fighter. Hurried trials were carried out at Farnborough and elsewhere with all manner of identification colour schemes, following which orders were issued for all Typhoons to be painted with prominent black and white chordwise stripes under the wings, and these were to remain a characteristic

feature of the aircraft for two years or more; the yellow stripe on the upper surface continued to be carried on many Typhoons until well into 1943.

Shortly before Nos. 56 and 266 Squadrons were declared operational a third Typhoon squadron started re-equipping at Duxford. No. 609 (West Riding) Squadron of the Auxiliary Air Force— which by this stage of the War retained few signs of its peacetime "weekend" character—moved to the Cambridgeshire airfield from Digby in Lincolnshire on 20 March with Spitfires under the command of Squadron Leader George Kemp ("Sheep") Gilroy, continuing to fly a diminishing number of patrols as the new fighters were delivered; by the end of April the Squadron was fully occupied in converting to Typhoons.

It was at this stage that the first accidents occurred, resulting from Typhoon tail units breaking off in flight (see page 40). As previously explained, once the cause had come to be diagnosed in August 1942 as a fracture of the elevator balance bracket, a local strengthening modification of this bracket was incorporated and accepted as a satisfactory interim remedy. Thereafter, at Duxford, the transport joint in the rear fuselage as well as

Typhoon IBs of No 56 Squadron pictured early in the autumn of 1942; each aircraft displays the yellow recognition stripe introduced that summer following instances in which RAF pilots mistook the Typhoons for Focke-Wulf Fw 190s. Most of the aircraft feature faired rear view mirrors, but only US-A has faired cannon barrels.

the offending balance brackets were frequently inspected, and no sign of cracking was detected.

A setback to this air of confidence, however, occurred when, on 21 October 1942, "Gerry" Sayer lost his life in a Typhoon. On that day the highly respected Gloster chief test pilot, visiting No. 1 Squadron (by then re-equipped with Typhoons, see below) at Acklington, took off in a Typhoon with strengthened elevator balance brackets to carry out gun firing in high-g turns over the North Sea, accompanied by a second Typhoon, flown by Pilot Officer P. N. Dobie for observation purposes. Neither pilot was ever seen again, nor was any distress call received.

The pundits immediately concluded that Sayer's aircraft had suffered tail breakage, and had somehow struck the other aircraft. Sanity prevailed, however, and a straightforward air collision, probably in cloud, was realized as being the most likely cause of the accident. Once this verdict was accepted, the Service concluded that it was also logical to accept the balance bracket reinforcement unreservedly—at least until evidence could be produced to suggest it was inadequate. While, as already explained, the programme to improve the longitudinal control continued for a further year, Typhoons now appeared with a ring of fishplates riveted round the rear transport joint (in place of the previous continuous steel strip), it being generally felt, in retrospect, that this measure was adopted as an outward indication of a "strengthened" tail joint for the reassurance of Service pilots; in reality the fishplates themselves would have contributed scarcely any reinforcement had structural failure occurred . . .

The first Typhoon Wing

As all three Duxford Squadrons struggled to maintain a semblance of operational capability during the summer of 1942, with aircraft being constantly withdrawn for inspection and modification, plans were laid to create a Duxford Typhoon Wing—intended to take its place alongside the famous Spitfire Wings in the South of England. This was considerably simplified by the creation of a "Typhoon Pool" on the station from which each squadron might "borrow" aircraft to make up the necessary Wing strength when required.

No. 609 Squadron, whose command passed to that famous Hurricane pilot, Squadron Leader Paul Henry Mills Richey DFC,[3] was declared operational on 30 June. It was also around this time that Flight Lieutenant 'Bee' Beamont (who had flown his last trials at Langley—for the time being—in May) also joined No. 609 as a flight commander and, as part of his own investigations into the Typhoon's suitability as a night fighter, flew a number of night patrols in *R7708*/PR-V from Duxford under Ground Controlled Interception (GCI)

No 266 Squadron's R7695/ZH-Z provides an interesting comparison with Gillam's R7698/ZZ, shown opposite. The shadows on the nose show the newly-introduced four-inch extended exhaust stubs—intended to alleviate CO contamination of the cockpit. The top cockpit panel is hinged open, illustrating why it was not possible to open the port car door for entry to the cockpit; both doors were however jettisonable. Note also the correct 50-inch A-type roundel, with traces of the previous roundel visible. Unlike R7698, R7695 did not fly on the Squadron's early operational sorties. (Photo: via R. C. Sturtivant)

radar supervision during the last week in July. With the exception of scathing criticism of the very poor windscreen and hood panels, Beamont judged the Typhoon to be perfectly suitable for short-range, clear-weather night interception and intruder operations—passing favourable comment on the Typhoon's lack of exhaust glare as well as its simple and straightforward landing characteristics.

During July and the first half of August, punctuating occasional operational sorties, the three Duxford squadrons flew practice exercises as a Wing, led by Wing Commander Denys Edgar Gillam (later Group Captain, DSO and two Bars, DFC and Bar, AFC) who was already gaining a reputation as one of the RAF's foremost specialists in ground attack tactics. However it must be emphasized that at this time the Typhoon was still officially regarded as a "dogfighter" with only a secondary ground attack rôle—on 9th August No. 266 Squadron destroyed a Junkers Ju 88 (the Typhoon's first air combat victory), and four days later shot down a Messerschmitt Me 210.

Then on the morning of 18 August the Duxford Wing Pilots were called together for a briefing on their first major operation. Addressed by Group Captain John Grandy (later Air Chief Marshal Sir John, GCB, KBE, DSO, and Chief of the Air Staff in 1971), commanding the Duxford Sector, the pilots were told that, bearing in mind the Typhoon still faced a number of problems with engine and airframe, it was for the Wing itself to decide whether or not it felt ready for its first "big show". When

---

[3] Whose book *Fighter Pilot*, describing his experiences early in the Second World War, must be regarded as a classic of its period.

Fresh from the Duxford "purgatory store", R7698/ZZ was the personal aircraft of the Duxford Wing Leader, Wg Cdr Denys Gillam, DSO, DFC, from June to December 1942. Listed on the strength of No 609 Squadron, the aircraft was flown by Gillam when he led No 266 Squadron on its first Typhoon operation on 20 June that year. Apart from the distinctive "ZZ" markings, the aircraft's rear fuselage band totally obscures the serial number, no recognition stripes were carried (they were only shortly to be introduced) and the fuselage roundel, being an adaptation of the earlier 60-inch Type A version, is non-standard. Note also the small faired rear-view mirror above the cockpit, then just being introduced. (Photo: via R. L. Ward, Farnborough)

Gillam outlined the nature of the operation, to cover a combined cross-Channel operation against Dieppe on the following day, the response was one of enthusiastic determination to participate.[4]

As preparations went ahead to make ready the Wing's aircraft for Operation "Jubilee", news arrived at No. 56 Squadron's dispersal that one of the Squadron's pilots, Sgt J. S. Jones, had crashed in *R7644* during an air firing practice near Sutton Bridge and had been killed.

Early on the 19th the Wing took off from Duxford to rendezvous with a formation of Defiants of an independent Flight—later to become No. 515 Squadron—which were equipped with "Moonshine" jamming equipment to create a screen intended to blind German radar as far as Ostend to the north-east of the Dieppe landings. After an uneventful sortie the Wing landed to refuel at West Malling, the Kent airfield from which the Typhoons would be flying during the operation. At 14:00 hr it took off once more, this time for a patrol over the landings themselves, crossing the Channel at full power and flying as a compact formation at 10,000 feet. As the French coast was crossed and the formation turned towards Dieppe, No. 56 Squadron climbed to provide top cover for the other two squadrons. Shortly before arriving over the landings a section from No. 266 Squadron spotted some Dornier Do 217 bombers which were promptly attacked by Flight Lieutenant R. H. L. Dawson and Pilot Officer W. S. Smithyson. Just as

Dawson called over his radio that he had shot down one of the bombers No. 56 Squadron was bounced from above and behind by a *Staffel* of Focke-Wulf Fw 190As, causing a moment's confusion as the covering Typhoons scattered. However, the German pilots continued their dive through No. 56 and made straight for the aircraft of Dawson and Smithyson, shooting down the latter and damaging Dawson's Typhoon. As Gillam ordered the Wing to retire, Flight Lieutenant A. C. Johnston managed to fire a burst at a Fw 190 and claimed it as probably destroyed.

Dawson's Typhoon was obviously badly crippled, with one wheel hanging down and his speed reduced to no more than 180 mph, and the other Wing pilots closed in to escort him back across the Channel. Just as one section of No. 609 Squadron broke away to attack some Fw 190s (claiming three of them as damaged), a Canadian squadron of Spitfire IXs carried out a snap attack on the remaining Typhoons, Dawson's aircraft being seen to dive vertically into the sea.

One further sweep by the Typhoons was flown in the evening—without any further sign of enemy aircraft—before the tired but exhilarated pilots landed back at Duxford.[5]

A prolonged analysis of the day's operation suggested that while the Typhoons had generally acquitted themselves adequately in combat, the fact that there had been three instances in which the Squadrons had been "bounced" from above and behind (including the attack by the Canadians) lent fuel to the clamour for the replacement of the Typhoon's wholly unsatisfactory cockpit canopy.

Some reports suggested that both Dawson's and Smithyson's aircraft had suffered tail failure, but this was later discounted. However, one aspect of the whole air operation, fairly widely recorded, was that a tactical aspect of Operation "Jubilee", formulated by the Air Staff, was to give the first Typhoon Wing and the first Spitfire IX Wing an opportunity to meet the Focke-Wulf Fw 190 in strength to discover just how the latest RAF fighter fared. There is little doubt but that had the Typhoon Wing failed to operate over Dieppe, the "hostile" lobby would have succeeded in having the aircraft abandoned altogether. Owing, however, to a somewhat inconsequential use of the new Spitfire IX, and a generally inept deployment of both new Wings, the trial of strength was seen to be inconclusive. It did nevertheless confirm a widely-held belief that the Typhoon was not a suitable "dogfighter" at altitudes above about 15,000 feet.

The verdict on "Jubilee" can only be one of planning incompetence for, while the RAF had provided a massive umbrella of Spitfire VBs, the air *support* element had been inadequate, incon-

[4] As recalled by Wing Commander Beamont in his recent book *Fighter Test Pilot* (Patrick Stephens Ltd., 1986).

[5] PRO/AIR 27/530, 531 and 1558

Sqn Ldr R. P. Beamont's Typhoon R7752/PR-G. The flying view shows the aircraft late in 1942 when at Manston; just obscured is Beamont's victory "tally" of 23 enemy trains destroyed, and the cannon are unfaired. The lower picture shows the aircraft at Manston in May 1943, with recognition stripes added and cannons faired. The nose panel, with squadron commander's pennant, squadron badge and victory score, is now displayed in the RAF Museum at Hendon. (Photos: (upper) via R. C. Sturtivant and (lower) Wg Cdr R. P. Beamont, CBE, DSO, DFC)

sistent and poorly co-ordinated. German air opposition, though by no means considerable, had been underestimated—the *Luftwaffe*'s fighters and fighter-bombers frequently choosing their opportunities to attack while they held the initiative. If the operation proved of any value at all, it served to demonstrate to the Allied Staffs just what depth of planning would be required for any future invasion across the English Channel. Ironically the Typhoon, an aeroplane whose future value had been widely questioned prior to the Dieppe landings, was now to embark on a phase of operations that would eventually place it in the forefront of that great invasion two years hence.

Battle at low altitude

While neither the Typhoon nor the Spitfire IX had been able to demonstrate their full potential over the Dieppe beaches, it now remained to discover how exactly their obvious potency could best be exploited. The new Spitfire—specifically introduced to recover the air superiority hard won by the earlier Mark VB in 1941—retained much of

that version's agility, and possessed a top speed roughly similar to that of the Typhoon, although its Merlin 61 was still not entirely free of teething troubles, having been rather hastily passed through its final development phase. Moreover the very attribute that characterized the new engine (a two-speed, two-stage supercharger) did not lend suitability for air combat at low altitude. Indeed it was an excellent dogfighter at just those altitudes where the Typhoon was virtually impotent.

Soon after the Dieppe landings the Duxford Wing was disbanded. No. 56 Squadron moved to the satellite airfield in north Norfolk at Matlaske on 24 August; on 18 September No. 609 Squadron travelled to that most famous of all fighter airfields—and home of an illustrious Spitfire Wing—Biggin Hill; and on 21 September No. 266 took station at Warmwell in Dorset, right on the South Coast. Meanwhile, no fewer than five new Typhoon squadrons were in the process of working up.

In July No. 1 Squadron, commanded by Squadron Leader James Archibald Findlay MacLachlan, DFC and Bar, had transferred from Tangmere to Acklington in Northumberland to re-equip with Typhoons, receiving its first aircraft on the 21st; however by the time the Squadron had acquired its full complement of Typhoons at the end of August command of No. 1 had passed to Squadron Leader Royce Clifford Wilkinson, DFM and Bar.

At High Ercall in Shropshire No. 257 Squadron, commanded by Squadron Leader Peter Guy Wykeham-Barnes, DFC and Bar, also received Typhoons in July and began training in the low-level interception rôle, preparatory to moving to the south of England in September. At Wittering in Northamptonshire the New Zealanders of No. 486 Squadron, having spent a frustrating period with Hurricane night fighters, changed to the day fighter rôle with Typhoons in July under the command of Squadron Leader Claude Lyttleton Collingwood Roberts, beginning a distinguished three-year association with the Typhoon and Tempest.

Two newly-formed squadrons received their Typhoons in September. No. 181 under Squadron Leader Dennis Crowley-Milling, DFC,[6] at Duxford, and No. 182 under Squadron Leader Thomas Patrick Pugh at Martlesham Heath; the former was to specialize initially in the low altitude interception of the tip-and-run raiders, and the latter began training in ground support operations with the Army.

[6] Crowley-Milling (later Air Vice-Marshal, CBE, DSO, DFC and Bar), a Pilot Officer during the Battle of Britain, had been shot down in a Spitfire over France while commanding No. 610 Squadron in 1941; he evaded capture by the Germans and made his way to Spain where he was promptly placed in a concentration camp. Eventually released, he returned to England, rejoining No. 610 Squadron with whom he fought over Dieppe, shooting down a Bf 109 to bring his score to six victories.

Thus by the end of 1942 eight Typhoon squadrons were operational in both offensive and defensive rôles. An end to the frustrating misfortunes was in sight, while the accident rate had been considerably reduced to something approaching that of other contemporary RAF fighters. The Sabre, however, continued to give a good deal of trouble, though by now seldom with fatal results.

No. 1 Squadron had suffered its first accident loss on 5 September when an Australian pilot, Sergeant A. E. Pearce, made a forced landing in Cumberland with a broken connecting rod; Pearce escaped unhurt but the aircraft was burnt out. The following day, however, a New Zealander, Pilot Officer D. P. Perrin, gained the Squadron's first victory when he destroyed a Messerschmitt Me 210 near Robin Hood's Bay, south of Whitby, while flying *R7922*; at much the same time Pilot Officer T. G. Bridges shot down another in *R7923* two miles south-west of Redcar.

On No. 181 Squadron Flight Lieutenant A. G. H. Lindsell, flying Typhoon IA *R7676* on 27 September was seen to make "one of his favourite steep turns" after take-off, but stalled and spun into the ground from 500 feet; two other aircraft, *R8932* (Sergeant G. E. Hadley) and *R8709* (Sergeant W. Grey), crashed on 8 and 11 November respectively. On the 13th No. 182 Squadron's CO suffered a tyre burst while taking off at Martlesham; seeing that he was likely to crash into parked aircraft he whipped up the undercarriage, causing the Typhoon to turn over on to its back— but arresting its forward progress most rapidly. Squadron Leader Pugh nevertheless escaped unhurt.

No. 56 Squadron, which had by now resumed offensive operations from Matlaske, flying frequent *Rhubarbs* over the Dutch coast, had at long last gained its first air victory on 14 September when Flight Lieutenant Ingle-Finch (now a flight commander) and Pilot Officer W. E. Coombes, RCAF, shot down a Junkers Ju 88 off the East Coast. The New Zealanders of No. 486 Squadron had, however, amassed the largest score of all the Typhoon squadrons by the end of the year, having despatched four Messerschmitt Bf 109Fs, a Focke-Wulf Fw 190A and two Dornier Do 217s. First of these victories, a Bf 109F, had been claimed by an English-born Sergeant Pilot, Francis Murphy; inevitably known on his squadron as "Spud" but thereafter as Frank, Murphy had emigrated to New Zealand only a few months before the outbreak of war and had promptly joined the RNZAF. Returning to England where he joined No. 486, he was commissioned early in 1943 after having destroyed a second Bf 109. Later as a Squadron Leader he was posted to Hawker Aircraft Ltd as a test pilot, remaining with the Company for many years to fly Typhoons, Tempests, Sea Furies, Sea Hawks and Hunters, ultimately

being appointed Chief Production Test Pilot.

While the old "R-serial" Typhoons were being returned to Gloster to have extensive modifications made to the rear fuselage to incorporate the Stage B canopies and flat windscreen quarter-lights (but still retaining the car doors), the first "DN-serial" Typhoons were beginning to appear on the squadrons before the end of the year. These featured the Stage B canopies from new, "letting much more light into the office". Nevertheless, although the new rear canopy was generally considered to be a great improvement and, indeed, resulted in a small improvement in speed by reason of reduced drag, pilots found that when straining to peer over their shoulder (round the edge of the armour behind the headrest), vision through the rear perspex at such an acute angle was so distorted that an aircraft within a 40 degree cone in the rear hemisphere was scarcely visible, let alone identifiable. An attempt to overcome this was made by adding a Desmo-type rear view mirror on top of the canopy, covered by a perspex blister. Although providing a marginal improvement in rear view, it was found that the turbulence around the small blister considerably increased cockpit noise, as well as cancelling the speed benefit of the new canopy.

Already however the entirely new "tear drop", single-piece sliding canopy was being tested at Langley and shown to be the ideal remedy. But, as already explained, this canopy demanded such extensive alterations (by eliminating the car doors) that it would be many months before it would appear on production Typhoons.

The last two months of 1942 saw four further Typhoon squadrons joining RAF Fighter Command, with No. 183 Squadron formed under Squadron Leader Arthur Vincent Gowers at Church Fenton in Yorkshire on 1 November, No. 195 Squadron at Duxford on the 16th under Squadron Leader Donald Murray Taylor, No. 197 Squadron at Turnhouse near Edinburgh on the 21st under Squadron Leader L. O. J. Prevot, DFC (a Belgian), and No. 198 Squadron at Digby in Lincolnshire under Squadron Leader John Wolferstan Villa on 8 December.[7]

*   ★   ★

Having described the activities of the various Typhoon squadrons up to the end of 1942, it is important at this point to explain at some length how the aircraft was being considered in the wider context of Fighter Command's operational philosophy at that time.

Following the disbanding of the Duxford Wing

---

[7] The average age of these four squadron commanders at the time of their appointments was 24 years and ten months; all had fought in the Battle of Britain 30 months previous, "Pancho" Villa alone destroying ten enemy aircraft.

Two views of ex-No 181 Squadron Typhoon R8836/EL-U on test with 500-lb bombs. (Photos: via R. C. Sturtivant)

in October, its component squadrons were dispersed and deployed in the low-level interception rôle against the German "sneak" raiders. When Beamont took command of No. 609 Squadron, and sought to have the Squadron included in the Biggin Hill Wing sweeps, the rebuff he received was in line with a policy generally adopted at the time, that the Typhoon was a low-level defensive interceptor, and not an "offensive dogfighter" compatible with operations being undertaken by the Spitfires.

It had been as the result of Beamont's personal approach to Air Vice-Marshal Hugh Saunders at No. 11 Group that he had been authorized to embark independently on the low-level *offensive* operations from Manston (in effect as an operational trial) that had demonstrated so convincingly the Typhoon's aptitude for such work, the results of which, including more than 100 attacks on enemy trains in less than three months, were submitted to No. 11 Group by Beamont in person.

When, in January 1943, Air Chief Marshal Sir Trafford Leigh-Mallory, now Commander-in-Chief, Fighter Command, called a conference at Bentley Priory to review the whole future of the Typhoon—against a background of widely held opinions, particularly among the Spitfire Wing Leaders, that the entire Typhoon programme be cancelled there and then—Beamont's was almost the only voice to be heard in the aircraft's favour. The achievements by No. 609 Squadron in the low-level *offensive* rôle, by day and night, were considered to be a powerful argument in support of a case to retain the Typhoon and, indeed, not only won the day but sowed the necessary seeds of

a whole new attitude towards the aircraft in the offensive rôle.

Be that as it may, once the decision to continue introducing the Typhoon into service had been confirmed, it was still necessary to employ a large proportion of the squadrons' efforts in defensive operations against the low-flying German fighter-bombers, against which the Spitfires were less effective. Nevertheless, throughout 1943, the necessary steps were to be taken to create—by means of specialist training—a powerful Typhoon ground attack/close support force which henceforth took an increasing part in the cross-Channel offensive. The first manifestation of this *volte-face* was an immediate release of substantial stocks of 500-lb bombs to the operational Typhoon squadrons.

Training got underway immediately, mainly on old Mark IA Typhoons (disposed of by operational squadrons), but soon "DN-serial" Mark IBs were arriving from No. 13 Maintenance Unit. Those squadrons either engaged in (Nos. 56, 181, 182 and 609) or working up for (Nos. 183, 195 and 198) ground attack operations were beginning to fly Typhoon Mark IB bombers—popularly referred to as "Bombphoons"—equipped initially to carry a pair of 250-lb bombs under the wings. Although clearance had been achieved to fly with 500-pounders, stocks of the heavier bombs were not yet sufficient to provide an adequate surplus beyond Bomber Command's requirements until February 1943.

The new year was one in which, with structural problems largely overcome and engine reliability considerably improved, Typhoon activity increased rapidly, so that by the spring *Rhubarbs* were being undertaken almost daily on every squadron.

Notwithstanding the Typhoon pilots' own confidence in their aircraft there remained considerable antipathy among some Spitfire Wing Leaders towards the Typhoon. When in October 1942, following a move to Biggin Hill, Squadron Leader Beamont (now commanding No. 609 Squadron) sought the inclusion of his Typhoons in the next Wing sweep, he had his request peremptorily refused with the remark that "Typhoons weren't suitable". Unabashed Beamont appealed successfully to No. 11 Group to be moved forward to the airfield at Manston, and was delighted to be able to operate with a large degree of autonomy, dividing the Squadron's effort between daylight defensive patrols between Ramsgate and Dungeness and trial night intruder operations. Beamont himself undertook a number of modifications to improve the gun sighting in the Typhoon, particularly for night work when the bright imagery of the reflector gunsight tended to obscure the target. Eventually he removed the gunsight reflector glass and brackets entirely so that the gunsight reflected directly on to the windscreen. In the course of nine day and night *Rhubarbs* between 17 and 23 December Beamont attacked and damaged 12 trains in Belgium and France.

During January 1943 No. 182 Squadron, now at Sawbridgeworth in Hertfordshire, was declared operational on New Year's Day, marking the occasion on the 3rd with a *Rhubarb* flown by Flight Lieutenant Manak and Sergeant C. T. G. Shields who dropped four 250-pounders on a target at Bruges. That month two further Squadrons started converting from Hurricanes to Typhoons: No. 245 at Charmy Down in Somerset under Squadron Leader S. S. Hordern, and No. 247 at High Ercall under Squadron Leader J. C. Melvill. On 1 February delivery of Typhoons started to No. 3 Squadron, then commanded by Squadron Leader F. de Soomer at Hunsdon in Hertfordshire. Nine days later No. 1 Squadron was ordered south from Acklington to Biggin Hill, but lost one of its new "DN" aircraft which turned over on landing at Southend *en route* following flap and brake failure; Sergeant H. Crawley escaped unhurt.

Four days later another No. 1 Squadron pilot, Sergeant R. W. Hornall, suffered engine failure during an exercise with Canadian ground forces but, rather than bale out and risk his aircraft falling among the crowded troops below, stayed in his cockpit and contrived to steer the failing aircraft to a very difficult crash landing without endangering their lives, and fortunately surviving unhurt himself. No. 1 Squadron, like Beamont's No. 609, had to divide its time between offensive and defensive operations, and it was during an intercept patrol on 6 March that a Canadian pilot, Pilot Officer G.

C. Whitmore, and an Australian Flight Sergeant H. R. Fraser, collided in cloud near Tonbridge, both men being killed. Sergeant Hornall again distinguished himself a week later when he shot down a Focke-Wulf Fw 190 off the coast near Brighton; on the same patrol Flight Lieutenant L. S. B. Scott destroyed another. Less than a month later Hornall accounted for his second Fw 190.

The *Luftwaffe* fighter-bomber raids against Southern England had been stepped up considerably with the creation of *Schnellkampfgeschwader 10* (SKG10, or Fast Bomber Wing), whose *IV. Gruppe* flew the Fw 190A-4/U-8 over Britain. This potent aeroplane was armed with a pair of fast-firing 20-mm cannon and two machine-guns, and could carry a 1,100-lb bomb in addition to drop tanks that enabled raids to be carried out as far north as Suffolk. Towns and ports throughout Southern England suffered frequent raids, with particularly damaging attacks on Ashford, Canterbury, Chelmsford, Eastbourne, Hastings and the Medway towns (as well as London of course) in the early months of 1943.

During the daylight raids the Typhoons managed to take a steady toll of the attackers, but even the British fighter found it extremely difficult to catch the very fast Focke-Wulfs, particularly if they had already bombed or jettisoned their loads.

Right, EJ967/DP-D of No 193 Squadron at Harrowbeer, Devon, in March 1943. (Photo: F. H. B. Hulbert). *Below*, bearing a tally of 18 trains destroyed during intruder operations, No 609 Squadron's DN406/PR-F is shown at Tangmere in May 1943. (Photo: Sydney Camm Collection)

Below, R8752/JX-L of No 1 Squadron was being flown by F/Sgt W. H. Ramsey (White 2) on a Rhubarb over Armentières when the aircraft struck an object on the ground and lost fuel from one of his drop tanks; struggling home with an intermittently-cutting engine he made a wheels-up landing at Lympne. (Photo: via R. L. Ward) *Left*, EK176/JX-K, also of No 1 Squadron at Lympne in July 1943. (Photo: Public Archives of Canada, Neg No PW 9151)

The Spitfire IXs were even less effective at low altitude, and not even a special low altitude version, the clipped-wing Mark XII with Rolls-Royce Griffon engine, did much to improve the situation. However it must be said that with fewer than 50 of the raiders lost from all causes (of which roughly half were claimed by the ground defences) during the course of more than 800 sorties in five months, the RAF fighter defences—which deployed more than 250 aircraft against the raiders—were largely ineffective, so much so that even 40 years on the penetration of radar, gun, missile and fighter defences by high speed aircraft flying at very low altitude is still regarded as the most effective form of short-range attack by manned aircraft.

As the German attacks by "sneak" raiders began to diminish in April 1943, so the Typhoon squadrons were permitted to apportion greater effort to offensive operations, defensive patrols being confined to a "duty squadron" on rotation. On 15 March four Typhoons of No. 56 Squadron attacked a merchant ship guarded by a pair of armed trawlers off the Dutch coast; cannon strikes were seen on all the vessels, but the aircraft flown by the new commanding officer, Squadron Leader Thomas Henry Vincent Pheloung, was hit and damaged by flak; struggling to bring the Typhoon home the pilot had perforce to bale out 35 miles off Happisburgh, but spent only half an hour in the water before being picked up by an air-sea rescue Walrus. No. 198 Squadron, which had enjoyed a relatively trouble-free working-up, was declared operational at Manston at the end of March and flew its first patrols on the 28th; three days later the Squadron suffered its first casualty when Sergeant Ansell crashed into the sea off Dover following engine failure. No. 486 Squadron was also ordered over to the offensive in April and began providing escorts for Typhoon bombers operating on *Ramrods* and *Roadsteads*, the fighter-bombers now almost invariably carrying the 500-pounders. The Squadron also flew a number of night *Rhubarbs* but achieved rather less success than No. 609 Squadron.

If the activities by the Focke-Wulfs over England were beginning to diminish, the increasing tempo of Typhoon operations over the *Luftwaffe's* airfields kept the German pilots fully and gainfully occupied. No. 3 Squadron, declared operational on 16th May, flew its first *Ramrod* against the marshalling yards at Eu that day without loss, but on its third such operation on the 18th against Poix airfield about 30 Fw 190s were airborne and waiting; no fewer than five of No. 3 Squadron's Typhoons (Flying Officers Gill and Hall, Pilot Officer Inwood and Sergeants Baily and Whitall) were shot down. A fortnight later Pilot Officer R. E. Barckley failed to return from a *Rhubarb* during which he was last seen attacking a train. Shortly afterwards, while escorting Typhoons on a *Roadstead* attack on a convoy of seven ships off the Hook of Holland, three more of No. 3 Squadron's pilots (Flying Officer A. T. Little, Pilot Officer C. G. Benjamin and Sergeant A. W. Lawrence) were shot down by Fw 190s, two of which were claimed damaged by Flight Lieutenant R. W. A. Mackichan and Flying Officer L. J. Foster. All the enemy ships were hit by bombs or cannon fire. On 5 September the Squadron lost its commanding officer, Squadron Leader S. R. Thomas, DFC, AFC, shot down during another *Roadstead*, being seen to crash land in Holland.

In the west of England No. 266 had moved from Warmwell to Exeter early in January to counter sneak raiders approaching the Devon and Cornish coasts. The Squadron claimed two Fw 190As destroyed in each of the first three months of the year, but once more these attacks began to tail off. On 17 June one of the Squadron's pilots, Flying Officer H. A. Cooper (in *R7915*) experienced disagreeable excitement of a different sort. He and another pilot, Flight Lieutenant J. D. Wright (in *EJ986*) were scrambled and, when flying at "nought feet" 25 miles off Start Point, Cooper's engine failed. Pulling up to 1,500 feet he baled out, but his parachute snagged on the Typhoon's radio

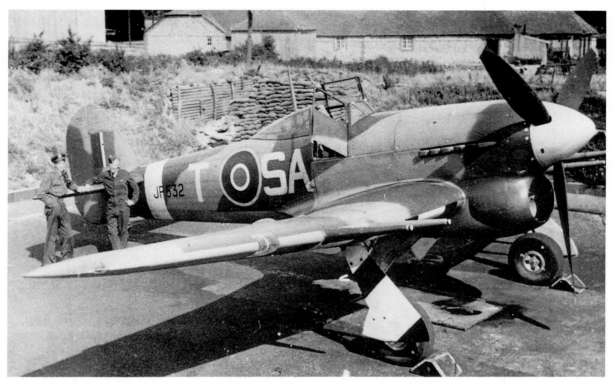

JP532/SA-T of No 486 Squadron, RNZAF, pictured in 1943; although shown here at Tangmere without bomb racks, this Typhoon was most frequently flown on Ramrods as a bomber. (Photo: via Richard Ward, Farnborough)

mast and he fell with the aircraft to 500 feet, at which height he managed to disconnect his "dog lead", thereby losing his dinghy pack. After hitting the sea he succeeded in inflating his Mae West lifejacket and remained afloat. Meanwhile, seeing his fellow pilot in the sea without a dinghy, Wright struggled to cut his own dinghy pack free with his knife (no simple task while flying the aircraft as the dinghy formed his seat "cushion") and eventually threw it out of the cockpit. Unfortunately the

Well-known, yet nonetheless superbly composed picture of Typhoon IB R8884/HF-L of No 183 Squadron at Gatwick in April 1943. This veteran aircraft was progressively modified following its early service at Duxford and is shown with bomb racks, faired rear view mirror and "strengthened" rear fuselage. (Photo: via D. J. Wells, Esq)

Aircraft of No 193 Squadron at Harrowbeer, Devon, lined up and awaiting a visit by the Brazilian Ambassador in October 1943. The nearest aircraft, JP919, carries the inscription "Bellows Brazil", indicating a Typhoon subscribed by that philanthropic group of ex-patriate Britons in that country, the Fellowship of the Bellows. (Photo: Sydney Camm Collection)

dinghy fouled the tailplane and remained lodged there, causing real control problems; nevertheless he remained circling the ditched pilot until relieved by another Section from the Squadron. Then an air-sea rescue Spitfire arrived and dropped a larger dinghy but Cooper, with little more than his head above the water, failed to spot it. In due course a Walrus alighted nearby and picked up the long-suffering pilot, but the amphibian itself could not take off owing to the high waves and so started to taxi back to the distant coast. A high-speed launch eventually took on board the pilot and landed him at Bolt Head, "exasperated and exhausted, but otherwise unharmed".

Four days later another 266 Squadron pilot, Pilot Officer N. V. Borland, baled out of *EJ931* following engine failure 12 miles east of Berry Head. This time the pilot only spent 15 minutes in the water before being picked up by a Walrus; it was only as the flying boat was taking off again that its pilot realized that he had alighted in the midst of a minefield!

Cooper was to survive another narrow escape on 30 July when, returning from a sortie in support of *Circus* No. 46 over Guipavas in *R8638*, he suffered yet another engine failure, this time just as he was crossing out over the French coast. No sooner had he jettisoned his hood and doors, preparatory to baling out, than his recalcitrant Sabre spluttered into life once more so that the Squadron was able to escort the faltering Typhoon back to Exeter. However finding that his stalling speed was now too high for a safe landing on the runway in use, he chose to put his aircraft down on a runway which was being repaired; the Typhoon overshot, ground-looped and crashed, but once more Cooper emerged unscathed!

Two ex-Hurricane bomber squadrons began converting to Typhoons in April, No. 174 at Gravesend (Squadron Leader W. W. McConnell, DFC) and No. 175 (Squadron Leader Alan William Pennington-Legh DFC). Both Squadrons received brand new aircraft—"EK" and "JP" serials—al-

though when No. 175 moved to Lasham on 29 May it left behind its new Typhoons to inherit No. 183 Squadron's elderly aircraft as the two units swapped airfields. No. 175 was declared operational first on 12 June, having moved on to the delightfully-named airfield of Appledram in West Sussex, and on that day Flight Lieutenants Murchie and Davies (in *EJ979* and *R8976* respectively) flew a *Rhubarb* to dive-bomb Abbeville airfield. The next day a second *Rhubarb* over Dieppe by Flying Officer Wise (in *EJ979*) and Pilot Officer Cockbone *(EK184)* encountered heavy flak, and the latter pilot was shot down.

It was No. 174 Squadron's turn on 14 July to fly its first operation as eight Typhoons carried out an attack with 500-lb bombs on French railway targets in *Ramrod* No. 136. On the next day Pilot Officer J. M. Chalifour in *EK228* of No.1 Squadron, flying from Lympne, probably suffered oxygen failure as his aircraft was seen to break formation at 10,000 feet and dive vertically into the sea.

A breathless account of a couple of *Rhubarbs*, flown by No. 185 Squadron 3 July, imparts an inkling of the increasing tempo of Typhoon operations at this time:

"Plt Off D. J. Webster *(R8938)* and F/Sgt T. H. McGovern RAAF *(DN315)* carried out a very successful *Rhubarb* on Zandaam, claiming three goods trains, a factory (*sic*) and an oil storage tank. F/Sgt N. Arbon *(EJ921)* and Sgt P. C. Mason RAAF *(EK223)* carried out one on De Honkes but saw nothing. Arbon hit a grass bank with his port wing tip trying to get under some high tension cables. Mason collided with a seagull. McGovern was hit in the nose tank and main oil feed—he arrived back with an inch of oil left in the tank . . ."[8]

As summer turned to autumn the pace of operations continued unabated. No. 3 Squadron, undeterred by the heavy losses suffered earlier in the

---

8 PRO/AIR 27/1164

year, flew 22 *Rhubarbs*, and participated in three *Rodeos*, eleven *Ramrods* and six *Roadsteads* in the space of six weeks. On 4 October one of the flight commanders, Flight Lieutenant G. L. Sinclair (not to be confused with Gordon Leonard Sinclair, DFC and Bar, the well-known Battle of Britain pilot who, in the previous month, had taken over command of No. 56 Squadron at Bradwell Bay), was posted Missing after a *Roadstead*. The next day a *Ramrod* by ten aircraft ran into German fighters which shot down the Squadron's newly-arrived CO, Squadron Leader Ronald Hawkins, MC, AFC, Flying Officer L. J. Foster (previously mentioned) and Warrant Officer J. La Rocque.

No. 1 Squadron, which had flown numerous escorts for Typhoon bombers and Whirlwinds in the course of *Ramrods* and *Roadsteads*, embarked on a phase of night intruder *Rhubarbs* with a solo night bombing attack on Abbeville airfield by Flight Lieutenant H. T. Mossip with 500-pounders, this pilot becoming regarded as an accomplished bombing expert on the Squadron.

By now Typhoons were flying as Wings in their own right, formations of anything up to 40 aircraft attacking targets in France and the Low Countries. In such raids two squadrons would provide the bombers—usually flying at 5,000 feet or below—while a pair of escorting Typhoon squadrons would fly overhead at between 7,000 and 10,000 feet. In one such attack by No. 124 Wing on 11 September No. 181 Squadron bombed Beauvais airfield as No. 175 flew top cover. The raid was intercepted by about 20 Fw 190s whose pilots shot down the Wing Leader, Wing Commander W. H. Ingle, as well as Flight Sergeant Murray of No. 175 Squadron; four Fw 190s were seen to be shot down.

It was during the closing months of 1943 that a sinister new target began to feature prominently in Typhoon operations with the identification of the first of the flying bomb launch sites in the Pas de Calais. Referred to as "No Ball" sites, these appeared at first as fairly elaborate complexes, and during early construction work the Germans forebore to deploy substantial flak defences on the sites for fear of attracting attention by British and American bombers. As the sites proliferated, however, and were accorded high priority for Allied air attack, so the gun defences were heavily reinforced; by the end of the year all calibres of flak were present, capable of throwing up a veritable curtain of fire over the launch sites.

Every type of raid was launched against the No-Ball sites, from daylight "carpet bombing" by the British and American medium and heavy bombers to low level sweeps and dive-bombing attacks by the fighter-bombers; it was in the latter category that Typhoons were thrown into the fray. Almost every one of the operational squadrons flew its share of No-Ball attacks during those winter months of 1943–44, but the realization slowly dawned that the 500-lb bomb scarcely caused any damage to the concrete ramps and neighbouring buildings except with direct hits, and even then such superficial scars only required a "barrowload of cement" to put matters aright. What were needed were heavier bombs and rocket projectiles but, so far as the Typhoon was concerned, these were still some weeks away at the end of 1943.

So, on the theory that constant attacks—even with cannon and 500-lb bombs—would all help to delay completion of the launching sites, the Typhoon pilots continued to perform the hated No-Ball sorties. No. 609 Squadron, which had enjoyed

JP504/OV-Z of No 197 Squadron at Tangmere in October 1943, equipped with bomb racks. The squadron commander, Sqn Ldr M. C. Holmes DFC poses in the aircraft, which carries his pennant on the car door. (Photo: Sydney Camm Collection)

a brief respite from operations in July while its Sabre engines underwent a series of remedial improvements, returned to the fray in October, though now with a new CO, Squadron Leader P. G. Thornton-Brown (Beamont having returned to Hawker for a further spell of test flying, this time on the new Tempest). Not all the Squadron's operations were confined to the flying bomb sites, and just occasionally its pilots found German bombers to attack: on 4 December the Squadron destroyed seven Dornier Do 217s in seven minutes! Before the end of the month however Thornton-Brown himself was shot down—by a USAAF P-47.

December was a hectic month for No. 1, whose activities were typified by *Ramrod* No. 336 on the 14th when the commanding officer, Squadron Leader A. Zwiegbergh, led eight aircraft to drop 16 500-pounders on a No-Ball site at Foresterberne. A week later Flight Sergeant S. D. Cunningham was shot down in *JR144* in another such attack, and the next day Pilot Office J. W. Sutherland in *JR237* failed to return . . .

★   ★   ★

Before passing on to the momentous events of 1944 it is worth setting out here the deployment of Fighter Command's Typhoon squadrons, including those new units which were, at the end of 1943, converting and working up to operational status:

HAWKER TYPHOON SQUADRONS, R.A.F. FIGHTER COMMAND, 31 DECEMBER 1943

Squadron	Base	Status	Commanding Officer
1	Lympne, Kent	Operational	Sqn Ldr A. Zwiegbergh
3	Swanton Morley, Norfolk	Operational	Sqn Ldr A. S. Dredge, DSO, DFC, AFC
56	Martlesham Heath, Suffolk	Operational	Sqn Ldr Gordon Leonard Sinclair, DFC and Bar
174	Westhampnett, Sussex	Operational	Sqn Ldr W. W. McConnell, DFC
175	Westhampnett, Sussex	Operational	Sqn Ldr M. R. Ingle-Finch, DFC
181	Odiham, Hampshire (moved this day from Merston, Sussex)	Operational	Sqn Ldr J. G. Keep
182	Odiham, Hampshire (moved this day from Merston, Sussex)	Operational	Sqn Ldr Michael Edward Reid
183	Predannack, Cornwall	Operational	Sqn Ldr W. Dring, DFC
184	Detling, Kent	Working-up (re-equipped 12–43)	Sqn Ldr Jack Rose, DFC
186	Ayr, Ayrshire	Working-up (re-equipped 11–43)	Sqn Ldr Francis Edward Goodenough Hayter
193	Harrowbeer, Devon	Operational	Sqn Ldr George William Petre, DFC, AFC
195	Fairlop, Essex	Operational	Sqn Ldr Donald Murray Taylor, DFC
197	Tangmere, Sussex	Operational	Sqn Ldr M. P. C. Holmes DFC
198	Manston, Kent	Operational	Sqn Ldr John Robert Baldwin, DSO, DFC and Bar
245	Westhampnett, Sussex	Operational	Sqn Ldr E. Haabjoern, DFC
257	Warmwell, Dorset	Operational	Sqn Ldr Ronald Henry Fokes, DFC, DFM
263	Ibsley, Hampshire	Working-up (re-equipped 12–43)	Sqn Ldr Gerald Bernard Warnes, DSO, DFC
266	Harrowbeer, Devon	Operational	Sqn Ldr Peter William Lefevre, DFC
486	Tangmere, Sussex	Operational	Sqn Ldr I. D. Waddy
609	Manston, Kent	Operational	Sqn Ldr John Christopher Wells, DSO, DFC and Bar

IN SUPPORT
OF LIBERATION

The dawn of 1944 found the Typhoon squadrons still plugging away at the No-Ball sites in Northern France, although poor or unsuitable weather reduced the effectiveness of the bombing attacks; these normally involved steep dives from at least 8,000 feet, demanding sight of the target from that altitude. Often fine weather over the Typhoon bases in Southern England would encourage several squadrons to take off, but then their pilots would find thick cloud building up over the French coast. Rather than risk killing innocent Frenchmen or attempting to land back with bombs still under their aircraft, most squadron commanders ordered their pilots to jettison the bombs (unfused) into the Channel.

While the majority of attacks were being carried out using the 500-lb bomb, No. 197 Squadron still flew most sorties with 250-pounders, this being the favourite weapon on *Rhubarbs* and because Manston still held sizeable stocks of the smaller bomb 197 was occasionally ordered off on "freelancing" *Rhubarbs* on the look-out for No-Ball sites—a particularly hazardous variation of the attacks; four of its aircraft attacked the launch site near Ligecourt on 3 January—a heavily gun-defended target—and Flight Sergeant N. F. Miles' aircraft (*JR150*) was seen to be hit by flak just as he released his bombs, and to crash within the ramp enclosure.

On No. 175 Squadron, at Westhampnett, New Year's Day was marked by the arrival of the first Typhoon with a sliding hood (*JP736*), and this was promptly appropriated by the CO! No. 181 Squadron moved into nearby Merston on 21 January with a new clutch of Typhoons with strengthened wings cleared to carry 1,000-lb bombs, but for the time being had to be content with 500-pounders as doubts were expressed as to whether the runway at Merston was adequate to cope with Typhoons taking off at over 13,000 lb. On this squadron

Flying Officer L. R. Allen (*JP968*) had a 500-lb bomb hang up during a No-Ball attack on the 25th; in attempting to avoid overflying the flak defences he was forced to turn steeply but, with a bomb under one wing he stalled and spun in.

January also saw two new Typhoon squadrons being re-equipped. No. 137 Squadron, commanded by Acting Squadron Leader J. R. Dennehey, DFC, at Colerne, had flown Whirlwinds until midway through the previous year but had since spent six months with Hurricane IVs so that its conversion training on Typhoons occupied less than a month. No. 164 Squadron, which moved to Fairlop in Essex in mid-January under Squadron Leader Humphrey à Becket Russell, DFC, received an assortment of much-used veterans and brand-new aircraft.

One of the squadrons that had started to re-equip with Typhoons, No. 186, in the previous November had had to contend with a move north from Ayr to Tain, and never really got to grips with the conversion, giving up their new aircraft and being supplied with aged Spitfire VBs (which in turn were only flown for a couple of months before the Squadron was disbanded to become No. 130 Squadron).

Meanwhile, as other Typhoon squadrons were approaching operational status after several weeks' training, and the No-Ball attacks continued, plans were being finalized to complete a reorganization of the Typhoon squadrons into Wings, not so much to bring them into line with the long-established Spitfire Wings whose identity had always been associated with specific RAF fighter stations, but to assemble specialist Typhoon squadrons into easily managed tactical formations.

The new Typhoon plan, the so-called Operation "Spartan", had foreshadowed the battle requirements of 2nd Tactical Air Force, which had come

Pilots and Typhoons of No 245 Squadron on the South Coast airfield at Westhampnett in February 1944. The Squadron was then flying Ramrods and Rangers with bombs and cannon, but two months later started training with rockets.

into existence at Bracknell on 1 June 1943, by which the squadrons would have to learn how to operate from relatively rudimentary (or "spartan") airfields with little or no hangarage and scarcely any permanent buildings. Groundcrews and pilots would have to live almost permanently under canvas and all maintenance would be carried out at the mercy of the elements; runways and taxytracks would be levelled and rolled by field engineers at little notice and then surfaced with wire matting or PSP (perforated steel planking). Some squadrons were fortunate in being moved on to fairly elaborate airfields to begin with in Southern England, but other sites gave a foretaste of "worse to come".

One of the preliminary elements of the Spartan Plan had involved the construction of a rudimentary airfield near Lydd, originally termed No. 121 Airfield in February 1943, this subsequently becoming the home of Nos. 174, 175 and 245 Squadrons. Thus in effect was born the first Tactical Typhoon Wing, No. 121 Wing and, in theory at any rate, wherever these squadrons moved they moved as No. 121 Wing—in May 1944 becoming No. 121 (Rocket Projectile) Wing. The first four Typhoon Spartan Wings were:

No. 121 Airfield, formed February 1943. Became No. 121 (Rocket Projectile) Wing, May 1944 (Nos. 174, 175 and 245 Squadrons)

No. 123 Airfield, formed April 1943. Became No. 123 (Rocket Projectile) Wing, May 1944 (Nos. 198 and 609 Squadrons)

No. 124 Airfield, formed April 1943. Became No. 124 (Rocket Projectile) Wing, May 1944 (Nos. 181, 182 and 247 Squadrons)

No. 143 Airfield, planned April 1943. Became No. 143 (Fighter-Bomber) Wing, RCAF, May 1944 (Nos. 438, 439 and 440 Squadrons, RCAF)

Seen in the company of German personnel, Typhoon JP577/HH-T of No 175 Squadron was shot down by flak while escorting 40 Bostons on a raid over France on 16th August 1943. The pilot, Sergeant Merlin, was presumably taken prisoner. (Photo: via R. C. Sturtivant)

No 137 Squadron only started receiving Typhoons in January 1944, and in March that year began training with rockets. It is not known exactly when the two photos above were taken, although the absence of any recognition stripes and the use of four-blade propellers suggest a date in 1945. (Photos: via Richard Ward, Farnborough)

During much of 1943 those Typhoon squadrons scheduled for close support operations had been subject to move at very short notice from their comfortable quarters to some distant, rudimentary airfield in the United Kingdom for a few days' operation in conditions of minimum maintenance facilities. The success with which these squadrons operated was carefully monitored by both Fighter Command and the Staff at 2nd Tactical Air Force, and the many lessons incorporated in orders and procedures adopted henceforth. However, much of the planned development and operational train-

ing by the Typhoon squadrons for tactical support of ground forces, which had been scheduled to start in earnest in October, had been delayed by the demands for attacks on the No-Ball sites, but when at the end of March 1944 RAF Bomber Command switched much of its effort to attacks on the French coast (and was able to send more of its aircraft against the launch sites) the Typhoon attacks gradually tailed off and reverted more and more to such targets as bridges, railways and road traffic—the sort of targets which pilots would be called on by the Army to attack when the invasion

In flight view of a No 183 Squadron Typhoon IB bomber, JR128/HF-L. As originally delivered to the Squadron it had featured the car door canopy but acquired the sliding hood early in 1944. The absence of underwing recognition stripes suggests that the photograph was taken shortly before the Normandy landings.

MN551 was extensively employed by Hawker and the A&AEE for external store clearance trials; it is shown here in June 1944 with a pair of supply containers. (Photo: A&AEE Neg No 1426)

of Europe was eventually launched.

Be that as it may, the dreaded No-Ball attacks continued to take their toll. No. 175 Squadron sent a Flight off on an "old-fashioned" fighter sweep in the Evreux area on 5 February, but this accidentally strayed too close to a No-Ball site whose alert gunners shot down Pilot Officer C. Tucker (in *JP385*) and Flight Sergeant D. A. Slack (*JP364*). No. 247 Squadron, now flying from Merston, carried out no fewer than five *Ramrods* in the last four days of the month, attacking flying bomb sites at Doullens, Esclavelles, Preeuseville, Beaumont-le-Hareng and Cormette. On the 28th Warrant Officer P. S. W. Daniel (*JP730*), on a weather patrol off Cherbourg, suffered engine failure and was seen to bale out near the island of Sark, but he could not be found by later patrols and was posted Missing.

Seen with a pair of 1,000-lb bombs at Needs Oar Point just before D-Day, MN598/FM-P of No 257 Squadron was to be transferred to No 609 Squadron, No 123 Wing, whose Wing Leader took it over as his 'personal' aircraft. This pilot, Wg Cdr W. Dring DFC, was to be killed in a flying accident while flying MN598 on 13 January 1945. Note the absence of all underwing recognition stripes—frequently removed from Typhoons engaged on low-level strikes before D-Day. (Photo: via Richard Ward, Farnborough)

In March No. 245 Squadron suffered casualties, Flying Officer C. E. Austin being lost during a *Ranger* east of Paris on the 16th, and on the 20th Flying Officer N. W. Crabtree failed to return from a *Ramrod* over the flying bomb site at Croisette. No. 164 Squadron at Thorney Island became operational on the 20th and on the same day flew a dive bombing attack with six Typhoons on the No-Ball site at Bonnieres, led by the CO, Squadron Leader Russell. No. 257 Squadron at Tangmere lost Pilot Officer J. B. Wood (in *JP510*) on a *Rhubarb* on the 16th during which he was last seen attacking a train with bombs and cannon.

Blinding the enemy

By April the tactical support Typhoon squadrons were assembling on the South Coast airfields from which they would ultimately operate in support of the great landing assault on the French coast. One major preliminary task had now to be attended to, a task almost exclusively undertaken by the Typhoons of the 2nd Tactical Air Force.

As mentioned in the previous Chapter, specially-equipped "Abdullah" Typhoons were intended to mark German *Würzburg* radars for attacks by other rocket-equipped aircraft. This radar, a gun-laying rather than a search-and-reporting radar, was but an element in an extensive screen established all along the enemy coast. Other radars existed in profusion, some 92 sites having been located (principally by photographic reconnaissance) on the French and Belgian coasts, including *Mammut*, *Wassermann*, *Freya*, "Giant" *Würzburg* (as distinct from the "standard" *Würzburg*, already referred to), and the naval *Seetakt* radar.

Although these 92 sites had all been pinpointed, and all would be attacked, it was accepted that some might escape complete destruction and might be able to "see" some of the approaching invasion forces, but it was necessary to attack every site so as not to disclose the exact point at which the Allies intended to land. Some radars overlooking the actual landing beaches were studiously avoided until the very last moment when, with clinical precision, they would be "taken out" in Typhoon strikes. Others, distant from the landing area, were also ignored, it being planned to mount a massive jamming operation against these by which it was intended to suggest to the Germans that that area was the one for which the invasion fleet was making.

The first such attack, intended to provide something of a pattern to be followed later, had already been carried out by No. 198 Squadron as early as 16 March when 12 Typhoons struck at the huge *Wassermann* radar near Ostende. That morning four of the fighters, each armed with 16 double-tiered 60-lb rockets, dived from 8,000 feet and let

The late Wing Commander W. Dring, DFC, seen here as a Flight Lieutenant. (Photo: Richard Ward, Whitstable)

was accordingly launched later the same day. However, it emerged that critical damage had indeed been inflicted during the first attack which prevented the great aerial array from being rotated, with the result that the entire structure had to be dismantled for repair—and the radar was still off the air when the Allies landed in Normandy almost three months later.

Taken in conjunction with handling and performance reports on the Typhoon when armed with 500- and 1,000-lb bombs, or eight and 16 rockets, attack procedures were evolved for the various target sites, some of which involved top cover by escorting fighters, particularly when the Typhoons were weighed down by the heavier bombs. Some of the prominent sites comprising multiple radars would require attacks to be repeated, while single attacks with accurately aimed bombs would suffice to destroy the delicate radar, or at least involve the Germans in lengthy recalibration before it could be brought back into operation.

loose their salvoes at the 150-foot tower just as the other eight Typhoons swept in at low level to strafe the surrounding flak positions. Although numerous hits were observed on the radar the tower still stood and appeared to be intact. A repeat strike

It later transpired that the Germans were experts at concealing the extent of damage caused to the equipment, knowing that the British monitoring receivers would be able to make some assessment by an absence of radar transmissions, at least

Wg Cdr R. T. P. Davidson DFC, the Canadian Wing Leader of No 143 Wing with his Typhoon MN518-018-RD displaying victory symbols for two German, two Italian and two Japanese aircraft shot down. This officer's unique wartime career embraced the Battle of Greece and the defence of Ceylon before coming to Britain where he led No 245 Squadron, No 121 Wing and No 143 (Canadian) Wing in succession. Suffering engine failure over France on 8 May 1944, he force landed but evaded capture, joining up with the French Resistance for four months before linking up with the advancing Allies after the Normandy landings. After the War he flew F-86 Sabre jet fighters over Korea with the USAF. He was to die peacefully on his farm near Ottawa on 22 November 1976. (Photo: via R. C. Sturtivant)

from broad-beamed radars. Transmitters would be brought into use immediately after an attack whose signals matched those of a working radar, even though the radar itself had been shattered; elsewhere a radar which had escaped serious damage would be switched off, if its area of search could be adequately covered by other radars. In other words the Germans contrived to operate an adequate but bare minimum of radar cover, and at the same time attempted to attract RAF attacks on stations which had already been rendered virtually useless. In this work of deception the Germans were partly successful and at least one extensive site accommodating a number of different radars—that at Cap d'Antifer, capable otherwise of watching the vital Côte Fleurie—attracted six attacks over a period of ten days, even though the very first strike had put almost every radar beyond repair.

Most of the Typhoon squadrons were detached from their South Coast airfields for a few days in March and April to carry out mock training attacks on specially prepared "target" sites, the pilots being given the opportunity to fire their rockets on practice ranges and to experience the Typhoon's handling when carrying the big 1,000-pounders and the two-tiered rockets.

On 8 May 2nd Tactical Air Force headquarters issued orders for the start of the attacks on enemy coastal radar, the first attack to be launched on the following day.[1] Two squadrons of the largest Typhoon Wing, No. 146—based on the forward airfield at Need's Oar Point in Hampshire, over-looking the Solent, and which had only started assembling one month previously—were to provide a force of eight aircraft to attack the radars at Caudecôte near Dieppe. In the event all aircraft were provided by No. 197 Squadron, being led on this occasion by Flight Lieutenant J. C. Button[2] (in *MN423*), all aircraft carrying 500-lb bombs with long-delay fuses. Although most of the bombs were seen to fall on or very close to the key buildings of the site the British monitoring service reported no apparent reduction in signals from the station, and it was considered necessary to send further strikes, even though later photographic reconnaissance confirmed that the delayed-action bombs had caused extensive damage.

Although Dieppe itself was some 70 miles from the planned invasion landing area its radar reached far across the Channel, while the big communications centre with its countless transmitter aerials at nearby Berneval-le-Grand constituted a vital target to be destroyed before the invasion; indeed so extensive was the latter that it required a raid by more than one hundred heavy bombers to demol-ish the entire centre.

Further sporadic attacks by the Typhoons fol-lowed during the next ten days, interspersed with strikes on other targets deeper into France, but these were not sufficient to indicate to the Germans that the RAF had indeed embarked on a concerted offensive against their radar, and there appeared no move to reinforce the coastal flak defences—already considered to be very heavy. The attack of the 9th, however, suggested to the RAF that either many more Typhoons would have to be committed to each strike, or that the 1,000-lb bombs and double-tiered rocket loads were essential.

The 2nd Tactical Air Force was evidently reluc-tant to risk large forces of Typhoons in single attacks, for while reserves of Typhoons were now plentiful, pilots highly trained in ground attack and close support operations were of the utmost value—and the invasion was still three weeks away. It was therefore decided to limit all immedi-ate attacks to two squadrons (often from different Wings so as to exploit the use of mixed weapons), not more than 30 aircraft being flown in a single strike; a maximum of eight aircraft in any attack were to carry the 1,000-pounders with a similar number armed with "double-stacked" rockets (al-though the latter limitation was soon waived). Whenever possible at least one squadron of dog-fighters—either British or American—was to be on hand nearby should the need arise to counter German interceptors, and air-sea rescue aircraft were to remain at two minutes' standby so long as any strike force was airborne.

The attacks re-started in earnest on the 22nd when No. 175 Squadron entered the fray as eight "double-stacked" Typhoons carried out strikes on the radar installations at Cap d'Antifer and Houl-gate covering the mouth of the Seine. Simul-taneously Nos. 181 and 247 Squadrons sent 28 Typhoons against the Dieppe radar complex, the force being divided between bomb-carrying and rocket-firing aircraft. The formation was led by the Norwegian, Wing Commander E. Haabjoern, DFC, whose aircraft (*MN542*) was hit by flak; the pilot came down in the sea only three miles off the enemy coast, yet was recovered unhurt by an air-sea rescue Walrus whose pilot made the 80-mile flight across the Channel to alight on the sea well within reach of German coastal guns.

At Arromanches, in the very centre of the planned invasion beachhead, the German radar station came in for a superbly executed 90-second attack by 20 Typhoons led by Wing Commander Green, eight Canadian aircraft of No. 440 Squad-ron planting their 1,000-pounders (11-second fused) directly on the transmitter buildings and aerials, all of which were later confirmed as demol-ished. The flak defences were evidently taken completely by surprise by the rocket-firing Ty-

---

[1] Not, as often stated, on the 10th.

[2] Later, as a Wing Commander and a Wing Leader in his own right, to lead Typhoon and Tempest Wings.

Gp Capt D. J. Scott, DSO, OBE, DFC, commanding No 123 Wing, with his Typhoon MN941/DJS, probably at Thorney Island during the summer of 1944 shortly before D-Day. (Photo: via R. C. Sturtivant)

phoons of No. 174 Squadron led by Squadron Leader W. Pitt-Brown at "nought feet", three sections of four aircraft converging from different directions almost simultaneously to lay a veritable carpet of shrieking rockets on the station as the big bombs dropped away from the diving Canadians overhead. Needless to say there was never any call to repeat the attack . . .

Now fully alerted to the intentions of the RAF (and, to a much lesser extent, the USAAF) to achieve systematic destruction of the French coastal radar stations and radio communications network, the Germans quickly moved flak reinforcements to the Channel Coast, and within 36 hours reconnaissance Spitfires and Mustangs were returning with evidence of this powerful build-up. When, on the 23rd, Nos. 183 and 197 Squadrons sent 23 Typhoons against Cap d'Antifer once more, the pilots reported flak that was heavier than any seen over a No-Ball site, with a dense curtain of fire from all calibres below 5,000 feet. Flying Officer J. Ralph of No. 183 Squadron was shot down and seen to crash into the sea only 200 yards off the coast, and could not be rescued; every aircraft that returned bore scars from the flak, three aircraft being subsequently written off. No. 197 Squadron also flew a smaller strike against the radar station at St Valery in the mouth of the Somme and not a dozen miles from the *Luftwaffe*'s fighter airfield at Abbeville; enemy fighters were not, however, seen.

On the next day Nos. 174 and 175 Squadrons carried out a co-ordinated attack on the radar station near Le Havre, the tactics found so success-

ful at Arromanches 24 hours earlier being repeated with equal effect. No. 174 also finished off the station at Houlgate. Nos. 197 and 198 Squadrons flew individual strikes, the former dive bombing the inland radar station at Pont-de-Percy in western Normandy without loss. No. 198 attacked the Jobourg station on the Cap de la Hague at the tip of the Cotentin peninsula, encountering alert flak defences which shot down the Canadian Flying Officer H. Freeman and Flight Sergeant L. Vallely, both of whom were seen to crash in flames.

The inland *Freya* radar at Fruges, about 20 miles south of St Omer, next came under attack on the 27th by Nos. 164 and 197 Squadrons, the former armed with rockets and the latter carrying out the dive bombing. Although the pilots reported the target as being "heavily damaged", subsequent signals detected from the station prompted another attack on the following day by No. 164. As was often the case in attacks where the defences were on the alert the flak concentrated on the leading Typhoon and the squadron commander, Squadron Leader Humphrey à Becket Russell, was seen to bale out after his aircraft was hit.[3]

Another commanding officer was lost when, on 2 June, 18 Typhoons of Nos. 198 and 609 Squadrons—all armed with rockets—attacked the gun-laying and fighter control radars at Caudecôte, near Dieppe. The strike was highly successful as more than 200 rockets blasted the buildings and

---

[3] Russell, a pre-War Regular officer, was taken prisoner but remained in the RAF after the War, retiring as a Wing Commander in 1958.

aerials, but once again the leading aircraft, *MN192* flown by Squadron Leader J. Niblett, DFC, of No. 198, was hit and seen to crash in a mass of flames.

One final "setpiece" attack was reserved for the eve of the invasion. It was suspected that among the radars on the Cap de la Hague that had in all probability survived intact was the *Seetakt* equipment, a radar that was capable of watching the Channel approaches to the entire invasion front. This attack had been scheduled for 4 June but, when the landings were postponed by 24 hours, this strike was in turn delayed until the 5th. Twenty-four Typhoons of No. 121 Wing (Nos. 174, 175 and 245 Squadrons), flying from Holmesley South and carrying nearly 200 rockets, swept the station with a storm of explosive, diving to attack from the landward and ending their runs with a shoot-out of cannon fire before making good their escape at wave-top height without loss.

That evening the British monitoring service detected scarcely any signals from German radar anywhere within 90 miles of the landing beaches. Of the 92 radio and radar stations known to have existed on the French and Belgian coasts three months earlier, only 16 were thought to have escaped complete destruction—none of them covering the invasion area or its approaches.

* * *

While the attacks on the German radar stations had occupied the larger proportion of the Typhoon squadrons' operational effort, with some 1,200 sorties flown in such attacks, numerous other routine operations had been flown, some of which had contributed to the campaign by the Allied Air Forces aimed at destroying the road and rail network in Northern France as a preliminary to the invasion. Others were flown against enemy shipping off the French, Belgian and Dutch coasts as *Channel Stop* operations were stepped up. No. 137 Squadron, whose recent traditions and training had been closely concerned with shipping strikes, took to flying off-shore *Rhubarbs*, and even solo patrols off the Dutch coast. More than once small, innocent-looking trawlers and coastal vessels turned out to be flak-packed picket boats whose gunners held their fire as the Typhoons started their attack, then opening up fiercely at the last moment to claim several unwary pilots; Warrant Officer J. W. Carter, an Australian, was lost in this manner near Flushing on 1 April, as was Flight Sergeant R. J. Easterbrook off the Hook of Holland on 5 May.

As part of the so-called "Transportation Plan", Typhoons were flown well into France for attacks on road and rail targets, usually involving *Rhubarb* sorties by aircraft carrying a pair of drop tanks and four rockets apiece. Occasionally a "plum" target would be spotted during photo reconnaissance as, for example, occurred early on 7 May when a large

number of railway fuel tank wagons was spotted concentrated in marshalling yards east of Le Mans. As speed of attack was essential, 24 Typhoons of No. 121 Wing were quickly loaded up with mixed drop tanks and rockets and set course on the 220-mile flight to the target. After only sporadic flak *en route* the Typhoons launched a spectacular strike in which an entire fuel train was destroyed and considerable damage inflicted on the rail tracks. (This was No. 245 Squadron's first operational sortie with rockets.) No. 184 Squadron, which had been declared operational on 24 April, flew eight Typhoons in a dive bombing strike on the railway bridge over a canal at Baupte in the Cotentin peninsula on the 28th, led by its CO, Squadron Leader J. Rose, DFC; a single direct hit served to cut the railway and block the canal, although both were repaired within a month.

As the pilots of No. 121 Wing landed at Holmesley South after their final setpiece attack on the radar installations on the Cap de la Hague on 5 June they were surprised to be called together for what appeared to be yet another briefing by the Wing's Commanding Officer. Yet this was to be a briefing with a difference. All over Southern England similar assemblies by members of the Allied forces were being given the news for which they had waited so long: the great invasion, Operation "Overlord", was to be launched that night.

In support of Overlord

Any attempt to describe in detail the events on the ground of that great day, 6 June 1944, would be superfluous in this work, save such that directly involved operations by the Typhoon squadrons, whose order of battle on that day is given in an accompanying table.

Long before first light the skies all over Southern England were alive with the sounds of hundreds of

Generally reputed to be a Typhoon of No 268 Squadron, this aircraft—displaying full "wrap-round" invasion stripes—would have been unusual in being fitted with rocket rails as the Squadron was almost exclusively engaged in fighter reconnaissance duties at the time of the Normandy landings. (Photo: via Sqn Ldr R. C. B. Ashworth)

aircraft, as bombers, transports and night fighters flew back and forth across the English Channel. Every one of the 2nd Tactical Air Force's Typhoon squadrons came to readiness, either for briefed attacks or for patrols behind the landing beaches. Only one Typhoon squadron was to remain on the ground throughout that day, No. 137 at Manston (a component of Air Defence of Great Britain), remaining at *Channel Stop* standby lest the Germans should attempt to sail E- or R-boats against the invasion armada. The Squadron was not needed.

The Typhoon operations over Normandy were in general to be confined to two types of sortie, namely setpiece attacks against specific targets which had not been attacked before D-Day for fear of disclosing the area in which the landings would take place, and armed reconnaissance patrols immediately behind the German battle line for attacks on targets of opportunity.

DEPLOYMENT OF TYPHOON SQUADRONS 6 June, 1944 (D-Day)			
Formation	*Base*	*Aircraft on Strength*	*Commanding Officer*
No. 83 GROUP			
No. 121 Wing			
No. 174 Squadron	Holmesley South	18	Sqn Ldr W. Pitt-Brown
No. 175 Squadron	Holmesley South	19	Sqn Ldr J. R. Pennington-Legh, DFC
No. 245 Squadron	Holmesley South	18	Sqn Ldr J. R. Collins, DFC and Bar
No. 124 Wing			Wg Cdr P. Webb, DFC
No. 181 Squadron	Hurn	16	Sqn Ldr C. D. North-Lewis, DFC
No. 182 Squadron	Hurn	18	Major D. H. Barlow, SAAF
No. 247 Squadron	Hurn	19	Sqn Ldr R. J. McNair, DFC
No. 129 Wing			
No. 184 Squadron	Westhampnett	19	Sqn Ldr J. Rose, DFC
No. 143 Wing, RCAF			
No. 438 Squadron	Funtington	17	Sqn Ldr F. G. Grant, DFC
No. 439 Squadron	Hurn	16	Sqn Ldr H. H. Norsworthy
No. 440 Squadron	Hurn	18	Sqn Ldr W. H. Pentland
No. 84 GROUP			
No. 123 Wing			Wg Cdr R. E. P. Brooker, DFC and Bar
No. 198 Squadron	Thorney Island	19	Sqn Ldr J. Niblett, DFC
No. 609 Squadron	Thorney Island	18	Sqn Ldr J. C. Wells, DFC
No. 136 Wing			
No. 164 Squadron	Thorney Island	18	Sqn Ldr P. H. Beake, DFC
No. 183 Squadron	Thorney Island	19	Sqn Ldr F. H. Scarlett
No. 146 Wing			Gp Capt D. E. Gillam, DSO and Bar, DFC and Bar, AFC
No. 193 Squadron	Need's Oar Point	19	Sqn Ldr D. G. Ross, DFC
No. 197 Squadron	Need's Oar Point	19	Sqn Ldr D. M. Taylor
No. 257 Squadron	Need's Oar Point	18	Sqn Ldr R. H. Fokes, DFM
No. 266 Squadron	Need's Oar Point	19	Sqn Ldr J. W. E. Holmes, DFC, AFC
Independent			
No. 1320 (Air Spotting) Flight		10	—

Note: In addition Air Defence of Great Britain, No. 10 Group fielded one Typhoon Squadron, No. 263, and No. 11 Group, another, No. 137 Squadron. The Fighter Interception Unit still possessed five of the "Abdullah" Typhoons. No. 268 Squadron had been warned to take on Fighter Reconnaissance Typhoons.

First attack of the day was a two-squadron effort by No. 146 Wing led by Wing Commander Baker in which Nos. 193 and 197 Squadrons were airborne at 07:10 hr to attack a German tank concentration spotted the previous day south-east of Bayeux. The tanks had still not moved when the 17 Typhoons swept in out of the morning mists to release their 500-lb bombs. Flak was reported to be slight and all aircraft returned safely; four tanks were claimed destroyed and five others seen to be damaged. At Holmsley South Nos. 174 and 175 Squadrons took off immediately afterwards to attack heavy gun positions (thought to be dug-in self-propelled guns) at Trevières west of Bayeux and behind the American "Omaha" landing beaches. Although numerous rocket strikes were seen to blanket the targets no positive claims were made; there was however no call for the attack to be repeated. The other 121 Wing Squadron, No. 245, also met with frustration when, briefed to attack the gun emplacements at Trouville with rockets, whose batteries were thought to be capable of reaching ships of the invasion fleet a dozen miles away, the pilots found the target area covered by a sea fret. Unable to spot suitable aiming points they turned inland and attacked a nearby encampment suspected as being used by the enemy gunners. In any case it is difficult to understand why this coastal battery had been chosen for attack by rocket-firing Typhoons for the big guns were heavily encased in concrete enclosures up to six feet thick, and not even six-inch rockets would have caused any significant damage.

Between 07:15 and 10:30 hr a total of seven Typhoon squadrons answered calls for attacks to be made on various fixed and mobile targets north of Caen. In the case of the former the British and Canadian forces were able to mark many of the targets by lobbing smoke bombs from mortars—so close were the guns to the beaches in front of Caen. In one instance some enemy guns turned out to be

about a dozen heavy tanks which the Germans chose to employ as dug-in artillery rather than send forward towards the beaches. First to arrive were 13 Typhoon bombers of No. 247 Squadron whose pilots placed all 26 250-pounders close to or on the tanks, claiming four destroyed. A second attack had been called up and No. 438 Squadron was approaching. However, when the controller in the British Sector's Fighter Direction ship was informed that the Canadians were carrying 1,000-pounders the attack was called off owing to the close proximity of ground forces to the target.

Instead No. 438 Squadron was diverted against a target that had been scheduled for a later attack. This was fortunate as the objective proved to be a battery of mobile 88-mm dual-purpose guns mounted behind embankments to the north-east of Caen and which had been in action for several hours. Although naval guns had shelled the battery to some effect earlier the ships had shifted target elsewhere as the troops went ashore. Now it was the turn of the Typhoons. Once again the ground forces were able to mark the target area with smoke shells, and the Canadian pilots carried out an excellent attack with their big bombs. The battery is believed to have lost only one gun, but there must have been many casualties as the remaining guns stayed silent for the rest of the day and were pulled out the following night.

Last of the preliminary "setpiece" attacks was led by Wing Commander R. E. P. Brooker in *MN570* at the head of 11 other Typhoons from No. 198 Squadron, all double-stacked with rockets. The Château le Meauffe, one of many large French mansions long since commandeered by the Germans for use as *Wehrmacht* headquarters, was heavily damaged in a copybook rocket attack and the surviving occupants hurriedly evacuated themselves elsewhere immediately afterwards. Such attacks caused widespread confusion amongst the German coastal defenders—if only for a matter of hours.

From late morning onwards on D-Day most of the Typhoon squadrons became involved in a long and sometimes arduous series of armed reconnaissance patrols, and this may be a convenient opportunity to explain briefly what these patrols (as distinct from the "cabrank" operations—to be introduced some days later) involved.

Occasionally still referred to by one or two Squadrons as "tactical *Rhubarbs*", the armed reconnaissance patrols usually followed briefings to cover a sector, often defined as a patrol line flown at between 3,000 and 5,000 feet between a number of easily identifiable towns behind the enemy lines, their main purpose being to keep a sharp look-out for road, rail and other surface movement by German forces attempting to move up to the front. In the event of spotting such forces the patrol leader would radio the sighting either to a forward

Typical store load carried by 2nd TAF Typhoons during armed reconnaissance patrols was a mix of drop tanks and rockets. (Photo: via Sqn Ldr R. C. B. Ashworth)

Armourers loading 60-lb rockets on MN317/ZY-B, an armoured Typhoon of No 247 Squadron shortly after D-Day, almost certainly at Hurn. Scarcely visible on the aircraft's nose are inscriptions CHINA BRITISH—the recognised courtesy title of No 247 Squadron—a small picture of a dog, and the legend "RADIATOR ARMOURED". Until the introduction of the Sabre IIB most of the armoured Typhoons retained three-blade propellers to keep the aircraft's cg within prescribed limits.

control van with the advanced Allied ground forces or, as on D-Day, to the Fighter Direction ship. Depending on the nature of the target and the weapons being carried by the Typhoons, the pilots might be instructed to attack, and in such an event a new patrol section would be ordered off as a back-up.

It should be remembered that on D-Day, and for some weeks following, the Allied beachhead occupied a relatively small area, so that the skies over and immediately around the ground battle could very quickly become congested with large numbers of aircraft, almost invariably British and American. To avoid confusion, particularly among the gunners on the ground, every aircraft likely to be flown anywhere over the invading forces—whether in Britain, at sea or in France—was painted with prominent black and white "invasion stripes" on upper and lower surfaces of wings and rear fuselage. (In the case of the Typhoons the "invasion stripes" were superimposed over the traditional recognition stripes, and were extended to the upper surfaces of the wings; later the upper surface segments were removed as it was felt that they compromised the normal camouflage required by the fighters and fighter-bombers at low altitude.)

In the first few days following D-Day, such was the degree of Allied air superiority, the Germans were scarcely able to move large forces of reinforcements by day and, certainly on D-Day itself,

most of the armed reconnaissance patrols were relatively uneventful. When small groups of vehicles did venture on to the roads they were indeed fortunate if they escaped attention by the British and American fighter-bombers.

The *Luftwaffe* was both slow and reluctant to react against the Normandy landings not, as is generally suggested, for reasons of weakness nor on account of any widespread damage to its airfields in the West—though both these circumstances contributed to the Germans' difficulties. For obvious reasons the *Luftwaffe* had preferred to deploy such strength that it could muster well back from the Channel coast, and as D-Day wore on these forces were moved piecemeal to airfields closer to the beachhead. Moreover the traditional rôle of the German air force had always been primarily to support the ground forces, so that orders had been given to the *Luftwaffe* to conserve its strength to support and cover the movement of *Wehrmacht* reinforcements as and when they could be brought up to the Channel coast. The difficulty facing the German command lay in doubts being expressed as to whether the Normandy landings did indeed constitute the Allies' main invasion effort.

Late on D-Day, as the British and Canadian forces in the east continued to consolidate and enlarge their foothold in Normandy, the Germans belatedly started to move reinforcements up towards Caen, and it was to locate these forces that the Typhoons' patrols were ordered. The first such column was spotted early in the afternoon as it set out from Falaise on the road to Caen, comprising about 30 tanks and half-tracked personnel carriers, and a score of trucks and other vehicles. Overhead the Typhoon pilots of No. 198 Squadron radioed their sighting and dived to the attack, loosing their rockets at the armoured vehicles and then sweeping the road with cannon fire. Seven tanks and half-tracks were knocked out (claimed as "flamers") and six damaged. Flak trucks put up some resistance but, weapons spent, No. 198 Squadron broke away and returned to base without loss.

Already six Typhoons of No. 183 Squadron, led by Squadron Leader F. H. Scarlett, were on their way from Thorney Island with orders to start an armed reconnaissance patrol south of Caen. They were immediately ordered to attack the remnants of the convoy east of Falaise but, before they could do so, another sighting report indicated a much larger German column approaching Caen from the south. Just as No. 183 spotted this new target and prepared to break port for a diving attack, 12 Messerschmitt Bf 109Gs bounced the Typhoons from above and behind, causing the pilots to jettison their bombs and to defend themselves. The German attack had been well timed and co-ordinated and as the Typhoons scattered each pilot found himself hemmed in by a pair of enemy fighters. Within seconds three Typhoons were shot down (Flight Lieutenant R. W. Evans and Flying Officers M. H. Gee and A. R. Taylor) and, although the remaining pilots attempted to fight it out, it was clear that, now without bombs or rockets, there was no good reason to stay. Hard pressed, they made good their escape at tree-top height.

On the ground, as its own fighter cover withdrew to replenish ammunition and refuel, the force of German tanks and transports split into several columns, each to make its way independently towards Caen. Soon afterwards one of these columns was found and attacked by Typhoons of No. 164 Squadron; this time the strike was well underway when some Focke-Wulfe Fw 190s, hurriedly summoned to relieve the Messerschmitts, put in a belated appearance. A brief fight followed and, although one Typhoon (Flying Officer A. E. Roberts, RAAF) was shot down, one of the German aircraft was also destroyed and seen to crash.

An hour later Typhoons of Nos. 181 and 182 found another of the columns as it neared Caen, this group thought to be composed of wireless vans with some flak trucks. The sky quickly filled with criss-crossing tracer as the Typhoons approached and contrived to aim their 500-pounders. Another Australian, Flight Sergeant G. J. Howard of No. 181, flying his first operational sortie, had his port aileron shot away by flak; attempting to pull up the Typhoon, Howard was evidently unable to prevent a stall, flicked and spun in; the pilot was not seen to bale out.

For the rest of the day the Typhoon Wings kept up a steady flow of patrols to the area south of Caen, sections of four or six aircraft—now mostly rocket-armed—searching out the scattered columns of German reinforcements while Spitfire squadrons were ordered to fly constant patrols overhead to keep watch for *Luftwaffe* fighters. One column of armoured personnel vehicles was caught in the village of St Leger by seven bomb-carrying aircraft of No. 245 Squadron; as the first three Typhoons approached, the German troops scrambled out of the vehicles and sought safety in nearby houses—which were promptly bombed to rubble by the last four aircraft in the Section; four of the half-tracks were claimed destroyed.

In No. 440 Squadron's third attack of the day the Canadians dive bombed a convoy of trucks with 1,000-pounders as it entered the suburbs of Caen; it encountered a determined barrage of flak which shot down Flying Officer L. R. Allman. Soon after 18:30 hr the survivors of the two groups of reinforcements reached Caen and found cover in the town. Two late evening patrols by Nos. 245 and 247 Squadrons were almost uneventful and few worthwhile targets were found.

And so the first day of the invasion drew to a close, and the skies over Normandy were left to the ministrations of the prowling night fighters. The tally taken by the 2nd Tactical Air Force showed that the Typhoon squadrons had flown a total of 414 sorties (or about eight per cent of the RAF's entire effort—which had included numerous attacks by medium and heavy bombers, radar feints, fighter patrols and sweeps, and, of course, considerable support of the airborne forces' attacks). Six Typhoons had been lost, four to German fighters and two to flak. They had shot down two enemy fighters and taken a fairly impressive toll of German vehicles, claiming the destruction of 17 tanks and ten other armoured vehicles, 22 guns of 88-mm calibre or larger, and 47 other vehicles; 21 tanks and 61 other vehicles were claimed to have been damaged. Yet it cannot be denied that some pilots expressed surprise and frustration that the actions over Normandy had not been more conclusive, that there had not been a much more spectacular response by the German ground and air forces. They were not to know that in the weeks to come, when the *Wehrmacht* succeeded in circumventing all the broken roads, railways and bridges—whose destruction had been so carefully achieved by the Allied air forces in the months before the invasion—the pace and heat of battle would come to live up to all expectations.

★　　★　　★

Among the mass of troops that had stormed ashore on 6 June had been the first elements of the RAF Airfield Construction Units, engineers whose job it would now be to prepare rudimentary airstrips—frequently under enemy fire—first to be used as emergency landing grounds by Allied fighters and fighter-bombers, and soon afterwards as full, though temporary, advanced bases for these aircraft. In the days immediately after D-Day all the essential earth-moving bulldozers, rollers, vast quantities of PSP matting, radio vans, fuel bowsers and other paraphernalia for these airstrips were trundled ashore from landing craft and taken a short distance inland.

For the time being, as German reinforcements began arriving in greater strength in Normandy, the Allies fought desperately to cling to the beach-heads. The Typhoons had, for almost two weeks, to operate from their bases in Southern England, although occasionally an aircraft would, within a week, be able to put down on one of the strips to have makeshift repairs carried out before returning home across the Channel.

On D+1 (7 June) the Typhoons were over the beachhead early once more, and from first light carried on with armed reconnaissance around Caen. The Germans had, however, managed during the night to rush forward two whole flak regiments along the road to Caen from Falaise and Argentan, with upwards of a score of 88-mm guns

with supporting light flak trucks stopping off in the villages of Potigny, Grainville and Lorguichon. When No. 184 Squadron pilots spotted what looked like suspicious activity near Grainville they went down to investigate, only to find that in fact they were fast approaching the newly dug-in flak positions. Before the Typhoons could turn away and escape, three aircraft were hit (Flight Lieutenant F. E. Holland, and Flight Sergeants L. Tidbury and J. J. Rowland) and crashed in flames; none of the pilots was seen to escape. An urgent call was radioed to the Fighter Direction ship to warn other pilots to be on the look-out for similar flak traps, but it is believed that Pilot Officer G. Rendle, RAAF, of No. 181 Squadron was hit by flak on a subsequent patrol; he reported a faltering engine and baled out near the ships off the Normandy beaches, but when picked up was found to have died.[4]

The real purpose of the flak traps became evident later in the day as the first major German armoured reinforcements began moving northwards towards Caen. By chance eight Typhoons of No. 245 Squadron, double-stacked with rockets (unusually for a briefed reconnaissance patrol), happened upon the mass of vehicles between Grainville and Caen, and carried out a splendidly

---

[4] Not to be confused with Warrant Officer J. Rendall, another Australian, also serving with No. 181 Squadron at the same time.

Rocket-equipped Typhoons of No 198 Squadron operating from dusty advanced landing grounds in Normandy shortly after the D-Day landings. (Photos: via Richard Ward, Whitstable)

No 198 Squadron's JP963/TP-T dispersed on the ALG of B.10 Plumetot in Normandy during July 1944 as a landmine is detonated by engineers in the background. The aircraft is fully armed-up with rockets and an extemporized shield has been wedged into the radiator intake to exclude the pervading limestone dust while on the ground. JP963 was to crash while taking off from another airstrip, B.7 Martragny, on 31 July, killing the pilot, Flt Lt Champion. (Photo: D. C. Ellingworth)

co-ordinated attack, four aircraft approaching from the beam as the other swept along the column from the rear—so confusing the flak gunners, each Typhoon firing ripple salvoes all along the line of tanks and hitting many in their less-heavily armoured rear. However as the attackers broke away, two were hit, Flying Officer L. J. Greenhalgh's Typhoon falling in a mass of flames, but Flying Officer K. J. A. Dickie being seen to force land nearby and run clear of his aircraft. The Squadron claimed 13 tanks and other armoured vehicles destroyed and more than 20 damaged.

Another Typhoon Squadron, No. 263—which had engaged in uneventful anti-shipping patrols on the previous day—now started a series of shipping strikes against ports fairly close to the invasion area, attacking E- and R-boats at St Peter Port in Guernsey and at St Malo on the 7th, and off Sark and St Malo again on the 8th. Alas, however, the Squadron's commanding officer, the Belgian Squadron Leader H. A. C. Gonay, was to be killed in action just six days later.

By 18 June the breakout from the beachhead had started, with the Americans successfully advancing westwards to reach the west coast of the Cotentin peninsula, thereby isolating the important port of Cherbourg to the north. Little progress had, however, been possible in the east where the British and Canadian forces were still firmly held in check in front of Caen. By now five of the British-built advanced landing grounds were in constant use by the Typhoon squadrons, although all squadrons had been returning to England in the evenings.

On the following day No. 174 Squadron was the first to move permanently to France where it took up residence on the dusty strip of B.2 in the west of the British sector about 15 miles east of Bayeux. On the 20th four more Squadrons moved across the Channel, Nos. 181, 182 and 247 being allocated to B. 6 at Coulombs—within sight of the "front line"—and No. 175 to B.3 nearer the coast in the centre of the British sector. On one occasion, when the Germans chose to launch an armoured thrust towards the beaches, aimed at cutting the British sector in two, the Typhoons of No. 124 Wing were being ordered into the air in full sight of the enemy tanks, having barely time to raise their wheels and release their rockets before turning downwind to rejoin the landing circuit to take on a fresh load of weapons. All the time the landing ground was under fire from 88-mm guns. Five Typhoons were lost to enemy shelling but no pilot or groundcrew member was killed or injured, and there was never any question of evacuating the landing ground at Coulombs—and the groundcrews kept working without let-up, refuelling and reloading the Typhoons without thought of taking shelter—so long as any aircraft demanded attention. The same night the *Luftwaffe* launched a sharp raid by low-flying Junkers Ju 88s, but only succeeded in tearing up a lot of runway planking, which was repaired at first light by the indefatigable engineers.

It was a suspicion raised by the increased appearance of German night fighters and bombers over the beachhead that led to an attack with 250-lb bombs by No. 197 Squadron on what was later confirmed as being a *Freya* radar station at Evreux on 23 June. Following this—for close on a fortnight at least—*Luftwaffe* air activity at night abated.

The gap at Falaise

By now "set piece" attacks by Typhoons were rarely being laid on, such were the demands on their services by the ground forces. The last to be carried out for several weeks had been flown on 10 June and, in keeping with the importance of the target, had involved 40 'double-stacked' rocket-firing Typhoons of Nos. 181, 182, 245 and 247 Squadrons. The target was the headquarters of *Panzer* Group West in the extensive complex of the Château de la Caine which suffered a simultaneous attack by 61 RAF Mitchell medium bombers of No. 2 Group which dropped about 300 500-lb bombs from 12,000 feet. Among the very large number of staff members killed was the German Chief of Staff, Generalmajor Ritter und Edler von Dawans.

In the west the Americans continued to make steady progress despite having to contend with occasional powerful German counter-attacks, and on several occasions the Typhoons were called on to mete out some of their characteristic brand of treatment against concentrations of German armour, in one attack near St Lô halting a powerful column of tanks by the simple expedient of blowing off the tracks of the leading vehicle, and then of the rearmost tank, before setting about those trapped between.

In the west of the British sector some advances were made and on 27 June No. 198 Squadron began operating "cabrank" patrols. This tactic—originated by the *Wehrmacht* some years before and later employed by the British Eighth Army in North Africa and Italy during 1943 with great success—involved more or less constant patrols by small formations of Typhoons over a small sector of the front, seldom more than ten miles long, their pilots in radio touch with a contact van among the leading elements of the ground forces. In the event that the advancing troops encountered enemy resistance that could not be quickly and economically overcome—be it a strongpoint or enemy armour—the contact controller would call up the patrolling fighters, passing a map reference and describing the target, while the ground forces would loose off coloured mortar bombs as target indicators. With increasing practice the Typhoon pilots became astonishingly adept at "taking out" such targets as defended farmhouses and enemy tanks concealed in the hedgerows of the bocage country.

Yet still the Germans in Caen resisted. Not even the devastating raids by RAF heavy bombers achieved much more than to create vast areas of rubble. Thousands of civilians were killed or injured, but still the *Wehrmacht* soldiers defied all attempts to dislodge them. While the Germans held on amid the ruins of Caen, the Americans continued to strike south in the Cotentin peninsula, beginning the classic right hook of a great outflanking movement. The British and Canadian forces struck powerfully south from Caumont and from the west of Caen towards Falaise. Then the American First Army attacked through Flers as the Third Army swung north from Alençon towards Argentan.

Throughout July the jaws of the pincers were forged as the Typhoons ranged all over Normandy. On the 8th No. 175 Squadron attacked a château near Caen, found to be occupied by a Hitler Youth battalion; the following day the same Squadron launched rockets against a concentration of self-propelled guns, claiming five destroyed but losing Flight Sergeant R. C. Dale to flak. Before the end of the month twelve Typhoon squadrons were flying constant strikes against 16 German divisions (including nine of *Panzers*) facing encirclement to the south-west. No. 182 Squadron was one of the most heavily engaged, flying almost 300 sorties in six days. Its commanding officer, the South African Major D. H. Barlow, was hit by flak while on a "cabrank" sortie on the 25th; German infantry had been seen to take refuge in a wood and the CO's aircraft (*MN891*) was hit as the Typhoons poured their rockets into the trees. He was, however, seen to bale out. Before the month was out the Squadron had lost another South African, Captain G. H. Kaufmann (a flight commander) as well as Flight Lieutenant A. C. Flood and Flight Sergeant H. C. B. Talalla.

On 7 August the Germans launched their final major counter-attack from the closing pocket, thrusting not north or south to relieve the pressure of the pincer jaws but westwards at Mortain, aiming to reach the sea at Avranches to isolate the American Third Army whose supply lines had become over-extended. On that day seven Typhoon squadrons were called upon to strike the

Flanked by battlefield graves, a German tank stands disabled and a half-track personnel carrier lies overturned after an attack by Allied aircraft in Normandy.

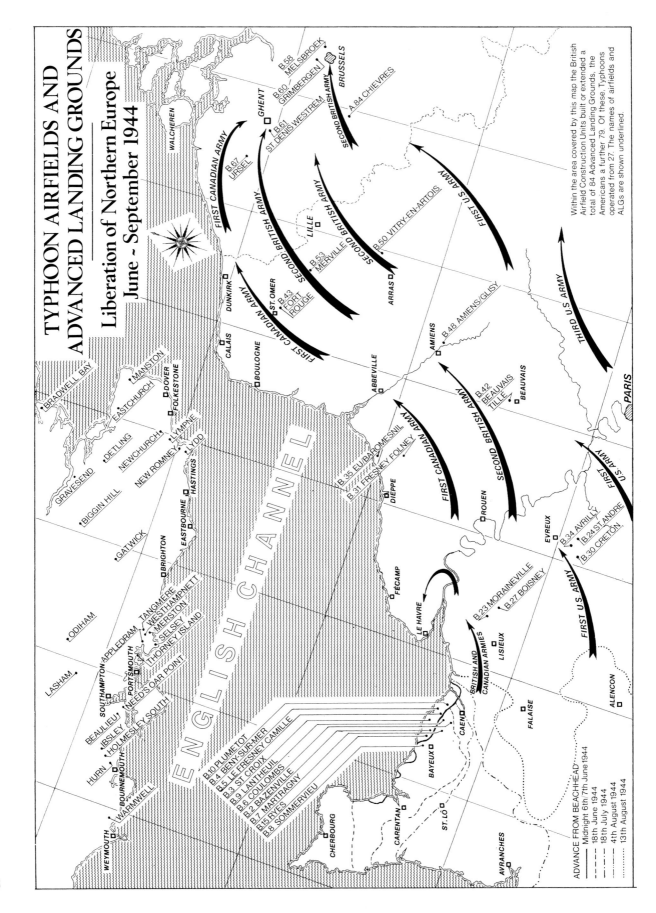

TYPHOON AIRFIELDS AND ADVANCED LANDING GROUNDS

Liberation of Northern Europe
June ~ September 1944

Within the area covered by this map the British Airfield Construction Units built or extended a total of 84 Advanced Landing Grounds, the Americans a further 79. Of these, Typhoons operated from 27. The names of airfields and ALGs are shown underlined.

WALCHEREN

B.58 MELSBROEK
B.60 GRIMBERGEN
BRUSSELS
GHENT
B.61 ST. DENIS WESTREM
A.84 CHIEVRES
SECOND BRITISH ARMY

FIRST CANADIAN ARMY

B.67 URSEL

SECOND BRITISH ARMY
LILLE
B.53 MERVILLE
VITRY-EN-ARTOIS
B.50 VITRY-EN-ARTOIS
SECOND BRITISH ARMY
FIRST US ARMY
ARRAS

FIRST CANADIAN ARMY
DUNKIRK
ST. OMER
B.43 FORT ROUGE

CALAIS
BOULOGNE
ABBEVILLE
AMIENS
B.48 AMIENS/GLISY

THIRD US ARMY

BRADWELL BAY
MANSTON
EASTCHURCH
DOVER
FOLKESTONE
DETLING
GRAVESEND
NEWCHURCH
LYMPNE
NEW ROMNEY
LYDD
BIGGIN HILL
HASTINGS
GATWICK
EASTBOURNE
BRIGHTON
TANGMERE
WESTHAMPNETT
MERSTON
APPLEDRAM
SELSEY
THORNEY ISLAND
SOUTHAMPTON
PORTSMOUTH
NEED'S OAR POINT
ODIHAM
LASHAM
BEAULIEU
IBSLEY
HOLMESLEY SOUTH
HURN
BOURNEMOUTH
WARMWELL
WEYMOUTH

SECOND BRITISH ARMY
BEAUVAIS
B.42 BEAUVAIS TILLE

FIRST CANADIAN ARMY
ROUEN
EVREUX
B.34 AVRILLY
B.24 ST. ANDRE
B.30 CRETON

B.35 EU/BAROMESNIL
B.31 FRESNEY FOLNEY
DIEPPE

FECAMP
LE HAVRE
B.23 MORAINEVILLE
B.27 BOISNEY
LISIEUX
FIRST US ARMY

ENGLISH CHANNEL

BRITISH AND CANADIAN ARMIES
CAEN
FALAISE
ALENCON

B.10 PLUMETOT
B.4 BENY-SUR-MER
B.5 LE FRESNEY CAMILLE
B.3 ST. CROIX
B.9 LANTHEUIL
B.6 COULOMBS
B.2 BAZENVILLE
B.7 MARTRAGNY
B.15 RYES
B.8 SOMMERVIEU

BAYEUX

CHERBOURG
CARENTAN
ST. LO
AVRANCHES

PARIS

ADVANCE FROM BEACHHEAD
———— Midnight 6th/7th June 1944
– – – – 18th June 1944
— - — - 18th July 1944
– - – - 4th August 1944
· · · · · · · 13th August 1944

Representing the ultimate production standard of Typhoon production examples, this aircraft, RB306, underwent a rigorous performance check flown by Frank Murphy at Langley in November 1944. It returned a maximum speed of 422 mph TAS at 12,800 feet in MS gear. The aircraft was later employed on external store clearance trials. (Photo: Sydney Camm Collection)

main German thrust being launched against elements of the American 30th Division. Their pilots found a concentration of 60 tanks and more than 200 support vehicles; in nine hours these squadrons flew 312 sorties, destroying about 30 tanks, a similar number of other armoured vehicles, four self-propelled guns and 50 supply trucks. Partway through the attacks in the west four of the squadrons were temporarily switched against a smaller German thrust in the British sector where five more tanks were knocked out.

The next day the Americans called for the Typhoons to "take out" a small wood near the village of Le Theil, south-east of Alençon, in which a German infantry battalion had sought refuge. Seven double-stacked Typhoons of No. 197 Squadron were on the scene in less than five minutes, led by the New Zealander, Squadron Leader A. H. Smith (in *MP119*), and, marked by red smoke from mortar bombs, the wood was systematically blasted to pieces, first by the rockets and then by cannon fire. The Americans stated afterwards that every one of the Germans who survived the ordeal was eager to surrender the moment the Typhoons departed.

Throughout the next week, as the jaws began to close, the massacre of German forces caught in the trap went on, yet still the *Wehrmacht* fought to keep open their escape route past Falaise. On the 17th, the day the Canadian First Army reached and cleared that town, No. 183 Squadron—the unit that had suffered most heavily on D-Day—again "caught a packet". Ordered up for an armed reconnaissance to the east of Falaise nine Typhoons, led by Flight Lieutenant H. A. Brownrigg (in *MN419*), were suddenly engulfed by about 50 Messerschmitt Bf 109Gs. In a short but vicious fight, in which the British pilots tried desperately to escape at ground level, four Typhoons were shot down (Flying Officer G. Campbell-Brown, War-

rant Officers W. Carragher and G. F. Humphrey and Flight Sergeant R. Gibson). There were no claims by the surviving pilots.

Three days later the Typhoons gained ample retribution. On that occasion, as the Polish Armoured Brigade faced an attack by the remnants of two German *Panzer* divisions near Vimoutiers, east of Falaise, 32 armoured Typhoons from Nos. 164, 183, 198 and 609 Squadrons, led by Wing Commander W. Dring, DFC, appeared on cue just as about a hundred German tanks emerged from a wood in front of the Poles. As the Wing Commander circled above, passing instructions to his pilots, the Typhoons "went briskly about their business with method and vigour", stopping the attack in its tracks and destroying 56 AFVs and damaging a score of others.

Let the achievements of August by just one Typhoon squadron—the hard-pressed No. 183—speak for all the others; its "scoreboard" that month included the destruction of 31 tanks, with 27 damaged; 11 other armoured vehicles were destroyed and 13 damaged; and some 50 trucks were also claimed as "flamers".

Photographs and the last battles

The crushing defeat inflicted on the *Wehrmacht* at and around Falaise spelled the end of any organized resistance in France. By no means all the German forces had been destroyed, but the survivors that managed to flee the trap eastwards had lost almost all their transport and armour, and were obliged to employ whatever bicycle, car or lorry that came readily to hand to convey them from the carnage of Normandy. Thousands on foot were rounded up by the pursuing Allies as they sped towards the Belgian border. For two or three weeks the pressure on the Typhoon squadrons eased as another task had to be faced—that of

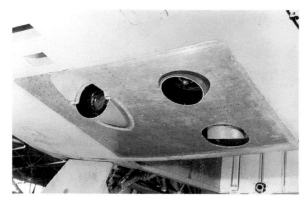

Above, the camera ports under the wing of a Typhoon PR IB. *Right*, the three-camera installation of a reconnaissance Typhoon, viewed looking forward. Nearest are the "split obliques", and beyond is the long-focus high-speed oblique camera. On the left is the inboard 20-mm cannon. (Photos: Hawker Aircraft Ltd., Neg Nos TYS/11 and TYS/14)

keeping up with the swiftly advancing armies. No sooner had orders been issued for this or that squadron to move forward to a particular airfield than the ground forces announced that they had occupied a town 50 miles further on. Between 20 August and mid-September there were no fewer than 90 squadron movements by the Typhoon squadrons alone in the course of an advance of 300 miles, each demanding maximum serviceability of aircraft, the speedy movement by road of ground-crews, their spares and tools, staff members, cooks, clerks and documents, bowsers, towing vehicles, "trolley-accs" and the thousand-and-one items that an operational unit demanded. Yet scarcely an occasion arose when the pilots, landing at their new airfield, had more than an hour or so to wait before the ground echelon caught up.

As autumn approached, leaving the dusty strips of Normandy far behind, the immediate aim was to get the 2nd Tactical Air Force into its winter quarters—the big, elaborate airfields of Belgium and Holland that had escaped the pulverizing of major ground battles. Long in advance the plans had been laid to bring the Typhoons up to such bases where once more they would regain the cohesion of autonomous Wings for the final assault on the German homeland.

★   ★   ★

Before however passing on to the operations of the autumn, it is necessary here to mention a new facet of Typhoon operations that had been introduced during the late summer of 1944, that of tactical photographic reconnaissance or, as it was initially undertaken, fighter reconnaissance.

Early in 1944 Hawker Aircraft Ltd had been instructed to carry out a trial installation, mounting a forward-facing camera in place of one of the Typhoon's cannon for use as a reconnaissance fighter. Soon afterwards the aircraft (*JR333*) underwent progressive modification at Boscombe Down and a Maintenance Unit until the aircraft

possessed three such cameras and but a single cannon. At the same time another scheme was evolved whereby, in place of the port wing fuel tank and port inner cannon, three reconnaissance cameras were mounted, comprising a pair of five-inch, split-oblique, high-speed cameras, angled downwards, and a long-focus, high-speed camera laid laterally, facing to the beam and angled down at 20 degrees. These aircraft, with a growing number of variations, came to be known as Typhoon Tac R Mark IBs, FR Mark IBs (when armoured) and PR Mark IBs (when not armoured). All subsequent conversions were undertaken by the Service, starting in May 1944, continuing until about September and involving around 120 aircraft.

First squadron to receive the reconnaissance Typhoons was No. 268 on 2 July, then based at Odiham and commanded by Squadron Leader (later Wing Commander) Albert Sydney Mann, DFC. It was the CO who, with Flying Officer (later Wing Commander) G. K. N. Lloyd, AFC, as his No. 2, flew the first reconnaissance sorties on 8th August over Normandy. The Squadron was also equipped with Tac R Mustangs, but the Typhoons tended to be employed on occasions when enemy fighter opposition could be expected, when their greater speed gave them a better chance of escape, for it should be emphasized that the task of these strictly reconnaissance sorties (as distinct from armed reconnaissance, as practised by the strike squadrons) was to bring home the photos, rather than to "mix it" with the opposition. Being an independent squadron—that is, not a component of a Typhoon strike Wing—No. 268 received its orders from, and was responsible to Group headquarters, being the unit charged with acquiring an overall picture of the battle area. During the great battles around Falaise the Squadron flew constantly for the benefit of the Supreme Command.

The reconnaissance sorties were carried out at heights between "ground level" and about 5,000 feet, seldom encountering enemy fighters but often having to contend with heavy flak; yet not one Typhoon was lost by the Squadron—although Flying Officer R. S. Clark had his canopy shot off on 18 August.

The Squadron ran into problems during the rapid advance across France as it was found that, given the relatively long lines of photographic patrols ordered, the Typhoons possessed insufficient range unless able to operate from airfields close up with the forward troops; moreover, as was perhaps to be expected, strike squadrons scrambling to the assistance of ground forces claimed priority of movement on the airfields. In early September No. 268 Squadron was based at Fort Rouge, near St Omer, at a time when leading elements of the British and Canadian armies were over a hundred miles to the east, and it was only on the 27th that space could be found for the Squadron at Ghent in Belgium. The Squadron carried out its last Typhoon sortie on 19 November before reverting exclusively to the Mustang.

A second photographic Typhoon squadron (which continued to fly Spitfire PRXIs at the same time) was No. 4, commanded by Squadron Leader C. D. Harris St John, DFC and Bar. The Squadron, based at St Denis Westrem in Belgium, took delivery of its first four Typhoons—officially designated as Typhoon PR Mark IBs with various oblique cameras fitted—on 1 October. This Squadron, cast in the mould of a conventional photographic reconnaissance unit, normally flew its Spitfires on high altitude operations, their extremely experienced pilots trained to fly carefully planned sorties deep into enemy territory, normally without too much fear of enemy interceptors. As the Allies now moved up for the final assault on Germany a new task was thrust upon No. 4 Squadron, that of medium altitude reconnaissance—heights that ex-

posed the pilots to greatest danger from flak and interception.

The Squadron's first setpiece operation was to provide a complete photographic commentary on the Allied air assault on the island of Walcheren in the mouth of the Scheldt on 11 October, when Bomber Command set out to attack heavy gun positions at Flushing and to breach the sea wall at Veere. Throughout the afternoon pairs of Ty-

Formerly a Typhoon FR Mark IB of No 268 Squadron, EE427/S with two-cannon armament became a PR Mark IB with No 4 Squadron late in 1944. (Photos: Sydney Camm Collection)

phoons kept up constant photographic surveillance, flying precisely planned runs over the island at 10,000 feet.

Similar operations were undertaken for several weeks over Holland, the pilots' post-sortie reports being of particular interest on account of the large number of sightings of German Messerschmitt Me 262 jet fighters, although none of the Typhoons was ever attacked. Another of the Squadron's tasks was to watch for the tell-tale trails from V-2 rockets being launched against England and Belgium from Holland so that it might be possible to pinpoint their launch sites. Only one Typhoon was lost when, on 18 November, Flight Lieutenant R. M. Cowell in *EK229* was shot down by flak while on a sortie over Bocholt, north-east of Essen; it later transpired that he was made a prisoner of war.

Fog over northern Germany and Holland severely curtailed photographic work by the Typhoons in December, and it was not until 16 January 1945 that it was resumed when Flight Lieutenant P. M. Sims carried out a reconnaissance sortie over Raamsdonkveer at 3,500 feet. Gradually however, as the final battles approached, the call for middle-altitude reconnaissance dwindled and No. 4 Squadron flew its last Typhoon sortie, in fact a low-level run over the Nijmegen area by Flight Lieutenants R. E. Wildin and I. H. Fryer, on 2 February.

★   ★   ★

As the Typhoon squadrons settled into their bases in Belgium and southern Holland in October 1944, the opportunity was taken to furnish them with replacement aircraft, fully modified to the final production standard—although there were many instances of "old favourites" being steadfastly retained on account of better-than-average service-

Top, flak damage to this 2 TAF Typhoon, JR427, included the severing of the rear wingspar and destruction of five wing ribs. *Above*, open air servicing of a Typhoon on a continental airfield among the debris of previous bombing. *Below*, Rocket-armed Typhoons of No 245 Squadron, 2 TAF. (Photos: via Richard Ward, Whitstable)

An interesting picture showing the astonishing lengths to which the Germans had gone to conceal the nature of buildings on their airfields, particularly in the Low Countries. Beyond the rocket-equipped Typhoon of No 137 Squadron (MN627/SF-N) a large hangar has been "camouflaged" by the construction of elaborate dummy buildings—with authentic architecture—over and around it. Such an airfield, believed to be B.58 Moelsbroek in Belgium, would have been frequently covered by Allied reconnaissance aircraft, yet the ruse appears to have succeeded—for no bomb damage is visible. (Photo: via T. Blundell)

ability record or some other quirk of exceptional performance.

Once more the call went out for setpiece attacks before the winter set in. During October alone the 2nd Tactical Air Force Typhoons were launched in more than a score of premeditated assaults on German headquarters of various sorts and sizes of which one, carried out by Nos. 197 and 266 Squadrons on 13 October was typical. In this, an attack on a *Wehrmacht* Corps headquarters near Breda in southern Holland, No. 197 Squadron led with 11 aircraft which dropped a full quota of 500-lb bombs and was followed by eight aircraft from No. 266 with rockets, flattening the building. Any occupant at the time of the attack could only have been rendered *hors de combat*.

It was however an attack carried out on the 24th that probably surpassed all previous setpiece strikes by Typhoons, a snap assault on the headquarters of the German Fifteenth Army, located in the Merwestein Park in the centre of the old Dutch city of Dordrecht, south-east of Rotterdam.

Warned by members of the Dutch Resistance movement that an important conference of *Wehrmacht* Generals and other senior staff officers was about to take place in the building, No. 84 Group came up with a hurriedly prepared but nevertheless meticulous plan to greet the visitors. Each of the Group's five component Typhoon Squadrons, Nos. 193, 197, 257, 263 and 266 (of No. 146 Wing)

would take part, led by Group Captain D. E. Gillam, DSO and two Bars, DFC and Bar, AFC. The attack passed off in copybook style as Gillam, flying ahead, dived from 6,000 feet with cannon blazing to drop a pair of 250-lb LC phosphorus marker bombs on the target building. Behind him the pilots of 48 Typhoons, flying in three formations line abreast, streaked in. As the two outer formations turned outwards to distract the flak gunners, the centre group of five aircraft flew straight at the building, hurling four 1,000-pounders and six 500-pounders at the building's façade.

General Dwight D. Eisenhower, Supreme Allied Commander, centre, in discussion with Gp Capt D. J. Scott, DSO, DFC, and Wg Cdr W. Dring, DFC, of No 123 Wing, on an airfield in Holland. (Photo: via Richard Ward, Whitstable)

Left, Wg Cdr F. G. Grant, DSO, DFC, Wing Leader of No 143 Canadian Wing, taxying at Eindhoven in about November 1944 in his "personal" Typhoon RB205/FGG with the help of a groundcrewman on each wing; the aircraft was one of those written off in the *Bodenplatte* attack. *Right*, Denys Gillam's second "personal" Typhoon MN587/ZZII, pictured between February 1944 and February 1945 when as a Group Captain, he commanded No 146 Wing. (Photo: Gp Capt D. E. Gillam, DSO, DFC, AFC)

Eleven seconds later the bombs, dropped from a height of 15 feet above the roof, exploded, collapsing the outer wall and bringing down almost every ceiling in the building. Following their feint, No. 263's Typhoons were first round again, firing 63 rockets into the slowly collapsing target; next came seven aircraft of No. 257 which dropped ten 1,000-pounders and four 500-pounders, followed by the 24 Typhoons of the other three squadrons which broadcast their rockets between the growing pile of rubble and the neighbouring flak posts. As the attack—said to have lasted less than a single minute—ended, the pilots reported that the target was scarcely recognizable as having been a building. While no Typhoon was lost, it emerged that a tragic accident had occurred (for which no planning could have allowed) when one of the bombs, so accurately released, had bounced off the ground and ricochetted over the target into a school almost a quarter mile beyond, in which a number of invalid children died.

Subsequent reports from the Dutch Resistance stated that two Generals, 17 senior staff officers and 55 of middle rank were among the Germans killed in the attack. When further news arrived that an elaborate funeral was planned for the *Wehrmacht* casualties a few days later, Gillam decided that it would be appropriate for No. 146 Wing to provide an explosive send-off, but Nature in the form of low cloud prevented the Typhoons' attendance.

It was the fog, low cloud and heavy rains that now persisted over the Low Countries which severely curtailed Allied air operations throughout December. When, however, the next setpiece attack occurred, it was to be the Typhoons themselves that were to be the principal target. Although the attack by the *Luftwaffe* was planned to strike at numerous bases occupied by Allied fighters and fighter-bombers, there can be little doubt that revenge against the Typhoon squadrons that had destroyed the numerous *Wehrmacht* headquarters and killed so many respected commanders, ranked high among the motives for, and determined the pattern of attack when it eventually materialized.

A Typhoon of No 439 Squadron, RCAF, taxying on a waterlogged airfield in the Low Countries. The Canadian Wing employed groundcrew personnel, perched on one or both wings, to assist pilots in taxying, a custom seldom observed in the RAF. (Photo: via Richard Ward, Whitstable)

Unternehmen "Bodenplatte'

Shortly after dawn on New Year's Day, 1945, the *Luftwaffe* launched a desperate, yet carefully planned major attack on the airfields of the Allied air forces based in the Low Countries and eastern France, the object being to destroy the largest possible number of British and American aircraft on the ground, thereby depriving the Allies of effective air support during the imminent ground assault on Germany.

The attack had originally been planned to co-incide with the opening of von Rundstedt's offensive in the Ardennes, which had been launched on 16 December, 1944. The persistent fog over the Allied airfields during the month had, however, forestalled the *Luftwaffe*'s great enterprise, although German aircraft had flown many hundreds of sorties in support of the ground offensive itself.

That the New Year's Day attacks achieved their immediate aim cannot be denied; surprise was exploited almost everywhere and the damage wrought was certainly impressive, particularly among the Typhoon squadrons. Yet for a number of reasons the Allies sought to play down the significance of the attack, and from the tone of the various reports and communiqués, issued immediately afterwards—and later quoted in numerous "histories"—it might have been thought that the Allies had won a major victory. Indeed the aircraft losses compiled for public consumption (quoted as 134 British and American aircraft destroyed and 62 damaged) are so wide of the true figure as to require some explanation.

In the first place, loss figures were called for by each Group in the evening of the day of the attack, resulting in a hurried assessment of aircraft "destroyed" and "damaged". However, what constituted a damaged aircraft under the circumstances prevailing in Northern Europe in the last winter of the War, with only very limited resources available for major repairs, was entirely different from that which might have escaped being written off a year earlier in England. Moreover, had a true picture of the damage suffered been submitted for scrutiny among, say, the Chiefs of Staff, there would likely have been wide-ranging, but ill-advised criticism of the commanders in the field for what might have been interpreted as a major lapse of vigilance and security. To have sought scapegoats and dismissals at this stage of the War could only have had a deleterious effect on the pattern of the ultimate assault on Germany. However, as will be shown, the situation faced by the Allied air forces deployed in the Low Countries during the winter of 1944–45 was such as to place the bases in a position of extreme vulnerability, and one that could not possibly have been mitigated by any commander on the spot.

Pilots and groundcrew of No 143 (Canadian) Wing struggle to remain operational despite severe flooding of their airfield early in 1945. (Photos: M. D. Howley, via Richard Ward, Farnborough)

Although the German order of battle for the operation, codenamed *Unternehmen "Bodenplatte"* (Operation "Baseplate"), is given in an accompanying table, only those parts of the attack as they involved the Typhoon squadrons are described here. And the ultimate loss figure for the Typhoon alone *on just one airfield* exceeded the total losses admitted by the Allies for all aircraft on all airfields!

★   ★   ★

In pursuit of the aim to launch a crippling pre-emptive strike against the Allied air force bases, the German High Command (OKL) instructed the 31-year-old Kommandierender General of *IX.(J) Fliegerkorps*, Generalmajor Dietrich Peltz, to prepare an overall plan by which some attack might be carried out. To do so involved assembling some 800 German fighters and fighter-bombers of 40 *Gruppen* from every war front, led by a high pro-

UNTERNEHMEN "BODENPLATTE", 1 January, 1945: THE ATTACKING FORCE

Unit	Commander	Force	Aircraft	Objective	Remarks
3.JAGDDIVISION	Generalmajor Walter Grabmann				
I.,II.,III./JG 1	Oberst Herbert Ihlefeld	69	Bf 109G–10, Bf 109K–4 Fw 190A–8, Fw 190D–9	St Denis Westrem	Lost 22 aircraft
I.,II.,III./JG 3	Oberstleutnant Heinz Bär	65	Bf 109G–10, Bf 109K–4	Eindhoven	Lost 17 aircraft
I.,II.,III./JG 6	Major Richard Leppla	64	Bf 109G–10, Fw 190D–9	Volkel	Lost "at least 12 aircraft".
I.,II.,III./JG 26	Oberst Josef Priller	60	Bf 109G–10, Bf 109K–4 Fw 190D–9	Brussels-Evere Grimbergen	Lost "at least 20 aircraft"; some reports
III./JG 54	—	17	Bf 109G–10, Bf 109K–4		state 22 aircraft.
I.,II.,III.,IV./JG 27	Major Ludwig Franzisket	55	Bf 109G–10, Bf 109K–4	Brussels-Melsbroek	Lost 29 aircraft (incl 21
IV./JG 54	—	17	Bf 109G–10, Fw 190D–9		over German territory).
I.,II.,III./JG 77	Oberstleutnant Erich Leie	57	Bf 109K–4	Antwerp-Deurne	Lost 11 aircraft (incl 5 over German territory).
5.JAGDDIVISION	(Oberst Harry von Bülow-Borthkamp)				
I.,II.,III./JG 53	Oberstleutnant Helmut Bennemann	55	Bf 109G–10, Bf 109K–4	Metz-Frascaty	Lost 19 aircraft (incl 11 to flak)
JAGDABSCHNITTS-FUHRER (Mittle-Rhein) I.,II.,III./JG 2	Oberst Handrick Oberstleutnant Kurt Bühligen	71	Bf 109G–10, Bf 109K–4 Fw 109A–8, Fw 190D–9	St Trond	Lost 18 aircraft
I.,II.,III./JG 4	Oberstleutnant Gerhard Michalski	66	Bf 109G–10, Bf 109K–4 Fw 190D–9	Le Culot	Lost 21 aircraft (incl 6 over German territory).
I.,II.,III./JG 11	Oberstleutnant Günther Specht	76	Bf 109G–10, Bf 109K–4 Fw 190A–8	Asch	Lost 12 aircraft (incl that of Geschw.Kdre.)
"PATHFINDERS" I./KG 51	Oberstleutnant Wolfgang Schenck	c.26	Me 262A–2a	—	Incl 4 aircraft to Eindhoven
I.,II.,III./SG 4	Oberstleutnant Ewald Janssen	27	Fw 190G–1	—	
NSGr. 20	Major Kurt Dahlmann	24	Fw 190G–1	—	Incl 4 aircraft to Eindhoven
Einsatzstaffel 104	Major Reinhard Seiler	9	Bf 109G–12	—	
NJG 1	Oberstleutnant Hans-Joachim Jabs	c.30	Ju 88G	—	Incl 4 aircraft to Eindhoven

portion of the *Luftwaffe*'s surviving pilots of considerable ability and experience. Detailed planning was undertaken well in advance of the originally-scheduled date of the attack (16 December, 1944), emphasis being laid on selecting flight routes that were thought to take the raiders well clear of known areas of heavy ground defence concentrations, the target airfields being selected as those on which Allied aircraft were known to exist in the largest numbers. As already stated the great attack was to be delayed by a fortnight—a period in which the Allied forces underwent some redeployment (particularly in the USAAF), and some areas were substantially reinforced by the repositioning of anti-aircraft gun defences. Because of the fog over the Low Countries few of these changes were detected by German aerial reconnaissance.

Such was the chronic shortage of fuel in Germany during the final six months of the War, scarcely any training could be undertaken to prepare the young, inexperienced line pilots who now constituted the greater part of the *Luftwaffe*, men in their late 'teens who would provide the main force of raiders in "*Bodenplatte*". These very young pilots would have to fly a long sortie at very low altitude so as to escape detection by Allied mobile radars and observer posts. Moreover, to preserve the utmost secrecy in the presence of almost continuous Allied reconnaissance patrols

over Germany, the assembly of the raiding forces on their "jumping off" airfields would not take place until the late evening of the day prior to the attack. Literally hundreds of young pilots with fewer than 60 flying hours in their logbooks were then given a detailed briefing to undertake a flight of such difficulty and hazard that would have taxed the skill and courage of many a seasoned veteran. To ease the burden of navigation a number of "pathfinding" aircraft, flown by exceptionally experienced pilots, would lead each formation, while ground flares would be discharged by *Wehrmacht* units to indicate the position of turning points *en route* to each target. Weapon loads would include relatively few high explosive bombs as these would severely reduce the raiders' performance, and roughly half the attacking aircraft would carry numerous small fragmentation bombs—the ideal weapon for use against parked aircraft—and great use would be made of machine-gun and cannon fire.

Each pilot was entreated to destroy "at least one enemy aircraft", and to emphasize the supreme importance of the attack the pilots were told that every strike would be led by famous holders of the Knight's Cross—as evidence of this such men as Herbert Ihlefeld, Heinz Bär, Kurt Bühligen and "Pips" Priller attended the briefings.

Meanwhile, on the airfields of the 2nd Tactical Air Force in Holland and Belgium, the RAF Wing and Squadron Commanders faced considerable difficulties, of which the greatest was one of aircraft congestion. Located on just four airfields were more than 500 aircraft, with no fewer than nine squadrons of Typhoons and Spitfires packed into the airfield at Antwerpe-Deurne, and eight Typhoon squadrons at Eindhoven. To add to their problems, not only had the airfields suffered heavily at the hands of British and American bombers during the years before liberation from the Germans, and been further damaged by demolition as the enemy departed, but the drainage systems—natural and man-made—had been so extensively damaged that they proved quite incapable of coping with anything but the lightest shower

of rain. There had been heavy rains during the early winter weeks and much of the dispersal area on the airfields was unable to accommodate aircraft, even with the aid of the perforated steel planking so beloved by Allied airfield engineers.

The destruction of almost all hangarage on the airfields meant that virtually all servicing and repair of aircraft had to be carried out in the open at the mercy of the winter elements. Serviceability among the Typhoons remained remarkably high although the spate of setpiece attacks against heavily defended targets in October and November had taken its toll. In short, although it had been anticipated that winter would find the 2nd Tactical Air Force comfortably ensconced in large "perma-

UNTERNEHMEN "BODENPLATTE", 1 January, 1945: THE TARGETS

Target Base (and number of aircraft located thereon)	Unit(s)	Aircraft	Commanding Officer	Remarks
B.61 St Denis Westrem, Belgium (Total of 51 aicraft)	No. 302 (Polish) Squadron	Spitfire IX	Sqn Ldr M. Duryasz	Aircraft losses not known.
	No. 308 (Polish) Squadron	Spitfire IX	Sqn Ldr K. Pniak	
	No. 317 (Polish) Squadron	Spitfire IX	Sqn Ldr M. Chelmecki	
B.78 Eindhoven, Holland (Total of 165 aircraft)	No. 137 Squadron	Typhoon IB	Sqn Ldr R. G. V. Barraclough	
	No. 168 Squadron	Typhoon IB	Sqn Ldr L. H. Lambert, DFC	
	No. 181 Squadron	Typhoon IB	Sqn Ldr D. R. Crawford	
	No. 182 Squadron	Typhoon IB	Sqn Ldr G. J. Gray, DFC	Total of 141 aircraft, all Typhoons, written off.
	No. 247 Squadron	Typhoon IB	Sqn Ldr J. H. Bryant, DFC	
	No. 438 Squadron (RCAF)	Typhoon IB	Sqn Ldr J. E. Hogg, RCAF	
	No. 439 Squadron (RCAF)	Typhoon IB	Sqn Ldr R. G. Crosby, RCAF	
	No. 440 Squadron (RCAF)	Typhoon IB	Sqn Ldr H. E. Gooding, RCAF	
B.80 Volkel, Holland (Total of 146 aircraft)	No. 3 Squadron	Tempest V	Sqn Ldr H. N. Sweetman, DFC	
	No. 56 Squadron	Tempest V	Sqn Ldr D. V. C. Cotes-Preedy, DFC & Bar, GM	
	No. 80 Squadron	Tempest V	Sqn Ldr R. L. Spurdle, DSO, DFC & Bar	Total of 13 aircraft, 11 Typhoons and 2 Tempests, written off.
	No. 274 Squadron	Tempest V	Sqn Ldr A. H. Baird, DFC	
	No. 174 Squadron	Typhoon IB	Sqn Ldr J. C. Melvill	
	No. 175 Squadron	Typhoon IB	Sqn Ldr R. W. Campbell	
	No. 184 Squadron	Typhoon IB	Sqn Ldr W. Smith, DFC	
B.70 Antwerp-Deurne, Belgium (Total of 162 aircraft)	No. 193 Squadron	Typhoon IB	Sqn Ldr C. D. Erasmus, DFC	
	No. 197 Squadron	Typhoon IB	Sqn Ldr A. H. Smith	
	No. 257 Squadron	Typhoon IB	Sqn Ldr D. P. Jenkins, DFC	
	No. 263 Squadron	Typhoon IB	Sqn Ldr R. D. Rutter, DFC	Total of 16 aircraft, 10 Typhoons and 6 Spitfires, written off.
	No. 266 Squadron	Typhoon IB	Sqn Ldr J. H. Deall	
	No. 74 Squadron	Spitfire IX	Sqn Ldr A. J. Reeves, DFC	
	No. 329 (French) Squadron	Spitfire IX	Comdt J. Ozanne	
	No. 341 (French) Squadron	Spitfire IX	Comdt C. Martell	
	No. 345 (French) Squadron	Spitfire IX	Comdt Guizard	
Metz-Frascaty, France (USAAF) (Total of c.66 aircraft)	356th Fighter Group (incl 386th, 387th and 388th Fighter Squadrons)	P–47D	Lieut-Col Donald A. Baccus	Aircraft lost said to be "a dozen aircraft".
Le Culot, Belgium (USAAF) (Total of c.140 aircraft)	36th Fighter Group (incl 22d, 23d and 53d Fighter Squadrons)	P–47D	Lieut-Col Van H. Slayden	Aircraft losses not known.
	373d Fighter Group (incl 410th, 411th and 412th Fighter Squadrons)	P–47D	Colonel James C. McGehee	Aircraft losses not known.
	363d Reconnaissance Group (161st, 162d and 380th Reconnaissance Squadrons)	F–5, F–6	Colonel James M. Smelley	Aircraft losses not known.
Saint Trond, Belgium (USAAF) (Total of c.78 aircraft)	48th Fighter Group (incl 55th, 56th and 57th Fighter Squadrons)	P–47D	Colonel James K. Johnson	Aircraft losses not known.
Asch, Belgium (USAAF) (Total of 58 aircraft)	366th Fighter Group (incl 389th, 390th and 391st Fighter Squadrons)	P–47D	Colonel Harold N. Holt	At least 15 P–47s written off.
Brussels-Evère (USAAF)	Aircraft in transit	—	—	22 aircraft written off (incl at least 9 C–47s).
Grimbergen, Belgium (USAAF)	Aircraft in transit	—	—	"At least 45" aircraft destroyed or written off.

nent'' air bases after months of leapfrogging over a succession of rudimentary, dusty landing strips, the squadrons found themselves herded together on a small number of huge waterlogged fields—each of which was familiar to, and accurately ''targeted'' by the enemy. Some of the airfields, particularly Deurne near Antwerp, had been hit by V-2 rockets.

The result of this general congestion and difficulty of movement—by both aircraft and personnel—was that the aircraft had frequently to be parked in large groups, often in the centre of the airfields or crammed together on hardstandings near the squadron crew rooms and vehicles. Having been in recent occupation of the airfields, the Germans were entirely familiar with their topography and, armed with this detailed knowledge the *Luftwaffe* pilots were able to approach their targets in such a manner as to achieve almost total surprise and maximum damage in their initial strafing runs.

It is true to say that "*Bodenplatte*" was launched without the slightest advanced knowledge by Allied intelligence; none of the sophisticated intelligence-gathering sources had detected the merest hint of an impending attack, for it would have been entirely feasible to order large numbers of Allied fighters to be on standing patrol in readiness. As it was, 2nd Tactical Air Force records show that at least a dozen routine operations had been ordered for the morning of New Year's Day and that all would have involved the loading of bombs, rockets or drop tanks, involving roughly 130 Typhoons and Tempests, none of which would

be in a position to intercept incoming raiders.

Flight planning by the Germans was carefully co-ordinated so that, although widely separated approach routes to the targets would be flown, the actual strikes would occur almost simultaneously at 09:20 hr. A remarkable degree of co-ordination was achieved in spite of the long and often complicated flights, and all reports indicate that the attacks on the various airfields opened between 09:10 and 09:20 hr.

The base at Eindhoven in southern Holland, home of no fewer than eight Typhoon squadrons with 165 aircraft, was to be hit by more than 80 attackers, including 65 Messerschmitt Bf 109Gs, led by four Me 262A–2a jets, four Junkers Ju 88Gs and about a dozen Focke-Wulfe Fw 190G-1s.

"B.78 Eindhoven. No. 247 Squadron. All pilots boarded the Squadron's transports and left early for the airfield as a long-range job was in the air. Then, out of the blue, came the whistle of bombs, the scream of diving planes, the chatter of machine guns, the heavier thump of cannon, and it seemed that the floodgates of hell had suddenly opened to release old Nick's devillish hoardes. First came the jet bombers and, after bombs away, the '109s and Ju 88s. Wave after wave they came in, strafing the airfield from end to end at a height of 50 feet, apparently concentrating on destroying aircraft. One 'Screamer' squadron (callsign of No. 143 (Canadian) Wing) was badly caught at the end of the runway, several aircraft being completely burned out and the rest damaged. Petrol dumps were set on fire, a bomb dump of No. 143 Wing was set on fire,

Bodenplatte, 1 January 1945. XM-K of No 182 Squadron was hit as it taxied out to take off, and the pilot sought safety after vacating his cockpit in a hurry. In the background is a pair of No 440 Squadron aircraft, also shot up as they moved out to take off; one of their pilots, Plt Off E. T. Flanagan, was seriously wounded. (Photo: M. D. Howley, via Richard Ward, Farnborough)

Bodenplatte, 1 January 1945. Moments after the *Luftwaffe* had left the occupants of Eindhoven to survey the damage. The two aircraft seen here belonged to No 439 Squadron, RCAF. (Photo: M. D. Howley, via Richard Ward, Farnborough)

with 1,000-lb bombs exploding every few minutes; individual aircraft in dispersal were set ablaze, rockets ignited and flashed in all directions . . . it has been estimated that, of 100-plus raiders that came over the airfield, 44 were claimed shot down. At the end of the day No. 247 Squadron had only five aircraft serviceable, No. 137 had 11, No. 181 had eight and all No. 182's aircraft were either destroyed or damaged.''

No. 247 Squadron's young chronicler may be forgiven for his rather breathless account of the attack, yet it conveys the pandemonium that reigned at Eindhoven during "*Bodenplatte*". In fact one Fw 190 was shot down by a Typhoon, five

Bf 109s were destroyed by the airfield ground defences, two Bf 109s were shot down by Tempests from Volkel which arrived towards the end of the attack, and four Bf 109s and two Fw 190Gs collided over or near the airfield; only one of the 14 German pilots was captured alive by Allied personnel in the area.

On No. 137 Squadron considerable damage was suffered among its dispersal buildings, a senior NCO being killed and a dozen other ground personnel wounded; Flight Sergeant L. A. V. Burrows was killed while taxying a Typhoon to dispersal; three Typhoons were destroyed and four damaged—all had to be written off.

Flight Lieutenant H. P. Gibbons on No. 168

Bodenplatte, 1 January 1945. Such was the congestion of aircraft at Eindhoven, with more than 160 Typhoons, that scarcely any dispersal was possible. These two No 439 Squadron aircraft (also pictured above) had been parked wing tip to wing tip; one received a direct hit and blew up, badly damaging its neighbour, seen on the right with its fin and rudder missing. (Photo: M. D. Howley, via Richard Ward, Farnborough)

Squadron was airborne on an air test in a Typhoon when the attack started and made straight for the pathfinders, shooting down a Fw 190G which fell on the airfield and exploded. He was immediately set on by Bf 109s and killed.

No. 181 Squadron had not been warned for operations during the morning, and fortunately there were few members at the dispersal; those who were present sought safety in a flooded shelter trench to watch as one aircraft was struck and destroyed by a fragmentation bomb and eight others badly damaged by splinters and gunfire.

No. 182 Squadron, also of No. 124 Wing, suffered much worse: "1–1–45. No. 182 Squadron. A Happy New Year, at least that is what we thought until the Hun descended on us shortly after 09:00 hr with some concentrated low level strafing for 23 minutes. The boys quickly sought cover and we were fortunate in only having two casualties (one airman killed and another had a foot blown off by a cannon shell). All the Squadron's aircraft were written off or damaged; a re-fitting party was therefore organized and flown off to England in a Dakota."

It was however to be the Canadian Wing, Nos. 438, 439 and 440 Squadrons, that seem to have suffered worst of all at Eindhoven, with 16 aircraft caught in the act of taking off when the attackers arrived.

"1–1–45. No. 438 Squadron. The Acting Squadron Commander, Flight Lieutenant P. Wilson, was taking off when the German attack started;

he aborted his take-off and stopped at the end of the runway. He was shot up and managed to get clear but was wounded in the stomach and died. The second aircraft, flown by Flying Officer R. W. Keller, got airborne but crashed just off the airfield, killing the pilot. Of the eight Squadron aircraft taking off, three were burned, one broke up, one was badly damaged, one beyond repair, and two undamaged. One of the other pilots was wounded, but five were able to jump out of their aircraft and sheltered."

Back in No. 438's dispersal five other Typhoons were destroyed and three badly damaged. No. 439 Squadron, warned for an operation later in the day, had been obliged to park its aircraft wingtip to wingtip beside a taxytrack, and these were being armed and fuelled when the raid started. It appears that this line of Typhoons attracted the first German strafing run across the airfield, with a number of well-placed high-explosive and fragmentation bombs hitting or narrowly missing the Typhoons. Although the groundcrews quickly scattered they were evidently some distance from shelter and suffered heavy casualties as a result. The Squadron records show that "one Typhoon was burned out and another damaged", yet photographs indicate that every one of No. 439's aircraft suffered numerous cannon and splinter strikes, and not one of the aircraft on charge the previous evening ever again featured in an operational report. (Seven aircraft, flown by the Squadron later in the day, had been "pooled" from other sur-

Just visible on the rear fuselage of this Typhoon are the codes FGG, identifying it as the aircraft flown by Wg Cdr F. G. Grant, Wing Leader of No 143 Wing at Eindhoven. The aircraft, RB205, was one of a large number of Typhoons that suffered various degrees of damage in the *Bodenplatte* attacks. In this instance the aircraft received many machine gun and cannon strikes and was declared a write off. The presence of snow in the picture dates it as having been taken on or about 4 January 1945. (Photo: via Richard Ward, Whitstable)

Prelude to tragedy. Each loaded with two 1,000-lb bombs, the Typhoons F3-T and F3-W of No 438 Squadron, RCAF, were taking off at Eindhoven when "T" burst its port tyre and swung broadside on the runway. As "W" taxied past, a groundcrewman arrived to assist the pilot of "T" to taxy clear. Unfortunately the landing gear collapsed, causing the port bomb to fall off, exploding moments later and killing both men and blowing the Typhoon to pieces. (Photo: via Richard Ward, Farnborough)

vivors on the Wing.)

"No. 440 Squadron suffered worst at Eindhoven. Eight aircraft were moving on to the runway to take off when Me 109s and long-nosed Fw 190s opened their attack. Two Typhoons were destroyed immediately and two badly damaged. One pilot, Pilot Officer E. T. Flanagan, was seriously wounded and many pilots and groundcrew received minor injuries. The Squadron dispersal was struck by a 1,100-kg bomb, but it "only" destroyed the orderly room. In the afternoon Wing Commander Grant (the Wing Leader, whose own Typhoon had been damaged and was written off) decided that No. 440 Squadron would be non-operational until replacement aircraft were delivered. The Squadron was declared operational once more on 4 January."

As a number of Tempests and Spitfires from Volkel arrived overhead at about 09:40 hr the Bf 109s attempted to reform into a cohesive formation to make good their escape (the pathfinder Ju 88s having remained in the area, ready to shepherd the single-seaters home). Of all the attacks that constituted "*Bodenplatte*", that on Eindhoven appears to have been by far the most successful, and the losses suffered by the attackers were roughly similar to those of the other formations. Yet the damage caused, ultimately assessed as the loss of 141 Typhoons at Eindhoven alone, would have ranked as one of the greatest single catastrophes suffered by the RAF during the War—in material terms. Miraculously the loss of life was much lower than might have been expected, a total of four pilots and eight groundcrewmen being killed, and three pilots and 104 groundcrew wounded.

The German attack at Volkel seems to have encountered much stiffer opposition and to have failed to achieve concentration in time and area. Many of the Tempests were engaged in offensive

patrols of their own, and it may well be that one of these ran into JG 6 as it was making for its target. None of the reports from ground observers mention Me 262 jets or Ju 88 pathfinders. Only No. 274 Squadron recorded combats, and it is likely that these were the ones that took place over or near Eindhoven; two Tempests were lost on the ground, together with 11 Typhoons, of which two belonged to No. 174 Squadron, one to No. 175 and two to No. 184 Squadron; the remainder were in the Wing repair pool and were damaged by cannon fire and subsequently written off.

Third of the Typhoon bases attacked was B.70 Antwerp-Deurne, but once again many of the aircraft were themselves away on patrol. No. 193 Squadron had three aircraft destroyed (apparently by fragmentation bombs); No. 257 Squadron reported that two aircraft were "damaged", although it is difficult to see how a Typhoon with most of its tail blown off and another collapsed on a shattered undercarriage could have been repaired on site! No. 266 Squadron reported the loss of a single Typhoon ("the most clapped-out aircraft on the Squadron"), but four others on the Wing strength were also written off, presumably while being serviced in the Wing pool.

Contrary to conflicting accounts published previously, this Typhoon (quoted as RB209 of No 168 Squadron) crashed when its pilot attempted to take off with full flap; realising that he would not get airborne, he braked too hard and locked the wheels, causing the aircraft to overturn. The error cost him his life. (Photo: via Richard Ward, Farnborough)

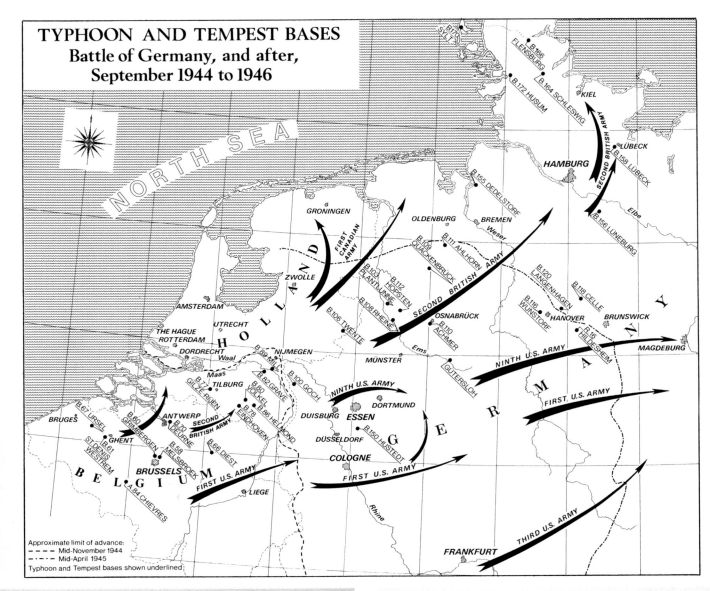

TYPHOON AND TEMPEST BASES
Battle of Germany, and after,
September 1944 to 1946

NORTH SEA

Approximate limit of advance:
--- Mid-November 1944
-·-·- Mid-April 1945
Typhoon and Tempest bases shown underlined

Left, rocket-laden Typhoon SW494/EL-F of No 181 Squadron taking off—probably at Eindhoven—early in 1945. *Right*, an aircraft of No 439 Squadron landing at Eindhoven; in the background is a "graveyard" of aircraft written off after the New Year's Day attack. (Photos: M. D. Howley, via Richard Ward, Farnborough)

Late production Typhoon bombers of No 440 Squadron, RCAF, undergoing engine maintenance at B.110 Osnabrück, Germany, in April 1945; SW452, shown on the right, was one of the aircraft delivered as a replacement following the Squadron's losses in *Bodenplatte* in January. (Photo: M. D. Howley, via Richard Ward, Farnborough)

As previously stated, the Allies were less than anxious to tell the world how effective "*Bodenplatte*" had been, and only by careful cross-checking between the various reports, as well as matching individual aircraft records, has it been possible to piece together what appears to be an accurate figure for Typhoon "write-offs". The total figure of 170 British aircraft lost is almost certainly about 30–40 on the low side, while a figure of 27 P-47s and 67 other American aircraft written off has been arrived at from semi-official accounts from only four of the nine American airfields targeted.

The loss of 183 German aircraft, taken from *Luftwaffe* records and *Geschwader* histories, is also likely to be an incomplete total as it is known that many of the "fledgling" pilots had not formally been taken on the established strength of the participating units, and so casualties among these young men were not administered by the unit involved. Nor have complete losses among the pathfinders been traced.

Yet the entire concept of "*Bodenplatte*", bold though it may have been, could never have seriously affected the outcome of the War, except perhaps to shorten the end for Germany. Apart from two Typhoon squadrons being withdrawn from operations for about three days, the scale of operations being undertaken by the Allied air forces was unaffected. Within six days every one of

the Typhoons and Tempests that had been written off had been replaced from stocks, while the stocks themselves would be replenished within a month.

While losses among the Allied pilots had been no higher than might have been expected in any one day of normal flying operations by the 2nd Tactical Air Force, those of the *Luftwaffe* were desperately more serious. They included Oberstleutnant Günther Specht, believed to have been shot down by flak near Brussels while leading JG11 against the American base at Asch; three *Gruppenkommandeur* and 32 *Staffelkapitäne* were also among the casualties, men whose places could not possibly be adequately filled in time for the approaching final battle for Germany. On the other hand, had it been possible to launch "*Bodenplatte*" six months earlier, before the Allies had broken out of their Normandy beachhead—when the *Luftwaffe* itself could have mustered an even larger force of aircraft, and when fuel stocks still

Running up prior to take-off with a pair of tail-fuzed 1,000-lb bombs at B.100 Goch, Germany, in April 1945 in RB389/I8-P (inscribed PULVERIZER IV) of No 440 Squadron, RCAF. (Photo: M. D. Howley, via Richard Ward, Farnborough)

existed to train the pilots—the result could have been disastrous for the whole Allied plan of invasion. As it was, the attacks on New Year's Day, 1945, caused not the slightest check in the Allied plans to assault the German homeland.

After "Bodenplatte"

If the German attack on 1 January came as an unpleasant surprise to the men of the 2nd Tactical Air Force, it was indeed little more than that. The various reports that appear in the squadron records do little to conceal the generally high morale that now permeated the Allied forces everywhere. The casualties were to be regretted, though far lower than were being daily borne by the fighting units of the Allied armies. Apart from the small effort to fetch a couple of hundred replacement Typhoons to the forward bases, there was much tidying up to be done, as well as running repairs to essential buildings, runways, taxytracks and vehicles. To most groundcrew members the attacks had merely relieved the monotony of a tedious and uncomfortable winter. It would not be long before they would be on the move forward once more.

Furthermore, it was not long before the Typhoons were being ordered off for the perpetual round of armed reconnaissance tasks, and more and more frequently the names of German airfields and towns came to feature in the patrol orders as the destinations of strikes and sweeps—although a fast growing proportion of these tasks now fell to the Tempests whose squadrons congregated at Volkel.

It was now also that that superb trio of long-

range American fighters came into its own, as the P-38, P-47 and P-51 were able to divert much more of their time to sweeps over airfields deep inside Germany. In the main the Typhoons were confined to patrols up to 50 miles into northern Germany, a growing proportion of their "armed reconnaissance" flights involving unrestricted attacks on targets of opportunity—particularly trains.

The German rail network had been largely created to cater for the needs of another war, in the middle of the last century and, perhaps more than any other system in Europe, was still to be relied

Referred to as being of "deplorably bad aerodynamic shape" by the Hawker test pilots, the 900-lb cluster bomb is here seen being carried by a Typhoon of No 143 (Canadian) Wing on an airfield in Germany early in 1945. (Photo: M. D. Howley, via Richard Ward, Farnborough)

upon to transport the military from one town or city to another. Not surprisingly, with the Allies banging on both the front and back doors, virtually every locomotive, passenger coach and rail wagon had been impressed for military use, so that any rail traffic spotted during the frequent patrols by Allied pilots could be attacked with rocket, bomb and cannon without conscience.

One or two of the Typhoon squadrons, notably No. 440 of the Canadian Wing, were given the task of "rail cutting", the job of simply tearing up the "permanent way" by dumping large numbers of 1,000-pounders on stretches of undefended track; but the German engineers were experts at making good such damage, and traffic was seldom inconvenienced for more than a few hours. Far more difficult to replace were the big locomotives, and these became favourite targets among the Typhoon pilots during the last four months of the War, although the *Wehrmacht* had an unwelcome habit of concealing the dreaded multiple-barrel 20-mm anti-aircraft guns among the trucks and coaches behind. These took a heavy toll of the unwary.

No. 175 Squadron was frequently ordered off on "railway patrols" during March and April, the line running south from Hengelo becoming an accustomed hunting ground until the losses began to climb fairly rapidly. This squadron alone lost six pilots (among them Squadron Leader M. Savage and Flight Lieutenant C. A. B. Slack) and seven aircraft in March, and three pilots and four aircraft in April, all to train flak.

For most squadrons, however, April brought a shift from road, rail and river targets as all-out efforts were now made to prevent the *Luftwaffe* from taking off to defend the cities as the Allied

The personal Typhoon RB431/JCB "ZIPP XI" of Wg Cdr J. C. Button, DSO, DFC, Wing Leader of No 123 Wing (after the death of Dring) in 1945. The segmented black and white spinner and matching propeller blades, and initials "JCB" on wheel fairings are noteworthy, as is the removal of the port inner cannon. (Photo: Raymond Rayner, via R. C. Sturtivant)

armies moved deeper into Germany. Attacks on airfields became commonplace as the Typhoons sought out the enemy fighters in their lairs. Worthwhile targets were now rare as the Germans took to using well-concealed air strips and otherwise innocent stretches of the *Autobahnen*, quickly dispersing the aircraft into nearby woods after sorties. Flight Sergeant R. B. Farmiloe of No. 197 Squadron was, however, sufficiently sharp-eyed to spot and destroy a Messerschmitt Me 262 jet on the airfield at Broekzetel near the German coast on 11 April.

The final couple of weeks of the War were punctuated for the Typhoon squadrons by a series of attacks off the German coast, both against ship-

Rocket-armed Typhoon ZX-W of No 247 Squadron gets airborne from its continental airfield shortly before the end of the War. (Photo: via Richard Ward, Farnborough)

The War was not yet over when this photo was taken (on 12 April 1945) of No 124 Wing's Typhoons on Twente/Enschede airfield in Holland. With the aircraft of No 181 Squadron in the foreground and those of No 137 beyond, each carries a pair of drop tanks and four rockets. Such was the degree of Allied air supremacy in the final weeks of the War that such concentrations of aircraft were commonplace—with no attempt made at dispersal. (Photo: Australian War Museum, Neg No UU2802)

ping seeking to escape to Norway, and concentrations of seaplanes being assembled for the same purpose. And it is perhaps an interesting little footnote to this Chapter to record that among the aircraft that took part in No. 184 Squadron's very last operation of the War—a shipping strike on 4th May 1945—was one of the very early R-serial Typhoons (*R8687*), an aeroplane that had suffered all manner of minor mishaps during its long Service career, but had always been repaired . . . and finished its War resplendent with all the final modifications, and as good as new!

★　　　★　　　★

Although the final weeks of the War were a period of routine operations, with few occasions of trauma or excitement, the Typhoon squadrons continued to make their presence felt right up to the moment of ultimate victory. Thereafter the task of distributing the Allied armies and air forces around Germany as powerful instruments of occupation became the order of the day.

For the time being few of the squadrons were disbanded, although an inevitable reduction in manpower quickly followed as the demobilization of personnel began to take effect. The return of squadrons to England and Wales for brief spells at the practice camps at Warmwell or Fairwood Common—which had started during the previous November and continued in rotation ever since—was maintained into the months of peace, although to many pilots the urgency to improve their skills at rocket firing all now seemed a trifle supperfluous.

In August 1945, however, the run-down of the Typhoons started in earnest, and in the following month the "Tiffy" was declared redundant for operational purposes: the last Squadron, No. 175, gave up its aircraft on disbandment on the last day of the month at Schleswig in Germany. Some of the squadrons, though temporarily deprived of their wartime identity, were soon to be restored—to join the growing force with Tempests, whose story must now be told.

6

ENTER THE TEMPEST

The process of reasoning that led ultimately to the development and introduction into RAF service of the Tempest was tortuous indeed, complicated on the one hand by Sydney Camm's acceptance that the Typhoon's wing—designed to be thick for all the right reasons in the first place—had compromised its high altitude performance long before it entered service, and on the other by pressing demands by the RAF for a fighter designed from the outset with a wing *and* armament capable of outperforming and destroying the new German fighters at altitude. The early Sabre engines were still proving unreliable in 1941, while Hawker itself was finding perfection of the big chin radiator elusive, bearing in mind the critical nature of the oil cooling demands by the engine. Moreover a further complication lay in the improving promise of the radial Centaurus installation in the Tornado that was beginning to suggest to Camm himself that he had perhaps been premature in ignoring that engine as a potentially realistic fighter powerplant during the early days of the War.

There must have been considerable temptation among Camm's senior design staff to abandon further development of the Typhoon altogether in 1941 and to move directly to an entirely new fighter design, perhaps powered by a Centaurus, or even the new Rolls-Royce Griffon. To do so, however, would have involved a delay of at least three years before production could start and, even if all went well, introduction into RAF service in mid- or late 1945. With Britain facing Germany on her own in 1941, and beset around by tragedies and the pressure of arms, who was to say that there would even by a Royal Air Force four years hence?

Be that as it may, Camm's project office had, in 1940, evolved a new wing, with a root thickness/chord ratio of 14.5 per cent decreasing to ten per cent at the tip, the maximum thickness occur-ring at 37.5 of the chord. This aerofoil section compared with a thickness/chord of some 18 per cent in the NACA 22-series wing on the Typhoon. With a root chord roughly the same as that of the Typhoon's wing, the new Hawker wing would be some five inches thinner at the root. Moreover, in place of straight taper on leading and trailing edges, the new wing was elliptical in plan culminating in a blunt elliptical tip, resulting in a considerably thinner wing at semi-span.

When members of the DTD visited Camm at Claremont in March 1941 to discuss a new fighter requirement, the Chief Designer put forward the idea of a "thin-wing" Typhoon which, to be powered by a new version of the Sabre—then known as the EC.107C—with wing-root radiators, promised to return a speed of 430 mph. When the DTD stated that this speed was required by the new fighter at 20,000 feet, together with an armament of four 20-mm Hispano cannon, Camm's draft design, which assumed an installed power output from the EC.107C of 2,400 hp, seemed capable of meeting the new requirement in full.

Following this meeting Camm was instructed to transfer all other project work associated with the Tornado (such as the development of a suitable Centaurus installation) to what came to be known for the time being as the Typhoon Mark II.

Further discussions followed during the summer of 1941, during which it was decided—in order to meet an in-service target date of December 1943—to employ as much of the Typhoon's fuselage and tail as possible. However from then on it was found increasingly necessary to diverge from the old design, particularly when it proved impossible to accommodate adequate fuel in the new, thin wing, so that a fuel tank had to be provided in the fuselage forward of the cockpit, thereby lengthening the fuselage by some 22 inches.

Views of the Tempest V HM595 during construction which clearly show the additional fuselage bay forward of the cockpit

Above and below, the prototype Tempest V, HM595, as it appeared on completion at Langley in September 1942, with Scheme B cockpit canopy and Typhoon-style fin and rudder. (Photos: Sydney Camm Collection)

The new Specification, F.10/41, was finally received by Hawker in the second week of August 1941, and on 18 November the Company was awarded a Contract, No. 1640/41/C.23a, for two Typhoon II prototypes, *HM595* and *HM599*. Two months later the name was changed to Tempest, and at that time the number of prototypes was increased to six, partly to take account of work being done on the Centaurus in the Tornado *HG641*, and partly as the result of Camm's scathing criticism of the Ministry's pernicious dependence upon inadequate orders for prototypes (pointing to the ridiculous situation that had arisen with the Typhoon). These prototypes were:

HM599 Tempest Mark I prototype with Sabre EC.107C (to become the Sabre IV) and wing-root radiators.

HM595 Tempest Mark V prototype with Sabre II and chin radiator.

LA602 and *LA607* Tempest Mark II prototypes with Centaurus IV engines.

LA610 and *LA614* Tempest Mark III with Rolls-Royce Griffon II engines, to be replaced later by the proposed Griffon 61 "power egg" to become the Tempest Mark IV. (Neither of these aircraft was completed as a Tempest; indeed only *LA610* was built and this became a Hawker Fury (monoplane) prototype.

Such was the promise shown by design calculations on the Tempest I that it was decided to push ahead and complete the less radical Tempest V prototype first in order to confirm wind tunnel data already being received on the new thin elliptical wing. Moreover, before any Tempest had flown Hawker was instructed to tool up for production in July 1942, and the following month received contracts for a total of 400 Tempest Is. In other words the Tempest V was at that time regarded as no more than simply a development stage in the evolution of the promising Mark I. (One could perhaps be forgiven for a feeling that history was in danger of being repeated, and that like the Typhoon pro-

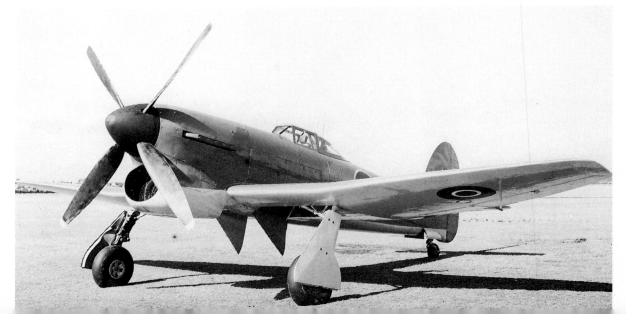

duction at Gloster in the previous year production of the Tempest might well prove premature, particularly as the provision of untried wing-root radiators could well compromise premature wing and fuselage production jigs.)

On 1 September 1942, *HM595* was wheeled out at Langley for Lucas to carry out a short series of taxying trials. Powered by a standard Sabre II, No. S1001, driving a four-blade de Havilland Hydromatic propeller (of which a similar example had been tested for several weeks on the Typhoon IA, *R9198*), the Tempest V prototype featured a new levered-suspension main undercarriage in place of the Typhoon's compression oleos, as well as tailwheel doors, but retained the Typhoon's tail unit with parallel-chord rudder trim tab; it also featured the current production Typhoon's all-transparent Scheme B cockpit canopy and car doors.

The following day Lucas took the new aircraft aloft on its maiden flight, attaining a maximum speed of 300 mph ASI at 10,000 feet. Limited manoeuvres were carried out, and check stalling at 5,000 feet at a flying weight of 10,550 lb gave a stalling speed of 90 mph with wheels and flaps down.

It was all too clear, however, that the aircraft possessed almost neutral directional stability with the rudder held central over the whole speed range, the nose tending to turn into a sideslip in one direction, and out of the sideslip in the other. When the rudder was released the effect was even worse. If a slight pressure was applied to the rudder bar a yaw developed, but on releasing the pressure the aircraft continued to yaw.

These impressions were confirmed by Lucas after handling flights on the 12th and 13th, so it was decided to fit a small 1.1 sq ft projection on the rudder, and this gave a small improvement. Before the end of the month a temporary dorsal fin extension of 2.7 sq ft was incorporated and this pro-

duced a marked improvement in the directional stability; at the same time the design of an entirely new fin and rudder was put in hand to incorporate a smoothly-contoured dorsal fin, also of 2.7 sq ft extra area, and a rudder increased by 0.4 sq ft.

The longitudinal stability was also criticized but, after both tailplane and elevators had been increased by 4.0 sq ft, this was regarded as satisfactory although Lucas complained that elevator control was extremely heavy, and found difficulty in getting the tail down on landing.

In other respects the new fighter was regarded as a considerable improvement over the Typhoon, the aileron control being very effective up to the highest speeds yet flown. Less tendency to swing to the right on take-off was encountered, and the engine—for some unexplained reason—was "remarkably free of vibration"!

There is little doubt that, having regard for the Tempest's length of nose, caused by the insertion of the new fuel tank, the deterioration of directional stability was to be expected. The view had, however, persisted that tests should be done to see if *HM595* could "get away" without major modification to the tail; the aircraft was, after all, intended at that time to do little more than prepare the ground for the proposed definitive Tempest I which, although featuring the lengthened nose, possessed no chin radiator, and calculations showed that increased fin area would not be required. Nevertheless Lucas insisted that the stability characteristics had so changed that it would not be possible to determine performance and handling readings at higher speeds and altitudes without the necessary modifications.

By October further changes had been carried out, increasing the fin area by another 1.44 sq ft (giving a total of 15.54 sq ft), reducing the rudder travel by ten per cent, and modifying the rudder trim tab. A preliminary performance check, car-

Front view of the Tempest V, HM595, emphasising the new thin wing; note the tailwheel doors. (Photo: Sydney Camm Collection)

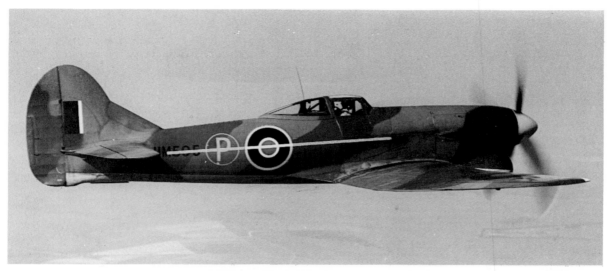

HM595 during flight trials at the A&AEE, Boscombe Down, in March 1943; the aircraft features an interim dorsal fin extension, and the white bar superimposed on the fuselage was applied to facilitate camera recording of the aircraft datum. (Photo: A&AEE, Neg No A/C135D, dated 12 March 1943)

ried out on 2 October, returned a maximum level speed of 430 mph TAS at 20,300 feet. Other minor adjustments were made throughout November, and attention turned to further improving the lateral control. Although all the Hawker pilots had remarked on the lightness and sensitivity of the Tempest's roll control, the "bent tab" (a small sheet of 14 or 18 gauge metal on the aileron's trailing edge which was simply bent up or down to provide neutral balance) could be, and often was accidentally distorted by groundcrew members, thereby significantly affecting the extremely sensitive aileron control. An entirely new trim system of differential tabs, controllable by the pilot, was put in hand, eventually giving way to the excellent spring tabs that were to be highly praised when the Tempest entered service.

On 12 December *HM595* was taken up for a full-throttle dive from 27,000 feet. Between 19,000 and 20,000 feet the aircraft reached a true airspeed of 575 mph (nearly Mach 0.76), Lucas reporting an increase in nose heaviness and a slight shaking of the whole aircraft as speed built up—the classic symptoms of the onset of compressibility. This was probably the highest speed so far attained by any British aircraft at that date. Unfortunately the engine failed during the dive and the starboard undercarriage unlocked, precipitating a forced landing at Langley.

An inspection of the engine failed to disclose the reason for the failure (although the inside of the cooling system was found to be coated with a deposit of copper, and tiny traces of metal found in the filters), but it was decided to fit a new Sabre, and on the 23rd *HM595* was flying at an all-up weight of 11,000 lb with engine No. S1137. A full-throttle dive with a third engine (No. S3165) was carried out on 26 January 1943, this time a speed of Mach 0.76 being reached at 20,000 feet

without experiencing further significant trouble. (The very high speeds attained in these dives did, however, spotlight an unsuspected weakness in the old car door design, with the starboard window sucking out of its frame; this was not regarded as being too serious as the new single-piece sliding hood on the Typhoon had already successfully completed its development trials and would be fitted in the Tempest during the coming weeks.)

After some delays in the delivery of the new Sabre IV engine, the Tempest Mark I prototype, *HM599*, was completed in mid-February 1943 and underwent ground handling and taxying tests on the 22nd. Two days later Philip Lucas flew the aircraft for the first time. As explained above, no dorsal fin extension had been thought necessary, and so it proved, Lucas reporting much better directional stability than on the Tempest V; most other aspects were also considered to be better, although elevator control deteriorated more rapidly at low speeds, disappearing completely below 110 mph ASI.

By March Napier had issued clearance for the Sabre IV to run at 4,000 rpm and with +9 lb boost, although the latter figure was not yet attainable in either of the two engines initially delivered for *HM599* (Nos. S 75 and 76). After S 75 had been removed for a 25-hour examination, S 76 completed about 20 hours before a crack was found in the cylinder block, causing it to be removed and a third engine, S 72, installed. While awaiting this engine during May the opportunity was taken to fit the new single-piece sliding hood. On 4 June Bill Humble (who had temporarily assumed the rôle as senior pilot during Lucas' absence in the Middle East for the Typhoon's tropical trials) flew *HM599* on the first of a series of performance measurement tests, recording a maximum level speed of 460 mph TAS at 24,000 feet in FS gear.

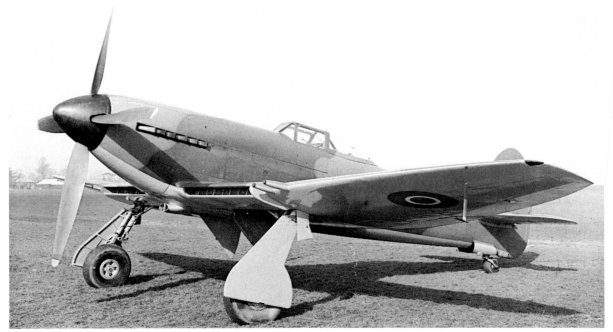

"Roll-out" photographs of the beautiful Tempest I, HM599, at Langley. (Photos: Author's Collection)

Bill Humble enjoying himself at the controls of the Tempest I. (Photos: Hawker Aircraft Ltd., Neg No ITF/16, lower)

Above, master exponent of the Tempest I was Bill Humble who seldom wore a flying helmet when airborne in the wartime fighters. *Right*, cockpit of the Tempest I, HM599, when still fitted with the Scheme B canopy and car doors. (Photos: via R. C. Sturtivant (*above*) and Author's Collection (*right*)

By dint of attention to minor airframe details the Tempest I's maximum speed was coaxed up to 472 mph by September 1943, partly due to the fitting of a tailplane of 11.5 per cent thickness/chord ratio; however, as will now be explained, much of this work was regarded as of academic interest only and, by December, no further development work was being covered by government contract.

The reason the Tempest I failed to attract continuing interest by the Air Ministry was largely due to the difficulties being experienced by Napier in achieving a satisfactory production standard in the Sabre IV. The engine running at 4,000 rpm was immensely powerful but, apart from a tendency to throw prodigious quantities of oil at any speed over 3,750 rpm, never managed to reach a time-between-inspections approaching 50 hours—this despite being virtually "hand built" from scratch. Nor could it be said that the engine was prone to any single design weakness, for the catalogue of failures cover a whole list of widely differing local causes. Nevertheless, apart from the oil throwing phenomenon, Hawker experienced very little trouble with the engine in the air, and it is likely that, given the benefit of more time and effort, the Sabre IV would have emerged as a quite outstanding engine. The beautiful Tempest Mark I, with its exceptionally finely contoured fuselage lines and wing radiators, proved to be very fast indeed—far exceeding the Air Ministry's fighter requirements of the day—and Bill Humble constantly extolled the aeroplane's superb handling virtues, *particularly above 20,000 feet*.

However, as usual, time was a commodity that war squandered. The German Focke-Wulf Fw 190A and Messerschmitt Bf 109G were only barely matched by Allied fighters at altitudes above 20,000 feet early in 1943, and the pressing demand was for an aircraft capable of a speed of at least 430 mph at around 25,000 feet *and* a four-cannon armament—and that was the basis of the first jet fighter Specifications being issued about that time. Only the Tempest V—in its prototype form at that—had demonstrated such an ability after only four months of flight trials, using an in-service engine. Thus, no sooner had an order for 400 Tempest Is been received by Hawker and preliminary jigs prepared than it was changed to encompass Tempest Vs[1].

Returning therefore to February 1943, one finds *HM595* fitted with yet another Sabre II (No. S 697) and the aircraft, after some "cleaning up" of the wing root fillet, returned a top speed of 438 mph TAS at 22,000 feet. After the fitting of an inertia device to the control column, all tendency to tighten up in turns up to 5g was eliminated. The aircraft was then flown to Boscombe Down to undergo evaluation as the new fighter for the RAF. When preliminary confirmation of the Hawker performance and handling characteristics was received by the Air Ministry the formal decision was taken to adopt the Tempest V for imme-

[1] This explains why one hundred JN-serial Tempest Vs were produced *before* 300 aircraft with EJ serial numbers; all had been scheduled for Sabre IVs and wing-root radiators, but the JN aircraft wing jigs had not yet been commenced.

When HM595 was fitted with a Sabre V and wing root oil cooler intakes it effectively became the Tempest VI prototype. (Photo: via R. C. Sturtivant)

diate production. (It is perhaps a little-known fact that when *HM595* returned to Langley in June the opportunity was taken to fit the Sabre IV (No. S 76) in the Tempest V prototype to furnish comparative performance and handling data with chin and wing radiators using the same engine; the maximum level speed attained on 17 June by Bill Humble was 459 mph TAS at 24,900 feet at an engine speed of 4,000 rpm; the aircraft was ballasted for guns and full ammunition, but the Chatellerault gun feed blisters were not fitted, these being calculated to reduce the speed by as much as seven to ten miles per hour. The tests were halted when the cockpit side windows "sucked out".)

Only eight weeks after the decision was taken to change production to the Tempest V the first pro-duction aircraft, *JN729*, was completed, and on 21 June Bill Humble carried out the first flight. Although this aircraft was fitted with the new sliding hood, Humble was only able to record a maximum speed of 422 mph, but Napier had already stated that the engine (No. S 3221), being an interim development unit prior to introduction of the Sabre IIA (about to be introduced also in the Typhoon), was down by some 55 bhp; moreover some hand-tooled engine panels were known to be badly fitting. The modified Sabre IIA, incorporating an oil system changed to suit a mixed-matrix coolant and oil radiator as well as dynamically-balanced crankshafts, was promised for delivery two months hence.

Now that *HM595* was no longer fully repre-

The first production Tempest V (Series 1), JN729: due to the urgency to introduce the aircraft into RAF service, this and several following aircraft were employed in development work alongside the prototype. (Photo: Hawker Neg No 5TG8)

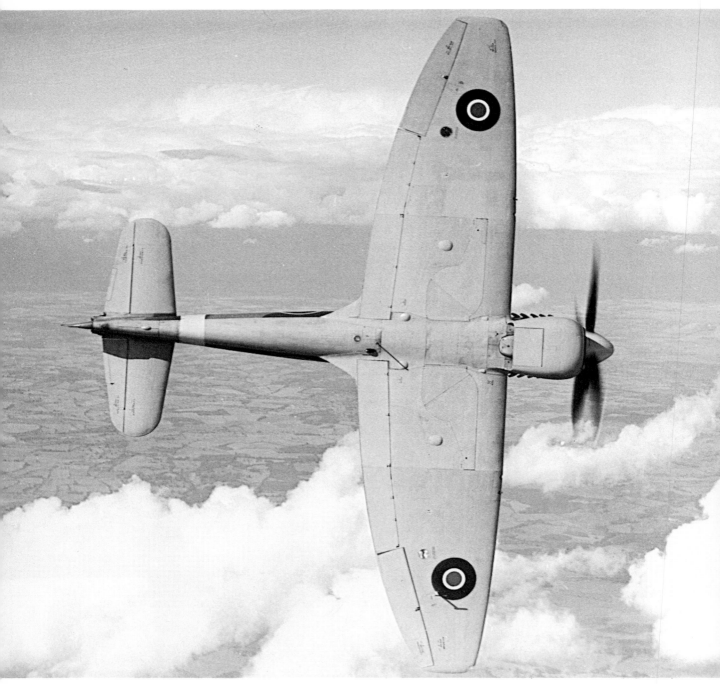

A magnificent flying study of a Tempest V Series 2. (Photo: Cyril Peckham (Hawker Aircraft Ltd), Neg No 5TF/18)

sentative of the proposed production Tempest V (and itself embarked on an independent programme that would lead to the Tempest Mark VI), the emphasis of development flying switched to *JN729*. By now of course—July 1943—Lucas had returned to Langley, but much of his time became devoted to the newly completed Tempest II prototype so that experimental flying of the Sabre-powered aircraft (including the Typhoon) was almost entirely undertaken by Humble and Squadron Leader R. P. Beamont. The latter pilot had re-

cently been seconded once more from the RAF (after having commanded No. 609 (West Riding) Squadron, and after flying Typhoons on operations for eight months), and not only brought to Hawker his valuable first-hand experience of operational use of the Typhoon but also "grew up" with the Tempest V from the start. This close association by an experienced officer with Fighter Command and a manufacturer, while not unique, resulted in an extraordinary degree of understanding between the Company and Service, for it was not simply confined to the personalities directly involved but was allowed to extend upwards in the higher echelons of both parties so that, for instance, Camm's design staff acquired a "feel" for the needs and preferences of Fighter Command's line pilots.

One detects the influential hand of Camm himself in the creation of this close association for, while always reflecting unqualified support for "his own" pilots, he would have been the first to acknowledge the tremendous contribution made by a Service pilot with recent combat experience in flying the Company's aircraft. By the end of July Beamont had already flown the Tempest I and V prototypes as well as the first production aeroplane, *JN729*, and in respect of the latter had helped to solve a problem involving the blowing off of coolant through the header tank relief valve while flying at high altitude.

By September three further production Tempest Vs (all fitted with the Sabre IIA engine) had flown and were involved in development flying, work being done largely on the perfection of aileron nose shape to correct overbalance at high speed, and to introduce a new tailwheel unit with a Dowty anti-shimmy wheel strut and a Marstrand twin-contact tyre. A performance check on the sixth production aircraft, *JN734*—regarded as the first wholly representative aircraft for Fighter Command—produced a maximum speed of 434 mph TAS at 22,800 feet, ballasted for full radio, gun armament and ammunition at an all-up weight of 11,300 lb, and a climb to 20,000 feet at 3,700 rpm and +7 lb boost in 6.6 minutes, figures that were confirmed at Boscombe Down. Two of the early production Tempests suffered forced landings before the end of the year, *JN732* by Bill Humble on 1 October following an engine failure, and *JN733* on 13 December for an unknown reason during a flight by a production pilot, Squadron Leader H. N. Sweetman, DFC; neither pilot was hurt and the aircraft were little damaged.

By the end of December the first 36 Tempest Vs had been completed and roughly half had been flown out of Langley on delivery to the Maintenance Units where full armament, gunsights, radio and other operational equipment was fitted, thereby exactly meeting the target delivery date originally demanded in the DTD requirement. As told in the following Chapter, deliveries to an operational squadron commenced the following month—though this was to prove somewhat premature.

The Tempest Mark II

As remarked above, the arrival in mid-1943 on the flight line at Langley of the first Bristol Centaurus-powered Tempest II prototype claimed an increasing proportion of the flying effort by the Hawker

pilots, and it is necessary once more to go back some months to describe the evolution that provided the transition from the Centaurus-powered Tornado to the Tempest II which, by its own continuing development and the Sea Fury derivative, carried the interceptor fighter right up to the end of the piston-engine era.

The supposed reluctance by Camm to countenance a high-performance fighter powered by a radial engine—particularly one the size of the 18-cylinder Bristol engine—has already been referred to, and the work done to develop the improved Centaurus installation in the Tornado *HG641*, had proceeded at snail's pace during 1942. With the cancellation of the Tornado programme it was certainly true of those that worked at Hawker that no one believed this work to have much relevance to a modern high performance interceptor fighter. The same could not be said of the engine manufacturers, who were committed to a development programme with the Centaurus—principally in the context of other aircraft—particularly when the German Focke-Wulf Fw 190A demonstrated so convincingly just what could be done when fitting a radial engine in a small high performance interceptor.

Although the Bristol engineers had begun to evolve a new exhaust system for the Centaurus (to replace the unwieldy front collector ring and outsize external exhaust pipe) sometime before 23 June 1942, when Oberleutnant Faber so obligingly presented the RAF with an intact Fw 190A to

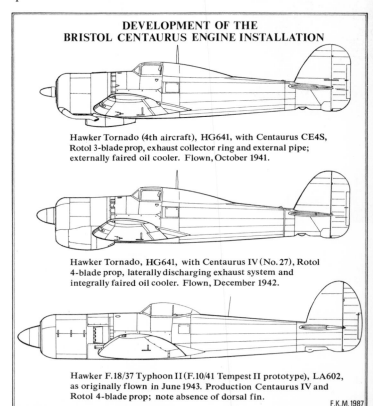

DEVELOPMENT OF THE BRISTOL CENTAURUS ENGINE INSTALLATION

Hawker Tornado (4th aircraft), HG641, with Centaurus CE4S, Rotol 3-blade prop, exhaust collector ring and external pipe; externally faired oil cooler. Flown, October 1941.

Hawker Tornado, HG641, with Centaurus IV (No. 27), Rotol 4-blade prop, laterally discharging exhaust system and integrally faired oil cooler. Flown, December 1942.

Hawker F.18/37 Typhoon II (F.10/41 Tempest II prototype), LA602, as originally flown in June 1943. Production Centaurus IV and Rotol 4-blade prop; note absence of dorsal fin.

F.K.M.1987

Centaurus engine for the prototype Tempest II, LA602. The photograph on the left illustrates the extent of plumbing necessary to achieve the grouped exhaust manifolds on the side of the fuselage. (Photos: Hawker Aircraft Ltd., Neg Nos 2TPS/8 and 2TPS/13)

examine and handle, such a system was not ready in time for *HG641* when it started its second programme of flying in December that year. Indeed that programme became superfluous as an entirely new design, owing a great deal to the BMW installation, was put in hand with considerable urgency during the late summer at Bristol, and shortly afterwards by Hawker in the first of the F.10/41 Centaurus-powered prototypes, *LA602*.

Although no complete general arrangement drawing appears to have survived, showing exactly how the Centaurus was originally intended to be installed in this aircraft—for manufacture of the airframe had certainly started long before the end of 1942—the newly evolving Centaurus installation must have resulted in extensive airframe alterations. To begin with, the movement aft of the relatively weighty exhaust system and the transfer of the oil coolers to the wing roots resulted in the entire engine being moved forward almost a foot for weight compensation (despite the Tempest's customary inclusion of the big fuselage fuel tank

Early photograph of the prototype Tempest II, LA602, when it still retained the Typhoon-style tail and the exhaust manifolds grouped in pairs. (Photo: Sydney Camm Collection)

forward of the centre of gravity—which had not been present in the Tornado *HG641*). By dispensing with the forward exhaust collector ring and the old ventral oil cooler it proved possible to achieve exceptionally clean engine cowling contours, while the grouping of individual exhaust pipes to discharge on the sides of the fuselage at least exploited the necessity for the ungainly "waisting" created by the difference in width of engine and centre fuselage.

The prototype was completed in June and, not surprisingly, was extensively instrumented for engine test purposes (far more so than in the Tempest I and V prototypes), with six cylinder head temperature gauges, six oil pressure gauges and four oil temperature gauges; strain gauges were also provided on all engine mountings, as well as Vibrograph equipment. The propeller fitted was an experimental Rotol constant-speed four-blader No. EH 294. Unlike the prototype Tempest I and V, the new single-piece sliding canopy was fitted from the outset, and no dorsal fin was included. All-up weight for the first flight, made by Lucas on 28 June 1943, was 10,963 lb.

To illustrate the manner in which *LA602* behaved during the first three flights, it is worth quoting here from Lucas' summaries:

"*LA602. Engine, Centaurus IV No. C 80023.*

"*Taxying.* Taxying tests were made on 26 June. The aircraft handled well on the ground. On opening up for take-off there is a strong tendency to swing to the right, but this is no worse than on the Tempest I and V. The view forward is very much the same as on the Tem-

pest V. It was noticed that the tail was rather slow coming up, although the acceleration of the aircraft when opening the throttle was reasonably good.

"*Engine Installation.* No trouble has been experienced with the cooling of the engine when running up to full throttle on the ground. The engine was running approximately 25 minutes during the first taxying tests and at no time did any of the cylinder temperatures rise above 210°C even during full-throttle runs across the aerodrome.

"There did not appear to be any difference in cylinder temperatures when taxying with the gills forward and open, or forward and closed. The oil temperatures were also well in hand.

"On the ground there is severe vibration at 1,800 rpm.

"*Flight Trials.* Three short flights only were made. On the first flight on 28 July the hydraulic pump failed soon after take-off when the undercarriage was down and, as it could not be pumped up, a landing had to be made. While in the air no fundamental faults could be detected. No difficulty was experienced in getting the tail down when landing. The engine installation is harsh and the vibration is similar to that experienced on the Centaurus Tornado. The radiator gill control was difficult to operate and both hands were required.

"On the second flight trouble was experienced with fumes in the cockpit, and a landing had to be made. It was suspected that these came either from the two lower exhaust pipes or through some gun-heater ducts leaking into the

The Tempest II, LA602, airborne with the standard Tempest fin. (Photo: Hawker Aircraft Ltd., Neg No 2TPF/16)

cockpit. Before the next flight the ducts were disconnected and two new bottom exhaust pipes were fitted with three-inch extensions.

"The third flight was made on 1 July and on this flight the cockpit was free from any smell or visible fumes. After climbing at 2,400 rpm to 10,000 feet a run was started at 2,400 rpm and +6 lb boost, but after one minute there was a loud 'clonk' and the engine started to vibrate badly. The aircraft was throttled down and landed on the aerodrome. On inspection of the engine after landing it was found that the sleeve valve drive to one of the cylinders had failed."

Because the failure experienced on the third flight caused extensive damage to the engine it was removed and replaced by a new Centaurus, No. 80133, which continued to run smoothly and entirely satisfactorily in *LA602* until December when it was removed for routine inspection after 73 hours' flying and 32 hours' ground running, much of this time being spent at full throttle.

In July *LA602* was flown a total of 19 times, with a wide range of tests being carried out. A full-throttle dive was flown, reaching Mach 0.75 at 10,000 feet, but recovery was effected immediately after some suspicious shaking of the aircraft was felt. Inspection after landing revealed fairly extensive damage at the rear of the fuselage where the tailwheel door rails and their mounting frame members had cracked, the metal skin below the tailplane had failed and fabric on both sides of the rudder had started to pull off the frames. Although this damage was repaired, subsequent flight disclosed further very severe vibration in the structure, suggesting that structural distortion during the high speed dive had been more serious than at first suspected, and extensive rebuilding was necessary. Because engine No. 80133 was not initially cleared to run with full supercharging, the first performance check returned a maximum level speed of no more than 432 mph TAS in MS gear at 9,100, 9,300 and 10,000 feet. Fuel consumption tests revealed some extraordinary figures for, while flying at 260 mph TAS at 10,000 feet, a figure of 6.15 miles per gallon was recorded. (Later, when flown at its optimum range setting, that is 200

mph IAS at about 17,000 feet, a figure of 7.4 miles per gallon was commonplace.)

During July and August a series of tests to measure the rate of roll on the various versions of the Tempest compared to that of the latest Typhoons was carried out. Flying each of these aircraft at 250, 300 and 400 mph IAS at 5,000, 10,000 and 18,000 feet, and correcting to an average stick force of 50 pounds, the following mean rates of roll were produced:

Typhoon IB (*EK122*) . . . 54 degrees per second
Tempest I (*HM599*) . . . 78 degrees per second
Tempest V (*JN729*) . . . 80 degrees per second
Tempest II (*LA602*) . . . 88 degrees per second

(The only comparative roll figures traced for the Spitfire (a Mark IX) at this time are perhaps misleading as the stick force quoted is on the basis of 40 lb; this gave a rate of roll of 66 degrees per second at 300 mph IAS at 15,000 feet.)

The marked improvement in the Tempests' roll rates was ascribed to their thinner wing section, the four per cent greater aileron area to total wing area, and the fact that the ailerons were closer to the wing tips.

Notwithstanding Lucas' early observations regarding engine vibration, which had been confined to ground running, the early Centaurus engines were in fact probably worse even than the Sabre in this respect, as an analysis during August disclosed. What made this vibration most disconcerting for the pilots was that the nature of the resonance changed markedly at different engine speeds as shown by the Vibrograph results:

Engine speed (rpm)	Nature of Vibration
1,600	Lateral vibration
1,820	Fore and aft and lateral
1,950	Very bad fore and aft
2,050	Bad fore and aft
2,200	Fore and aft
2,400	High frequency fore and aft, and vertical

Flying view of the second Tempest II prototype, LA607

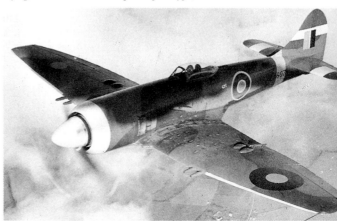

It was also shown that the bad fore and aft vibration frequency was at a resonance of twice engine speed, and was regarded as being particularly dangerous in that this form of vibration had been shown to encourage fatigue and structural failure in the Typhoon. The Hawker pilots also complained of local resonances in the pilot's seat armour, the top exhaust pipes and the exhaust shield panel.

Because similar vibration had been encountered in other Centaurus-powered aircraft (notably the Centaurus IV-powered Bristol Buckingham prototypes), the second Tempest II prototype, *LA607*, was completed with stiffened engine mountings but, although this resulted in a general improvement in the vibration characteristics, there were still certain engine speeds at which the installation was unacceptable.

The second Tempest II prototype was flown on 18 September 1943, and when this joined the flight programme the opportunity was taken to return Centaurus No. 80133 to *LA602*, now fitted with a flexible mounting, incorporating a facility to vary the degree of stiffening. In November the investigation into vibration was widened to include the use of a five-blade Rotol propeller, but this gave no all-round improvement. That month however, by carefully balancing the mounting stiffness in each of the engine pick-ups, the transmitted vibration was reduced to acceptable values, and henceforth the Tempest IIs were able to proceed to other areas of development.

In February 1944 *LA602* was fitted with the standard Tempest V tail (with dorsal fin exten-

The Tempest II, LA607, given spurious "Squadron codes" for a public flying display. (Photo: via R. C. Sturtivant)

sion—*LA607* had been so fitted from the outset), and considerable attention was paid to improving still further the fuel consumption of the Centaurus, it now being suggested for the first time that the Tempest II would likely be required for service in the Far East where it was intended ultimately to replace the Hurricane and Spitfire; service in that theatre would place much emphasis on the range capabilities of the Tempest.

On 7 July *LA607*, having been brought up to the proposed Mark II production standard, was flown with a Centaurus V (No. 81071) and during that and the following month performance tests confirmed the figures for the in-service version: maximum speed, 448 mph TAS at 19,100 feet in FS gear and an all-up take-off weight of 11,950 lb (ballasted for full gun armament); climb to 20,00 feet, 6.7 minutes; maximum rate of climb at sea level, 5,100 feet/minute; range (still air) at 14,000 feet on full internal fuel, 1,150 statute miles at 235 mph in

An early production Hawker-built Tempest II, MW742, with the distinctive tail and nose bands adopted by the early aircraft. This example was later to be transferred to the Royal Indian Air Force. (Photo: Hawker Neg No 2TF/109)

As MW742 banks away from the photographic aircraft, the attachment points for rocket installation can be seen under the wings—this despite the fact that the aircraft was initially prepared for service as an interceptor fighter. *Below*, the busy flight line at Langley shortly after the War when the Tempest II was required to equip the RAF in India.

Above, production Tempest FB Mark II, PR806, with underwing bomb pylons (Photo: via R. C. Sturtivant). *Right*, close-up of a 1,000-lb bomb under the wing of a Tempest (Photo: Hawker Aircraft Ltd., Neg No 5TPG/51)

MS gear; maximum endurance for patrol loiter, 5 hours 20 minutes. When flown with a pair of 45-gallon drop tanks, the maximum speed was measured at 424 mph TAS, and the sea level rate of climb at 4,300 feet/minute. The still air range increased to 1,740 miles at 225 mph, and the maximum endurance to 8 hours 25 minutes. Among British wartime fighters such figures were outstanding.

Large scale production of the Tempest II for the RAF was planned early in 1944, it being intended that this would be undertaken exclusively at the Bristol Aeroplane Company's Ministry of Aircraft Production Shadow factory at Old Mixon, Weston-super-Mare in Somerset. However, with the running out of Hurricane production at Langley in September that year, Hawker opted to set up a production in its own factory with an initial batch of 100 aircraft, with 300 being contracted with Bristol. These first 400 Tempests were intended to be "pure fighters" as further Contracts were raised (330 aircraft by Bristol and 800 by Hawker) to cover aircraft with wings strengthened to take a pair of 1,000-lb bombs, up to 16 60-lb three-inch rocket projectiles, or a pair of 90-gallon drop tanks, the latter extending the maximum ferry

Flown here by Bill Humble, PR533 was the first Tempest FB Mark II stressed to carry a pair of 1,000-lb bombs.

range for reinforcement purposes to 2,410 miles.

In the event the ending of the War in the Far East brought widespread cancellations, and Bristol only completed 50 aircraft (as well as components of a further 20, which were transferred to Langley), while the parent Company completed 402. The former were produced as fighters, although most were retrospectively modified to carry bombs, while all the Langley aircraft were completed with the strengthened wings from the outset.

The first production aircraft, a Hawker-built example *MW735*, was flown by Bill Humble on 4 October 1944, fitted temporarily with a Centaurus IV, and was followed by the Centaurus V-powered *MW736* on 9 December (although shortly afterwards an experimental Centaurus VII with rubber engine mountings was installed briefly). These two aircraft were used for development work exclusively.

Early in 1945, when it was clear that the war in Europe was drawing to an end, Hawker was instructed to carry out a trial conversion of a Tempest V to a Mark II to investigate the cost and feasibility, as well as to determine the extent of alterations to the Tempest V production line. An early standard Mark V, *JN750*, was returned to Langley for the conversion and, after five weeks of re-jigging the fuselage and wing centre-section, emerged complete with Centaurus V, Rotol propeller and tropical intakes, and was first flown by Humble on 23 March. No subsequent conversion order was placed and *JN750* remained at Langley for about a year as something of a hybrid with numerous minor Tempest V features remaining; it

was, however, employed in several interesting trials, including the installation of four 305-lb Triplex rocket projectiles (also being flown on some Tempest Vs); it also took a major part in the programme to clear both the Tempest II and VI for tropical service.

As plans continued for the establishing of a Tempest II Wing at Chilbolton (to be commanded by Wing Commander R. P. Beamont (now DSO and Bar, DFC and Bar) who had left Langley for the last time in February 1944 to form and command the first Tempest V Wing, No. 150, initially at Castle Camps and ultimately Newchurch) to accompany Tiger Force to the Far East, one final

Above right, Tempest V Series 1, JN740, with eight rockets on Mark II rails. *Right*, Tempest V Series 2, NV946 with Mark VIII "zero-length" rocket rails (Photo: Sydney Camm Collection). *Below*, close-up of the Mark VIII rocket installation (Photo: Hawker Aircraft Ltd., Neg No TPRP/3)

Penultimate production Tempest V, SN354 was set aside for a trial installation of the fast-firing Vickers "P" 40-mm anti-armour gun towards the end of 1945. As on the Hurricane IID anti-tank aircraft of the Second World War, a single gun was mounted under each of the Tempest's wings. Performance trials were carried out at Langley before the aircraft went to Boscombe Down for Service evaluation, but it was not long before official interest in the gun waned, promising though it may have been. (Photo: Hawker Aircraft Ltd., Neg No 5TG/ARM7)

trial was conducted on the Tempest II. Following undercarriage stress calculations which had confirmed that the aircraft could be taken off from a 2,000-yard runway at an all-up weight of 14,400 lb in hot, sea level conditions, the Air Ministry asked for the "Far East" Tempests to be fitted with a belly rack capable of mounting a single 90-gallon drop tank, it being intended to mount a pair of 1,000-lb underwing bombs as well—although ammunition for the outer cannon would be omitted in this configuration; thus loaded a standard Tempest II bomber would gross 14,280 lb and be capable of a radius of action of at least 1,000 miles with adequate reserves.

A production Langley-built Tempest II, *PR550*, was flown with the belly tank in November 1945,

but by then of course the war in the Far East had also ended, and with it the plans for the Tempest II Wing. The ventral rack trials continued for over a year on *PR550* and in the meantime provision for the rack's inclusion was made in Tempest VIs for the Middle East. As it was, as far as is known, no Tempest ever took off at a weight of over 14,000 lb; nevertheless there are references in other records to a range check flight, carried out by Humble in *PR550* during May 1946 carrying a total of 430 gallons of fuel, internally and externally, which returned a maximum range figure of 2,950 statute miles at a take-off weight of 13,850 lb. As will be told in the following Chapter, the Tempest II was to remain in squadron service with the Royal Air Force until June 1951.

An early production Tempest VI, NX135, at Langley early in 1946. (Photo: Hawker Aircraft Ltd.)

Above and below, further views of the Tempest VI, this time a late production aircraft, NX201, with full tropical equipment, photographed in August 1946. As explained in the text, production of the version had all but finished by the time it entered RAF service in December that year, such was the prolonged vacillation by government and Air Ministry over the level of British presence in the Middle East. The front view, *above*, shows to good effect the asymmetric arrangement of the wing root intakes. (Photos: Sydney Camm Collection)

The Tempest VI

Too late to enjoy service during the Second World War, the Sabre V-powered Tempest VI was in effect a version intended for service in the tropics, with oil coolers moved to the wing roots, enlarged radiator with tropical filter, a Rotol propeller and spring tabs.

Development was entirely straightforward, but prolonged. As a prototype, the original Mark V *HM595* was converted when this aeroplane became redundant in the original Tempest development programme, being fitted with Sabre V No. S 5055 and flown by Humble on 9 May 1944 (just as the first Tempest Vs were about to go into action with the RAF). A speed check, carried out by R. V. Muspratt on 2 June, returned a maximum speed of 452 mph TAS at 19,600 feet though, with a new engine fitted, Humble recorded 462 mph in

September; he also took the aircraft to Warmwell two months later for a short spell of gun firing and reported that on one occasion he aimed and fired the guns during a dive at 560 mph, the aircraft remaining "as steady as a rock".[2] A second Tempest VI, *EJ841* (converted from a production Mark V) joined the test programme at Langley in September that year to assist in clearing the aircraft for tropical service at just about the time the first production examples were emerging from the factory.

It was to be more than a year before these aircraft were to join the RAF in the Middle East, languishing at Maintenance Units while the government and Air Ministry squabbled and bick-

---

[2] As evidence of this gun-firing steadiness, Wing Commander Beamont flying a Tempest V from Volkel, Holland, on 2 October 1944, shot down a Focke-Wulf Fw 190D while flying at 530 mph IAS.

ered over the level of British military presence necessary in the Eastern Mediterranean. Once the decision was taken to equip two squadrons of Tempest VIs (later raised to five), further delays were occasioned while a Maintenance Unit in Egypt was provided with the necessary spares. In the meantime the production order for 300 aircraft had been drastically cut to 142, so that by 1949 there were inadequate stocks of aircraft to maintain the squadrons at full strength, and some Tempest Vs were retained long past their allotted lifespan. Although a small number of trial conversions of Tempest Vs to VIs was undertaken, the process of converting them for tropical service was considered too lengthy and the scheme was abandoned, and most surplus Tempest Vs underwent a substantial programme for conversion to target-towing duties, continuing in this menial but essential rôle until the mid-'fifties.

Prototype conversion of the Tempest TT Mark 5 target tug, SN329, pictured in July 1948. The close-up view *below* illustrates the underwing towing winch pod with access panels removed. (Photos: Author's Collection)

Logical continuation of the annular radiator and cooling fan trials with the Typhoon (see page 42) involved conversion of Tempest V, EJ518, to incorporate the annular radiator, *above*. This aircraft suffered a forced landing following engine failure and its place was taken by NV768. The new installation, with improved cooling air in-flow round the enlarged spinner prompted Napier to experiment with an enormous ducted spinner (shown opposite). Unfortunately the greatly increased weight of the installation offset any improvement in performance and the trials remained of academic interest only. Although the oil cooler air intakes were moved to the wing roots, as on the Tempest Mark VI, both EJ518 and NV768 always remained Mark Vs, contrary to some sources. (All photos: D. Napier & Sons)

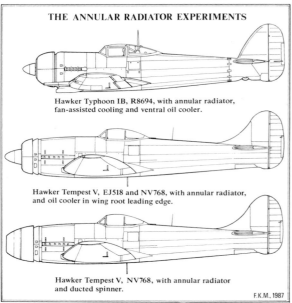

THE ANNULAR RADIATOR EXPERIMENTS

Hawker Typhoon IB, R8694, with annular radiator, fan-assisted cooling and ventral oil cooler.

Hawker Tempest V, EJ518 and NV768, with annular radiator, and oil cooler in wing root leading edge.

Hawker Tempest V, NV768, with annular radiator and ducted spinner.

F.K.M., 1987

NV768 in company with another Napier test Tempest V, EJ823, used to flight test the wing root oil cooler intakes.

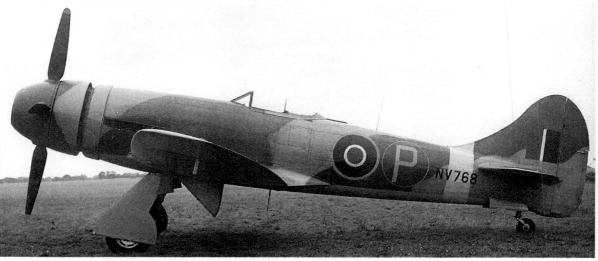

Above, one of the massive Tempest wing jigs at Langley. *Left*, Tempest front fuselage sections in the finishing shop at Perivale prior to delivery to Hawker. *Below*, fuselage assembly at Langley. *Bottom*, the stockpile of Tempest front fuselage sections at Langley in the summer of 1944, caused by a labour dispute at the factory. (Photos: Hawker)

7

TEMPESTS SUPREME

To suggest that the Tempest was the best Allied single-seat fighter of the Second World War might be contested by advocates of one or two other aeroplanes, and would demand qualification. The American P-51 was almost certainly the finest long-range escort fighter, while the Spitfire—worshipped by those who flew it—was always a superlative dogfighter. Other magnificent aircraft were about to enter service when the War ended. Yet the Tempest, and by this only the Tempest Mark V is relevant, was the aircraft that earned the greatest respect of its opponents in the final year of the War, faster than the Spitfire and the P-51, even in their later variants, and capable of much greater punch than either, and supremely strong and agile. Alas for the victory scoreboards, the popular cri-

Cockpit of the Tempest V. It is not generally appreciated that the Tempest was the only single-seat fighter to enter RAF service during the War which dispensed with the inclined gunsight reflector glass, the gunsight ring image being projected directly on to the windscreen in which the very highest quality of non-distorting armoured glass was used.

The Tempest V Series 1, JN735, was the first production aircraft fully representative of operational squadron examples, although one or two earlier aircraft were retrospectively modified up to that standard and delivered. Indeed, flown by Plt Off S. B. Feldman, JN735 shot down a flying bomb on 26 June 1944. The aircraft is shown here at Langley in December 1943. (Photo: Hawker Aircraft Ltd., Neg No 5TG17)

teria for "greatness", the Tempest arrived when the *Luftwaffe* had shrunk to a shadow of its former power yet, for all that, the air combats were no less vicious and hardfought. As the *Luftwaffe* stated, after a captured Tempest had been evaluated by the Germans, only the Me 262 was faster than the Tempest—yet it was only the Tempest that could, and did catch the German jet by diving on it. When it fired its guns at such high speeds the Tempest alone was always rock steady.

★　　★　　★

As told in the previous Chapter, production Tempest Vs of the JN-serial batch started delivery to RAF Maintenance Units before the end of 1943. These were subsequently defined as Mark V Series 1 aircraft with Hispano Mark I cannon, whose long barrels extended forward of the wing leading edge, to differentiate them from the Series 2 variant (which began deliveries early in 1944) with Mark V cannon whose shorter barrels were scarcely visible forward of the wing. Moreover none of the early aircraft possessed spring tabs, having yet to gain full approval by the A&AEE at Boscombe Down.

The purpose for which the Tempest was originally introduced was as a battlefield air superiority fighter (in modern parlance), an aircraft intended

to dominate the skies over the invasion forces, capable of countering the anticipated *Luftwaffe* reaction to the assault on *Festung Europa*. Its high performance and armament of four cannon was exactly what was deemed necessary to keep the skies clear over the ground attack Typhoons, while at the same time being a superb ground attack aircraft in its own right *with cannon armament only*. For it must be remembered that when the Tempest first reached the RAF in December 1943 it had not been cleared to carry rockets and bombs.

As events turned out, the *Luftwaffe* did not, or could not react violently over Normandy as anticipated, while another, more sinister threat developed nearer home, claiming the Tempests' undivided attention for a couple of months, to counter which the particular attributes possessed by the new fighter were exploited to the full.

The first Tempest Wing

Meanwhile the formation of the new Tempest Wing, No. 150, had gone ahead in March 1944, with headquarters at Castle Camps. Wg Cdr R. P. Beamont, DSO, DFC and Bar, was ordered to form this Wing by the Air Officer Commanding, No. 11 Group, ADGB, Air Vice-Marshal H. W. L.

A pilot climbs aboard Tempest V JN768/QO-N of No 3 Squadron at Newchurch in May 1944 as three Typhoons fly overhead. This early Series 1 Tempest was the aircraft in which F/Sgt R. W. Cole shot down a flying bomb on 17 June, and in which Wg Cdr R. P. Beamont was shot down in the Rheine area on 12 October that year before being taken prisoner. (Photo: Sydney Camm Collection)

("Dingbat") Saunders (later Air Chief Marshal Sir Hugh, GCB, KBE, MC, DFC and Bar, MM), using the New Zealand Squadron, No. 486, at Castle Camps, No. 3 at Bradwell Bay and No. 56 at Acklington. The primary operational task would be to gain and maintain air superiority over the sector between Brussels and the Seine Bay, Beamont being offered the choice between Friston, Gatwick, Headcorn and Newchurch as his Wing airfield—all in south-east England—from which

he selected the last-named, having inspected each in a Typhoon.

From the outset, therefore, it can be seen that Fighter Command appreciated the emphasis of the Tempest's superior performance in air combat potential; however, despite the priority afforded to the air superiority task, the ground attack rôle was still to be pursued when opportunities arose.

By March about 55 Tempests had reached or passed through the Maintenance Units, of which

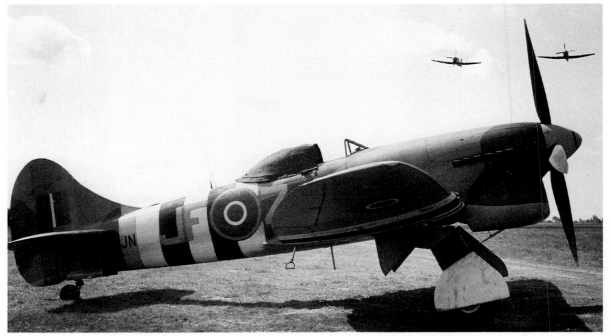

Another Tempest V of No 3 Squadron, this time a Series 2 aircraft; the application of fuselage "invasion stripes" indicates that this photo was taken at Newchurch after 6 June. (Photo: RAF Museum, Neg No CH14095)

Tempests of the New Zealand Squadron, No 486, at Beaulieu, before the formation of the Newchurch Wing. In the lower photograph the wartime censor has attempted to obliterate the ventral IFF blade aerial, this despite the fact that Typhoons, similarly equipped, had been lost over enemy territory in fairly large numbers for more than a year! (Photo: Sydney Camm Collection)

some 36 had been fully prepared for operations. No. 486 Squadron, which had first received some of the latter while based at Beaulieu in January, had been pre-occupied with attacks on the flying bomb sites and had been unable to get down to the job of converting to Tempests, and their aircraft stood around scarcely flown. In February the Squadron was ordered to hand over these aircraft to No. 3 Squadron, then at Manston, but once more the priority afforded to the "No-Ball" attacks had delayed the task of conversion.

Saunders now moved these two squadrons "out of the line", No. 486 to Castle Camps and No. 3 to Bradwell Bay, and, working from Castle Camps, Beamont set about working up the two units on Tempests. With almost all available aircraft now allocated, it was decided that No. 56 Squadron would have to wait some weeks before being re-equipped. (The Squadron was due to hand over its

Typhoons to 2nd Tactical Air Force prior to the Normandy landings, and in the event had to make do with elderly Spitfire Vs over the invasion area—a task performed with great success.)

In working up his two squadrons, Beamont paid considerable attention to formation practice and night operation, and on 6 April took them north to Ayr for an eight-day armament practice camp where the Tempest's air-to-ground gunnery qualities became immediately evident—Beamont himself gaining scores of 71 and 65 per cent on the 15-foot square target in consecutive sorties.

Beamont had however been privy to 'top level' fears of a flying bomb assault on Southern England, an eventuality then regarded as top secret on account of possible interference with the assembly of forces for the coming invasion assault by a precipitate evacuation of the civilian population. Throughout the period of No. 150 Wing's work-

Air-to-air view of a Tempest V, JN766/SA-N, of No 486 Squadron, RNZAF, during the Squadron's conversion training period

ing-up, he had always in mind the likelihood of being called on to forsake the offensive rôle to engage in air defence responsibilities. Because Saunders always saw in the Tempest his cornerstone of defence, No. 150 Wing was steadfastly retained within ADGB and not transferred to 2nd Tactical Air Force (until later) although, so long as the flying bomb attack did not materialize, the Tempests *would* be made available for air support over the invasion area.

On 14 April Nos. 3 and 486 moved south to Newchurch, to be joined a fortnight later by No. 56 Squadron with a mixed complement of Spitfire Vs and Typhoons. No. 3 was declared operational

under Squadron Leader K. A. Wigglesworth, DFC, with the New Zealanders under Squadron Leader J. H. Iremonger following suit on 1 May. *Ramrods* and *Rangers* over France and Belgium started immediately, Beamont frequently leading formations of between eight and 12 aircraft; on 28 May, for instance, flying *JN751*, he led a *Ranger* by eight aircraft over Cormeilles airfield where two Junkers Ju 188s were found and destroyed on the ground.

On D-Day itself the Wing Leader himself led ten Tempests over the beachhead in a dusk sweep which continued until after dark; no enemy aircraft were encountered, but on return the pilots

Camera-gun frames from Wg Cdr R. P. Beamont's Tempest shot during a train strike on 22 May 1944 over Northern France as part of the pre-invasion efforts to destroy the railway network behind the planned beachhead. In the photo on the left Beamont's first locomotive's boiler is seen exploding having been hit by cannon fire. On the right a second train is shown being hit in an attack on Doullens marshalling yards. Beamont went on to make two further successful train attacks on the same sortie. On that day the Tempest Wing attacked more than 40 trains without loss. (Photo: Wg Cdr R. P. Beamont)

Top, a photo reconnaissance picture of the airfield at Cormeilles-en-Vexin taken on the day after the Tempest attack of 28 May 1944, showing the position of three Ju 188s destroyed. *Above*, Beamont's camera-gun film shows his attack on a Ju 188 at Cormeilles; he states that the next frame showed a large piece of the German aircraft being hurled into the air; "it went over my head". (Photos: Wg Cdr R. P. Beamont)

COMBAT REPORTS   APPENDIX 'A'

PILOTS:- W/C R. Beamont, D.S.O., D.F.C. & Bar, P/O SLADE-BETTS,
F/S McKERRAS, F/S FOSTER, F/S DOMANSKI (Polish).
150 WING. 28th May, 1944.

At 16.55 hours nine Tempest V of 3 Sqdn took off for CORMEILLE-
EN-VEXIN Airfield, as information had been received that FW 190s
and ME 410s were seen on a P.R.U. sortie that morning. Owing to a
variety of technical troubles 4 of the Tempests came back before
reaching the French target. The remaining pilots closed up to a loose
formation with W/C Beamont leading, a section to port: P/O Slade-Betts,
and F/Sgt McKerras, and a section to starboard: F/Sgt Foster and
F/Sgt Domanski.

They crossed in a AULT at 8,000 feet and went straight to CORMEILLE-
EN-VEXIN, passing to the right of the Airfield. In bays on the East
side of the South dispersal five twin-engine aircraft were seen, so W/C
Beamont led the formation into a diving turn out of the sun, opening
fire at about 485 mph, range about 800 yds. The W/C's attack was from
¼ head-on and his target and those of the other two sections were identified as Ju 88's, possibly Ju 188s, painted black all over.

In the turn and dive P/O Slade-Betts and F/Sgt McKerras had pulled
over to starboard but got into position, and P/O Slade-Betts took the
aircraft in the bay on the right of the W/C's target, and F/Sgt McKerras
took the next on the right, both observing strikes.

F/Sgt Foster came down behind W/C Beamont, but as his windshield was
oiled up he could not select a target and fired a very short burst at
the same target as the leader. F/Sgt Domanski came down last, and
picking the next aircraft on the right not previously attacked, gave
it a burst, observing strikes.

As W/C Beamont pulled away he saw a piece of his target fly off and
the aircraft burning, and F/Sgt Domanski saw this and another target
burning. As he crossed the E. dispersal, F/Sgt McKerras gave a burst
at some huts and saw strikes.

It was only as the section was at the intersection of the runway
that inaccurate fire was opened by light guns. The formation stayed
low down for 2 or 3 miles and then climbed. Smoke from two fires was
seen from the target up to a distance of six miles. The formation
passed BEAUVAIS Airfield where no aircraft were seen, but there were
many unfilled bomb craters and damaged hangars. They crossed out at
AULT at 8,000 feet, landing at base at 1805 hours.

----------oOo----------

150 WING   COMBAT REPORT

W/CDR R.P. BEAMONT D.S.O. D.F.C. PILOT   8th June 1944

I was leading the Newchurch Tempest Wing on a fighter sweep to
the Caen area of the beachhead via Rouen, Bernay and Argentan. We
took off from Newchurch at 12.25 hours, and crossed the French
coast at Pte d'Ailly at 10,000 ft. When we were a few miles to the
West of Rouen at 12.50 hours over scattered cloud, I saw five
aircraft in line astern at about 5,000 ft, turning from East to
North. Leaving 486 (N.Z.) Squadron up above as top cover, I took
No. 3 Squadron down to investigate. I closed in behind the aircraft
at 370 I.A.S., and recognised them as ME.109Gs. They were travelling
at approximately 300 m.p.h. and did not realise they were being
bounced until just before I had opened fire, when the e/a broke to
port and dived for cloud with violent evasive action. I selected
the fourth or last e/a, I am not sure which, and opened fire with
a 2/3 second burst, starting with 30° deflection, and changing
according to the e/a's evasive action.

I opened fire at about 500 yards range closing to pointblank, and
saw strikes at the end of the burst on the starboard side of the
fuselage. The e/a immediately poured smoke and flames. I had to
break to starboard in order to avoid collision and then to port
when I saw clearly the enemy aircraft enveloped in flames in an
inverted dive.

I broke to starboard as I finished my attack and heard a loud
bang and saw a strike on my starboard wing. My No. 2, who subsequently saw my e/a disintegrate and the starboard wing break off,
saw two ME 109s diving down out of sun at him and myself. My U/C
warning lights went on so I handed over to S/Ldr. Dredge, on No. 3
Squadron, and set course for base where I landed at 13.30 hrs.

The aircraft I destroyed was camouflaged mottled chocolate and
brown and no national markings were visible.

I claim one ME.109G destroyed.

Rounds fired:- 60 rounds 20 mm each gun, H.E.I. and S.A.P.I.

No stoppages.

Facsimile transcripts of the combat reports covering the attack on Cormeilles airfield of 28 May 1944 and Beamont's air combat with Messerschmitt Bf 109Gs on 8 June. (By courtesy of Wg Cdr R. P. Beamont)

found the weather too bad for a landing at New-church. Beamont therefore led his pilots to an-other airfield where, despite being short of fuel and with many other aircraft waiting to land, all the Tempests got down safely. Two days later No. 150 Wing met a formation of Bf 109Gs over Rouen, one of them being shot down by the Wing Leader (flying *JN751*—thus the first Tempest to destroy an enemy aircraft), one by Flight Lieutenant A. R. Moore and a third by Pilot Officer G. A. Whitman, all without loss.

The flying bomb attack

Thus far the two Tempest Squadrons had been performing exactly the task for which No. 150 Wing had been created, although it would be some time before the third component Squadron, No. 56, would receive its first Tempests.

Then, on the night of 15/16 June, the crew of a Mosquito night fighter reported shooting down an unknown type of aircraft over the English Channel. Indeed the first flying bomb to land in England in the early hours of 13 June at Swanscombe, near Gravesend, had been followed by a small number of others—none of which had been detected by the coastal radar.

These small aircraft, complete with wings and powered by pulse-jets, were projected from inclined ramps—the launch sites that had commanded so much attention during the previous eight months—and propelled on their way towards London and elsewhere, being stabilized by gyros and flying at speeds between 380 and 420 miles per hour at heights up to around 5,000 feet. After a predetermined time the pulse-jet would cut out,

Photo reconnaissance picture of a flying bomb launch site in Northern France. (Photo: Wg Cdr R. P. Beamont, CBE, DSO, DFC)

Close-up view of a Newchurch Wing Tempest. (Photo: RAF Museum Neg No E1356)

leaving the bomb to crash to the ground.

No. 150 Wing at Newchurch was brought to Readiness on the evening of 15 June and warned for defensive operations at dawn the following day. During that night numerous flying bombs reached south-east England, but only in the early hours of the 16th was the first bomb shot down by the Mosquito referred to above. Before full light Wing Commander Beamont, in *JN751*, and Flight Sergeant R. W. Cole (21)[1] of No. 3 Squadron were ordered off and intercepted a flying bomb in cloudy conditions and light rain just south of Folkestone, this being shot down by the Wing Leader at Faversham.

On that first day of co-ordinated patrols by the Tempests No. 3 Squadron sent off 19 standing patrols, each by a pair of pilots, the next to destroy a V-1 being Flight Sergeant M. J. A. Rose (12) in *JN760*, with a further ten shot down by the Squad-

ron later in the day. On the 17th, bombs were destroyed by Beamont (30), Flight Lieutenant Van Lierde, DFC (40, a Belgian), Flying Officer M. F. Edwards (8), Flight Sergeant R. W. Cole, Flight Sergeant M. J. A. Rose and Flight Sergeant C. W. Orwin.

On the 20th No. 3 Squadron scored its first "double-barrelled" victory when the American pilot, Pilot Officer S. B. Feldman (9), destroyed two bombs in daylight, an achievement bettered by Van Lierde on the 23rd who destroyed three. On the 28th, after only 13 days, the Squadron shot down its 100th bomb. By that date the Newchurch Tempests were operating around the clock, Beamont being the first to destroy two V-1s on a single night sortie (one at Tenterden and one north of Hastings on 28 July—while flying *JN751*).

No. 3 Squadron suffered its first casualty on Tempests on 1 July (a month in which it shot down a further 146 bombs) when Flying Officer G. E. Kosh crashed near Rye, having last been seen chasing a V-1 into low cloud; two days later Flight

---

[1] Figures given in parentheses in the remainder of this Chapter indicate the total number of flying bombs—five or more—destroyed by the pilot named.

Camera-gun film from a Newchurch Tempest as it destroys a flying bomb. As one may appreciate, the violence with which these bombs detonated in the air forced the attacking pilot to take instant avoiding action if his aircraft was to escape serious damage from flying debris; as it was, some aircraft and pilots were lost and many aircraft returned to base with extensive damage. (Photos: Wg Cdr R. P. Beamont)

Sergeant S. Domanski[2] was killed in an accident, and on 6 August Flight Sergeant D. J. Mackerras[2] was also killed while chasing a bomb.

The New Zealanders of No. 486 Squadron also fought a magnificent battle against the V-1s and soon began to take a toll matching that of No. 3, the highest tally of 28 being gained by Squadron Leader H. E. Umbers, DFC (later the Squadron

Commander), with no fewer than 24 pilots gaining scores of five or more bombs; the Squadron also suffered heavily, losing six pilots killed and two injured. By the end of the first three months of the V-1 attacks, when No. 486 moved to the continent, it had destroyed 223 flying bombs.

The third Squadron, No. 56, started converting to Tempests on 24 June, and after only eight days was declared operational on the new aircraft. The following day Flight Lieutenant D. V. C. Cotes-Preedy, DFC, GM, gained the Squadron's first Tem-

---

[2] Both these pilots had taken part in the successful attack on Comeilles on 28 May.

A pair of Tempest Vs of the Newchurch Wing take off for a patrol during the flying bomb attacks. (Photo: Sydney Camm Collection)

139

pest score. On 7 July Sergeant G. H. Wylde (5) shot down a bomb off Beachy Head, but then his engine failed and he had to bale out; he was picked up unhurt. Flight Sergeant A. C. Drew destroyed a pair of bombs on the 26th; having used up all his ammunition on the first target he spotted another bomb, flew alongside it and, with his own wing tip, nudged the V-1's wing upwards, thereby toppling its gyros and causing it to crash south-east of Ashford. Drew was to lose his life three days later when he flew into the ground in low cloud.

★   ★   ★

Before moving on to the achievements of other Tempest squadrons in the flying bomb "campaign" it is necessary here to mention the influence which Beamont himself was able to bring to bear on the manner in which the defence against the flying bombs was developed, as well as to summarize the successes achieved by his Wing. It should be stated that in almost all operational respects the nature of a Wing Leader's appointment brought— and had always brought—a considerable degree of authority and influence for, despite the rank of Wing Commander, he was given a remarkably free hand in operational matters and autonomy in interpreting orders from Group and Command "above". Only in matters that significantly affected other commands was prior conference with senior authority required.

Thus, as early as 20 June, when it was clear to Beamont that some fighters were confusing the defences without gaining results, he approached No. 11 Group with a suggestion that a corridor within the area bounded between Hastings, London and Folkestone be declared restricted for the sole defence by the Newchurch Tempests, two Spitfire squadrons (of Mark XIIs and Mark XIVs) and a Wing of P-51 Mustangs. All other freelancing aircraft were to be kept clear of this area as being too slow to achieve worthwhile results. Within a matter of days this plan was adopted and put into effect, and straightaway the Tempests began to take a fast-mounting toll of the bombs:

29 June No. 150 Wing's 200th bomb destroyed
7 July No. 150 Wing's 300th bomb destroyed
14 July No. 150 Wing's 400th bomb destroyed
26 July No. 150 Wing's 500th bomb destroyed

Against this background of tremendous success, Beamont himself was working to improve the Tempest in its rôle of bomb-destroyer. On 3 July he carried out a trial using 150-grade fuel and 11 lb boost, this giving a speed of 415 mph at 500 feet (indicated)—and being introduced immediately throughout the Wing. On the 27th he shot down two bombs (at Bexhill and Tenterden) using point harmonization of his cannon—as distinct from spread harmonization, normally adopted—with considerable effect; this unauthorized practice created some friction with No. 11 Group as it had not been cleared officially, but Beamont nevertheless went ahead and ordered its adoption throughout his Wing, again with outstanding success.

On 26 August the Wing Leader tried his hand at flying a Meteor I, belonging to No. 616 Squadron

---

From: Air Commodore C.A. Bouchier, C.B.E., D.F.C.

HEADQUARTERS NO. 11 GROUP,
ROYAL AIR FORCE
UXBRIDGE.
9th September, 1944.

Dear Beamont,

    Air Marshal Sir Roderic Hill, K.C.B., M.C., A.F.C., has received a letter from Sir Ernest Gowers, K.C.B., K.B.E., London Regional Defence Commissioner, of which the following is an extract:-

    " At a recent meeting of my Standing Committee of Town Clerks of the London Region a spontaneous and unanimous request was made to me that I should convey to you, on behalf of the Local Authorities in the Region, their deep sense of obligation to the Pilots under your Command whose skill and devotion are doing so much to mitigate London's present ordeal. I gladly do this. We are filled with admiration of their magnificent achievements, and I hope you will find it possible to convey this tribute to them so that they may know how fully and gratefully London realises its debt to them. "

    I feel the foregoing should be brought to the notice of all Wing Leaders, Squadron Commanders and Pilots concerned, not forgetting the splendid work also done by Control Staffs both at Sector and G.C.I. Stations.

Yours sincerely

(C. Bouchier)

Wing Commander R.P. Beamont, D.S.O., D.F.C.,
R.A.F. Station,
NEWCHURCH.

FROM   A O C 11 GROUP   232250B
TO   WING COMMANDER BEAMONT   NEWCHURCH
INFO   BIGGIN HILL, ADGB

23/JUNE HEARTIEST CONGRATULATIONS TO YOU AND OFFICERS COMMANDING NOS 3 - 486 AND 56 SQUADRONS AND ALL PILOTS FORMING THE NEWCHURCH WING IN SHOOTING DOWN THE FIRST HUNDRED FLYING BOMBS. A SPLENDID ACHIEVEMENT AND FINE SHOOTING. KEEP IT UP AND BANG THEM DOWN.   BOUCHIER

FROM   A O C NO 11 GROUP
TO   NEWCHURCH FOR W/CDR BEAMONT
INFO   ADGB BIGGIN HILL

29/JUNE
PLEASE ACCEPT FOR YOURSELF AND CONVEY TO OFFICERS COMMANDING NO 3, 486 AND 56 SQUADRONS AND ALL PILOTS OF THE NEWCHURCH WING THE HEARTIEST CONGRATULATIONS OF ALL MEMBERS OF MY STAFF AND MYSELF UPON THE DESTRUCTION BY THEM OF THEIR 200TH PILOTLESS AIRCRAFT. SPECIAL CONGRATULATIONS ALSO TO NO 3 SQUADRON ON GETTING THEIR FIRST HUNDRED BY THEMSELVES. WE FOLLOW EACH DAY WITH ADMIRATION THE TRULY SPLENDID WORK YOU ARE DOING WITH SUCH SKILL AND UNTIRING DETERMINATION.

— BOUCHIER —

Group photo of No 501 Squadron's officers beside one of the Squadron's unpainted Tempests, EJ533/SD-R, at Bradwell Bay in November 1944. Shown in the photo are, left to right, W/Off Wojynski, Capt Payne (Army Liaison Officer), Flt Lt Robb, Flt Lt Hansen, Sqn Ldr A. Parker-Rees, DFC (CO), Flt Lt Willis, Flt Lt Birks, W/Off Balam, Flt Lt Langdon-Down, Fg Off Grottick and Fg Off Harte; behind, left to right, Fg Off Panter, Fg Off Maday, Fg Off Johnson, Flt Lt Burton, Flt Lt R. C. Stockburn, Fg Off Polley, Flt Lt Porter, Flt Lt Raymond and Fg Off Bennett. (Photo: Flt Lt R. C. Stockburn)

at Manston, to see how the new jet compared with the Tempest when flown against the flying bomb; his verdict was that "it was not much good". The thrust of the Rolls-Royce Welland turbojets was so puny that the relatively big Meteor possessed scarcely any acceleration. Not surprisingly the Meteors gained very little success against the bombs.

★   ★   ★

Next to convert to Tempests was No. 501 (County of Gloucester) Squadron at Westhampnett. It had been decided, after No. 150 Wing had reached its full establishment and with deliveries of new aircraft now accelerating—at least from the Maintenance Units, if not from the manufacturers—to start re-equipping those squadrons that had been flying older fighters and No. 501, which had still flown Spitfire VBs over Normandy, was the first in line (after No. 56). Series 2 Tempest Vs, complete with spring tabs, were delivered to Westhampnett and were greeted with enthusiasm by all. Under the command of Squadron Leader M. G. Barnett the Squadron was declared operational by day after only three days' conversion training. On 2 August it moved to Manston where it immediately started flying bomb patrols.

As command then passed to Squadron Leader J. Berry, DFC and Bar (61.33),[3] newly arrived from No. 3 Squadron at Newchurch, training started in night interception of the bombs, to become a night specialist squadron with a secondary daylight rôle. It had been thought that the intermittent spurts of light from the flying bomb's pulse-jet would make

both locating the target and aiming the guns simple, but in the latter the assumption was incorrect. To begin with, the flash of the pulse-jet tended to destroy the Tempest pilot's night vision and, being unable then to see the bomb itself as the fighter approached from astern, and therefore unable to judge the range accurately (with no wing span reference), pilots found themselves opening fire much too close, and when the bombs exploded in the air they did so with a shattering detonation; at least three pilots were indeed lost when their aircraft were engulfed. The problem was resolved in two ways. To begin with the Tempest pilots closed in below the bomb until directly underneath, and then fell back about 300 yards before climbing to open fire. Soon afterwards a simple optical rangefinder, developed at the RAE, Farnborough, was introduced.

Although the Tempest possessed a sizeable margin of speed over the bombs, No. 501 Squadron received several aircraft that had been left unpainted, these being found to possess a maximum

---

[3] This pilot attained by far the highest score of bombs destroyed by any RAF pilot, losing his life in October. The award of one of his DFCs for his success against the V-1s seems paltry indeed. The eight highest scoring Tempest pilots (out of the RAF's "top ten") were:

Sqn Ldr J. Berry (Nos. 3 and 501 Squadrons)	61.33	(1)
Flt Lt R. Van Lierde (No. 3 Squadron)	40	(2)
Wg Cdr R. P. Beamont (No. 150 Wing)	30	(3)
Flt Lt A. E. Umbers (No. 3 Squadron)	28	(6)
Fg Off R. W. Cole (No. 3 Squadron)	21.66	(7)
Flt Lt A. R. Moore (No. 3 Squadron)	21.5	(8)
Fg Off R. H. Clapperton (No. 3 Squadron)	21	(9=)
Fg Off R. Dryland (No. 3 Squadron)	21	(9=)

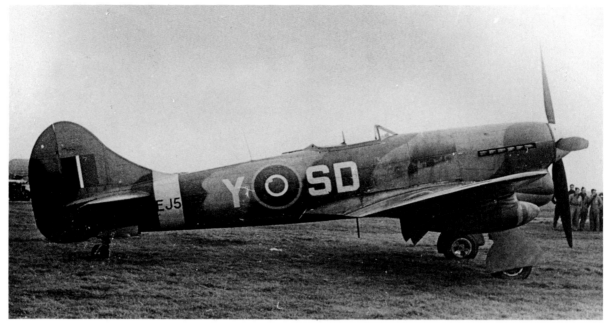

Tempest V EJ555-018-SD-Y of No 501 Squadron with drop tanks, introduced in October 1944. (Photo: Richard Ward, Farnborough)

Three Tempest Vs with representative armament provision. The nearest aircraft, JN328, is equipped with Mark II rocket installation, next is a late production aircraft, SN108, with underwing bomb racks, and further (carrying No 501 Squadron codes SD-Z), EJ884, a "clean" fighter with cannon armament only. (Photo: via R. C. Sturtivant)

A pair of Tempest Vs take off on patrol. The style of AEF recognition stripes suggests that the picture was taken in about October 1944; by that date the use of wing drop tanks was commonplace on the Tempest Squadrons. (Photo: via R. L. Ward, Whitstable)

speed about five miles an hour greater than those painted overall. Any expedient that would reduce the tail-chase, especially if the bomb could be caught and destroyed while still over the Channel, was considered worth investigating; the small gain achieved by the unpainted aircraft was, however, not deemed worthwhile and they were not generally adopted.

No. 501 was to remain in action against the flying bombs longest of all the Tempest squadrons, moving to Bradwell Bay on 22 September whence it operated against Heinkel He 111 aircraft which started air-launching V-1s when the Allies overran the remaining launch sites in the Pas de Calais in September 1944.

Fifth of the Tempest squadrons to be equipped before the ground-launched V-1 attacks ended was another ex-Spitfire unit, No. 274 Squadron, to whom Squadron Leader Barnett, DFC, transferred his command on leaving No. 501 in August. Once more this officer achieved a very fast conversion, No. 274 operating its first flying bomb patrol from West Malling on 12 August after only three days on Tempests, Flying Officer J. W. Lyne and Flying Officer G. G. G. Walkington flying an uneventful sortie that day. The next day the Squadron suffered its first Tempest casualty when Flight Sergeant R. W. Ryman flew into a hill near Elham, north of Folkestone, and was killed. The first bomb destroyed by the Squadron fell two miles north-east of Sittingbourne on the 15th, shot down by Flight Lieutenant O. E. Willis, this pilot gaining

the second victory when he destroyed a bomb the next day two miles north of Maidstone. Later that day a Canadian, Flight Lieutenant J. Malloy, "bagged a brace".

However, by the time No. 274 Squadron entered the battle, the supply of bombs to the French launching sites was beginning to dwindle as the Allies broke eastwards from the battlefields of Normandy, and the Squadron, now under orders to confine its patrols to the Channel, had less opportunity to combat the bombs. As a result its pilots, though no less capable than those of the other Squadrons, did not feature among the top scorers.

Sadly, history has hitherto been less than generous to the achievements of the Royal Air Force in holding in check the full effects of the flying bomb menace, preferring to shrug aside the attacks as "a last desperate fling by a defeated enemy". In truth they had constituted a powerful and premeditated campaign which, but for the success in destroying, and preventing the completion of so many of the launching sites beforehand, could have employed as many as 200 sites, each capable of discharging at least 20 bombs every day against England. The casualties and damage from such enormous salvoes would have been catastrophic to the Allies, quite apart from the carnage among the civilian population.

And when the attack did materialize it was the pilots and aircraft of fewer than a dozen Fighter Command squadrons that took the greater toll. In

143

Ground and flight views of the second production Tempest V, JN730, which was employed for several months in clearance trials of the new streamlined drop tanks that were to become such a feature of Tempest operations during the last eight months of the War. (Photos: Hawker Aircraft Ltd.)

the first month of the attacks the Newchurch Tempests destroyed 600 bombs, compared to some 260 by all the guns of Anti-Aircraft Command. Even at the end of the ground-launched attacks in September the total of 1,460 gained by the guns (compared to those by the fighters of 1,772) was only achieved after the fighters had, as a result of blurred arguments, been confined to absurdly narrow margins of patrol. As was acknowledged partway through the attacks, the guns were wrongly sited, and many were outdated and quite useless against small, fast, low-flying targets— even though these flew level and in straight lines. Only late in the attacks, when many of the guns were provided with radar directors and VT fuses for their ammunition (and the fighters "cleared out of the way") did the ground defences make significant headway. Even Churchill seemed disinclined to voice appreciation of Fighter Command's superlative efforts, said to be an attitude adopted to bolster the flagging morale of the gunners—an astonishing attitude when the morale of those few pilots was no less important!

Bearing in mind that so many Allied airmen were committed to the support of the Normandy invasion to ensure that the hard-won foothold on the continent was never lost, it seems extraordinary that history has not chosen to accord some lasting testimonial to the vigilance and skill of the men of Fighter Command in that difficult summer over south-east England.

At grips with the Luftwaffe again

While the Tempest squadrons of the Newchurch Wing continued to mount flying bomb patrols at the end of August the German armies were retreating eastwards across northern France, and, as the launch sites were overrun by the British and Canadian forces, so the number of bombs being sent across the Channel diminished. This in turn allowed No. 150 Wing to turn its attention increasingly to operations over the continent once more, while still maintaining a reduced scale of flying bomb patrols.

On 26 August Beamont, flying *JN751*, led No. 486 Squadron on a ground support sortie, finding and attacking a column of AFVs and motorized transport near St Omer; the Wing Leader himself damaged three AFVs, suffering hits from ground fire in an elevator and the main wingspar, but the Tempests returned without loss. Two days later Beamont, this time flying a No. 3 Squadron aircraft (JF-E) as *JN751* was still being repaired, led Nos. 56 and 486 Squadrons on a radar suppression attack on the *Freya* at Cassel near St Omer, claiming good results; one of the New Zealanders suffered minor flak damage.

The Wing Leader, flying a No. 486 Squadron Tempest (*JN792*/SA-H) on 6 September, took aircraft of Nos. 3 and 486 on a sweep to the Dutch border in support of a daylight raid on Emden, this time without excitement. He was again airborne on the 10th in SA-H, leading Nos. 3 and 486 Squadrons on a ground attack sortie against rail and river targets in the vicinity of The Hague.

The following day 36 aircraft of the three New-church Wing squadrons flew to the Ruhr in support of a daylight raid by 200 Lancasters, Beamont now flying a new Tempest, coded RP-B. This was the first occasion that Tempests flew over Germany and also the first operation on which the drop tanks were used, the sortie involving a flight of 600 miles; the tanks were jettisoned when empty.[4]

On 13 September Beamont, again flying RP-B, led 24 Tempests of Nos. 3 and 486 Squadrons in an attack on a "Big Ben" (V-2) launch site that had

---

[4] This was to become normal practice on Tempest operations for about four months. By the end of the year, however, with an average daily "usage" of about 60 drop tanks, a shortage was threatened and for the remainder of the War pilots were usually instructed to bring their empty tanks home, unless faced with air combat or an emergency.

been positively pinpointed near The Hague. As the Tempests dived to attack with cannon Squadron Leader K. A. Wigglesworth, DFC, may have been hit by flak for he failed to recover and crashed into the target area. The attackers, however, evidently hit either a V-2 rocket or a fuel store for there was a massive explosion on the ground which completely engulfed the launch site.[5]

As the ground-launched phase of the V-1 campaign petered out in September 1944, No. 150 Wing made preparations to move to the continent, the three Squadrons spending a week or so away from the operational airfields in the south-east so that working parties could give the aircraft a thorough going-over after the strains of past weeks when they had been flown at (and beyond) the normally permitted limits for long periods as the pilots had striven to catch V-1s approaching heavily populated areas. Most of the JN-batch aircraft were withdrawn to be brought up to the latest modification standard, and EJ-serial aircraft issued.

On 28 September Wing Commander Beamont (now with a Bar to his DSO) led a massed formation of 48 Tempests of Nos. 3, 56 and 486 Squadrons to B.60 Grimbergen, just to the north of Brussels. Now, as No. 122 Wing of 2nd Tactical Air Force, it was ordered over on to the offensive, its tasks

---

[5] As recounted by Wing Commander Beamont to the writer.

A Wing formation of Tempest Vs led by eight aircraft of No 80 Squadron. AEF recognition stripes cannot be detected in the original photograph, suggesting that the picture was taken early in 1945. (Photo: via R. L. Ward, Whitstable)

A Tempest V, W2-R, of No 80 Squadron at Wunstorf, Germany, in 1945. The bell insignia on the aircraft's fin commemorates the Squadron's first commanding officer on the Western Front in 1918, Major V. D. Bell. (Photo: via Richard Ward, Farnborough)

being numerous, varied and wideranging, from escort of Allied medium and heavy bombers attacking targets in Belgium, Holland and Western Germany, to carrying out offensive sweeps over *Luftwaffe* airfields and targets specified by the British and Canadian armies. Now that the V-2 rocket attacks had started in earnest against England and Brussels, patrols were ordered to locate the launching pads from which the missiles rose, this task being part of Operation "Big Ben". Another cryptic instruction was to keep a sharp look out for Messerschmitt Me 262 jet fighters and bombers, now being encountered in growing numbers; attacks were to be made against the new German aircraft whenever possible, as much as anything to determine how best they might be tackled by the Tempest and to discover what tactics the Germans had evolved, especially at low level.

Grimbergen proved to be no more than a temporary location for the Wing, and on 1 October the three squadrons were ordered to move to the large airfield of B.80 Volkel in Holland. So close was this to the front line at that time that some of the pilots on their landing circuit found themselves under fire from German flak batteries, and Warrant Officer F. M. Reid, AFM, was shot down and killed, and the Wing Leader's RP-B was hit in the starboard tailplane while approaching to land.

During the first fortnight in which the Wing was in residence at Volkel there were no fewer than six sightings from the ground of low-flying Me 262 bombers within a dozen miles of the base. On at least a couple of occasions pairs of Tempests were scrambled in attempts to catch the German aircraft, but the jets were long gone by the time the Tempests had got airborne. So preoccupied had the Allies become with the German aircraft that a system was introduced by which ground observer posts (of which many were dotted about in Belgium and southern Holland) would fire off coloured signal flares—the colour denoting the rough direction in which the enemy aircraft was flying. Any Tempest pilot, already airborne on patrol with fuel and ammunition remaining, who spotted the flares was encouraged to go after the intruder, or "rat" as the low-flying jets were now termed.

The first Messerschmitt Me 262 fell to the guns of Pilot Officer R. W. Cole of No. 3 Squadron who, alerted by the ground flares, spotted the jet streaking north towards Nijmegen at low level. Opening up to full boost, Cole put the nose of the Tempest down and went after the "rat", quickly reaching about 530 mph and closing to 200 yards before opening fire. Hit in one engine, the Me 262 suddenly started trailing a long plume of white

A late production Tempest V, SN179/JJ-P, probably at Quackenbr-211-ck, Germany. (Photo: Ralph Stockburn DFC)

Starboard side view of SN179/JJ-P. (Photo: Ralph Stockburn DFC)

smoke (usually signifying that one engine had flamed out), pulled up steeply and then crashed near Grave; the pilot baled out and landed nearby by parachute.

It had been suspected for some time that the Me 262s were operating over the northern sector of the front line from the airfield at Rheine, roughly halfway between Osnabrück and the German frontier with Holland. Already the first armed reconnaissance patrols by Tempests were being ordered to this area, and it was on such a sortie on 26 November that Cole was shot down by flak. Indeed, the attention paid by the RAF to this base prompted the Germans to deploy a very large concentration of light and heavy flak around it, leaving only a narrow corridor for taking off and landing.

Alas, Pilot Officer Cole was not the first victim of the flak in the area of Rheine. Wing Commander Beamont, who had shot down his tenth enemy aircraft (a Focke-Wulf Fw 190D, at over 530 mph) near Arnhem on 2 October, had put himself down to lead an armed reconnaissance by No. 3 Squadron on 12 October. After a delayed take-off, caused when a Messerschmitt Me 262 attacked Volkel itself and hit the flying control tented site, the Tempests made for the area of Rheine where the pilots spotted a train on the Münster line. While attacking this target Beamont's aircraft, *JN768*, was hit by flak and the pilot was forced down in enemy territory.

Beamont, who was taken prisoner, had only the previous day received the offer of a test flying post with Hawker Aircraft Ltd at the end of his third tour of operations, but had decided to complete one hundred fighter operations over enemy territory before deciding whether to accept. He was to be shot down on his 95th . . . after a total of 630 operational hours on fighters.

In the meantime the fourth Tempest Squadron, No. 274, had joined No. 122 Wing at Volkel. Like the squadrons of the old No. 150 Wing, No. 274 had gone north after the initial flying bomb attacks had abated, and then moved, first to Deurne near Antwerp, and then to Grave at the beginning of October. On the 7th it arrived at Volkel. It had already lost an aircraft on the 5th when Flying Officer G. T. Kinnell, RNZAF, crash landed *EJ709* in No Man's Land after a patrol near Münster, but had been reported safe. However, the Squadron's new commanding officer, Squadron Leader J. R. Heap, was to be killed on 21 November attempting to force land after engine failure during a patrol over Venlo.

Although the bad weather of December re-

Sqn Ldr Bruce Cole as commanding officer of No 3 Squadron at the end of the War, with his boxer bitch. Bruce became Chief Flying Instructor at Cranwell in the late 1940s, and the Author recalls the frequent distractions caused by his dog in the otherwise decorous routine of the College. Sadly this magnificent pilot was killed in a flying accident shortly afterwards. (Photo: Flt Lt Pitt, via M. A. Garbett)

stricted flying by the 2nd Tactical Air Force, No. 122 Wing managed to put up numerous patrols and sweeps, and Flight Lieutenant R. B. Cole, DFC, and Flying Officer G. Mann of No. 274 Squadron claimed a Messerschmitt Me 262 damaged ten miles north of Rheine on the 5th. This Squadron obtained its first confirmed victories over piloted enemy aircraft (as distinct from the flying bombs) when it ran into a formation of Bf 109Gs near Emmerich, two being shot down by the American, Flight Lieutenant D. C. Fairbanks, RCAF, and another by Flight Lieutenant W. J. Hibbert. On Christmas Eve Squadron Leader E. D. Mackie, DFC and Bar, RNZAF (who was flying supernumerary to the Squadron, not its CO, and of whom more will be told in due course) shot down a Fw 190D six miles south of Eindhoven.

On the 28th No. 3 Squadron had a brush with Bf 109Gs and Ks which shot down Flight Lieutenant M. F. Edwards (8); the other flight commander, Flight Lieutenant K. F. Thiele, DSO, DFC and two Bars, evened the score by destroying one of the enemy fighters.

The fifth Tempest V squadron to join No. 122 Wing was No. 80 which, under Squadron Leader R. L. Spurdle, DSO, DFC and Bar, had given up Spitfire IXs in favour of Tempests at West Malling early in August and, moving to Manston later, carried out flying bomb patrols before going over to the offensive.

At first, as part of Operation "Big Ben", No. 80 Squadron carried out sweeps over Holland (carrying drop tanks) to spot and attack V-2 launch pads, but these were soon seen to be virtually fruitless as the German crews and launch equipment were highly mobile and little time was spent on any pad before de-camping to another. On 16 September, in an attack on a train thought to be carrying rockets north of Arnhem, the Australian pilot,

Pilot Officer W. E. Maloney (in *EJ662*) was seen to be hit by flak and crash land nearby. The next day the Squadron lost three aircraft during Operation "Market" (the ill-fated airborne attack at Arnhem) when it was ordered out to suppress flak batteries on the island of Walcheren. The three aircraft were all hit as they swept low over the heavy defences, one being seen to crash in flames on land while another (*EJ519*), flown by Warrant Officer P. L. Godfrey, was seen to crash off the coast as the pilot attempted to ditch. Flight Lieutenant E.E.O. Irish in *EJ657* baled out and was rescued. The following day, once again supporting the Arnhem air drops with anti-flak sweeps over Flushing, the Squadron lost two pilots, with Flying Officer R. H. Hannay (in *EJ607*) posted missing and Flying Officer P. S. Haw, hit by flak, being drowned when forced to bale out too low over the sea.

No. 80 Squadron arrived at Volkel on 7 October and took its turn with the other four Tempest squadrons in flying armed reconnaissance patrols. One such sortie to Rheine was rewarded with outstanding success when four Tempests (flown by Flight Lieutenant R. W. A. MacKichan, DFC, Flying Officers D. S. Angier and J. W. Garland, RCAF, and Warrant Officer G. W. Dopson) ran into four Focke-Wulf Fw 190Ds near the enemy airfield on 27 December, and shot them all down, the Tempest pilots claiming one apiece. The flak had held fire owing to the presence of friendly aircraft . . .

Meanwhile, with Tempest production and deliveries to the RAF in England enjoying a surge—following a slow-down in the late summer—two new squadrons, Nos. 33 and 222, had disposed of Spitfire IXs to take on Tempests at Predannack, Cornwall, in mid-December; it was, however, to be late February before these Squadrons joined the 2nd Tactical Air Force.

* * *

If the increasing tempo of events late in 1944 had given a foretaste of the vicious battles to come, as the War entered its last few months it was perhaps ironic that the big Tempest Wing at Volkel should escape relatively lightly in the drama of "*Bodenplatte*", only a couple of aircraft being destroyed on the ground. No. 122 Wing ended the day with honours more than evened as Tempests destroyed at least two of the attackers near Eindhoven, while Flying Officer Garland of No. 80 Squadron caught and shot down two Focke-Wulf Fw 190s near Münster.

On the 4th the Volkel Wing carried out a full programme of armed reconnaissance patrols north of the Ruhr, one such sortie involving a fight with Bf 109s well inside Germany near Bielefeld, Flying Officer D. E. Ness, RCAF, and Flight Lieutenant J. H. Ryan of No. 56 Squadron each shooting down

One of the Tempest pilots whose personal victory score accelerated rapidly in the closing weeks of the War, Flt Lt Ralph Stockburn, seen in the cockpit of his aircraft shortly after VE-Day

one of the enemy. Twelve miles north-west of Rheine Pilot Officer N. J. Rankin, RAAF, and Flight Sergeant L. B. Crook of No. 80 shared a Focke-Wulf Fw 190D; this Squadron was, however, to lose Flying Officer A. W. D. MacLachlan, RAAF, on the 13th when he had to force land *EJ774* near Stavelot in enemy territory to the south of the British sector after being hit by flak; the pilot was seen to walk away from his Tempest, apparently unhurt.

The following day No. 56 Squadron, on a sweep to Paderborn, south of Bielefeld—80 miles into Germany—had a running fight with about 20 Fw190s, of which Flying Officer J. J. Payton shot down one, with another being shared by Flight Lieutenant Ryan and Pilot Officer J. E. Hughes. On the 16th the Squadron lost Pilot Officer H. Shaw (9) in *EJ772*; during an attack on a train the locomotive's boiler exploded and the Tempest was seen to be struck by the debris and crash nearby. In an attack on German road transport on the 20th Pilot Officer J. S. Ferguson (also of No. 56), evidently leaving his breakaway too late, turned too sharply, suffered high-speed stall, flicked over and crashed—the Tempest blowing up on impact. Two days afterwards Flying Officer MacLaren (5) destroyed a Bf 109G in the vicinity of Neede.

23 January was to be a red letter day for the Volkel Tempest Wing as a big sweep was laid on for 48 Tempests, flying in three groups some ten miles apart, covering the route Rheine–Osnabrück–Bielefeld–Münster–Hengelo. Unless attacked by very superior numbers of German aircraft, each formation was expected to fend for itself before continuing the sweep on its own. The day started well when Flight Lieutenant F. L. MacLeod of No. 56 Squadron chanced upon a low-flying Me 262 near Paderborn which he despatched "after having pushed the Tempest through the gate". As the Squadron approached Rheine the German flak remained ominously inactive—a sure sign that the *Luftwaffe* was airborne in the area. Suddenly a mixed formation of Bf 109s and Fw 190s was spotted to the north-west; in a fight that lasted less than a couple of minutes Flying Officers Payton and MacLaren each destroyed a Focke-Wulf and Flying Officer V. L. Turner, RAAF, got a Messerschmitt.

Soon afterwards, near Gütersloh, No. 274 ran into another mixed group of German fighters as Flight Lieutenant L. A. Wood and Flying Officer C. G. Scriven each shot down Fw 190s and Flight Lieutenant Mann a Bf 109. No. 80 Squadron had a couple of fights; in one near Münster Flight Sergeant Crook destroyed a '190 and a '109, as the Rhodesian pilot, Flight Lieutenant A. Seager, shot down another Fw 190 and Flight Lieutenant L. R. G. Smith got a 109.

Later, in something of a "Commonwealth benefit match", Squadron Leader Eval Dall Mackie,

A silver-painted Tempest V, SN330/J5-H of No 3 Squadron landing at Geilenkirchen, Germany, after the War. (Photo: via Richard Ward, Farnborough)

the New Zealander from Otorohanga, generally known as "Rosie" and recently appointed to command No. 80 Squadron, shot down one of a formation of Bf 109s near Münster, his tenth victory and one that brought the award of the DSO. In the same fight the Canadian Flight Lieutenant D. L. Price and the Australian Pilot Officer F. A. Lang shared a '109.

Thus the day ended on which at least half the Volkel pilots had been in action against German fighters, and shot down 13 without loss. In each instance cine cameras had confirmed the claims, and seven of the German pilots had been seen to bale out, one or two of them at very low altitude. Most of the RAF pilots seemed to consider their German opponents lacked flying experience, some making the classic combat mistake of turning away when attacked, thereby presenting an easier target for the Tempest pilots. This view was to be expressed ever more frequently during the following weeks.

No. 80 Squadron was to claim a further pair of Bf 109s the next day between Bielefeld and Münster, the successful pilots being Flight Lieutenant D. L. Price, RCAF, and Flying Officer R. J. Holland.

February brought no respite in the air battles and, although the spate of successes continued, they were bought more dearly, each of the squadrons suffering fairly heavy losses.

On the 1st the distinguished pilot, Squadron Leader K. F. Thiele, DSO, DFC and two Bars, was appointed to command No. 3 Squadron but, alas, his command was shortlived; ten days later he was to be shot down by flak near Rheine and taken prisoner. On that first day of February No. 274 Squadron lost Flight Lieutenant G. Bruce, RCAF, shot down by Fw 190s during an armed reconnaissance between Hamm and Gütersloh, Flight Lieutenant Hibbert (in *NV722*) gaining revenge by downing one of the enemy fighters. The next day Squadron Leader Mackie on No. 80 Squadron suffered engine failure and force landed *NV657* in

149

friendly territory, fortunately without injury. Elsewhere Sergeant J. K. Holden on No. 56 was missing after an attack on a train; he is thought to have failed to recover from his dive and crashed nearby.

On the 3rd No. 274 Squadron came across relatively unfamiliar opponents during a patrol towards Bremen, finding a formation of Messerschmitt Me 410s near Vechta; three of these were damaged by the squadron commander, Squadron Leader A. R. Baird, DFC, while one was shot down by Flying Officer R. E. Mooney. Nos. 80 and 274 Squadrons carried out co-ordinated sweeps one hundred miles into Germany on the 8th, the former finding a small formation of Fw 190s 20 miles south-east of Bremen, Pilot Officer R. S. E. Verran shooting down one of them. Thirty miles to the south, near Minden, 274 Squadron had a short, sharp fight with some '109s which shot down the CO, Squadron Leader Baird, but lost three of their number to Flying Officers T. A. Sutherland, W. J. B. Stark and F. W. Mossing, RCAF.

A couple of pilots on No. 80 Squadron had narrow escapes on 10 February as Flight Sergeant Crook (in *NV654*) had his engine seize while in the landing circuit at Volkel; diving crosswind he just succeeded in reaching the airfield where he made a distinctly hurried landing, wheels up, wrecking the aircraft but escaping injury to himself. Flying Officer G. F. Royds in *EJ776* struck high tension power cables during a sweep near Hamm, but succeeded in bringing his damaged Tempest back to base. Both were examples of fine airmanship where lesser pilots could so easily have lost their heads, their lives *and* their aircraft.

Both Nos. 3 and 274 Squadrons now had new commanding officers appointed to them, Squadron Leader Bruce Cole, DFC, to the former, and Squadron Leader David Charles Fairbanks, DFC, RCAF, to the latter. And Fairbanks it was who celebrated his new appointment by flying straight to Rheine the next day and shooting down a Messerschmitt 262! Five days later he destroyed a pair of '109s near Hildesheim; on the 22nd (having been awarded a Bar to his DFC) he shot down a pair of Fw 190s near Hamm. On the 28th, while leading eight Tempests near Rheine, he was caught in a trap and bounced by about 40 Focke-Wulf Fw 190Ds which shot down the American (in his favourite Tempest, *NV943*) and Flying Officer J. B. Spence in *EJ771*.

While No. 274 Squadron had shot down 13 German aircraft during February for the loss of six pilots—including two COs and two flight commanders—No. 56 had destroyed nine of the enemy for the loss of two Tempests. No. 80 Squadron had increased its score by six aircraft shot down, also losing six and three pilots; Royds and Angier were both posted missing on the 14th, and Flight Lieutenant Price, RCAF, had been seen to bale out safely

German locomotives hit by Tempests; both have been crippled by cannon fire. The upper example—inscribed with its rail route from Utrecht to Hengelo and with German military insignia—has also been struck by a rocket, probably from a Typhoon. (Photos: Richard Ward, Whitstable)

after being hit by flak while escorting Typhoons in an attack on an oil installation on the 25th.

By the end of February both No. 33 and 222 Squadrons had arrived in Holland, being based at B.77 Gilze-Rijen. No. 33 had already suffered its first loss on the 25th when Flying Officer A. Harman was posted missing after a sweep to Rheine.

Henceforth, as with the Typhoons, railways would come under increasing attack by the Tempests, it being a favourite tactic for these aircraft to go for the locomotive, aiming with their cannons to bring it to a halt at least, and then to call up a nearby patrol of rocket-armed Typhoons to blast the line of trucks or coaches with more suitable weapons.

It was of course impossible for the *Luftwaffe* to mount any sort of defence over these trains, and their defence was left entirely to the accompanying flak. That is not to say that air fighting diminished in any way during March and April, but that such encounters with German fighters occurred whenever patrols clashed, the RAF pilots on the look-out for likely targets on the ground or under orders to patrol between two or more points. The Germans had simply to look for Allied aircraft.

March opened for No. 80 Squadron with the loss of a Norwegian pilot, Captain O. Ullestad, on the 2nd, shot down by enemy fighters near Rheine; five days later Squadron Leader Mackie, flying *NV700*, shot down a Focke-Wulf Fw 190D near Hanover. On the 22nd eight Tempests from No. 56 and a similar number from No. 80 Squadron carried out a combined sweep over Hesepe and surprised a dozen Fw 190s, Flight Lieutenants G. B. Milne and J. T. Hodges, Flying Officer Turner, RAAF, and Sergeant P. C. Brown of No. 56 Squadron, and Flight Lieutenant R. C. Cooper and Flying Officer G. A. Bush of No. 80 each destroyed an enemy fighter, all without loss. During the month, when No. 222 Squadron was also declared operational, a total of 88 enemy aircraft (all but nine of them fighters) were shot down for the loss of 21 Tempests and 17 pilots, at least nine of whom had been seen to leave their aircraft safely, either in the air or on the ground.

On 2 April, during an armed reconnaissance by No. 80 Squadron between Rheine and Osnabrück, Flying Officer R. J. Holland and Pilot Officer R. A. Horsey were both shot down by flak. The latter pilot was flying a brand new Tempest, *SN139*,

fitted with the new ranging gunsight and the latest IFF equipment and, although the pilot was not seen to leave the aircraft, there was no fire and it seemed likely that the new equipment might fall into enemy hands intact; the following day therefore No. 80 Squadron returned to ensure that the Tempest was destroyed by fire. It was later learned that both pilots had died in their cockpits, and had been recovered by the Germans.

No. 33 Squadron had a hard month with Flight Sergeant P. W. C. Watton and Sergeant S. Staines both lost near Hamburg on the 12th, Flight Sergeant C. Peters posted missing after a patrol between Husum and Kiel on the 23rd, and three pilots shot down near Lübeck the next day, the Dutch pilot, Flying Officer D. J. ter Beck, plus Flight Lieutenant R. J. Hetherington, RNZAF, and Flight Sergeant J. E. Fraser.

Air fighting on the 15th and 16th was particularly fierce, with No. 56 Squadron's Flight Lieutenant J. A. McCairns, DFC and two Bars, sharing the destruction of an Me 262 with Flight Lieutenant N. D. Cox near Hamburg on the first day, as No. 80 Squadron's Squadron Leader Mackie shared a Fw 190 with Sergeant W. F. Turner, and Flight Lieutenant A. Seager destroyed another in the same area.

On the 16th Wing Commander R. E. P. Brooker, the Wing Leader, headed an armed re-

No 274 Squadron Tempest V, EJ596/JJ-K "JOYCE" at B.155 Dedelstorf, Germany, in June 1945. Note the post-War re-appearance of the underwing serial number and of No 274 Squadron's "flash" (previously applied to the Squadron's Hurricanes in the Middle east during the War); locating the marking below the windscreen quarterlight was unique. (Photo: Flt Lt Ralph Stockburn DFC)

connaissance to Neuruppin, only 30 miles from Berlin. Not surprisingly the Tempests encountered both flak and fighters, Flight Lieutenant M. P. Kilburn, DFC, destroying a Fw 190 and Flight Lieutenant R. B. Prickett another—both pilots of No. 80 Squadron. Four of the Wing's aircraft did not return, including that of the Wing Leader, whose fate could not be established. That evening Squadron Leader Mackie, RNZAF, was promoted Wing Commander and appointed Wing Leader; his place at the head of No. 80 Squadron was taken by the South African, Major R. A. Henwick, DFC, SAAF.

The last week of the War was more kaleidoscopic than ever. There could be no pattern of events for the Tempests, as patrols were ordered off at moments' notice, only to be recalled as news of a more important target was received and a new briefing prepared. By the end of April six of the squadrons were dispersed between Fassberg (Nos. 3, 56 and 486) and Quackenbrück (Nos. 33, 222 and 274)—with No. 80 back in England for a brief respite. If indeed chaos reigned, it existed in the echelons of the *Luftwaffe*, as the surviving commanders sought desperately to shepherd the remaining *Staffeln* from airfield to airfield in search of fuel with which they might still fly to defend their cities. In the RAF, pilots who had had to wait patiently for the opportunity to score against the enemy now found themselves confronted by numerous targets, as Wings were ordered off against large groups of German aircraft, in the air or on the ground, being assembled for the last battles. Much of the Tempests' work (like that of the Typhoons) was to be done on the German coast and, being conveniently based, the squadrons flew numerous sweeps over the area of Kiel and Lübeck, on the lookout for German flying boats and seaplanes in the two large bays.

Most of the former *Luftwaffe* fighter airfields, not least that at Rheine (Hopsten), had been overrun; No. 80 Squadron had spent a brief period on that airfield—whose defences had claimed so many Tempests and Typhoons—before moving on to keep up with the advancing armies. On No. 3 Squadron a relatively unknown French pilot, Flight Lieutenant Pierre Clostermann, DFC, had been finding the Tempest much to his liking after a long spell on Spitfires, his tally of enemy now increasing rapidly. During the last three months he served on both Nos. 56 and 274 Squadrons as a flight commander and in April, promoted to Acting Squadron Leader, he joined No. 3 as supernumerary to Bruce Cole.

On No. 274 Squadron, ordered to patrol the Hamburg area day after day in late April, one of the flight commanders, Flight Lieutenant R. C. Stockburn, DFC, shot down a Fw 190, three Ju 88s and a He 111, and damaged three Ju 88s in the space of four sorties. No. 56 Squadron, covering the Lübeck Bay area on 2 May, destroyed seven German aircraft including three Fw 190s, two Fi 156s, a Bv 138 and a Ju 52/3mW floatplane. The following day Clostermann alone shot down a Ju 252 transport, two Do 24 flying boats, a Fw 190 and shared a Fw 190 and a Bf 109, as well as destroying two Ar 232 transports on the ground and a Bv 138 on the water. Highest-scoring Tempest pilot (a position he had assumed after the loss of Fairbanks), Clostermann's ultimate tally—including some previously shot down while flying Spitfires—included 19 Fw 190s, seven Bf 109s, two Do 24s, and single Fi 156, He 111, Ju 88, '252 and '290; of these 33 aircraft, 23 had been destroyed in the last three months.

Thus the Tempest's war ended on notes of a crescendo. Losses among aircraft had been heavy, but in most instances the pilots had been able to bring their fighters home to a forced landing, the Tempest often being summarily written off simply because replacements were now streaming in from the Maintenance Units in England. On the airfield at Fassberg during the last week, where there was little attempt at dispersal—even if space existed— there were well over one hundred Tempests, of which more than 40 were more or less severely damaged and unairworthy, as the groundcrews struggled to give the Wing a full complement of aircraft for the final spate of operations.

After the War

Unlike the Typhoon, the Tempest was to remain in service with the Royal Air Force for many more years—despite the introduction of the new jet fighters, the Meteor and Vampire.

With the end of the War in Europe and plans well underway to create a Wing of Tempest IIs for the Far East, it was anticipated that the remaining production of Tempest Vs would be adequate to equip those squadrons surviving disbandment in the 2nd Tactical Air Force with the forces of occupation. Of the total of eight squadrons with the

This veteran Tempest V, EJ598/JF-F, begins to show its age late in 1945. (Photo: via Sqn Ldr R. C. B. Ashworth)

Tempest V, six (Nos. 3, 33, 56, 80, 274 and 486) were to remain in Germany for the time being, and the other two, Nos. 222 and 501, returned to or remained in Britain, the former to start re-equipping with Meteors in October 1945 and the latter already disbanding at the end of the War.

Life for the Tempest squadrons immediately after the War was one of anti-climax and boredom, as pilots and groundcrews, who were not due for immediate demobilization, kept the minimum number of aircraft required for "Group efforts" serviceable. There was at first a number of Victory flypasts, an unaccustomed stint of close formation flying in large groups—intended as much to press home to the population of Germany the full meaning of the word "defeat" as to lend encouragement to the people of Denmark, Holland and Belgium now struggling to pick up the pieces of their shattered homes. Unfortunately these huge flypasts proved neither popular nor exhilarating among the pilots; nor were those on the ground, whose job it was to route the unwieldy formations over the spectators, aware of just how difficult it was for the formations themselves to manoeuvre. There was a number of collisions (beginning with one involving four Tempests, in which three pilots died, on 12 May) and, after no fewer than fifteen aircraft had been destroyed with further pilot losses and civilian casualties, this activity was discontinued.

Gradually the number of pilots available to staff the Tempest squadrons dwindled as the relatively large number of "Free Europeans"—the French, Dutch, Belgians, Norwegians, Danes, Poles and Czechs—left the RAF to return to their own home countries. The Commonwealth pilots remained a little longer, but that fine band of New Zealanders in No. 486 Squadron disbanded in October, having "handed in" their Tempests the previous month at Dunsfold, Surrey. No. 274 Squadron, during a stint at Armament Practice Camp in Britain during September, disbanded to become No. 174, and continued as such (with the same Tempests) in Germany until it disbanded for good in March 1946.

No. 33 Squadron gave up its Tempest Vs in November to convert to Spitfire XVIEs, and No. 56 exchanged its Tempests for Meteors in March and April, 1946. Both Nos. 3 and 80 Squadrons soldiered on with Tempests in Germany, the former changing to Vampires in April 1948 and the latter to Spitfire 24s in January that year.

Many of the Tempest V fighters that became redundant in 1946 and 1947 were re-issued to a new squadron, No. 16, which re-equipped at Fassberg in April 1946 and continued with these aircraft for a year, while others were returned to Maintenance Units in Britain and eventually to Langley. From 1948 onwards they were re-issued to the RAF in a new, though humble guise, that of target tug. Although an underwing target winch

Tempest V NV708/JCB was the "personal" aircraft of Wg Cdr J. C. Button, Wing Commander (Flying), at Wunstorf, Germany, in 1946–47. The aircraft came to grief on 7 January 1947 when its port landing gear folded up while taxying. (Photos, P. H. Dobbs, via R. C. Sturtivant).

was developed by Hawker and ML Aviation Ltd for the Tempest (and other aircraft)—and was indeed used for several years at the Armament Practice Stations—the more common procedure of simply towing the target banner off the ground on a fixed, ie, unwinched, cable, came to be adopted, and the Tempest TT Mark 5 survived in RAF service,[6] particularly with the new Operational Conversion Units, until the mid-1950s when they gave place to Mosquitos and Meteors.

The Tempest Marks II and VI

The war against Japan was just ending in August 1945 when the first Centaurus-powered Tempest Mark IIs were delivered from Maintenance Units to the first RAF squadron scheduled to take them to the Far East, No. 247. Within a fortnight all plans for Tiger Force were dropped, and future ideas for No. 247 scrapped as a completely new approach to the Tempest II was considered.

Central to these plans was the situation in India where the Imperial status of the sub-continent was due to end in 1947. It was recognized that the likely process of dismantling the 200-year-old machinery of British administration might be difficult without a continuing military presence by the British Army

[6] From 1948 RAF aircraft nomenclature was changed to the use of Arabic numerals in place of Roman for Mark numbers.

Top left, rocket-armed Tempest IIs of No 5 Squadron at Yelahanka in November 1946; the nearest aircraft is PR530/OQ-D and displays the Squadron's maple leaf badge on the engine cowling. *Above*, another Tempest II, PR836, probably of No 30 Squadron at Agra. *Upper left*, an ex-RAF Tempest II PR605, shortly after being handed over to No 11 Squadron, Royal Indian Air Force. *Lower left and below*, Indian Tempests awaiting delivery to India at Langley in 1947

and the Royal Air Force, both suffering the inevitable pressures of demobilization, particularly in the Commonwealth forces. It was therefore decided to go ahead with the delivery of Tempest IIs (which had in any case been cleared for use in the Far East), and with these aircraft to maintain a small number of squadrons on a "war footing", thereby continuing the close ties with the Royal Indian Air Force—to whom it was planned to transfer the Tempests when finally the British rule ended.

Thus it was that No. 5 Squadron, formerly flying Thunderbolts against the Japanese and now based at Bhopal, was warned to re-equip with Tempest IIs, and on 5 March, 1946, the first arrived, flown out by Hawker's Squadron Leader Frank Murphy who, three days later, gave a scintillating aerobatic display for the edification of the resident pilots. After normal conversion training, No. 5 got

Tempest II, A128 (ex-PR866 of the RAF) awaiting delivery to Pakistan at Langley in about 1948. (Photo: Hawker Aircraft Ltd.)

straight down to the business of learning the skills of rocket attacks—this being the appropriate deterrent in the event of terrorist attacks or civil rioting during the run-up to the transfer of administration.

Three further squadrons, No. 20 (ex-Spitfire XIVs), 30 (ex-Thunderbolts) and 152 (ex-Spitfire XIVs), converted to Tempest IIs in India during June and July, but with the RIAF now pressing for re-equipment with modern aircraft, Nos. 30 and 152 Squadrons handed over their aircraft to the Indians at the end of 1946 and were disbanded.

Both Nos. 5 and 20 Squadrons retained their Tempests until August 1947, moving between various airfields in the meantime. There was a number of alarms during the final weeks of the British presence, and on one occasion the Indian authorities asked for a detachment of rocket-armed Tempests to be based at an advanced landing ground at Miranshah as it was feared that local insurgents would resort to acts of terrorism against the new Indian administration. Four such Tempests (of No. 5 Squadron) were indeed despatched, and they may have represented adequate deterrent as no violence occurred. The Squadrons were eventually disbanded and their remaining Tempests handed over to No. 3 Squadron of what would soon simply be termed the Indian Air Force (having carried the "Royal" prefix for just two years).

In addition to about 50 ex-RAF Tempests transferred in India to the indigenous Service, an undertaking by the British government to supply 90 aircraft from stocks in the United Kingdom was given in 1947 for delivery during that and the following year. Capable of supporting a rather smaller air force, Pakistan negotiated to receive 24 aircraft at much the same time and these equipped Nos. 5, 9 and 14 Squadrons of a fighter-bomber Wing of the Royal Pakistan Air Force based at Lahore, Miranshah and Peshawar until replaced by Hawker Fury fighter-bombers in 1951, when

Upper, a converted Tempest FB II, MW798/HF-M, of No 54 Squadron, shown flying over Britain in 1946. *Lower*, silver-painted, rocket-equipped Tempest II PR674, pictured at Tangmere (Photo: Peter Cook, via Sqn Ldr R. C. B. Ashworth)

they were relegated to the training rôle.

Elsewhere the Tempest II continued to serve with the Royal Air Force for some years. Another squadron, intended for transfer to the Far East with Tiger Force, had been No. 183 Squadron which, like No. 247, received the first of its aircraft at Chilbolton in Hampshire during August 1945. It continued desultory training until November that year when it was disbanded and was renumbered No. 54. This became the only fully-operational, home-based Tempest II squadron when, in June 1946, it moved to Odiham. However, influence in high places was brought to bear by "old boys" of this long-established Regular Squadron and soon resulted in the Tempests being replaced by jets, and in October that year No. 54 began converting to Vampires.

Three Germany-based squadrons received Tempest IIs, Nos. 16, 26 and 33; the first-named flew the aircraft until December 1947, while No. 26 persevered until April 1949 when it too changed to Vampires.

No. 33 Squadron was the only Tempest II squadron in the RAF to fire its weapons in anger. Re-equipped with the aircraft at Fassberg in October 1946 (having only flown its Spitfire XVIEs for 11 months), the Squadron remained in Germany until July 1949 when it was ordered to pack up and sail to the Far East, taking its Tempests with it, this time to Singapore following the declaration of a state of emergency in Malaya the previous year. Recognizing the excellent reputation of the Tempest in the ground attack rôle, particularly with rockets, the Air Ministry saw fit to commit No. 33 Squadron to the thoroughly difficult and hazardous task of attacking the terrorists operating in the thick jungle environment of Malaya. Arriving at Changi on Singapore island in August, the Squadron moved north to the base of Butterworth the following month, and to Kuala Lumpur in April 1950. Numerous patrols were flown and, so far as anything could be described as successful, the Tempests operated effectively during rocket strikes on terrorist bands in the jungle. It soon became obvious, however, that patrols, which were often carried out long distances from base over extremely dense jungle, were chancy in a single-engine fighter and in due course No. 33 Squadron gave up the Tempests—in June 1951—in favour of the excellent and very popular twin-engine de Havilland Hornet.

★   ★   ★

Right, Tempest II, PR779/5R-D of No 33 Squadron, probably at Gutersloh. *Below left*, Tempest FB 2s (nearest aircraft, PR685/XC-U), of No 26 Squadron at Gutersloh in 1948. *Below right*, No 33 Squadron Tempest 2s in May 1948

The third version of the Tempest to join the RAF was the Sabre V-powered Tempest VI which, as already related, had languished almost a year while government and Air Ministry pondered a decision on the level of RAF presence appropriate in the Middle East.

Once more the problems of manning in the theatre, which in effect extended from Malta in the west to Iraq in the east, and from Cyprus in the north to Kenya in the south, gave rise to all manner of difficulties, not least in manning the numerous bases occupied in Egypt, Palestine and elsewhere, as well as the supporting Maintenance Units. Another complication was that posed by introducing an entirely new engine, the Sabre, to the theatre at just the time when any experienced engine fitter in the Service was in all likelihood eagerly awaiting his return home for "demob".

Notwithstanding these difficulties, the first Tempests were flown out to Egypt late in 1946 and were delivered in December to Nos. 6 and 249 Squadrons, the former lately arrived at Nicosia in Cyprus, and the latter at the big RAF base at Habbaniya in Iraq.

No. 6, the RAF's oldest "desert veteran", having served in the Middle East since July 1919, gave up the last of its Hurricanes, of which it had flown every main variant since 1941, in January 1947 and in July that year moved to Shallufa in Egypt as part of the Canal Zone fighter defence force. In November detachments were sent to Nairobi and Mogadishu as a precaution against civil

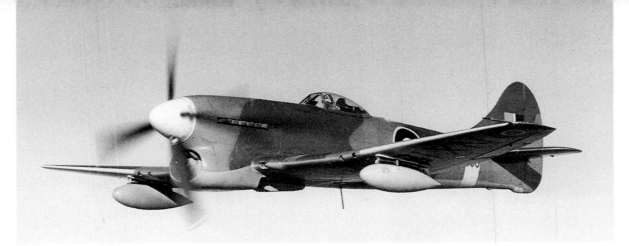

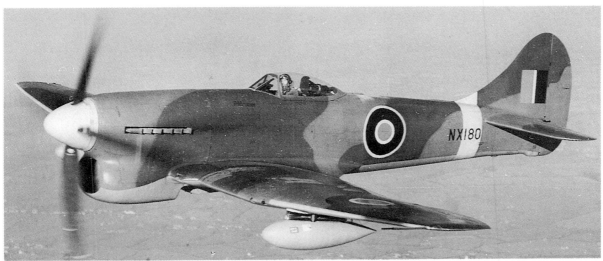

In-flight views of the Tempest VI NX180, flown by the A&AEE to clear the use of drop tanks on a "tropical" aircraft.

Tempest VIs of No 6 Squadron in the Middle East. *Below left*, NX191 displays the Squadron's "flying can-opener" badge on the side of the radiator; *below right*, NX204 sports the "gunner's stripe" down the leading edge of the fin. *Bottom left*, NX135 in natural metal finish features the "gunners stripe" flanking the Squadron Badge on the fin and, *bottom right*, the demise of JV-G, destroyed in a landing accident at Mafraq on 23 June 1950 when the undercarriage fouled a fence on the landing approach. (Photos: G. H. Bettger, J. D. R. Rawlings, A. Rosier and R. C. Sturtivant)

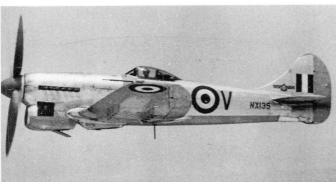

Above, a crashed No 6 Squadron Tempest VI is recovered by a tracked trailer. (Photos: G. H. Bettger)

Above, two views of No 249 Squadron Tempest 6s (NX143/GN-H and NX126/GN-A) at Habbaniya, Iraq (Photos, Richard Ward, Farnborough, and R. C. Sturtivant). *Below*, No 249 Squadron aircraft at Nicosia. The crashed aircraft, *below right*, displays the segmented spinner adopted by the Squadron.

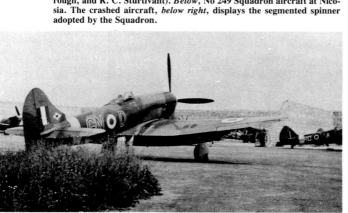

disturbances in Somalia and, although the Squadron was to have its permanent base in Egypt, No. 6 continued to move around the Middle East as detachments visited all the RAF bases in the area. It eventually started converting to Vampires in October 1949.

No. 249 Squadron, given a few Tempest Vs for a short time, retained F.6s at Habbaniya until 1949 when in April it moved to Deversoir in Egypt where it also changed to Vampires in March 1950. No. 213 Squadron, equipped with Tempest VIs at Nicosia in January 1947, followed much the same path as No. 6, changing to Vampires at the end of 1949, while No. 8—another very long established "Middle East squadron"—flew its Tempest F.6s at Khormaksar, Aden, until July 1949 when it converted to Bristol Brigands.

Last of the Tempest Mark 6 Squadrons was No. 39, newly re-formed at Nairobi/Eastleigh in Kenya on 1 April 1948; it, however, only retained the single-engine aircraft until February the following year when it prepared to move to Egypt to convert to night fighting with Mosquitos.

Thus by 1951 the last Tempests were finally disappearing from "front line" service with the Royal Air Force. Since the War they had, however, served on a number of training units and establishments, despite a pervading parsimony by the Exchequer towards the air force which imposed considerable difficulties with regard to complex engines such as the Sabre and Centaurus—particularly at a time when the euphemistically described "simple" jet engine was demanding and receiving every possible priority.

Nevertheless, so long as Tempests remained in service with operational squadrons, they were required to train both new pilots and to convert those of longer experience when changing squadron. Apart from the late wartime use of a few Tempest Vs by the anti-aircraft co-operation squadron, No 287, based mainly at Hornchurch, Mark Vs performed target-towing duties with Nos. 1, 2 and 3 Armament Practice Stations at Fairwood Common, Acklington and Charter Hall respectively between the end of 1945 and—in the case of Acklington—the mid-1950s, and also at the Sylt gunnery training station. The Central Gunnery School also employed TT Mark 5s from about 1948 at Leconfield.

For training future squadron and flight commanders, newly posted to the operational squadrons, the Central Fighter Establishment at West Raynham in Norfolk flew a number of both Tempest 2s and 5s between 1947 and 1949, while on an even more "advanced" level the Mark 2 was one of the favourite fighters with the Empire Test Pilots' School at Farnborough during the late 1940s.

Finally, as well as some Mark Vs flown by No. 17 Operational Training Unit at Silverstone and Swinderby during 1945 and 1946, the Tempest was widely used by the Operational Conversion Units which came into existence shortly after the War,

namely No. 226 OCU at Stradishall in Suffolk, No. 229 at Chivenor in North Devon and No. 233 at Pembrey in South Wales.

★   ★   ★

The Typhoon and Tempest left an indelible mark on the pages of RAF history. Neither was an aeroplane that had ever suffered fools gladly, yet each endeared itself to the pilot faced with a hazardous task to perform—and none was so perilous as the work undertaken low over the battlefields of Europe in the last two years of the War, whether it involved the destruction of an enemy tank or headquarters, or a vicious air battle with the excellent fighters of a desperate enemy.

And when peace eventually returned, the superb Tempest carried the Royal Air Force forward through the lean years of transition from piston engine to jet, going about the often humdrum business of the Service, whether patrolling the uneasy skies of a divided Germany or searching out a tiny band of elusive bandits in the far-off jungles of Malaya.

Sadly there is but a handful of surviving examples of aircraft, none currently airworthy, to remind one of this departed pair of classic aeroplanes. It is indeed to be hoped that care and perseverance will be rewarded for those who labour to return such an aircraft back to its appropriate element. No mere words and pictures can possibly convey the sight and sound of those "mighty fighters".

Not airworthy, yet well preserved Tempest survivor, NV778 (ex-SN217), seen at Abingdon on 14 June 1968. (Photo: Richard Ward, Farnborough, Neg Ref Q23/35)

A PICTURE MISCELLANY

While every effort has been made in the course of the foregoing Chapters to illustrate aircraft referred to in the text it is inevitable that to do so in every instance would involve lengthy interruptions in the narrative. In the following pages is shown a variety of pictures illustrating "fringe aspects" of the narrative, as well as additional close-up and complementary views of the aircraft themselves.

Front view of the Tornado HG641 as it was originally completed in 1941 with the Bristol Centaurus radial in its archaic installation, see page 24. With its enormous oil cooler fairing and crude high-mass flow exhaust pipe, it is not difficult to understand Sydney Camm's reluctance to pursue the development of radial engine single-seat fighters in the late 'thirties. (Photo: Sydney Camm Collection, dated October 1941)

HG641 as it reappeared in November 1942, with attempts made to improve the engine cowling. The white band round the rear fuselage is in fact the temporary "strengthening" strip bonded on the transport joint pending investigation of the loss of tail units by Typhoons at that time. As with the majority of experimental aircraft, the Tornado was painted yellow underneath (though depicted as black in this "ortho" film photograph); in the interests of wartime security, recognition diagrams issued to the Observer Corps and anti-aircraft gunners did not carry the names of the aircraft but were simply referred to by numbered experimental aircraft—the Centaurus Tornado was accorded the number 154. (Photo: Sydney Camm Collection, dated November 1942)

Close-up views of the Typhoon IB, R8694, with annular radiator and fan-assisted cooling, see page 42. It is worth noting that Napier achieved a much neater exhaust system in this installation than in the standard Typhoon. (Photos: D. Napier & Sons, Neg Nos 166OW, 166OWA and 166OWB)

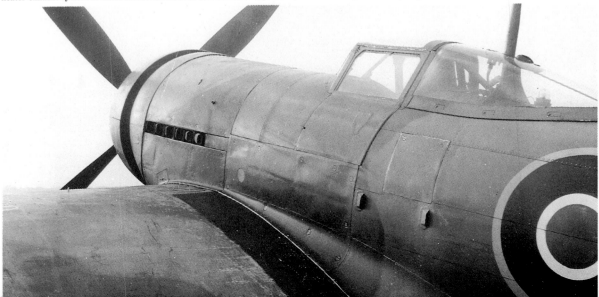

The pilots of No 56 Squadron, the first to be equipped with Typhoons. Although the names of all the Squadron's pilots are known it has unfortunately proved impossible to put "names to faces", and the exact date on which the photographs were taken is not known, although the configuration of the aircraft with faired cannon and yellow wing band suggests late 1942 or early 1943. (Photos: Author's Collection)

Prototype trial installation of the Stage B (sometimes referred to as Scheme B) canopy on a DTD Typhoon at Langley; the port car door is open, necessitating closure of the overhead panel. Retention of some struts and frames under the rear canopy still restricted the pilot's rearward field of vision, although this was progressively improved. (Photo: Hawker Aircraft Neg No TS19L dated 2 August 1941)

Sqn Ldr A. C. Johnstone's Typhoon IB, EK183/US-A of No 56 Squadron at Matlaske, Norfolk, in 1943; the yellow recognition stripe is just visible on the port wing. (Photo: via Sqn Ldr R. C. B. Ashworth)

Typhoon IB EJ927 of No 257 Squadron at Warmwell in 1943. Like the aircraft on the left it features the Scheme B canopy and both have faired rear-view mirrors. (Photo: via Sq Ldr R. C. B. Ashworth)

Starboard view of Wing Commander Denys Gillam's Typhoon "ZZ" in company with an aircraft of No 266 Squadron at Duxford in 1942; see pages 62–63. (Photo: via R. Ward, Whitstable)

163

Armourers loading a Typhoon with 500-lb bombs. The aircraft is unusual in possessing Oerlikon rather than Hispano cannon with forward recoil springs. (Photo: Martin P. Pegg, via R. Ward, Farnborough)

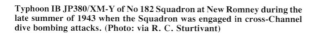

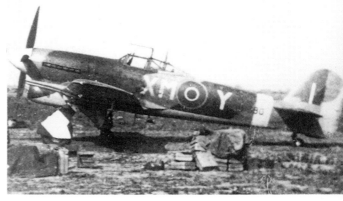

Typhoon IB JP380/XM-Y of No 182 Squadron at New Romney during the late summer of 1943 when the Squadron was engaged in cross-Channel dive bombing attacks. (Photo: via R. C. Sturtivant)

Canadian personnel carrying out major servicing on Typhoon MN716/F3-A of No 438 Squadron, RCAF, on a forward airfield on the continent, probably early in 1945. (Photo: M. D. Howley, via R. Ward, Farnborough)

Maintenance work on another No 438 Squadron Typhoon. With support sorties frequently ordered at very short notice, it was common practice to stock bombs (like the 1,000-pounders, seen here) around the dispersal bays rather than having to wait for them to be brought from a central bomb dump. (Photo: via R. Ward, Farnborough)

Close-up of the personal markings on the starboard side of Wing Commander Gillam's Typhoon. As explained on page 63, the aircraft acquired modified fuselage roundels, and presumably the remainder of the aircraft was repainted at the same time, with rough tape masking over the wing commander's personal insignia—the name "Penny" and a knight mounted on a white winged horse. (Photo: Author's Collection)

Pilot and groundcrew with Typhoon R8835 of No 181 Squadron. The photograph was probably taken in 1943 when the Squadron was converting to the ground attack rôle, as practice bomb carriers can just be discerned on the underwing pylon. The aircraft is an early example with Stage B canopy and unfaired cannon barrels, and the retention of the yellow wing band—visible behind the inboard cannon—without underwing black-and-white stripes is interesting. (Photo: via R. Ward, Whitstable)

Among the measures adopted as part of "Operation Spartan" as the time of the Normandy landing approached was to create repair units in the field, so as to avoid lengthy delays in returning lesser damaged aircraft to maintenance units in the rear. No 511 Forward Repair Unit was one such. On the right is shown Typhoon EK128 which had suffered Category B damage with No 174 Squadron on 30 January 1944. *Below right*, JR501 after repair by No 511 FRU; this aircraft had suffered Category B damage with No 198 Squadron and went on to serve with Nos 184 and 175 Squadrons. *Above*, No 511 FRU's unofficial "badge", stencilled on the fin of repaired aircraft.

As a means of training ground fitters, aircraft with "flying hours expired" were delivered to the Schools of Technical Training. The aircraft shown on the left, formerly JR135 and carrying the codes PA-H of No 55 OTU, was re-serialled 5345M as a Ground Instruction Machine and was in all likelihood employed to train engine fitters. (Photo: via R. C. Sturtivant)

Right, twilight of the gods. Typhoons wearing the unit codes of No 56 OTU (SW638/HQ-E and SW593 are identifiable) dumped at the edge of an airfield in Britain in 1945 to await the salvage of radio, instruments, armament and engine, before being scrapped. (Photo: via Sqn Ldr R. C. B. Ashworth)

A Typhoon bomber, JR128/HF-L, of No 183 Squadron. The aircraft features the exhaust manifold fairing introduced retrospectively at maintenance units in 1943 in an attempt to "tidy up" the airflow round the stubs. Although a slight improvement in performance was achieved, some squadrons discarded the fairings owing to the complication imposed on removal of the engine panels for maintenance. (Photo: Author's Collection)

Providing comparison with the aircraft in the upper photograph is this later Typhoon, MN524, possibly seen during a manufacturer's test flight; the exhaust fairings are not fitted. The picture also gives an excellent indication of the much improved field of vision bestowed by the single-piece sliding canopy. (Photo: via R. C. Sturtivant)

Ground level view of MN882/TP-E of No 198 Squadron on a continental airfield, probably late in 1944. The aircraft, equipped with rocket rails and four-blade propeller, has had its AEAF recognition stripes reduced to the undersides only (ordered in September that year), and the individual aircraft letter is repeated at the top of the fin and below the spinner; this particular aircraft also repeats the Squadron codes on the fin. (Photo: via R. Ward, Whitstable)

The Typhoon's Sabre was always a tricky engine to start, and freezing weather didn't help matters. In this picture groundcrewmen are blowing hot air from a generator truck through the radiator and oil cooler matrices during the winter of 1944–45. (Photo: via R. Ward, Whitstable)

Fine weather and foul with the Canadian Wing in 1945. The upper picture shows armourers struggling with heavy belts of 20-mm ammunition through the quagmire that became such a feature of Dutch and Belgian airfields during the winter of 1944–45. *Above*, Canadian groundcrew of No 440 Squadron relax in the sun. Just visible beyond the fuselage of the Typhoon MN720 is a damaged aircraft lying on its belly; indeed this is the same aircraft as that depicted below, being removed from the runway after a wheels-up landing. Such was the replacement situation that the aircraft was almost certainly written off without any attempt at repair. (Photos: RAF Museum, Hendon)

The annular radiator/ducted spinner Tempest V, NV768, pictured during a rare visit to Langley from Napier. (Photo: Author's Collection)

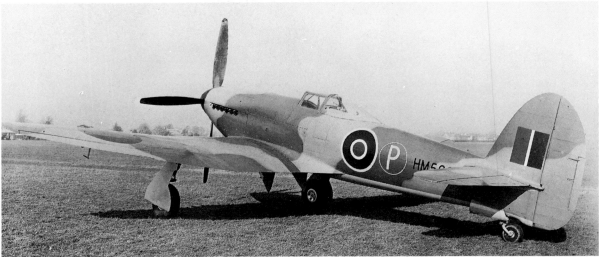

Tempest I metamorphosis. *Above*, two views of the aircraft, HM599, in February 1944 showing to good effect the generous wing radiators and the much modified Stage B canopy originally fitted. This, the fastest Tempest of all, gave promise of tremendous potential but arrived just too late to confirm the interest originally demonstrated by the Air Ministry, and by 1946 the aircraft was languishing in a protective cocoon (*seen below*) prior to being scrapped. (Photos: *Above*, Hawker Aircraft Ltd., *below*, via Sqn Ldr R. C. B. Ashworth)

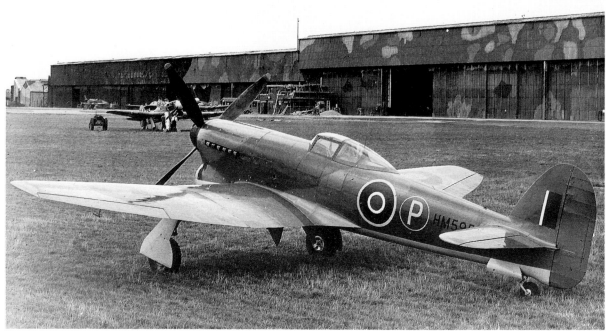

The prototype Tempest V, HM595, outside the Langley flight sheds in 1942 when still fitted with the Typhoon-style tail unit. In the background may be seen the new watch office and control tower in the course of construction—surely one of the worst-sited control towers ever conceived; it was widely referred to as the "blind flying watch office", two-thirds of the airfield circuit being invisible.

An aerial view of Langley taken on 22 September 1945, showing early Tempest VIs and the Fury (monoplane) prototype NX802 outside the final assembly shops and flying control building. In the right foreground may be seen the Tempest V SN354 prior to installation of the Vickers 40-mm P-guns—note the single wing blisters. (Photo: Author's Collection)

Two fine in-flight views of an early Tempest V Series 1, JN757, probably the work of Cyril Peckham who did much contract photography for Hawker Aircraft Limited for over twenty years. (Photos: Sydney Camm Collection)

TEMPEST 6 AIRCRAFT OF THE MIDDLE EAST SQUADRONS

Above, a Tempest 6 of No 6 Squadron in silver finish fires a pair of three-inch rockets (with concrete practice heads) over an armament range in the Middle East. (Photo: via Sqn Ldr R. C. B. Ashworth). *Right*, a No 6 Squadron Tempest 6, NX154/JD-K; just visible are two Mark 8 "zero-length" rocket rails under the starboard wing. (Photo: A. Tozier, via J. D. R. Rawlings)

Above and right, two grief-stricken Tempests of No 39 Squadron at Khartoum in the Sudan in 1948 or 1949. (Both photos: D. Howley, via R. L. Ward, Farnborough, Neg Refs F26C/5/5A and F26C/6/22A)

Above and right, two views of a Tempest 6 at Dijon, France, in July 1950. Scarcely visible is the elephant marking of No 249 Squadron; this Squadron had given up Tempests the previous March and the use of drop tanks suggests that the aircraft was being ferried home when the photos were taken. Note also the segmented spinner, a feature adopted by No 249 Squadron. (Photo: E. Mihaly, via Sqn Ldr R. C. B. Ashworth)

Contributing in no small degree to the Tempest V's manoeuvrability and sensitivity of control were the new aileron spring tabs, introduced in place of the Typhoon's "bent tabs". In this picture of the first production aircraft, JN729, being flown by Bill Humble, the port spring tab can be seen as an unpainted strip on the aileron. Late production aircraft also featured such tabs in the rudder. (Photo: Author's Collection)

Apart from affording interest in the Hawker F.2/43 Fury prototype NX802—itself a direct development of the Tempest II—this 1946 Langley photograph also includes a No 33 Squadron Tempest V, SN213/5R-S, in silver finish (*background, left*) and, visible over the Fury's nose, the Tempest V JN876, coded RH, formerly the personal aircraft of Air Marshal Sir Roderick M. Hill, KCB, MC, AFC, when AOC-in-C Fighter Command the previous year. (Photo: Author's Collection)

Top, close-up view of the ML target winch under the port wing of the prototype Tempest TT 5 SN329 (see page 123). *Above left*, cockpit of SN329 with the winch control panel, windmill speed and cable pay-out indicators. *Above right*, the target tug's tail unit, showing the protective cables (on all Tempest tugs, whether employing fuselage or underwing winch installation) intended to prevent the banner cable from fouling the tail controls. *Below*, front view of SN329 with target winch under the port wing and a drop tank under the starboard. (Photos: Author's Collection)

Right, a Tempest TT 5, NV960, with under-fuselage target cable installation; just visible on the right is the tail of a Hawker Sea Fury 20 target tug. (Photo: via Sqn Ldr R. C. B. Ashworth)

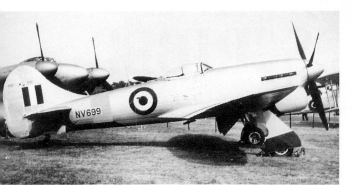

Left, another Tempest TT 5, NV699, this time at a post-War air display; the colour scheme featured silver upper surfaces and black and yellow diagonal bars underneath; the band round the rear fuselage was also in "training yellow". (Photo: Author's Collection)

Right, a Tempest TT 5, SN261, carrying the codes of the Central Gunnery School in 1949. (Photo: Arthur Pearcy, via Sqn Ldr R. C. B. Ashworth)

Left, Tempest TT 5. SN260/WH-17, of the Armament Practice Station, Sylt. (Photo: M. C. Gray, via R. C. Sturtivant)

Right, a Tempest TT 5, SN346, crashed on take-off at Sylt on 5 January 1953, probably as the result of having failed to get airborne from an icy runway while towing a flag target. (Photo: via R. Ward, Farnborough)

THE TYPHOON AND TEMPEST DESCRIBED

The Hawker Typhoon was a single-engine, single-seat low-wing monoplane fighter with retractable undercarriage. Construction was of all-metal and power was provided by a 2,200-hp Napier Sabre II liquid-cooled in-line engine driving a three- or four-blade de Havilland constant-speed propeller.

Fuselage

The primary construction of the centre and front fuselage comprised a rectangular section of box structure with rigidly braced steel tubes interconnected by riveted flat plate joints and machined metal pressings. To these tubes were welded numerous pick-up points with which external light alloy, detachable panels engaged with rotating studs. At the front of the box structure were a pair of extended triangular cantilever fabricated assemblies extending forward on the left- and right-hand sides, terminating with two heavy-duty mounting pads which constituted the front engine bearers; the rear engine mounting feet were semi-flexibly attached to extension lugs at the upper main wing spar attachments. A single bulkhead was located aft of the engine and between this and the upper frame carrying the front of the windscreen structure was located the engine oil tank. Aft of this was located the cockpit compartment.

Early Typhoons featured a double frame behind the pilot's seat forming the front contour of the canopy fairing; to this frame was attached the pilot's armour backplate; these aircraft featured front-hinged doors on each side of the fuselage, each door incorporating wind-down transparent panels; the overhead transparent panel was hinged on the port side to open upwards, fastening closed along the top edge of the starboard door; both doors and overhead panel were jettisonable, and access to the cockpit was normally through the starboard door.

Later aircraft had the fuselage frames reduced in height so as to omit the structure of a hood fairing; the car doors were omitted and a single-piece, transparent sliding hood was fitted, engaging in rails on the cockpit sills and a central rail on top of the rear fuselage.

The rear fuselage structure was of monocoque construction employing oval-shaped former frames and near-straight longitudinal stringers to which light alloy sheet was flush-riveted. The front and rear primary structures were joined together by four heavy-duty, quickly removable bolts. The rearmost section of the fuselage was a separately constructed unit, permanently attached on a transport joint comprising a pair of heavy gauge frames, the skin sheets butting together, flush-riveted by four rows of rivets and covered at the joint by further flush-riveted fish plates. The rearmost fuselage section incorporated the vertical fin integrally.

The forward-retracting tailwheel, without enclosing doors, was mounted on a pair of crosswise tubes attached at locally strengthened points to the bottom fuselage formers at the location where the fin front spar extended through the rear fuselage bulkhead, with access panels on either side of the fuselage beneath the tailplane.

Wings

The mainplanes were constructed on two main spars, front and rear, and comprised slightly anhedralled centre-sections and dihedralled outer sections. In the centre-section both spars were heavy-gauge T-beams webbed with a fabricated N-truss of box-section members. The front wing spar was attached to the fuselage on the lower members of the primary structure forward of the main front bulkhead, and the rear wing spar was attached to a multiple-member joint in the fuselage primary structure just forward of the front frame of the monocoque section.

The wing centre-sections accommodated the main landing gear units which, hinged at a point just inboard of the wing joint with the outer sections, retracted into bays between the centre-section wing spars. Two fuel tanks were located immediately aft of the wheel bays and two more forward of the front spars.

The outer wing section spars were of plain web manufacture, pierced with multiple, circular lightening holes; nose formers were attached to the front of the mainspar, with interspar ribs interrupted to accommodate the gun bays; to provide additional wing rigidity an intermediate spanwise spar was incorporated at the front of the gun bays. Wing skinning was riveted to the flanges of multiple spanwise stringers.

The two gun bays each accommodated a pair of Hispano Mark I 20-mm cannon, each gun being fed from magazines outboard. The gun barrels projected through the front spar and extended prominently forward of the wing leading edge.

Strongpoints, wiring and piping were provided to permit the carriage of two 44-gallon drop tanks or bombs of 250-lb, 500-lb, or 1,000-lb on auxiliary rack fairings, attachable to the outer wing undersurfaces immediately outboard of the inner and outer wing joints; up to 16 rocket projectiles (three-inch with 60-lb warheads) could be carried on Mark I RP rails attachable under the outer wing sections. A range of other external stores, including smoke tanks, napalm bombs, supply containers etc, could be carried on the store racks.

The metal ailerons were hinged to the rear of the outer wing rear spar, with landing flaps extending inboard from the ailerons to the fuselage, split at the joint between wing centre and outer sections. The Frise ailerons incorporated a ground-adjustable trim tab.

Tail surfaces

The vertical fin was a multiple-spar structure manufactured integrally with the rearmost fuselage section. To the rearmost spar, an extension of the fuselage sternpost member, was hinged the fabric-covered rudder which incorporated a large, parallel-chord servo trim tab.

The cantilever tailplane was a two-spar structure with interspar ribs and nose formers, the interconnected metal-covered elevators being hinged to the rear spar, each including a servo trim tab.

Main landing gear

The main landing gear comprised Vickers oleopneumatic shock-absorber legs terminating in mountings for inboard wheels with Dunlop tyres. Adjustably-attached fairings retracted with the wheel units to seal the landing gear in its bays, the wheels being covered by separate D-doors hinged

on either side of the centreline of the under-fuselage. Retraction was by hydraulic operation with an electrical sequencing unit to ensure the D-doors closed last to cover the wheels.

Powerplant and ancillary services

Power was provided by a single 2,200-hp Napier Sabre IIA or 2,200-hp Sabre IIB, 24-cylinder sleeve-valve, liquid-cooled, two-speed supercharged, side-canted H-type in-line engine, mounted on and between the cantilever extensions forward of the front fuselage primary structure. The engine exhausted through six twin-branched stub manifolds on each side of the aircraft's nose. (See below for detailed engine specification.)

The engine drove a three- or four-blade de Havilland propeller, pitch-changing for constant-speeding being effected hydraulically and automatically.

The large coolant radiator was mounted rigidly, suspended in double metal straps from the engine mounting cantilever structure. Cooling air passed through the radiator matrix and discharged through an aperture duct whose exit carried a controllable shutter flap. Incorporated as a central core of the coolant radiator was the engine oil cooler.

An engine-charged hydraulic system operated the flaps and landing gear retraction, with a manually-operated emergency sub-system. An engine-pressurized pneumatic system provided power for the mainwheel brakes and for gun cocking.

Napier Sabre II

The engine consisted of two single-piece, cast light alloy cylinder blocks, left and right, each with 12 parallel-bore cylinders; these cylinder blocks each bolted to a left and right half of a cast light alloy crankcase which bolted together vertically on the centreline of the engine.

Cylinders

Bore, 5.0 inches; stroke 4.75 inches; total engine capacity 2,240 cu in (36.65 litres). Compression ratio, 7:1. Each cylinder bank had separate induction faces above and below, and an exhaust face between the upper and lower cylinder banks. Twelve jacketed passages led from the exhaust ports to six ejector-type exhaust stubs attached to the cylinder block between the cylinder heads. Each cylinder had three inlet and two exhaust ports and a compound sleeve scraper ring. Coolant jackets round cylinders were provided with drilled passages between them. There were coolant galleries on each side of the induction faces above and below each block, with coolant U-channels connecting outer galleries cast on the front of the blocks. The inner side of each block was grooved along the centreline to accommodate the sleeve-drive worm-shaft.

Cylinder heads

Each cylinder head was a light alloy casting with coolant jacketing. It was provided with a compression ring and two phosphor-bronze sparking plug adaptors and was attached to the cylinder block by seven studs. There were also holes in the head flange for two of the long crankcase studs which passed through the cylinder block to the head. Four coolant jacket transfer holes and the head itself were sealed by rubber composition rings.

Sleeves

The steel sleeves each incorporated four ports—two inlet, one exhaust and one combined inlet/exhaust; the sleeves were strengthened locally at the inner ends for the driving pins.

Sleeve drive

A case-hardened hollow-steel drive-shaft ran in 14 bearings in the groove in the inner side of each cylinder block; each shaft was in two halves, joined by flanged coupling in the form of an external sleeve, and there were three worm gears machined on each half of the shaft. A drive gear bolted to the front end of the shaft meshed with an idler gear which was in turn driven by an engine reduction gear pinion. Between each pair of upper and lower cylinders there was a light alloy pedestal housing a wormwheel and two horizontal crank arms with ball and socket joints into which the driving pins of the upper and lower sleeves fitted. The bronze wormwheels which drove the sleeve cranks were held in position by twin roller bearing races mounted in each pedestal housing. The cranks, being solid, necessitated split ball joints. The entire assembly was positively lubricated by the low pressure oil system circuit.

Pistons

The pistons were machined from light alloy; each was provided with one compression and one compression-cum-scraper ring above the gudgeon pin, and one wedge-action scraper ring below it. Hollow, fully-floating gudgeon pins were retained by hardened steel washers and circlips.

Connecting rods

The steel H-section forked and plain connecting rods were assembled in horizontally-opposed pairs, each pair having a common split steel-backed lead-bronze bearing. The fixed bronze small-end bearings were lubricated by splash only.

Crankshafts

The engine incorporated two interchangeable six-throw crankshafts, one above the other, with a lead-coated lead-bronze lined bearing between each throw. The crank webs were drilled and the seven journals and six crankpins were bored to provide oil passages. A spur pinion was shrunk on the forward end of each shaft, these driving four compound gears in the propeller reduction gear; the rear ends of the shafts were flanged and bolted to the upper shaft flange was a spur gear driven by the starter through an idler gear in the crankcase.

Crankcase

Each half of the crankcase was stiffened by five cross webs, the front and rear walls and the five webs providing housings for the propeller shaft rear bearing and the crankshaft bearings. Facings for the upper auxiliary unit cover and the starter hand turning gear casing were provided above, and for bottom cover unit and oil sump below. The front cover unit housed the propeller shaft, reduction gear and sleeve drive gears, and comprised the gear carrier and the truncated cone-shaped propeller shaft cover which were attached to the front faces of the crankcase halves by equally-spaced bolts and studs. The supercharger unit was attached to the rear end of the crankcase halves by a series of bolts and studs.

The crankcase halves were assembled together by bolts and studs arranged in four rows, the outer rows each having six crankcase bolts passing through both halves, and each inner row having six long tie-bolts which passed through both crankcase and cylinder blocks. The central cross web also took eight centre-bearing bolts disposed in four rows. In the front web there were four internal steel studs to secure the propeller shaft's rear bearing.

Reduction gear

Gear ratio, 0.2742:1. The propeller shaft helical gear was located on the centreline of the engine with four compound reduction gears disposed symmetrically around it; spur pinions on the front ends of the crankshafts meshed with the rear gears of the upper and lower pairs of reduction gears.

Induction

A special Hobson injector-type carburettor was mounted on the side of the intake bend of the supercharger; this injector incorporated the fuel-entering valve, boost control, accelerator pump and a pressure regulating valve. The fuel was supplied to the nozzle from the injector, the nozzle being situated inside the spinner which, being fitted on the end of the impeller shaft, fed the fuel into the eye of the impeller in a fine spray.

Fuel pump

Fuel was supplied to the injector by a Pesco pump of the vane type which was bolted to the underside of the sump; a relief valve, embodied in the pump, was differentially controlled to compensate for variations in atmospheric pressure.

THE HAWKER TYPHOON Mk. IB

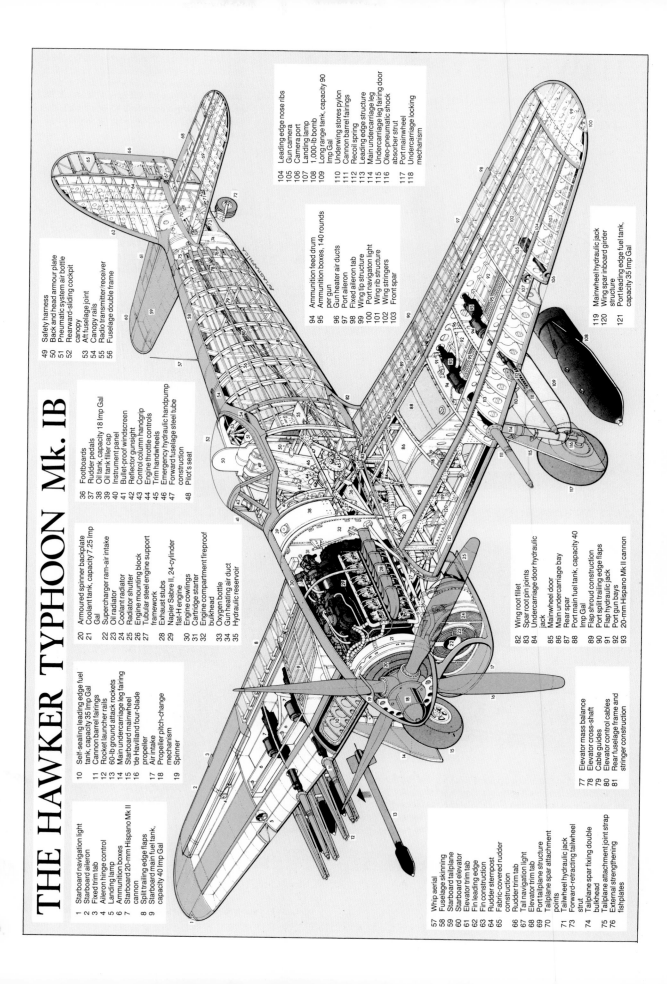

1 Starboard navigation light
2 Starboard aileron
3 Fixed trim tab
4 Aileron hinge control
5 Landing lamp
6 Ammunition boxes
7 Starboard 20-mm Hispano Mk II cannon
8 Split trailing edge flaps
9 Starboard main fuel tank, capacity 40 Imp Gal

10 Self-sealing leading edge fuel tank, capacity 35 Imp Gal
11 Cannon barrel fairings
12 Rocket launcher rails
13 60-lb ground attack rockets
14 Main undercarriage leg fairing
15 Starboard mainwheel
16 de Havilland four-blade propeller
17 Air intake
18 Propeller pitch-change mechanism
19 Spinner

20 Armoured spinner backplate
21 Coolant tank, capacity 7.25 Imp Gal
22 Supercharger ram-air intake
23 Oil radiator
24 Coolant radiator
25 Radiator shutter
26 Engine mounting block
27 Tubular steel engine support framework
28 Napier Sabre II, 24-cylinder flat-H engine
29 Exhaust stubs
30 Engine cowlings
31 Cartridge starter
32 Engine compartment fireproof bulkhead
33 Oxygen bottle
34 Gun heating air duct
35 Hydraulic reservoir

36 Footboards
37 Rudder pedals
38 Oil tank, capacity 18 Imp Gal
39 Oil tank filler cap
40 Instrument panel
41 Bullet-proof windscreen
42 Reflector gunsight
43 Control column handgrip
44 Engine throttle controls
45 Trim handwheels
46 Emergency hydraulic handpump
47 Forward fuselage steel tube construction
48 Pilot's seat

49 Safety harness
50 Back and head armour plate
51 Pneumatic system air bottle
52 Rearward-sliding cockpit canopy
53 Aft fuselage joint
54 Canopy rails
55 Radio transmitter/receiver
56 Fuselage double frame

57 Whip aerial
58 Fuselage skinning
59 Starboard tailplane
60 Starboard elevator
61 Elevator trim tab
62 Fin leading edge
63 Fin construction
64 Rudder sternpost
65 Fabric-covered rudder construction
66 Rudder trim tab
67 Tail navigation light
68 Elevator trim tab
69 Port tailplane structure
70 Tailplane spar attachment points
71 Tailwheel hydraulic jack
73 Forward-retracting tailwheel strut
74 Tailplane spar fixing double bulkhead
75 Tailplane attachment joint strap
76 External strengthening fishplates

77 Elevator mass balance
78 Elevator cross-shaft
79 Cable guides
80 Elevator control cables
81 Rear fuselage frame and stringer construction

82 Wing root fillet
83 Spar root pin joints
84 Undercarriage door hydraulic jack
85 Mainwheel door
86 Main undercarriage bay
87 Rear spar
88 Port main fuel tank, capacity 40 Imp Gal
89 Flap shroud construction
90 Port split trailing edge flaps
91 Flap hydraulic jack
92 Port gun bays
93 20-mm Hispano Mk II cannon

94 Ammunition feed drum
95 Ammunition boxes, 140 rounds per gun
96 Gun heater air ducts
97 Port aileron
98 Fixed aileron tab
99 Wing tip structure
100 Port navigation light
101 Wing rib structure
102 Wing stringers
103 Front spar

104 Leading edge nose ribs
105 Gun camera
106 Camera port
107 Landing lamp
108 1,000-lb bomb
109 Long range tank, capacity 90 Imp Gal
110 Underwing stores pylon
111 Cannon barrel fairings
112 Recoil spring
113 Leading edge structure
114 Main undercarriage leg
115 Undercarriage leg fairing door
116 Oleo-pneumatic shock absorber strut
117 Port mainwheel
118 Undercarriage locking mechanism

119 Mainwheel hydraulic jack
120 Wing spar inboard girder structure
121 Port leading edge fuel tank, capacity 35 Imp Gal

HAWKER TYPHOON IB

Rocket-armed ground-attack fighter as flown over Northern France in June and July 1944

Aircraft 'T-Tommy', JP963, of No 198 Squadron based at Funtington, Sussex, and Hurn, Hants, June 1944. Depicted here armed with eight rocket projectiles with 60-lb warheads, JP963 accompanied the Squadron to Normandy the following month but was lost on operations in August.

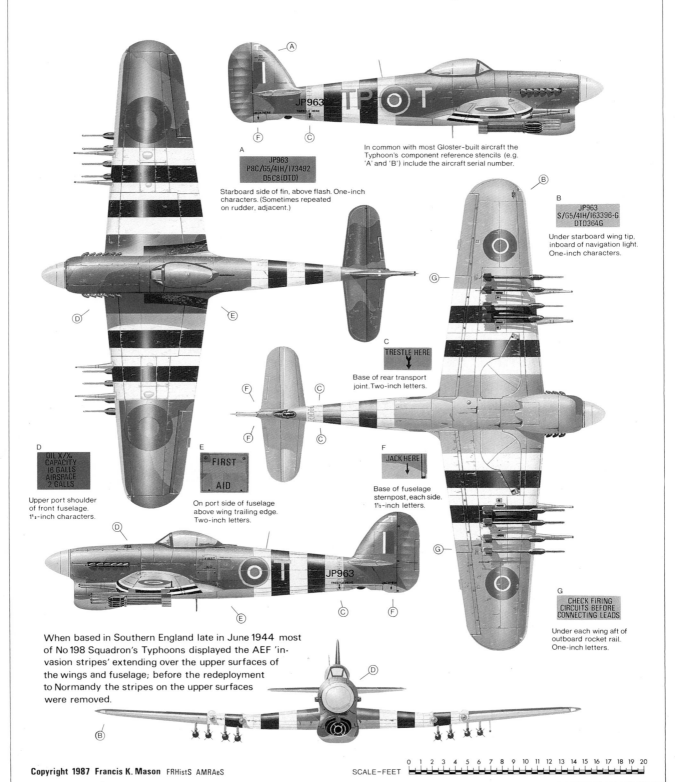

In common with most Gloster-built aircraft the Typhoon's component reference stencils (e.g. 'A' and 'B') include the aircraft serial number.

A
JP963
P8C/G5/4IH/I73492
D5C8(DTD)

Starboard side of fin, above flash. One-inch characters. (Sometimes repeated on rudder, adjacent.)

B
JP963
S/G5/4IH/I63396-G
DTD364G

Under starboard wing tip, inboard of navigation light. One-inch characters.

C
TRESTLE HERE ↓

Base of rear transport joint. Two-inch letters.

D
OIL X/X
CAPACITY
16 GALLS
AIRSPACE
2 GALLS

Upper port shoulder of front fuselage. 1½-inch characters.

E
FIRST AID

On port side of fuselage above wing trailing edge. Two-inch letters.

F
JACK HERE ↓

Base of fuselage sternpost, each side. 1½-inch letters.

G
CHECK FIRING
CIRCUITS BEFORE
CONNECTING LEADS

Under each wing aft of outboard rocket rail. One-inch letters.

When based in Southern England late in June 1944 most of No 198 Squadron's Typhoons displayed the AEF 'invasion stripes' extending over the upper surfaces of the wings and fuselage; before the redeployment to Normandy the stripes on the upper surfaces were removed.

SCALE–FEET   0 1 2 3 4 5 6 7 8 9 10 11 12 13 14 15 16 17 18 19 20

HAWKER TEMPEST V

As flown as interceptor fighter against the V-1 flying bombs in July 1944

Aircraft 'Z-Zebra', JN808, of No 3 (Fighter) Squadron was an early production Tempest V, upgraded to Series 2 standard with short-barrel 20-mm Hispano cannon. Commanded by Sqn. Ldr. A.S. Dredge, DSO, DFC, AFC, No 3 Squadron alone destroyed 176 of the flying bombs during July 1944 while operating as a component unit of the Newchurch Wing.

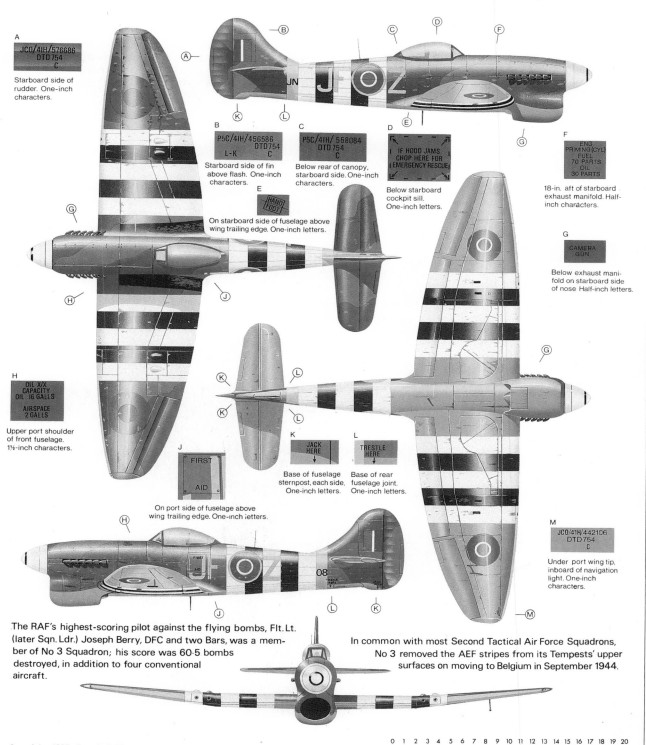

A

JCO/41H/576686
DTD 754
C

Starboard side of rudder. One-inch characters.

B

P5C/41H/456586
DTD 754
L-K   C

Starboard side of fin above flash. One-inch characters.

C

P5C/41H/ 558084
DTD 754
C

Below rear of canopy, starboard side. One-inch characters.

D

IF HOOD JAMS
CHOP HERE FOR
EMERGENCY RESCUE

Below starboard cockpit sill. One-inch letters.

E

HAND|
FOOT

On starboard side of fuselage above wing trailing edge. One-inch letters.

F

ENG.
PRIMING (CYL)
FUEL
70 PARTS
OIL.
30 PARTS

18-in. aft of starboard exhaust manifold. Half-inch characters.

G

CAMERA
GUN.

Below exhaust manifold on starboard side of nose. Half-inch letters.

H

OIL X/X
CAPACITY
OIL 16 GALLS
AIRSPACE
2 GALLS

Upper port shoulder of front fuselage. 1½-inch characters.

J

FIRST
AID

On port side of fuselage above wing trailing edge. One-inch letters.

K

JACK
HERE

Base of fuselage sternpost, each side. One-inch letters.

L

TRESTLE
HERE

Base of rear fuselage joint. One-inch letters.

M

JCO/41H/442106
DTD 754
C

Under port wing tip, inboard of navigation light. One-inch characters.

The RAF's highest-scoring pilot against the flying bombs, Flt. Lt. (later Sqn. Ldr.) Joseph Berry, DFC and two Bars, was a member of No 3 Squadron; his score was 60·5 bombs destroyed, in addition to four conventional aircraft.

In common with most Second Tactical Air Force Squadrons, No 3 removed the AEF stripes from its Tempests' upper surfaces on moving to Belgium in September 1944.

SCALE-FEET   0 1 2 3 4 5 6 7 8 9 10 11 12 13 14 15 16 17 18 19 20

Hawker Tornado, Typhoon and Tempest

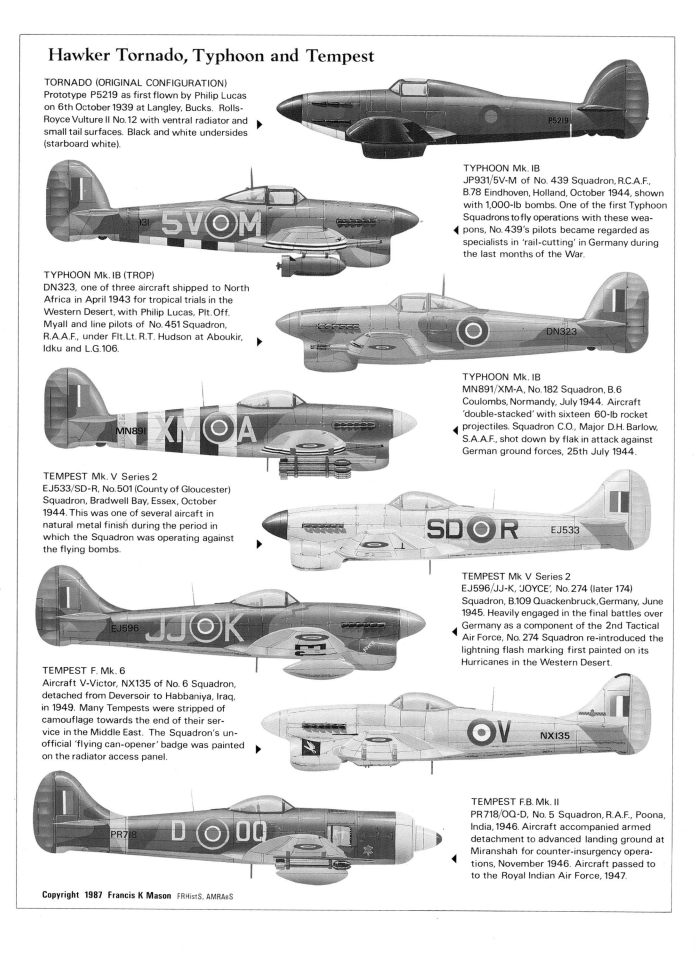

TORNADO (ORIGINAL CONFIGURATION)
Prototype P5219 as first flown by Philip Lucas on 6th October 1939 at Langley, Bucks. Rolls-Royce Vulture II No. 12 with ventral radiator and small tail surfaces. Black and white undersides (starboard white).

TYPHOON Mk. IB
JP931/5V-M of No. 439 Squadron, R.C.A.F., B.78 Eindhoven, Holland, October 1944, shown with 1,000-lb bombs. One of the first Typhoon Squadrons to fly operations with these weapons, No. 439's pilots became regarded as specialists in 'rail-cutting' in Germany during the last months of the War.

TYPHOON Mk. IB (TROP)
DN323, one of three aircraft shipped to North Africa in April 1943 for tropical trials in the Western Desert, with Philip Lucas, Plt. Off. Myall and line pilots of No. 451 Squadron, R.A.A.F., under Flt. Lt. R.T. Hudson at Aboukir, Idku and L.G.106.

TYPHOON Mk. IB
MN891/XM-A, No. 182 Squadron, B.6 Coulombs, Normandy, July 1944. Aircraft 'double-stacked' with sixteen 60-lb rocket projectiles. Squadron C.O., Major D.H. Barlow, S.A.A.F., shot down by flak in attack against German ground forces, 25th July 1944.

TEMPEST Mk. V Series 2
EJ533/SD-R, No. 501 (County of Gloucester) Squadron, Bradwell Bay, Essex, October 1944. This was one of several aircraft in natural metal finish during the period in which the Squadron was operating against the flying bombs.

TEMPEST Mk V Series 2
EJ596/JJ-K, 'JOYCE', No. 274 (later 174) Squadron, B.109 Quackenbruck, Germany, June 1945. Heavily engaged in the final battles over Germany as a component of the 2nd Tactical Air Force, No. 274 Squadron re-introduced the lightning flash marking first painted on its Hurricanes in the Western Desert.

TEMPEST F. Mk. 6
Aircraft V-Victor, NX135 of No. 6 Squadron, detached from Deversoir to Habbaniya, Iraq, in 1949. Many Tempests were stripped of camouflage towards the end of their service in the Middle East. The Squadron's unofficial 'flying can-opener' badge was painted on the radiator access panel.

TEMPEST F.B. Mk. II
PR718/OQ-D, No. 5 Squadron, R.A.F., Poona, India, 1946. Aircraft accompanied armed detachment to advanced landing ground at Miranshah for counter-insurgency operations, November 1946. Aircraft passed to to the Royal Indian Air Force, 1947.

Supercharger

Hydraulically-operated two-speed single-entry centrifugal type. MS (low) gear ratio, 4.68:1. FS (high) gear ratio, 5.83:1. The change-speed clutch was located inside the supercharger casing between the impeller and the crankcase. From the impeller the mixture passed through a ring of fixed diffuser blades and thence to four volutes cast in the supercharger casing. Each volute supplied mixture to one bank of cylinders through one of four manifolds, two above and two below the top and bottom banks of cylinders.

Lubrication

The lubrication system comprised one main pressure pump, a large main pressure oil filter, a main scavenge pump with supercharger scavenge pump above it, and the front scavenge pump. The main pressure filter was located on the left side of the engine, while the pumps, the high pressure relief valve and two gauze scavenge filters were located in the bottom cover unit. Pressure oil lubricated the main and big-end bearings, the propeller shaft rear bearing and reduction gear balance arms; it was also directed through numerous jets to the propeller shaft reduction gears. Two pressure reducing valves in the main pressure circuit fed a low pressure circuit which directed oil to the sleeve drives, the upper auxiliary unit and the bottom cover unit. The sleeves, pistons, cylinder bores and connecting rods' small-ends were lubricated by splash oil from the crankshaft main and connecting rod big-end bearings. The oil, after completing its main and low-pressure circuits collected in the front portion of the bottom cover unit, and was transferred by the front scavenge pump to the sump when it was drawn by the main scavenge pump and returned to the supply tank via the carburettor throttle spindles and the supercharger inlet volute jacket.

Ignition

Two BTH type C1 SE-ES duplex magnetos, mounted opposite one another on the upper auxiliary drive casing, were driven by the upper auxiliary drive shaft, together with two BTH distributors similarly mounted and driven. Each distributor was wholly energized by one magneto and fired 24 plugs. Each cylinder was provided with two plugs and fully screened and armoured harness.

Auxiliary drives

The auxiliary drives were located in the upper and lower auxiliary unit covers. The upper main drive shaft was driven by a pinion on the front end of the upper crankshaft through an idler gear in the top front portion of the crankcase. The accessories on the upper cover included the duplex magnetos and distributors, the ignition servo control unit, the propeller governor control unit, the air compres-

sors, the hydraulic and vacuum pumps, and the electric generator. The lower shaft, driven by the lower crankshaft through an idler gear, drove the two coolant pumps, the main and supercharger scavenge pumps, the front scavenge pump, and the oil and fuel pumps.

Coolant system

The engine coolant was circulated under pressure. Two centrifugal pumps circulated the coolant from the ring-type header tank in the nose of the cowling through the engine and radiator; thermostatic valves prevented the coolant being circulated to the radiator until the predetermined temperature was reached.

Starter

In the Typhoon and Tempest the Sabre was started by a Coffman Type L.4S cartridge starter, which drove on to the upper crankshaft rear pinion through an idler gear; the starter itself was mounted on the upper crankcase.

Propeller drive

Left-hand tractor. The propeller shaft embodied oil pressure ducts for operating the propeller pitch-change in conjuction with the propeller governor unit (constant speed unit). The control of the governor was interconnected with the ignition servo control unit.

Engine dimensions and weight

Overall length, 6 ft 10¼ in. *Overall width*, 3 ft 4 in. *Overall height*, 3 ft 10 in. *Net dry weight*, 2,470 lb.

Engine performance at take-off and rated altitude

Rated power, MS gear, 2,120 hp at 3,650 rpm at 6,300 ft; FS gear, 1,910 hp at 3,600 rpm at 15,500 ft. Maximum power (combat) rating, 5 minutes maximum, MS gear, 2,590 hp at 3,800 rpm at 2,500 ft; FS gear, 2,400 hp at 3,850 rpm at 13,000 ft. Maximum take-off power, MS gear, 5 minutes maximum, 2,400 hp at 3,850 rpm at sea level.

THE TEMPEST MARK V

The Hawker Tempest was a substantially developed derivative of the Typhoon, possessing an entirely new wing. This wing, of basic two-spar configuration, was of elliptical plan-form, laminar-flow section with blunt elliptical tips. Maximum thickness occurred at 37.5 per cent of chord. The wing centre-section, which featured no dihedral, accommodated the wide-track, inwards-retracting main landing gear, inter-spar fuel tanks and a fuel tank in the leading edge of the port wing.

Split landing flaps on the trailing edge of the wing extended from the Frise ailerons inboard to the fuselage, and the outer wing sections also accommodated the gun bays with four Hispano Mark V 20-mm cannon whose barrels were wholly con-

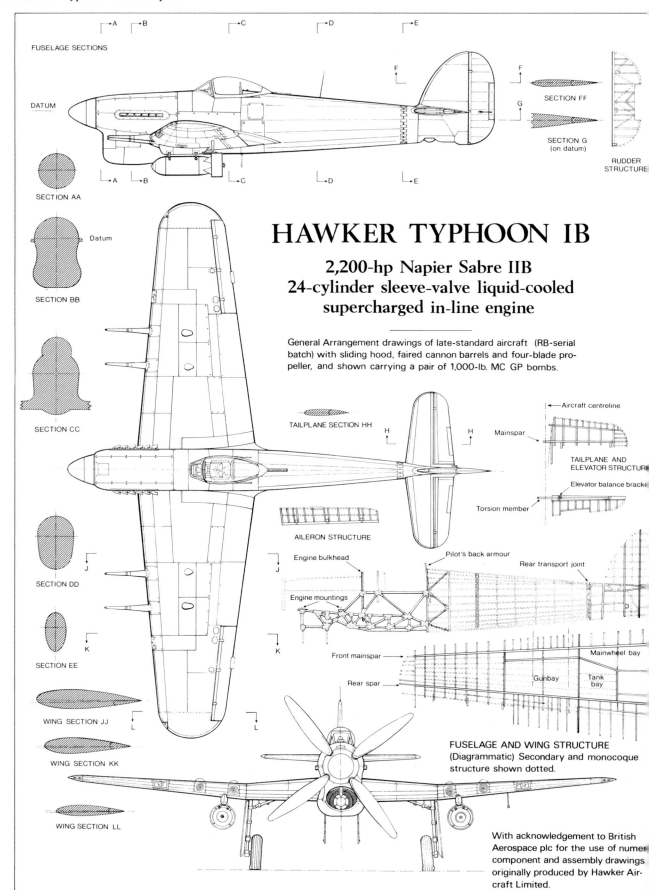

FUSELAGE SECTIONS

A B C D E

DATUM

F F

SECTION FF

G

SECTION G
(on datum)

RUDDER
STRUCTURE

SECTION AA

SECTION BB

Datum

SECTION CC

HAWKER TYPHOON IB

2,200-hp Napier Sabre IIB
24-cylinder sleeve-valve liquid-cooled
supercharged in-line engine

General Arrangement drawings of late-standard aircraft (RB-serial
batch) with sliding hood, faired cannon barrels and four-blade propeller, and shown carrying a pair of 1,000-lb. MC GP bombs.

TAILPLANE SECTION HH

Aircraft centreline

Mainspar

H H

TAILPLANE AND
ELEVATOR STRUCTURE

Elevator balance bracket

Torsion member

AILERON STRUCTURE

Engine bulkhead

Pilot's back armour

Rear transport joint

Engine mountings

SECTION DD

J J

SECTION EE

K K

Front mainspar

Mainwheel bay

Rear spar

Gunbay

Tank
bay

WING SECTION JJ

L L

WING SECTION KK

FUSELAGE AND WING STRUCTURE
(Diagrammatic) Secondary and monocoque
structure shown dotted.

WING SECTION LL

With acknowledgement to British
Aerospace plc for the use of numer
component and assembly drawings
originally produced by Hawker Aircraft Limited.

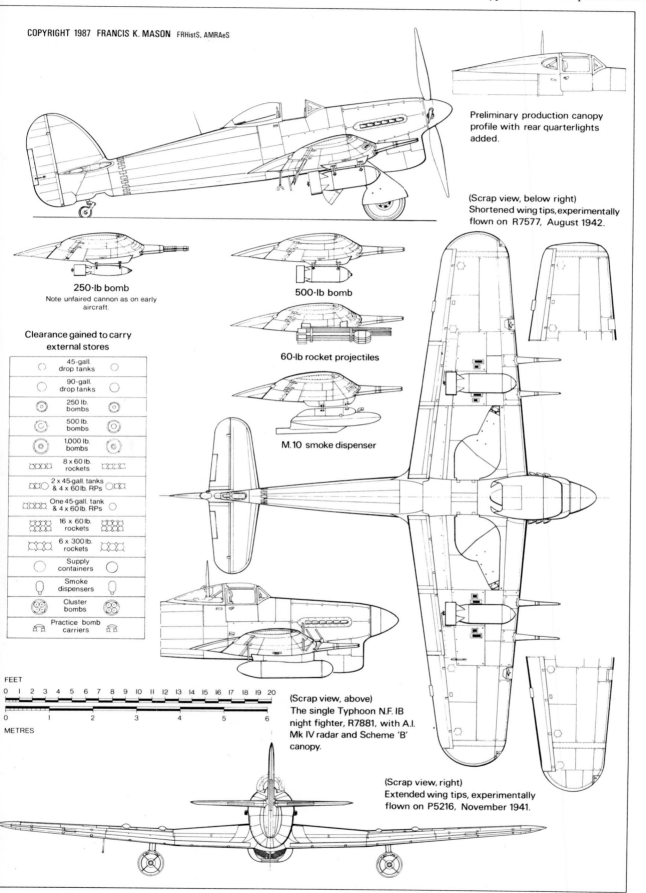

COPYRIGHT 1987 FRANCIS K. MASON FRHistS, AMRAeS

Preliminary production canopy profile with rear quarterlights added.

(Scrap view, below right)
Shortened wing tips, experimentally flown on R7577, August 1942.

250-lb bomb
Note unfaired cannon as on early aircraft.

500-lb bomb

60-lb rocket projectiles

M.10 smoke dispenser

Clearance gained to carry external stores

○ 45-gall. drop tanks ○	
○ 90-gall. drop tanks ○	
◎ 250 lb. bombs ◎	
◎ 500 lb. bombs ◎	
◎ 1,000 lb. bombs ◎	
8 x 60 lb. rockets	
2 x 45-gall. tanks & 4 x 60 lb. RPs	
One 45-gall. tank & 4 x 60 lb. RPs	
16 x 60 lb. rockets	
6 x 300 lb. rockets	
○ Supply containers ○	
Smoke dispensers	
Cluster bombs	
Practice bomb carriers	

FEET
0 1 2 3 4 5 6 7 8 9 10 11 12 13 14 15 16 17 18 19 20

0 1 2 3 4 5 6
METRES

(Scrap view, above)
The single Typhoon N.F. IB night fighter, R7881, with A.I. Mk IV radar and Scheme 'B' canopy.

(Scrap view, right)
Extended wing tips, experimentally flown on P5216, November 1941.

tained within the wings (on the Tempest Mark V Series 2).

The fuselage approximated to that of the Typhoon, but incorporated an additional bay forward of the cockpit to include an additional (main) fuel tank. The Napier Sabre (Mark IIB), driving a four-blade de Havilland Hydromatic propeller, was retained, its rear mountings now being located forward of the Typhoon's position to cater for the additional fuel tank bay. A single-piece sliding cockpit canopy was included.

The main structure of the tail unit remained the same as in the Typhoon although tailplane, elevator and rudder areas were marginally increased. A new dorsal fin fairing was included, fairing the fin leading edge to a concave curve.

The main landing gear incorporated Dowty levered-suspension oleo legs (in contrast to the Typhoon's compression oleos), and wheel doors were provided over the retracting tailwheel.

Overall Geometric Data
Typhoon Wing span, 41 ft 7 in; length, 31 ft 11 in; height, 15 ft 3½ in; wing area, 279 sq ft.
Tempest V Wing span, 41 ft 0 in; length, 33 ft 8 in; height, 16 ft 1 in; wing area, 302 sq ft.

Performance
It has not proved practical to quote detailed performance figures for either the Typhoon or Tempest V on account of the widely differing standards of airframe preparation and ratings of the various versions of the Sabre II engine. Reference to the text will permit judgement of how the performance of representative standards of aircraft was affected by progressive modification.

The following may be regarded as being generally accurate for aircraft in good external condition with engines fully rated.

Typhoon Mark IB. (Napier Sabre IIA, four-blade propeller, sliding cockpit canopy, faired cannon barrels, whip aerial and no external stores)
Maximum speed, 422 mph at 12,500 feet; time to 12,500 feet, 3.2 minutes; normal range, 980 miles; service ceiling, 31,800 feet.

Tempest Mark V. (Napier Sabre IIB, and no external stores)
Maximum speed, 442 mph at 20,500 feet; time to 20,500 feet, 6.1 minutes; normal range, 820 miles; service ceiling, 33,200 feet.

1. TYPHOONS

NO. 1 SQUADRON

(Received first Typhoon, 21 July 1942; declared operational, September 1942; disposed of Typhoons, April 1944)

Airfields

Acklington, Northumberland	from 8–7–42
Biggin Hill, Kent	from 9–2–43
Lympne, Kent	from 15–3–43
Martlesham Heath, Suffolk	from 15–2–44
North Weald, Essex	from 2–4–44

Commanding Officers

Sqn Ldr J. A. F. MacLachlan, DSO, DFC and Bar	7–41 to 8–42
Sqn Ldr R. C. Wilkinson, OBE, DFM and Bar	8–42 to 5–43
Sqn Ldr A. Zweighburgk, DFC	5–43 to 4–44

NO. 3 SQUADRON

(Received first Typhoon, 1 February 1943; declared operational, 16 May 1943; disposed of Typhoons, April 1945)

Airfields

Hunsdon, Hertfordshire	from 21–8–42
West Malling, Kent	from 14–4–43
Manston, Kent	from 11–6–43
Swanton Morley, Norfolk	from 28–12–43
Manston, Kent	from 14–2–44
Bradwell Bay, Essex	from 6–3–44
Ayr, Ayrshire	from 6–4–44
Bradwell Bay, Essex	from 14–4–44

Commanding Officers

Sqn Ldr F. de Soomer	9–42 to 8–43
Sqn Ldr S. R. Thomas, DFC, AFC	8–43 to 9–43
Sqn Ldr R. Hawkins, MC, AFC	9–43 to 10–43
Sqn Ldr K. A. Wigglesworth, DFC	10–43 to 8–44

NO. 4 SQUADRON

(Received first Typhoon, 1 October 1944; declared operational, 11 October 1944; disposed of Typhoons, February 1945)

Airfields

B.61 St Denis Westrem, Belgium	from 27–9–44
B.70 Deurne, Belgium	from 11–10–44
B.77 Gilze-Rijen, Holland	from 23–11–44

Commanding Officer

Sqn Ldr C. D. Harris St John, DFC

NO. 56 SQUADRON

(Received first Typhoon, 11 September 1941; declared operational, 29 May 1942; disposed of Typhoons, May 1944)

Airfields

Duxford, Cambridgeshire	from 26–6–41
Snailwell, Cambridgeshire	from 30–3–42
Matlaske, Norfolk	from 24–8–42
Manston, Kent	from 22–7–43
Martlesham Heath, Suffolk	from 6–8–43
Manston, Kent	from 15–8–43
Bradwell Bay, Essex	from 23–8–43
Martlesham Heath, Suffolk	from 4–10–43
Scorton, Yorkshire	from 15–2–44
Acklington, Northumberland	from 23–2–44
Scorton, Yorkshire	from 7–3–44
Ayr, Ayrshire	from 7–4–44
Newchurch, Kent	from 28–4–44

Commanding Officers

Sqn Ldr P. P. Hanks, DSO, DFC, AFC	6–41 to 12–41
Sqn Ldr H. S. L., Dundas, DSO and Bar, DFC	12–41 to 11–42
Sqn Ldr A. C. Johnstone	12–42 to 6–43
Sqn Ldr T. H. V. Pheloung	1–43 to 6–43
Sqn Ldr C. J. Donovan	6–43 to 9–43
Sqn Ldr G. L. Sinclair, DFC and Bar	9–43 to 5–44

NO. 137 SQUADRON

(Received first Typhoon, January 1944; declared operational, 8 February 1944; disposed of Typhoons to No. 174 Sqn., August 1945)

Airfields

Colerne, Wiltshire	from 2–1–44
Lympne, Kent	from 4–2–44
Manston, Kent	from 1–4–44
B.6 Coulombs, France	from 13–8–44
B.30 Creton, France	from 29–8–44
B.48 Amiens/Glissy, France	from 3–9–44
B.58 Melsbroek, Belgium	from 6–9–44
B.78 Eindhoven, Holland	from 22–9–44
B.86 Helmond, Holland	from 13–1–45
B.106 Twente, Holland	from 11–4–45
B.112 Hopsten, Germany	from 13–4–45
B.120 Langenhagen, Germany	from 17–4–45
B.156 Luneburg, Germany	from 30–4–45
B.118 Celle, Germany	from 7–5–45
B.160 Kastrup, Germany	from 11–4–45
B.172 Husum, Germany	from 21–6–45
B.158 Lubeck, Germany	from 11–7–45
Warmwell, Dorset	from 20–8–45

Commanding Officers

Sqn Ldr J. R. Dennehey, DFC	12–43 to 4–44
Sqn Ldr G. Piltingrud, DFC	4–44 to 9–44
Sqn Ldr E. T. Brough, DFC	9–44 to 12–44
Sqn Ldr R. G. V. Barraclough, DFC	12–44 to 3–45
Sqn Ldr D. Murray, DFC	3–45 to 8–45

NO. 164 SQUADRON

(Received first Typhoon, January 1944; declared operational, 20 March 1944; disposed of Typhoons, June 1945)

Airfields

Twinwood Farm, Bedfordshire	from 4–1–44
Fairlop, Essex	from 13–1–44
Twinwood Farm, Bedfordshire	from 11–2–44
Acklington, Northumberland	from 8–3–44
Thorney Island, Hampshire	from 22–4–44
Llanbedr, Merioneth	from 11–4–44
Thorney Island, Hampshire	from 22–4–44
Funtington, Sussex	from 17–6–44
Hurn, Hampshire	from 21–6–44
B.8 Sommervieu, France	from 17–7–44
B.7 Martragny, France	from 20–7–44
B.23 Moraineville, France	from 3–9–44
B.35 Baromesnil, France	from 6–9–44
B.53 Merville, France	from 13–9–44
B.67 Ursel, Belgium	from 30–10–44
B.77 Gilze-Rijen, Holland	from 26–11–44
Fairwood Common, Glamorgan	from 17–12–44
B.77 Gilze-Rijen, Holland	from 29–12–44
B.84 Chievres, Belgium	from 1–1–45
B.77 Gilze-Rijen, Holland	from 19–1–45
B.91 Kluis, Holland	from 21–3–45
B.103 Plantlunne, Germany	from 17–4–45
B.116 Wunstorf, Germany	from 26–5–45
Turnhouse, Midlothian	from 12–6–45

Commanding Officers

Sqn Ldr H. à B. Russell, DFC	9–43 to 5–44
Sqn Ldr P. H. Beake, DFC	5–44 to 8–44
Sqn Ldr R. van Lierde, DFC and Bar	8–44 to 1–45
Sqn Ldr P. L. Bateman-Jones	1–45 to 8–45

NO. 168 SQUADRON

(Received first Typhoon, 23 September 1944; declared operational, 12 October 1944; disposed of Typhoons, February 1945)

Airfields

B.66 Diest, Belgium	from 20–9–44
B.78 Eindhoven, Holland	from 2–10–44

Commanding Officer

Flt Lt C. A. M. Barbour

NO. 174 SQUADRON

(Received first Typhoon, 8 April 1943; declared operational, 14 July 1943; disposed of Typhoons, September 1945)

Airfields

Gravesend, Kent	from 5–4–43
Merston, Sussex	from 12–6–43
Lydd, Kent	from 1–7–43
Westhampnett, Sussex	from 10–10–43
Eastchurch, Kent	from 21–1–44
Westhampnett, Sussex	from 4–2–44
Holmesley South, Hampshire	from 1–4–44
B.2 Bazenville, France	from 19–6–44
B.24 St André, France	from 27–8–44
B.42 Beauvais, France	from 1–9–44
B.50 Vitry-en-Artois, France	from 4–9–44
B.70 Deurne, Belgium	from 17–9–44
B.80 Volkel, Holland	from 30–9–44
Warmwell, Dorset	from 10–11–44
B.80 Volkel, Holland	from 21–11–44
B.100 Goch, Germany	from 20–3–45
B.158 Lubeck, Germany	from 26–8–45
Warmwell, Dorset	from 9–9–45

Commanding Officers

Sqn Ldr W. W. McConnell, DFC	8–42 to 2–44
Sqn Ldr W. Pitt-Brown, DFC and Bar, AFC	2–44 to 8–44
Sqn Ldr J. C. Melvill	8–44 to 1–45
Sqn Ldr D. T. N. Kelly	1–45 to 3–45
Sqn Ldr R. R. Monk, DFC	3–45 to 4–45
Sqn Ldr D. Murray, DFC	8–45 to 9–45

NO. 175 SQUADRON

(Received first Typhoon, 10 April 1943; declared operational, 12 June 1943; disposed of Typhoons, September 1945)

Airfields

Colerne, Wiltshire	from 8–4–43
Lasham, Hampshire	from 24–5–43
Appledram, Sussex	from 2–6–43
Lydd, Kent	from 1–7–43
Westhampnett, Sussex	from 9–10–43
Eastchurch, Kent	from 24–2–44
Westhampnett, Sussex	from 8–3–44
Holmesley South, Hampshire	from 1–4–44
B.3 St Croix, France	from 20–6–44
B.5 Le Fresney, France	from 24–6–44
B.42 Beauvais, France	from 2–9–44
B.50 Vitry-en-Artois, France	from 4–9–44
B.70 Deurne, Belgium	from 17–9–44
B.80 Volkel, Holland	from 30–9–44
Warmwell, Dorset	from 21–11–44
B.80 Volkel, Holland	from 4–12–44
B.100 Goch, Germany	from 21–3–45
B.110 Achmer, Germany	from 11–4–45
B.150 Hustedt, Germany	from 19–4–45
Warmwell, Dorset	from 28–5–45
Manston, Kent	from 11–6–45
B.164 Schleswig, Germany	from 16–6–45
B.160 Kastrup, Germany	from 22–8–45
B.164 Schleswig, Germany	from 5–9–45

Commanding Officers

Sqn Ldr J. R. Pennington-Legh, DFC and Bar	3–42 to 7–43
Sqn Ldr R. T. P. Davidson	7–43 to 9–43
Sqn Ldr M. R. Ingle-Finch, DFC	9–43 to 11–44
Sqn Ldr R. W. Campbell	11–44 to 9–45

NO. 181 SQUADRON

(Received first Typhoon, 7 September 1942; declared operational, 10 February 1943; disposed of Typhoons, September 1945)

Airfields

Duxford, Cambridgeshire	from 1–9–42
Snailwell, Cambridgeshire	from 10–12–42
Cranfield, Bedfordshire	from 1–3–43
Snailwell, Cambridgeshire	from 8–3–43
Gravesend, Kent	from 24–3–43
Lasham, Hampshire	from 5–4–43
Appledram, Sussex	from 2–6–43
New Romney, Kent	from 2–7–43
Merston, Sussex	from 8–10–43
Odiham, Hampshire	from 31–12–43
Merston, Sussex	from 13–1–44

Eastchurch, Kent	from 6–2–44
Merston, Sussex	from 21–2–44
Hurn, Hampshire	from 1–4–44
B.6 Coulombs, France	from 20–6–44
B.30 Creton, France	from 31–8–44
B.48 Amiens/Glisy, France	from 3–9–44
B.58 Melsbroek, Belgium	from 6–9–44
B.78 Eindhoven, Holland	from 23–9–44
Warmwell, Dorset	from 13–2–45
B.86 Helmond, Holland	from 3–3–45
B.106 Enschede, Holland	from 11–4–45
B.112 Hopsten, Germany	from 13–4–45
B.120 Langenhagen, Germany	from 18–4–45
B.156 Luneburg, Germany	from 1–5–45
B.158 Lubek, Germany	from 7–5–45
B.160 Kastrup, Germany	from 6–7–45
Manston, Kent	from 20–7–45
Warmwell, Dorset	from 21–7–45
B.160 Kastrup, Germany	from 3–8–45
B.166 Flensburg, Germany	from 5–9–45
B.164 Schleswig, Germany	from 8–9–45

Commanding Officers

Sqn Ldr D. Crowley-Milling, DSO, DFC and Bar	9–42 to 8–43
Sqn Ldr F. W. M. Jensen, DFC and Bar, AFC	8–43 to 11–43
Sqn Ldr J. G. Keep	11–43 to 8–44
Sqn Ldr C. D. North-Lewis, DSO, DFC and Bar	5–44 to 8–44
Sqn Ldr A. E. S. Vincent, DFC	8–44 to 12–44
Sqn Ldr W. H. B. Short, DFC	12–44
Sqn Ldr D. R. Crawford	12–44 to 2–45
Sqn Ldr H. Ambrose, DFC and Bar	2–45 to 8–45

NO. 182 SQUADRON

(Received first Typhoon, 16 September 1942; declared operational, 3 January 1943; disposed of Typhoons, September 1945)

Airfields

Martlesham Heath, Suffolk	from 25–8–42
Sawbridgeworth, Herts	from 7–12–42
Snailwell, Cambridgeshire	from 17–1–43
Sawbridgeworth, Herts	from 20–1–43
Martlesham Heath, Suffolk	from 30–1–43
Middle Wallop, Hampshire	from 1–3–43
Zeals, Wiltshire	from 12–3–43
Middle Wallop, Hampshire	from 13–3–43
Fairlop, Essex	from 5–4–43
Lasham, Hampshire	from 29–4–43
Appledram, Sussex	from 2–6–43
New Romney, Kent	from 2–7–43
Wigtown, Wigtownshire	from 18–9–43
New Romney, Kent	from 22–9–43
Merston, Sussex	from 12–10–43
Odiham, Hampshire	from 31–12–43
Eastchurch, Kent	from 5–1–44
Merston, Sussex	from 21–1–44
Hurn, Hampshire	from 1–4–44
B.6 Coulombs, France	from 20–6–44
Holmesley South, Hampshire	from 22–6–44
B.6 Coulombs, France	from 3–7–44
B.30 Creton, France	from 30–8–44
B.48 Amiens/Glisy, France	from 3–9–44
B.58 Melsbroek, Belgium	from 6–9–44
B.78 Eindhoven, Holland	from 22–9–44
B.86 Helmond, Holland	from 13–1–45
Warmwell, Dorset	from 3–2–45
B.86 Helmond, Holland	from 21–2–45
B.106 Enschede, Holland	from 11–4–45
B.108 Rheine, Germany	from 13–4–45
B.120 Langenhagen, Germany	from 17–4–45
B.156 Luneburg, Germany	from 1–5–45
B.158 Lubeck, Germany	from 7–5–45
B.160 Kastrup, Germany	from 11–7–45
Warmwell, Dorset	from 5–8–45
B.160 Kastrup, Germany	from 19–8–45
B.166 Flensburg, Germany	from 5–9–45
B.164 Schleswig, Germany	from 8–9–45

Commanding Officers

Sqn Ldr T. P. Pugh, DFC	9–42 to 8–43
Sqn Ldr D. R. Walker	8–43 to 10–43
Sqn Ldr M. E. Reid	10–43 to 4–44
Major D. H. Barlow, SAAF	4–44 to 7–44
Sqn Ldr G. J. Gray, DFC and Bar	8–44 to 3–45
Sqn Ldr J. D. Derry, DFC	3–45 to 9–45

NO. 183 SQUADRON

(Received first Typhoon, 1 November 1942; declared operational,
April 1943; disposed of Typhoons, June 1945)

Airfields

Church Fenton, Yorkshire	from 1–11–42
Cranfield, Bedfordshire	from 1–3–43
Snailwell, Cambridgeshire	from 8–3–43
Church Fenton, Yorkshire	from 12–3–43
Colerne, Wiltshire	from 26–3–43
Gatwick, Surrey	from 8–4–43
Lasham, Hampshire	from 3–5–43
Colerne, Wiltshire	from 30–5–43
Harrowbeer, Devon	from 5–6–43
Tangmere, Sussex	from 4–8–43
Perranporth, Cornwall	from 18–9–43
Predannack, Cornwall	from 13–10–43
Tangmere, Sussex	from 1–2–44
Manston, Kent	from 15–3–44
Thorney Island, Hampshire	from 1–4–44
Funtington, Sussex	from 18–6–44
Hurn, Hampshire	from 22–6–44
Eastchurch, Kent	from 14–7–44
B.7 Martragny, France	from 25–7–44
B.23 Morainville, France	from 3–9–44
B.35 Baromesnil, France	from 6–9–44
B.53 Merville, France	from 11–9–44
B.67 Ursel, Belgium	from 29–10–44
B.77 Gilze-Rijen, Holland	from 25–11–44
A.84 Chievres, Belgium	from 1–1–45
B.77 Gilze-Rijen, Holland	from 19–1–45
B.91 Kluis, Holland	from 21–3–45
B.103 Plantlunne, Germany	from 17–4–45
B.116 Wunstorf, Germany	from 27–4–45
Milfield, Northumberland	from 16–6–45

Commanding Officers

Sqn Ldr A. V. Gowers, DFC	11–42 to 10–43
Sqn Ldr W. Dring, DFC	10–43 to 4–44
Sqn Ldr F. W. Scarlett	4–44 to 7–44
Sqn Ldr R. W. Mulliner, DFC	7–44 to 1–45
Sqn Ldr H. M. Mason	1–45 to 2–45
Sqn Ldr J. R. Cullen, DFC	2–45 to 10–45

NO. 184 SQUADRON

(Received first Typhoon, 24 December 1943; declared operational,
25 April 1944; disposed of Typhoons, September 1945)

Airfields

Detling, Kent	from 12–10–43
Odiham, Hampshire	from 6–3–44
Eastchurch, Kent	from 11–3–44
Odiham, Hampshire	from 3–3–44
Westhampnett, Sussex	from 23–4–44
Holmesley South, Hampshire	from 13–5–44
Westhampnett, Sussex	from 20–5–44
Holmesley South, Hampshire	from 17–6–44
B.10 Plumetot, France	from 27–6–44
B.5 Le Fresney, France	from 14–7–44
B.24 St André, France	from 28–8–44
B.42 Beauvais, France	from 2–9–44
B.50 Vitry-en-Artois, France	from 4–9–44
B.70 Deurne, Belgium	from 17–9–44
B.80 Volkel, Holland	from 30–9–44
B.100 Goch, Germany	from 21–3–45
B.110 Achmer, Germany	from 11–4–45
B.150 Hustedt, Germany	from 19–4–45
Warmwell, Dorset	from 7–5–45
B.164 Schleswig, Germany	from 28–5–45
B.160 Kastrup, Germany	from 2–8–45
B.166 Flensburg, Germany	from 5–9–45

Commanding Officers

Sqn Ldr J. Rose, DFC	12–42 to 8–44
Sqn Ldr J. W. Wilson, DFC	8–44 to 11–44
Sqn Ldr W. Smith, DFC	11–44 to 8–45

NO. 186 SQUADRON

(Received first Typhoon, 16 November 1943; was not declared
operational; disposed of Typhoons, February 1943)

Airfields

Ayr, Ayrshire	from 3–8–43
Tain, Ross and Cromarty	from 7–1–44

Commanding Officers

Sqn Ldr F. E. G. Hayter	8–43 to 1–44
Sqn Ldr W. H. Ireson	1–44 to 4–44

NO. 193 SQUADRON

(Received first Typhoon, 22 January 1943; declared operational,
1 April 1943; disposed of Typhoons, August 1945)

Airfields

Harrowbeer, Devon	from 18–12–42
Gravesend, Kent	from 17–8–43
Harrowbeer, Devon	from 18–9–43
Fairlop, Essex	from 20–9–43
Thorney Island, Hampshire	from 15–3–44
Llanbedr, Merioneth	from 6–4–44
Need's Oar Point, Hampshire	from 11–4–44
Hurn, Hampshire	from 3–7–44
B.15 Ryes, France	from 11–7–44
B.3 St Croix, France	from 15–7–44
Manston, Kent	from 8–9–44
B.51 Lille, France	from 11–9–44
Fairwood Common, Glamorgan	from 18–9–44
B.70 Deurne, Belgium	from 6–10–44
B.89 Mill, Holland	from 8–2–45
B.111 Ahlhorn, Germany	from 30–4–45
R.16 Hildesheim, Germany	from 8–6–45

Commanding Officers

Sqn Ldr W. H. A. Wright	12–42 to 1–43
Sqn Ldr G. W. Petre, DFC, AFC	1–43 to 2–44
Sqn Ldr D. G. Ross, DFC	2–44 to 6–44
Sqn Ldr J. C. Button, DSO, DFC	6–44 to 8–44
Sqn Ldr J. M. G. Plamondon	8–44 to 11–44
Sqn Ldr C. D. Erasmus, DFC	11–44 to 3–45
Sqn Ldr D. M. Taylor, DFC	4–45 to 8–45

NO. 195 SQUADRON

(Received first Typhoon, 27 November 1942; declared operational,
8 March 1943; disposed of Typhoons, February 1944)

Airfields

Duxford, Cambridgeshire	from 16–11–42
Hutton Cranswick, Yorkshire	from 21–11–42
Woodvale, Lancashire	from 12–2–43
Ludham, Norfolk	from 13–5–43
Matlaske, Norfolk	from 31–7–43
Coltishall, Norfolk	from 21–8–43
Fairlop, Essex	from 23–9–43

Commanding Officers

Sqn Ldr D. M. Taylor, DFC	11–42 to 1–44
Sqn Ldr C. A. Harris	1–44 to 2–44

NO. 197 SQUADRON

(Received first Typhoon, 27 November 1942; declared operational,
31 January 1943; disposed of Typhoons, August 1945)

Airfields

Drem, East Lothian	from 25–11–42
Tangmere, Sussex	from 28–3–43
Manston, Kent	from 15–3–44
Tangmere, Sussex	from 1–4–44
Need's Oar Point, Hampshire	from 10–4–44
Manston, Kent	from 2–9–44
B.51 Lille, France	from 11–9–44
B.70 Deurne, Belgium	from 2–10–44
B.89 Mill, Holland	from 8–2–45
B.105 Drope, Germany	from 16–4–45
B.111 Ahlhorn, Germany	from 30–4–45
R.16 Hildesheim, Germany	from 8–6–45

Commanding Officers

Sqn Ldr P. O. Prevot, DFC	11–42 to 6–43
Sqn Ldr A. H. Corkett	6–43 to 7–43
Sqn Ldr M. P. C. Holmes, DFC	7–43 to 1–44
Sqn Ldr D. M. Taylor, DFC	1–44 to 7–44
Sqn Ldr A. H. Smith	7–44 to 1–45
Sqn Ldr R. C. Curwen, DFC	1–45 to 2–45
Sqn Ldr K. J. Harding, DFC	2–45 to 8–45

NO. 198 SQUADRON
(Received first Typhoon, 8 December 1942; declared operational, 28 March 1943; disposed of Typhoons, September 1945)

Airfields

Digby, Lincolnshire	from 8–12–42
Ouston, Durham	from 23–1–43
Acklington, Northumberland	from 9–2–43
Manston, Kent	from 24–3–43
Woodvale, Lancashire	from 15–5–43
Martlesham Heath, Suffolk	from 5–6–43
Bradwell Bay, Essex	from 19–8–43
Manston, Kent	from 23–8–43
Tangmere, Sussex	from 17–3–44
Llanbedr, Merioneth	from 30–3–44
Thorney Island, Hampshire	from 6–4–44
Funtington, Sussex	from 18–6–44
Hurn, Hampshire	from 22–6–44
B.5 Le Fresney, France	from 1–7–44
B.10 Plumetot, France	from 11–7–44
B.7 Martragny, France	from 29–7–44
B.23 Morainville, France	from 3–9–44
B.35 Baromesnil, France	from 6–9–44
B.53 Merville, France	from 11–9–44
B.67 Ursel, Belgium	from 30–10–44
Fairwood Common, Glamorgan	from 6–11–44
B.67 Ursel, Belgium	from 21–11–44
B.77 Gilze-Rijen, Holland	from 26–11–44
A.84 Chievres, Belgium	from 31–12–44
B.77 Gilze-Rijen, Holland	from 19–1–45
B.91 Kluis, Holland	from 21–3–45
B.103 Plantlunne, Germany	from 17–4–45
B.116 Wunstorf, Germany	from 27–5–45

Commanding Officers

Sqn Ldr J. W. Villa, DFC and Bar	12–42 to 5–43
Sqn Ldr J. Manak	5–43 to 8–43
Sqn Ldr J. M. Bryan, DFC and Bar	8–43 to 11–43
Sqn Ldr J. Baldwin, DSO, DFC and Bar	11–43 to 4–44
Sqn Ldr J. M. Bryan, DFC and Bar	4–44 to 5–44
Sqn Ldr J. Niblett, DFC	5–44 to 6–44
Sqn Ldr I. J. Davies, DFC	6–44
Sqn Ldr Y. P. E. H. Ezano, C de G	8–44 to 10–44
Sqn Ldr A. W. Ridler	10–44 to 12–44
Sqn Ldr N. J. Durrant	12–44 to 9–45

NO. 245 SQUADRON
(Received first Typhoon, 31 December 1942; declared operational, 28 February 1943; disposed of Typhoons, August 1945)

Airfields

Charmy Down, Somerset	from 26–10–42
Peterhead, Aberdeenshire	from 29–1–43
Gravesend, Kent	from 31–3–43
Fairlop, Essex	from 28–5–43
Selsey, Sussex	from 1–6–43
Lydd, Kent	from 30–6–43
Westhampnett, Sussex	from 10–10–43
Holmesley South, Hampshire	from 1–4–44
Eastchurch, Kent	from 25–4–44
Holmesley South, Hampshire	from 30–4–44
Eastchurch, Kent	from 12–5–44
Holmesley South, Hampshire	from 22–5–44
B.5 Le Fresney, France	from 27–6–44
B.24 St André, France	from 28–8–44
B.42 Beauvais, France	from 2–8–44
B.50 Vitry-en-Artois, France	from 4–9–44
B.70 Deurne, Belgium	from 17–9–44
B.80 Volkel, Holland	from 1–10–44
Warmwell, Dorset	from 24–12–44
B.80 Volkel, Holland	from 6–1–45
B.100 Goch, Germany	from 21–3–45
B.110 Achmer, Germany	from 11–4–45
B.150 Celle, Germany	from 19–4–45
B.164 Schleswig, Germany	from 28–5–45
Warmwell, Dorset	from 16–6–45
B.164 Schleswig, Germany	from 3–7–45

Commanding Officers

Sqn Ldr S. S. Hordern	10–42 to 9–43
Sqn Ldr J. R. Collins, DFC and Bar	9–43 to 8–44
Sqn Ldr A. Zweighbergk, DFC	10–44 to 8–45

NO. 247 SQUADRON
(Received first Typhoon, 11 January 1943; declared operational, c. 11 March 1943; disposed of Typhoons, August 1945)

Airfields

High Ercall, Shropshire	from 21–9–42
Middle Wallop, Hampshire	from 1–3–43
Fairlop, Essex	from 5–4–43
Gravesend, Kent	from 28–5–43
Bradwell Bay, Essex	from 4–6–43
New Romney, Kent	from 10–7–43
Attlebridge, Norfolk	from 7–8–43
New Romney, Kent	from 13–8–43
Merston, Sussex	from 11–10–43
Snailwell, Cambridgeshire	from 23–10–43
Merston, Sussex	from 5–11–43
Odiham, Hampshire	from 31–12–43
Merston, Sussex	from 13–1–44
Eastchurch, Kent	from 1–4–44
Hurn, Hampshire	from 24–4–44
B.6 Coulombs, France	from 20–6–44
Hurn, Hampshire	from 23–6–44
B.30 Creton, France	from 30–8–44
B.48 Amiens/Glisy, France	from 3–9–44
B.58 Melsbroek, Belgium	from 6–9–44
B.78 Eindhoven, Holland	from 22–9–44
B.86 Helmond, Holland	from 13–1–45
Warmwell, Dorset	from 21–2–45
B.86 Helmond, Holland	from 7–3–45
B.106 Twente, Holland	from 12–4–45
B.112 Hopsten, Germany	from 13–4–45
B.120 Langenhagen, Germany	from 17–4–45
B.156 Luneburg, Germany	from 2–5–45
B.158 Lubeck, Germany	from 6–5–45
Chilbolton, Hampshire	from 20–8–45

Commanding Officers

Sqn Ldr J. C. Melvill	5–42 to 8–43
Sqn Ldr E. Haabjoern, DFC	8–43 to 1–44
Sqn Ldr R. J. McNair, DFC	1–44 to 8–44
Sqn Ldr B. G. Stapleton, DFC	8–44 to 12–44
Sqn Ldr J. H. Bryant, DFC	1–45 to c.6–45(?)

NO. 257 SQUADRON
(Received first Typhoons, 15 July 1942; declared operational, 31 August 1942; disposed of Typhoons, March 1945)

Airfields

High Ercall, Shropshire	from 6–6–42
Exeter, Devon	from 21–9–42
Warmwell, Dorset	from 8–1–43
Gravesend, Kent	from 12–8–43
Warmwell, Dorset	from 17–9–43
Beaulieu, Hampshire	from 20–1–44
Tangmere, Sussex	from 31–1–44
Need's Oar Point, Hampshire	from 10–4–44
Hurn, Hampshire	from 2–7–44
B.3 St Croix, France	from 15–7–44
Fairwood Common, Glamorgan	from 11–8–44
B.3 St Croix, France	from 30–8–44
B.23 Morainville, France	from 6–9–44
B.51 Lille/Seclin, France	from 11–9–44
B.70 Deurne, Belgium	from 2–10–44
B.89 Mill, Holland	from 8–2–45

Commanding Officers

Sqn Ldr P. G. Wykeham-Barnes, DSO and Bar, OBE, DFC and Bar, AFC	5–42 to 9–42
Sqn Ldr G. A. Brown, DFC	9–42 to 4–43
Sqn Ldr C. L. C. Roberts	4–43 to 5–43
Sqn Ldr P. H. Lee	5–43 to 7–43
Sqn Ldr R. H. Fokes, DFC, DFM	7–43 to 6–44
Sqn Ldr W. C. Ahrens	6–44 to 7–44
Sqn Ldr W. J. Johnston, DFC and Bar	7–44 to 10–44
Sqn Ldr D. P. Jenkins, DFC	10–44 to 1–45
Sqn Ldr A. G. Todd, DFC	1–45 to 3–45

NO. 263 SQUADRON
(Received first Typhoon, 2 December 1943; declared operational, 1 February 1944; disposed of Typhoons, August 1945)

Airfields

Warmwell, Dorset	from 12–7–43
Ibsley, Hampshire	from 5–12–43
Fairwood Common, Glamorgan	from 5–1–44
Beaulieu, Hampshire	from 23–1–44
Warmwell, Dorset	from 6–3–44
Harrowbeer, Devon	from 19–3–44
Bolt Head, Devon	from 19–6–44
Hurn, Hampshire	from 10–7–44
Eastchurch, Kent	from 23–7–44
B.3 St Croix, France	from 6–8–44
Manston, Kent	from 6–9–44
B.51 Lille/Vendeville, France	from 11–9–44
B.70 Deurne, Belgium	from 2–10–44
Fairwood Common, Glamorgan	from 13–1–45
B.89 Mill, Holland	from 10–2–45
B.105 Drope, Germany	from 16–4–45
B.111 Ahlhorn, Germany	from 30–4–45
R.16 Hildesheim, Germany	from 10–6–45

Commanding Officers

Sqn Ldr G. B. Warnes, DSO, DFC	12–43 to 2–44
Sqn Ldr H.. A. C. Gonay (Belgian)	2–44 to 6–44
Sqn Ldr R. D. Rutter, DFC	6–44 to 1–45
Sqn Ldr M. T. S. Rumbold	1–45 to 8–45

NO. 266 SQUADRON

(Received first Typhoon, 5 January 1942; declared operational, 29 May 1942; disposed of Typhoons, July 1945)

Airfields

King's Cliffe, Northants	from 24–10–41
Duxford, Cambridgeshire	from 29–1–42
Warmwell, Dorset	from 21–9–42
Exeter, Devon	from 2–1–43
Gravesend, Kent	from 7–9–43
Exeter, Devon	from 10–9–43
Harrowbeer, Devon	from 21–9–43
Bolt Head, Devon	from 7–3–44
Harrowbeer, Devon	from 12–3–44
Acklington, Northumberland	from 15–3–44
Tangmere, Sussex	from 22–3–44
Need's Oar Point, Hampshire	from 10–4–44
Snaith, Yorkshire	from 27–4–44
Need's Oar Point, Hampshire	from 6–5–44
Eastchurch, Kent	from 29–6–44
Hurn, Hampshire	from 13–7–44
B.3 St Croix, France	from 17–7–44
B.23 Morainville, France	from 6–9–44
Manston, Kent	from 8–9–44
Tangmere, Sussex	from 9–9–44
B.51 Lille/Vendeville, France	from 11–9–44
B.70 Deurne, Belgium	from 2–10–44
B.89 Mill, Holland	from 8–2–45
B.105 Drope, Germany	from 16–4–45
Fairwood Common, Glamorgan	from 27–4–45
B.111 Ahlhorn, Germany	from 4–6–45
R.16 Hildesheim, Germany	from 8–6–45

Commanding Officers

Sqn Ldr C. L. Green, DFC	10–41 to 7–43
Sqn Ldr A. S. Macintyre	7–43 to 8–43
Sqn Ldr P. W. Lefevre, DFC	8–43 to 2–44
Sqn Ldr J. W. E. Holmes, DFC, AFC	3–44 to 7–44
Sqn Ldr J. D. Wright, DFC	7–44 to 10–44
Sqn Ldr J. H. Deall	10–44 to 3–45
Sqn Ldr R. A. G. Sheward	3–45 to 7–45

NO. 268 SQUADRON

(Received first Typhoon, 2 July, 1944; declared operational, 8 August 1944; disposed of Typhoons, December 1944)

Airfields

Odiham, Hampshire	from 27–6–44
B.10 Plumetot, France	from 10–8–44
B.4 Beny-sur-Mer, France	from 13–8–44
B.27 Boisney, France	from 1–9–44
B.31 Fresney Folney, France	from 5–9–45
B.43 Fort Rouge, France	from 11–9–44
B.61 St Denis Westrem, Belgium	from 27–9–44
B.70 Deurne, Belgium	from 11–10–44
B.77 Gilze-Rijen, Holland	from 25–11–44

Commanding Officers

Sqn Ldr A. S. Mann, DFC	
(Sqn Ldr K. K. Majumdar, DFC)	

NO. 438 SQUADRON RCAF

(Received first Typhoon, 12 January 1944; declared operational, March 1944; disposed of Typhoons, August 1945)

Airfields

Ayr, Ayrshire	from 1–44
Hurn, Hampshire	from 3–44
Funtington, Sussex	from 4–44
B.9 Lantheuil, France	from 6–44
B.24 St André, France	from 8–44
B.48 Amiens/Glisy, France	9–44
B.58 Melsbroek, Belgium	9–44
B.78 Eindhoven, Holland	from 9–44
Warmwell, Dorset	from 3–45
B.100 Goch, Germany	4–45
B.110 Osnabrück, Germany	4–45
B.150 Celle, Germany	from 4–45
B.166 Flensburg, Germany	from 5–45

Commanding Officers

Sqn Ldr F. G. Grant, DSO, DFC	11–43 to 7–44
Sqn Ldr J. R. Beirnes	7–44 to 10–44
Sqn Ldr R. F. Reid	10–44 to 12–44
Flt Lt P. Wilson	12–44
Sqn Ldr J. E. Hogg	1–45 to 3–45
Sqn Ldr J. R. Beirnes, DFC	3–45 to 6–45
Sqn Ldr R. A. Brown	6–45
Sqn Ldr P. Bissky	6–45
Sqn Ldr M. Harrison	6–45

NO. 439 SQUADRON RCAF

(Received first Typhoon, February 1944; declared operational, March 1944; disposed of Typhoons, August 1945)

Airfields

Ayr, Ayrshire	from 1–44
Hurn, Hampshire	from 3–44
Funtington, Sussex	4–44
Hurn, Hampshire	from 4–44
Hutton Cranswick, Yorkshire	5–44
Hurn, Hampshire	from 5–44
B.9 Lantheuil, France	from 6–44
B.24 St André, France	from 8–44
B.48 Amiens/Glisy, France	9–44
B.58 Melsbroek, Belgium	9–44
B.78 Eindhoven, Holland	from 9–44
B.100 Goch, Germany	from 3–45
Warmwell, Dorset	4–45
B.150 Celle, Germany	from 4–45
B.166 Flensburg, Germany	from 5–45

Commanding Officers

Sqn Ldr W. M. Smith	1–44 to 3–44
Sqn Ldr H. H. Norsworthy	3–44 to 9–44
Sqn Ldr K. J. Fiset, DFC	9–44 to 12–44
Sqn Ldr R. G. Crosby	12–44 to 1–45
Sqn Ldr J. H. Beatty	1–45 to 8–45

NO. 440 SQUADRON RCAF

(Received first Typhoon, February 1944; declared operational, March 1944; disposed of Typhoons, August 1945)

Airfields

Ayr, Ayrshire	from 2–44
Hurn, Hampshire	from 3–44
Funtington, Sussex	4–44
Hurn, Hampshire	from 4–44
B.7 Martragny, France	6–44
B.9 Lantheuil, France	from 6–44
B.24 St André, France	from 8–44
B.48 Amiens/Glisy, France	9–44
B.58 Melsbroek, Belgium	9–44
B.78 Eindhoven, Holland	from 9–44
B.100 Goch, Germany	from 3–45
B.110 Osnabrück, Germany	4–45
B.150 Celle, Germany	4–45
Warmwell, Dorset	from 4–45
B.150 Celle, Germany	5–45
B.166 Flensburg, Germany	from 5–45

Commanding Officers

Sqn Ldr W. H. Pentland	2–44 to 10–44
Sqn Ldr A. E. Monson	10–44 to 12–44
Sqn Ldr H. O. Gooding	12–44 to 3–45
Sqn Ldr R. Coffey	3–45 to 7–45
Sqn Ldr A. E. Monson, DFC	8–45

NO. 485 SQUADRON, RNZAF

(Received first Typhoon, March 1945; did not achieve operational status; disposed of Typhoons, April 1945)

Airfield

Predannack, Cornwall	2–45 to 4–45

Commanding Officer

Sqn Ldr K. J. McDonald, OBE, DFC	2–45 to 7–45

NO. 486 SQUADRON, RNZAF

(Received first Typhoon, July 1942; declared operational, September 1942; disposed of Typhoons, April 1944)

Airfields

Wittering, Northants	from 4–42
North Weald, Essex	from 9–42
West Malling, Kent	10–42
Tangmere, Sussex	10–42
Beaulieu, Hampshire	from 1–44
Castle Camps, Cambridgeshire	3–44
Ayr, Ayrshire	3–44
Castle Camps, Cambridgeshire	from 3–44

Commanding Officers

Sqn Ldr C. L. C. Roberts	3–42 to 4–43
Sqn Ldr D. J. Scott, DSO, OBE, DFC	4–43 to 9–43
Sqn Ldr I. D. Waddy	9–43 to 1–44
Sqn Ldr J. H. Iremonger, DFC	1–44 to 12–44

NO. 609 (WEST RIDING) SQUADRON, AAF

(Received first Typhoon, April 1942; declared operational, 30 June 1942; disposed of Typhoons, September 1945)

Airfields

Duxford, Cambridgeshire	from 30–3–42
Bourn, Cambridgeshire	from 26–8–42
Duxford, Cambridgeshire	from 30–8–42
Biggin Hill, Kent	from 18–9–42
Manston, Kent	from 2–11–42
Matlaske, Norfolk	from 22–7–43
Lympne, Kent	from 18–8–43
Manston, Kent	from 14–12–43
Fairwood Common, Glamorgan	from 6–2–44
Manston, Kent	from 20–2–44
Tangmere, Sussex	from 16–3–44
Acklington, Northumberland	from 21–3–44
Thorney Island, Hampshire	from 1–4–44
B.2 Bazenville, France	from 18–6–44
Hurn, Hampshire	from 22–6–44
B.10 Plumetot, France	from 1–7–44
B.7 Martragny, France	from 19–7–44
B.23 Morainvile, France	from 3–9–44
B.35 Baromesnil, France	from 6–9–44
B.53 Merville, France	from 11–9–44
B.67 Ursel, Belgium	from 30–10–44
B.77 Gilze-Rijen, Holland	from 26–11–44
A.84 Chievres, Belgium	from 31–12–44
B.77 Gilze-Rijen, Holland	from 19–1–45
B.91 Kluis, Holland	from 21–3–45
B.103 Plantlunne, Germany	from 17–4–45
B.116 Wunstorf, Germany	from 27–5–45
Lasham, Hampshire	from 2–6–45
Fairwood Common, Glamorgan	from 4–6–45
B.116 Wunstorf, Germany	from 23–6–45

Commanding Officers

Sqn Ldr G. K. Gilroy, DSO, DFC and Bar	7–41 to 6–42
Sqn Ldr P. H. M. Richey, DFC	6–42 to 10–42
Sqn Ldr Beamont, DSO, DFC and Bar	10–42 to 5–43
Sqn Ldr A. Ingle, DFC, AFC	5–43 to 8–43
Sqn Ldr P. G. Thornton-Brown	8–43 to 12–43
Sqn Ldr J. C. Wells, DFC and Bar	12–43 to 6–44
Sqn Ldr L. E. J. Geerts (Belgian)	6–44 to 8–44
Sqn Ldr R. A. F. Lallemant, DFC (Belgian)	8–44 to 9–44
Sqn Ldr T. Y. Wallace, DFM	9–44 to 11–44
Sqn Ldr C. J. G. de Moulin, DFC (Belgian)	11–44 to 12–44
Sqn Ldr E. R. A. Roberts, DFC	12–44 to 3–45
Sqn Ldr L. W. F. Stark, DFC and Bar, AFC	3–45 to 9–45

OPERATIONAL TYPHOON SQUADRONS OF THE R.A.F. AND COMMONWEALTH AIR FORCES

SQUADRONS	1941	1942	1943	1944	1945
1	HURRICANE IIC			SPITFIRE IX	
3		HURRICANE IIC		TEMPEST V	
4 (FR/PR)				SPITFIRE XI SPITFIRE XI SPITFIRE XI	
56	HURRICANE IIB			TEMPEST V	
137			WHIRLWIND		BECAME No 174 SQDN
164			HURRICANE IV		SPITFIRE IX
168 (FR)				MUSTANG DISBANDED	
174		HURRICANE IIB			TEMPEST V
175		HURRICANE IIB			DISBANDED
181		NEWLY FORMED			DISBANDED
182		HURRICANE I			DISBANDED
183		NEWLY FORMED			SPITFIRE IX
184			HURRICANE IV		DISBANDED
186			HURRICANE IV SPITFIRE VB		
193		HURRICANE IIC			DISBANDED
195		NEWLY FORMED	DISBANDED		
197		NEWLY FORMED		DISBANDED	
198		NEWLY RE-FORMED		DISBANDED	
245		HURRICANE IIB			METEOR III
247		HURRICANE IIC			TEMPEST II
257	SPITFIRE VB			DISBANDED	
263			WHIRLWIND		METEOR III
266	SPITFIRE VB			DISBANDED	
268 (FR)				MUSTANG MUSTANG	
438 (RCAF)			HURRICANE IV		DISBANDED
439 (RCAF)			HURRICANE IV		DISBANDED
440 (RCAF)			HURRICANE IV		DISBANDED
485 (RNZAF)				TEMPEST V SPITFIRE IX	
486 (RNZAF)		HURRICANE IIB		TEMPEST V	
609 (West Riding)	SPITFIRE V				DISBANDED

2. TEMPESTS

NO. 3 SQUADRON

(Received first Tempest Mark V, 9 March 1944; declared operational, 23 April 1944; disposed of Tempests, April 1948)

Airfields

Bradwell Bay, Essex	from 6–3–44
Ayr, Ayrshire	from 6–4–44
Bradwell Bay, Essex	from 14–4–44
Newchurch, Kent	from 28–8–44
Matlaske, Norfolk	from 21–9–44
B.60 Grimbergen, Belgium	from 28–9–44
B.80 Volkel, Holland	from 1–10–44
Warmwell, Dorset	from 2–4–45
B.112 Hopstein, Germany	from 17–4–45
B.152 Fassburg, Germany	from 26–4–45
B.160 Kastrup, Germany	from 21–6–45
B.156 Luneburg, Germany	from 18–7–45
B.159 Lubeck, Germany	from 8–8–45
B.155 Dedelstorf, Germany	from 5–9–45
B.170 Sylt, Germany	from 6–10–45
B.152 Fassburg, Germany	from 27–10–45
Wunstorf, Germany	from 21–1–46
Gatow, Germany	from 27–3–46
Dedelstorf, Germany	from 6–5–46
Manston, Kent	from 1–6–46
Dedelstorf, Germany	from 12–6–46
Wunstorf, Germany	from 21–9–46

Commanding Officers

Sqn Ldr A. S. Dredge, DSO, DFC, AFC	10–43 to 8–44
Sqn Ldr K. A. Wigglesworth, DFC	8–44 to 9–44
Sqn Ldr H. N. Sweetman, DFC	9–44 to 1–45
Sqn Ldr K. F. Thiele, DSO, DFC and Bar	1–45 to 2–45
Sqn Ldr R. B. Cole, DFC	2–45 to 4–47
Sqn Ldr C. H. Macfie, DFC	5–47 to 11–49

NO. 5 SQUADRON

(Received first Tempest Mark II, 5 March 1946; disposed of Tempests, August 1947. All Tempest service in India)

Airfields

Bhophal, India	from 17–2–46
Poona, India	from 1–6–46
Peshawa, India	from 22–1–47
Mauripur, India	from 3–7–47

Commanding Officers

Sqn Ldr L. H. Dawes, DFC	2–45 to 5–46
Sqn Ldr F. Rothwell, DFC, TD	5–46 to 8–47

NO. 6 SQUADRON

(Received first Tempest Mark VI, December 1946; disposed of Tempests, December 1949. All Tempest service in Mediterranean, Middle East and East Africa)

Airfields

Nicosia, Cyprus	from 3–10–46
Khartoum, Sudan	from 26–11–47
Fayid, Egypt	from 5–5–48
Deversoir, Egypt	from 1–9–48

(with frequent detachments throughout the Middle East and East Africa)

Commanding Officers

Sqn Ldr C. K. Gray, DFC	12–46 to 11–47
Sqn Ldr D. Crowley-Milling, DSO, DFC and Bar	11–47 to 7–50

NO. 8 SQUADRON

(Received first Tempest Mark VI, April 1947; disposed of Tempests, July 1948. All Tempest service at Aden)

Airfield

Khormaksar, Aden	from 1–9–46

Commanding Officers
(Not known)

NO. 16 SQUADRON

(Received first Tempest Mark V, April 1946; received first Tempest Mark II, April 1947; disposed of Tempests, December 1948. All Tempest service in Germany)

Airfields

Fassburg, Germany	from 1–4–46
Gütersloh, Germany	from 1–12–47

Commanding Officers

Sqn Ldr D. C. Usher, DFC, DFM	4–46 to 1–48
Sqn Ldr R. E. Mooney	1–48 to 6–48
Wg Cdr L. A. Malins, DSO, DFC	6–48 to 7–49

NO. 20 SQUADRON

(Received first Tempest Mark II, June 1946; disposed of Tempests, August 1947. All Tempest service in India)

Airfield

Agra, India	from 5–46
	(until disbanded on 1–8–47)

Commanding Officers (not known)

NO. 26 SQUADRON

(Received first Tempest Mark II, January 1947; disposed of Tempests, April 1949. All Tempest service in Germany.)

Airfields

Fassburg, Germany	from 11–46
Güterlosh, Germany	from 19–11–47

Commanding Officers

Sqn Ldr H. Ambrose, DFC and Bar	1–47 to 5–47
Sqn Ldr J. Brandt	5–47 to 12–47
Sqn Ldr A. D. Mitchell, CVO, DFC and Bar, AFC	12–47 to 6–48
Sqn Ldr J. W. Frost, DFC	6–48 to 9–48
Sqn Ldr J. F. McPhie, AFC	9–48 to 5–51

NO. 30 SQUADRON

(Received first Tempest Mark II, June 1946; disposed of Tempests, December 1946. All Tempest service in India)

Airfield

Agra, India	from 6–46
	(until disbanded, 1–12–46)

Commanding Officer
Not known.

NO. 33 SQUADRON

(Received first Tempest Mark V, December 1944; declared operational, February 1945; disposed of Tempest Mark Vs, November 1945. Received first Tempest Mark IIs, October 1946; disposed of Tempest IIs, June 1951)

Airfields

Predannack, Cornwall	from 15–12–44
B.77 Gilze-Rijen, Holland	from 20–2–45
B.91 Kluis, Holland	from 7–4–45
B.109 Quackenbrück, Germany	from 20–4–45
B.155 Dedelstorf, Germany	from 19–6–45
B.106 Twente, Holland	from 14–9–45
B.170 Sylt, Germany	from 17–9–45
B.155 Dedelstorf, Germany	from 6–10–45
B.152 Fassburg, Germany	from 23–10–45
Gütersloh, Germany	from 1–12–47
(Moved to Far East with Tempests	7–49)
Changi, Singapore	from 8–49
Butterworth, Malaya	from 9–49
Changi, Singapore	from 10–49
Kuala Lumpur, Malaya	from 4–50
Butterworth, Malaya	from 6–50
Kuala Lumpur, Malaya	from 9–50

Commanding Officers (where known)

Sqn Ldr I. G. S. Matthews, DFC	9–44 to 3–45
Sqn Ldr A. W. Bower, DFC	from 3–45

NO. 39 SQUADRON

(Received first Tempest F Mark 6s, April 1948; disposed of Tempests, February 1949. All Tempest service in East Africa)

Airfield

Nairobi and Eastleigh, Kenya	from 1–4–48 to 28–2–49

Commanding Officer
Not known

NO. 54 SQUADRON

(Received first Tempest Mark II, November 1945; disposed of
Tempests, October 1946)

Airfields

Chilbolton, Hampshire	from 15–11–45
Odiham, Hampshire	from 28–6–46
Molesworth, Northants	from 5–9–46
Odiham, Hampshire	from 30–9–46

Commanding Officer

Sqn Ldr F. W. M. Jenson, OBE, DFC and Bar, AFC   12–45 to 10–46

NO. 56 SQUADRON

(Received first Tempest Mark V, 24 June 1944; declared operational, 2 July 1944; disposed of Tempests, March 1946)

Airfields

Newchurch, Kent	from 28–4–44
Matlaske, Norfolk	from 23–9–44
B.60 Grimbergen, Belgium	from 28–9–44
B.80 Volkel, Holland	from 1–10–44
B.112 Hopsten, Germany	from 11–4–45
B.152 Fassburg, Germany	from 26–4–45
Warmwell, Dorset	from 8–5–45
B.152 Fassburg, Germany	from 23–5–45
B.160 Kastrup, Germany	from 22–6–45
B.164 Schleswig, Germany	from 22–8–45
B.155 Dedelstorf, Germany	from 5–9–45
B.152 Fassburg, Germany	from 23–10–45
B.170 Sylt, Germany	from 31–12–45
Fassburg, Germany	from 22–1–46
Gatow, Germany	from 22–2–46
Fassburg, Germany	from 25–3–46

Commanding Officers

Sqn Ldr A. R. Hall	5–44 to 9–44
Sqn Ldr D. V. Cotes-Preedy, DFC and Bar, GM	9–44 to c.12–44
Sqn Ldr R. R. St Quentin, DFC	c.1–45

NO. 80 SQUADRON

(Received first Tempest Mark Vs, 8 August 1944; declared operational, 1 September 1944; disposed of Tempests, January 1948)

Airfields

West Malling, Kent	from 5–7–44
Manston, Kent	from 29–8–44
Coltishall, Norfolk	from 20–9–44
B.70 Deurne, Belgium	from 29–9–44
B.82 Grave, Holland	from 1–10–44
B.80 Volkel, Holland	from 7–10–44
B.112 Hopsten, Germany	from 12–4–45
Warmwell, Dorset	from 18–4–45
B.152 Fassburg, Germany	from 7–5–45
B.160 Kastrup, Germany	from 24–6–45
B.158 Lubeck, Germany	from 6–9–45
Wunstorf, Germany	from 31–1–46
Gatow, Germany	from 3–6–47
Duxford, Cambridgeshire	from 2–9–47

Commanding Officers

Sqn Ldr R. L. Spurdle, DSO, DFC and Bar	7–44 to 1–45
Sqn Ldr E. D. Mackie, DSO, DFC and Bar	1–45 to 4–45
Major R. A. Henwick, DFC, SAAF	4–45 to 11–45
Sqn Ldr A. H. B. Friendship, DFM and Bar	11–45 to 5–46
Sqn Ldr H. E. Walmsley, DFC and Bar	5–46 to 11–47
Sqn Ldr R. A. Newberry	11–47 to 11–48

NO. 152 SQUADRON

(Received first Tempest Mark IIs, July 1946; disposed of Tempests,
January 1947. All Tempest service in India)

Airfield

Risalpur, India	from 18–6–46 to 31–1–47

Commanding Officer

Sqn Ldr C. T. A. Douglas, DFC   6–46 to 1–47

NO. 174 SQUADRON

(Received first Tempest Mark V, September 1945; disposed of
Tempests, March 1946. All Tempest service in Germany)

Airfields

B.155 Dedelstorf, Germany	from 19–9–45
Gatow, Germany	from 19–10–45
B.152 Fassburg, Germany	from 26–11–45

Commanding Officer

Sqn Ldr D. C. Usher, DFC, DFM   9–45 to 3–46

NO. 183 SQUADRON

(Received first Tempest Mark II, August 1945; disposed of Tempests, November 1945)

Airfields

Chilbolton, Hampshire	from 17–6–46
Fairwood Common, Glamorgan	from 8–10–45

Commanding Officers

Sqn Ldr J. R. Cullen, DFC	2–45 to 10–45
Sqn Ldr F. W. M. Jenson, OBE, DFC and Bar, AFC	10–45 to 11–45

NO. 213 SQUADRON

(Received first Tempest Mark VI, January 1947; disposed of Tempests, January 1950. All Tempest service in Mediterranean, Middle
East and East Africa)

Airfields

Nicosia, Cyprus	from 25–9–46
Shallufa, Egypt	from 3–9–47
Khartoum, Sudan	from 22–10–47
Mogadishu, Italian Somaliland	from 17–8–48
Deversoir, Egypt	from 21–10–48

Commanding Officers

Not known.

NO. 222 SQUADRON

(Received first Tempest Mark V, December 1944; disposed of
Tempests, October 1945)

Airfields

Predannack, Cornwall	from 17–12–44
B.77 Gilze-Rijen, Holland	from 21–2–45
B.91 Kluis, Holland	from 7–4–45
B.109 Quackenbruck, Germany	from 20–4–45
Fairwood Common, Glamorgan	from 4–6–45
Boxted, Essex	from 9–6–45
Exeter, Devon	from 12–6–45

Commanding Officers

Sqn Ldr J. B. Rigby, DFC and Bar	7–44 to 1–45
Sqn Ldr E. B. Lyons, DFC	1–45 to 5–45
Sqn Ldr R. M. Matheson	5–45 to 10–45

NO. 247 SQUADRON

(Received first Tempest Mark IIs, August 1945; disposed of Tempests, May 1946)

Airfield

Chilbolton, Hampshire	from 20–8–45 to 27–6–46

Commanding Officers

Not known.

NO. 249 SQUADRON

(Received first Tempest Mark V, December 1946 (later joined by
Tempest F Mark VIs); disposed of Tempests, March 1950. All
Tempest service in the Middle East)

Airfields

Habbaniya, Iraq	from 6–46
Deversoir, Egypt	from 1–4–49

Commanding Officer

Not known

NO. 274 SQUADRON

(Received first Tempest Mark V, July 1944; declared operational,
12 August 1944; disposed of Tempests, September 1945)

Airfields

West Malling, Kent	from 5–7–44
Manston, Kent	from 17–8–44
Coltishall, Norfolk	from 20–9–44
B.70 Deurne, Belgium	from 29–9–44
B.82 Grave, Holland	from 2–10–44
B.80 Volkel, Holland	from 7–10–44
B.91 Kluis, Holland	from 17–3–45

B.109 Quackenbruck, Germany   from 20–4–45
B.155 Dedelstorf, Germany   from 20–6–45
Warmwell, Dorset   from 3–9–45
Commanding Officers
Sqn Ldr J. F. Edwards, DFC, DFM   3–44 to 8–44
Sqn Ldr M. G. Barnett, DFC   8–44 to 9–44
Sqn Ldr J. R. Heap, DFC   9–44 to 11–44
Sqn Ldr A. H. Baird, DFC   11–44 to 2–45
Sqn Ldr D. C. Fairbanks, DFC and Bar
(American, RCAF)   2–45
Sqn Ldr W. J. Hibbert   3–45 to 4–45
Sqn Ldr D. C. Usher, DFC, DFM   4–45 to 9–45

NO. 287 SQUADRON

(Anti-aircraft co-operation; received first Tempest Mark V, November 1944; disposed of Tempests, June 1945)
Airfields
Gatwick, Surrey   from 27–8–44
Redhill, Surrey   from 20–1–45
Hornchurch, Essex   from 3–5–45
Commanding Officers
Not known.

NO. 349 SQUADRON (BELGIAN)

(Received first Tempest Mark V, February 1945; but training abandoned; disposed of aircraft, April 1945)
Airfield
Predannack, Cornwall   from 21–2–45
    until 19–4–45

Commanding Officers
Sqn Ldr A. A. Van der Velde (Belgian)   7–44 to 3–45
Sqn Ldr R. A. Lallemant, DFC and Bar (Belgian)   3–45 to 12–45

NO. 485 SQUADRON, RNZAF

(Received first Tempest Mark V, February 1945; but training abandoned; disposed of Tempests, March 1945)
Airfield
Predannack, Cornwall   from 2–45
    until 4–45

Commanding Officer
Sqn Ldr K. J. Macdonald   2–45 to 7–45

NO. 486 SQUADRON, RNZAF

(Received first Tempest Mark V, January 1944; declared operationa, May 1944; disposed of Tempests, September 1945)
Airfields
Beaulieu, Hampshire   from 1–44
Newchurch, Kent   from 4–44
Matlaske, Norfolk   9–44
B.60 Grimbergen, Belgium   from 9–44
B.80 Volkel, Holland   from 10–44
B.112 Hopsten, Germany   4–45
B.152 Fassburg, Germany   from 4–45
B.150 Celle, Germany   5–45
B.160 Kastrup, Germany   from 5–45
B.158 Lubeck, Germany   from 7–45
B.166 Flensburg, Germany   9–45
Dunsfold, Surrey   from 9–45 to 10–45

Commanding Officers
Sqn Ldr J. H. Iremonger, DFC   1–44 to 12–44
Sqn Ldr A. E. Umbers, DFC   12–44 to 2–45
Sqn Ldr K. G. Taylor-Cannon   2–45 to 4–45
Sqn Ldr W. E. Schrader, DFC   4–45 to 5–45
Sqn Ldr C. J. Sheddan, DFC   5–45 to 10–45

NO. 501 (COUNTY OF GLOUCESTER) SQUADRON, AAF

(Received first Tempest Mark V, July 1944; declared operational, August 1944; disposed of Tempests, April 1945)
Airfields
Westhampnett, Sussex   from 2–7–44
Manston, Kent   from 2–8–44
Bradwell Bay, Essex   from 22–9–44
Hunsdon, Hertfordshire   from 3–3–45
Commanding Officers
Sqn Ldr M. G. Barnett   10–43 to 8–44
Sqn Ldr J. Berry, DFC and Bar   8–44 to 10–44
Sqn Ldr A. Parker-Rees, DFC   10–44 to 4–45

TEMPEST SQUADRONS OF THE R.A.F. AND COMMONWEALTH AIR FORCES

Legend: ▨ -Tempest V   ▨ -Tempest II   ▨ -Tempest VI

SQUADRONS	1944	1945	1946	1947	1948	1949	1950	1951
3		Tempest V			VAMPIRE I			
5	TYPHOON	THUNDERBOLT		SPITFIRE XVI				
6			SPITFIRE IX			VAMPIRE 5		
8			MOSQUITO VI			BRIGAND		
16		SPITFIRE XVI			VAMPIRE 5			
20		SPITFIRE XIV		DISBANDED				
26			SPITFIRE XIV			VAMPIRE 5		
30		THUNDERBOLT	DISBANDED					
33	SPITFIRE IX		SPITFIRE XVI					
39				RE-FORMED		MOSQUITO NF		HORNET 3
54	SPITFIRE IX	SPITFIRE VIII		VAMPIRE I				
56			METEOR III					
80					SPITFIRE 24			
152	SPITFIRE IX		SPITFIRE XVI	DISBANDED				
174	TYPHOON		DISBANDED					
183		SPITFIRE IX	DISBANDED					
213				MUSTANG IV			VAMPIRE 5	
222	SPITFIRE IX		METEOR III					
247	TYPHOON		VAMPIRE I					
249	SPITFIRE IX		MOSQUITO 26				VAMPIRE 5	
274			DISBANDED					
287 *	VARIOUS		VARIOUS					
349 (Belgian) **	SPITFIRE IX	SPITFIRE XVI						
485 (RNZAF) **	SPITFIRE IX	TYPHOON						
486 (RNZAF)			DISBANDED					
501	SPIT. IX		DISBANDED					

* Not an operational squadron.
** Did not achieve operational status with Tempests

APPENDIX B
Summary of Flight Test and Development Work on Hawker Tornado, Typhoon and Tempest aircraft at Langley (Hawker)

Flight Report	Aircraft	Test	Date	Engine	Airscrew	Weight	Pilot
1	F.18/37 P5219	Preliminary taxying trials	1–10–39	Vulture II No 12	DB330/A/1	8,785	P. G. Lucas
2	F.18/37 P5219	Third taxying trial	3–10–39	Vulture II No 12	DB330/A/1	8,749	P. G. Lucas
3	F.18/37 P5219	First handling flights	6/7–10–39	Vulture II No 12	DB330/A/1	9,127	P. G. Lucas
4	F.18/37 P5219	Third handling flight	12–10–39	Vulture II No 12	DB330/A/1	9,127	P. G. Lucas
5	F.18/37 P5219	Handling	18–10–39	Vulture II No 12	DB330/A/1	9,127	P. G. Lucas
6	F.18/37 P5219	Handling	27–10–39	Vulture II No 12	DB330/A/1	9,127	P. G. Lucas
7	F.18/37 P5219	Handling	9/10–11–39	Vulture II No 12	DB330/A/1	9,127	P. G. Lucas
9	F.18/37 P5219	Levels and intake pressures	19–11–39	Vulture II No 12	Rotol 14′ Magnesium 665	9,251	P. G. Lucas
10	F.18/37 P5219	Handling and levels	28–11–39	Vulture II No 12	Rotol 14′	9,251	P. G. Lucas
11	F.18/37 P5219	Levels with modified intake; pressure drop across oil cooler	6–12–39	Vulture II No 12	Rotol 14′	9,115	P. G. Lucas
12	F.18/37 P5219	General handling Wheel flaps added	11/20–1–40	Vulture II No 12	Rotol 14′	9,115	P. G. Lucas
13	F.18/37 P5219	General handling; wheel flaps deleted	14/15–2–40	Vulture II No 12	Rotol 14′	9,127	P. G. Lucas
14	Typhoon P5212	Taxying trials	23–2–40	Sabre 95009	DH Hydr.23FX	9,546	P. G. Lucas
15	Typhoon P5212	First flight	24–2–40	Sabre 95009	DH Hydr.23FX	9,546	P. G. Lucas
16	Typhoon P5212	Second flight (part of intake carried away)	1–3–40	Sabre 95009	DH Hydr.23FX	9,546	P. G. Lucas
17	Tornado P5219	Handling with modified wheel fairings	29–2–40	Vulture II No 12	Rotol 14′	9,115	P. G. Lucas
18	Tornado P5219	FS-gear climb and levels	2–3–40	Vulture II No 12	Rotol 14′	9,115	P. G. Lucas
19	Tornado P5219	FS-gear climb and levels	2–3–40	Vulture II No 12	Rotol 14′	9,115	P. G. Lucas
21	Tornado P5219	General handling	6–3–40	Vulture II No 12	Rotol 14′	9,115	P. G. Lucas
22	Typhoon P5212	General handling	9–3–40	Sabre 95009	DH Hydr.23FX	9,546	P. G. Lucas
23	Typhoon P5212	General handling	15–3–40	Sabre 95009	DH Hydr.23FX	9,546	P. G. Lucas
24	Typhoon P5212	General handling	18–3–40	Sabre 95009	DH Hydr.23FX	9,546	P. G. Lucas
25	Typhoon P5212	General handling; fuel system observations	21–3–40	Sabre 95009	DH Hydr.23FX	9,546	P. G. Lucas
26	Tornado P5219	General handling	27–3–40	Vulture II No 12	Rotol 14′	9,115	P. G. Lucas
27	Tornado P5219	General handling	2–4–40	Vulture II No 12	Rotol 14′	9,115	P. G. Lucas
29	Typhoon P5212	Modified fuel system; FS levels	4–4–40	Sabre 95009	DH Hydr.23FX	9,115	P. G. Lucas
30	Tornado P5219	Extended intake above nose	4/5–4–40	Vulture II No 12	Rotol 14′	9,115	P. G. Lucas
31	Typhoon P5212	New engine and mounting; handling	7–5–40	Sabre 95007	DH.33 Ex-2	9,546	P. G. Lucas
32	Typhoon P5212	RAE Vibrograph; airframe failure and forced landing following	9–5–40	Sabre 95007	DH.33 Ex-2	9,850	P. G. Lucas
33	Tornado P5219	Directional stability tests	16–5–40	Vulture II No 12	Rotol 14′	9,115	P. G. Lucas
34	Tornado P5219	Levels with tailwheel doors	12–6–40	Vulture II No 12	Rotol 14′	9,115	P. G. Lucas
59	Typhoon P5212	First flight after accident; engine failed	7–7–40	Sabre 95007	DH Hydr. 14′	9,410	R. C. Reynell
64	Tornado P5219	FS-gear climb and levels	14–7–40	Vulture II No 132	Rotol 530	9,115	P. G. Lucas
65	Tornado P5219	MS-gear levels	15–7–40	Vulture II No 132	Rotol DR530	9,115	P. G. Lucas
66	Tornado P5219	FS-gear levels	17–7–40	Vulture II No 132	Rotol DR530	9,115	P. G. Lucas
68	Typhoon P5212	Handling to trace ignition trouble and fuel consumption	19–7–40	Sabre 95007	DH Hydr. 14′	9,410	P. G. Lucas
71	Tornado P5219	Partial at 20,500 ft	22–7–40	Vulture II No 132	Rotol DR330	10,225	R. C. Reynell
73	Tornado P5219	Full-load climb	27–7–40	Vulture II No 132	Rotol DR330	10,225	P. G. Lucas
74	Tornado P5219	Full-load climb and levels	29–7–40	Vulture II No 132	Rotol DR330	10,225	P. G. Lucas
75	Tornado P5219	Climb and levels; forced landing after engine trouble	31–7–40	Vulture II No 132	Rotol DR330	10,225	R. C. Reynell
79	Typhoon P5212	Preliminary test of modified radiator and fabric rudder	2–8–40	Sabre 95013	DH 65522 14′	9,410	P. G. Lucas
80	Typhoon P5212	Max rate turns and directional stability with 12″ chord rudder	2–8–40	Sabre 95013	DH 65522 14′	9,410	P. G. Lucas
83	Typhoon P5212	MS and FS-gear levels	6–8–40	Sabre 95013	DH 65522 14′	9,410	P. G. Lucas
85	Typhoon P5212	Levels: standard intake	12–8–40	Sabre 95013	DH 65522 14′	9,410	P. G. Lucas
86	Typhoon P5212	Levels: small intake	12–8–40	Sabre 95013	DH 65522 14′	9,410	P. G. Lucas
88	Typhoon P5212	Oil & water suitability with varying RPM and boost	13–8–40	Sabre 95013	DH 65522 14′	9,410	P. G. Lucas
89	Typhoon P5212	Fuel consumption in MS-gear	15–8–40	Sabre 95013	DH 65522 14′	9,410	P. G. Lucas
91	Typhoon P5212	Oil & water suitability with enlarged oil cooler	24–8–40	Sabre 95013	DH 5804 14′	9,410	P. G. Lucas
97	Typhoon P5212	Handling and levels with multi-stub exhausts and new flap operation	17–9–40	Sabre 95018	DH 65622 14′	9,850	P. G. Lucas
98	Typhoon P5212	Climb and levels with DH faired-root blades	18–9–40	Sabre 95018	DH 65858 14′	9,850	P. G. Lucas
119	Tornado P5224	First taxying and handling flights	5, 6, 7. 15–12–40	Vulture II No 132	Rotol DES.6215 13′ 2½″ dia.	9,600	P. G. Lucas
123	Tornado P5224	Light-load climb and handling	2–1–41	Vulture II No 132	Rotol DES.6215	9,600	P. G. Lucas
126	Tornado P5224	Full-throttle climb to 28,000 ft; in MS-gear, and partials	17–1–41	Vulture II No 132	Rotol DES.6215	10,579	P. G. Lucas
129	Typhoon P5212	Engine test with new engine having 12″ impeller	2, 7–2–41	Sabre 95015	DH faired roots	10,600	P. G. Lucas
130	Tornado P5224	Full-throttle climb & levels with new magnetos	10–2–41	Vulture II No 132	Rotol DES.6215	10,579	P. G. Lucas
132	Typhoon P5212	Engine test with automatic boost control out of action	10–2–41	Sabre 95015	DH faired roots	10,600	P. G. Lucas
135	Tornado P5224	Climb and levels	15–2–41	Vulture II No 132	Rotol/Jablo	10,579	P. G. Lucas
144	Tornado P5224	Climb and levels	22–2–41	Vulture II No 132	Rotol/Jablo	10,579	P. G. Lucas
147	Typhoon P5212	Check on rated altitudes, MS and FS-gears	21–2–41	Sabre 95022	DH 50011	10,600	P. G. Lucas

Flight Report	Aircraft	Test	Date	Engine	Airscrew	Weight	Pilot
148	Typhoon P5212	Flexible engine mounting	21–2–41	Sabre 95022	DH 50011	10,600	P. G. Lucas
150	Typhoon P5212	Oil cooler pressures and temperature test	25–2–41 26–2–41 }	Sabre 95022	DH 50011	10,600	P. G. Lucas
151	Tornado P5224	Undercarriage malfunction	5–3–41	Vulture II No 132	Rotol/Jablo	10,579	K. G. Seth-Smith
155	Typhoon P5212	Comparative climbs at 3,500 and 4,000 rpm	5–3–41	Sabre 95022	DH 52016	10,600	P. G. Lucas
156	Typhoon P5212	Propeller test (DH 52016)	7–3–41	Sabre 95022	DH 52016	10,600	P. G. Lucas
159	Tornado P5224	Air intake readings, forward intake	4–3–41 5–3–41 }	Vulture II No 132	Rotol/Jablo	10,579	P. G. Lucas
160	Tornado P5224	Trimming tab control	c.9–3–41	Vulture II No 132	Rotol/Jablo	10,579	P. G. Lucas
163	Tornado P5224	Forced landing following engine failure	21–3–41	Vulture II No 132	Rotol/Jablo	10,579	P. G. Lucas
165	Tornado P5224	Air intake cut back 5″	21–3–41	Vulture II No 132	Rotol/Jablo	10,579	P. G. Lucas
166	Typhoon P5212	Level speeds and Vibrograph records	28–3–41	Sabre 95022	Rotol RA.4066	10,600	P. G. Lucas
170	Tornado P5219	Level speeds (new engine)	31–3–41	Vulture V No 164	Rotol DR960	10,491	K. G. Seth-Smith
171	Tornado P5219	Level speeds (new engine)	31–3–41	Vulture V No 164	Rotol DR960	10,491	K. G. Seth-Smith
172	Typhoon P5212	Climb & levels in MS & FS gear	30–3–41	Sabre 95022	Rotol EE137	10,600	P. G. Lucas
176	Tornado P5219	Climb and levels in FS-gear	4–4–41	Vulture V No 164	Rotol DR960	10,491	P. G. Lucas
177	Typhoon P5212	Fuel tank distribution tests	4–4–41	Sabre 95022	Rotol EE137	10,600	K. G. Seth-Smith
182	Tornado P5219	Oil loss from engine breather	12–4–41	Vulture V No 164	Rotol DR960	10,491	K. G. Seth-Smith
184	Tornado P5219	Air intake pressures	15–4–41	Vulture V No 164	Rotol DR960	10,491	K. G. Seth-Smith
185	Tornado P5219	Climb and levels in MS-gear	16–4–41	Vulture V No 164	Rotol DR960	10,491	K. G. Seth-Smith
186	Tornado P5219	Levels in MS-gear	16–4–41	Vulture V No 164	Rotol DR960	10,491	K. G. Seth-Smith
187	Tornado P5219	Full climb to ceiling	17–4–41	Vulture V No 164	Rotol DR960	10,491	P. G. Lucas
190	Tornado P5219	Full climb to ceiling	21–4–41	Vulture V No 164	Rotol DR533	10,390	K. G. Seth-Smith
191	Tornado P5219	Level speeds	21–4–41	Vulture V No 164	Rotol DR533	10,390	K. G. Seth-Smith
193	Tornado P5219	Level speeds	26–4–41	Vulture V No 164	Rotol DR533	10,390	K. G. Seth-Smith
202	Typhoon P5216	First handling; four-cannon gun-bay readings	3–5–41 4–5–41 }	Sabre 95023	DH A52016	10,735	P. G. Lucas
203	Tornado P5219	Level speeds in MS-gear	5–5–41	Vulture V No 164	Rotol DR960	10,390	K. G. Seth-Smith
204	Tornado P5219	Climb and levels in MS-gear	10–5–41	Vulture V No 164	Rotol DR960	10,390	K. G. Seth-Smith
GT1	Typhoon R7576	Taxying trials (at Gloster)	26–5–41	Sabre I S45/153237	DH Hydr.A52017	10,307	M. Daunt
GT2	Typhoon R7576	Handling report on 3 flights	27,28–5–41	Sabre I S45/153237	DH Hydr.A52017	10,307	M. Daunt
211	Tornado P5219	Levels in MS-gear and oil test	11–6–41	Vulture V No 164	Rotol DR.533	10,390	K. G. Seth-Smith
213	Tornado P5224	Test of new engine installation	11–6–41	Vulture V No 126	Rotol DR.960	—	K. G. Seth-Smith
215	Typhoon R7576	Handling on 1st production Typhoon	12–6–41	Sabre I S45/152237	DH Hydr.A52017	10,307	P. G. Lucas
219	Typhoon P5216	Levels with cutaway head fairing	15–6–41	Sabre 95018	Rotol EE137	10,600	P. G. Lucas
220	Typhoon P5216	Full throttle climb	17–6–41	Sabre II 95018	Rotol EE137	10,600	H. S. Broad
221	Tornado P5219	Full-throttle levels	17–6–41	Vulture V No 164	Rotol DR533	10,390	P. G. Lucas
223	Typhoon P5216	Full-throttle climb for oil suitability	17–6–41	Sabre II 95018	DH A50011	10,735	P. G. Lucas
224	Typhoon P5216	Full-throttle climb with insulating sleeve in intake	18–6–41	Sabre II 95018	DH A50011	10,735	P. G. Lucas
226	Tornado P5219	Levels & oil slinging checks	19–6–41	Vulture V No 164	Rotol DR.533	10,390	W. Humble
227	Tornado P5219	Level speeds	16–6–41	Vulture V No 164	Rotol DR.533	10,390	H. S. Broad
228	Tornado P5219	Level speeds	18–6–41	Vulture V No 164	Rotol DR.533	10,390	W. Humble
229	Tornado P5219	Level speeds	17–6–41	Vulture V No 164	Rotol DR.533	10,390	W. Humble
230	Typhoon P5216	Full-throttle climb and levels in MS-gear	20–6–41	Sabre II 95018	DH A52016	10,735	P. G. Lucas
232	Tornado P5219	Oil cooling test	20–6–41	Vulture V No 164	Rotol DR.533	10,390	P. G. Lucas
235	Tornado P5219	Oil cooling with original tank	27–6–41	Vulture V No 164	Rotol DR.533	10,390	K. G. Seth-Smith
237	Tornado P5219	Oil slinging and cooling	28–6–41	Vulture V No 164	Rotol DR.533	10,390	K. G. Seth-Smith
238	Typhoon P5212	Levels with fairing cutaway	27–6–41	Sabre II 95018	Rotol EE137	10,600	P. G. Lucas
239	Typhoon IA R7577	Oil cooling test: large cone	29–6–41	Sabre I S49/153241	DH Hydr.PX.512	10,281	P. G. Lucas
240	Typhoon IA R7577	Oil cooling test: medium cone	29–6–41	Sabre I S49 /153241	DH Hydr.PX.512	10,281	P. G. Lucas
241	Typhoon IA R7577	Oil cooling test: large cone	1–7–41	Sabre I S49/153241	DH Hydr.PX.512	10,281	P. G. Lucas
242	Typhoon IA R7577	Oil cooling test: medium cone	30–6–41	Sabre I S49/153241	DH Hydr.PX.512	10,281	P. G. Lucas
243	Typhoon IA R7577	Oil cooling test: large cone	2–7–41	Sabre I S49/153241	DH Hydr.PX.512	10,281	P. G. Lucas
244	Typhoon IA R7577	Oil cooling test: no cone	2–7–41	Sabre I S49/153241	DH Hydr.PX.512	10,281	P. G. Lucas
245	Typhoon IA R7577	Oil cooling test: no cone	4–7–41	Sabre I S49/153241	DH Hydr.PX.512	10,281	P. G. Lucas
246	Typhoon P5212	MS-gear Level speeds	2–7–41	Sabre II 95018	Rotol EE137	10,600	K. G. Seth-Smith
247	Tornado P5219	Oil tank test	3–7–41	Vulture V No 164	Rotol DR.532	10,390	K. G. Seth-Smith
251	Tornado P5224	Climb and levels	7–7–41	Vulture V No 126	Rotol DR.960	10,430	K. G. Seth-Smith
252	Typhoon P5212	Take-off tests	8–8–41	Sabre II 95026	Rotol EE137	10,605	K. G. Seth-Smith
256	Typhoon IA R7577	Oil cooling: large cone and spoiler	6–7–41	Sabre I S49/153241	DH Hydr.PX.512	10,281	K. G. Seth-Smith
274	Tornado P5224	Ignition and oil slinging test	14–8–41	Vulture V No 132	Rotol EE112	10,340	K. G. Seth-Smith
275	Tornado P5224	Pressurized oil and fuel tanks; Heenan type oil tank	7–8–41 11–8–41 }	Vulture V No 132	Rotol EE112	10,340	P. G. Lucas
276	Tornado P5224	Climb, levels and ignition test	16–8–41	Vulture V No 132	Rotol EE112	10,430	K. G. Seth-Smith
277	Typhoon P5212	Vibration tests	14–8–41	Sabre II 95018	Rotol EE137	10,605	K. G. Seth-Smith
278	Typhoon IA R7577	Radiator suitability climb	18–8–41	Sabre I S64	DH Hydr.PX512	10,281	K. G. Seth-Smith
281	Typhoon IA R7577	Radiator suitability climb	19–8–41	Sabre I S64	DH Hydr.PX512	10,281	K. G. Seth-Smith
283	Tornado P5224	Engine test	19–8–41	Vulture V	Rotol	10,400	K. G. Seth-Smith
284	Typhoon IA R7577	Maintenance of fuel pressure	31–8–41	Sabre I S64	DH Hydr.PX512	10,281	H. S. Broad
285	Tornado I R7936	Light load handling test	31–8–41	Vulture V No 4252	Rotol DR.534	10,051	P. G. Lucas
290	Typhoon IA R7577	Ceiling climb and gun bay heating	11–9–41	Sabre I S64	DH Hydr.PX512	10,770	K. G. Seth-Smith
291	Typhoon IA R7577	Level speeds in FS-gear	11–9–41	Sabre I S64	DH Hydr.PX512	10,770	K. G. Seth-Smith
296	Typhoon IA R7577	Take-off tests	25–9–41	Sabre I S64	DH Hydr.PX512	10,770	K. G. Seth-Smith
297	Typhoon IA R7577	Level speeds	27–9–41	Sabre I S64	DH Hydr.PX512	10,770	K. G. Seth-Smith
299	Typhoon IA R7577	Climb and levels in MS-gear	10–10–41	Sabre II S177	DH Hydr.PX512	10,770	P. G. Lucas
300	Typhoon IA R7577	Climb and levels in FS-gear	10–10–41	Sabre II S177	DH Hydr.PX512	10,770	K. G. Seth-Smith
304	Typhoon IA R7577	Test of door by Fox & Nicholls	16–10–41	Sabre II S177	DH Hydr.PX512	10,770	P. G. Lucas
306	Typhoon IA R7577	Level speeds in FS-gear	20–10–41	Sabre II S177	DH Hydr.PX512	10,770	K. G. Seth-Smith
308	Tornado I R7936	Production climb and levels	16–10–41	Vulture V No 4252	Rotol RS6/1	10,550	K. G. Seth-Smith
309	Typhoon IA R7577	Level speeds in FS-gear and climb at 3,700 rpm	21–10–41	Sabre II S177	DH Hydr.PX512	10,770	P. G. Lucas
310	Typhoon IA R7577	Counter-balance elevator control	27–10–41	Sabre II S177	DH Hydr.PX512	10,770	P. G. Lucas
311	Tornado HG641	Preliminary handling tests	23–10–41	Centaurus CE45 No 19	Rotol HX.63	9,658	P. G. Lucas
314	Typhoon IA R7577	Take-off tests with 4-blade DH propeller	27–10–41	Sabre II S177	DH 4-bl. 50004	10,890	K. G. Seth-Smith

Flight Report	Aircraft	Test	Date	Engine	Airscrew	Weight	Pilot
315	Typhoon IA R7577	Climb in MS-gear and partials in FS-gear	28–10–41	Sabre II S177	DH 4-bl. 50004	10,890	K. G. Seth-Smith
316	Typhoon IA R7577	Ceiling climb in FS-gear	29–10–41	Sabre II S177	DH 4-bl. 50004	10,890	K. G. Seth-Smith
317	Tornado HG641	Level speeds and handling	29–10–41	Centaurus CE45 No 19	Rotol HX.63	9,658	P. G. Lucas
318	Tornado HG641	Carbon monoxide test	31–10–41	Centaurus CE45 No 19	Rotol HX.63	9,658	P. G. Lucas
319	Tornado R7936	Level speeds in FS-gear	1–11–41	Vulture V No 4252	Rotol RS6/1	10,550	K. G. Seth-Smith
320	Typhoon IA R7577	Carbon monoxide analyser	1–11–41	Sabre II S177	DH 4-bl. 50004	10,890	P. G. Lucas
321	Tornado P5219	Cockpit and gun-bay heating	5–11–41	Vulture V No 164	Rotol EE175	10,500	W. Humble
324	Typhoon P5216	Handling with extended wing tips and modified rear-view canopy	9–11–41	Sabre II 95018	DH Hydr.PX512	9,890	P. G. Lucas(?)
325	Typhoon IA R7577	Levels in FS and MS-gear	9–11–41	Sabre II S177	DH 4-bl. 50004	10,890	P. G. Lucas
326	Typhoon IA R7577	Counterbalance elevator control	12–11–41	Sabre II S177	DH 4-bl. 50004	10,890	P. G. Lucas
328	Typhoon P5216	Levels in FS-gear	18–11–41	Sabre II 95018	DH Hydr.PX512	10,346	K. G. Seth-Smith
330	Typhoon IA R7577	Dive from FS M.P.A. (Maximum Permissible Altitude)	23–11–41	Sabre II S 177	DH 4-bl. 50004	10,890	K. G. Seth-Smith
331	Tornado HG641	Carbon monoxide test	27–11–41	Centaurus CE 45	Rotol HX.63	9,658	P. G. Lucas
332	Typhoon IA R8198	First flight, Langley Typhoon	26–11–41	Sabre II S 98	DH Hdr. 52046	10,402	P. G. Lucas
333	Typhoon IA R7591	Carbon monoxide test (No 56 Squadron aircraft)	21–11–41	Sabre II	DH Hydr.	—	P. G. Lucas
334	Typhoon P5216	Rudder angles and levels in FS-gear	7–12–41	Sabre II 95018	DH Hydr. PX512	10,346	K. G. Seth-Smith
336	Tornado HG641	Air intake pressures and levels	7–12–41	Centaurus CE.4S	Rotol HX.63	9,658	P. G. Lucas
337	Tornado P5224	Dive to 150 kts ASI	9–12–41	—	—	10,550	P. G. Lucas
338	Typhoon IA R7595	Modified rear view, Scheme B	11–12–41	—	—	—	P. G. Lucas
339	Typhoon IA R8198	Carbon monoxide test	11–12–41	—	—	—	P. G. Lucas
341	Tornado P5219	Cockpit and gun bay heating	11–12–41	Vulture V No 164	Rotol EE175	10,500	W. Humble
342	Tornado HG641	Air intake investigation	11–12–41	Centaurus CE.19	Rotol HX.63	9,658	K. G. Seth-Smith
343	Typhoon IA R7577	Cockpit ventilation and subsequent forced landing	12–12–41	Sabre II S 177	DH 4-bl. 50004	10,890	P. G. Lucas
344	Tornado P5219	Cockpit heating	15–12–41	Vulture V No 164	Rotol EE175	10,500	W. Humble
347	Typhoon IA R8198	Cockpit heating and CO test	15–12–41	Sabre II S 98	DH Hydr. 52046	10,402	K. G. Seth-Smith
348	Typhoon IA R8198	FS-climb and CO test	15–12–41	Sabre II S 98	DH Hydr. 52046	10,402	K. G. Seth-Smith
350	Typhoon IA R8198	Climb to check oil temps	17–12–41	Sabre II S 98	DH Hydr. 52046	10,402	K. G. Seth-Smith
351	Typhoon IA R8198	MS climb to check oil temps	18–12–41	Sabre II S 98	DH Hydr. 52046	10,402	K. G. Seth-Smith
353	Typhoon IA R8198	Climb to check oil temps and pressure without valve bellows	17–12–41	Sabre II S 98	DH Hydr. 52046	10,402	K. G. Seth-Smith
355	Typhoon P5216	Carburettor check, levels and dive	23–12–41	Sabre II 95018	DH Hydr.PX512	10,346	K. G. Seth-Smith
357	Typhoon IA R7595	Cockpit temperature check	28–12–41	—	—	—	K. G. Seth-Smith
360	Typhoon IA R7577	Cockpit and gun bay heating	6–1–42	Sabre II S 215	DH Hydr.PX512	10,770	K. G. Seth-Smith
361	Typhoon IA R8198	Oil check with de-aerator	6–1–42	Sabre II S 98	DH Hydr. 52046	10,500	K. G. Seth-Smith
363	Tornado P5219	Gun bay and cockpit heating	6–1–42	Vulture V No 164	Rotol EE175	10,500	K. G. Seth-Smith
364	Typhoon IA R7577	Fuel system tests with float valves fitted	8–1–42	Sabre II S 215	DH Hydr. 55/2	—	W. Humble
366	Typhoon IA R8198	Oil checks on FS-climb	8–1–42	Sabre II S 98/A153290	DH Hydr. 52046	10,500	K. G. Seth-Smith
367	Typhoon IA R7577	Oil and fuel system check in dive	25–1–42	Sabre II S 215	DH Hydr. 55/2	—	K. G. Seth-Smith
368	Typhoon IA R8198	Oil pressure and levels with extended exhausts	25–1–42	Sabre II S 98	DH Hydr. 52046	10,500	P. G. Lucas
369	Typhoon IA R7577	FS-climb and fuel system test	25–1–42	Sabre II S 215	DH Hydr. 55/2	10,770	K. G. Seth-Smith
371	Typhoon P5216	Carburettor test in weak mixture	25–1–42	Sabre II 95018	DH Hydr. 5004	10,346	P. G. Lucas
372	Typhoon IA R8198	FS climb and oil check	28–1–42	Sabre II S 98	DH Hydr. 52046	10,500	K. G. Seth-Smith
373	Typhoon IA R7577	FS climb and oil check	28–1–42	Sabre II S 215	DH Hydr. 52016	10,770	P. G. Lucas
374	Typhoon IA R7577	Fuel tank draining; flap blow-up speed; rate of roll measurement	27–1–42	Sabre II S 215	DH Hydr. 52016	10,770	K. G. Seth-Smith
377	Typhoon IA R8198	Pressure readings in wheel wells	7–2–42	Sabre II S 98	DH Hydr. 52046	10,500	K. G. Seth-Smith
378	Typhoon IA R8198	Oil check on FS climb	7–2–42	Sabre II S 98	DH Hydr. 52046	10,500	K. G. Seth-Smith
380	Typhoon P5216	10° dive	8–2–42	Sabre II 95018	DH Hydr. PX512	10,346	K. G. Seth-Smith
381	Typhoon P5216	Oil pressure check on FS climb	11–2–42	Sabre II 95018	DH Hydr. PX512	10,346	K. G. Seth-Smith
382	Typhoon IA R8198	FS climb and MS levels with 4″ extended exhausts	11–2–42	Sabre II S 98	DH Hydr. 52046	10,500	Not known
384	Typhoon P5216	Rudder angles	13–2–42	Sabre II 95018	DH Hydr. PX512	—	W. Humble
386	Typhoon IA R8198	Oil pressure check on FS climb	13–2–42	Sabre II S 98	DH Hydr. 52046	10,500	K. G. Seth-Smith
388	Typhoon P5216	FS level speeds	14–2–42	Sabre II 95018	DH Hydr.PX512	10,346	K. G. Seth-Smith
389	Typhoon IA R7577	Carburation test	16–2–42	Sabre II S 283	DH Hydr.55/2	10,770	K. G. Seth-Smith
390	Typhoon IA R7577	Climb to check oil temperature	16–2–42	Sabre II S 283	DH Hydr.55/2	10,770	K. G. Seth-Smith
391	Typhoon IA R7577	FS climb to check oil temperature	19–2–42	Sabre II S 283	DH Hydr.55/2	10,770	K. G. Seth-Smith
392	Typhoon IA R7577	Climb at 2,600 rpm and FS cruise	20–2–42	Sabre II S 283	DH Hydr.55/2	10,770	K. G. Seth-Smith
393	Typhoon IA R8198	Climb to check oil pressures	19–2–42	Sabre II S 98	DH Hydr.PX512	10,500	P. G. Lucas
394	Typhoon IA R8198	FS climb to check oil pressures	21–2–42	Sabre II S 98	DH Hydr.PX512	10,500	K. G. Seth-Smith
395	Typhoon IA R8198	FS climb to check oil pressures	22–2–42	Sabre II S 98	DH Hydr.PX512	10,500	K. G. Seth-Smith
396	Typhoon IA R7577	Climb at 2,800 rpm with radiator shutter open	22–2–42	Sabre II S 283	DH Hydr.52016	10,770	W. Humble
398	Typhoon IA R7577	FS climb to check oil pressures	22–2–42	Sabre II S 283	DH Hydr.52016	10,770	K. G. Seth-Smith
399	Typhoon P5216	MS Levels to check oil temps	22–2–42	Sabre II 95018	DH Hydr.PX512	10,346	P. G. Lucas
400	Typhoon P5216	Ground warming with grease-filled thermostat	22–2–42	Sabre II 95018	DH Hydr.PX512	10,346	P. G. Lucas
401	Typhoon P5216	Modified Dunlop wheel and brakes	23–2–42	Sabre II 95018	DH Hydr.PX512	9,770	P. G. Lucas
403	Typhoon IA R8198	Oil pressure check with thermostatic valve	23–2–42	Sabre II S 98	DH Hydr.52046	10,500	K. G. Seth-Smith
404	Typhoon IA R7577	Calibration of fuel flow meter	24–2–42	Sabre II S 283	DH Hydr.55/2	10,770	J. A. Crosby-Warren
405	Typhoon IA R7577	Oil temps on FL climb and level	25–2–42	Sabre II S 283	DH Hydr.55/2	10,770	J. A. Crosby-Warren
406	Typhoon IA R8198	Oil checks with thermostat valve	25–2–42	Sabre II S 98	DH Hydr.52046	10,500	K. G. Seth-Smith
407	Typhoon IA R7577	Climb to check oil temperatures	27–2–42	Sabre II S 283	DH Hydr.52016	10,770	W. Humble
409	Typhoon IA R7577	Oil temperatures and stick forces	27–2–42	Sabre II S 283	DH Hydr.52016	10,770	K. G. Seth-Smith
411	Typhoon IA R8198	Climb to check oil temperature	27–2–42	Sabre II S 98	DH Hydr.52046	10,500	K. G. Seth-Smith
412	Typhoon P5216	Climb and level to check oil shuttle valve. Flap check.	27–2–42	Sabre II S 95018	DH Hydr.PX512	10,346	K. G. Seth-Smith

Flight Report	Aircraft	Test	Date	Engine	Airscrew	Weight	Pilot
413	Typhoon IA R8198	Oil temp with 1″ 240° blank	28–2–42	Sabre II S 98	DH Hydr.52046	10,500	J. A. Crosby-Warren
414	Typhoon IA R7577	Oil temp with ³/₄″ 240° blank	28–2–42	Sabre II S 283	DH Hydr.52016	10,770	J. A. Crosby-Warren
415	Typhoon IA R8198	Oil temps; standard cone	3–3–42	Sabre II S 98	DH Hydr.52046	10,500	J. A. Crosby-Warren
416	Typhoon IA R7577	Climb to check 1″ 360° blank	3–3–42	Sabre II S 283	DH Hydr.52016	10,770	K. G. Seth-Smith
417	Tornado I R7936	General handling stability and dive	3–3–42	Vulture V No 4252	Rotol RS6/1	9,694	P. G. Lucas
419	Typhoon P5216	Carburettor test	28–3–42	Sabre II 95018	DH Hydr.PX512	10,346	K. G. Seth-Smith
420	Typhoon IA R7577	Oil check: .35″ 360° blank	8–3–42	Sabre II S 283	DH Hydr.55/2	10,770	K. G. Seth-Smith
421	Typhoon IA R7577	Oil check: 1″ 180° blank	8–3–42	Sabre II S 283	DH Hydr.55/2	10,770	K. G. Seth-Smith
422	Typhoon P5216	Oil check: 1″ 240° blank	8–3–42	Sabre II 95018	DH Hydr.PX512	10,346	K. G. Seth-Smith
423	Typhoon R8198	Climb to check oil temps	8–3–42	Sabre II S 98	DH Hydr.52046	10,500	W. Humble
424	Typhoon IA R7577	MS levels with short exhausts	8–3–42	Sabre II S 283	DH Hydr.52016	10,770	P. G. Lucas
425	Typhoon P5216	Carburettor test and levels	8–3–42	Sabre II 95018	DH Hydr.PX512	10,346	K. G. Seth-Smith
426	Typhoon IA R7577	Oil temps, 1.5″ 240° blank; levels with 4″ ext. exhausts	10–3–42	Sabre II S 283	DH Hydr.52016	10,770	W. Humble
427	Typhoon P5216	FS levels and 4″ ext. exhausts	9–3–42	Sabre II 95018	DH Hydr.PX512	10,346	K. G. Seth-Smith
428	Typhoon IA R8198	Non-return valve in Live-Line centrifuge pump	11–3–42	Sabre II S 98	DH Hydr.52046	10,500	P. G. Lucas
430	Typhoon IA R7577	Carburettor test	14–3–42	Sabre II S 283	DH Hydr.52016	10,770	P. G. Lucas
431	Typhoon IA R8198	Forced landing with engine failure	14–3–42	Sabre II S 98	DH Hydr.52046	10,500	P. G. Lucas
432	Typhoon P5216	Levels; 4″ extended exhausts	14–3–42	Sabre II 95018	DH Hydr.PX512	10,346	W. Humble
434	Typhoon IA R8199	Special production tests	14–3–42	Sabre II S 299	DH Hydr.52159	10,100	W. Humble
435	Typhoon IA R8199	Special production tests	15–3–42	Sabre II S 299	DH Hydr.52159	10,100	K. G. Seth-Smith
436	Typhoon P5216	Hydraulic pressures and temps; 4″ extended exhausts	20–3–42	Sabre II 95018	DH Hydr.PX512	10,346	W. Humble
439	Typhoon IA R8200	Special production tests	15–3–42	Sabre II S 303	DH Hydr.	10,100	R. P. Beamont
440	Typhoon IA R8199	Special production tests	23–3–42	Sabre II S 88	DH Hydr.52149	10,100	P. G. Lucas
441	Typhoon IA R8200	Special production tests	—	—	—	10,100	P. G. Lucas
442	Typhoon P5216	Levels in FS-gear	23–3–42	Sabre II 95018	DH Hydr.PX512	10,346	K. G. Seth-Smith
445	Typhoon IA R8199	Production tests: 1″ 180° blank	25–3–42	Sabre II S 88	DH Hydr.52149	10,100	P. G. Lucas
446	Typhoon IA R8199	Special production tests	25–3–42	Sabre II S 88	DH Hydr.52149	10,100	P. G. Lucas
447	Typhoon IA R7577	Oil cooling climb; gun heating; carburation	25–3–42	Sabre II S 337	DH Hydr.52016	10,770	K. G. Seth-Smith
448	Typhoon IA R7577	Oil cooling climb; carburation	26–3–42	Sabre II S 337	DH Hydr.52016	10,770	K. G. Seth-Smith
451	Typhoon IA R7675	Special production test	28–3–42	Sabre II S 107	DH Hydr.52139	10,100	P. G. Lucas
452	Typhoon IA R7644	Special production test	26–3–42	Sabre II S 313	DH Hydr.52096	10,100	W. Humble
453	Typhoon IA R7646	Special production test	28–3–42	Sabre II S 166	DH Hydr.52118	10,300	P. G. Lucas
455	Typhoon IA R7653	Special production test	28–3–42	Sabre II S 307	DH Hydr.52102	10,100	W. Humble
456	Typhoon IA R7577	Oil cooling tests	28–3–42	Sabre II S 337	DH Hydr.52016	10,770	K. G. Seth-Smith
457	Typhoon IA R7577	Carburation test	28–3–42	Sabre II S 337	DH Hydr.52016	10,770	K. G. Seth-Smith
458	Typhoon IA R7585	Special production test	29–3–42	Sabre II S 154	DH Hydr.52029	10,100	R. P. Beamont
459	Typhoon IB R7646	Cannon heating in IB-wing	29–3–42	Sabre II S 166	DH Hydr.52118	10,300	K. G. Seth-Smith
460	Typhoon IA R7652	Special production test	25–3–42	Sabre II S 313	DH Hydr.52092	10,100	R. P. Beamont
461	Typhoon IA R7654	Special production test	26–3–42	Sabre II S 207	DH Hydr.52137	10,100	W. Humble
463	Typhoon IA R7644	Oil suitability climb	29–3–42	Sabre II S 314	DH Hydr.52059	10,100	K. G. Seth-Smith
465	Typhoon IB R7646	Climb and cockpit heating	30–3–42	Sabre II S 166	DH Hydr.52118	10,300	W. Humble
466	Typhoon IA R8220	Standard production test	30–3–42	Sabre II S 303	DH Hydr.52172	10,100	R. P. Beamont
467	Typhoon IA R7577	Climb and carburation	30–3–42	Sabre II S 337	DH Hydr.52016	10,770	K. G. Seth-Smith
468	Typhoon IA R7575	Special production tests	30–3–42	Sabre II S 107	DH Hydr.52139	10,100	R. P. Beamont
469	Typhoon IA R7585	Special production tests	29–3–42	Sabre II S 154	DH Hydr.52029	10,100	W. Humble
470	Typhoon IA R7577	Oil suitability climb	1–4–42	Sabre II S 337	DH Hydr.52016	10,770	K. G. Seth-Smith
471	Typhoon IA R7577	Test of 'Stanbury' cooler	1–4–42	Sabre II S 337	DH Hydr.52016	10,770	K. G. Seth-Smith
472	Typhoon IB R7646	Oil test on 3,300 rpm climb	1–4–42	Sabre II S 166	DH Hydr.52118	10,300	K. G. Seth-Smith
473	Typhoon IA R7577	Climb with high starting temps	1–4–42	Sabre II S 337	DH Hydr.52016	10,770	K. G. Seth-Smith
474	Typhoon IA R7577	Climb and cruise; oil temps	2–4–42	Sabre II S 337	DH Hydr.52016	10,770	K. G. Seth-Smith
476	Typhoon IA R7618	Standard production test	2–4–42	Sabre II S 257	DH Hydr.52088	10,100	W. Humble
477	Typhoon IA R8220	Special production test	1–4–42	Sabre II S 303	DH Hydr.52172	10,100	W. Humble
478	Typhoon IA R7672	Standard production test	3–4–42	Sabre II S 179	DH Hydr.52179	10,100	W. Humble
479	Typhoon IA R7645	Special production test	3–4–42	Sabre II S 99	DH Hydr.52099	10,100	R. P. Beamont
480	Typhoon IA R7654	Special production test	3–4–42	Sabre II S 174	DH Hydr.52137	10,100	R. P. Beamont
481	Typhoon IA R7618	Oil cooler modified with oil way	4–4–42	Sabre II S 257	DH Hydr.52088	10,100	W. Humble
482	Typhoon IA R7651	Special production test	7–4–42	Sabre II S 295	DH Hydr.52030	10,100	W. Humble
483	Typhoon IA R7545	Special production test	7–4–42	Sabre II S 99	DH Hydr.52165	10,100	R. P. Beamont
484	Typhoon IA R7630	Special production test	7–4–42	Sabre II S 328	DH Hydr.52061	10,100	W. Humble
485	Typhoon IA R7628	Special production test	8–4–42	Sabre II S 45	DH Hydr.52125	10,100	W. Humble
486	Typhoon IA R7675	Special production test	1–4–42	Sabre II S 107	DH Hydr.52139	10,100	W. Humble
487	Typhoon P5216	Oil cooling climb and FS level	9–4–42	Not known	DH Hydr.PX512	10,346	K. G. Seth-Smith
488	Typhoon IA R7618	Special production test	8–4–42	Sabre II S 257	DH Hydr.52088	10,100	R. P. Beamont
489	Typhoon IA R7630	Standard production test	8–4–42	Sabre II S 328	DH Hydr.52061	10,100	F. H. S. Fox
490	Typhoon IA R7647	Special production test	10–4–42	Sabre II S 161	DH Hydr.52097	10,100	R. P. Beamont
491	Tornado P5219	MS levels; rad shutter up, down and removed	10–4–42	Vulture V No 164	Rotol EE175	10,500	P. G. Lucas
492	Typhoon IB R7692	Special production test	10–4–42	Sabre II S 87	DH Hydr.52093	10,300	W. Humble
494	Typhoon P5216	Oil cooling climb	11–4–42	Sabre II 95026	DH Hydr.PX512	10,346	K. G. Seth-Smith
495	Typhoon IA R7647	Special production test	13–4–42	Sabre II S 161	DH Hydr.52097	10,100	W. Humble
496	Typhoon IB R7692	Special production test	13–4–42	Sabre II S 85	DH Hydr.52093	10,300	R. P. Beamont
497	Typhoon IA R7681	Special production test	13–4–42	Sabre II S 209	DH Hydr.52129	10,100	W. Humble
498	Typhoon P5216	Oil cooling test	12–4–42	Sabre II 95026	DH Hydr.PX512	10,346	K. G. Seth-Smith
500	Typhoon IA R7647	Special production test	14–4–42	Sabre II S 161	DH Hydr.52097	10,100	W. Humble
502	Typhoon IB R7673	Special production test	14–4–42	Sabre II S 332	DH Hydr.52143	10,300	W. Humble
503	Typhoon IB R7692	Special production test	14–4–42	Sabre II S 85	DH Hydr.52093	10,300	W. Humble
504	Typhoon IA R7680	Special production test	15–4–42	Sabre II S 213	DH Hydr.52103	10,100	W. Humble
505	Typhoon IA R7632	Special production test	15–4–42	Sabre II S 137	DH Hydr.52086	10,100	F. H. S. Fox

Flight Report	Aircraft	Test	Date	Engine	Airscrew	Weight	Pilot
506	Typhoon IA R7647	Special production test	15–4–42	Sabre II S 161	DH Hydr.52097	10,100	R. P. Beamont
507	Typhoon P5216	Oil cooling climb and cruise; check of hydraulic temperatures	14–4–42	Sabre II 95026	DH Hydr.PX512	10,346	K. G. Seth-Smith
509	Typhoon IA R7577	Oil cooling climb; carburation	15–4–42	Sabre II S 157	DH Hydr.52016	10,770	K. G. Seth-Smith
510	Typhoon IA R7577	Oil cooling and carburettor test	15–4–42	Sabre II S 157	DH Hydr.52016	10,770	K. G. Seth-Smith
511	Typhoon P5216	Level speeds, FS-gear	16–4–42	Sabre II 95026	DH Hydr.PX512	10,346	K. G. Seth-Smith
512	Typhoon IB R7692	Special production test	15–4–42	Sabre II S 85	DH Hydr.52093	10,300	F. H. S. Fox
513	Typhoon IA R7680	Investigation of low oil pressure after take-off	16–4–42	Sabre II S 213	DH Hydr.52103	10,100	W. Humble
514	Typhoon IA R7632	Investigation of low oil pressure	16–4–42	Sabre II S 137	DH Hydr.52086	10,100	W. Humble
515	Typhoon IA R7640	Special production test	16–4–42	Sabre II S 214	DH Hydr.52095	10,100	W. Humble
516	Typhoon IB R7673	Special production test	17–4–42	Sabre II S 332	DH Hydr.52143	10,300	R. P. Beamont
517	Typhoon IA R7577	Oil cooling climb; carburation	17–4–42	Sabre II S 157	DH Hydr.52016	10,770	K. G. Seth-Smith
518	Typhoon IA R7577	Fuel consumption at 25,000 ft	18–4–42	Sabre II S 157	DH Hydr.52016	10,770	W. Humble
519	Typhoon IA R8198	Oil cooling climb	19–4–42	Sabre II S 324	DH Hydr.52158	10,500	K. G. Seth-Smith
521	Typhoon IA R8198	Oil cooling climb and cruise	19–4–42	Sabre II S 324	DH Hydr.52158	10,500	K. G. Seth-Smith
522	Typhoon IA R7632	Oil suitability climb	19–4–42	Sabre II S 137	DH Hydr.52086	10,100	R. P. Beamont
523	Typhoon IA R8198	Oil suitability climb	6–4–42	Sabre II S 324	DH Hydr.52046	10,500	P. G. Lucas
524	Typhoon IA R8198	Oil suitability climb	8–4–42	Sabre II S 324	DH Hydr.52046	10,500	K. G. Seth-Smith
525	Typhoon IA R8198	Oil cooling test	12–4–42	Sabre II S 324	DH Hydr.52046	10,500	K. G. Seth-Smith
526	Typhoon IA R8198	Oil temperatures and pressures	16–4–42	Sabre II S 324	DH Hydr.52046	10,500	K. G. Seth-Smith
527	Typhoon IA R8198	Oil cooling climb	17–4–42	Sabre II S 324	DH Hydr.52046	10,500	P. G. Lucas
528	Typhoon IA R7577	Oil suitability climb	20–4–42	Sabre II S 157	DH Hydr.52016	10,770	P. G. Lucas
529	Typhoon IA R7632	Oil suitability climb	21–4–42	Sabre II S 137	DH Hydr.52086	10,100	P. G. Lucas
530	Typhoon IA R7577	Oil suitability climb	21–4–42	Sabre II S 157	DH Hydr.52016	10,770	W. Humble
531	Typhoon IA R8198	Oil suitability; oscillograph recordings	21–4–42	Sabre II S 324	DH Hydr.52158	10,500	W. Humble
532	Typhoon IA R8198	Ground warming test	22–4–42	Sabre II S 324	DH Hydr.52158	10,500	P. G. Lucas
533	Typhoon IA R8198	Axial flow oil cooler	22–4–42	Sabre II S 324	DH Hydr.52158	10,500	W. Humble
535	Typhoon IA R7632	Plates in oil cooler	22–4–42	Sabre II S 137	DH Hydr.52086	10,100	W. Humble
536	Typhoon IA R7673	Semi-sinuous flow oil cooler	22–4–42	Sabre II S 332	DH Hydr.52143	10,300	K. G. Seth-Smith
537	Typhoon IB R7673	Semi-sinuous flow oil cooler	22–4–42	Sabre II S 332	DH Hydr.52143	10,300	P. G. Lucas
539	Typhoon IB R7673	Semi-sinuous flow oil cooler	24–4–42	Sabre II S 332	DH Hydr.52143	10,300	K. G. Seth-Smith
540	Typhoon IA R7577	Oil suitability climb	24–4–42	Sabre II S 157	DH Hydr.52016	10,770	K. G. Seth-Smith
541	Typhoon IA R7577	Perforated baffles in oil cooler	24–4–42	Sabre II S 157	DH Hydr.52016	10,770	K. G. Seth-Smith
542	Typhoon IA R8198	Oil suitability; radiator shutter closed; oscillograph recording	24–4–42	Sabre II S 324	DH Hydr.52158	10,500	P. G. Lucas
543	Typhoon IB R7646	Gun heating; carburation and misting of windows	24–4–42	Sabre II S 166	DH Hydr.52118	10,300	W. Humble
544	Typhoon IA R7577	Carburation test	24–4–42	Sabre II S 157	DH Hydr.52016	10,770	K. G. Seth-Smith
545	Typhoon IA R7632	Oil suitability; 5-flow cooler	25–4–42	Sabre II S 137	DH Hydr.52016	9,770	W. Humble
546	Typhoon IB R7646	Cannon heating; carburation	26–4–42	Sabre II S 166	DH Hydr.52118	10,300	R. P. Beamont
547	Typhoon IA R7577	Oil suitability; 10-flow cooler	26–4–42	Sabre II S 157	DH Hydr.52016	10,770	W. Humble
549	Typhoon P5216	Full throttle level speeds	27–4–42	Sabre II S 322	DH Hydr.PX512	10,350	W. Humble
550	Typhoon IB R7646	Cannon heating	28–4–42	Sabre II S 166	DH Hydr.52118	10,330	W. Humble
551	Typhoon IB R7646	Fuel system pressurization	28–4–42	Sabre II S 166	DH Hydr.52118	10,330	W. Humble
552	Typhoon IA R7577	Oil suitability; 10-flow cooler	27–4–42	Sabre II S 157	DH Hydr.52016	10,770	K. G. Seth-Smith
553	Typhoon IB R7646	Cannon heating	29–4–42	Sabre II S 166	DH Hydr.52118	10,330	R. P. Beamont
555	Typhoon IA R8198	Oil suitability; 10-flow cooler	1–5–42	Sabre II S 324	DH Hydr.52046	10,500	W. Humble
556	Typhoon IA R7632	Carburation test	1–5–42	Sabre II S 137	DH Hydr.52086	9,770	K. G. Seth-Smith
557	Typhoon IB R7673	Oil suitability: 8-flow cooler	3–5–42	Sabre II S 332	DH Hydr.52143	10,300	R. P. Beamont
558	Typhoon IA R7595	Special production tests	4–5–42	Sabre II S 270	DH Hydr.52037	10,100	R. P. Beamont
559	Typhoon IB R7673	Oil suitability: 8-flow cooler	5–5–42	Sabre II S 332	DH Hydr.52143	10,300	K. G. Seth-Smith
560	Typhoon IA R8198	Oil suitability: 10-flow cooler	30–4–42	Sabre II S 324	DH Hydr.52046	10,500	K. G. Seth-Smith
561	Typhoon IB R7673	Carburation and oil flow tests	2–5–42	Sabre II S 332	DH Hydr.52143	10,300	W. Humble
562	Typhoon IA R7632	Modified Dunlop wheels/brakes	8–5–42	Sabre II S 137	DH Hydr.52086	9,770	P. G. Lucas
563	Typhoon IB R7646	Forced landing at Cranwell	4–5–42	Sabre II S 166	DH Hydr.52118	10,300	W. Humble
564	Typhoon IA R7632	Oil cooling checks	5–5–42	Sabre II S 137	DH Hydr.52086	10,580	W. Humble
565	Typhoon IB R7673	Report on engine failure	8–5–42	Sabre II S 332	DH Hydr.52143	10,300	K. G. Seth-Smith
566	Tornado P5219	Level speeds with and without tailwheel doors	8–5–42 } 10–5–42	Vulture V No 164	Rotol EE175	10,500	W. Humble
567	Typhoon IA R7632	Oil cooler investigation	7–5–42	Sabre II S 137	DH Hydr.52086	10,580	W. Humble
568	Typhoon P5216	Carburettor test	9–5–42	Sabre II S 322	DH Hydr.HX512	10,350	P. G. Lucas
569	Typhoon IA R8198	FT climb and carburation	11–5–42	Sabre II S 324	DH Hydr.52158	10,500	W. Humble
570	Tornado P5219	MS levels with blast tubes covered	12–5–42	Vulture V No 164	Rotol EE175	10,500	W. Humble
571	Typhoon IA R8198	Oil suitability: 10-flow cooler	10–5–42	Sabre II S 324	DH Hydr.52158	10,500	P. G. Lucas
572	Typhoon IA R7632	Oil suitability: Gallay cooler	13–5–42	Sabre II S 137	DH Hydr.52086	10,580	K. G. Seth-Smith
573	Typhoon IA R7632	Oil suitability: 10-flow cooler	14–5–42	Sabre II S 137	DH Hydr.52086	10,580	P. G. Lucas
574	Typhoon IA R7632	Various radiator shutter posns.	15–5–42	Sabre II S 137	DH Hydr.52086	10,580	W. Humble
575	Tornado P5219	FT and throttled levels	16–5–42	Vulture V No 164	Rotol EE175	10,500	W. Humble
578	Typhoon IB R7673	Carburation test	17–5–42	Sabre II S 178	DH Hydr.52143	10,300	K. G. Seth-Smith
579	Typhoon IB R7673	Fuel consumption tests	18–5–42	Sabre II S 178	DH Hydr.52143	10,300	K. G. Seth-Smith
580	Typhoon IA R7632	Radiator shutter 2⁵/₈-inch down	19–5–42	Sabre II S 137	DH Hydr.52086	10,580	W. Humble
582	Typhoon IB R7673	Fuel consumption at 15,000 ft	19–5–42	Sabre II S 178	DH Hydr.52143	10,830	K. G. Seth-Smith
583	Typhoon IA R7632	Radiator shutter neutral	20–5–42	Sabre II S 137	DH Hydr.52086	10,580	K. G. Seth-Smith
584	Typhoon IB R7673	Fuel consumption tests	22–5–42	Sabre II S 178	DH Hydr.52143	10,830	W. Humble
585	Typhoon IA R8198	Flight with DH 4-blade airscrew	22–5–42	Sabre II S 324	DH 4-bl.50004	10,570	K. G. Seth-Smith
586	Typhoon IB R7673	Oil suitability: 8-flow cooler	28–5–42	Sabre II S 178	DH Hydr.52143	10,830	W. Humble
587	Typhoon IB R7646	Gun bay and cockpit heating	28–5–42	Sabre II S 418	DH Hydr.52118	10,300	W. Humble
588	Tornado P5219	Levels with tailwheel doors	27–5–42	Vulture V No 164	Rotol EE175	10,500	K. G. Seth-Smith
589	Typhoon P5216	Levels with ducted exhausts	27–5–42	Sabre II S 322	DH Hydr.PX512	10,350	W. Humble
590	Typhoon IB R7646	Behaviour of whip aerials	28–5–42	Sabre II S 418	DH Hydr.52118	10,300	W. Humble
591	Typhoon IA R8198	Test of DH 4-blade airscrew	29–5–42	Sabre II S 324	DH 4-bl.50004	10,750	K. G. Seth-Smith
592	Typhoon IB R7673	Fuel consumptions at 25,000 and 20,000 ft	29–5–42	Sabre II S 178	DH Hydr.52143	10,830	W. Humble
593	Typhoon IB R7673	Level speed with rear view mirror blister	1–6–42	Sabre II S 178	DH Hydr.52143	10,830	{ P. G. Lucas { W. Humble

Flight Report	Aircraft	Test	Date	Engine	Airscrew	Weight	Pilot
594	Typhoon IA R7632	Timed climb to 30,000 ft	30–5–42	Sabre II S 137	DH Hydr. 52086	10,580	W. Humble
595	Typhoon IA R7577	Levels with internal rudder mass balance	30–5–42	Sabre II S 305	DH Hydr. 52046	10,350	W. Humble
596	Typhoon IB R7673	Fuel consumption at 20,000 ft	30–5–42	Sabre II S 178	DH Hydr. 52143	10,830	W. Humble
597	Typhoon P5216	Levels with ducted exhausts	30–5–42	Sabre II S 322	DH Hydr. 52018	10,350	K. G. Seth-Smith
598	Typhoon IA R7632	Timed climb to 30,000 ft	1–6–42	Sabre II S 137	DH Hydr. 52086	10,580	W. Humble
599	Typhoon P5216	MS levels with ducted exhausts	1–6–42	Sabre II S 322	DH Hydr. 52018	10,350	W. Humble
600	Typhoon IA R7577	Levels with internal rudder mass balance	2–6–42	Sabre II S 305	DH Hydr. 52046	10,350	P. G. Lucas
601	Typhoon IB R7673	Levels with and without rear view mirror blister	2–6–42	Sabre II S 178	DH Hydr. 52143	10,830	W. Humble
602	Typhoon P5216	Level speeds with and without ducted exhaust pipes	2–6–42	Sabre II S 322	DH Hydr. 52018	10,350	K. G. Seth-Smith
603	Typhoon P5216	Levels with 4″ extended exhausts	3–6–42	Sabre II S 322	DH Hydr. 52018	10,350	W. Humble
604	Typhoon IA R7632	Timed climb: rad. flap down	3–6–42	Sabre II S 137	DH Hydr. 52086	10,580	K. G. Seth-Smith
605	Typhoon IA R7632	Timed climb to 30,000 ft in weak mixture; rad. shutter open	3–6–42	Sabre II S 137	DH Hydr. 52086	10,580	P. G. Lucas
606	Typhoon IA R7632	Timed climb: rad. flap neutral	2–6–42	Sabre II S 137	DH Hydr. 52086	10,580	K. G. Seth-Smith
607	Typhoon IA R7632	Timed climb: rad. flap 2/3 down	3–6–42	Sabre II S 137	DH Hydr. 52086	10,580	K. G. Seth-Smith
608	Typhoon IA R7632	Timed climb: rad. flap 1/3 down	3–6–42	Sabre II S 137	DH Hydr. 52086	10,580	P. G. Lucas
609	Typhoon IA R7632	Timed climb: rad. flap open	4–6–42	Sabre II S 137	DH Hydr. 52086	10,580	W. Humble
610	Typhoon P5216	Levels with 4″ extended exhausts	5–6–42	Sabre II S 322	DH Hydr. 52018	10,350	K. G. Seth-Smith
611	Typhoon IA R7577	Levels with standard rudder	7–6–42	Sabre II S 305	DH Hydr. 52046	10,350	W. Humble
612	Typhoon P5216	Hobson Engine Control Box	9–6–42	Sabre II S 322	DH Hydr. 52018	10,350	P. G. Lucas
613	Typhoon IB R7673	Rear view mirror	9–6–42	Sabre II S 178	DH Hydr. 52143	10,830	P. G. Lucas
614	Typhoon IA R7577	Sprung seat	9–6–42	Sabre II S 305	DH Hydr. 52046	10,350	P. G. Lucas
615	Typhoon IA R7632	Infiltration of fumes into cockpit	6–6–42	Sabre II S 137	DH Hydr. 52086	10,580	W. Humble
616	Typhoon IA R7577	Handling with enclosed rudder mass balance	12–6–42	Sabre II S 305	DH Hydr. 52046	10,350	P. G. Lucas
617	Typhoon IA R7577	Climb and level with increased rating. Max corrected TAS 446 mph at 20,000 ft	13–6–42	Sabre II S 305 (rating increased)	DH Hydr. 52046	10,620	P. G. Lucas
618	Typhoon P5216	Levels with 27 1/2″ whip aerial	11–6–42	Sabre II S 322	DH Hydr. 52018	10,350	W. Humble
619	Typhoon IA R7577	Climb and levels at increased rating; TAS 446 mph at 20,600 mph	11–6–42	Sabre II S 305 (rating increased)	DH Hydr. 52046	10,620	K. G. Seth-Smith
620	Typhoon IA R7577	Climb with increased rating	11–6–42	Sabre II S 305	DH Hydr. 52046	10,620	P. G. Lucas
621	Typhoon P5216	20° dive; camera recorded	13–6–42	Sabre II S 322	DH Hydr. 52018	10,350	W. Humble
622	Typhoon P5216	Timed full-throttle climb	13–6–42	Sabre II S 322	DH Hydr. 52018	10,350	W. Humble
623	Typhoon IA R7577	FT climb, 3,700 lb, +7 lb boost	16–6–42	Sabre II S 305	DH Hydr. 52046	10,620	W. Humble
624	Typhoon IA R7577	Full-throttle MS levels	17–6–42	Sabre II S 305	DH Hydr. 52046	10,620	W. Humble
625	Typhoon IA R7577	Ceiling climb, 3,900 rpm	16–6–42	Sabre II S 305	DH Hydr. 52046	10,620	K. G. Seth-Smith
626	Typhoon IA R8198	FT levels with 4-blade prop	16–6–42	Sabre II S 233	DH 4-bl. 50004	10,570	W. Humble
627	Typhoon IA R8198	FT, FS-gear levels and climb	17–6–42	Sabre II S 233	DH 4-bl. 50004	10,570	W. Humble
628	Typhoon IA R7632	Climb and levels with modified rad shutter (rear hinge)	16–6–42	Sabre II S 137	DH Hydr. 52086	10,580	P. G. Lucas
629	Typhoon IA R8198	Fore and aft stability with 4-blade prop	17–6–42	Sabre II S 233	DH 4-bl. 50004	10,570	P. G. Lucas
630	Typhoon IA R7673	Oil cooling: 10-flow cooler	16–6–42	Sabre II S 178	DH Hydr. 52143	10,830	K. G. Seth-Smith
631	Typhoon P5216	30° dive; camera recorded	16–6–42	Sabre II S 322	DH Hydr. 52018	10,350	W. Humble
632	Typhoon IB R7673	Fuel consumption test	16–6–42	Sabre II S 178	DH Hydr. 52143	10,830	K. G. Seth-Smith
633	Typhoon IA R8198	Levels with 4-blade prop	17–6–42	Sabre II S 233	DH 4-bl. 50004	10,570	K. G. Seth-Smith
634	Typhoon IB R7646	SU carburettor on sprint engine	20–6–42	Sabre II S 418	DH Hydr. 52118	10,300	W. Humble
635	Typhoon IB R7673	Fuel consumption tests	20–6–42	Sabre II S 178	DH Hydr. 52143	10,830	K. G. Seth-Smith
636	Typhoon IA R7577	FT climb, 3,700 rpm, 7+ boost	17–6–42	Sabre II S 305	DH Hydr. 52046	10,620	P. G. Lucas
637	Typhoon P5216	Mod to prevent wheel doors pulling off in dive	20–6–42	Sabre II S 322	DH Hydr. 52018	10,350	K. G. Seth-Smith
638	Typhoon IB R7673	Fuel consumption test	21–6–42	Sabre II S 178	DH Hydr. 52143	10,830	W. Humble
639	Typhoon IA R8198	Level speeds (rating increased); 4-blade prop; max corrected TAS 454 mph at 20,500 ft; engine failed on landing.	22–6–42	Sabre II S 523 (rating increased)	DH 4-bl. 50004	10,350	W. Humble
640	Typhoon P5216	Levels and elevator tab movement	23–6–42	Sabre II S 322	DH Hydr. 52018	10,350	W. Humble
641	Typhoon IA R8198	Tank pressurization climb	23–6–42	Sabre II S 233	DH 4-bl. 50004	10,570	K. G. Seth-Smith
642	Typhoon IA R7577	Levels at various rpm	23–6–42	Sabre II S 305	DH Hydr. 52046	10,620	W. Humble
643	Typhoon IA R7577	FT climb, 3,700 rpm, +7 lb boost	23–6–42	Sabre II S 305	DH Hydr. 52046	10,620	K. G. Seth-Smith
645	Typhoon P5216	FS levels, oil cooling	26–6–42	Sabre II S 322	DH Hydr. 52018	10,350	W. Humble
646	Typhoon IA R8198	Ceiling climb, 3-blade prop	26–6–42	Sabre II S 233	DH Hydr. 52158	10,720	K. G. Seth-Smith
647	Typhoon IA R8198	MS climb and fuel pressures	29–6–42	Sabre II S 233	DH Hydr. 52158	10,720	K. G. Seth-Smith
648	Typhoon P5216	10° dive, 3,700 rpm, +7 lb boost	27–6–42	Sabre II S 322	DH Hydr. 52018	10,350	W. Humble
649	Typhoon P5216	30° dive, 3,700 rpm, +7 lb boost	27–6–42	Sabre II S 322	DH Hydr. 52018	10,350	W. Humble
650	Typhoon IA R7617	Vibration with balanced crankshaft	1–7–42	—	—	—	K. G. Seth-Smith
652	Typhoon P5216	Nose heaviness in 30° dive	1–7–42	Sabre II S 322	DH Hydr. 52018	10,350	K. G. Seth-Smith
653	Typhoon IA R8198	FS-gear levels, 3-blade prop	1–7–42	Sabre II S 233	DH Hydr. 52158	10,720	W. Humble
654	Typhoon P5216	10° dive, 3,150 rpm, +4 1/2 lb boost	29–6–42	Sabre II S 322	DH Hydr. 52018	10,350	W. Humble
655	Typhoon IA R8198	Level speed with 3-blade prop	5–7–42	Sabre II S 233	DH Hydr. 52158	10,720	W. Humble
656	Typhoon IA R8198	MS levels with 4-blade prop	8–7–42	Sabre II S 233	DH 4-bl. 50004	10,800	W. Humble
658	Typhoon IA R7577	Partial climbs	24–7–42	Sabre II S 305	DH Hydr. 52046	10,620	W. Humble
659	Typhoon IB R7692	Spinning; operation of tail parachute	24–7–42	Sabre II	DH Hydr.	10,830	K. G. Seth-Smith
660	Typhoon IB R7673	Carburation stability with 4-blade prop	6–7–42	Sabre II S 178	DH 4-blade	10,830	K. G. Seth-Smith
661	Typhoon IA R7577	Partial climbs, light load	14–7–42	Sabre II S 211	DH Hydr. 52046	9,700	K. G. Seth-Smith
662	Typhoon IA R8198	Climbs with 4-blade prop	14–7–42	Sabre II S 233	DH 4-bl. 50004	10,800	K. G. Seth-Smith
663	Typhoon IA R7632	Test of extended rad flap	15–7–42	Sabre II S 137	DH Hydr. 52086	10,580	W. Humble
666	Typhoon IA R7632	Take-off at various flap angles	20–7–42	Sabre II S 137	DH Hydr. 52086	9,730	K. G. Seth-Smith
667	Typhoon IA R7577	Ceiling climb at light load	19–7–42	Sabre II S 211	DH Hydr. 52046	9,700	K. G. Seth-Smith
668	Typhoon P5216	Trim change in 30° dive	19–7–42	Sabre II S 257	DH Hydr. 52158	10,350	P. G. Lucas
669	Typhoon IA R8198	FS levels with 4″ extended exhausts and fairings	21–7–42	Sabre II S 233	DH Hydr. 52158	10,500	K. G. Seth-Smith
670	Typhoon IA R7577	Rate of roll, standard wing tips	24–7–42	Sabre II S 211	DH Hydr. 52046	10,600	W. Humble
671	Typhoon P5216	20° dive from 30,300 ft	24–7–42	Sabre II S 257	DH Hydr. 52018	10,350	P. G. Lucas
672	Typhoon P5216	30° dives, 3,700 rpm, +7 lb boost	24–7–42	Sabre II S 257	DH Hydr. 52018	10,350	W. Humble
673	Typhoon IA R8198	Climb and levels with 4-blade prop	25–7–42	Sabre II S 233	DH 4-bl. 40811	10,780	P. G. Lucas

Flight Report	Aircraft	Test	Date	Engine	Airscrew	Weight	Pilot
674	Typhoon IB R7673	Fuel consumptions	26–7–42	Sabre II S 291	DH Hydr.52143	10,830	W. Humble
675	Typhoon IA R7577	Levels and stalling speed with square wing tips	27–7–42	Sabre II S 211	DH Hydr.52016	10,600	W. Humble
677	Typhoon IA R8198	General test of 4-blade prop	28–7–42	Sabre II S 233	DH 4-bl.40811	10,780	P. G. Lucas
679	Typhoon IB R7692	Spinning: CG normal	19–7–42	Sabre II	DH Hydr.	11,070	K. G. Seth-Smith
680	Typhoon IB R7692	Spinning: CG extended aft	28–7–42	Sabre II	DH Hydr.	11,070	K. G. Seth-Smith
681	Typhoon IB R7673	Fuel consumption at 5,000 ft	31–7–42	Sabre II S 291	DH Hydr.52143	10,830	W. Humble
682	Typhoon IB R7638	Test of 4-blade prop	5–8–42	Sabre II S 191	DH 4-bl.40811	9,700	W. Humble
683	Typhoon IA R8198	Test of 4-blade prop	31–7–42	Sabre II S 233	DH 4-bl.40811	10,700	P. G. Lucas
684	Typhoon IB R7638	Test of 4-blade prop	9–8–42	Sabre II S 191	DH 4-bl.40811	10,830	K. G. Seth-Smith
685	Typhoon IA R7577	FT levels, square wing tips	9–8–42	Sabre II S 211	DH Hydr.52016	10,600	K. G. Seth-Smith
686	Typhoon IB R7673	Fuel consumptions	15–8–42	Sabre II S 291	DH Hydr.52143	10,830	W. Humble
687	Typhoon IB R8198	FT climb and MPA levels	17–8–42	Sabre II S 233	DH Hydr.52158	10,680	W. Humble
688	Typhoon IB R7673	Fuel cons. at 10,000 & 15,000 ft	16–8–42	Sabre II S 291	DH Hydr.52143	10,830	W. Humble
689	Typhoon IA R8198	MS climbs and FS levels	20–8–42	Sabre II S 233	DH Hydr.52158	10,680	W. Humble
690	Typhoon IB R7638	Cut-back radiator duct	7–42	Sabre II S 191	DH Hydr.	9,700	P. G. Lucas
691	Typhoon IA R7577	Wooltufts on fin, rudder and tailplane	8–42	Sabre II S 211	DH Hydr.52016	10,600	W. Humble
692	Typhoon IA R7632	Oil suitability: 10-flow cooler	24–8–42	Sabre II S 54	DH Hydr.52086	10,580	W. Humble
693	Typhoon IA R8198	D-section tailwheel tread	19–8–42	Sabre II S 233	DH 4-bl.40811	10,680	W. Humble
694	Typhoon IA R7632	Oil suitability: 10-flow cooler	26–8–42	Sabre II S 54	DH Hydr.52086	10,580	W. Humble
696	Tempest V HM595	Taxying tests	1–9–42	Sabre II S 1001	DH 4-bl.50004	10,932	P. G. Lucas
697	Tempest V HM595	First flight	2–9–42	Sabre II S 1001	DH 4-bl.50004	10,932	P. G. Lucas
699	Typhoon IB R7646	Clear view rear hood fairing	6–9–42	Sabre II S 418	DH Hydr.52118	—	W. Humble
		(*Note:* On 5–9–42 T. B. Fitzgerald taxied Hurricane Z2399 into Typhoon IA R8198)					
700	Typhoon IA R7577	Test of sprung rudder pedals	9–42	Sabre II S 211	DH Hydr.52016	9,700	W. Humble
701	Typhoon IB R7638	Various cabin tops	6–9–42	Sabre II S 191	DH Hydr.	—	W. Humble
702	Tempest V HM595	Preliminary handling report	12–9–42	Sabre II S 1001	DH 4-bl.50004	10,932	P. G. Lucas
703	Typhoon IB R7646	Handling: Two 500-lb bombs	8–9–42	Sabre II S 418	DH Hydr.52118	12,176	P. G. Lucas
704	Tempest V HM595	Directional stability tests	13–9–42	Sabre II S 1001	DH 4-bl.50004	10,932	P. G. Lucas
705	Typhoon IB R7646	Handling: Two 500-lb bombs with and without fairings	12–9–42	Sabre II S 418	DH Hydr.52118	12,176	P. G. Lucas
706	Typhoon IB R7638	CO test with short pipes	7–9–42	Sabre II S 191	DH Hydr.	—	W. Humble
707	Typhoon IA R7632	Behaviour of carburettor	13–9–42	Sabre II S 54	DH Hydr.52086	10,580	W. Humble
708	Typhoon IB R7638	CO contamination, short exhausts	10–9–42	Sabre II S 191	DH Hydr.	9,700	M. S. C. Hymans
709	Tempest V HM595	Handling with modified horn-balanced rudder	15–9–42	Sabre II S 1001	DH 4-bl.50004	10,390	P. G. Lucas
710	Typhoon IB R8222	Special production tests	15–9–42	Sabre II S 421	DH Hydr.56113	10,630	T. B. Fitzgerald
711	Typhoon IB R7638	CO test with short exhausts	15–9–42	Sabre II S 191	DH Hydr.	9,700	W. Humble
712	Typhoon P5216	Oil suitability: 10-flow cooler	19–9–42	Sabre II S 257	DH Hydr.52018	10,350	W. Humble
713	Typhoon P5216	Oil suitability: axial cooler	19–9–42	Sabre II S 257	DH Hydr.52018	10,350	W. Humble
714	Tempest V HM595	Handling with modified fin (increased area)	24–9–42	Sabre II S 1001	DH 4-bl.50004	10,390	P. G. Lucas
715	Typhoon IB R7638	CO tests with short exhausts	23–9–42	Sabre II S 191	DH Hydr.	9,700	W. Humble
716	Typhoon P5216	Ceiling climb	24–9–42	Sabre II S 257	DH Hydr.52018	10,380	W. Humble
717	Typhoon P5216	Levels and elevator angles	24–9–42	Sabre II S 257	DH Hydr.52018	10,380	W. Humble
718	Typhoon P5216	Carburettor tests	24–9–42	Sabre II S 257	DH Hydr.52018	10,380	W. Humble
719	Typhoon IB R7638	Diving tests	27–9–42	Sabre II S 191	DH Hydr.	9,700	W. Humble
720	Tempest V HM595	Handling. Rudder cords below geared tab; rad pressures	27–9–42	Sabre II S 1001	DH 4-bl.50004	10,930	P. G. Lucas
721	Typhoon IB R7617	Vibration test with balanced crankshaft	29–9–42	Sabre II S 158	DH Hydr.	10,520	W. Humble
722	Typhoon P5216	Ceiling climb; FT levels	1–10–42	Sabre II S 257	DH Hydr.52018	10,350	W. Humble
723	Tempest V HM595	Stability test with modified elevators	2–10–42	Sabre II S 1001	DH 4-bl.50004	10,930	P. G. Lucas
724	Tempest V HM595	Suitability climb and levels	2–10–42	Sabre II S 1001	DH 4-bl.50004	10,932	P. G. Lucas
725	Typhoon P5216	Climb to ceiling and levels	2–10–42	Sabre II S 257	DH Hydr.52018	10,350	W. Humble
730	Typhoon IA R8198	Pressures on rad bath nosing	8–10–42	Sabre II S 233	DH Hydr.	—	P. G. Lucas
731	Tempest V HM595	Handling tests	11–10–42	Sabre II S 1001	DH 4-bl.50004	10,932	P. G. Lucas
732	Typhoon IA R8198	CO tests with short exhausts	9–10–42	Sabre II S 233	DH Hydr.	—	W. Humble
733	Typhoon IB R7617	Rotol 4-blade propeller	12–10–42	Sabre II S 158	Rotol 4-bl.215	10,520	P. G. Lucas
735	Tempest V HM595	Handling and trim measurements	16–10–42	Sabre II S 1001	DH 4-bl.50005	10,932	P. G. Lucas
736	Typhoon IA R7577	Sprung rudder pedals	20–10–42	Sabre II S 211	DH Hydr.52016	10,600	W. Humble
737	Typhoon IB R7617	DH light 4-blade propeller	21–10–42	Sabre II S 158	DH 4-bl.40811	10,530	J. A. Crosby-Warren
738	Tempest V HM595	Carbon monoxide tests	17–10–42	Sabre II S 1001	DH 4-bl.50005	10,932	P. G. Lucas
739	Tempest V HM595	Rudder trim tab altered	24–10–42	Sabre II S 1001	DH 4-bl.50005	10,932	P. G. Lucas
741	Typhoon IB R8925	MS and FS-gear levels	21–10–42	Sabre II S 511	DH Hydr.	9,700	M. S. C. Hymans
742	Typhoon IB R8762	Handling: 44-gallon drop tanks	25–10–42	Sabre II	DH Hydr.	11,770	W. Humble
743	Typhoon P5216	.322 gear ratio, 3-blade prop	27–10–42	Sabre II S 95018	DH Hydr.52018	—	P. G. Lucas
744	Tornado I R7936	Handling with Rotol contraprop	23–10–42	Vulture	Rotol 11′ dia contraprops	—	P. G. Lucas
745	Typhoon P5216	Levels: .322 gear ratio	31–10–42	Sabre II S 95018	DH 4-bl.50004	10,420	W. Humble
747	Typhoon IB R7673	Spinning trials	6–11–42	Sabre II S 291	DH Hydr.	11,040	W. Humble
748	Typhoon IA R8198	FT levels, Napier shrouds	8–11–42	Sabre II S 233	DH Hydr.52158	10,680	W. Humble
749	Typhoon IA R7577	Test with DH light 4-bl. prop	8–11–42	Sabre II S 211	DH 4-bl.40811	—	P. G. Lucas
750	Typhoon IA R8198	MS and FS-gear levels	10–11–42	Sabre II S 233	DH Hydr.52158	10,680	W. Humble
751	Tempest V HM595	Directional stability; extended dorsal fin	17–11–42	Sabre II S 1001	DH 4-bl.50005	10,932	P. G. Lucas
752	Typhoon IA R8198	CO contamination with Napier exhaust shrouds	17–11–42	Sabre II S 233	DH Hydr.52158	10,680	W. Humble
753	Typhoon P5216	FT levels: .322 gear ratio	17–11–42	Sabre II S 95018	DH 4-bl.50004	10,560	W. Humble
754	Typhoon P5216	Camera-recorded climb	16–11–42	Sabre II S 95018	DH 4-bl.50004	10,560	W. Humble
755	Typhoon P5216	Timed climb: .322 gear ratio	18–11–42	Sabre II S 95018	DH 4-bl.50004	10,560	M. S. C. Hymans
756	Typhoon Trop IB R8925	Preliminary handling tests with tropical air intake	18–11–42	Sabre II S 1104	DH Hydr.56807	—	W. Humble
757	Typhoon Trop IB R8925	Forced landing report	18–11–42	Sabre II S 1104	DH Hydr.56807	—	M. S. C. Hymans
758	Typhoon IA R7577	Levels: DH light 4-bl. prop	20–11–42	Sabre II S 211	DH 4-bl.40811	10,800	W. Humble

Flight Report	Aircraft	Test	Date	Engine	Airscrew	Weight	Pilot
759	Typhoon IA R7577	Handling: DH light 4-bl. prop	20–11–42	Sabre II S 211	DH 4-bl.40811	10,800	W. Humble
760	Typhoon IA R8198	FT levels without shrouds	22–11–42	Sabre II S 233	DH Hydr.52158	10,680	W. Humble
761	Tempest V HM595	Handling and stability	22–11–42	Sabre II S 1001	DH 4-bl.50005	10,932	P. G. Lucas
762	Typhoon Trop IB R8889	Handling and stability	27–11–42 30–11–42 }	Sabre II S 1107	DH Hydr.	10,760	M. S. C. Hymans
763	Typhoon IB R7617	Test of Rotol 4-blade prop	24–11–42	Sabre II S 257	Rotol 4-bl.215	—	W. Humble
764	Typhoon IB R7617	Vibration with sprung engine mounting	11–42	Sabre II S 257	Rotol 4-bl.215	10,520	P. G. Lucas
765	Typhoon IA R7577	Behaviour of CSU under sudden throttle applications	11–42	Sabre II S 211	DH 4-bl.40811	10,800	W. Humble
766	Typhoon P5216	Timed climbs: .320 gear ratio	1–12–42	Sabre II 95018	DH 4-bl.50004	10,560	M. S. C. Hymans
767	Typhoon IA R7577	Timed climb to 30,000 ft	2–12–42	Sabre II S 211	DH 4-bl.40811	10,800	M. S. C. Hymans
768	Typhoon IA R7577	Vibration tests	2–12–42	Sabre II S 211	DH 4-bl.40811	10,800	P. G. Lucas
769	Typhoon IB R7617	Vibration tests	2–12–42	Sabre II S 257	Rotol 4-bl.215	10,520	W. Humble
770	Typhoon IA R7577	Timed climb to 30,000 ft	12–12–42	Sabre II S 211	DH 4-bl.40811	10,800	M. S. C. Hymans
771	Typhoon IA R8198	Full throttle level speeds	15–12–42	Sabre II S 1145	DH Hydr.52158	10,680	W. Humble
772	Tempest V HM595	Comparative directional stability: normal & narrow rudder	23–12–42	Sabre II S 1137	DH 4-bl.50005	11,000	P. G. Lucas
773	Typhoon P5216	Needle bearings in elevator countershaft	20–12–42	Sabre II 95018	DH 4-bl.50004	10,560	P. G. Lucas
774	Tornado HG641	First handling flight; new engine installation	23–12–42 24–12–42 }	Centaurus IV CE.27	Rotol 4-bl.263	10,094	P. G. Lucas
775	Typhoon IA R7577	Timed climb and FS levels	23–12–42	Sabre II S 211	Rotol 4-bl.EH215	10,800	M. S. C. Hymans
776	Typhoon IB DN340	FT levels; cleaned-up prodn.	22–12–42	Sabre II S 599	DH Hydr.	9,800	W. Humble
777	Tempest V HM595	Dive with cords on rudder	24–12–42	Sabre II S 1137	DH 4-bl.40005	11,000	P. G. Lucas
778	Tornado HG641	Cyl temperatures, cruising	29–12–42	Centaurus IV CE.27	Rotol 4-bl.EH263	10,094	P. G. Lucas
779	Tornado HG641	Carbon monoxide contamination	30–12–42	Centaurus IV CE.27	Rotol 4-bl.EH263	10,094	P. G. Lucas
780	Typhoon IB DN323	Landing accident	31–12–42	Sabre II	DH Hydr.	—	M. S. C. Hymans
781	Tornado HG641	Fuel consumptions	29–12–42	Centaurus IV CE.27	Rotol 4-bl.EH263	10,094	P. G. Lucas
782	Typhoon IB R7617	DH 4-bl prop overspeeding	22–12–42	Sabre II S 211	DH 4-bl.40811	—	W. Humble
784	Tornado HG641	CO test; MSA recorder	2–1–43	Centaurus IV CE.27	Rotol 4-bl.EH263	10,094	P. G. Lucas
785	Typhoon IA R7577	Timed climb, DH 3-bl. Hydr.	8–1–43	Sabre II S 211	DH Hydr.	10,600	W. Humble
786	Tornado HG641	Performance; cyl temps and fuel consumptions	8–1–43	Centaurus IV CE.27	Rotol 4-bl.EH263	10,094	P. G. Lucas
787	Typhoon P5216	Elevator trims curves, CG fwd	8–1–43	Sabre II S 1135	DH Hydr.	9,400	W. Humble
788	Tornado HG641	Performance and fuel consumption	9–1–43	Centaurus IV CE.27	Rotol 4-bl.EH263	10,094	P. G. Lucas
789	Typhoon P5216	Elevator trim curves, CG aft	11–1–43	Sabre II S 1135	DH Hydr.	9,500	M. S. C. Hymans
790	Tornado HG641	Functioning of Rotol prop	17–1–43	Centaurus IV CE.27	Rotol 4-bl.EH263	10,094	P. G. Lucas
791	Tempest V HM595	Level speeds	15–1–43	Sabre II S 3165	DH 4-bl.50004	11,100	P. G. Lucas
792	Typhoon P5216	Elevator trim curves, CG extended aft	13–1–43	Sabre II S 1135	DH Hydr.	9,550	W. Humble
793	Tornado HG641	Carbon monoxide contamination	9–1–43	Centaurus IV CE.27	Rotol 4-bl.EH263	10,090	W. Humble
794	Typhoon R8809	Provisional report on sliding hood	17–1–43	Sabre II	DH Hydr.	—	P. G. Lucas
796	Typhoon IB R7617	Reverse action DH 4-bl prop	15–1–43	Sabre II S 211	DH 4-bl.40812	—	W. Humble
797	Typhoon IB R8809	Flight test of sliding hood	17–1–43	Sabre II	DH Hydr.	—	W. Humble
798	Typhoon IB R7577	Oil suitability tests	26–1–43	Sabre II S 211	DH Hydr.	10,600	W. Humble
800	Tempest V HM595	Increased area dorsal fin	26–1–43	Sabre II S 3165	DH 4-bl.40812	11,780	P. G. Lucas
801	Typhoon IB R8809	Handling with sliding hood	26–1–43	Sabre II S 58	DH Hydr.	9,700	P. G. Lucas
802	Typhoon IB R8809	Handling with sliding hood	29–1–43	Sabre II S 58	DH Hydr.	9,700	W. Humble
803	Typhoon IB R7577	Oil suitability tests	1–2–43	Sabre II S 211	DH Hydr.	10,600	W. Humble
804	Tornado HG641	CO tests; modified bottom panel	2–2–43	Centaurus IV CE.27	Rotol 4-bl.EH263	10,090	P. G. Lucas
805	Typhoon P5216	Elevator trim curves; enlarged tailplane; CG extended aft	4–2–43	Sabre II S 1135	DH Hydr.	9,480	W. Humble
806	Tornado HG641	Combat climb; FS levels	3–2–43	Centaurus IV CE.27	Rotol 4-bl.EH263	10,094	P. G. Lucas
807	Tempest V HM595	Pressures on U/c fairing	5–2–43	Sabre II S 3165	DH 4-bl.40812	11,080	W. Humble
808	Typhoon P5216	Elevator trim curves; enlarged tailplane; CG forward	6–2–43	Sabre II S 158	DH Hydr.	9,520	W. Humble
809	Tempest V HM595	Test of main tanks contents gauge	5–2–43	Sabre II S 3165	DH 4-bl.40812	11,080	W. Humble
810	Typhoon IA R8198	FT MS level speeds	10–2–43	Sabre II S 37	DH Hydr.52158	10,680	W. Humble
811	Typhoon P5216	Trim change with throttle movement	9–2–43	Sabre II S 211	DH Hydr.	9,350	W. Humble
812	Typhoon P5216	Elevator trim curves: CG fwd	10–2–43	Sabre II S 211	DH Hydr.	9,350	W. Humble
813	Typhoon P5216	Directional stability	11–2–43	Sabre II S 211	DH Hydr.	9,480	P. G. Lucas
814	Typhoon P5216	Elevator trim curves. Large-chord tailplane: CG aft	11–2–43	Sabre II S 211	DH Hydr.	9,480	W. Humble
815	Typhoon IA R8198	Full-throttle levels	11–2–43	Sabre II S 37	DH Hydr.52128	10,680	W. Humble
816	Tempest V HM595	Dives with oleo fairing locks	13–1–43	Sabre II S 3165	DH 4-bl.40812	11,700	P. G. Lucas
817	Tempest V HM595	Inertia balance on control column; longitudinal stability	13–2–43	Sabre II S 3165	DH 4-bl.40812	11,700	P. G. Lucas
818	Typhoon IA R7577	Full-throttle level speeds	14–2–43	Sabre II S 211	DH Hydr.	10,600	W. Humble
819	Typhoon IA R8198	MS and FS-gear level speeds	15–2–43	Sabre II S 37	DH Hydr.	10,680	W. Humble
821	Tempest V HM595	Undercarriage retraction	13–2–43	Sabre II S 3165	DH 4-bl.40812	11,730	P. G. Lucas
822	Typhoon IB R8809	Functioning of sliding hood	16–2–43	Sabre II S 58	DH Hydr.	9,700	W. Humble
823	Tempest V HM595	Dive from 11,000 feet	13–2–43	Sabre II S 3165	DH 4-bl.40812	11,730	P. G. Lucas
824	Tempest V HM595	Dive from 27,500 feet	13–2–43	Sabre II S 3165	DH 4-bl.40812	11,730	P. G. Lucas
825	Typhoon IA R8809	Full-throttle level speeds	18–2–43	Sabre II S 37	DH Hydr.	10,680	W. Humble
826	Typhoon P5216	Rudder trim at 10,000 feet	18–2–43	Sabre II S 158	DH Hydr.	10,060	W. Humble
827	Tempest V HM595	Partials at combat rating	19–2–43	Sabre II S 3165	DH 4-bl.40811	11,700	W. Humble
828	Tempest V HM595	Dive from 27,000 feet	13–2–43	Sabre II S 3165	DH 4-bl.40812	11,700	P. G. Lucas
830	Tempest I HM599	Taxying trials	22–2–43	Sabre IV S 75	DH 4-bl.50004	11,050	P. G. Lucas
831	Tempest I HM599	First handling flights	24–2–43	Sabre IV S 75	DH 4-bl.50004	11,050	P. G. Lucas
832	Typhoon IB R8809	Levels with sliding hood	24–2–43	Sabre II S 58	DH Hydr.	9,700	W. Humble
833	Typhoon P5216	Directional trim at 20,000 and 30,000 feet	24–2–43	Sabre II S 158	DH Hydr.	10,060	W. Humble
834	Typhoon P5216	Dynamic longitudinal stability	26–2–43	Sabre II S 158	DH Hydr.	10,060	W. Humble
835	Typhoon P5216	Rudder trim with throttle changes	26–2–43	Sabre II S 158	DH Hydr.	10,060	W. Humble
836	Typhoon P5216	Dynamic longitudl stability	26–2–43	Sabre II S 158	DH Hydr.	9,480	W. Humble
838	Typhoon P5216	Rudder bar forces	4–3–43	Sabre II S 158	DH Hydr.	10,060	W. Humble
842	Tornado I R7936	Test of Rotol contraprops	3–43	Vulture	Rotol contraprop	—	P. G. Lucas
843	Typhoon P5216	Directional stability	3–3–43	Sabre II S 158	DH Hydr.	9,980	W. Humble

201

Flight Report	Aircraft	Test	Date	Engine	Airscrew	Weight	Pilot
844	Typhoon IB R7617	Vibration report on special DH Hydromatic props	2–43	Sabre II S 211	DH Hydr. (various)	—	Various
849	Typhoon IA R8198	Levels with exhaust fairings	3–43	Sabre II S 37	DH Hydr.52158	10,680	W. Humble
850	Typhoon IB DN340	Rudder mass balance decreased	3–43	Sabre II S 599	DH 4-bl.40811	—	W. Humble
851	Typhoon IB DN340	Handling: Two 1,000-lb bombs	17–3–43	Sabre II S 599	DH 4-bl.40811	13,248	W. Humble
852	Typhoon P5216	Rudder trim loads	22–3–43	Sabre II S 158	DH Hydr.	9,980	W. Humble
853	Typhoon IB R7881	Night Fighter: general test	23–3–43	Sabre II S 373	DH 4-bl.50004	11,900	P. G. Lucas
854	Typhoon IB R7617	Sprung engine mounting and production exhaust shrouds	23–3–43	Sabre II	DH Hydr.	—	W. Humble
855	Tempest I HM599	Handling and levels	26–3–43	Sabre IV S 76	DH 4-bl.50004	11,050	P. G. Lucas
857	Typhoon IB R7646	FT levels in FS and MS-gear	29–3–43	Sabre II S 1079	DH 4-bl.50006	10,840	P. G. Lucas
858	Typhoon IB R7646	Radiator suitability	26–3–43	Sabre II S 1079	DH 4-bl.50006	10,840	W. Humble
859	Typhoon IA R7577	Elevator trim tab gear boxes	29–3–43	Sabre II S 211	DH Hydr.	—	P. G. Lucas
860	Tempest I HM599	Fuel consumptions	28–3–43	Sabre IV S 76	DH 4-bl.50003	11,050	W. Humble
861	Typhoon IB R8809	Sliding hood with new rails	1–4–43	Sabre II S 58	DH Hydr.	—	W. Humble
862	Tempest I HM599	Engine handling	30–3–43	Sabre IV S 76	DH 4-bl.50003	11,050	W. Humble
864	Typhoon IB R7881	Night fighter: turbulence investigation	1–4–43	Sabre II S 373	DH 4-bl.50004	11,450	W. Humble
865	Tempest I HM599	Performance and handling	3–43	Sabre IV S 76	DH 4-bl.50003	11,050	P. G. Lucas
868	Typhoon IB R7881	Night fighter: turbulence with long range tanks	1–4–43	Sabre II S 333	DH 4-bl.50004	11,450	W. Humble
871	Tornado P5219	Carbon monoxide contamination	6–4–43	Vulture	Rotol 3-bl.	—	W. Humble
874	Tempest I HM599	Handling with forward-facing intake removed	12–4–43	Sabre IV S 76	DH 4-bl.50004	11,050	P. G. Lucas
875	Tempest I HM599	Determination of fwd CG limit	16–4–43	Sabre IV S 76	DH 4-bl.50004	11,050	P. G. Lucas
876	Tempest V HM595	Speed comparisons with and without gun blisters	12–4–43	Sabre II S 697	DH 4-bl.40812	11,700	P. G. Lucas
881	Typhoon P5216	Comparison of Kollsman leading edge pitot with std head	13–4–43	Sabre II S 158	DH Hydr.	9,980	P. G. Lucas
883	Typhoon IB R8809	Diving and directional stability tests	17–4–43	Sabre II	DH Hydr.	—	P. G. Lucas
886	Tempest V HM595	Comparisons with and without gun blisters	14–4–43	Sabre II S 697	DH 4-bl.40812	11,700	W. Humble
887	Typhoon P5216	Differential fuel pressure warning light	4–43	Sabre II S 158	DH Hydr.	9,980	W. Humble
889	Typhoon P5216	Comparison of Mark VIIIB l.e. pitot head with standard	19–4–43	Sabre II S 158	DH Hydr.	9,980	W. Humble
892	Typhoon IB R7646	Suitability climb	27–4–43	Sabre II S 1079	DH 4-bl.50006	10,860	W. Humble
893	Typhoon IB R7646	Tropical air intake	1–5–43	Sabre II S 1079	DH 4-bl.50006	10,860	W. Humble
895	Typhoon IB R7646	Tropical; air temps behind radiator matrix	28–4–43	Sabre II S 1079	DH 4-bl.50006	10,860	W. Humble
897	Typhoon IB R7646	Tropical; radiator temps	3–5–43	Sabre II S 1079	DH 4-bl.50006	10,860	W. Humble
898	Tornado P5219	CO contamination	4–43	Vulture V	Rotol 3-bl	—	W. Humble
899	Typhoon IB R7617	CO contamination	3–5–43	Sabre II S 211	DH Hydr.	—	W. Humble
900	Typhoon IB R7646	Fuel pressure readings	4–5–43	Sabre II S 1079	DH 4-bl.50006	10,860	W. Humble
902	Typhoon IB R7646	Radiator suitability	9–5–43	Sabre II S 1079	DH 4-bl.50006	10,860	W. Humble
904	Typhoon IB R7646	Tropical intake; FT levels	11–5–43	Sabre II S 1079	DH 4-bl.50006	10,860	W. Humble
905	Tornado I R7536	Test of DH contra-props	11–5–43	Vulture V	DH contraprop	—	W. Humble
907	Typhoon IB EK229	Full-throttle level speeds	18–5–43	Sabre II S 722	DH Hydr.56074	9,700	R. P. Beamont
908	Typhoon IB EK229	CO contamination	18–5–43	Sabre II S 722	DH Hydr.56074	9,700	R. P. Beamont
911	Tornado I R7536	Direction stability with increased fin area	25–5–43	Vulture V No 132	DH 11′3″ cont/prop	—	W. Humble
914	Typhoon IB EK229	CO contamination	5–43	Sabre II S 722	DH Hydr.56074	9,700	W. Humble
915	Typhoon IB EK229	Drop tanks (paper)	5–43	Sabre II S 722	DH Hydr.56074	10,320	R. P. Beamont
916	Tempest I HM599	Level speeds	4–6–43	Sabre IV S 72	DH 4-bl.40812	10,890	W. Humble
917	Typhoon IA R7577	Effect of inertia weight on control column	6–43	Sabre II S 211	DH 4-bl.50004	11,055	R. P. Beamont
918	Typhoon IA R7577	Lightened elevator mass balance weight	6–43	Sabre II S 211	DH 4-bl.50004	11,055	W. Humble
919	Tempest I HM599	Level speeds	6–6–43	Sabre IV S 72	DH 4-bl.40813	10,890	R. P. Beamont
920	Typhoon IA R7577	3-flow Gallay oil cooler	6–6–43	Sabre II S 211	DH 4-bl.50004	11,055	R. P. Beamont
921	Tempest V HM595	Full-throttle level speeds	7–6–43	Sabre IV S 76	DH 4-bl.50006	11,800	W. Humble
922	Typhoon IB EK229	High-pressure tyres	6–43	Sabre II S 722	DH Hydr.56074	11,900	R. P. Beamont
923	Tempest V HM595	Engine behaviour	8–6–43	Sabre IV S 76	DH 4-bl.50006	11,800	W. Humble
924	Typhoon IB EK229	Cockpit ventilation	6–43	Sabre II S 722	DH Hydr.56074	11,900	R. P. Beamont
925	Tempest V HM595	FT levels in MS-gear	9–6–43	Sabre IV S 76	DH 4-bl.50006	11,800	R. P. Beamont
926	Tempest I HM599	Timed climb and FT levels	11–6–43	Sabre IV S 72	DH 4-bl.40812	10,890	W. Humble
927	Tempest I HM599	Fuel tank pressures	11–6–43	Sabre IV S 72	DH 4-bl.40812	10,890	R. P. Beamont
928	Tempest V HM595	Full throttle level speeds	16–6–43	Sabre IV S 76	DH 4-bl.50006	11,800	R. P. Beamont
930	Tempest V HM595	Cooling climb	17–6–43	Sabre IV S 76	DH 4-bl.	11,800	W. Humble
931	Typhoon IB EK229	Cockpit ventilation	6–43	Sabre II S 722	DH Hydr.56074	11,900	R. P. Beamont
932	Tempest I HM599	Full-throttle level speeds	6–43	Sabre IV S 72	DH 4-bl.40812	10,890	R. P. Beamont
933	Tempest I HM599	Carburation	20–6–43	Sabre IV S 72	DH 4-bl.40812	10,890	R. P. Beamont
935	Typhoon IA R7577	Suitability climb and levels	20–6–43	Sabre II S 211	DH 4-bl.50004	10,955	W. Humble
936	Tempest V JN729	First production Tempest V; climb and level speeds	21–6–43	Sabre II S 3221	DH 4-bl.50003	11,324	W. Humble
937	Tempest V JN729	Full-throttle level speeds	21–6–43	Sabre II S 3221	DH 4-bl.50003	11,324	W. Humble
938	Tempest V JN729	General handling	25–6–43	Sabre II S 3221	DH 4-bl.50003	11,324	W. Humble
939	Tempest V JN729	Control column	25–6–43	Sabre II S 3221	DH 4-bl.50003	11,324	W. Humble
940	Typhoon IB EK229	Tests of inertia weight	21–6–43	Sabre II S 722	DH 4-bl.56074	11,900	W. Humble
941	Typhoon IB EK229	Elevator with l.e. mass balance	21–6–43	Sabre II S 722	DH Hydr.56074	11,900	W. Humble
942	Typhoon IB R7577	Suitability levels and cruises	6–43	Sabre II S 211	DH Hydr.	10,955	R. P. Beamont
943	Tempest I HM599	Full-throttle level speeds	23–6–43	Sabre IV S 72	DH 4-bl.40812	10,810	W. Humble
944	Tempest I HM599	Pressures on air intake	24–6–43	Sabre IV S 72	DH 4-bl.40812	10,810	R. P. Beamont
945	Typhoon IB EK229	High pressure tyres, 58 psi.	6–43	Sabre II S 722	DH Hydr.56074	11,160	W. Humble
946	Tempest V HM595	Partial climbs 11–15,000 ft	21–6–43	Sabre IV S 76	DH Hydr. 3-bl.	11,800	W. Humble
947	Tempest V HM595	Emergency u/c locking gear	17–6–43	Sabre IV S 76	DH Hydr. 3-bl.	11,800	W. Humble
949	Tempest II LA602	Taxying and preliminary handling report	26–6–43 1–7–43 }	Centaurus IV C 80023	Rotol 4-bl.EH294	10,963	P. G. Lucas
950	Typhoon IB EK229	Nose balanced elevators	6–43	Sabre II S 722	DH Hydr.56074	11,260	W. Humble
952	Tempest II LA602	Cylinder and oil temperatures	9–7–43	Centaurus IV C 80133	Rotol 4-bl.EH294	10,963	P. G. Lucas
954	Tempest II LA602	Cylinder and oil temperatures	12–7–43	Centaurus IV C 80133	Rotol 4-bl.EH294	10,960	W. Humble

Flight Report	Aircraft	Test	Date	Engine	Airscrew	Weight	Pilot
955	Typhoon IB EK497	Suitability climb and cruise	13–7–43	Sabre II S 1054	DH Hydr. 3-bl.	11,670	R. P. Beamont
		(Note: Sabre II S 722 failed in Typhoon IB EK229 on 15–7–43)					
956	Tempest V HM595	MS-gear levels	15–7–43	Sabre IV S 76	DH 4-bl.50006	11,800	R. P. Beamont
957	Typhoon IB EK497	Level speeds and dive	14–7–43	Sabre II S 1054	DH Hydr. 3-bl.	11,670	W. Humble
958	Typhoon IB EK497	PE comparisons	14–7–43	Sabre II S 1054	DH Hydr. 3-bl.	11,670	W. Humble
959	Typhoon IB EK497	Climb and levels without stone guard	16–7–43	Sabre II S 1054	DH Hydr. 3-bl.	11,670	R. P. Beamont
960	Tempest V HM595	Time to roll 360°	7–43	Sabre IV S 76	DH 4-bl.50006	11,800	R. P. Beamont
961	Tempest II LA602	Handling and fuel flows	7–43	Centaurus IV C 80133	Rotol 4-bl.EH294	10,963	P. G. Lucas
962	Typhoon IB EK497	Levels and forced landing after engine failure	16–7–43	Sabre II S 1054	DH Hydr. 3-bl.	11,670	R. P. Beamont
963	Tempest II LA602	Handling and fuel flows	10–7–43	Centaurus IV C 80133	Rotol 4-bl.EH294	10,963	P. G. Lucas
964	Tempest II LA602	Climb at rated rpm and boost	19–7–43	Centaurus IV C 80133	Rotol 4-bl.EH294	11,040	P. G. Lucas
965	Typhoon IB EK229	Longitudinal stability	7–43	Sabre II S 722	DH 4-bl.40812	11,215	W. Humble
968	Typhoon IB R7595	Summary of Strain Gauge tests	11–4–43	—	—	—	Various
969	Tempest V JN729	Cooling climb	27–7–43	Sabre II S 3334	DH 4-bl.40235	10,930	R. P. Beamont
970	Typhoon IB EK497	Suitability climb and cruises	26–7–43	Sabre II S 4857	DH Hydr. 3-bl.	12,180	R. P. Beamont
971	Typhoon IB EK497	Climb, cruises and levels	28–7–43	Sabre II S 4857	DH Hydr. 3-bl.	12,180	R. P. Beamont
973	Typhoon IB R7646	Climb, cruises and levels	26–7–43	Sabre II S 3250	DH 4-bl.50003	10,895	R. P. Beamont
974	Tempest V JN729	Cooling climb	27–7–43	Sabre II S 3250	DH 4-bl.40235	10,930	R. P. Beamont
975	Typhoon IB EK497	Full-throttle MS levels	27–7–43	Sabre II S 4857	DH Hydr. 3-bl.	11,540	W. Humble
976	Typhoon IB EK497	Full-throttle MS levels	27–7–43	Sabre II S 4857	DH Hydr. 3-bl.	11,275	W. Humble
977	Typhoon IB R7646	Suitability climb and levels	30–7–43	Sabre II S 3250	DH 4-bl.50003	10,895	W. Humble
978	Tempest II LA602	Bendix Stromberg carburettor defect report	29–7–43	Centaurus IV C 80133	Rotol 4-bl.EH282	—	P. G. Lucas
979	Tempest II LA602	Handling with Rotol prop	19–7–43	Centaurus IV C 80133	Rotol 4-bl.EH282	11,040	P. G. Lucas
980	Typhoon IB EK497	Full-throttle MS levels	28–7–43	Sabre II S 4857	DH Hydr. 3-bl.	11,540	W. Humble
981	Tempest V JN729	Cooling climb	28–7–43	Sabre II S 3335	DH 4-bl.40235	10,930	R. P. Beamont
982	Typhoon IB EK229	Elevator trim curves	29–7–43	Sabre II S 3348	DH 4-bl.40097	11,340	R. P. Beamont
983	Tempest V JN729	FT cooling climb	29–7–43	Sabre II S 3334	DH 4-bl.40235	10,930	P. G. Lucas
984	Tempest V JN729	FT cooling climb	29–7–43	Sabre II S 3334	DH 4-bl.40235	10,930	W. Humble
985	Typhoon IB EK229	Elevator trim curves	3–8–43	Sabre II S 3348	DH 4-bl.40097	11,340	R. P. Beamont
986	Typhoon IB EK497	Rocket projectile installation: full-throttle levels	29–7–43	Sabre II S 4857	DH Hydr. 3-bl.	11,540	W. Humble
987	Tempest II LA602	Report on high oil temps and low oil pressures	4–8–43	Centaurus IV C 80133	Rotol 4-bl.EH282	11,040	P. G. Lucas
988	Tempest V JN729	Cooling climb	30–7–43	Sabre II S 3334	DH 4-bl.40235	10,930	R. P. Beamont
990	Typhoon IB EK122	Pressure plotting wing; summary of records	5–8–43	Sabre II	DH Hydr. 3-bl.	Various	Various
991	Typhoon IB EK122	Pressure plotting wing; 2nd summary of records	5–8–43	Sabre II	DH Hydr. 3-bl.	Various	P. G. Lucas
992	Typhoon IB EK229	High pressure tyres, FE. 30 × 9.00 — 15	5–8–43	Sabre II S 3348	DH 4-bl.40097	11,340	W. Humble
994	Typhoon P5216	Push-pull elevator control	6–8–43	Sabre II S 170	DH Hydr. 3-bl.	10,050	P. G. Lucas
995	Tempest V JN729	Cooling climb	4–8–43	Sabre II S 3334	DH 4-bl.40235	10,930	R. P. Beamont
996	Typhoon IB R7646	Tropical. Suitability climbs	5–8–43	Sabre II S 2350	DH 4-bl.50003	10,895	W. Humble
998	Typhoon IB EK229	Stability with and without 8-lb inertia weight	7–8–43	Sabre II S 3348	DH 4-bl.40097	11,340	W. Humble
999	Tempest II LA602	Vibration records, cyl temps and oil cooling	8–43	Centaurus IV C 80133	Rotol 4-bl.EH282	10,980	P. G. Lucas
1000	Tempest II LA602	Cyl temps, climb and levels	9–8–43	Centaurus IV C 80133	Rotol 4-bl.EH282	10,980	P. G. Lucas
1001	Typhoon IB R7646	Functioning of air cleaner	6–8–43	Sabre II S 2350	DH 4-bl.50003	10,895	R. P. Beamont
1002	Tempest II LA602	Lateral control	12–8–43	Centaurus IV C 80133	Rotol 4-bl.EH282	10,890	P. G. Lucas
1003	Typhoon P5216	Comparison of static vent and underwing pitot	7–8–43	Sabre II S 170	DH Hydr. 3-bl.	10,050	W. Humble
1004	Typhoon P5216	Comparison of static vent and leading edge pitot	11–8–43	Sabre II S 170	DH Hydr. 3-bl.	10,050	R. P. Beamont
1005	Typhoon IB EK229	Stability with and without 8-lb inertia weight	13–8–43	Sabre II S 3348	DH 4-bl.40097	10,060	W. Humble
1006	Tempest V JN729	Handling: stick force under g	15–8–43	Sabre II S 3334	DH 4-bl.40235	11,415	R. P. Beamont
1007	Tempest V JN729	Handling: aileron over-balance	15–8–43	Sabre II S 3334	DH 4-bl.40235	11,415	R. P. Beamont
1008	Tempest II LA602	Cyl temps and fuel consumption with power enrich. jet	15–8–43	Centaurus IV C 80133	Rotol 4-bl.EH282	10,980	W. Humble
1009	Typhoon P5216	Comparison between leading edge pitot and static vent	16–8–43	Sabre II S 170	DH Hydr. 3-bl.	10,050	W. Humble
1010	Tempest V JN729	Cockpit ventilation	18–8–43	Sabre II S 3334	DH 4-bl.40235	11,415	R. P. Beamont
1012	Tempest V JN729	Suitability climb and levels	18–8–43	Sabre II S 3334	DH 4-bl.40235	11,415	R. P. Beamont
1013	Tempest II LA602	Cylinder temperatures and fuel consumptions	17–8–43	Centaurus IV C 80133	Rotol 4-bl.EH282	10,980	P. G. Lucas
1014	Tempest V JN729	Suitability climb and levels	18–8–43	Sabre II S 3334	DH 4-bl.40235	11,415	W. Humble
1015	Tempest II LA602	Cyl temps and fuel consump.	18–8–43	Centaurus IV C 80133	Rotol 4-bl.EH282	10,980	R. P. Beamont
1016	Typhoon IB EK122	Summary of wing pressure plotting records	17–8–43	Sabre II	DH Hydr. 3-bl.	Various	P. G. Lucas
1017	Tempest V JN729	FT levels, FS-gear	19–8–43	Sabre II S 3334	DH 4-bl.40235	11,415	P. G. Lucas
1018	Typhoon P5216	Comparison of l.e. pitot, static vent and std. pitot	19–8–43	Sabre II S 170	DH 3-bl. Hydr.	10,050	R. P. Beamont
1019	Tempest V JN729	Cannon heating	19–8–43	Sabre II S 3334	DH 4-bl.40235	11,415	W. Humble
1020	Tempest V JN729	Investigation of aileron circuit stretch	21–8–43	Sabre II S 3334	DH 4-bl.40235	11,415	P. G. Lucas
1021	Tempest V JN729	Timed climbs	20–8–43	Sabre II S 3334	DH 4-bl.40235	11,415	R. P. Beamont
1023	Tempest V JN729	Suitability climb	23–8–43	Sabre II S 3334	DH 4-bl.40235	11,415	W. Humble
1024	Tempest I HM599	Forward air intake carburettor flange pressures	19–8–43	Sabre IV S 2904	DH 4-bl.40031	—	R. P. Beamont
1026	Tempest I HM599	FT levels, MS and FS-gear	24–8–43	Sabre IV S 2904	DH 4-bl.40031	10,955	P. G. Lucas
1027	Typhoon P5216	Comparison of pitot heads	25–8–43	Sabre II S 170	DH 3-bl. Hydr.	10,050	W. Humble
1028	Typhoon IB EK229	Directional stability	26–8–43	Sabre II S 3348	DH 4-bl. Hydr.	10,470	W. Humble
1030	Typhoon IB EK229	Directional stability with 4-blade prop and full load	27–8–43	Sabre II S 3348	DH 4-bl. Hydr.	11,330	W. Humble
1031	Typhoon IB EK229	Anti-shimmy tailwheel	28–8–43	Sabre II S 3348	DH 4-bl. Hydr.	11,330	W. Humble
1032	Typhoon P5216	Comparison of pitot heads	31–8–43	Sabre II S 170	DH 3-bl. Hydr.	10,050	W. Humble
1033	Tempest I HM599	Suitability climb	30–8–43	Sabre IV S 2904	DH 4-bl.40031	10,875	W. Humble
1034	Tempest V JN729	Suit. climb and timed climb	2–9–43	Sabre II S 3334	DH 4-bl.40235	11,415	W. Humble
1036	Tempest V JN729	Aileron angles for over-balance	30–8–43	Sabre II S 3334	DH 4-bl.40235	11,415	R. P. Beamont

Flight Report	Aircraft	Test	Date	Engine	Airscrew	Weight	Pilot
1037	Typhoon IB EK229	Increased elevator mass balance	11–9–43	Sabre II S 3348	DH 4-bl. Hydr.	10,470	Not known
1038	Tempest I HM599	FS-gear level speeds	16–9–43	Sabre IV S 2904	DH 4-bl.40031	10,875	W. Humble
1039	Typhoon IB R7646	Tropical. Suit. climb	16–9–43	Sabre II S 3250	DH 3-bl. Hydr.	10,780	R. P. Beamont
1040	Tempest I HM599	Full throttle level speeds	18–9–43	Sabre IV S 2904	DH 4-bl.40031	10,875	W. Humble
1041	Typhoon IB R7771	Suitability, mixed matrix rad, Sabre IIA installation	18–9–43	Sabre IIA S 3336*	DH Hdr. 3-bl.	9,770	R. P. Beamont

Note: Many Sabres were modified with the mixed matrix radiators and henceforth termed Sabre IIAs.

Flight Report	Aircraft	Test	Date	Engine	Airscrew	Weight	Pilot
1042	Tempest II LA607	Second prototype. 1st Flight.	18–9–43	Centaurus IV C 80145	Rotol 4-bl.EH282	11,370	P. G. Lucas
1043	Typhoon IB R7771	FT levels, mixed matrix rad.	18–9–43	Sabre IIA S 3336	DH Hydr. 3-bl.	9,770	R. P. Beamont
1044	Tempest I HM599	Elevator control; low speeds	22–9–43	Sabre IV S 2904	DH Hydr. 4-bl.	10,875	W. Humble
1045	Typhoon IB JP752	Longitudinal instability with 4-blade prop	26–9–43	Sabre II	DH Hydr. 4-bl.	—	P. G. Lucas
1047	Typhoon IB EK229	Tempest tailplane; 4-bl prop	26–9–43	Sabre IIA S 3348	DH Hydr. 4-bl.	10,470	P. G. Lucas
1049	Typhoon IB R7771	FT levels, 'S' gear	23–9–43	Sabre IIA S 3336	DH Hydr. 3-bl.	10,825	W. Humble
1051	Tempest V JN732	Prodn. aircraft; forced landing	1–10–43	Sabre IIA	DH Hydr. 4-bl.	—	W. Humble
1052	Typhoon IB R7771	Suitability cruises, S-gear	1–10–43	Sabre IIA S 3336	DH Hydr. 3-bl.	10,825	W. Humble
1053	Tempest II LA607	Fuel cons. and cyl temps	24–9–43	Centaurus IV C 80145	Rotol 4-bl.EH282	11,370	P. G. Lucas
1056	Tempest V	Aileron tests	18–10–43	Sabre IIA	DH Hydr. 4-bl.	—	P. G. Lucas
1057	Tempest V JN729	Longitudinal stability	6–10–43	Sabre IIA S 3334	DH Hydr. 4-bl.	11,435	P. G. Lucas
1058	Typhoon IB EK122	Test with armour plating	6–10–43	Sabre IIA	DH Hydr. 3-bl.	11,815	P. G. Lucas
1060	Tempest I HM599	Full-throttle levels	7–10–43	Sabre IV S 2904	DH Hydr. 4-bl.	10,955	R. P. Beamont
1061	Typhoon IB EK229	Longitudinal stability with 16 lbs on control column	8–10–43	Sabre IIA S 3348	DH Hydr. 4-bl.	10,700	P. G. Lucas
1062	Tempest II LA607	Fuel cons. and cyl temps	7–10–43	Centaurus IV C 80145	Rotol 4-bl.EH282	11,370	R. P. Beamont
1063	Tempest V JN730	2nd prodn. aircraft; special coolant header tank	12–10–43	Sabre IIA S 3335	DH Hydr. 4-bl.	11,520	P. G. Lucas
1064	Tempest II LA602	First flight with sprung engine mounting	8–10–43	Centaurus IV C 80133	Rotol 4-bl.EH294	11,250	P. G. Lucas
1065	Typhoon IB JP752	Handling: 16-lb inertia weight	Various	Sabre IIA	DH Hydr. 3-bl.	—	W. Humble
1066	Tempest V	Dowty u/c; inflation pressure	15–10–43	Sabre IIA	DH Hydr. 3-bl.	—	P. G. Lucas
1067	Tempest V JN731	3rd prodn; aileron overbal.	13–10–43	Sabre IIA	DH Hydr. 4-bl.	—	W. Humble
1068	Typhoon IB EK152	Yaws from trimmed dives	16–10–43	Sabre IIA	DH Hydr. 3-bl.	—	R. P. Beamont
1069	Tempest V JN729	Take-offs & landing, CG fwd	Various	Sabre IIA S 3334	DH Hydr. 4-bl.	10,695	W. Humble
1070	Tempest V JN729	Partial climbs	16–10–43	Sabre IIA S 3334	DH Hydr. 4-bl.	11,400	R. P. Beamont
1071	Tempest V JN731	CO contamination	19–10–43	Sabre IIA	DH Hydr. 4-bl.	—	H. S. Broad
1072	Typhoon IB EK229	Dowty anti-shimmy Tempest tailwheel	Various	Sabre IIA	DH Hydr. 4-bl.	—	P. G. Lucas
1073	Tempest II LA602	Engine vibration tests	18–10–43	Centaurus IV C 80133	Rotol 4-bl.EH282	11,250	P. G. Lucas
1075	Tempest V JN731	Modified aileron noses	22–10–43	Sabre IIA	DH Hydr. 4-bl.	—	P. G. Lucas
1076	Typhoon IB DN248	Sliding hood and 4-bl prop	26–10–43	Sabre IIA	DH Hydr. 4-bl.	12,250	W. Humble
1077	Tempest II LA602	New throttle box	27–10–43	Centaurus IV C 80133	Rotol 4-bl.EH282	11,250	P. G. Lucas
1078	Tempest V JN729	Take-off & landing, CG norm.	Various	Sabre IIA S 3334	DH Hydr. 4-bl.	11,400	W. Humble
1079	Tempest II LA602	Vibration with stiffened engine mounting	Various	Centaurus IV C 80133	Rotol 4-bl.EH282	11,250	P. G. Lucas
1080	Tempest II LA602	Vibration, sprung engine and Rotol 5-blade propeller	4–11–43	Centaurus IV C 80145	Rotol 5-bl.EH318	10,760	W. Humble
1081	Typhoon	Typhoon aircraft fitted with 4-blade props: Report	6–11–43	Sabre IIA	DH 4-bl. Hydr.	Various	P. G. Lucas
1082	Tempest II LA607	General report of 5-bl. prop	13–11–43	Centaurus IV C 80145	Rotol 5-bl.EH318	10,760	P. G. Lucas
1084	Typhoon IB DN248	Stability with 16-lb inertia and 8-lb mass balance weight	11–11–43	Sabre IIA	DH 4-bl. Hydr.	—	W. Humble
1085	Tempest II LA607	Cyl temps and 7,000 cc power enrichment jet	12–11–43	Centaurus IV C 80145	Rotol 5-bl.EH318	10,760	R. P. Beamont
1087	Tempest II LA607	Failure of hydraulic system and emergency lowering of u/c	13–11–43	Centaurus IV C 80145	Rotol 5-bl.EH318	10,760	P. G. Lucas
1088	Typhoon IB EK122	30 hr test of armour installn.	15–11–43	Sabre IIA	DH 3-bl. Hydr.	11,815	P. G. Lucas
1089	Tempest I HM599	Full-throttle level speeds	18–11–43	Sabre IV S 2904	DH 4-bl.40031	10,875	R. P. Beamont
1090	Tempest II LA602	Engine mounting vibration test	19–11–43	Centaurus IV C 80133	DH 4-bl. Hydr.	—	P. G. Lucas
1092	Tempest I HM599	Full-throttle level speeds	19–11–43	Sabre IV S 2904	DH 4-bl.40031	10,875	W. Humble
1093	Tempest I HM599	Full-throttle level speeds	24–11–43	Sabre IV S 2904	DH 4-bl.40031	10,875	W. Humble
1094	Tempest II LA607	Vibration: 4-bl. wooden prop	25–11–43	Centaurus IV C 80145	Rotol 4-bl.EH319	11,330	P. G. Lucas
1095	Tempest II LA602	Flexible engine mounting and Rotol 4-blade wooden prop	26–11–43	Centaurus IV C 80133	Rotol 4-bl.EH319	11,140	P. G. Lucas
1096	Tempest II LA602	Rotol 4-blade wooden prop	25–11–43	Centaurus IV C 80133	Rotol 4-bl.EH319	10,720	P. G. Lucas
1097	Typhoon IB JR333	Stability: sliding hood, 4-bl prop, inertia and bal. wgts.	29–11–43	Sabre IIA	DH 4-bl.Hydr.	11,350	R. P. Beamont
1098	Tempest V JN729	Suitability climb	26–11–43	Sabre IIA S 3334	DH 4-bl.40002	11,400	W. Humble
1100	Tempest V JN729	Full throttle level speeds	1–12–43	Sabre IIA S 3334	DH 4-bl.40002	11,400	R. P. Beamont
1101	Tempest V JN729	Timed climbs, M and S gear	2–12–43	Sabre IIA S 3334	DH 4-bl.40002	11,400	R. P. Beamont
1102	Tempest II LA602	Engine mount vibration tests	5–12–43	Centaurus IV C 80191	Rotol 5-bl.EH318	10,760	P. G. Lucas
1103	Typhoon IB EK152	Fin and rudder pressure plots	12–12–43	Sabre IIA	DH 3-bl.Hydr.	10,700	P. G. Lucas
1104	Typhoon IB JR333	Full-throttle level speeds	14–12–43	Sabre IIA S 1914	DH 3-bl. Hydr.	11,295	R. P. Beamont
1105	Typhoon IB JR333	General handling	15–12–43	Sabre IIA S 1914	DH 3-bl. Hydr.	11,295	W. Humble
1106	Tempest V JN733	Forced landing	13–12–43	Sabre IIA	DH 4-bl.Hydr.	—	H. N. Sweetman
1107	Typhoon IB JR333	Vibration of reflector sight	15–12–43	Sabre IIA S 1914	DH 3-bl. Hydr.	11,295	W. Humble
1108	Typhoon IB JR333	Full-throttle level speeds	20–12–43	Sabre IIA S 1914	DH 3-bl. 56986	11,295	W. Humble
1109	Tempest V JN729	Propeller vibration tests	21–12–43	Sabre IIA S 3334	DH 4-bl. Hydr.	—	R. P. Beamont
1110	Tempest V JN729	Elevator control investigation	10–1–44	Sabre IIA S 3334	DH 4-bl. Hydr.	—	P. G. Lucas
1111	Tempest II	Single lever carburettor	23–12–43	Centaurus IV	Rotol 4-bl.	—	P. G. Lucas
1112	Tempest II LA602	Comparison of 4-blade props with metal and wooden blades	Various	Centaurus IV C 80191	Rotol 4-bl.EH319 / Rotol 4-bl.EH282	10,720 / 11,280	W. Humble
1114	Tempest II LA607	Cyl temps, 7,000 cc jet	27–12–43	Centaurus IV C 80145	Rotol 4-bl.EH282	11,450	R. P. Beamont
1115	Tempest II LA607	Cyl temps, 7,000 cc jet	30–12–43	Centaurus IV C 80145	Rotol 4-bl.EH282	11,450	P. G. Lucas
1116	Tempest II LA607	Cyl temps; timed climb	22–12–43	Centaurus IV C 80145	Rotol 4-bl.EH282	11,450	W. Humble
1118	Typhoon IB JR333	Vibration: sprung engine mount	6–1–44	Sabre IIA	DH Hydr. 3-bl.	11,295	Not known
1119	Typhoon IB JR333	Aileron handling report	6–1–44	Sabre IIA	DH Hydr. 3-bl.	11,295	W. Humble
1120	Typhoon IB EK122	Neg G oil tank: Handling	6–1–44	Sabre IIA	DH Hydr. 3-bl.	11,300	W. Humble
1121	Typhoon IB EK497	Level speeds in MS-gear	4–1–44	Sabre IIA S 4857	DH Hydr. 3-bl.	9,800	W. Humble

Flight Report	Aircraft	Test	Date	Engine	Airscrew	Weight	Pilot
1122	Tempest II LA607	Cyl temps: timed climbs	30–12–43	Centaurus IV C 80145	Rotol 4-bl.EH282	11,450	W. Humble
1123	Tempest II LA607	Timed climbs, +8 lb boost	31–12–43	Centaurus IV C 80145	Rotol 4-bl.EH282	11,450	P. G. Lucas
1124	Typhoon IB EK122	Generator cooling	8–1–44	Sabre IIA	DH Hydr. 3-bl.	10,450	R. P. Beamont
1125	Tempest II LA607	Oil pressures on climb	14–1–44	Centaurus IV C 80145	Rotol 4-bl.EH282	11,450	W. Humble
1126	Tempest II LA607	Oil pressures on climb	20–1–44	Centaurus IV C 80145	Rotol 4-bl.EH282	11,450	R. P. Beamont
1127	Tempest V JN747	Report on accident	20–1–44	Sabre IIA S 4917	DH 4-bl. 41745	9,800	P. E. Raw
1128	Tempest V JN729	U/c emergency assister; report	21–1–44	Sabre IIA S 3334	DH 4-bl. Hydr.	10,950	R. V. Muspratt
1129	Tempest V JN749	Forced landing	23–1–44	Sabre IIA	DH 4-bl. Hydr.	9,900	R. V. Muspratt
1130	Tempest II LA607	Fuel consumption and cyl temps	25–1–44	Centaurus IV C 80145	Rotol 4-bl.EH282	11,450	W. Humble
1131	Tempest II LA607	Fuel consumption and cyl temps	27–1–44	Centaurus IV C 80145	Rotol 4-bl.EH282	11,450	R. P. Beamont
1132	Tempest II LA607	Oil cooler suitability, 15,000 ft	27–1–44	Centaurus IV C 80145	Rotol 4-bl.EH282	11,450	W. Humble
1133	Typhoon IB R7646	Tropical air intake	24–1–44	Sabre IIA S 3250	DH 3-bl. Hydr.	10,700	R. P. Beamont
1134	Tempest V JN729	Handling: aileron spring tabs	28–1–44	Sabre IIA S 3334	DH 4-bl. Hydr.	10,850	P. G. Lucas
1135	Tempest II LA602	Vibration with flex. engine mounting	28–1–44	Centaurus IV C 80191	Rotol 4-bl.EH319	11,185	P. G. Lucas
1136	Typhoon IB R7646	Tropical air intake	1–2–44	Sabre IIA S 3250	DH 3-bl. Hydr.	10,780	W. Humble
1137	Tempest V JN729	Take-off measurements	28–1–44	Sabre IIA S 3334	Reverse action DH	11,360	R. P. Beamont
1138	Typhoon IB EK497	Mk III RP instn; level speeds	27–1–44	Sabre IIA S 620	DH 3-bl. Hydr.	10,200	R. P. Beamont
1139	Tempest V JN730	FT Levels: overload tanks	3–2–44	Sabre IIA S 3335	DH 4-bl. Hydr.	11,520	W. Humble
1140	Typhoon IB EK497	Level speeds	4–2–44	Sabre IIA S 620	DH 3-bl. Hydr.	10,200	R. P. Beamont
1142	Tempest V JN730	FT Levels: no overload tanks	25–1–44	Sabre IIA S 3335	DH 4-bl. Hydr.	11,420	P. G. Lucas
1143	Tempest V JN736	Levels with 3-blade propeller	5–2–44	Sabre IIA S 4978	Std. Typhoon 3-bl.	11,370	W. Humble
1144	Tempest V JN730	Overspeeding prop on take-off	9–2–44	Sabre IIA S 3335	DH 4-bl. Hydr.	11,420	P. G. Lucas
1145	Tempest II LA602	Oil pressure fluctuations	8–2–44	Centaurus IV C 80191	Rotol 4-bl.EH319	11,175	R. P. Beamont
1146	Tempest II LA607	Oil pressure fluctuations	8–2–44	Centaurus IV C 80145	Rotol 4-bl.EH282	11,450	R. P. Beamont
1147	Typhoon IB EK497	Flying accident	4–2–44	Sabre IIA S 620	DH 3-bl. Hydr.	—	W. Humble
1148	Tempest V JN730	Vibration: 3-blade propeller	13–2–44	Sabre IIA S 4978	Std. Typhoon 3-bl.	11,370	W. Humble
1149	Tempest II LA602	Oil pressure investigation	10–2–44	Centaurus IV C 80191	Rotol 4-bl.EH319	10,840	W. Humble
1150	Tempest II LA602	Oil suitability climb	12–2–44	Centaurus IV C 80191	Rotol 4-bl.EH319	10,840	R. P. Beamont
1151	Tempest V JN730	Cruise with full overload tanks	11–2–44	Sabre IIA S 3335	DH 4-bl. Hydr.	12,180	W. Humble
1152	Tempest I HM599	Levels and cruise; fuel cons. with new engine type	8–2–44	Sabre V S 5051	DH 4-bl. Hydr.	11,110	W. Humble
1153	Tempest I HM599	Levels with new engine	11–2–44	Sabre V S 5051	DH 4-bl. Hydr.	11,110	P. G. Lucas
1154	Tempest II LA602	Dorsal fin added	17–2–44	Centaurus IV C 80191	Rotol 4-bl.EH319	10,900	P. G. Lucas
1155	Tempest I HM599	Handling report on Sabre V	18–2–44	Sabre V S 5051	DH 4-bl. Hydr.	11,110	P. G. Lucas
1156	Tempest II LA602	Coring of oil cooler	28–2–44	Centaurus IV C 80191	Rotol 4-bl.EH319	10,900	P. G. Lucas
1157	Tempest V JN730	Levels: paper overload tanks	24–2–44	Sabre IIA S 3335	DH 4-bl. Hydr.	11,610	W. Humble
1158	Tempest II LA602	Fuel consumption, 7,000 cc jet	24–2–44	Centaurus IV C 80191	Rotol 4-bl.EH319	11,185	P. G. Lucas
1159	Typhoon IB	Tailplane vibration	29–2–44	Sabre IIA	DH 3-bl. Hydr.	—	P. G. Lucas
1160	Typhoon IB MN254	ARI.5613 installation	28–2–44	Sabre IIA	DH 4-bl. Hydr.	—	W. Humble
1161	Tempest II LA602	Oil cooler tests	1–3–44	Centaurus IV C 80191	Rotol 4-bl.EH319	11,185	P. G. Lucas
1162	Tempest II LA602	Fuel consumption and oil temps	29–2–44	Centaurus IV C 80191	Rotol 4-bl.EH319	11,185	P. G. Lucas
1164	Tempest V JN729	Vibration: 4-blade prop	Various	Sabre IIA S 5043	DH 4-bl.40194	11,360	W. Humble
1165	Tempest V JN730	Functioning of drop tank jettison	4–3–44	Sabre IIA S 3335	DH 4-bl. Hydr.	11,810	P. G. Lucas
1166	Typhoon IB MN315	Test of rudder trim gear	5–3–44	Sabre IIA	DH 4-bl. Hydr.	—	Not known
1167	Typhoon IB R7646	Tropical air intake: max boost	9–3–44	Sabre IIA S 3250	DH 3-bl. Hydr.	10,780	P. G. Lucas
1168	Tempest I HM599	Report on minor air collision	9–3–44	Sabre V S 5051	DH 4-bl. Hydr.	11,110	P. G. Lucas
1169	Tempest V JN729	Sliding hood assister	12–3–44	Sabre IIA S 5043	DH 4-bl.40194	11,360	P. G. Lucas
1170	Tempest V JN730	Cruises: Fuel consumptions	4–3–44	Sabre IIA S 3335	DH 4-bl. Hydr.	12,245	P. G. Lucas
1171	Tempest I HM599	Levels: Fuel consumptions	8–3–44	Sabre V S 5051	DH 4-bl. Hydr.	11,190	W. Humble
1172	Tempest V JN730	Cruise cons: Overload tanks	12–3–44	Sabre IIA S 3335	DH 4-bl. Hydr.	12,245	W. Humble
1173	Typhoon IB JR333	Vibration of gunsight	18–3–44	Sabre IIA	DH 3-bl. Hydr.	—	W. Humble
1174	Typhoon IB MN315	Vibration with 3-blade prop	17–3–44	Sabre IIA	DH 3-bl. Hydr.	—	W. Humble
1175	Tempest II LA602	Unusual vibration	17–3–44	Centaurus IV C 80191	Rotol 4-bl.EH319	11,330	P. G. Lucas
1176	Tempest II LA602	Carburation and fuel flows	17–3–44	Centaurus IV C 80191	Rotol 4-bl.EH319	11,330	P. G. Lucas
1177	Tempest II LA602	Performance with metal blades	17–3–44	Centaurus IV C 80191	Rotol 4-bl.EH282	11,330	W. Humble
1178	Tempest II LA602	Climb with de-aerators (Note: this engine now declared 'dud')	13–3–44	Centaurus IV C 80191	Rotol 4-bl.EH282	11,130	P. G. Lucas
1179	Typhoon IB JR333	Drop tank jettison trials	26–3–44	Sabre IIA S 1914	DH 3-bl. Hydr.	11,615	(Various)
1180	Typhoon IB EK497	Performance with bomb racks	17–3–44	Sabre IIA S 620	DH 3-bl. Hydr.	11,315	W. Humble
1181	Tempest II LA602	Performance: wooden prop blades	28–3–44	Centaurus IV C 80445	Rotol 4-bl.EH319	11,330	P. G. Lucas
1182	Tempest II LA602	Carburation: 6,400 cc jet	24–3–44	Centaurus IV C 80445	Rotol 4-bl.EH319	11,175	P. G. Lucas
1183	Tempest II LA602	Carburation: 6,400 cc jet	25–3–44	Centaurus IV C 80445	Rotol 4-bl.EH319	11,175	P. G. Lucas
1184	Tempest II LA602	Performance: wooden prop blades	26–3–44	Centaurus IV C 80445	Rotol 4-bl.EH319	11,175	P. G. Lucas
1185	Tempest II LA602	Climbs: wooden prop blades	26–3–44	Centaurus IV C 80445	Rotol 4-bl.EH319	11,175	P. G. Lucas
1186	Typhoon IB MN399	Stability: 4-bl. prop and 20-lb lead weight in tail	24–3–44	Sabre IIA S 2084	DH 4-bl. Hydr.	11,455	W. Humble
1187	Tempest II LA602	Climbs and level speeds	28–3–44	Centaurus IV C 80445	Rotol 4-bl.EH282	11,315	G. C. Brunner
1188	Tempest II LA602	Longitudinal stability	25–3–44	Centaurus IV C 80445	Rotol 4-bl.EH319	11,175	G. C. Brunner
1189	Tempest II LA602	Longitudinal stability	26–3–44	Centaurus IV C 80445	Rotol 4-bl.EH319	10,810	G. C. Brunner
1190	Tempest I HM599	Performance and fuel cons.	28–3–44	Sabre V S 5051	DH 4-bl. Hydr.	11,140	W. Humble
1191	Tempest II LA602	Performance with metal prop	30–3–44	Centaurus IV C 80445	Rotol 4-bl.EH282	11,315	P. G. Lucas
1192	Tempest II LA602	Vibration during dives	3–4–44	Centaurus IV C 80445	Rotol 4-bl.EH319	10,810	W. Humble
1193	Tempest I HM599	Position error comparisons	9–3–44	Sabre V S 5051	DH 4-bl. Hydr.	11,140	W. Humble
1194	Tempest I HM599	Unusual vibration	11–4–44	Sabre V S 5051	DH 4-bl. Hydr.	11,140	W. Humble
1195	Tempest I HM599	Carburation of Sabre V	11–4–44	Sabre V S 5051	DH 4-bl. Hydr.	11,140	W. Humble
1196	Tempest V JN730	Fuel performance, overload tanks	4–4–44	Sabre IIA S 3335	DH 4-bl. Hydr.	12,245	P. G. Lucas
1197	Tempest V JN729	Take-off: fine pitch angle increased to 38 degrees	15–4–44	Sabre IIA S 5048	DH 4-bl.40194	11,360	W. Humble
1198	Typhoon IB MN290	High frequency vibration	17–4–44	Sabre IIA	DH 4-bl. Hydr.	—	W. Humble
1199	Typhoon IB MN232	High frequency vibration	18–4–44	Sabre IIA	DH 4-bl. Hydr.	—	W. Humble
		(Note: This test also involved Typhoon IB JR210 – which was painted 'TR210' in error)					
1200	Typhoon IB	Two 500-lb cluster bombs	19–4–44	Sabre IIA	DH 4-bl. Hydr.	—	P. G. Lucas
1201	Tempest V JN730	Fuel consumption and cruises	18–4–44	Sabre IIA S 3335	DH 4-bl. Hydr.	12,245	P. G. Lucas
1202	Tempest V JN730	Range test	24–4–44	Sabre IIA S 3335	DH 4-bl. Hydr.	11,490	P. G. Lucas

Flight Report	Aircraft	Test	Date	Engine	Airscrew	Weight	Pilot
1203	Tempest II LA602	Carburation and performance	18–4–44	Centaurus IV C 80477	Rotol 4-bl.EH282	11,330	P. G. Lucas
1204	Tempest II LA602	Carburation: 5,600 cc jet	18–4–44	Centaurus IV C 80477	Rotol 4-bl.EH282	11,330	P. G. Lucas
1205	Tempest II LA602	Oil cooler suitability on climb	20–4–44	Centaurus IV C 80477	Rotol 4-bl.EH282	11,330	P. G. Lucas
1206	Tempest I HM599	Carburation in FS-gear	22–4–44	Sabre V S 5051	DH 4-bl. Hydr.	11,140	W. Humble
1207	Tempest II LA602	Oil cooler suitability on climb	21–4–44	Centaurus IV C 80477	Rotol 4-bl.EH282	11,330	W. Humble
1208	Tempest V JN730	Drop tank jettison test	26–4–44	Sabre IIA S 3335	DH 4-bl. Hydr.	—	W. Humble
1209	Tempest V JN729	Handling: spring tab ailerons	29–4–44	Sabre IIA S 5048	DH 4-bl.40194	11,360	P. G. Lucas
1210	Typhoon IB JP974	Mark III gunsight vibration	22–4–44	Sabre IIA	DH 3-bl. Hydr.	—	W. Humble
1211	Tempest I HM599	Level speeds	27–4–44	Sabre V S 5051	DH 4-bl. Hydr.	11,140	W. Humble
1212	Tempest II LA602	Performance; oil cooler test	28–4–44	Centaurus IV C 80477	Rotol 4-bl.EH282	11,110	P. G. Lucas
1213	Tempest V JN740	Levels in MS-gear with Mark III RP rails	28–4–44	Sabre IIA S 4900	DH 4-bl. Hydr.	11,890	W. Humble
1214	Tempest V JN740	Levels in MS-gear; no RP rails	1–5–44	Sabre IIA S 4900	DH 4-bl. Hydr.	11,680	P. G. Lucas
1215	Tempest V JN740	Levels in MS-gear with Mark III RP rails and fairings	2–5–44	Sabre IIA S 4900	DH 4-bl. Hydr.	12,660	W. Humble
1216	Typhoon/Tempest	Control wire tensiometer	5–5–44	Sabre IIA	DH 4-bl. Hydr.	—	P. G. Lucas
1217	Typhoon IB MN267	Vibration investigation	10–5–44	Sabre IIA	DH 4-bl. Hydr.	—	W. Humble
1218	Tempest II LA607	New engine with auto gills	5–5–44	Centaurus IV C 80421	Rotol 4-bl.EH319	11,890	P. G. Lucas
1219	Tempest II LA607	Ditto; metal propeller	8–5–44	Centaurus IV C 80421	Rotol 4-bl.EH321	11,980	P. G. Lucas
1220	Tempest II LA607	Ditto; pressure fuel transfer	9–5–44	Centaurus IV C 80421	Rotol 4-bl.EH321	11,980	P. G. Lucas
1221	Tempest VI HM595	First flight. Level speeds	9–5–44	Sabre V S 5055	DH 4-bl. Hydr.	11,930	W. Humble
1222	Tempest VI HM595	Second flight. Level speeds	12–5–44	Sabre V S 5055	DH 4-bl. Hydr.	11,930	W. Humble
1223	Tempest II LA607	Cyl temps, auto gills	12–5–44	Centaurus IV C 80421	Rotol 4-bl.EH321	11,980	R. V. Muspratt
1224	Tempest II LA607	Full-throttle climbs, auto gills	12–5–44	Centaurus IV C 80421	Rotol 4-bl.EH321	11,980	W. Humble
1225	Tempest II LA607	Full-throttle climb, auto gills	15–5–44	Centaurus IV C 80421	Rotol 4-bl.EH321	11,980	R. V. Muspratt
1226	Typhoon IB EK497	Diving with Mk III RP rails and RPs with 60-lb warheads	22–5–44	Sabre IIA	DH 3-bl. Hydr.	12,660	P. G. Lucas
1227	Typhoon IB JR333	Hose connection	18–5–44	Sabre IIA S 1914	DH 3-bl. Hydr.	11,615	W. Humble
1228	Tempest V JN798	Levels with bomb racks and fairings	19–5–44	Sabre IIA S 4973	DH 4-bl. Hydr.	11,285	W. Humble
1229	Tempest II LA607	Auto-gill positions and temps	19–5–44	Centaurus IV C 80421	Rotol 4-bl.EH321	11,700	W. Humble
1230	Tempest VI HM595	Suitability climb and levels	23–5–44	Sabre V S 5055	DH 4-bl. Hydr.	11,930	W. Humble
1231	Tempest V JN729	Fuel pressure warning light	19–5–44	Sabre IIA S 5048	DH 4-bl.40194	11,360	R. V. Muspratt
1232	Tempest I HM599	Timed climb: Combat rating	22–5–44	Sabre V S 5051	DH 4-bl. Hydr.	11,110	R. V. Muspratt
1233	Typhoon IB MN315	Camera bay temperatures	22–5–44	Sabre IIA S 2213	DH 4-bl. Hydr.	11,265	W. Humble
1234	Tempest V JN798	Level speeds: clean aircraft	23–5–44	Sabre IIA S 4973	DH 4-bl. Hydr.	11,240	W. Humble
1235	Typhoon IB R7646	Tropical radiator (modified)	30–5–44	Sabre IIA S 6591	DH 3-bl. Hydr.	10,780	R. V. Muspratt
1236	Tempest V JN798	Level speeds: with and without cannon fairings	30–5–44	Sabre IIA S 4973	DH 4-bl. Hydr.	11,240	R. V. Muspratt
1237	Tempest V JN798	Level speeds with bomb racks	30–5–44	Sabre IIA S 4973	DH 4-bl. Hydr.	11,285	R. V. Muspratt
1238	Tempest I HM599	Carburation in FS-gear	1–6–44	Sabre V S 5051	DH 4-bl. Hydr.	11,110	W. Humble
1239	Tempest VI HM595	Carburation in FS-gear	2–6–44	Sabre V S 5055	DH 4-bl. Hydr.	11,930	W. Humble
1240	Tempest V JN740	Level speeds: clean aircraft	30–5–44	Sabre IIA S 591	DH 4-bl. Hydr.	11,680	W. Humble
1241	Tempest V JN740	Handling with Mk III RP rails	Various	Sabre IIA S 591	DH 4-bl. Hydr.	Various	R. V. Muspratt
1242	Typhoon IB JR210	Vibration investigation	7–6–44	Sabre IIA	DH 4-bl. Hydr.	—	W. Humble
1243	Tempest II LA607	Cylinder temps, auto-gills	8–6–44	Centaurus IV C 80421	Rotol 4-bl.EH321	11,700	P. G. Lucas
1244	Tempest II LA607	Oil suitability; 20,000 feet	10–6–44	Centaurus IV C 80421	Rotol 4-bl.EH321	11,700	W. Humble
1245	Tempest VI HM595	Air intake pressures	10–6–44	Sabre V S 5055	DH 4-bl. Hydr.	11,930	W. Humble
1246	Tempest I HM599	Static pressure rad duct exit	14–6–44	Sabre V S 5051	DH 4-bl. Hydr.	11,110	W. Humble
1247	Tempest VI HM595	Carburation in FS-gear	14–6–44	Sabre V S 5055	DH 4-bl. Hydr.	11,930	W. Humble
1248	Tempest I HM599	Speeds compared HM599 and HM595	16–6–44	Sabre V S 5051	DH 4-bl. Hydr.	11,110	P. G. Lucas
1250	Tempest II LA607	Throttle calibration	17–6–44	Centaurus IV C 80421	Rotol 4-bl.EH321	11,700	P. G. Lucas
1251	Tempest II LA607	Level speeds	17–6–44	Centaurus IV C 80421	Rotol 4-bl.EH321	11,700	P. G. Lucas
1252	Tempest V JN741	Modified windscreen frame	14–6–44	Sabre IIA	DH 4-bl. Hydr.	—	P. W. S. Bulman
1253	Tempest II LA607	Throttle calibration	20–6–44	Centaurus IV C 80421	Rotol 4-bl.EH321	11,700	W. Humble
1254	Tempest V JN798	Levels with and without exhaust shrouds	Various	Sabre IIA S 4973	DH 4-bl. Hydr.	11,240	P. G. Lucas
1255	Tempest V JN798	Level with Smoke Curtain Instns.	24–6–44	Sabre IIA S 4973	DH 4-bl. Hydr.	12,035	W. Humble
1256	Typhoon IB MN686	Modified oil cooler	4–7–44	Sabre IIA S 1279	DH 4-bl. Hydr.	11,590	W. Humble
1257	Typhoon IB JR333	Reconnaissance fighter; handling with one drop tank	4–7–44	Sabre IIA S 1914	DH 3-bl. Hydr.	—	P. G. Lucas
1258	Typhoon IB JR333	Performance with Vokes air filter	4–7–44	Sabre IIA S 1914	DH 3-bl. Hydr.	11,335	F. Murphy
1259	Typhoon IB JR333	Level speeds: clean aircraft	5–7–44	Sabre IIA S 1914	DH 3-bl. Hydr.	11,325	W. Humble
1260	Typhoon IB JR333	Performance, Napier momentum cleaner	6–7–44	Sabre IIA S 1914	DH 3-bl. Hydr.	11,325	P. G. Lucas
1261	Tempest V JN798	Performance: 150-grade fuel	4–7–44	Sabre IIA S 4972	DH 4-bl. Hydr.	11,490	P. G. Lucas
1262	Tempest II LA607	Cyl temps, Centaurus V	7–7–44	Centaurus V C 81071	Rotol 4-bl.73207	11,800	P. G. Lucas
1263	Tempest V JN798	Level speeds with M10 containers	12–7–44	Sabre IIA S 4972	DH 4-bl. Hydr.	12,475	W. Humble
1264	Tempest II LA607	Oil cooler suitability	13–7–44	Centaurus IV 81071	Rotol 4-bl.73207	11,800	W. Humble
1265	Tempest V JN798	Handling with 2 × 500-lb SCI, 2 × M10, and 2 × 500-lb bombs	28–7–44	Sabre IIA S 4972	DH 4-bl. Hydr.	12,475	W. Humble
1267	Tempest V JN798	Crutch adjustments	17–7–44	Sabre IIA S 4972	DH 4-bl. Hydr.	12,475	W. Humble
1268	Tempest V JN798	Levels: Two 500-lb bombs	17–7–44	Sabre IIA S 4972	DH 4-bl. Hydr.	12,535	F. Murphy
1269	Tempest II LA607	Oil cooler suitability	15–7–44	Centaurus V C 81071	Rotol 4-bl.73207	11,800	P. G. Lucas
1270	Tempest II LA607	Weak mixture climb: cyl temps	16–7–44	Centaurus V C 81071	Rotol 4-bl.73207	11,800	W. Humble
1271	Tempest II LA607	Cyl temps with large oil cooler	18–7–44	Centaurus V C 81071	Rotol 4-bl.73207	11,800	P. G. Lucas
1272	Tempest II LA607	Weak mixture climb to 30,000 ft	18–7–44	Centaurus V C 81071	Rotol 4-bl.73207	11,800	W. Humble
1273	Tempest V EJ590	Hood jettison tests	20–7–44	Sabre IIA	DH 4-bl. Hydr.	—	P. G. Lucas
1274	Tempest V EJ592	Level speed in unpainted state	18–7–44	Sabre IIA S 6576	DH 4-bl.40450	11,620	F. Murphy
1275	Tempest II LA607	Air intake pressures	19–7–44	Centaurus V C 81071	Rotol 4-bl.73207	11,800	P. G. Lucas
1276	Tempest II LA607	Neg G oil tank; combat climb	21–7–44	Centaurus V C 81071	Rotol 4-bl.73207	11,800	W. Humble
1277	Tempest V EJ592	Control circuit tension	21–7–44	Sabre IIA S 6576	DH 4-bl.40450	11,620	W. Humble
1278	Typhoon IB EK439	Vibration check	28–7–44	Sabre IIA	DH 4-bl. Hydr.	—	W. Humble
1279	Tempest II LA607	Wing root fillet pressures	27–7–44	Centaurus V C 81071	Rotol 4-bl.73207	11,800	P. G. Lucas
1280	Tempest V EJ592	Levels with flash eliminators	9–8–44	Sabre IIA S 6576	DH 4-bl.40450	11,620	W. Humble
1281	Tempest V JN729	Spring tab on rudder	18–8–44	Sabre IIA S 5048	DH 4-bl.40194	11,360	P. G. Lucas
1282	Typhoon IB JR333	Fuel consumption tests	17–8–44	Sabre IIA S 1914	DH 3-bl. Hydr.	11,335	F. Murphy
1283	Tempest II LA607	Auto oil cooler shutter control	23–8–44	Centaurus IV C 80421	Rotol 4-bl.73207	11,800	W. Humble
1284	Tempest II LA607	Levels: Throttle calibration	26–8–44	Centaurus IV C 80421	Rotol 4-bl.73207	11,800	W. Humble

Flight Report	Aircraft	Test	Date	Engine	Airscrew	Weight	Pilot
1285	Tempest V EJ592	Performance with Vokes cleaner	18–8–44	Sabre IIA S 6576	DH 4-bl.40450	11,620	F. Murphy
1286	Tempest V JN798	Performance with two 1,000 lb bombs	10–8–44 } 6–9–44	Sabre IIA S 4973	DH 4-bl. Hydr.	13,535	F. Murphy
1287	F.2/43 NX798	Preliminary handling, 1st flight	5–9–44	Centaurus XII C80473	Rotol 4-bl.73215	11,150	P. G. Lucas
1288	Tempest V JV729	Diving incident	12–9–44	Sabre IIA S 5043	DH 4-bl. Hydr.	11,340	F. Murphy
1289	Tempest II LA607	Transfer fuel system	11–9–44	Centaurus IV C 80421	Rotol 4-bl.73207	11,800	W. Humble
1290	F.2/43 NX798	Loss of oil pressure	13–9–44	Centaurus XII C 80473	Rotol 4-bl.73215	11,150	P. G. Lucas
1291	Tempest V EJ592	Gyro Gunsight Mk IID	15–9–44	Sabre IIA S 6576	DH 4-bl.40450	—	Not known
1292	F.2/43 NX798	Weak mixture climb: cyl temps	25–9–44	Centaurus XII C 80473	Rotol 4-bl.73215	11,150	W. Humble
1293	F.2/43 NX798	FT levels, M and S gears	26–9–44	Centaurus XII C 80473	Rotol 4-bl.73215	11,150	P. G. Lucas
1294	Tempest VI HM595	Rated climb, levels and cruises with Rotol 4-blade prop.	23–9–44	Sabre V S 5063	Rotol 4-bl.EH379	11,930	W. Humble
1295	Tempest V EJ759	Tropical aircraft: Performance	25–9–44	Sabre IIA S 33	DH 4-bl. Hydr.	11,680	W. Humble
1296	F.2/43 NX798	Handling report	28–9–44	Centaurus XII C 80473	Rotol 4-bl.73215	11,150	P. G. Lucas
1297	Tempest VI HM595	Engine handling report	28–9–44	Sabre V S 5063	Rotol 4-bl.EH379	11,930	F. Murphy
1298	Tempest VI HM595	MS-gear level speeds	26–9–44	Sabre V S 5063	Rotol 4-bl.EH379	11,930	F. Murphy
1299	F.2/43 NX798	Timed climb at combat rating	30–9–44	Centaurus XII C 80473	Rotol 4-bl.73215	11,150	P. G. Lucas
1301	Tempest VI HM595	Airscrew surging	5–10–44	Sabre V S 5063	Rotol 4-bl.EH379	11,930	F. Murphy
1302	Tempest VI HM595	Levels: Vokes dry cleaner	5–10–44	Sabre V S 5063	Rotol 4-bl.EH379	11,930	F. Murphy
1303	Tempest V EJ592	Suitability climb and fuel cons.	5–10–44	Sabre IIA S 6576	DH 4-bl.40450	11,620	W. Humble
1304	Tempest V EJ592	Level speeds: aircraft painted	6–10–44	Sabre IIA S 6576	DH 4-bl. 40450	11,620	W. Humble
1305	Tempest II MW735	First production aircraft	4–10–44	Centaurus IV C 80481	Rotol 4-bl.73294	11,590	W. Humble
1306	Tempest II MW735	Performance measurements	4–10–44	Centaurus IV C 80481	Rotol 4-bl.73294	11,590	P. G. Lucas
1307	Tempest VI HM595	Suitability climb and fuel cons.	10–10–44	Sabre V S 5063	Rotol 4-bl.EH379	11,930	F. Murphy
1308	Tempest V JN741	Spinning trials	17–10–44	Sabre IIA S 4877	DH 4-bl. Hydr.	—	P. G. Lucas
1309	F.2/43 NX798	Handling with exhaust fairings	17–10–44	Centaurus XII C 80473	Rotol 4-bl.73215	11,930	P. G. Lucas
1310	Tempest VI HM595	Level speeds: fuel consumption	17–10–44	Sabre V S 5063	Rotol 4-bl.EH379	11,930	W. Humble
1311	F.2/43 NX798	Handling with l.e. fillets	18–10–44	Centaurus XII C 80473	Rotol 4-bl.73265	11,185	P. G. Lucas
1312	F.2/43 NX798	Handling: spring tab rudder	18–10–44	Centaurus XII C 80473	Rotol 4-bl.73265	11,185	P. G. Lucas
1313	F.3/43 NX798	Overspeeding Rotol prop	18–10–44	Centaurus XII C 80473	Rotol 4-bl.73265	11,185	P. G. Lucas
1314	Tempest II LA607	Dynamometer tests	19–10–44	Centaurus V C 80421	Rotol 4-bl.73207	11,800	W. Humble
1315	Tempest II MW735	CO contamination	10–10–44	Centaurus IV C 80481	Rotol 4-bl.73294	11,590	W. Humble
1316	Tempest II MW735	Handling and vibration	10–44	Centaurus IV C 80481	Rotol 4-bl.73294	11,590	W. Humble
1317	Tempest II MW735	Level speed measurements	31–10–44	Centaurus IV C 80481	Rotol 4-bl.73294	11,590	F. Murphy
1318	Tempest VI HM595	FS-gear combat climb and cruises	27–10–44	Sabre V S 5063	Rotol 4-bl.EH379	11,930	F. Murphy
1319	Tempest II MW735	Rough engine running	9–11–44	Centaurus IV C 80481	Rotol 4-bl.73294	11,590	F. Murphy
1320	Tempest I HM599	Airscrew surging	6–11–44	Sabre V S 5058	DH 4-bl. Hydr.	—	F. Murphy
1321	Tempest VI HM595	Propeller tip loss check	4–11–44	Sabre V S 5063	Rotol 4-bl.EH379	11,930	F. Murphy
1322	Tempest V EJ592	Timed climbs at low rating	10–11–44	Sabre IIA S 6576	DH 4-bl. Hydr.	11,645	W. Humble
1323	Tempest I HM599	Engine surge	13–11–44	Sabre V S 5058	DH 4-bl. Hydr.	—	F. Murphy
1324	Tempest VI HM595	Combat climb, levels and cruises	13–11–44	Sabre V S 5063	Rotol 4-bl.EH379	11,930	W. Humble
1325	Tempest V JN730	Low pressure shock absorber	23–11–44	Sabre IIA	DH 4-bl. Hydr.	11,500	W. Humble
1326	Tempest V EJ592	Prodn. spring tab ailerons	23–11–44	Sabre IIA S 6576	DH 4-bl.40450	11,620	W. Humble
1327	Tempest VI HM595	Combat climb, levels and cruises	23–11–44	Sabre V S 5063	Rotol 4-bl.EH379	11,930	W. Humble
1328	Tempest I HM599	Suitability climb and cruises	23–11–44	Sabre V S 5058	DH 4-bl. Hydr.	11,110	F. Murphy
1329	Typhoon IB RB306	Levels with various cluster bombs	24–11–44	Sabre IIA S 3704	DH 4-bl. Hydr.	12,240	F. Murphy
1330	Tempest VI HM595	Rated climb and cruises	29–11–44	Sabre V S 5063	Rotol 4-bl.EH379	11,930	P. G. Lucas
1331	Tempest VI HM595	Suitability climb	29–11–44	Sabre V S 5063	Rotol 4-bl.EH379	11,930	W. Humble
1332	Typhoon IB RB306	Handling: various cluster bombs	1–12–44	Sabre IIA S 3704	DH 4-bl. Hydr.	12,240	F. Murphy
1333	Tempest V JN730	4-blade prop overspeeding	5–12–44	Sabre IIA S 7760	Various	11,800	W. Humble
1334	Tempest V	Goodyear tailwheel tyre	6–12–44	Sabre IIA	DH 4-bl. Hydr.	11,800	W. Humble
1335	F.2/43 NX798	Carbon monoxide check	2–12–44	Centaurus XII C 80473	Rotol 4-bl.73265	11,185	W. Humble
1336	F.2/43 NX798	General handling	7–12–44	Centaurus XII C 80473	Rotol 4-bl.73265	11,185	P. G. Lucas
1337	Tempest VI HM595	Suitability: rated climb	1–12–44	Sabre V S 5063	Rotol 4-bl.EH379	11,930	F. Murphy
1338	Tempest V JN730	Balanced fuel float valves	2–12–44	Sabre IIA	DH 4-bl. Hydr.	11,500	Not known
1339	Typhoon IB RB306	Level speeds: bomb racks only	4–12–44	Sabre IIA S 3704	DH 4-bl. Hydr.	11,560	F. Murphy
1340	Tempest II MW736	Standard production. Handling	9–12–44	Centaurus V C 80544	Rotol 4-bl.	11,220	P. G. Lucas
1341	Tempest I HM599	Engine surge report	5–12–44	Sabre V S 5058	DH 4-bl. Hydr.	11,110	F. Murphy
1342	F.2/43 LA610	Taxying and handling: Griffon engine and Rotol contraprop	27–11–44	Griffon 85 No 1258	Rotol Contra CR312	10,895	P. G. Lucas
1343	Tempest I HM599	Engine surge report	18–12–44	Sabre V S 5059	DH 4-bl. Hydr.	11,110	F. Murphy
1344	Typhoon IB RB306	Handling with supply containers	14–12–44	Sabre IIA S 3704	DH 4-bl. Hydr.	11,650	F. Murphy
1345	F.2/43 LA610	Suitability rated climb and forced landing	18–12–44	Griffon 85 No 1258	Rotol Contra CR312	10,895	P. G. Lucas
1346	F.2/43 LA610	Blanks over cooling ducts	22–12–44	Griffon 85 No 1258	Rotol Contra CR312	10,895	P. G. Lucas
1347	Tempest II MW736	Vibration with rubber mounting	22–12–44	Centaurus V C 80544	Rotol 4-bl.	11,220	P. G. Lucas
1348	Tempest V EJ592	Spring tab rudder	30–12–44	Sabre IIA S 6576	DH 4-bl. Hydr.	11,645	W. Humble
1349	Tempest II LA607	Engine cutting at 12 lb boost	28–12–44	Centaurus V C 80060	Rotol 4-bl.	11,800	P. G. Lucas
1350	Tempest V NV668	Adjustable leg fairings	9–1–45	Sabre IIA	DH 4-bl. Hydr.	—	W. Humble
1351	Tempest VI HM595	Propeller overspeeding	5–1–45	Sabre V S 5063	Rotol 4-bl.	11,930	W. Humble
1352	Tempest II MW736	Loss of fuselage side panel	17–1–45	Centaurus V C 80544	Rotol 4-bl.	11,220	W. Humble
1353	F.2/43 NX798	General handling	18–1–45	Centaurus XII C 103	Rotol 4-bl.	11,200	W. Humble
1354	Tempest VI HM595	New oil cooler fitted	19–1–45	Sabre V S 5063	Rotol 4-bl.	11,930	F. Murphy
1355	Tempest II MW736	Vibration with rubber mounting	Various	Centaurus VII C 86085	Rotol 4-bl.	11,220	P. G. Lucas
1356	Tempest V JN730	New chined sliding hood	22–1–45	Sabre IIA	DH 4-bl. Hydr.	—	W. Humble
1357	Tempest V JN730	New type plastic seat	29–1–45	Sabre IIA	DH 4-bl. Hydr.	—	W. Humble
1358	Tempest II MW736	Behaviour of engine throttling	Various	Centaurus VII C 86065	Rotol 4-bl.	11,220	W. Humble
1359	Tempest V JN730	U/c red lights showing under high g	6–2–45	Sabre IIA	DH 4-bl. Hydr.	—	W. Humble
1360	Tempest V NV961	Sabre IIB engine; overspeeding	Various	Sabre IIB S 7824	DH 4-bl. Hydr.	—	H. S. Broad
1361	F.2/43 LA610	Handling with increased fin area	13–2–45	Griffon 81 No 2052	Rotol Contra CR312	10,880	W. Humble
1362	F.2/43 NX798	Stalling with and without exhaust fairings	7–2–45	Centaurus XII C 103	Rotol 4-bl.73215	10,970	W. Humble
1363	Typhoon IB RB306	Dives with practice bombs	21–2–45	Sabre IIA S 3704	DH 4-bl. Hydr.	11,410	F. Murphy
1364	Tempest V NV946	Levels with clean aircraft	14–2–45	Sabre IIA S 2629	DH 4-bl. Hydr.	11,550	W. Humble
1365	Tempest II MW739	Pressure transfer fuel system	14–2–45	Centaurus V C 40487	Rotol 4-bl.73338	11,320	F. Murphy
1366	Tempest II MW736	Cannon heating	Various	Centaurus V C 86085	Rotol 4-bl.	11,300	W. Humble
1367	Tempest II MW736	Tropical cockpit vents	8–2–45	Centaurus V C 86085	Rotol 4-bl.	11,220	W. Humble

Flight Report	Aircraft	Test	Date	Engine	Airscrew	Weight	Pilot
1368	Tempest V NV946	Zero-length RP rails	9–2–45	Sabre IIA S 2629	DH 4-bl. Hydr.	11,410	F. Murphy
1369	Tempest II LA607	90-gallon drop tanks	13–2–45	Centaurus V C 80060	Rotol 4-bl.73207	12,100	F. Murphy
1370	Tempest V JN730	Fuel float valves with counterbalance	9–2–45	Sabre IIA	DH 4-bl. Hydr.	—	F. Murphy
1371	Tempest VI HM595	Suitability climbs and levels	9–2–45	Sabre V S 5073	Rotol 4-bl.	11,930	W. Humble
1372	Tempest II MW736	Tropical cockpit vents	8–2–45	Centaurus V C 86085	Rotol 4-bl.	11,220	W. Humble
1373	Tempest V NV946	Levels and dives; zero-length RP rails	13–2–45	Sabre IIA S 2629	DH 4-bl. Hydr.	11,250	F. Murphy
1374	Tempest V NV761	Test of alternative brake linings	12–2–45	Sabre IIB S 7824	DH 4-bl. Hydr.	—	W. Humble
1375	Tempest II MW736	Flexible gun heating pipes	16–2–45	Centaurus V C 86085	Rotol 4-bl.	—	W. Humble
1376	Tempest II LA607	Levels with clean aircraft	13–2–45	Centaurus V C 80060	Rotol 4-bl.73207	12,100	F. Murphy
1377	Tempest II LA607	Oil suitability	13–2–45	Centaurus V C 80060	Rotol 4-bl.73207	12,100	W. Humble
1379	Fury I NX798	Handling with various fairings	24–2–45	Centaurus XII C 103	Rotol 4-bl.73215	11,200	P. G. Lucas
1380	Fury I NX798	Stalling speeds	24–2–45	Centaurus XII C 103	Rotol 4-bl.73215	11,200	P. G. Lucas
1381	Tempest V JN730	Handling in weak mixture	5–3–45	Sabre IIA	DH 4-bl. Hydr.	11,600	W. Humble
1382	Sea Fury X SR661	Vibration assessment	5–3–45	Centaurus XII C 101	Rotol 4-bl.EH321	11,200	P. G. Lucas
		(Note: The Sea Fury prototype having flown, all references to Furies and Sea Furies are henceforth omitted)					
1383	Tempest V EJ592	Levels: Vokes rosette filter	2–3–45	Sabre IIA S 6576	DH 4-bl. Hydr.	11,650	W. Humble
1384	Tempest V SN127	Levels at various ratings	2–3–45	Sabre IIB S 7836	Rotol 4-bl.79591	11,750	W. Humble
1385	Tempest II MW736	Levels with production Centaurus	28–1–45	Centaurus V C 86085	Rotol 4-bl.	11,220	F. Murphy
1386	Tempest I HM599	Rated climbs with rad shutter	2–3–45	Sabre V S 5058	DH 4-bl.45707	11,150	F. Murphy
1389	Tempest VI HM595	Suitability levels	10–3–45	Sabre V S 5073	Rotol 4-bl.EH379	11,930	F. Murphy
1390	Tempest V EJ592	Levels with clean aircraft	7–3–45	Sabre IIA S 6576	DH 4-bl. Hydr.	11,640	F. Murphy
1391	Tempest V EJ756	(Napier aircraft) Rough running with Sabre V engine	5–3–45	Sabre V S 5072	DH 4-bl. Hydr.	—	F. Murphy
1392	Tempest VI HM595	Rough running with Sabre V engine	14–3–45	Sabre V S 5073	Rotol 4-bl.EH379	11,930	F. Murphy
1393	Tempest V EJ592	Suitability climb	12–3–45	Sabre IIA S 6576	DH 4-bl. Hydr.	11,650	F. Murphy
1394	Tempest II LA607	Fuel consumptions	14–3–45	Centaurus V C 80060	Rotol 4-bl.73207	12,600	F. Murphy
1395	Tempest I HM599	Effect of shutter on trim	15–3–45	Sabre V S 5058	DH 4-bl.45707	11,150	F. Murphy
1396	Tempest V EJ592	Spring tab investigation	20–3–45	Sabre IIA S 6576	DH 4-bl. Hydr.	11,650	W. Humble
1397	Tempest II LA607	Fuel consumptions	15–3–45	Centaurus V C 80060	Rotol 4-bl.73207	12,600	W. Humble
1398	Tempest VI HM595	Roughness investigation	15–3–45	Sabre V S 5073	Rotol 4-bl.EH379	11,930	F. Murphy
1399	Tempest V EJ837	Climb, levels and handling	14–3–45	Sabre IIA S 6714	DH 4-bl. Hydr.	11,700	F. Murphy
1400	Tempest II MW736	Gun heating trials	Various	Centaurus V C 86085	Rotol 4-bl.	11,220	W. Humble
1402	Tempest II JN750	Tropical air intake	23–3–45	Centaurus V C 86212	Rotol 4-bl.	11,850	W. Humble
1404	Tempest I HM599	Dive recoveries	3–3–45	Sabre V S 5058	DH 4-bl. Hydr.	11,150	F. Murphy
1405	Tempest VI HM595	Suitability combat climb	27–3–45	Sabre V S 5073	DH 4-bl.	11,930	F. Murphy
1406	Tempest II LA607	Oil suitability	3–4–45	Centaurus V C 80060	Rotol 4-bl.	12,400	W. Humble
1407	Tempest II MW762	Levels and cruise performance	3–4–45	Centaurus V C 86029	Rotol 4-bl.73253	11,890	P. G. Lucas
1408	Tempest II MW741	Oil cooler flap functioning	Various	Centaurus V C 80064	Rotol 4-bl.	11,890	F. Murphy
1409	Tempest II LA607	Investigation of rough running	26–4–45	Centaurus V C 80060	Rotol 4-bl.	—	W. Humble
1410	Tempest II MW762	Torquemeter	Various	Centaurus V C 86029	Rotol 4-bl.73253	11,890	W. Humble
1411	Tempest II LA607	Automatic supercharger gear change	3–5–45	Centaurus V C 80060	Rotol 4-bl.	—	P. G. Lucas
1415	Tempest V EJ592	Levels with visor cleaner open	Various	Sabre IIA S 6576	DH 4-bl. Hydr.	11,650	F. Murphy
1416	Tempest V EJ837	Levels with strut thermometer	Various	Sabre IIA S 6714	DH 4-bl. Hydr.	11,700	F. Murphy
1417	Tempest V EJ837	Levels without strut thermometer	15–5–45	Sabre IIA S 6714	DH 4-bl. Hydr.	11,700	F. Murphy
1418	Tempest V EJ837	Levels with strut thermometer	17–5–45	Sabre IIA S 6714	DH 4-bl. Hydr.	11,700	R. V. Muspratt
1419	Tempest II	Fuel flow measurements	29–5–45	Centaurus V C 86212	Rotol 4-bl.	11,550	R. V. Muspratt
1420	Tempest II MW765	Carbon monoxide contamination	7–6–45	Centaurus V C 86043	Rotol 4-bl.	12,200	H. S. Broad
1421	Tempest II MW766	Carbon monoxide contamination	6–6–45	Centaurus V C 86046	Rotol 4-bl.	12,200	P. G. Lucas
1422	Tempest V EJ592	Levels: production standard	4–6–45	Sabre IIA S 6576	DH 4-bl. Hydr.	11,640	R. V. Muspratt
1423	Tempest II	Tropical air intake	Various	Centaurus V C 86212	Rotol 4-bl.	11,550	R. V. Muspratt
1424	Tempest V EJ592	Suitability climb and levels	29–5–45	Sabre IIA S 6576	DH 4-bl. Hydr.	11,640	W. Humble
1425	Tempest V NV934	Standard and Napier oil tanks	11–6–45	Sabre IIA S 1480	DH 4-bl. Hydr.	11,600	F. Murphy
1427	Tempest II LA607	Cruises and fuel flows	4–6–45	Centaurus V C 80060	Rotol 4-bl.73207	11,800	W. Humble
1428	Tempest II LA607	Level speeds in MS-gear	8–6–45	Centaurus V C 80060	Rotol 4-bl.73207	11,800	R. V. Muspratt
1430	Tempest V EJ592	Levels with visor cleaner closed	19–6–45	Sabre IIA S 6576	DH 4-bl. Hydr.	11,650	R. V. Muspratt
1431	Tempest V EJ592	Suitability: visor cleaner open	20–6–45	Sabre IIA S 6576	DH 4-bl. Hydr.	11,650	W. Humble
1432	Tempest V EJ592	Fuel flows with visor cleaner	20–6–45	Sabre IIA S 6576	DH 4-bl. Hydr.	11,650	W. Humble
1433	Tempest V EJ592	Fuel flows with visor cleaner	26–6–45	Sabre IIA S 6576	DH 4-bl. Hydr.	11,650	R. V. Muspratt
1437	Tempest II LA607	Vibration with torque-balanced propellers	7–7–45	Centaurus V C 80060	Rotol 4-bl.	11,800	W. Humble
1438	Typhoon IB SW555	Handling with rudder bias cables	7–7–45	Sabre IIA	DH 4-bl. Hydr.	—	W. Humble
1439	Tempest II MW765	Carbon monoxide contamination	10–7–45	Centaurus V C 86043	Rotol 4-bl.	12,200	N. F. Duke
1441	Tempest II PR533	Levels and dives: two 1,000 lb bombs	30–6–45	Centaurus V C 86076	Rotol 4-bl.	13,765	R. V. Muspratt
1442	Tempest II PR533	Levels: clean aircraft	6–7–45	Centaurus V C 86076	Rotol 4-bl.	11,775	R. V. Muspratt
1443	Tempest V NV668	Air injection emerg. u/c release	18–7–45	Sabre IIA S 7754	DH 4-bl. Hydr.	—	R. V. Muspratt
1444	Tempest II MW767	Carbon monoxide contamination	19–7–45	Centaurus V C 86088	Rotol 4-bl.	—	N. F. Duke
1445	Tempest V EJ592	Fuel flows with visor cleaner	12–7–45	Sabre IIA S 6576	DH 4-bl. Hydr.	11,650	R. V. Muspratt
1446	Tempest II PR554	Oil pressure fluctuation check	2–8–45	Centaurus V C 86217	Rotol 4-bl.	—	H. S. Broad
1447	Tempest II MW765	Carbon monoxide contamination	16–7–45	Centaurus V C 86043	Rotol 4-bl.	12,200	R. V. Muspratt
1448	Tempest II MW765	Cockpit temperatures	20–7–45	Centaurus V C 86043	Rotol 4-bl.	12,200	R. V. Muspratt
1449	Tempest V EJ740	Undercarriage functioning	13–8–45	Sabre IIA	DH 4-bl. Hydr.	—	W. Humble
1450	Tempest II	Loss of boost pressure	27–7–45	Centaurus V C 86212	Rotol 4-bl.	11,900	W. Humble
1451	Tempest V EJ756	Check on engine roughness	Various	Sabre V S 5067	DH 4-bl. Hydr.	11,600	F. Murphy
1453	Tempest II MW762	Water-methanol injection test	18–7–45	Centaurus V C 86029	Rotol 4-bl.	11,700	R. V. Muspratt
1455	Tempest II LA607	Drop-tank pressure relief valve	31–8–45	Centaurus V C 80060	Rotol 4-bl.73207	11,950	P. G. Lucas
1456	Tempest V EJ592	Fuel flow measurements	21–8–45	Sabre IIA S 6576	DH 4-bl. Hydr.	11,650	Not known
1457	Tempest V EJ740	Undercarriage functioning	27–8–45	Sabre IIA	DH 4-bl. Hydr.	—	R. V. Muspratt
1458	Tempest II MW409	Handling: Bristol prodn. aircraft	8–45	Centaurus V	Rotol 4-bl.	—	F. Murphy
1459	Tempest II PR533	Wing flap relief valve pressure	23–8–45	Centaurus V C 86076	Rotol 4-bl.	11,775	R. V. Muspratt
1463	Tempest I HM599	Oil compression tailwheel strut	31–8–45	Sabre V S 5058	DH 4-bl. Hydr.	11,180	W. Humble
1465	Tempest VI EJ841	Handling at forward CG limit	11–9–45	Sabre V S 5121	Rotol 4-bl.	10,970	W. Humble
1467	Tempest VI EJ841	Suitability: rated climb	7–9–45	Sabre V S 5121	Rotol 4-bl.	10,970	W. Humble
1468	Tempest II MW762	Performance with water-methanol	19–9–45	Centaurus V C 86029	Rotol 4-bl.	11,915	N. F. Duke
1473	Tempest VI EJ841	Suitability combat climb	17–9–45	Sabre V S 5121	Rotol 4-bl.	11,750	R. V. Muspratt
1474	Tempest VI EJ841	Levels and fuel consumption	20–9–45	Sabre V S 5121	Rotol 4-bl.	11,750	W. Humble
1478	Tempest V EJ637	Dive recovery flap trials	27–9–45	Sabre IIA S 6714	DH 4-bl. Hydr.	11,210	W. Humble

Flight Report	Aircraft	Test	Date	Engine	Airscrew	Weight	Pilot
1479	Tempest II PR662	Thermal setting gill control	19–9–45	Centaurus V C 86409	Rotol 4-bl.	11,600	N. F. Duke
1480	Tempest VI EJ841	Combat suitability climb	28–9–45	Sabre V S 5121	Rotol 4-bl.	11,750	W. Humble
1484	Tempest VI EJ841	Carbon monoxide contamination	9–10–45	Sabre V S 5121	Rotol 4-bl.	11,750	R. V. Muspratt
1485	Tempest V EJ592	Performance with Maclaren grid	11–10–45	Sabre IIA S 6576	DH 4-bl. Hydr.	11,650	R. V. Muspratt
1487	Tempest VI EJ841	Dive with steel filter box	11–10–45	Sabre V S 5121	Rotol 4-bl.	11,750	R. V. Muspratt
1489	Tempest V EJ592	Climb with Maclaren grid	17–10–45	Sabre IIA S 6575	DH 4-bl. Hydr.	11,650	R. V. Muspratt
1490	Tempest VI NX117	Production aircraft; suitability climb and levels	17–10–45	Sabre V S 5115	Rotol 4-bl.	12,100	W. Humble
1491	Tempest VI NX117	Suitability climb and cruises	19–10–45	Sabre V S 5115	Rotol 4-bl.	12,100	W. Humble
1492	Tempest V EJ592	Combat climb with Maclaren grid	22–10–45	Sabre IIA S 6576	DH 4-bl. Hydr.	11,650	R. V. Muspratt
1493	Tempest V EJ592	Combat climb with Maclaren grid	24–10–45	Sabre IIA S 6576	DH 4-bl. Hydr.	11,650	W. Humble
1494	Tempest VI NX118	Suitability climb and cruises	17–10–45	Sabre V S 5101	Rotol 4-bl.	12,100	N. F. Duke
1495	Tempest VI NX113	Suitability climb and levels	19–10–45	Sabre V S 5083	Rotol 4-bl.	12,100	F. Silk
1496	Tempest VI NX121	Suitability climb and levels	19–10–45	Sabre V S 5123	Rotol 4-bl. 79791	12,100	M. S. Hymans
1497	Tempest VI NX122	Suitability climb and cruises	24–10–45	Sabre V S 5103	Rotol 4-bl.	12,100	Not known
1498	Tempest VI NX115	Suitability climb and levels	23–10–45	Sabre V S 5126	Rotol 4-bl.	12,100	Not known
1499	Tempest V EJ592	Levels with Maclaren grid	26–10–45	Sabre IIA S 6576	DH 4-bl. Hydr.	11,650	R. V. Muspratt
1500	Tempest VI NX118	Suitability climb and levels	23–10–45	Sabre V S 5101	Rotol 4-bl.	12,100	F. Silk
1501	Tempest VI NX116	Suitability climb and cruises	27–9–45	Sabre V S 5125	Rotol 4-bl.	12,100	H. S. Broad
1502	Tempest V SN354	Levels with 40-mm P-guns	19–10–45	Sabre IIB S 7075	Rotol 4-bl.	11,750	W. Humble
1503	Tempest VI EJ841	Shutter with no side fairings	1–11–45	Sabre V S 5121	Rotol 4-bl.	11,750	R. V. Muspratt
1504	Tempest VI EJ841	Shutter with side fairings	31–10–45	Sabre V S 5121	Rotol 4-bl.	11,750	N. F. Duke
1506	Tempest V JN800	Rated suitability climb	6–11–45	Sabre IIB S 7246	Rotol 4-bl.	11,600	R. V. Muspratt
1507	Tempest V JN800	MS and FS-gear levels	9–11–45	Sabre IIB S 7246	DH 4-bl. Hydr.	11,600	N. F. Duke
1509	Tempest II PR550	Jettison tests with 90-gallon belly drop tank	16–11–45	Centaurus V C 86170	Rotol 4-bl.	11,750	R. V. Muspratt
1510	Tempest VI NX124	1st production spring tab ailerons	19–11–45	Sabre V S 5084	Rotol 4-bl.	11,760	H. S. Broad
1513	Tempest II PR784	New type of wheelbrake lining	11–45	Centaurus V	Rotol 4-bl.	—	Not known
1515	Tempest II PR550	Levels with 90-gallon drop tank	19–11–45	Centaurus V C 86170	Rotol 4-bl.	11,750	F. Murphy
1516	Tempest II PR550	Levels without 90-gallon drop tank	27–11–45	Centaurus V C 86170	Rotol 4-bl.	11,750	F. Murphy
1517	Tempest VI NX113	Suitability climb and cruise	27–11–45	Sabre V S 5083	Rotol 4-bl.	12,100	F. Murphy
1518	Tempest VI NX121	Suitability climb and cruise	27–11–45	Sabre V S 5123	Rotol 4-bl.	12,100	R. V. Muspratt
1519	Tempest VI EJ841	Suitability climb and levels	6–12–45	Sabre V S 5121	Rotol 4-bl.	11,750	R. V. Muspratt
1520	Tempest VI NX121	Climb with rad shutter closed	1–12–45	Sabre V S 5123	Rotol 4-bl.	12,100	R. V. Muspratt
1521	Tempest VI NX117	Suitability: Oil System	2–12–45	Sabre V S 5115	Rotol 4-bl.	11,975	W. Humble
1522	Tempest II PR622	Tailwheel locking trials	7–12–45	Centaurus V	Rotol 4-bl.	11,890	R. V. Muspratt
1524	Tempest II MW766	Carbon monoxide contamination	3–12–45	Centaurus V C 86217	Rotol 4-bl.	11,900	R. V. Muspratt
1526	Tempest VI NX113	Suitability: Oil coolers	13–12–45	Sabre V S 5083	Rotol 4-bl.	11,975	R. V. Muspratt
1527	Tempest VI NX113	Suitability: Oil coolers	15–12–45	Sabre V S 5083	Rotol 4-bl.	11,975	R. V. Muspratt
1528	Tempest II MW762	Handling: Horn-balanced elevators	18–12–45	Centaurus V C 86029	Rotol 4-bl.	11,887	W. Humble
1529	Tempest VI NX113	Suitability: Oil coolers	18–12–45	Sabre V S 5083	Rotol 4-bl.	11,975	R. V. Muspratt
1531	Tempest II PR599	Investigation of oil fluctuation	21–12–45	Centaurus V C 86118	Rotol 4-bl.	11,800	W. Humble
1532	Tempest II MW 737	Carbon monoxide contamination	1–1–46	Centaurus V C 86120	Rotol 4-bl.	11,800	R. V. Muspratt
1533	Tempest II MW409	Aileron tests	3–1–46	Centaurus V	Rotol 4-bl.	11,800	R. V. Muspratt
1534	Tempest II PR550	Airframe vibration checks	8–1–46	Centaurus V C 86170	Rotol 4-bl.	11,850	W. Humble
1536	Tempest II MW762	Carbon monoxide contamination	10–1–46	Centaurus V C 86029	Rotol 4-bl.	11,887	R. V. Muspratt
1537	Tempest VI NX113	Seven gills in oil cooler	10–1–46	Sabre V S 5083	Rotol 4-bl.	11,980	R. V. Muspratt
1538	Tempest II MW762	Stick force with g	10–1–46	Centaurus V C 86029	Rotol 4-bl.	11,759	W. Humble
1539	Tempest II MW762	Stability at high Mach nos	18–1–46	Centaurus V C 86029	Rotol 4-bl.	11,759	W. Humble
1540	Tempest VI NX113	De-aerator pressure check	16–1–46	Sabre V S 5083	Rotol 4-bl.	11,975	R. V. Muspratt
1542	Tempest VI NX113	Brief handling check	16–1–46	Sabre V S 5083	Rotol 4-bl.	11,970	W. Humble
1548	Tempest II MW740	Carbon monoxide contamination	5–2–46	Centaurus V	Rotol 4-bl.	—	W. Humble
1549	Tempest II MW737	Performance measurement: levels	13–12–45	Centaurus V C 86120	Rotol 4-bl.	11,703	R. V. Muspratt
1550	Tempest II MW762	Stick force with g	18–2–46	Centaurus V C 86029	Rotol 4-bl.	11,887	R. V. Muspratt
1551	Tempest VI NX113	Five gill/inch oil cooler	19–2–46	Sabre V S 5083	Rotol 4-bl.	11,980	R. V. Muspratt
1552	Tempest II PR871	Fuel level warning light	26–2–46	Centaurus V	Rotol 4-bl.	11,850	R. V. Muspratt
1554	Tempest II PR622	Fuel consumption test	1–3–46	Centaurus V C 86409	Rotol 4-bl.	11,870	W. Humble
1555	Tempest II PR622	Directional stability on landing	14–3–46	Centaurus V C 86409	Rotol 4-bl.	11,870	W. Humble
1558	Tempest II MW762	Stick forces with g	18–3–46	Centaurus V C 86029	Rotol 4-bl.	11,759	R. V. Muspratt
1559	Tempest VI NX133	Performance of standard aircraft	18–3–46	Sabre V S 5223	Rotol 4-bl.	11,650	H. S. Broad
1560	Tempest II PR550	Level speeds with belly drop tank	9–3–46	Centaurus V C 86170	Rotol 4-bl.	11,950	'J.B.'
1561	Tempest V SN352	Handling with four 305-lb Triplex rocket projectiles	19–3–46	Sabre IIB	Rotol 3-bl.	—	R. V. Muspratt
1562	Tempest VI NX113	Seven gill/inch oil cooler	21–3–46	Sabre V S 5083	Rotol 4-bl.	11,980	W. Humble
1563	Tempest II PR622	Fuel consumption (new carburettor)	22–3–46	Centaurus V C 86409	Rotol 4-bl.	11,870	W. Humble
1565	Tempest II PR909	Test of blow-back valves	21–3–46	Centaurus V C 86621	Rotol 4-bl.	11,900	'J.B.'
1566	Tempest VI EJ841	Air intake pressures	30–3–46	Sabre V S 5121	Rotol 4-bl.	—	W. Humble
1567	Tempest VI NX113	Seven gill/inch oil cooler	1–4–46	Sabre V S 5083	Rotol 4-bl.	11,980	W. Humble
1569	Tempest II PR871	Modified exhaust pipe mounting	3–46	Centaurus V	Rotol 4-bl.	11,850	W. Humble
1570	Tempest VI NX133	Suitability: seven gill oil cooler	4–4–46	Sabre VA S 5223	Rotol 4-bl.	11,950	W. Humble
1571	Tempest II PR550	Fuel transfer with belly tank	5–4–46	Centaurus V C 86555	Rotol 4-bl.	11,950	'J.B.'
1572	Tempest II PR662	Fuel consumption; old carburettor	4–4–46	Centaurus V C 86409	Rotol 4-bl.	11,800	R. V. Muspratt
1574	Tempest II PR550	Levels: belly drop tank	12–4–46	Centaurus V C 86555	Rotol 4-bl.	11,950	R. V. Muspratt
1576	Tempest II PR550	Shift of belly tank on mounting	11–4–46	Centaurus V C 86555	Rotol 4-bl.	11,950	R. V. Muspratt
1577	Tempest II PR550	Handling with two 90-gall wing drop tanks	13–4–46	Centaurus V C 86555	Rotol 4-bl.	13,250	'J.B.'
1579	Tempest II JN750	Directional stability on landing	18–4–46	Centaurus V	Rotol 4-bl.	—	W. Humble
1580	Tempest II MW762	Spinning trials	26–5–46	Centaurus V C 86029	Rotol 4-bl.	11,640	W. Humble
1581	Tempest VI NX155	Oil pressure check	29–4–46	Sabre VA S 3586	Rotol 4-bl.	11,950	H. S. Broad
1583	Tempest II PR550	Handling: 90-gallon belly drop tank	27–4–46	Centaurus V C 86555	Rotol 4-bl.	12,530	'J.B.'
1587	Tempest II PR550	Shift of belly tank on mounting	3–5–46	Centaurus V C 86555	Rotol 4-bl.	12,530	'J.B.'
1588	Tempest II PR550	Levels with two 90-gallon tanks	16–4–46	Centaurus V C 86555	Rotol 4-bl.	13,250	R. V. Muspratt
1590	Tempest II PR905	Endurance trials: Hawker shutter	8–5–46	Centaurus V C 86667	Rotol 4-bl.	11,640	W. Humble
1594	Tempest II PR550	Fuel system check: belly drop tank	5–46	Centaurus V C 86555	Rotol 4-bl.	13,250	W. Humble
1599	Tempest II PR905	Wet element filter functioning	14–5–46	Centaurus V C 86667	Rotol 4-bl.	11,640	R. V. Muspratt
1600	Tempest VI NX119	Gyro gunsight and camera	9–5–46	Sabre VA	Rotol 4-bl.	11,950	W. Humble
1603	Tempest VI NX144	Levels with two 45-gallon drop tanks	28–5–46	Sabre VA S 5248	Rotol 4-bl.	13,000	R. V. Muspratt

Flight Report	Aircraft	Test	Date	Engine	Airscrew	Weight	Pilot
1604	Tempest VI NX144	Levels with clean aircraft	1–6–46	Sabre VA S 5248	Rotol 4-bl.	12,245	W. Humble
1605	Tempest VI NX188	Prevention of inadvertent selection of coarse pitch	30–5–46	Sabre VA S 3871	Rotol 4-bl.	12,250	Not known
1606	Tempest II JN750	Hawker shutter box	1–6–46	Centaurus V C 86667	Rotol 4-bl.	—	Not known
1607	Tempest II PR905	Strengthened wing drop tank points	13–6–46	Centaurus V	Rotol 4-bl.	—	Not known
1609	Tempest VI NX144	Timed combat climb	17–6–46	Sabre VA S 5248	Rotol 4-bl.	12,245	R. V. Muspratt
1611	Tempest VI NX144	Timed rated climbs	18–6–46	Sabre VA S 5248	Rotol 4-bl.	12,245	W. Humble
1615	Tempest II JN750	Hawker shutter box strengthened	5–7–46	Centaurus V	Rotol 4-bl.	—	Not known
1616	Tempest VI NX144	Fuel consumption and FS levels	9–7–46	Sabre VA S 5248	Rotol 4-bl.	12,245	W. Humble
1619	Tempest VI NX144	Handling at forward cg limit	12–7–46	Sabre VA S 5248	Rotol 4-bl.	12,245	R. V. Muspratt
1630	Tempest V	Overspeeding test of DH prop	17–7–46	Sabre IIA	DH 4-bl. (special)	—	R. V. Muspratt
1633	Tempest II PR905	Take-off with 1,000-lb bombs	1–8–46	Centaurus V C 86667	Rotol 4-bl.	13,300	R. V. Muspratt
1636	Tempest V NV767	General handling flight	12–8–46	Sabre IIB S 2059	D.H. 4-bl. Hydr.	11,900	W. Humble
1637	Tempest V NV939	Performance with high drag stores	21–8–46	Sabre IIB	D.H. 4-bl. Hydr.	12,700	'J.B.'
1640	Tempest II PR905	Performance with supply containers	5–9–46	Centaurus V C 86667	Rotol 4-bl.	13,450	F. Murphy
1641	Tempest VI NX113	Two full 90-gallon drop tanks	12–9–46	Sabre V S 5083	Rotol 4-bl.	13,400	R. V. Muspratt
1642	Tempest VI NX113	Distortion of rad tubes under 5g	13–9–46	Sabre V S 5083	Rotol 4-bl.	12,650	F. Murphy
1646	Tempest II PR550	Drop tank trials	17–9–46	Centaurus V C 86555	Rotol 4-bl.	—	W. Humble
1648	Tempest VI NX113	Wing cooler performance	4–10–46	Sabre V S 5083	Rotol 4-bl.	12,650	W. Humble
1652	Tempest V EJ837	Change of trim on glide	4–11–46	Sabre IIB S 7274	D.H. 4-bl. Hydr.	12,700	F. Murphy
1653	Tempest V EJ837	Test of dive recovery flaps	29–10–46	Sabre IIB S 7274	D.H. 4-bl. Hydr.	12,820	W. Humble
1655	Tempest V EJ837	Dive to M=0.76, recovery flaps up	8–11–46	Sabre IIB S 7274	D.H. 4-bl. Hydr.	12,820	W. Humble
1657	Tempest V EJ837	Dive with recovery flaps down	13–11–46	Sabre IIB S 7274	D.H. 4-bl. Hydr.	12,820	R. V. Muspratt
1659	Tempest V EJ837	Dive and recovery using flap	18–11–46	Sabre IIB S 7274	D.H. 4-bl. Hydr.	12,820	R. V. Muspratt
1660	Tempest II PR550	Jettison trials of 90-gal. belly drop tank	12–11–46	Centaurus V C 86555	Rotol 4-bl.	12,750	R. V. Muspratt
1663	Tempest V EJ837	Trim change in level flight when selecting dive recovery flaps	22–11–46	Sabre IIB S 7274	D.H. 4-bl. Hydr.	12,820	F. Murphy
1666	Tempest V EJ837	Levels with dive recovery flaps	3–12–46	Sabre IIB S 7274	D.H. 4-bl. D3/446	12,820	R. V. Muspratt
1667	Tempest II PR550	Forced landing; oil system failure	3–12–46	Centaurus VII C 86555	Rotol 4-bl.	12,750	R. V. Muspratt
1671	Tempest II PR905	Modified air intake trunking	29–11–46	Centaurus V C 86667	Rotol 4-bl.	T.S.L.	R. V. Muspratt
1673	Tempest II PR622	Paratroop supply container dropping trials at Airborne Forces Experimental Establishment, Beaulieu	5–12–46	Centaurus V	Rotol 4-bl.	13,050	F. Murphy
1676	Tempest VI NX262	Cooling tests with radiator blanks	12–46	Sabre V S 3972	Rotol 4-bl.	T.S.L.	R. V. Muspratt
1680	Tempest II PR905	Modified air intake trunking	2–1–47	Centaurus V C 86667	Rotol 4-bl.	T.S.L.	R. V. Muspratt
1687	Tempest V EJ837	High Mach No dive with recovery flaps	23–1–47	Sabre IIB S 7274	D.H. 4-bl. D3/446	12,820	R. V. Muspratt
1693	Tempest VI NV268	Cooling tests with radiator blanks	26–2–47	Sabre V S 3983	Rotol 4-bl.	T.S.L.	W. Humble
1694	Tempest V EJ837	Elevator angles at the stall	3–3–47	Sabre IIB S 7274	D.H. 4-bl. D3/446	12,820	R. V. Muspratt
1697	Tempest II PR550	Flap blow-up tests	10–4–47	Centaurus VII C 86555	Rotol 4-bl.	12,250	W. Humble
1698	Tempest II PR550	Handling with 100/1000-lb bomb carriers	11–4–47	Centaurus VII C 86555	Rotol 4-bl.	—	W. Humble
1703	Tempest II PR550	Hawker 100/1000-lb bomb carriers	11–4–47	Centaurus VII C 86555	Rotol 4-bl.	12,370	R. V. Muspratt
1709	Tempest V EJ837	High Mach No dive; recovery flaps	25–4–47	Sabre IIB S 7274	D.H. 4-bl. D3/446	12,820	R. V. Muspratt
1713	Tempest VI NX113	Cooling with radiator duct blisters	29–4–47	Sabre V S 5083	Rotol 4-bl.	T.S.L.	R. V. Muspratt
1717	Tempest VI NX113	Cooling with radiator duct blisters	13–5–47	Sabre V S 5083	Rotol 4-bl.	T.S.L.	F. Murphy
1725	Tempest VI NX113	Cooling; no radiator duct blisters	28–5–47	Sabre V S 5083	Rotol 4-bl.	T.S.L.	R. V. Muspratt
1727	Tempest VI NX113	Cooling with radiator duct blisters	29–5–47	Sabre V S 5083	Rotol 4-bl.	T.S.L.	R. V. Muspratt
1728	Tempest VI NX113	Cooling with radiator duct blisters	29–5–47	Sabre V S 5083	Rotol 4-bl.	T.S.L.	R. V. Muspratt
1729	Tempest II PR550	Functioning of 100/1,000-lb carriers with 1,000-lb MC bombs	30–5–47	Centaurus VII C 86555	Rotol 4-bl.	13,600	R. V. Muspratt
1738	Tempest VI NX288	Cooling in high Mach no dives	29–6–47	Sabre VA S 3990	Rotol 4-bl.	12,285	W. Humble
1739	Tempest VI NX288	Modified intake filter louvre	14–7–47	Sabre VA S 3990	Rotol 4-bl.	12,650	F. Murphy
1747	Tempest VI NX288	Spinning trials at rear cg posn.	11–8–47	Sabre VA S 3990	Rotol 4-bl.	T.S.L.	R. V. Muspratt
1748	Tempest VI NX288	Spinning trials at fwd. cg posn.	11–8–47	Sabre VA S 3990	Rotol 4-bl.	T.S.L.	W. Humble
1750	Tempest VI NX288	High altitude spins, cg fwd.	15–8–47	Sabre VA S 3990	Rotol 4-bl.	T.S.L.	F. Murphy
1752	Tempest V EJ837	Dive with recovery flaps down	25–8–47	Sabre IIB S 7839	D.H. 4-bl. D3/446	T.S.L.	R. V. Muspratt
1757	Tempest V EJ837	Dive recovery using recovery flaps	26–8–47	Sabre IIB S 7839	D.H. 4-bl. D3/446	T.S.L.	W. Humble
1760	Tempest V EJ837	Dive recovery using recovery flaps	3–10–47	Sabre IIB S 7839	D.H. 4-bl. D3/446	T.S.L.	F. Murphy
1785	Tempest VI NX288	Flexible radiator mountings	21–1–48	Sabre VA S 3990	Rotol 4-bl.	12,400	T. S. Wade
1801	Tempest VI NX288	Landings to test RP shear pins	27–2–48	Sabre VA S 3990	Rotol 4-bl.	T.S.L.	E. S. Morell
1812	Tempest VI NX144	Proving test of rectangular rad.	18–3–48	Sabre VA S 5248	Rotol 4-bl.	T.S.L.	E. Murphy
1826	Tempest II PR871	Forced landing: engine failure	8–4–48	Centaurus VII	Rotol 4-bl.	T.S.L.	E. S. Morell
1827	Tempest VI NX144	Oil cooling with rectangular rad.	8–4–48	Sabre VA S 5248	Rotol 4-bl.	T.S.L.	F. Murphy
1847	Tempest VI NX144	Cooler back pressure tests	13–5–48	Sabre VA S 5248	Rotol 4-bl.	T.S.L.	F. Murphy

Note: Aircraft loaded weights were seldom recorded for Tempest aircraft from 1947; T.S.L. = 'Typical Service Load'.

Flight Report	Aircraft	Test	Date	Engine	Airscrew	Weight	Pilot
1863	Tempest 5 SN329	General handling with Malcolm target-towing winch	23–6–48	Sabre IIC S 6864	DH 4-bl.	—	T. S. Wade
1865	Tempest 6 NX144	Handling: Two 90-gal. drop tanks	24–6–48	Sabre VA S 5248	Rotol 4-bl.	T.S.L.	E. S. Morell
1867	Tempest 5 SN329	Malcolm target-towing winch	25–6–48	Sabre IIC S 6864	DH 4-bl.	—	F. Murphy
1868	Tempest 5 SN329	Malcolm target-towing winch	6–7–48	Sabre IIC S 6864	DH 4-bl.	—	T. S. Wade
1870	Tempest 5 SN329	Malcolm targer-towing winch	9–7–48	Sabre IIC S 6864	DH 4-bl.	—	T. S. Wade
1873	Tempest 5 SN329	Malcolm target-towing winch	13–7–48	Sabre IIC S 6864	DH 4-bl.	—	T. S. Wade
1890	Tempest 6 SN329	Malcolm winch and 500-lb bomb	27–8–48	Sabre IIC S 6864A	DH 4-bl.	13,150	F. Murphy
1919	Tempest 6 NX288	Reduced rudder cable tension	26–10–48	Sabre VA S 3990	Rotol 4-bl.	T.S.L.	N. Duke
1925	Tempest 6 NX288	Reduced rudder cable tension	3–11–48	Sabre VA S 3990	Rotol 4-bl.	T.S.L.	E. S. Morell
1931	Tempest II A128	(Pakistani aircraft) Power fluctuation investigation	12–11–48	Centaurus V	Rotol 4-bl.	T.S.L.	T. S. Wade
1934	Tempest 2 PR871	Boost and RPM fluctuation	25–11–48	Centaurus VII	Rotol 4-bl.	T.S.L.	F. Murphy
1940	Tempest II A129 (Pakistani)	Further investigation of power fluctuation	3–12–48	Centaurus V	Rotol 4-bl.	T.S.L.	T. S. Wade
1995	Tempest II HA566 (Indian)	Forced landing report	20–4–49	Centaurus V	Rotol 4-bl.	T.S.L.	F. Murphy

Notes of explanation

This Appendix includes details of Service and development (experimental) aircraft, with emphasis upon the operational fortunes of each. Every aircraft produced is listed in the relevant introductory paragraphs, with historical details of representative aircraft from each consecutive serial batch. Little mention is therefore made of aircraft at training units.

It would have been possible, had space been available, simply to reproduce the contents of the individual aircraft history cards (AHCs, available for public scrutiny at the Public Records Office) but to have done so would have resulted in a mass of sterile matter, almost entirely concerned with the *movement* of aircraft between Maintenance Units, stations and Wings. It is felt that more interest lies in the achievements of pilots and the fate of the aircraft, and these aspects—which are virtually absent from the AHCs—provide the basis of this Appendix. (Moreover it is generally accepted that from about May 1943 onwards the accuracy of much information in the AHCs is suspect in that dates are often incorrect by weeks, even months, owing to the creation of the Typhoon Wings and the movement by aircraft between component squadrons not being notified to the movement clerks.)

Reliance has therefore been placed more upon Squadron, Wing and Group returns and records, as well as the manufacturers' Service Department record cards, together with individual combat reports and pilots' logbooks. While reference *has* occasionally been made to AHCs for some checking purposes, where a discrepancy has arisen the accuracy of personal records has been accepted in preference to that of uncorroborated statistical matter.

To illustrate this, the example of the reconnaissance Typhoons may be quoted, about which little has previously been published, probably because these aircraft are seldom referred to as such in the AHCs. They were produced by incorporating a number of modifications at two maintenance units with installation kits delivered from several Contractors, together with bought-out items issued from Service stores. The aircraft themselves are therefore scarcely identifiable in the AHCs, and then only by the Modification numbers, making differentiation between FR and PR aircraft difficult. Only by reference to Unit charge returns and to squadron sortie details (logbooks and Forms 541 and 1151) can one be fairly confident of identifying the aircraft correctly.

HAWKER F.18/37 TORNADO

Two prototypes, P5219 and P5224, designed to Air Ministry Specification F.18/37, ordered under Contract No. 815124/38 and manufactured under Works Order No. 5264 dated 3 March 1938 at Langley, Bucks.

P5219 Ff 6–10–39, P. G. Lucas. Vulture II No. 12; AUW 9,127 lb; ventral radiator. Ff with nose radiator, 6–12–39; wheel flaps added, 1–40; tailwheel doors added, 6–40; engine failure and forced landing, 31–7–40. Vulture V No. 164, 3–41.

P5224 Ff 15–12–40, P. G. Lucas. Vulture II No. 132; AUW 9,600 lb. Extended trials on radiator fairing, 2–41, at Napiers, Luton, 2–41. Returned to HAL, Langley, 3–41; engine failure and forced landing, 21–3–41. Vulture V No. 126, 6–41; Vulture V No. 132, 8–41.

HAWKER TORNADO I

Order for one prototype and 200 production aircraft placed with A. V. Roe & Co Ltd., Woodford, placed in 1939 but cancelled early in 1941. Only prototype R7936 completed.

R7936 Avro-built. Ff at Langley, 31–8–41, P. G. Lucas. Vulture V No. 4252; AUW 10,051 lb. Performance tests, HAL, 8–41 to 3–42; thereafter trials at A&AEE, RAE and Rolls-Royce, and trials as propeller test bed with de Havilland and Rotol.

R7937 Not completed. Components used in **HG641** (see below).

R7938 Not completed. Components used as spares for **R7936** and **HG641**.

One further aircraft, **HG641**, completed by Hawker in 1941 employing components from **R7937** (see above) for use as test airframe for Bristol Centaurus radial engine. Ordered by Air Ministry under Contract No. 21392/41 and covered by Works Order No. 8517.

HG641 Ff at Langley, 23–10–41, P. G. Lucas. Centaurus CE4S No. 19. Hawker-built from Avro-manufactured components. Cowling, oil cooler and exhaust modifications with Centaurus IV No. 27; ff at Langley, 23–12–42, P. G. Lucas.

198 Tornado aircraft cancelled: **R7939–R7975, R7992–R8036, R8048–R8091, R8105–R8150, R8172–R8197.**

HAWKER 18/37 TYPHOON

Two prototypes, P5212 and P5216, designed to Air Ministry Specification F.18/37, ordered under Contract No. 815124/38 and manufactured under Works Order No. 5232 dated 3 March 1938 at Langley, Bucks.

P5212 Ff 24–2–40, P. G. Lucas; part of radiator fairing lost on 2nd flight, 1–3–40; Sabre I No. 95009. Structural failure in flight, 9–5–40, flying with Sabre No. 95007; Sabre No. 95013, 8–40; Sabre No. 95018, 9–40; Sabre No. 95015, 2–41; Sabre No. 95022, 2–41; Sabre No. 95018, 7–41; Sabre No. 95026, 8–41; Sabre No. 95018 (as Sabre II), 27–6–41; Sabre No. 95026 (as Sabre II), 11–4–42; production Sabre II No. S.322, 5–42. Provision for twelve Browning guns.

P5216 Ff 3–5–41, P. G. Lucas. First flown with extended wing tips, 9–11–41. Sabre No. 95018 (became Sabre II), 15–6–41; Sabre No. 95026 (as Sabre II), 4–42; production Sabre II No. S.322, 27–4–42.

One additional F.18/37 prototype, **LA594**, to be powered by Bristol Centaurus IV, ordered under Contract No. 21392/41 and commenced manufacture under Works Order No. 3862 during 1941. Designated Centaurus Typhoon II, but not completed; components employed in Tempest II prototype **LA602** (*qv*).

Note: All Typhoon production was centred on Gloster Aircraft Company Ltd., Brockworth, Gloucester. However, a single production batch of 15 aircraft (employing components common to the Typhoon and the Avro-produced Tornado) was produced by Hawker at Langley, being intended as trials aircraft; some were however delivered to the RAF. Although these Typhoons were not completed until the Gloster deliveries were well under way, they are shown here for convenience.

R8198 Mk IA. Ff 26–11–41 at Langley. Extended trials at Langley from 12–41; 4-inch extended exhausts, 1–42; oil cooler trials from 2–42; engine failed 14–3–42.

R8199 Mk IA. Trials at Langley from 3–42. To No. 56 Sqn., Manston, 29–5–42, for low-level raider interception; shot down by Spitfires of No. 401 Sqn., RCAF, 1–6–42; Sgt. Stuart-Turner killed.

R8200 Mk IA. Special production tests at Langley, 3–42. No. 56 Sqn., Duxford, 'US-K'; Snailwell, 6–42; Matlaske, 10–42.

R8220 Mk IA. Special production tests at Langley, 4–42. No. 56 Sqn., Snailwell, 6–42; Matlaske, 5–43.

R8221 Mk IA. Purgatory Store, Duxford.
R8222 Mk IB. No. 609 Sqn., Biggin Hill, 10–42.
R8223 Mk IB. No. 56 Sqn., Matlaske, 'US-J', 10–42.
R8224 Mk IB. No. 56 Sqn., Matlaske, 5–43.
R8225 Mk IB. Pergatory Store, Duxford.
R8226 Mk IB. Pergatory Story, Duxford.
R8227 Mk IB. No. 56 Sqn., Matlaske, 'US-Z', 10–42. No. 197 Sqn., Drem, 'OV-W', 2–43.
R8228 Mk IB.
R8229 Mk IB.
R8230 Mk IB.
R8231 Mk IB.

211

HAWKER TYPHOON I

First production batch of 250 Mark IAs and IBs produced by Gloster Aircraft Co Ltd, Brockworth, Gloucester. R7576–R7599, R7613–R7655, R7672–R7721, R7738–R7775, R7792–R7829, R7845–R7890, R7913–R7923. Deliveries commenced September 1941, completed June 1942; average rate of production, approximately one aircraft per day.

R7576 Mk IA. Ff 27–5–41, M. Daunt, at GAC; ff 12–6–41, P. G. Lucas, at HAL. Performance and handling trials, Langley, 8–41. Became Ground Instruction Machine **4638M**.

R7577 Mk IA. Performance and handling trials, HAL, 6–41, No. 609 Sqn., Duxford, 3–42, **'PR–A'**.

R7578 Mk IA. Engine handling trials, Napiers, Luton, 9–41.

R7579 Mk IA. Type evaluation, A & AEE, Boscombe Down, 9–41, Later to CFS, Upavon.

R7580 Mk IA. No. 56 Sqn., Duxford, 9–41.

R7581 Mk IA. Became Ground Instruction Machine, **3514M**.

R7582 Mk IA. No. 56 Sqn., Duxford, 9–41, **'US-Z'**.

R7583 Mk IA. No. 56 Sqn., Duxford, 9–41, **'US-W'**. Was first Typhoon delivered to an RAF Squadron, 11–9–41.

R7584 Mk IA. No. 56 Sqn., Duxford, **'US-S'**; deld 23–10–41.

R7585 Mk IA. Performance and handling trials, GAC and HAL, 9–41. No. 56 Sqn., Snailwell, 6–42. Became Ground Instruction Machine **4637M**.

R7586 Mk IA. No. 56 Sqn., Duxford, **'US-Y'**, later **'US-P'**; deld 2–10–41. Became Ground Instruction Machine **3521M**.

R7587 Mk IA. Performance and handling trials, GAC and HAL, 9–41. No. 56 Sqn., Duxford, **'US-D'**, 10–41. Became Ground Instruction Machine **3518M**.

R7588 Mk IA. No. 56 Sqn., Duxford, deld 3–10–41; **'US-X'** later **'US-N'**.

R7589 Mk IA. No. 56 Sqn., Duxford, deld 12–10–41, **'US-T'**. No. 181 Sqn., Duxford, 9–42. Directional stability trials, RAE, Farnborough, date unknown.

R7590 Mk IA. No. 266 Sqn., Duxford, 2–42.

R7591 Mk IA. No. 56 Sqn., Duxford, 11–41, **'US-T'**. Returned to HAL for CO contamination tests, 21–11–41.

R7592 Mk IA. No. 56 Sqn., Duxford; deld 28–10–41, **'US-L'**.

R7593 Mk IA. No. 56 Sqn., Duxford; deld 30–10–41, **'US-A'**.

R7594 Mk IA. No. 56 Sqn., Duxford; deld 31–10–41, **'US-B'**. Became Ground Instruction Machine **3527M**.

R7595 Mk IA. No. 56 Sqn., Duxford, 11–41. (Intermittent performance checks, HAL and GAC, 10–41 to 12–41).

R7596 Mk IA. No. 56 Sqn., Duxford, 11–41, **'US-M'**.

R7597 Mk IA. No. 56 Sqn., Duxford, 11–41.

R7598 Mk IA. No. 56 Sqn., Duxford, 12–41, **'US-O'**.

R7599 Mk IA. No. 56 Sqn., Duxford, 12–41, **'US-L'**.

R7613 Mk IA. No. 56 Sqn., Duxford, 12–41, **'US-E'**.

R7614 Mk IA. Armament trials, A & AEE, Boscombe Down, 1–42.

R7615 Mk IA. No. 56 Sqn., Duxford, 12–41, **'US-J'**.

R7616 Mk IA. No. 56 Sqn., Duxford, 12–41, **'US-F'**. Became Ground Instruction Machine, **3520M**.

R7617 Performance and handling trials, GAC, HAL and A & AEE, 12–41.

R7618 Mk IA. Engine handling trials, Napiers, Luton, 1–42; engine vibration investigation, HAL, A & AEE and RAE, 1942.

R7619 Mk IA. No. 56 Sqn., Duxford, 1–42, **'US-O'**. No. 266 Sqn., Duxford, 2–42.

R7620 Mk IA. No. 56 Sqn., Duxford, 1–42.

R7621 Mk IA. No. 56 Sqn., Duxford, 1–42, **'US-H'**; Snailwell, 6–42, **'US-S'**.

R7622 Mk IA. No. 56 Sqn., Duxford, 1–42, **'US-Q'**. No. 266 Sqn., Duxford, 2–42, **'UO-Q'**.

R7623 Mk IA. No. 56 Sqn., Duxford, 1–42. No. 266 Sqn., Duxford, 2–42. Became Ground Instruction Machine **3519M**.

R7624 Mk IA. No. 266 Sqn., Duxford, 2–42. No. 182 Sqn., Martlesham Heath, 9–42, **'XM-D'**.

R7625 Mk IA. Crashed during delivery to No. 266 Sqn., 12–41; repaired and delivered to No. 266 Sqn., Duxford, 3–42, **'UO-C'**.

R7626 Mk IA. No. 266 Sqn., Duxford, 2–42, **'UO-W'**, Became Ground Instruction Machine **3515M**.

R7627 Mk IA. No. 266 Sqn., Duxford, 2–42, **'UO-L'**. No. 181 Sqn., Duxford, 9–42.

R7628 Performance and handling trials, GAC, HAL and A & AEE, 1–42. No. 56 Sqn., Duxford, 1–42.

R7629 Mk IA. No. 56 Sqn., Duxford, 1–42, **'US-P'**. No. 182 Sqn., Martlesham Heath, 9–42.

R7630 Performance and handling trials, GAC, HAL and A & AEE, 1–42.

R7631 Mk IA. No. 266 Sqn., Duxford, 2–42; flew Squadron's first operational sortie, 28–5–42, when Plt Off G. Elcombe was scrambled for intercept (of Spitfire). No. 181 Sqn., Duxford, No. 183 Sqn., Church Fenton, deld 1–12–42; badly damaged in landing accident, 12–12–42; Sgt. Collins unhurt. Became Ground Instruction Machine **4639M**.

R7632 Performance and handling trials, GAC, HAL and A & AEE, 2–42.

R7633 Mk IA. No. 56 Sqn., Duxford, 2–42, **'US-C'**. No. 266 Sqn., Duxford, 3–42. No. 56 Sqn., Snailwell, 6–42.

R7634 Mk IA. No. 266 Sqn., Duxford, 2–42, **'UO-D'**.

R7635 Mk IA. No. 266 Sqn., Duxford, 2–42, **'UO-V'**.

R7636 Mk IA. No. 266 Sqn., Duxford, 3–42. Became Ground Instruction Machine **3513M**.

R7637 Mk IA. No. 266 Sqn., Duxford, 3–42.

R7638 Mk IA. Engine handling trials, Napiers, Luton, 3–42. To Rotol Ltd for propeller trials, 5–42. Became Ground Instruction Machine **4568M**.

R7639 Mk IA. No. 266 Sqn., Duxford, 3–42.

R7640 Performance and handling trials, GAC, HAL and A & AEE, 3–42.

R7641 Mk IA. No. 266 Sqn., Duxford, 2–42, **'UO-A'**, later **'ZH-A'**.

R7642 Mk IA. No. 266 Sqn., Duxford, 2–42.

R7643 Mk IA. No. 266 Sqn., Duxford, 2–42.

R7644 Mk IA. Oil cooling trials, HAL, Langley, 2–42. No. 56 Sqn., Duxford, 8–42; crashed near Sutton Bridge, 18–8–42; Sgt J. S. Jones killed.

R7645 Mk IA. Fuel system trials, HAL, Langley, 2–42. No. 266 Sqn., Duxford, 3–42; took part in *Rodeo* No. 78 over Dunkirk, 23–6–42, as **'ZH-B'**.

R7646 Mk IA. Stability trials, HAL, Langley; crash landed at Cranwell, 4–5–42; repaired with four-cannon wings and transparent hood, Langley, 1942–43. Tropical conversion; completed 28–4–43. Set aside for possible shipment to North Africa.

R7647 Mk IA. Oil cooling trials, HAL, 3–42.

R7648 Mk IA. No. 56 Sqn., Duxford, 2–42. No. 266 Sqn., Duxford, 3–42. No. 56 Sqn., Snailwell, 6–42, **'US-A'**.

R7649 Mk IA. No. 266 Sqn., Duxford, 3–43, **'UO-U'**. No. 183 Sqn., Church Fenton, 11–42.

R7651 Mk IA. MAP engine evaluation programme, Napiers, Luton, 4–42.

R7652 Mk IA. DH propeller trials, HAL, 4–42. No. 56 Sqn., Snailwell, 6–42, **'US-W'**.

R7653 Mk IA. DH propeller trials, HAL, 5–42. No. 56 Sqn., Matlaske, 10–42, **'US-U'**. No. 198 Sqn., Digby, 12–42; aircraft crashed and burnt out, 26–2–43, following engine failure; F/Sgt Freitag escaped with minor burns.

R7654 Performance and handling trials, GAC, HAL and A & AEE, 3–42.

R7672 Mk IA. Radiator suitability trials, HAL, 3–42. Special production tests, Langley, 4–42.

No. 266 Sqn., Duxford, 6–42; took part in Squadron's first operation, *Circus* No. 193, 20–6–42.

R7673 Mk IA. Armament trials, A & AEE, 3–42.

R7674 Mk IA. No. 266 Sqn., Duxford, 3–42.

R7675 Mk IA. Engine vibration investigation, HAL, and Napier, Luton, 4–42.

R7676 Mk IA. No. 266 Sqn., Duxford, 3–42, **'UO-Q'**; took part in *Rodeo* No. 78 over Dunkirk, 23–9–42. No. 181 Sqn., Duxford, deld 25–9–42; Flt Lt A. G. H. Lindsell spun into the ground at Duxford after take-off and killed, 27–9–42.

R7677 Mk IB. No. 609 Sqn., Duxford, 4–42. No. 182 Sqn., Martlesham Heath, 9–42, **'XM-L'**.

R7678 Mk IB. No. 56 Sqn., Duxford, 4–42; to Manston, 5–42, to combat tip-and-run raiders; shot down by Spitfires of No. 401 Sqn., RCAF, 1–6–42; Plt Off P. H. Duego, RCAF, injured.

R7679 Mk IB. No. 56 Sqn., Snailwell, 3–42, **'US-L'**; Matlaske, 10–42.

R7680 Mk IB. Special production tests, HAL, Langley, 4–42.

R7681 Mk IA. No. 609 Sqn., Duxford, 4–42, **'PR-P'**.

R7682 Mk IB. No. 56 Sqn., Snailwell, 3–42; Matlaske, 10–42.

R7683 Mk IB. No. 56 Sqn., Snailwell, 3–42; No. 195 Sqn., Hutton Cranswick, 12–42.

R7684 Mk IA. No. 56 Sqn., Snailwell, 3–42; Duxford 25–4–42 to 22–1–42, coded JG and flown by Gp Capt John Grandy, DSO, Station Commander.

R7686 Mk IA. No. 266 Sqn., Duxford, 3–42, **'UO-G'**; took part in *Rodeo* No. 78 over Dunkirk, 23–6–42.

R7687 Mk IA. No. 266 Sqn., Duxford, 3–42, **'UO-V'**; Sqn Ldr C. L. Green led Squadron's first *Circus* (No. 193) from Mardych to Cap Gris Nez, 20–6–42.

R7688 Mk IA. No. 609 Sqn., 4–42, **'PR-K'**. No. 195 Sqn., Hutton Cranswick, 12–42.

R7689 Mk IA. No. 266 Sqn., Duxford, 3–42, **'UO-F'**.

R7690 Mk IA. No. 609 Sqn., Duxford, 4–42, **'PR-C'**.

R7691 Mk IA. No. 609 Sqn., Duxford, 4–42, **'PR-N'**.

R7692 Mk IA. Oil system trials, HAL, Langley, 3–42.

R7694 Mk IB. No. 56 Sqn., Snailwell, 3–42.

R7695 Mk IB. No. 266 Sqn., Duxford, 3–42, **'ZH-Z'**.

R7696 Mk IB. No. 266 Sqn., Duxford, 3–42; took part in *Rodeo* No. 78 over Dunkirk, 23–6–42. No. 181 Sqn., Duxford, 9–42.

R7698 Mk IB. No. 609 Sqn., Duxford, 3–42. Coded **'ZZ'**, flown by Duxford Wing Leader, Wg Cdr Denys E. Gillam, DSO and Bar, DFC and Bar, AFC, 6–42 to 12–42; Gillam led No. 266 Sqn's first full Typhoon operation, *Circus* No. 193 sweep over Cap Gris Nez, 20–6–42.

R7700 Mk IA. Armament trials, A & AEE, Boscombe Down, 4–42.

R7701 Became Ground Instruction Machine **3524M**.

R7702 Mk IA. No. 56 Sqn., Snailwell, 6–42, **'US-M'**; Matlaske, 10–42, **'US-N'**.

R7703 Mk IA. No. 609 Sqn., Duxford, 4–42.

R7704 Mk IA. No. 266 Sqn., Duxford, 3–42.

R7706 Mk IA. No. 609 Sqn., Duxford, 4–42, **'PR-J'**. No. 197 Sqn., Drem, deld 27–11–42, **'OV-L'**.

R7707 Mk IA. No. 266 Sqn., Duxford, 4–42.

R7708 Mk IB. No. 609 Sqn., Duxford, 4–42, **'PR-V'**.

R7710 Mk IA. No. 609 Sqn., Duxford, 4–42.

R7711 Mk IB. No. 56 Sqn., Snailwell, 3–42, **'US-M'**, later **'US-N'**.

R7712 Mk IB. Engine handling trials, Napiers, Luton, 4–42.

R7713 Mk IB. No. 56 Sqn., Snailwell, 3–42, **'US-Z'**. No. 609 Sqn., Duxford, 4–42.

R7714 Mk IB. No. 56 Sqn., Snailwell, 6–42; shot down during *Rhubarb* over Holland, 10–4–43; Sgt F. Nettleton killed.

Note: Henceforth all aircraft are Mark IBs unless stated

R7739 No. 56 Sqn., Snailwell, 6–42; Matlaske, 10–42.
R7741 No. 56 Sqn., Matlaske, 10–42.
R7744 No. 56 Sqn., Snailwell, 6–42.
R7751 No. 609 Sqn., Duxford, 4–42.
R7752 No. 609 Sqn., Duxford, 4–42.
R7755 Became Ground Instruction Machine **3726M**.
R7760 Became Ground Instruction Machine **4272M**.
R7762 Became Ground Instruction Machine **3722M**.
R7765 Became Ground Instruction Machine **3438M**.
R7771 Sabre IIA engine with mixed-matrix radiator; trials at Napiers, Luton, 5–42.
R7772 Became Ground Instruction Machine **3729M**.

R7797 Became Ground Instruction Machine **3522M**.
R7799 No. 266 Sqn., Duxford, 5–42.
R7800 No. 266 Sqn., 5–42; took part in Squadron's first Typhoon operation, *Circus* No. 193, sweep from Mardych to Cap Gris Nez, 20–6–42.
R7804 No. 266 Sqn., Duxford, 5–42; Exeter, 3–43.
R7813 No. 266 Sqn., Duxford, 5–42; Plt Off W. S. Smithyman shot down and killed by Canadian-flown Spitfire during Dieppe operation, 19–8–42.
R7814 No. 266 Sqn., Duxford, 5–42; took part in Sqn's first Typhoon operation, *Circus* No. 193, a sweep from Mardych to Cap Gris Nez, 20–6–42.
R7815 No. 266 Sqn., Duxford, 5–42; took part in Sqn's first Typhoon operation, *Circus* No. 193, 20–6–42; on 19–8–42 (Dieppe operation) Flt Lt R. H. L. Dawson was shot down and killed by Canadian-flown Spitfire.
R7816 No. 266 Sqn., Duxford, 5–42.
R7817 No. 266 Sqn., Duxford, 5–42.
R7818 No. 266 Sqn., Duxford, 5–42.
R7819 No. 266 Sqn., Duxford, 5–42, '**UO-S**'; took part in Sqn's first Typhoon operation, *Circus* No. 193, 20–6–42. Fighter Interception Unit, Ford, 1943; night fighter trials.
R7820 No. 266 Sqn., Duxford, 5–42; took part in Sqn's first Typhoon operation, *Circus* No. 193, 20–6–42.
R7821 No. 266 Sqn., Duxford, 5–42; took part in Sqn's first Typhoon operation, *Circus* No. 193, 20–6–42.
R7822 No. 266 Sqn., Duxford, 5–42; took part in Sqn's first Typhoon operation, *Circus* No. 193, 20–6–42.
R7823 No. 56 Sqn., Manston, 5–42, '**US-O**'; Matlaske, 10–42, '**US-S**'.
R7824 No. 56 Sqn., Manston, 5–42; Snailwell, 6–42.
R7825 No. 56 Sqn., Manston, 5–42.
R7826 No. 56 Sqn., Manston, 5–42; Snailwell, 6–42.
R7828 No. 266 Sqn., Duxford, 5–42.
R7829 No. 266 Sqn., Duxford, 5–42; Exeter, 3–43.

R7845 No. 609 Sqn., Duxford, 5–42.
R7846 No. 56 Sqn., Manston, 5–42. Experimentally fitted with tropical air filter, HAL, Langley, 7–42; returned to standard, 8–42. No. 56 Sqn., Matlaske, 10–42, '**US-R**'.
R7847 No. 56 Sqn., Manston, 5–42.
R7849 No. 609 Sqn., Duxford, 5–42.
R7850 Napier engine flight test bed, Luton.
R7851 No. 1 Sqn., Acklington, 7–42; Lympne, 7–43.
R7852 No. 1 Sqn., Lympne, 4–43; F/Sgt W. H. Ramsey suffered battle damage at Armentieres during *Rhubarb*, 2–4–43, but returned to crash landing at Lympne, unhurt.
R7853 No. 56 Sqn., Manston, 5–42; Matlaske, 12–42; crashed at Brinton, Norfolk, 17–1–43; Sgt F. W. Sullivan killed.
R7855 Mk IA. No. 609 Sqn., Duxford, 5–42, '**PR-D**'.
R7856 No. 1 Sqn., Acklington; deld 22–7–42.
R7861 No. 1 Sqn., Acklington; deld 25–7–42.
R7862 No. 1 Sqn., Acklington; deld 25–7–42.

R7863 No. 1 Sqn., Acklington; was first Typhoon on the Squadron, deld 21–7–42.
R7864 No. 1 Sqn., Acklington, 7–42; crashed following engine failure, 13–2–43; Sgt R. W. Hornall stayed in aircraft to prevent it falling among Canadian troops; pilot unhurt but aircraft destroyed.
R7865 No. 1 Sqn., Acklington, 7–42.
R7868 No. 1 Sqn., Acklington, 7–42.
R7869 Mk IA. No. 56 Sqn., Matlaske, 10–42. No. 183 Sqn., Church Fenton, deld 7–12–42.
R7870 No. 609 Sqn., Duxford, 6–42, '**PR-O**'.
R7872 No. 609 Sqn., Duxford, 6–42.
R7873 No. 609 Sqn., Duxford, 6–42, '**PR-T**'.
R7874 No. 609 Sqn., Duxford, 6–42, '**PR-U**'.
R7875 No. 609 Sqn., Duxford, 6–42, '**PR-V**'.
R7876 No. 1 Sqn., Acklington; deld 27–7–42.
R7877 No. 1 Sqn., Acklington; deld 27–7–42; Lympne, 7–43.
R7878 Became Ground Instruction Machine **3721M**.
R7879 No. 257 Sqn., High Ercall, 8–42.
R7880 No. 266 Sqn., Duxford, 7–42, '**UO-C**'.
R7881 NF Mk IB. AI-equipped night fighter. Fighter Interception Unit, Ford, *c.*10–42; subsequently powered by Sabre IIA and IIB engines driving four-blade propeller. Trials with several RAF squadrons, 1943, and RAE, Farnborough, 1943–44.
R7882 No. 266 Sqn., Duxford, 7–42, '**UO-J**'; Exeter, 3–43.
R7883 No. 609 Sqn., Duxford, 7–42.
R7886 No. 266 Sqn., Duxford, 7–42, '**UO-R**'. No. 609 Sqn., Duxford, 8–42, '**PR-R**'.

R7914 No. 195 Sqn., Hutton Cranswick, 12–42; Ludham, 6–43.
R7915 DTD aircraft. Retained by GAC for trial installations, 1942. No. 266 Sqn., Exeter, 3–43; suffered engine failure 25 miles south of Start Point and crashed into the sea, 17–6–43; Fg Off H. A. Cooper baled out and rescued unhurt.
R7918 No. 266 Sqn., Duxford, 7–42, '**UO-V**'.
R7919 No. 1 Sqn., Acklington, 7–42.
R7921 No. 266 Sqn., Duxford, 7–42, '**UO-K**'. No. 1 Sqn., Acklington, 8–42.
R7922 No. 1 Sqn., Acklington, 7–42; Plt Off D. P. Perrin, RNZAF, destroyed Me 210 at Robin Hood's Bay, 6–9–42; Sgt R. H. Hornall destroyed Fw 190A off Brighton, 13–3–43.
R7923 No. 56 Sqn., Snailwell, 7–42. No. 1 Sqn., Acklington, 7–42; Plt Off T. G. Bridges destroyed Me 210 two miles SW of Redcar, 6–9–42.

Second production batch of 250 Mark IAs and IBs produced by Gloster Aircraft Co Ltd., Brockworth, Gloucester. R8630–R8663, R8680–R8722, R8737–R8781, R8799–R8845, R8861–R8900, R8923–R8947, R8966–R8981. Deliveries commenced 6–42, completed 9–42. Average rate of production, approximately 2.6 aircraft per day.

R8630 No. 1 Sqn., Acklington, 7–42. No. 257 Sqn., High Ercall, 8–42.
R8631 No. 1 Sqn., Acklington, 7–42. No. 257 Sqn., High Ercall, 8–42. No. 1 Sqn., Lympne, 7–43.
R8632 No. 257 Sqn., High Ercall, 8–42; Exeter, 9–42; Warmwell, 2–43.
R8633 No. 257 Sqn., High Ercall, 8–42.
R8634 No. 1 Sqn., Acklington, 7–42.
R8635 To RAE, Farnborough, for trials, 7–42.
R8636 No. 257 Sqn., High Ercall, 8–42.
R8637 No. 257 Sqn., High Ercall, 8–42.
R8638 No. 257 Sqn., High Ercall, 8–42; Warmwell, 2–43. No. 266 Sqn., Exeter, 7–43; crashed on return from *Circus* over Guipavas, 30–7–43; Fg Off H. A. Cooper unhurt.
R8639 No. 257 Sqn., High Ercall, 8–42; Warmwell, 2–43.
R8640 No. 47 MU., Sealand; airframe packing training.
R8642 No. 257 Sqn., High Ercall, 8–42.
R8646 No. 257 Sqn., High Ercall; deld 24–7–42; crashed 29–7–42.
R8648 Retained by GAC for trial installations, 7–42.

R8650 No. 257 Sqn., High Ercall, 8–42; Exeter, 11–42; Plt Off J. F. McEwen crash landed following engine failure, but unhurt, 29–11–42.
R8651 No. 257 Sqn., High Ercall, 8–42.
R8652 Mk IA. No. 257 Sqn., High Ercall, 8–42; Exeter, 11–42; Plt Off P. G. Scotchman, scrambled from Bolt Head, 3–11–42, shot down one Fw 190A low-level raider into the sea; first confirmed air victory by Typhoon IA.
R8653 No. 257 Sqn., High Ercall, 8–42.
R8654 No. 257 Sqn., High Ercall, 8–42.
R8655 No. 257 Sqn., High Ercall, 8–42.
R8656 No. 257 Sqn., High Ercall, 8–42; Exeter, 9–42; Plt Off M. J. Coombe (with F/Sgt Addington in **R8658**) gained Squadron's first Typhoon victory, 28–9–42, a Ju 88 shot down 30 miles east of Bolt Head.
R8658 No. 257 Sqn., High Ercall, 8–42; Exeter, 9–42; F/Sgt A. J. Addington (with Plt Off Coombe in **R8656**) gained Squadron's first Typhoon victory, 28–9–42, a Ju 88 shot down 30 miles east of Bolt Head.
R8659 No. 257 Sqn., High Ercall, 8–42; Warmwell, 2–43.
R8660 No. 486 Sqn., RNZAF, Wittering, 8–42.
R8661 Mk. IA. No. 257 Sqn., High Ercall, 8–42; Warmwell, 2–43.
R8663 No. 257 Sqn., High Ercall, 8–42.

R8680 No. 257 Sqn., High Ercall, 8–42.
R8681 No. 486 Sqn., RNZAF, Wittering, 8–42.
R8682 No. 486 Sqn., RNZAF, Wittering, 8–42.
R8683 No. 486 Sqn., RNZAF, Wittering, 8–42.
R8684 No. 486 Sqn., RNZAF, Wittering, 8–42.
R8685 No. 257 Sqn., High Ercall, 8–42; Warmwell, 2–43.
R8687 Typhoon Pool, Duxford, 7–42. No. 245 Sqn., Middle Wallop, 2–43, '**ZY-P**'. No. 184 Sqn., Odiham, 3–44. No. 175 Sqn., B.80 Volkel, Holland, 2–45. No. 184 Sqn., B. 110 Achmer, Germany, 5–45; flew the Squadron's last wartime operation, a shipping strike, 4–5–45.
R8688 RAE, Farnborough; propeller trials, 8–42 to 10–42.
R8690 No. 1 Sqn., Acklington, 8–42.
R8691 No. 257 Sqn., High Ercall, 8–42.
R8692 No. 486 Sqn., RNZAF, Wittering, 8–42.
R8693 To RAE, Farnborough, and A & AEE, Boscombe Down; trials of camouflage and recognition schemes, 8–42.
R8694 To Napiers, Luton, for flight trials with Sabre IV and VI engines, with and without annular radiator, from 9–42.
R8696 No. 486 Sqn., RNZAF, Wittering, 8–42.
R8697 No. 486 Sqn., RNZAF, Wittering, 8–42.
R8698 No. 486 Sqn., RNZAF, Wittering, 8–42.
R8699 No. 486 Sqn., RNZAF, Wittering, 8–42.
R8700 No. 486 Sqn., RNZAF, Wittering, 8–42.
R8701 No. 486 Sqn., RNZAF, Wittering, 8–42.
R8703 No. 257 Sqn., High Ercall, 8–42.
R8704 No. 486 Sqn., RNZAF, Wittering, 8–42.
R8705 Crashed during manufacturers' test flight, 15–8–42; disposed of by No. 50 MU.
R8706 No. 486 Sqn., RNZAF, Wittering, 8–42.
R8707 Typhoon Pool, Duxford, 8–42. No. 486 Sqn., RNZAF, Wittering, 8–42, '**SA-V**'. Became Ground Instruction Machine **3701M**.
R8708 No. 1 Sqn., Acklington, 9–42; Lympne, 7–43.
R8709 Mk IA. Typhoon Pool, Duxford, 8–42. No. 181 Sqn., Snailwell, 11–42; Sgt W. Grey crashed on take-off, 10–11–42.
R8710 Typhoon Pool, Duxford, 8–42.
R8711 No. 257 Sqn., Exeter, 9–42; Plt Off D. R. Kenward crashed into local GCI station while landing at Exeter, 29–9–42, but escaped with minor injuries; aircraft destroyed.
R8712 No. 486 Sqn., RNZAF, Wittering, 8–42.
R8713 Typhoon Pool, Duxford, 8–42. No. 486 Sqn., RNZAF, North Weald, 9–42, '**SA-T**'.
R8714 Became Ground Instruction Machine **4288M**.
R8715 Typhoon Pool, Duxford. No. 609 Sqn., Duxford, 8–42.
R8720 Collided with Typhoon **R8756**, 8–42, and disposed of by No. 50 MU.
R8721 No. 56 Sqn., Matlaske, 8–42, 5–43.

213

R8737 Became Ground Instruction Machine **4110M.**

R8740 Became Ground Instruction Machine **4271M.**

R8741 No. 486 Sqn., RNZAF, North Weald, 9–42, **'SA–R'**.

R8742 No. 181 Sqn., Snailwell, 3–43, **'EL–A'**.

R8743 No. 266 Sqn., Exeter, 3–43.

R8744 No. 486 Sqn., RNZAF, North Weald, 9–42.

R8745 No. 56 Sqn., Matlaske, 10–42. Became Ground Instruction Machine **4268M.**

R8746 No. 486 Sqn., RNZAF, North Weald, 9–42, **'SA–P'**. Became Ground Instruction Machine **4277M.**

R8752 No. 1 Sqn., Acklington, 9–42.

R8756 Collided with Typhoon **R8720**, 8–42, and disposed of by No. 50 MU.

R8760 No. 195 Sqn., Hutton Cranswick; was the Squadron's first Typhoon, deld 27–11–42.

R8762 Trials with HAL, GAC and A & AEE with Hurricane-type 44-gallon drop tanks, 9–42.

R8767 No. 266 Sqn., Warmwell, 9–42; Exeter, 3–43.

R8768 No. 257 Sqn., Warmwell, 1–43.

R8769 Crashed during delivery to the RAF, 19–9–42; believed written off.

R8772 No. 266 Sqn., Warmwell, 9–42, No. 181 Sqn., Duxford, 11–42. No. 266 Sqn., Exeter, 2–43.

R8775 Became Ground Instruction Machine **4251M.**

R8781 No. 486 Sqn., RNZAF, North Weald, 9–42, No. 257 Sqn., Warmwell, 1–43.

R8799 No. 56 Sqn., Snailwell, 9–42, **'US-P'**. No. 182 Sqn., Martlesham Heath, 11–42.

R8800 No. 486 Sqn., RNZAF, North Weald, 9–42.

R8801 No. 486 Sqn., RNZAF, North Weald, 9–42.

R8802 No. 181 Sqn., Duxford, 10–42. No. 266 Sqn., Exeter, 3–43.

R8803 To Napiers, Luton, 9–42, for engine trials.

R8804 No. 266 Sqn., Warmwell, 9–42; air defence patrols.

R8805 Became Ground Instruction Machine, **3704M.**

R8809 No. 247 Sqn., High Ercall, 1–43; offensive sweeps.

R8810 No. 609 Sqn., Biggin Hill, 9–42; air defence patrols.

R8811 No. 266 Sqn., Warmwell, 9–42; air defence patrols.

R8812 No. 609 Sqn., Biggin Hill, 9–42; air defence patrols.

R8813 No. 266 Sqn., Warmwell, 9–42; Exeter, 3–43; air defence patrols.

R8814 No. 486 Sqn., RNZAF, North Weald, 9–42; air defence patrols.

R8815 No. 609 Sqn., Biggin Hill, 9–42; air defence patrols.

R8816 No. 486 Sqn., RNZAF, North Weald, 9–42; air defence patrols.

R8819 Typhoon Pool, Duxford, 8–42. No. 195 Sqn., Hutton Cranswick, 12–42; Matlaske, 7–43.

R8821 No. 486 Sqn., RNZAF, North Weald, 9–42; air defence patrols.

R8822 No. 56 Sqn., Matlaske, 8–42; *Rhubarbs* and *Roadsteads* over Dutch coast.

R8823 No. 266 Sqn., Warmwell, 9–42; air defence patrols.

R8824 No. 56 Sqn., Matlaske, 8–42, **'US-O'**, 5–43; *Rhubarbs* and *Roadsteads* over Dutch coast.

R8825 No. 56 Sqn., Matlaske, 8–42; *Rhubarbs* over Dutch coast.

R8826 No. 56 Sqn., Matlaske, 10–42, **'US-A'**; usually flown by Sqn Ldr H. S. L. Dundas, DSO and Bar, DFC; *Rhubarbs* over Dutch coast. No. 181 Sqn., Duxford, 10–42. No. 182 Sqn., Martlesham Heath, 12–42.

R8827 No. 56 Sqn., Snailwell, 9–42, **'US-Z'**. No. 181 Sqn., Duxford, 10–42. No. 56 Sqn., Matlaske, 5–43, **'US-Z'**.

R8828 No. 181 Sqn., Duxford, 10–42; Snailwell, 2–43.

R8829 No. 181 Sqn., Duxford, 10–42; Snailwell, 2–43.

R8830 No. 181 Sqn., Duxford, 10–42.

R8831 No. 181 Sqn., Cranfield and Snailwell, 3–43, **'EL-U'**. Became Ground Instruction Machine, **3694M.**

R8832 No. 257 Sqn., Warmwell, 2–43; *Rhubarbs* over French airfields.

R8833 No. 182 Sqn., Martlesham Heath, 11–42, **'XM-A'**. No. 181 Sqn., Cranfield and Snailwell, 3–43, **'EL-D'**.

R8834 No. 182 Sqn., Martlesham Heath, 11–42, **'XM-M'**.

R8835 No. 181 Sqn., Duxford, 12–42. No. 3 Sqn., West Malling, 5–43, **'QO-M'**; shot down by Fw 190s during *Ramrod*, 18–5–43; Fg Off Gill missing.

R8836 No. 182 Sqn., Martlesham Heath, 11–42, **'XM-B'**. No. 181 Sqn., Duxford, 12–42.

R8837 No. 609 Sqn., Biggin Hill, 9–42; air defence patrols.

R8838 No. 609 Sqn., Biggin Hill, 9–42; air defence patrols.

R8840 No. 182 Sqn., Appledram, 6–43, **'XM-L'**. No. 164 Sqn., Fairlop, 1–44, **'FJ-B'**.

R8841 No. 609 Sqn., Biggin Hill, 9–42; air defence patrols. No. 247 Sqn., Gravesend, 5–43; *Rhubarbs* and *Rodeos* over French coast.

R8843 Purgatory Store: airframe snags, 5–43. No. 486 Sqn., RNZAF, Tangmere, No. 10 Group, 16–9–43 to 19–1–44; coded **'DJS'** and flown by Wg Cdr (later Gp Capt) D. J. Scott, DSO, OBE, DFC and Bar, RNZAF.

R8845 Purgatory Store: airframe snags due to faulty manufacture.

R8861 No. 266 Sqn., Warmwell, 9–42; air defence patrols.

R8862 No. 1 Sqn., Acklington, 8–42; air defence patrols. No. 182 Sqn., Martlesham Heath, 12–42, **'XM-C'**.

R8863 No. 182 Sqn., Martlesham Heath, 12–42; conversion training on Typhoons.

R8864 No. 266 Sqn., Warmwell, 10–42; Exeter, 3–43; *Rhubarbs* over French coast.

R8865 No. 56 Sqn., Matlaske, 10–42, **'US-T'**; *Rhubarbs* and *Roadsteads* over Dutch coast.

R8866 No. 181 Sqn., Snailwell, 2–43; *Roadsteads* off Dutch coast.

R8867 No. 181 Sqn., Duxford, 12–42. No. 247 Sqn., High Ercall, 1–43; conversion training on Typhoons.

R8868 No. 181 Sqn., Duxford, 12–42; conversion training on Typhoon.

R8869 No. 181 Sqn., Duxford, 12–42; conversion training on Typhoon.

R8870 No. 181 Sqn., Duxford, 12–42; conversion training on Typhoon.

R8871 No. 181 Sqn., Duxford, 12–42; conversion training on Typhoon.

R8872 No. 257 Sqn., Exeter, 11–42; Fg Off G. F. Ball, scrambled from Bolt Head, 3–11–42, shot down one Fw 190A low-level raider over the sea.

R8873 No. 56 Sqn., Matlaske, 10–42, **'US-N'**; defensive patrols and *Rhubarbs* over Holland.

R8874 No. 609 Sqn., Biggin Hill, 10–42; defensive patrols along Kent coast.

R8876 No. 56 Sqn., Matlaske, 10–42; defensive patrols and *Rhubarbs* over Holland.

R8877 No. 181 Sqn., Duxford, 12–42; conversion training on Typhoon; Snailwell, 2–43.

R8878 No. 266 Sqn., Warmwell, 10–42; air defence patrols.

R8879 No. 181 Sqn., Duxford, 12–42. No. 3 Sqn., West Malling, 5–43; took part in Squadron's third operation, *Ramrod* bombing attack on Poix airfield, 18–5–43, and was shot down by Fw 190As; Sgt Baily missing.

R8880 No. 181 Sqn., Snailwell, 2–43; was Squadron's first operational loss when Flt Lt P. S. C. Lovelace crashed into the sea, 19–2–43, in thick fog during *Roadstead*, four miles off the Hook of Holland.

R8881 No. 486 Sqn., RNZAF, West Malling, 10–42; air defence patrols.

R8882 Purgatory Store with manufacturing faults. No. 1 Sqn., Lympne, 12–43; Sqn Ldr A. Zweigbergk led *Ramrod* No. 336, 14–

12–43, dropping 500-lb bombs on V-1 launch site at Foresterberne.

R8883 No. 609 Sqn., Biggin Hill, 10–42; trials for night intruder operations.

R8884 No. 56 Sqn., Matlaske, 8–42, **'US-L'**. No. 18 MU, 12–42. No. 183 Sqn., Church Fenton, **'HF-L'**; deld 3–1–43.

R8885 No. 183 Sqn., Cranfield, 3–43, **'HF-E'**; training exercises with ground forces, SE England.

R8886 No. 183 Sqn., Snailwell, 3–43, **'HF-V'**; training exercises with ground forces, SE England.

R8888 No. 609 Sqn., Biggin Hill, 10–43; trials for night intruder operations. No. 182 Sqn., Martlesham Heath, 12–42; conversion training on Typhoon.

R8889 Trials at GAC and HAL with various hoods and radio aerial masts, 10–42. Converted for tropical trials with Vokes "interim" filter; to North Africa, 4–43. No. 451 Sqn., RAAF, LG. 106, Western Desert, 6–43.

R8891 DTD aircraft. Handling and performance checks, HAL, 6–11–42; converted to tropical aircraft and held for possible shipment to Middle East, 6–43. Returned to standard.

R8892 No. 182 Sqn., Martlesham Heath, 12–42; conversion training on Typhoon.

R8893 No. 182 Sqn., Martlesham Heath, 12–42; conversion training on Typhoon.

R8894 Purgatory Store with airframe faults, 11–42. No. 247 Sqn., High Ercall, 1–43; conversion training on Typhoon.

R8895 No. 182 Sqn., Martlesham Heath, 12–42; conversion training on Typhoon. No. 181 Sqn., Snailwell, 2–43; *Roadsteads* off Dutch coast. No. 3 Sqn., Hunsdon, 2–43, **'QO-A'**, later **'QO-E'**.

R8896 No. 181 Sqn., Duxford, 12–42; conversion training on Typhoons.

R8897 Purgatory Store with manufacturing faults. No. 439 Sqn., RCAF, Dunsfold, 3–44.

R8898 No. 609 Sqn., Biggin Hill, 10–42; trials for night intruder operations.

R8899 No. 609 Sqn., Biggin Hill, 10–42; trials for night intruder operations.

R8900 Purgatory Store as rogue aircraft, 12–42. No. 198 Sqn., Thorney Island, 5–44, **'TP-R'** .

R8923 No. 56 Sqn., Matlaske, 10–42. No. 257 Sqn., Warmwell, 1–43; air defence patrols. No. 263 Sqn., Ibsley, 12–43, **'HE-U'**; conversion training on Typhoons.

R8924 No. 182 Sqn., Martlesham Heath, 12–42, **'XM-E'** ; conversion training on Typhoons.

R8925 DTD aircraft, 11–42. Converted as tropical aircraft and held for possible shipment to the Middle East, 1943. Became Ground Instruction Machine **3486M.**

R8926 Purgatory Story with overstressed airframe. No. 439 Sqn., RCAF, Dunsfold, 3–44, **'5V–B'**. No. 183 Sqn., B.67 Ursel, Belgium, 10–44; Capt A. Lens took part in rocket and cannon attack in support of assault on Walcheren, 1–11–44. No. 164 Sqn., B.91 Kluis, Holland, 3–45.

R8927 No. 181 Sqn., Snailwell, 2–43; *Roadsteads* off Dutch coast. No. 263 Sqn., Ibsley, 12–43, **'HE-V'** ; conversion training on Typhoons.

R8929 No. 181 Sqn., Duxford, 12–42; conversion training on Typhoons.

R8930 No. 182 Sqn., Martlesham Heath, 12–42; conversion training on Typhoons.

R8932 No. 181 Sqn., Snailwell, 11–42; conversion training on Typhoons; crashed, 8–11–42, Sgt G. E. Hadley escaped unhurt. Aircraft repaired, 1943. Delivered as replacement after *Bodenplatte* to No. 245 Sqn., 2–45; B. 86 Helmond, Holland, 3–45.

R8933 No. 183 Sqn., Gatwick, 4–43, **'HF-F'**; training exercises with ground forces, SE England.

R8936 No. 266 Sqn., Warmwell, 10–42; air defence operations.

R8937 No. 226 Sqn., Exeter, 4–43, **'ZH-L'**; air defence operations; crashed at Exeter, 8–4–43.

R8938 No. 195 Sqn., Hutton Cranswick, 12–42;

Matlaske, 7–43; *Rhubarbs* over Holland; Plt Off D. J. Webster (with F/Sgt McGovern in **DN315**) destroyed three trains, a small factory and an oil storage tank during *Rhubarb* over Zandaam, 3–7–43.

R8940 No. 609 Sqn., Biggin Hill, 10–42; night intruder operations.

R8941 No. 486 Sqn., RNZAF, West Malling, 10–42; air defence operations.

R8942 No. 609 Sqn., Biggin Hill, 10–42; trials for night intruder operations. No. 1 Sqn., Biggin Hill, 3–43; collided with Typhoon **DN615**, near Tonbridge; Plt Off G. C. Whitmore (Canadian) killed, 6–3–43.

R8943 From No. 13 MU to RAE, Farnborough, 12–42, for propeller overspeeding trials.

R8944 No. 183 Sqn., Church Fenton; deld 22–12–42 for conversion training on Typhoons; aircraft was the Squadron's first operational casualty when on 14–5–43 Plt Off E. Berrisford ran out of fuel over English Channel, baled out and was presumed drowned.

R8946 No. 3 Sqn., Manston, 6–43, '**QO-L**'; shot down by Fw 190As during *Roadstead* off Hook of Holland, 7–43; Fg Off A. Little missing.

R8947 No. 182 Sqn., Martlesham Heath, 12–42; conversion training on Typhoons.

R8966 No. 182 Sqn., Martlesham Heath, 12–42; conversion training on Typhoons.

R8967 Purgatory store; modifications lapsed.

R8968 No. 247 Sqn., High Ercall, 1–43; conversion store; modifications lapsed.

R8969 No. 56 Sqn., Matlaske, 9–42, '**US-T**'. Purgatory store; modifications lapsed.

R8970 No. 183 Sqn., B.7 Martragny, France, 8–44; F/Sgt R. Gibson shot down by Bf 109Gs, 17–8–44, during armed reconnaissance in Evreux area.

R8971 Purgatory store; modifications lapsed.

R8972 Purgatory store; rogue aircraft.

R8973 No. 56 Sqn., Matlaske, 9–42, '**US-B**'. No. 183 Sqn., Thorney Island, 6–44; shot down on D-Day (6–6–44) during RP attack on German tank column; Fg Off A. R. Taylor missing.

R8974 No. 182 Sqn., Martlesham Heath, 12–42; New Romney, 7–43; *Rhubarbs* and *Ramrods* over France.

R8975 No. 182 Sqn., Martlesham Heath, 12–42; New Romney, 7–42; *Rhubarbs* and *Ramrods* over France.

R8976 No. 183 Sqn., Snailwell, 3–43, '**HF-T**'; No. 175 Sqn., Appledram, 6–43; carried out Squadron's first operation (with **EJ979**), 3–6–43; Flt Lt Davies dive-bombed Abbeville airfield.

R8977 No. 439 Sqn., RCAF, Dunsfold, 3–44, '**5V-D**' .

R8978 No. 183 Sqn., Church Fenton, 12–42; conversion training on Typhoons; Gatwick, 5–43; '**HF-R**' ; *Rhubarbs* and *Rodeos* over France.

R8979 No. 182 Sqn., Appledram, 7–43, '**XM-D**'; *Rhubarbs* over France.

R8980 No. 257 Sqn., Warmwell, 1–43; air defence operations.

R8981 No. 1 Sqn., Acklington, 10–42; air defence operations.

Third production batch of 700 aircraft produced by Gloster Aircraft Co Ltd., Brockworth, Gloucester. Deliveries commenced 20–9–42, completed 5–4–43; average rate of production, approximately 3.6 aircraft per day. All Mark IBs.

Part 1. 300 aircraft. DN241-DN278, DN293-DN341, DN356-DN389, DN404-DN453, DN467-DN513, DN529-DN562, DN576-DN623.

DN241 No. 1 Sqn., Acklington, 1–43; landing accident at Southend, 9–2–43, during Squadron move to Biggin Hill; Sgt H. Crawley unhurt but aircraft written off.

DN245 No. 257 Sqn., Warmwell, 2–43; air defence operations.

DN246 No. 182 Sqn., Martlesham Heath, 10–42, '**XM-J**' ; *Rhubarbs* over Belgium and France. No. 3 Sqn., Manston, 5–43, '**QO-A**'; shot down by Fw 190As during *Ramrod* over Poix airfield, 16–5–43; Sgt Whitall missing.

DN248 No. 183 Sqn., B. 67 Ursel, Belgium, 10–44; Lt A. G. Hill, SAAF, took part in rocket and cannon attack in support of assault on Walcheren, 1–11–44.

DN249 No. 13 MU., 12–42. No. 183 Sqn., Church Fenton; deld 22–12–42; conversion training on Typhoons.

DN252 No. 247 Sqn., High Ercall, 1–43, '**ZY-N**'; conversion training on Typhoons.

DN253 No. 3 Sqn., Manston, 6–43, '**QO-T**'; *Ramrods* over France.

DN256 No. 193 Sqn., Harrowbeer, 1–43; shipping reconnaissance operations.

DN259 No. 181 Sqn., Snailwell, 2–43; *Roadsteads* off Dutch coast.

DN261 No. 182 Sqn., Martlesham Heath, 10–42, '**XM-L**' ; conversion training on Typhoons.

DN262 No. 266 Sqn., Warmwell, 10–42; Exeter, 3–43; air defence operations.

DN263 No. 175 Sqn., No. 121 Airfield, near Lydd, 7–43; *Rhubarbs* and *Rodeos* over France.

DN264 No. 197 Sqn., Drem, 1–43 '**OV-G**' ; Flt Lt R. H. Hyde claimed one Bf 109G probably destroyed while escorting raid on Triqueville airfield (*Ramrod* No. 61)

DN265 No. 56 Sqn., Matlaske, 12–42; *Rhubarbs* over Holland.

DN266 No. 195 Sqn., Hutton Cranswick, 12–42; conversion training on Typhoons.

DN267 No. 175 Sqn., Holmesley South, 6–44; flew rocket attack against gun positions on D-Day (6–6–44).

DN268 No. 183 Sqn., Snailwell, 3–43, '**HF-J**'; exercises with ground forces in SE England.

DN270 No. 56 Sqn., Matlaske, 5–43; *Rhubarbs* and *Roadsteads* over Dutch coast.

DN271 No. 13 MU., 11–42. No. 183 Sqn., Church Fenton; deld 9–12–42, '**HF-M**' ; conversion training on Typhoons.

DN273 No. 13 MU., 11–42. No. 183 Sqn., Church Fenton; deld 2–12–42, '**HF-N**'; Snailwell, 3–43; exercises with ground forces, SE England.

DM275 No. 13 MU., 11–42. No. 183 Sqn., Church Fenton; deld 2–12–42, '**HF-B**'; Snailwell, 3–43; exercises with ground forces, SE England.

DN277 No. 56 Sqn., Matlaske, 10–42, '**US-T**' ; *Rhubarbs* over Holland.

DN278 No. 247 Sqn., High Ercall, 1–43, '**ZY-D**'. No 183 Sqn., Church Fenton, 2–43; written off in forced landing, 21–2–43.

DN293 No. 245 Sqn., Charmy Down, 12–42; conversion training on Typhoon.

DN295 No. 257 Sqn., Warmwell, 2–43; Flt Lt Burfield, a Fighter Command flying instructor visiting the Squadron, crashed at Beddington, 28–2–43, and killed.

DN296 No. 266 Sqn., Warmwell, 11–42, '**ZH-K**'; Exeter, 3–43; air defence operations.

DN297 No. 13 MU., 11–42. No. 183 Sqn., Church Fenton; deld 2–12–42; conversion training on Typhoons.

DN301 No. 197 Sqn., Drem, 11–42, '**OV-H**' ; Tangmere, 3–43; *Ramrods* over France.

DN306 No. 195 Sqn., Hutton Cranswick; deld 12–42; Ludham, 6–43; F/Sgt T. H. McGovern, RAAF (with Plt Off Webster in **R8938**), destroyed three trains, a small factory and an oil storage tank during *Rhubarb* over Zandaam, 3–7–43.

DN307 No. 56 Sqn., Matlaske, 12–42, '**US-L**' ; *Rhubarbs* over Holland.

DN309 No. 197 Sqn., Tangmere, 3–43; *Ramrods* over France.

DN314 No. 195 Sqn., Hutton Cranswick; deld 12–42; Ludham, 6–43.

DN315 No. 195 Sqn., Hutton Cranswick; deld 12–42; Ludham, 6–43; F/Sgt T. H. McGovern, RAAF (with Plt Off Webster in **R8938**) destroyed three trains, a small factory and an oil storage tank during *Rhubarb* over Zandaam, 3–7–43.

DN316 No. 195 Sqn., Ludham, 6–43; *Rhubarbs* over Holland.

DN317 No. 56 Sqn., Matlaske, 12–42, '**US-C**' ; *Rhubarbs* over Holland.

DN318 No. 257 Sqn., Exeter, 11–42; Warmwell, 3–43; air defence operations.

DN319 No. 182 Sqn., Martlesham Heath, 11–42, '**XM-X**' ; conversion training on Typhoons.

DN320 No. 197 Sqn., Tangmere, 3–43; *Ramrods* over France.

DN321 No. 197 Sqn., Drem, 1–43; conversion training on Typhoons, then air defence operations.

DN323 Converted to tropicalized aircraft; shipped to North Africa for trials, 4–43. No. 451 Sqn., RAAF, LG.106, Western Desert, 6–43.

DN328 No. 195 Sqn., Hutton Cranswick, 12–42; conversion training on Typhoons.

DN330 No. 56 Sqn., Matlaske; deld 1–12–42, '**US-N**', 5–43; *Rhubarbs* over Holland.

DN331 No. 195 Sqn., Hutton Cranswick; deld 30–11–42; Ludham, 6–43; *Rhubarbs* over Holland.

DN333 No. 257 Sqn., Exeter, 11–42. No. 197 Sqn., Drem, 1–43, '**OV-K**'; conversion training on Typhoons, then air defence operations.

DN334 No. 183 Sqn., Snailwell, 3–43, '**HF-D**' ; exercises with ground forces, SE England.

DN335 No. 1 Sqn., Acklington, 1–43; air defence operations.

DN337 No. 181 Sqn., Duxford, 11–42; Snailwell, 2–43; *Roadsteads* off Dutch coast.

DN338 No. 247 Sqn., High Ercall, 1–43; conversion training on Typhoons.

DN339 No. 56 Sqn., Matlaske, 11–42, '**US-L**' ; *Rhubarbs* over Holland.

DN340 Armament trials (cannon and 500-lb bombs), HAL, Langley, 1–43.

DN341 No. 198 Sqn., Digby, 12–42, '**TP-E**'; conversion training on Typhoons.

DN358 No. 181 Sqn., Duxford, 11–42, '**EL-B**'. No. 195 Sqn., Hutton Cranswick, 12–42; collided with AM Works lorry while taxying, 29–1–43; civilian driver killed; Sgt D. E. F. Potter unhurt and cleared of responsibility.

DN359 No. 266 Sqn., Exeter, 3–43; air defence operations.

DN361 No. 195 Sqn., Hutton Cranswick, 12–42, '**JE-M**' ; Ludham, 6–43; *Rhubarbs* over Holland and Belgium.

DN362 No. 197 Sqn., Drem, 1–43, '**OV-U**'; Tangmere, 3–43; *Rhubarbs* and *Ramrods* over France.

DN363 No. 197 Sqn., Tangmere, 3–43, '**OV-B**'; Fg Off Turton claimed one Fw 190A probably destroyed while escorting raid on Triqueville airfield (*Ramrod* No. 61).

DN370 No. 195 Sqn., Hutton Cranswick, 12–42; conversion training on Typhoons.

DN371 No. 197 Sqn., Drem, 1–43, '**OV-I**' ; conversion training on Typhoons.

DN373 No. 195 Sqn., Hutton Cranswick, 12–42; conversion training on Typhoons.

DN374 No. 56 Sqn., Matlaske, 3–43; aircraft hit by flak during attack on two armed trawlers off Dutch coast, 15–3–43; Sqn Ldr V. Phelong (CO) baled out 35 miles off Happisburgh and was rescued unhurt.

DN375 No. 195 Sqn., Ludham, 6–43; *Rhubarbs* over Holland and Belgium.

DN376 No. 197 Sqn., Drem 1–43; conversion training on Typhoons.

DN377 No. 183 Sqn., Church Fenton, 12–42, '**HF-P**' ; conversion training on Typhoons.

DN380 No. 56 Sqn., Matlaske, 5–43; *Rhubarbs* and *Roadsteads* over Dutch coast.

DN381 No. 247 Sqn., High Ercall, 1–43; New Romney, 9–43; flying escorts for Typhoon bombers.

DN382 No. 247 Sqn., High Ercall, 1–43; conversion training on Typhoons.

DN385 No. 1 Sqn., Acklington, 1–43; air defence operations.

DN389 No. 195 Sqn., Hutton Cranswick, 12–42, '**JE-F**' ; conversion training on Typhoons.

DN404 No. 247 Sqn., High Ercall, 1–43; conversion training on Typhoons.

DN405 No. 183 Sqn., Church Fenton, 12–42; **'HF-T'** ; conversion training on Typhoons.
DN406 No. 609 Sqn., Manston, 12–43, **'PR-F'**; night intruder operations and air defence operations. No. 56 Sqn., Matlaske, 3–43, **'US-F'**; *Roadsteads* off Dutch coast.
DN407 No. 197 Sqn., Drem, 1–43; conversion training on Typhoons.
DN408 No. 175 Sqn., No. 121 Airfield, near Lydd, 7–43; crashed into sea after engine failure on take-off, 1–7–43; F/Sgt Kelsick baled out and was rescued unhurt.
DN409 No. 3 Sqn., Manston, 6–43; *Ramrods* and *Rodeos* over France and Belgium.
DN410 No. 197 Sqn., Tangmere, 3–43; *Ramrods* and *Rodeos* over France.
DN411 No. 56 Sqn., Matlaske, 2–43; crashed in spin during formation practice, 24–2–43; Sgt K. Jenner presumed drowned.
DN412 No. 195 Sqn., Hutton Cranswick, 12–42; conversion training on Typhoons.
DN420 No. 247 Sqn., High Ercall, 1–43; conversion training on Typhoons.
DN421 No. 181 Sqn., Cranfield, 3–43; *Roadsteads* off Dutch coast.
DN424 No. 195 Sqn., Woodvale, 4–43; aircraft struck a railway signal during authorised low-flying, 9–4–43, and crashed; Sgt W.A. Dixon, RAAF, killed.
DN429 No. 247 Sqn., High Ercall, 1–43; conversion training on Typhoons. No. 137 Sqn., Colerne, 1–44, **'SF-W'** ; conversion training on Typhoons.
DN430 No. 247 Sqn., High Ercall, 1–43; conversion training on Typhoons.
DN431 No. 247 Sqn., High Ercall, 1–43; New Romney, 9–43; flying escorts for Typhoon bombers.
DN432 No. 1 Sqn., Acklington and Lympne, 1–43 until 12–43. No. 164 Sqn., Fairlop, 1–44, **'FJ-F'** ; conversion training on Typhoons.
DN435 No. 245 Sqn., High Ercall, 1–43; conversion training on Typhoons.
DN438 No. 198 Sqn., Woodvale, 5–43; crashed into the sea off St Annes.
DN441 No. 195 Sqn., Duxford, 1–43; conversion training on Typhoons.
DN442 No. 257 Sqn., Warmwell, 2–43. Later to No 55 OTU
DN443 No. 197 Sqn., Drem, 1–43, **'OV-F'**; conversion training on Typhoons.
DN444 No. 247 Sqn., High Ercall, 1–43; crashed at Madeley, Shropshire, while low flying, 19–3–43.
DN447 No. 56 Sqn., Matlaske, 5–43, **'US-V'**; *Rhubarbs* over Holland.
DN449 No. 175 Sqn., B.150 Hustedt, Germany, 4–45; rocket attacks on transportation targets in Germany.
DN451 No. 1 Sqn., Acklington, 1–43; air defence operations.
DN453 No. 247 Sqn., High Ercall, 1–43; conversion training on Typhoons.

DN471 No. 184 Sqn., Detling, 12–43; dive bombing attacks on flying bomb sites in France.
DN473 No. 197 Sqn., Drem, **'OV-E'** , 1–43; conversion training on Typhoons.
DN474 No. 195 Sqn., Woodvale, 3–43; aircraft crashed, 9–3–43; F/Sgt F. H. Jones, RAAF slightly injured.
DN478 No. 56 Sqn., Matlaske, 2–43, **'US-U'**; *Rhubarbs* over Holland.
DN484 No. 182 Sqn., Martlesham Heath, 2–43; *Rhubarbs* over Belgium.
DN487 No. 247 Sqn., High Ercall, 1–43; conversion training on Typhoons.
DN488 No. 56 Sqn., Matlaske, 5–43, **'US-S'**; *Rhubarbs* and *Roadsteads* over Dutch coast.
DN490 No. 1 Sqn., Lympne, 3–43; *Rhubarbs* over Northern France.
DN491 No. 56 Sqn., Matlaske, 5–43, **'US-R'**; *Rhubarbs* and *Roadsteads* over Dutch coast.
DN492 No. 137 Sqn., Colerne, 1–44, **'SF-W'**; conversion training on Typhoons.
DN493 No. 247 Sqn., High Ercall, 1–43; conversion training on Typhoons.
DN494 No. 197 Sqn., Drem, 2–43, **'OV-N'**; air defence operations.

DN497 No. 197 Sqn., Drem, 1–43; Sgt Barnard flew the Squadron's first operational sortie, 31–1–43 (with Plt Off Pearson in DN536), an uneventful scramble.
DN502 No. 1 Sqn., Lympne, 7–43; *Rhubarbs*, shipping escorts and escorts for Typhoon bombers.
DN503 Became Ground Instruction Machine 4652M .

DN531 No. 247 Sqn., High Ercall, 1–43; conversion training on Typhoons
DN534 No. 247 Sqn., Middle Wallop, 3–43; flying escorts for Typhoon bombers.
DN535 No. 56 Sqn., Matlaske, 3–43, **'US-M'** ; *Rhubarbs* over Holland.
DN536 No. 197 Sqn., Drem, 1–43; Plt Off Pearson flew the Squadron's first operational sortie, 31–1–43 (with Sgt Barnard in DN497), an uneventful scramble.
DN537 No. 174 Sqn., Gravesend, 4–43; conversion training on Typhoons.
DN538 No. 174 Sqn., Lydd, 7–43; took part in Squadron's first Typhoon operation, 14–7–43, *Ramrod* No. 136, a bombing attack on French railways.
DN539 No. 247 Sqn., High Ercall, 1–43; conversion training on Typhoons.
DN540 No. 247 Sqn., High Ercall, 1–43; conversion training on Typhoons.
DN543 No. 247 Sqn., High Ercall, 1–43; conversion training on Typhoons.
DN545 No. 197 Sqn., Drem, 1–43, **'OV-J'** ; air defence operations.
DN547 No. 55 OTU.
DN548 No. 197 Sqn., Drem 1–43. No. 175 Sqn., B.150 Hustedt, Germany, 4–45; flew rocket attacks on transportation targets in Germany.
DN553 No. 174 Sqn., Lydd, 7–43; took part in Squadron's first Typhoon operation, 14–7–43, *Ramrod* No 136, a bombing attack on French railways.
DN558 No. 197 Sqn., Drem, 1–43; air defence operations.
DN559 No. 197 Sqn., Drem, 1–43; air defence operations.
DN562 No. 266 Sqn., Need's Oar Point, 6–44; flew dive bombing attack on gun position near Bayeux on D-Day (6–6–44).

DN576 No. 197 Sqn., Tangmere, 4–43, **'OV-Y'** ; *Ramrods* over France.
DN578 No. 175 Sqn., Colerne, 4–43; conversion training on Typhoons.
DN580 No. 174 Sqn., Gravesend, 4–43; Lydd, 7–43; took part in the Squadron's first Typhoon operation, *Ramrod* No. 136, on 14–7–43, a bombing attack on French railways.
DN582 No. 609 Sqn., Manston, 4–43; *Roadsteads* and night intruder operations.
DN583 No. 56 Sqn., Matlaske, 3–43, **'US-H'**; *Rhubarbs* over Holland.
DN585 No. 1 Sqn., Biggin Hill, 3–43; Flt Lt L. S. B. Scott shot down a Fw 190A off Brighton, 13–3–43.
DN589 No. 3 Sqn., Manston, 6–43, **'QO-A'**; usually flown as a bomber; shot down by Fw 190As off Hook of Holland, 7–43; Plt Off C. G. Benjamin missing.
DN590 No. 3 Sqn., Manston, 6–43, **'QO-K'**; usually flown as a bomber; Flt Lt R. W. A. Mackichan damaged a Fw 190A, 7–43.
DN591 No. 245 Sqn., Gravesend, 4–43; air defence patrols off South Foreland.
DN597 No. 182 Sqn., New Romney, 7–43; *Rhubarbs* with 500-lb bombs.
DN599 No. 245 Sqn., Gravesend, 4–43, **'MR-D'**; air defence patrols off South Foreland.
DN601 No. 609 Sqn., Manston, 4–43; *Roadsteads* and night intruder operations.
DN605 Became Ground Instruction Machine 4654M
DN606 No. 175 Sqn., Colerne, 4–43; conversion training on Typhoons.
DN609 No. 3 Sqn., Hunsdon, 4–43; Sgt E. Ticklepenny suffered fuel pump failure during bombing practice at Leysdown, 28–4–43; force landed near Billericay. Pilot slightly hurt but aircraft written off.

DN610 No. 175 Sqn., Colerne, 4–43; conversion training on Typhoons.
DN615 No. 1 Sqn., Biggin Hill and Lympne, 3–43; crashed after collision in cloud with Typhoon R8942 near Tonbridge, 6–3–43; F/Sgt H. R. Fraser, Australian, killed.
DN619 No. 438 Sqn., RCAF, Ayr, 1–44; conversion training on Typhoons.

Part 2. 400 aircraft. EJ900–EJ934, EJ946–EJ995, EK112–EK154, EK167–EK197, EK208–EK252, EK266–EK301, EK321–EK348, EK364–EK413, EK425–EK456, EK472–EK512, EK535–EK543.

EJ901 No. 175 Sqn., Colerne, 4–43; conversion training on Typhoons.
EJ902 No. 175 Sqn., Colerne; deld 10–4–43, the first Typhoon on the Squadron; conversion training on Typhoons.
EJ905 PR Mark IB. (With twin split 5–inch oblique cameras.) No. 268 Sqn., B.70 Deurne, Belgium, 11–44; Flt Lt R. I. Mackintosh flew the last Typhoon PR sortie, 19–11–44; PR cover of attack by No. 146 Wing Typhoon bombers.
EJ906 Tropicalized aircraft. Shipped to North Africa for trials, 4–43. No. 451 Sqn., RAAF, LG.106, Western Desert, 6–43.
EJ910 No. 195 Sqn., Ludham, 6–43; *Rhubarbs* over Holland. No. 175 Sqn., B.80 Volkel, Holland, 2–45; RP attacks on German targets in support of ground forces.
EJ911 No. 247 Sqn., Middle Wallop, 2–43, **'ZY-Z'**; conversion training on Typhoons.
EJ914 No. 3 Sqn., West Malling, 5–43, **'QO-Z'**; shot down by Fw 190As during *Ramrod* over Eu, 18–5–43; Plt Off Inwood missing.
EJ917 No. 266 Sqn., Exeter, 3–43; air defence operations.
EJ919 No. 257 Sqn., Gravesend, 8–43; air defence operations.
EJ921 No. 195 Sqn., Ludham, 6–43; F/Sgt N. Arbon flew a *Rhubarb* over De Honkes, 3–7–43.
EJ924 No. 266 Sqn., Exeter, 3–43; air defence operations.
EJ925 No. 266 Sqn., Exeter, 3–43; air defence operations
EJ926 No. 257 Sqn., Warmwell, 2–43, **'FM-L'**; air defence operations. No. 184 Sqn., Detling, 12–43; conversion training on Typhoons; B. 110 Achmer, Germany, 4–45; armed reconnaissance operations and shipping strikes.
EJ927 No. 257 Sqn., Gravesend, 8–43; air defence operations.
EJ928 No. 197 Sqn., Drem, 2–43, **'OV-A'**; air defence operations.
EJ929 FR Mark IB. No. 4 Sqn., B.61 St Denis Westrem, Belgium, 10–44; low-level photo surveillance of the ground battle zone, Belgium and Holland.
EJ930 No. 3 Sqn., Hunsdon, 2–43, **'QO-P'**. No. 198 Sqn., Acklington, 3–43, **'TP-P'**; conversion training on Typhoons.
EJ931 No. 266 Sqn., Exeter, 3–43; air defence operations; suffered engine failure 12 miles east of Berry Head, 21–6–43; Plt Off N. V. Borland baled out and was rescued unhurt.
EJ932 No. 266 Sqn., Exeter, 3–43; air defence operations.
EJ934 No. 175 Sqn., Colerne, 4–43; conversion training on Typhoons.

EJ946 No. 175 Sqn., Colerne, 4–43; conversion training on Typhoons.
EJ947 No. 175 Sqn., Colerne, 4–43; conversion training on Typhoons.
EJ948 No. 486 Sqn., RNZAF, Tangmere, 2–43, **'SA-Z'**; air defence operations.
EJ950 No. 3 Sqn., Manston, 6–43, **'QO-X'**; *Roadsteads* off French and Belgian coasts by bomb-carrying aircraft.
EJ952 No. 182 Sqn., Martlesham Heath, 2–43, **'XM-S'**; *Rhubarbs* by bomb-carrying aircraft.
EJ955 No. 266 Sqn., Exeter, 3–43, **'ZH-Q'**; air defence operations. Converted to **FR Mark IB**, 1944. No. 4 Sqn. B.77 Gilze-Rijen, Holland, 1–45; Flt Lt I. H. Fryer flew Squadron's last low-level PR sortie (Nijmegen area),

2–2–45.

EJ958 No. 3 Sqn., Manston, 6–43, **'QO-Y'**; *Roadsteads* off French and Belgian coasts by bomb-carrying aircraft.

EJ961 No. 3 Sqn., Manston, 6–43, **'QO-H'**; shot down by flak during *Roadstead* off Dunkirk, 29–6–43; Plt Off R. M. Purdon missing.

EJ962 No. 56 Sqn., Matlaske, 3–43, **'US-R'**; *Rhubarbs* over Holland.

EJ964 No. 3 Sqn., Manston, 6–43, **'QO-G'**; *Roadsteads* off French and Belgian coasts by bomb-carrying aircraft.

EJ967 No. 193 Sqn., Harrowbeer, 3–43, **'DP-D'**; conversion training on Typhoons.

EJ968 No. 3 Sqn., Hunsdon, 3–43, **'QO-W'**; conversion training on Typhoons.

EJ970 No. 3 Sqn., Manston, 6–43, **'QO-M'**; shot down by Fw 190As during *Roadstead* off Hook of Holland, 7–43; Sgt. A. W. Lawrence missing.

EJ971 No. 245 Sqn., Gravesend, 4–43; weapon training with RPs.

EJ972 No. 137 Sqn., Colerne, 1–44; conversion training on Typhoons.

EJ973 No. 486 Sqn., RNZAF, Tangmere, 3–43, **'SA-B'**; air defence operations.

EJ974 No. 1 Sqn., Biggin Hill, 4–43; **'JX-T'**; air defence operations.

EJ978 No. 56 Sqn., Matlaske, 5–43, **'US-U'**; *Rhubarbs* and *Roadsteads* over Dutch coast.

EJ979 No. 175 Sqn., Appledram, 6–43; flew on the first Typhoon operation by the Squadron; Flt Lt Murchie (in company with *R8976*) dive bombed Abbeville airfield, 3–6–43.

EJ980 No. 175 Sqn., Woodvale, 3–43, **'JE-S'**; conversion training on Typhoons.

EJ982 No. 1 Sqn., Biggin Hill and Lympne, 3–43; *Rhubarbs* and escorts for Typhoon bombers, 7–43.

EJ983 No. 1 Sqn., Biggin Hill and Lympne; 3–43; *Rhubarbs* and escorts for Typhoon bombers, 7–43.

EJ984 No. 175 Sqn., Appledram, 6–43; shot down during *Rhubarb* over Dieppe, 19–6–43; Plt Off Cockburn missing.

EJ986 No. 266 Sqn., Exeter, 3–43; air defence operations.

EJ987 No. 3 Sqn., Hunsdon, 3–43, **'QO-M'**. No. 184 Sqn., Acklington, 3–43, **'TP-M'**; air defence operations. No. 164 Sqn., Fairlop, 1–44; B.91 Kluis, Holland, 3–45; RP attacks against German barge traffic on the Rhine.

EJ989 No. 3 Sqn., Manston, 6–43, **QO-S'**; usually flown as bomber.

EJ990 No. 55 OTU.

EJ991 No. 247 Sqn., Middle Wallop, 3–43, **'ZY-E'**; conversion training on Typhoons.

EJ992 No. 1 Sqn., Biggin Hill, 4–43, **'JX-M'**; *Rhubarbs* against rail targets in France.

EJ993 No. 174 Sqn., Gravesend, 4–43; conversion training on Typhoons.

EJ995 No. 175 Sqn., Colerne, conversion training on Typhoons, 4–43.

EK113 No. 1 Sqn., Lympne, 9–43; flying escorts for Typhoon bombers on *Ramrods* over France.

EK115 No. 164 Sqn., Fairlop, 1–44, **'FJ-L'**; conversion training on Typhoons.

EK121 No. 609 Sqn., Manston, 3–43; *Roadsteads* off French and Belgian coasts.

EK122 Pressure plotting wing; trials at HAL, Langley, 2–43.

EK128 No. 174 Sqn., Lydd, 7–43; took part in Squadron's first Typhoon operation, 14–7–43, *Ramrod No 136*, a bombing attack on French railway targets. No. 137 Sqn., B.86 Helmond, Holland, 3–45; rocket attacks in support of ground forces.

EK133 No. 175 Sqn., Colerne, 4–43; conversion training on Typhoons.

EK134 No. 174 Sqn., Lydd, 7–43; took part in Squadron's first Typhoon operation, 14–7–43, *Ramrod No 136*, a bombing attack on French railway targets.

EK138 No. 175 Sqn., Colerne, 4–43; conversion training on Typhoons.

EK139 No. 175 Sqn., Colerne, 4–43; conversion training on Typhoons.

EK144 No. 56 Sqn., Matlaske, 5–43, **'US-N'**;

Rhubarbs over Holland.

EK149 No. 3 Sqn., Manston, 6–43, **'QO-B'** ; usually flown as bomber on *Ramrods* over France.

EK150 Became Ground Instruction Machine **5611M** .

EK152 External store trials (with 500-lb bombs and 44-gallon drop tanks), HAL, Langley, and A&AEE, Boscombe Down, 3–43.

EK153 No. 175 Sqn., Colerne, 4–43; conversion training on Typhoon.

EK154 Miscellaneous trials at RAE, Farnborough, 1943. Became Ground Instruction Machine **5880M**

EK169 Miscellaneous trials at RAE, Farnborough, 1943.

EK171 No. 175 Sqn., Colerne, 4–43; conversion training on Typhoons.

EK172 No. 257 Sqn., Warmwell, 4–43, **'FM-M'**; Gravesend, 8–43; air defence operations.

EK173 No. 56 OTU.

EK176 No. 1 Sqn., Lympne, 7–43; *Rhubarbs* over Northern France.

EK179 No. 56 Sqn., Matlaske, 5–43, **'US-P'** ; *Rhubarbs* over Holland.

EK180 FR Mark IB. No. 268 Sqn., B.10 Plumetot, France, 8–44. Twin split oblique cameras added, 10–44, to become **PR Mark IB** . No. 4 Sqn., B.61 St Denis Westrem, Belgium, 10–44; Flt Lt D. J. Speares flew photo sortie over Walcheren, 11–10–44; B.77 Gilze-Rijen, Holland, 2–45; Flt Lt R. E. Wildin flew Squadron's last low level PR sortie (in company with *EJ995*) in Nijmegen area, 2–2–45.

EK181 No. 56 Sqn., Matlaske, 4–43, **'US-X'** ; *Rhubarbs* over Holland.

EK183 No. 56 Sqn., Matlaske, 4–43, **'US-A'**; *Rhubarbs* over Holland.

EK184 No. 181 Sqn., Lasham, 4–43, **'EL-U'**; *Roadsteads* off Dutch and Belgian coasts.

EK187 No. 3 Sqn., Hunsdon, 4–43, **'QO-K'**; conversion training on Typhoons. No. 198 Sqn., Manston, 5–43, **'TP-X'**; air defence operations. No. 609 Sqn., Manston, 6–43; *Rhubarbs* and *Roadsteads* over French and Belgian coasts.

EK189 No. 56 Sqn., Matlaske, 5–43, **'US-T'**; *Rhubarbs* over Holland.

EK190 No. 247 Sqn., Fairlop, 4–43, **'ZY-X'**; escorts for Typhoon bombers over France.

EK191 FR Mark IB. No. 268 Sqn.; flown from various forward landing grounds in France and Belgium between 9–44 and 12–44; providing Tac R for ground forces.

EK196 FR Mark IB. No. 268 Sqn., B.10 Plumetot, France, 8–44; flew Tac R sorties in Caen, Falaise and Le Mans area for ground forces.

EK209 No. 56 Sqn., Matlaske, 5–43, **'US-P'**; *Rhubarbs* over Holland.

EK210 No. 1 Sqn., Lympne, 7–43; flew escorts for Typhoon and Whirlwind fighter-bombers on *Roadsteads* off French coast.

EK212 FR Mark IB. No. 268 Sqn., B.10 Plumetot, France, 8–44; flew Tac R sorties in Caen, Falaise and Le Mans area for ground forces.

EK217 No. 3 Sqn., West Malling, 5–43, **'QO-N'**; shot down by Fw 190As during *Ramrod* over marshalling yards at Eu, 18–5–43; Fg Off Hall missing.

EK219 No. 168 Sqn., B.78 Eindhoven, Holland, 10–44. No. 439 Sqn., RCAF, B.78 Eindhoven, Holland, 12–44, **'5V-X'**; B.150 Celle, Germany, 5–45.

EK220 No. 184 Sqn., B.110 Achmer, Germany, 4–45; shipping and airfield strikes with RPs over Germany.

EK221 No. 181 Sqn., Lasham, 5–43, **'EL–Q'**; *Roadsteads* off French and Belgian coasts.

EK223 No. 195 Sqn., Ludham, 5–43; Sgt P. C. Mason, RCAF, flew *Rhubarb* over De Honkes, 3–7–43.

EK225 No. 609 Sqn., Manston, 4–43, **'PR-H'**; *Roadsteads* off Belgian coast.

EK226 No. 182 Sqn., New Romney, 7–43; *Rhubarbs* with 500-lb bombs over Northern France.

EK227 No. 3 Sqn., West Malling, 5–43 to 6–43,

'QO-D'; shot down during attack on enemy train, 2–6–43; Plt Off R. E. Barckley missing.

EK228 No. 1 Sqn., Lympne, 7–43; Plt Off J. M. Chalifour killed when aircraft suffered loss of tail unit at 10,000 feet and dived into the ground, 15–7–43.

EK229 External store trials (500-lb bombs and 44-gallon drop tanks), HAL, Langley, and A&AEE, Boscombe Down, 6–43.

EK232 No. 55 OTU.

EK233 No. 164 Sqn., Thorney Island, 3–44; took part in Squadron's first Typhoon operation, 20–3–44, a dive bombing attack on flying bomb launch site at Bonnieres.

EK240 FR Mark IB. No. 268 Sqn., B.10 Plumetot, France, 8–44; flew Tac R sorties in Caen, Falaise and Le Mans areas.

EK245 No. 266 Sqn., Exeter, 4–43. No. 175 Sqn., Colerne, 4–43; conversion training on Typhoons.

EK247 FR Mark IB. No. 268 Sqn., B.10 Plumetot, France, 8–44; flew Tac R sorties in Caen, Falaise and Le Mans areas. Twin split oblique cameras fitted, 10–44. No. 4 Sqn., B.61 St Denis Westrem, Belgium, 10–44. Flt Lt M. R. Cowell flew photo sortie over Walcheren, 11–10–44.

EK267 FR Mark IB. No. 268 Sqn., Odiham, 7–44; Sqn Ldr A. S. Mann flew the first Typhoon Tac R sortie (with Fg Off G. K. N. Lloyd in *EK272*) over Normandy, 8–8–44.

EK268 No. 56 Sqn., Matlaske, 4–43, **'US-X'**; *Rhubarbs* over Holland.

EK269 No. 56 Sqn., Matlaske, 4–43, **'US-K'**; *Rhubarbs* over Holland.

EK270 No. 137 Sqn., Colerne, 1–44; conversion training on Typhoons. No. 247 Sqn., B.86 Helmond, Holland, 3–45 (replacement aircraft after *Bodenplatte*)

EK272 FR Mark IB. No. 268 Sqn., Odiham, 7–44; Fg Off G. K. N. Lloyd flew the first Typhoon Tac R sortie (with Sqn Ldr A. S. Mann in *EK267*) over Normandy, 8–8–44. Aircraft converted to **PR Mark IB** with twin split oblique cameras added, *c*.10–44.

EK273 No. 195 Sqn., Ludham, 6–43; *Rhubarbs* over Holland and Belgium.

EK280 No. 181 Sqn., Lasham, 4–43, **'EL-G'**; *Roadsteads* and *Rhubarbs* over Dutch and Belgian coast.

EK285 No. 56 Sqn., Matlaske, 4–43, **'US-B'**; 2–44, **'US-T'**; *Rodeos*, *Ramrods* and *Roadsteads* over Dutch and Belgian coasts.

EK289 No. 56 Sqn., Matlaske, 4–43, **'US-D'**; *Rhubarbs* over Holland.

EK321 No. 56 Sqn., Matlaske, 4–43, **'US-L'**; *Rhubarbs* over Holland.

EK322 No. 257 Sqn., Warmwell, 4–43, **'FM-Q'**; air defence operations. No. 609 Sqn., Manston, 5–43; *Roadsteads* off Belgian coast.

EK326 No. 56 Sqn., Matlaske, 4–43, **'US-L'**; 2–44, **'US-E'**; *Rodeos* and *Ramrods* over Holland and Belgium.

EK327 Miscellaneous trials, RAE, Farnborough, 5–43.

EK369 No. 174 Sqn., Lydd, 7–43; took part in Squadron's first Typhoon operation, 14–7–43, *Ramrod No. 136*, a bombing attack on French railway targets.

EK371 No. 3 Sqn., Hunsdon, 4–43, **'QO-N'**. No. 247 Sqn., Bradwell Bay, 6–43, **'ZY-P'**. Reissued to No. 247 Sqn., B.86 Helmond, Holland, 3–45, as a replacement aircraft after *Bodenplatte*.

EK372 FR Mark IB. No. 268 Sqn., B.10 Plumetot, France, 8–44. No. 4 Sqn., B.61 St Denis Westrem, Belgium, 10–44; Flt Lt D. J. Speares flew low-level fighter reconnaissance over Raamsdonkveer, 16–1–45.

EK379 No. 174 Sqn., Fairlop, 1–44, **'FJ-J'**; conversion training on Typhoons.

EK380 PR Mark IB. No. 268 Sqn., B.70 Deurne, Belgium, 11–44; Flt Lt A. R. Hill, DFC, flew the Squadron's last PR sortie, 19–11–44; photo cover of an attack by No. 146 Wing Typhoons. No. 4 Sqn., B.77 Gilze-Rijen, Holland, 11–44; low level photo reconnaissance in Apeldoorn area.

EK382 No. 175 Sqn., Colerne, 4–43; conversion training on Typhoons. No. 168 Sqn., B. 78 Eindhoven, Holland, 10–44. No. 175 Sqn., B. 80 Volkel, Holland, 2–45; Flt Lt C. A. B. Slack hit the ground during an attack on a train near Munster, 30–3–45; aircraft exploded.

EK383 No. 438 Sqn., RCAF, Ayr, 1–44, '**F3–H**'; conversion training on Typhoons.

EK384 No. 168 Sqn., B.78 Eindhoven, Holland, 10–44; flying fighter cover for Typhoon bombers.

EK388 No. 182 Sqn., Middle Wallop, 4–43, '**XM-F**'; *Rhubarbs* with 500–lb bombs over France.

EK390 FR Mark IB. No. 4 Sqn., B. 77 Gilze–Rijen, Holland, 1–45; Flt Lt P. M. Sims flew low–level fighter reconnaissance over Raamsdonkveer, 16–1–45.

EK395 No. 182 Sqn., New Romney, 8–43. Sqn Ldr T. P. Pugh killed during dive bombing attack on German destroyers in Dunkirk harbour, 2–8–43; flak seen to hit starboard bomb before release, which exploded.

EK413 No. 55 OTU.

EK427 FR Mark IB. No. 4 Sqn., B. 61 St Denis Westrem, Belgium, 10–44; flew low level fighter reconnaissance sorties in areas of Bocholt and Apeldoorn.

EK428 FR Mark IB. No. 268 Sqn., B. 10 Plumetot, France, 8–44; flew Tac R sorties in areas of Bretteville–sur–Laize and Mezidon.

EK429 PR Mark IB Fitted with twin split five–inch oblique cameras. No. 4 Sqn., B. 61 St Denis Westrem, 10–44. Flt Lt R. M. Cowell shot down by flak, 18–11–44, during photo sortie at 10,000 feet near Bocholt (and made POW).

EK432 No. 168 Sqn., B. 78 Eindhoven, Holland, 10–44; flew cover for Typhoon bombers.

EK436 FR Mark IB. No. 268 Sqn., B. 10 Plumetot, France, 8–44; flew Tac R sorties over Northern France, 8–44. Fitted with twin split five–inch oblique cameras, 10–44. No. 4 Sqn., B. 61 St Denis Westrem, 10–44. Flt Lt D. A. J. Draper flew Squadron's first Typhoon operation (with Flt Lt H. D. Leventon in **JP372**), a photo sortie over Walcheren.

EK440 FR Mark IB. No. 4 Sqn., B. 61 St Denis Westrem, Belgium; low–level Tac R and FR sorties over Holland.

EK447 No. 175 Sqn., Colerne, 4–43, '**HH-B**'; conversion training on Typhoons.

EK455 No. 175 Sqn., Colerne, 4–43, '**HH-D**'; conversion training on Typhoons.

EK481 No. 438 Sqn., RCAF, Ayr, 1–44, '**F3-N**'; conversion training on Typhoons.

EK495 No. 3 Sqn., Hunsdon, 4–43, '**QO-L**'; conversion training on Typhoons.

EK497 External store trials, HAL, Langley, and A&AEE, Boscombe Down, 5–42. No. 183 Sqn., B.67 Ursel, Belgium, 10–44; Flt Lt E. W. Harbutt took part in rocket and cannon attack in support of assault on Walcheren, 1–11–44; Fg Off D. Webber shot down by USAAF P–51 Mustang while landing at Chievres during "*Bodenplatte*", 1–1–45.

EK498 No. 183 Sqn., B. 67 Ursel, Belgium, 10–44; Flt Lt E. R. Roberts, DFC, took part in rocket and cannon attack in support of assault on Walcheren, 1–11–44.

EK505 No. 197 Sqn., Tangmere, 4–43, '**OV-D**'; air defence operations.

EK511 No. 486 Sqn., RNZAF, Tangmere, 4–43, '**SA-T**'; *Ramrods* and *Roadsteads* over French coast.

Fourth production batch of 600 aircraft produced by Gloster Aircraft Co Ltd., Brockworth, Gloucester, JP361–JP408, JP425–JP447, JP480–JP516, JP532–JP552, JP576–JP614, JP648–JP689, JP723–JP756, JP784–JP802, JP836–JP861, JP897–JP941, JP961–JP976, JR125–JR152, JR183–JR223, JR237–JR266,

JR289–JR338, JR360–JR392, JR426–JR449, JR492–JR535. **Napier Sabre IIA engines fitted from new; many aircraft modified with Sabre IIB engines in 1944. Later aircraft featured sliding hood from new; majority of earlier aircraft retrospectively modified. Deliveries commenced (to RAF Maintenance Units), 5–4–43, completed c.7–12–43; average rate of production, 2.5 aircraft per day. All aircraft Mark IBs.**

JP361 Performance and handling tests, GAC and HAL, 4–43. Deld to RAF, 5–43.

JP367 No. 184 Sqn., Detling, 12–43; conversion training on Typhoons. No. 164 Sqn., Fairlop, 1–44, '**FJ-J**'.

JP369 No. 175 Sqn., No. 121 Airfield, Lydd, 7–43; shot down by flak during fighter sweep near Evreux, 5–2–44; F/Sgt D. A. Slack posted missing.

JP370 No. 182 Sqn., New Romney, 7–43; dive bombing *Rodeos* over France.

JP371 FR Mark IB. No. 268 Sqn., Odiham, 7–44; B. 10 Plumetot, France; flew Tac R sorties in support of invasion ground forces in Normandy.

JP372 PR Mark IB. Fitted with twin split five–inch oblique cameras. No. 4 Sqn., B. 61 St Denis Westrem, Belgium, 10–44; Flt Lt H. D. Leventon (with Flt Lt D. A. J. Draper in **EK436**) carried out Squadron's first Typhoon PR operation, 11–10–44; photo cover of Walcheren.

JP373 FR Mark IB. No. 268 Sqn., B. 10 Plumetot, France, 8–44; Fg Off R. S. Clark had his canopy shot off by flak during Tac R sortie, 18–8–44, over Normandy. No. 4 Sqn., B. 61 St Denis Westrem, Belgium, 10–44. Sqn Ldr C. D. Harris St. John, DFC and Bar, flew sortie on PR over Walcheren, 11–10–44.

JP376 No. 175 Sqn., No. 121 Airfield, Lydd; dive bombing attacks on French airfields, and providing escorts for Typhoon bombers.

JP378 No. 175 Sqn., No. 121 Airfield, Lydd, 7–43; dive bombing attacks on French airfields, and providing escorts for Typhoon bombers.

JP379 No. 175 Sqn., No. 121 Airfield, Lydd, 7–43; dive bombing attacks on French airfields and other targets.

JP380 No. 182 Sqn., Appledram, 6–43, '**XM–Y**'; *Ramrods* and dive bombing attacks on coastal targets in France.

JP381 No. 182 Sqn., New Romney, 8–43; took part in *Ramrod* No. 209, an offensive sweep in the Amiens area, 19–8–43.

JP382 No. 183 Sqn., Harrowbeer, 6–43, '**HF-M**'; dive bombing attacks on French airfields. No. 175 Sqn., Holmesley South, 6–44; flew RP attacks against German gun positions near landing beaches on D-Day (6–6–44).

JP385 No. 175 Sqn., No. 121 Airfield, Lydd, 7–43; shot down, probably by flak, during fighter sweep near Evreux, 5–2–44; Plt Off C. Tucker posted missing, but thought to have survived.

JP387 No. 175 Sqn., No. 121 Airfield, Lydd, 7–43; *Circuses*, *Ramrods* and *Rodeos* over France.

JP389 No. 182 Sqn., New Romney, 7–43. Converted to **FR Mark IB.** No. 268 Sqn., B. 10 Plumetot, France, 8–44; Tac R sorties in support of invasion ground forces. No. 4 Sqn., B. 61 St Denis Westrem, Belgium, 10–44; Fg Off M. Urban and Flt. Lt. I. H. Fryer flew photo sorties over Walcheren, 11–10–44.

JP391 No. 182 Sqn., New Romney, 7–43; took part in *Ramrod* No. 209, an offensive sweep in the Amiens area, 19–8–43.

JP394 No. 182 Sqn., Appledram, 6–43, '**HH-E**'; No. 121 Airfield, Lydd, 7–43; dive bombing attacks on French airfields.

JP395 No. 182 Sqn., Appledram, 6–43, '**XM-H**'; Hurn, 6–44; flew armed reconnaissance sorties over Normandy beachhead, D-Day (6–6–44).

JP396 No. 175 Sqn., Appledram, 6–43; No. 121 Airfield, Lydd, 7–43; flying escorts for Typhoon bombers on *Rodeos*.

JP397 No. 182 Sqn., Appledram, 6–43, '**XM-S**'; No. 121 Airfield, Lydd, 7–43; dive bombing attacks against French coastal targets.

JP400 No. 182 Sqn., New Romney, 7–43; flying escorts for Typhoon bombers over France.

JP401 No. 182 Sqn., New Romney, 7–43; took part in *Ramrod* No. 209, an offensive sweep over Poix–Amiens–Berck, on 19–8–43. No. 439 Sqn., RCAF, Ayr, 3–44; conversion training on Typhoons.

JP403 No. 182 Sqn., New Romney, 7–43; flying escorts for Typhoon bombers over France.

JP406 Became Ground Instruction Machine **5305M**.

JP407 No. 195 Sqn., Ludham, 5–43, '**JE-L**', *Rhubarbs* over Belgium and Holland. No. 164 Sqn., Thorney Island, 3–44; Sqn Ldr H. A. B. Russell led the Squadron on its first Typhoon operation, 20–3–44, a dive bombing attack on flying bomb launch site at Bonnieres.

JP408 No. 266 Sqn., Exeter, 5–43; air defence operations. No. 3 Sqn., West Malling, 6–43, '**QO-G**'; *Roadsteads* and *Rhubarbs* over French and Belgian coasts. No. 266 Sqn., B. 70 Deurne, Belgium, 10–44; W/Off Henderson took part in No. 146 Wing's bombing attack on German 15th Army HQ in Dordrecht, 24–10–44.

JP425 No. 609 Sqn., Manston, 5–43; *Roadsteads* off French and Belgian coasts.

JP426 No. 3 Sqn., Manston, 11–43; shot down on *Ramrod* over flying bomb launch site, Cap Gris Nez, 10–11–43; Fg Off R. M. Walmsley believed killed.

JP429 No. 175 Sqn., No. 121 Airfield, Lydd; usually flown as bomber in attacks on French airfields.

JP432 No. 245 Sqn., Fairlop, 5–43, '**MR-S**'; air defence operations along Kent coast.

JP437 No. 195 Sqn., Fairlop, 1–44; usually flown as bomber in *Roadsteads* off French and Belgian coasts.

JP440 No. 184 Sqn., Westhampnett, 6–44; flew RP attacks against German armour on D-Day (6–6–44).

JP441 No. 175 Sqn., No. 121 Airfield, Lydd, 7–43; flew dive bombing attacks on French airfields. No. 266 Sqn., B.70 Deurne, Belgium, 10–44; flown by Fg Off Miller in rocket attack on German HQ south of Breda, 13–10–44.

JP443 No. 174 Sqn., No. 121 Airfield, Lydd, 8–43; took part in dive bombing attack at Amiens/Glissy, 16–8–43. No. 164 Sqn., Fairlop, 1–44, '**FJ-T**', later '**FJ-G**'; conversion training on Typhoons.

JP444 No. 174 Sqn., No. 121 Airfield, Lydd, 8–43; shot down by flak during dive bombing attack at Amiens/Glissy, 16–8–43; Flt Lt Sterne, DFC, seen to bale out and believed made POW.

JP445 No. 174 Sqn., No. 121 Airfield, Lydd, 8–43; took part in dive bombing attack at Amiens/Glissy, 16–8–43.

JP446 No. 56 Sqn., Matlaske, 5–43, '**US-U**'. No. 257 Sqn., Gravesend, 8–43. No. 164 Sqn., Fairlop, 1–44; conversion training on Typhoons.

JP447 No. 257 Sqn., Warmwell, 6–43, '**FM-C**'; air defence operations; Gravesend, 8–43; Fg Off M. J. Coombe baled out over sea following engine failure, 7–11–43, but assumed to have drowned.

JP480 No. 174 Sqn., No. 121 Airfield, Lydd, 8–43; took part in dive bombing attack at Amiens/Glissy, 16–8–43. No. 182 Sqn., Hurn, 6–44; flew armed reconnaissance sorties with RPs on D-Day (6–6–44).

JP482 No. 247 Sqn., New Romney, 9–43; flew escorts for Typhoon bombers.

JP483 No. 1 Sqn., Lympne, 9–43; flew shipping escorts, escorts for Typhoon and Whirlwind bombers and *Rhubarbs* over French coast.

JP484 No. 174 Sqn., No. 121 Airfield, Lydd, 8–43; took part in dive bombing attack at Amiens/Glissy, 16–8–43.

JP487 No. 247 Sqn., Bradwell Bay, 6–43, '**ZY-Y**'; flew escorts for Typhoon bombers.

JP488 No. 247 Sqn., New Romney, 9–43; flew escorts for Typhoon bombers; Newchurch,

JP489 No. 164 Sqn., Thorney Island, 3–44; took part in Squadron's first Typhoon operation, 20–3–44, a dive bombing attack on flying bomb launch site at Bonnieres.

JP490 No. 257 Sqn., Gravesend, 8–43; *Roadsteads* off French coast.

JP491 No. 257 Sqn., Gravesend, 8–43; *Roadsteads* off French coast.

JP494 No. 257 Sqn., Gravesend, 8–43, '**FM-D**'; *Roadsteads* off French coast; Warmwell, 1–44; air defence operations.

JP496 No. 175 Sqn., Lydd, Westhampnett and Eastchurch, 7–43 to 9–43; '**HH-W**', then '**RB**' when flown by Wg Cdr R. T. P. Davidson, DFC, Wing Leader, No. 121 Wing, 9–43; shot down by Fw 190As while escorting Typhoons of No. 181 Sqn., in raid on Beauvais, 11–9–43; F/Sgt Murray missing.

JP498 No. 1 Sqn., Lympne, 9–43; flew shipping escorts, escorts for Typhoon and Whirlwind bombers and *Rhubarbs* over French coast.

JP503 No. 198 Sqn., Martlesham Heath, 6–43, '**TP-F**'; defensive patrols. No. 195 Sqn., Fairlop, 1–44; *Roadsteads* off French and Belgian coasts. No. 198 Sqn., Thorney Island, 5–44, '**TP-F**'; aircraft crashed in flames during attack on radar station at Joubourg, 24–5–44; F/Sgt L. Valleley missing.

JP504 No. 197 Sqn., Tangmere, 6–43, '**OV-Z**'; air defence patrols.

JP505 No. 247 Sqn., Bradwell Bay, 6–43, '**ZY-R**'; flying escorts for Typhoon bombers.

JP510 No. 257 Sqn., Gravesend, 8–43; Plt Off J. B. Wood missing on *Rhubarb* near Fécamp, 16–3–44.

JP511 No. 184 Sqn., B. 80 Volkel, Holland, 1–45; flew RP and cannon attacks on German MT columns in Holland.

JP512 No. 266 Sqn., Exeter, 6–43; air defence operations. No. 175 Sqn., B. 80 Volkel, Holland, 1–45; flew RP attacks on German river traffic.

JP515 No. 181 Sqn., Odiham, 1–44; dive bombing attacks on flying bomb launch sites on French coast. No. 168 Sqn., B. 78 Eindhoven, Holland, 10–44; flew cover for Typhoon bombers.

JP532 No. 486 Sqn., RNZAF, Tangmere, c.7–43, '**SA-T**'; normally flown as bomber on *Roadsteads* off French coast.

JP535 No. 174 Sqn., Merston, 6–43, '**XP-W**'; conversion training on Typhoons.

JP538 No. 247 Sqn., B. 86 Helmond, Holland, 3–45; replacement aircraft after *Bodenplatte*.

JP540 No. 182 Sqn., Hurn, 6–44; flew armed reconnaissance sorties over beachhead in Normandy on D-Day (6–6–44).

JP541 No. 174 Sqn., Holmesley South, 6–44; took part in rocket attack on radar station at Arromanches, Northern France, 22–5–44.

JP544 No. 247 Sqn., New Romney, 9–43; flew escorts for Typhoon bombers.

JP549 No. 174 Sqn., Lydd, 8–43; took part in bombing attack at Amiens/Glissy, 18–8–43.

JP550 No. 174 Sqn., Lydd, 7–43; took part in Squadron's first Typhoon operation, 14–7–43, *Ramrod* No. 136, a bombing attack on French railway targets.

JP551 No. 181 Sqn., Odiham, 1–44; dive bombing attacks on flying bomb launch sites.

JP552 No. 182 Sqn., New Romney, 8–43; took part in *Ramrod* No. 209, a sweep in Amiens area, 19–8–43; F/Sgt R. L. H. Dench missing in action.

JP577 No. 175 Sqn., No. 121 Airfield, Lydd, 8–43; shot down by flak while escorting 40 Bostons over France, 16–8–43; Sgt Merlin missing.

JP578 No. 247 Sqn., Bradwell Bay, 6–43, '**ZY-Z**'. No. 55 OTU, '**EH-P**'.

JP579 No. 181 Sqn., Odiham, 1–44; dive bombing attacks on flying bomb launch sites. No. 198 Sqn., B. 103 Plantlunne, Germany, '**TP-E**', 4–45; RP attacks on German road traffic.

JP581 No. 247 Sqn., New Romney, 9–43; flew escorts for Typhoon bombers.

JP583 No. 137 Sqn., Colerne, 1–44; conversion training on Typhoons.

JP584 No. 175 Sqn., Appledram, 6–43, '**HH-C**'; Lydd, 10–43; crashed into sea during *Rhubarb*, 26–10–43; F/Sgt Shanks killed.

JP585 No. 3 Sqn., Manston, 8–43; Sqn Ldr S. R. Thomas, DFC, AFC, (CO), shot down during *Roadstead*, 5–9–43; seen to crash land in Holland.

JP588 No. 247 Sqn., Bradwell Bay, 6–43, '**ZY-Z**'; flew escorts for Typhoon bombers.

JP592 No. 1 Sqn., Lympne, 9–43; flew escorts, escorts for Typhoon and Whirlwind bombers, and *Rhubarbs* over French coast.

JP601 No. 183 Sqn., Harrowbeer, 6–43, '**HF-L**'; bombing operations against French airfields.

JP602 No. 174 Sqn., No. 121 Airfield, Lydd, 8–43; took part in dive bombing attack at Amiens/Glissy, 16–8–43.

JP604 No. 181 Sqn., Appledram, 6–43; Odiham, 1–44; F/Sgt G. J. Howard, RAAF, crashed with flak damage suffered during attack on enemy MT near Caen on D-Day (6–6–44).

JP606 No. 56 Sqn., Matlaske, 6–43, '**US-A**'; Acklington, 2–44.

JP607 No. 195 Sqn., Fairlop, 1–44; *Roadsteads* off Belgian coast. Aircraft passed to No. 164 Squadron.

JP612 No. 182 Sqn., Appledram, 6–43, '**XM-F**'; Hurn, 6–44; flew armed reconnaissance sorties over roads leading to landing beaches on D-Day (6–6–44).

JP614 No. 175 Sqn., B. 80 Volkel, Holland, 2–45; armed reconnaissance sorties over roads and railways in Germany.

JP648 No. 195 Sqn., Ludham, 6–43, '**JF-D**'; *Rhubarbs* over Holland and Belgium.

JP649 No. 247 Sqn., New Romney, 9–43; flying escorts for Typhoon bombers.

JP651 No. 56 Sqn., Matlaske, 6–43, '**US-M**'; *Rhubarbs* over Holland.

JP653 No. 247 Sqn., New Romney, 9–43; aircraft crashed into sea between Dymchurch and Hythe following engine failure, 23–9–43, during sortie to attack targets at St Omer; Flt Lt C. E. Brayshaw baled out and was rescued unhurt.

JP654 No. 182 Sqn., Appledram, 6–43, '**XM-P**'; flying escorts for Typhoon bombers.

JP655 No. 198 Sqn., Thorney Island, 6–44, '**TP-P**'; took part in rocket attack on Château le Meauffe on D-Day (6–6–44).

JP656 No. 184 Sqn., Westhampnett, 6–44; flew rocket attacks on German armoured columns on evening of D-Day (6–6–44).

JP659 No. 184 Sqn., Westhampnett, 6–44; flew rocket attacks on German armoured columns on evening of D-Day (6–6–44).

JP660 No. 245 Sqn., Selsey, 6–43, '**MR-S**'; air defence patrols and ground support exercises with Army in SE England.

JP661 No. 247 Sqn., New Romney, 7–43, '**ZY-P**'; flying escorts for Typhoon bombers, 9–43.

JP663 No. 137 Sqn., Colerne, 1–44; conversion training on Typhoons.

JP667 No. 198 Sqn., Martlesham Heath, 7–43, '**TP-M**'; *Rhubarbs* and flying escorts for Typhoon bombers.

JP671 No. 174 Sqn., No. 121 Airfield, Lydd, 7–43, '**XP-R**'; dive bombing attacks on targets in Northern France.

JP672 No. 247 Sqn., New Romney, 9–43; flying escorts for Typhoon bombers.

JP675 No. 247 Sqn., New Romney, 9–43; flying escorts for Typhoon bombers.

JP679 No. 1 Sqn., Lympne, 9–43; carried out Squadron's first Typhoon night intruder sortie with 500-lb bombs against Abbeville airfield; pilot, Fg Off H. T. Mossip, c.10–43.

JP680 No. 1 Sqn., Lympne, 9–43; 12–43; *Rhubarbs* and bombing attacks on flying bomb launch sites in Northern France.

JP681 No. 56 Sqn., Matlaske, 7–43, '**US-F**'; *Rhubarbs* over Holland.

JP682 No. 56 Sqn., Matlaske, 7–43, '**US-L**'; *Rhubarbs* over Holland.

JP684 No. 3 Sqn., Manston, 2–44; F/Sgt N. J. McCook, RNZAF, missing on *Roadstead* off Den Helder, Holland, 8–2–44.

JP685 No. 1 Sqn., Lympne, 7–43; 12–43, '**JX-O**'; *Ramrods* and *Rhubarbs*; bombing attacks on flying bomb launch sites.

JP688 No. 182 Sqn., New Romney, 7–43, '**XM-F**'. No. 247 Sqn., New Romney, 8–43, '**ZY-R**'; flying escorts for Typhoon bombers.

JP689 No. 486 Sqn., RNZAF, Tangmere, 7–43, '**SA-P**'; night intruder sorties and daylight *Roadsteads* off French coast.

JP726 Fighter Leaders' School, 1945.

JP728 No. 56 Sqn., Matlaske, 7–43, '**US-G**'; *Rhubarbs* over Holland.

JP730 No. 247 Sqn., Merston, 2–44; W/Off P. S. W. Daniel baled out after engine failure 3 miles east of Sark during weather reconnaissance over Cherbourg, 28–2–44; was posted missing when patrols failed to find him.

JP733 No. 3 Sqn., Manston, 10–43; Sqn Ldr R. Hawkins, MC, AFC, (CO) missing on *Ramrod*, 5–10–43.

JP736 No. 175 Sqn., Westhampnett; deld 1–44; was Squadron's first Typhoon with sliding hood, and usually flown by Sqn Ldr M. R. Ingle–Finch; flew RP strikes against German gun positions and MT on D-Day (6–6–44).

JP738 No. 1 Sqn., Lympne, 8–43; '**JX-N**'; *Rhubarbs* over France.

JP739 No. 181 Sqn., Odiham, 1–44; bomb and rocket strikes on shipping in English Channel.

JP741 No. 3 Sqn., Manston, 8–43, '**QO-U**'; *Roadsteads* off Dutch and Belgian coasts.

JP742 No. 257 Sqn., Gravesend, 8–43, '**FM–R**'; *Roadsteads* off French coast.

JP743 No. 197 Sqn., Need's Oar Point, 5–44; took part in attack on radar station near Dieppe, 9–5–44. No. 183 Sqn., B. 103 Plantlunne, Germany, 4–45; armed reconnaissance during final advance in Germany.

JP744 No. 3 Sqn., Manston, 11–43; shot down during *Ramrod* over flying bomb launch site, Cap Gris Nez, 10–11–43.

JP749 No. 56 Sqn., Martlesham Heath, 8–43, '**US-V**'; *Rhubarbs* over Belgium.

JP752 No. 266 Sqn., Need's Oar Point, 6–44; flew armed reconnaissance sorties around Caen on D-Day (6–6–44).

JP753 No. 175 Sqn., No. 121 Airfield, Lydd, 8–43, '**HH-S**'; flew escorts for Typhoon bombers in attacks on targets in France.

JP754 No. 56 Sqn., Martlesham Heath, 8–43, '**US-N**', later '**US-S**'; *Rhubarbs* over Belgium.

JP756 No. 3 Sqn., Manston, 11–43; shot down during *Ramrod* over flying bomb launch site, Cap Gris Nez, 10–11–43.

JP785 No. 247 Sqn., New Romney, 9–43; flying escorts for Typhoon bombers.

JP786 No. 247 Sqn., Attlebridge, 8–43, '**ZY-A**'; flying escorts for Typhoon bombers.

JP793 No. 183 Sqn., Tangmere, 8–43; '**HF-E**'; *Ramrods* over German airfields in France.

JP795 No. 1 Sqn., Lympne, 12–43; dive bombing attacks on flying bomb launch sites in Northern France.

JP802 No. 193 Sqn., Gravesend, 8–43; flying *Rhubarbs* and escorts for Typhoon bombers. No. 245 Sqn., Westhampnett, 10–43, '**MR-M**'; flew *Ramrods* over France and, from 11–43, bombing attacks against flying bomb launch sites.

JP842 No. 3 Sqn., Manston, 11–43; shot down during *Ramrod* over flying bomb launch site, Cap Gris Nez, 10–11–43.

JP843 No. 197 Sqn., Tangmere, 9–43, '**OV-Y**'; flying escorts for Typhoon and medium bombers and, from 10–43, converted to the bombing rôle.

JP844 No. 198 Sqn., B. 103 Plantlunne, Germany, 4–45, '**TP-H**'; flying armed reconnaissance patrols with RP during the final advance in Germany.

JP847 No. 1 Sqn., Lympne, 12–43; bombing attacks on flying bomb launch sites. No.3

Sqn., Manston, 2–44; sweeps over German airfields to cover withdrawal of American bombing raids.

JP849 No. 195 Sqn., Fairlop, 1–44; *Roadsteads* over Belgian coast; aircraft passed to No. 164 Sqn.

JP851 No. 609 Sqn., Lympne, 9–43, '**PR-Q**'; local flying (non–operational) pending engine modifications.

JP853 No. 266 Sqn., Exeter and Gravesend, 9–43, '**ZH–K**'. No. 486 Sqn., RNZAF, Tangmere, 10–43, '**SA–K**'; *Roadsteads* off French coast.

JP855 No. 195 Sqn., Fairlop, 9–43, '**JE–W**'; *Rhubarbs* over France and Belgium.

JP856 No. 183 Sqn., B. 7 Martragny, France, 8–44; W/Off G. F. Humphrey shot down by Bf 109Gs, 17–8–44, during armed reconnaissance over Evreux area.

JP857 No. 3 Sqn., Manston, 10–43; Fg Off J. L. Foster missing in action, 5–10–43.

JP859 No. 55 OTU, 1944.

JP900 No. 197 Sqn., Need's Oar Point, 5–44; took part in attack on radar station near Dieppe, 9–5–44.

JP901 No. 486 Sqn., RNZAF, Tangmere, 9–43, '**SA–N**'; *Roadsteads* off French coast and night intruder sorties.

JP908 No. 195 Sqn., Fairlop, 9–43, '**JE-H**'; *Rhubarbs* over France and Belgium.

JP913 No. 182 Sqn., New Romney, 9–43, '**XM–B**'; Hurn, 6–44; flew armed reconnaissance sorties over roads leading to landing beaches on D-Day (6–6–44).

JP915 No. 56 Sqn., Bradwell Bay, 9–43, '**US-X**'; *Roadsteads* off Belgian coast.

JP917 No. 181 Sqn., New Romney, 9–43, '**EL–O**'; *Rhubarbs* and *Rodeos* over France.

JP918 No. 174 Sqn., No. 121 Airfield, Lydd, 9–43; *Roadsteads* and *Rhubarbs* over French coast.

JP919 No. 193 Sqn., Gravesend, 9–43; *Roadsteads* and *Rhubarbs* over Belgian coast. No. 257 Sqn., Beaulieu, 1–44, '**FM-B**'; bombing attacks on flying bomb launch sites. No. 168 Sqn., B. 78 Eindhoven, Holland, 10–44; flew escorts for RP– and bomb–armed Typhoons over Northern Europe.

JP920 No. 181 Sqn., New Romney, 9–43, '**EL-E**'; *Rhubarbs* and *Rodeos* over France. No. 168 Sqn., B. 78 Eindhoven, Holland, 10–44; flew escorts for RP– and bomb–armed Typhoons over Northern Europe.

JP921 No.3 Sqn., Manston, 10–43; Flt Lt G. L. Sinclair missing on *Roadstead*, 4–10–43.

JP923 No. 181 Sqn., New Romney, 9–43, '**EN-N**'; *Rhubarbs* and *Rodeos* over France.

JP926 No. 3 Sqn., Manston, 10–43; W/Off J. La Rocque missing on *Ramrod*, 5–10–43.

JP931 No. 439 Sqn., RCAF, Hurn, 3–44, '**5V-M**'; attacks with 1,000-lb bombs on flying bomb launch sites in Northern France.

JP934 No. 266 Sqn., Gravesend, 9–43; escort for Typhoon bombers on *Roadsteads* off French and Belgian coasts.

JP961 No. 1 Sqn., Lympne, 12–43; attacks with 500–lb bombs on flying bomb launch sites in Northern France.

JP963 No. 198 Sqn., B. 7 Martragny, 7–44, '**TP-C**'; crashed on take–off, 31–7–44, killing pilot, Flt Lt Champion.

JP967 No. 197 Sqn., Tangmere, 10–43, '**OV-F**'; dive bombing attacks on flying bomb launch sites in Northern France.

JP968 No. 181 Sqn., Merston, 1–44; Flt Lt L. R. Allen believed to have spun in from tight turn during rocket attack on flying bomb launch site and killed, 25–1–44.

JP969 No. 183 Sqn., B. 67 Ursel, Belgium, 10–44; Fg Off F. B. Lawless took part in rocket and cannon attack in support of assault on Walcheren, 1–11–44.

JP970 No. 183 Sqn., Perranporth, 10–43, '**HF-C**'. No. 56 OTU, 1944, '**FE-F**'.

JP974 No. 609 Sqn., Lympne, 10–43, '**PR-U**'. No. 266 Sqn., Harrowbeer, 12–43. To HAL, Langley, 1944, for tests with Mark III gunsight.

JR125 No. 56 Sqn., Bradwell Bay, 10–43, '**US–S**'; *Roadsteads* off Belgian coast.

JR126 No. 1 Sqn., Lympne, 10–43, '**JX-H**'; *Rhubarbs* with 500–lb bombs over France.

JR127 No. 182 Sqn., Merston, 10–43, '**XM-P**'; *Rhubarbs* with 500–lb bombs over France.

JR128 No. 183 Sqn., Perranporth, 10–43, '**HF-S**'; flew escorts for Mosquito aircraft operating over the Brest peninsula.

JR131 No. 186 Sqn., Ayr; deld 22–11–43; conversion training on Typhoons, but did not progress to combat duties with them.

JR132 No. 186 Sqn., Ayr; deld 16–11–43; conversion training on Typhoons, but did not progress to combat duties with them.

JR135 No. 266 Sqn., Harrowbeer, 11–43; *Rhubarbs* with 500–lb bombs over France.

JR137 No. 181 Sqn., Odiham, 1–44; dive bombing attacks on flying bomb launch sites in Northern France.

JR138 No. 197 Sqn., Need's Oar Point, 5–44; took part in rocket attack on radar station near Dieppe, 9–5–44.

JR139 No. 164 Sqn., Thorney Island, 3–44; took part in Squadron's first Typhoon operation, 20–3–44, a dive bombing attack on flying bomb launch site at Bonnieres.

JR141 No. 198 Sqn., B. 7 Martragny, France, 8–44; Fg Off G. Campbell–Brown shot down by Bf 109Gs, 17–8–44; during armed reconnaissance over Evreux area.

JR144 No. 1 Sqn., Lympne, 12–43; lost in action, 21–12–43; F/Sgt S. D. Cunningham missing.

JR148 No. 186 Sqn., Ayr; deld 22–11–43; conversion training on Typhoons, but did not progress to combat duties with them.

JR149 No. 195 Sqn., Fairlop, 11–43, '**JE-Y**'; No. 56 OTU, '**FE-V**'.

JR150 No. 197 Sqn., Fairlop, 1–44; F/Sgt N. F. Miles missing on *Rhubarb* over Licgecourt, 3–1–44; believed hit by flak and crashed in the target area.

JR152 No. 486 Sqn., RNZAF, Tangmere, 11–43, '**SA-Y**'; *Roadsteads* off French coast.

JR185 No. 55 OTU, '**EH-H**'.

JR188 No. 3 Sqn., Manston, 2–44; aircraft suffered engine failure during *Roadstead* on 3–2–44; W/Off J. C. Earle attempted to ditch the Typhoon but was drowned.

JR189 No. 184 Sqn., B. 5 Le Fresny Camille, France, 8–44; Flt Lt D. H. Gross, RCAF, was shot down during RP attack on German AFVs near Trun, 18–8–44.

JR193 No. 182 Sqn., Merston, 10–43, '**XM-U**'; *Rhubarbs* with 500–lb bombs over France.

JR194 No. 184 Sqn., Detling, 12–43; conversion training on Typhoons. No. 175 Sqn., B. 80 Volkel, Holland, 2–45; armed reconnaissance sorties over Germany.

JR195 No. 174 Sqn., Holmesley South, 5–44; took part in rocket attack on radar station at Arromanches, 22–5–44.

JR196 No. 263 Sqn., Beaulieu, 2–44; flown by Plt Off H. M. Proctor on Squadron's first *Ramrod*, No. 128, against flying bomb launch site, 3–2–44.

JR197 No. 56 Sqn., Bradwell Bay, 10–43, '**US-G**'. No. 198 Sqn., Manston, 12–43, '**TP-T**'; Thorney Island, 6–44; took part in rocket attack on Château le Meuffe on D-Day, 6–6–44.

JR199 No. 186 Sqn., Ayr; deld 22–11–43; conversion training on Typhoons, but did not progress to combat duties with them.

JR200 No. 186 Sqn., Ayr; was the first Typhoon delivered, on 15–11–43, to the Squadron, which did not progress to combat status with these aircraft. **JR200** was also the only aircraft lost by the Squadron when F/Sgt F. L. East collided with a Spitfire of No. 130 Sqn., while landing in 11–43; the Spitfire pilot was killed but East escaped unhurt.

JR205 No. 247 Sqn., Merston, 10–43, '**ZY-B**'; flew escorts for Typhoon bombers.

JR207 No. 247 Sqn., Merston, 10–43, '**ZY-L**'; flew escorts for Typhoon bombers.

JR208 No. 247 Sqn., Merston, 10–43, '**ZY-C**'; flew escorts for Typhoon bombers.

JR209 No. 183 Sqn., Perranporth, 10–43, '**HF-G**'; flew escorts for Mosquito aircraft operating over the Brest peninsula.

JR210 Rogue aircraft. Investigation of excessive engine vibration, HAL, RAE and A & AEE; aircraft was marked 'TR210' in error.

JR214 No. 197 Sqn., Tangmere, 10–43, '**OV-J**'. No. 247 Sqn., Odiham, 12–43, '**ZY-C**'; attacks with 500–lb bombs on flying launch sites.

JR216 No. 56 Sqn., Martlesham Heath, 10–43, '**US-N**'; *Roadsteads* off Belgian coast.

JR217 No. 486 Sqn., RNZAF, Tangmere, 10–43, '**SO-U**'; limited night intruder sorties over France.

JR218 No. 186 Sqn., Ayr; deld 17–11–43; conversion training on Typhoons, but Squadron did not progress to combat status with them.

JR220 No. 182 Sqn., Merston, 10–43, '**XM-X**'; Hurn, 6–44; flew armed reconnaissance sorties over roads leading to landing beaches in Normandy, D-Day (6–6–44).

JR222 No. 164 Sqn., Thorney Island, 3–44; took part in Squadron's first operation, 20–3–44, a dive bombing attack on flying bomb launch site at Bonnieres.

JR223 No. 195 Sqn., Fairlop, 1–44; *Roadsteads* over Belgian coast. Trial installations at RAE, Farnborough, later in 1944.

JR237 No. 1 Sqn., Lympne, 12–43; Plt Off J. W. Sutherland missing in action, 22–12–43.

JR240 No. 186 Sqn., Ayr; deld 18–11–43; conversion training on Typhoons, but Squadron did not progress to combat status with them.

JR241 No. 198 Sqn., B. 103 Plantlunne, Germany, 4–45, '**TP-D**'; close support, and airfield and shipping strikes.

JR243 No. 164 Sqn., Fairlop, 1–44; conversion training on Typhoons.

JR244 No. 181 Sqn., Merston, 10–43, '**EL-Q**'; shipping strikes with rockets. No. 168 Squadron, B. 78 Eindhoven, Holland, 10–44, '**QC-S**'; flew fighter cover for Typhoon bombers.

JR247 No. 137 Sqn., B. 86 Helmond, Holland, 3–45; armed reconnaissance patrols in support of ground forces.

JR248 No. 197 Sqn., Need's Oar Point, 5–44; took part in attack on radar station near Dieppe, 9–5–44; B.51 Lille/Vendeville, France, 9–44; Cabrank operations, usually with 250–lb bombs.

JR249 No. 186 Sqn., Ayr; deld 29–11–43; conversion training on Typhoon, but Squadron did not progress to combat status with them.

JR250 No. 186 Sqn., Ayr; deld 29–11–43; conversion training on Typhoons, but Squadron did not progress to combat status with them.

JR251 No. 263 Sqn., Ibsley, 12–43; conversion training on Typhoons.

JR253 No. 263 Sqn., Beaulieu, 2–44; flown by Plt Off W. E. Watkins on Squadron's first *Ramrod*, No. 128, against flying bomb launch site, 3–2–44.

JR255 No. 182 Sqn., Merston, 10–43, '**XM-Y**'; Hurn, 6–44; flew armed reconnaissance sorties over roads leading to landing beaches in Normandy, D-Day (6–6–44).

JR260 No. 183 Sqn., Predannack, 11–43, '**HF-J**'; flew escorts for Mosquito aircraft operating over the Brest peninsula.

JR261 No. 181 Sqn., Odiham, 1–44; dive bombing attacks on flying bomb launch sites, Northern France. No. 137 Sqn., Colerne, 1–44; conversion training on Typhoons. No. 174 Sqn., Holmesley South, 5–44; took part in rocket attacks on radar station at Arromanches, 22–5–44.

JR262 No. 56 Sqn., Martlesham Heath, 11–43, '**US-J**'; *Roadsteads* off Belgian coast.

JR263 No. 56 Sqn., Martlesham Heath, 11–43, '**US-O**'; *Roadsteads* off Belgian coast. No. 183 Sqn., Predannack, 1–44, '**HF-Z**'; flew escorts for Mosquito aircraft operating over Brest peninsula; B. 103 Plantlunne, Germany, 4–45; armed reconnaissance sorties over Germany.

JR264 No. 186 Sqn., Ayr; deld 16–11–45; conversion training on Typhoons, but Squadron

did not progress to combat status with them.
JR265 No.1 Armament Practice Station, Fairwood Common, 10–45.

JR288 No. 266 Sqn., Harrowbeer, 11–43; *Rhubarbs* with 500–lb bombs over France.
JR292 No. 181 Sqn., Odiham, 1–44; bombing attacks on flying bomb launch sites.
JR293 No. 182 Sqn., Merston, 11–43, '**XM-C**'; *Rhubarbs* with 500–lb bombs over France.
JR294 No. 181 Sqn., Merston, 11–43, '**EL-C**'. No. 609 Sqn., Manston, 12–43; air defence patrols and limited attacks on flying bomb launch sites in the Pas de Calais.
JR297 No. 181 Sqn., Merston, 11–43, '**EL-B**'; shipping attacks with rockets.
JR298 No. 186 Sqn., Ayr; deld 15–11–43; conversion training on Typhoons. No. 198 Sqn., B. 103 Plantlunne, Germany, '**TP-N**', 4–45; close support, and airfield and shipping strikes.
JR299 No. 439 Sqn., RCAF, Hurn, 3–44, '**5V-S**'; conversion training on Typhoons.
JR303 No. 266 Sqn., B. 70 Deurne, Belgium, 10–44; flown by F/Sgt Laing in No. 146 Wing's bombing attack on the German 15th Army HQ at Dordrecht, 24–11–44.
JR304 No. 263 Sqn., Beaulieu, 2–44; flown by Plt Off R. C. Beaumont on Squadron's first *Ramrod*, No. 128, against flying bomb launch site, 3–2–44.
JR305 No. 137 Sqn., B. 86 Helmond, Holland, 3–45; close support operations with rockets.
JR308 No. 175 Sqn., B. 42 Beauvais–Tillé, France, '**HH-D**'; close support operations and strikes with RPs against German river traffic. No. 168 Sqn., B. 78, Eindhoven, Holland, 10–44; flew cover for Typhoon bombers.
JR310 No. 184 Sqn., Westhampnett, 6–44; flew sorties wtih RPs against German armour on D-Day (6–6–44).
JR311 No. 245 Sqn., Westhampnett, 11–43, '**MR-G**'; flew *Rhubarbs* and *Roadsteads* with 500–lb bombs over French coast.
JR312 No. 609 Sqn., Manston, 11–43; air defence patrols and limited offensive patrols over French coast.
JR313 No. 186 Sqn., Ayr; deld 22–11–43; conversion training on Typhoons, but Squadron did not progress to combat status with them.
JR314 No. 3 Sqn., Manston, 2–44; *Roadsteads* off Dutch coast; also sweeps over France to cover withdrawal of USAAF raids.
JR317 No. 181 Sqn., Manston, 11–43, '**EL-J**'; shipping strikes with rockets.
JR318 No. 186 Sqn., Ayr; deld 22–11–43; conversion training on Typhoons. No. 197 Sqn., 1944, '**OV-L**'.
JR320 No. 257 Sqn., Need's Oar Point, 4–44; dive bombing attacks on flying bomb launch sites and other targets in France.
JR324 No. 186 Sqn., Ayr; deld 18–11–43; conversion training on Typhoons, but Squadron did not progress to combat status with them.
JR326 No. 247 Sqn., Merston, 11–43, '**ZY-T**'; flew escorts for Typhoon bombers over France.
JR327 No. 137 Sqn., Colerne, 1–44; conversion training on Typhoons. No. 175 Sqn., B. 150 Hustedt, Germany, 4–45; armed reconnaissance and attacks on German road and rail targets.
JR329 No. 486 Sqn., RNZAF, Tangmere, 11–43, '**SA-R**'; offensive strikes over French coast.
JR330 No. 263 Sqn., Ibsley, 12–43; conversion training on Typhoons.
JR332 No. 168 Sqn., B. 78 Eindhoven, Holland, 10–44; bombing strikes with 1,000–lb bombs.
JR334 No. 486 Sqn., RNZAF, Tangmere, 2–44; offensive strikes over French coast.
JR335 No. 186 Sqn., Ayr; deld 17–11–43; conversion training on Typhoons, but Squadron did not reach combat status with them.
JR336 No. 197 Sqn., Tangmere, 12–43, '**OV-N**'; *Ramrods* over flying bomb launch sites.
JR337 No. 184 Sqn., Detling, 12–43, '**BR-Z**'; conversion training on Typhoons.
JR338 No. 197 Sqn., Tangmere, 12–43, '**OV-S**';

Ramrods over flying bomb launch sites.

JR360 No. 56 Sqn., Martlesham Heath, 11–43, '**US-P**'; *Roadsteads* off Belgian coast. No. 175 Sqn., B. 3 St Croix, France, 6–44; close support of ground forces in Normandy.
JR362 No. 439 Sqn., RCAF, Hurn, 3–44, '**5V-F**'; flew dive bombing sorties on D-Day (6–6–44).
JR363 No. 164 Sqn., B. 77 Gilze–Rijen, Holland, 2–45; rocket strikes against German barges on the Rhine.
JR366 No. 198 Sqn., Manston, 12–43, '**TP-C**'; Thorney Island, 6–44; took part in rocket attack against Château le Meauffe, D-Day (6–6–44).
JR368 No. 266 Sqn., Fairwood Common, 4–45; armament practice camp.
JR371 No. 59 OTU, 1944, '**II-J**'.
JR372 No. 247 Sqn., Hurn, 6–44; took part in rocket attack on gun position north of Caen, D-Day (6–6–44).
JR376 No. 197 Sqn., Tangmere, 12–43, '**OV-U**'; *Ramrods* over flying bomb launch sites. No. 175 Sqn., B. 80 Volkel, Holland, 2–45. W/Off R. W. Ashman (Jamaican) missing in action, 27–2–45.
JR377 No. 164 Sqn., Thorney Island, 3–44; took part in Squadron's first Typhoon operation, 20–3–44, a dive bombing attack on flying bomb launch site at Bonnieres.
JR379 No. 609 Sqn., Manston, 12–43; bombing attacks on flying bomb launch sites in the Pas de Calais.
JR381 No. 181 Sqn., Odiham, 12–43, '**EL-Z**'; *Roadsteads* with rockets off the French coast.
JR382 No. 263 Sqn., Beaulieu, 2–44; flown by Flt Lt D. G. Ross on Squadron's first *Ramrod*, No. 128, against flying bomb launch site, 3–2–44.
JR384 No. 247 Sqn., Odiham, 12–43, '**ZY-X**'; bombing attacks with 500–lb bombs against flying bomb launch sites.
JR392 No. 183 Sqn., B. 67 Ursel, Belgium, 10–44; Fg Off T. J. Lee–Warner took part in rocket and cannon attack in support of assault on Walcheren, 1–11–44.

JR427 No. 182 Sqn., Merston, 12–43, '**XM-S**'; bombing attacks with 500–lb bombs against flying bomb launch sites.
JR428 No. 164 Sqn., B. 77 Gilze–Rijen, Holland, 2–45; rocket strikes against German barges on the Rhine.
JR429 No. 249 Sqn., Westhampnett, 12–43; bombing attacks with 500–lb bombs against flying bomb launch sites.
JR431 No. 183 Sqn., B.103 Plantlunne, Germany, 4–45; armed reconnaissance sorties over Germany.
JR434 No. 263 Sqn., Beaulieu, 2–44; flown by Fg Off N. P. Blacklock on Squadron's first *Ramrod*, No. 128, against flying bomb launch site, 3–2–44.
JR437 No. 137 Sqn., Lympne, 2–44; flew bomber escorts and *Ramrods* with 500–lb bombs.
JR440 No. 263 Sqn., Beaulieu, 2–44; Sqn Ldr G. B. Warnes, DSO, DFC, led Squadron on its first *Ramrod*, No. 128, against flying bomb site, 3–2–44.
JR442 No. 56 Sqn., Martlesham Heath, 12–43, '**US-W**'; bombing attacks on flying bomb launch sites.
JR443 No. 55 OTU, '**EH-Q**'.
JR444 No. 439 Sqn., RCAF, Hurn, 3–44, '**5V-J**'. No. 168 Sq., B. 78 Eindhoven, Holland, 10–44; flew cover for Typhoon bombers.
JR446 No. 3 Sqn., Swanton Morley, 12–43; *Roadsteads* off Dutch coast.
JR448 No. 3 Sqn., Swanton Morley, 12–43; *Roadsteads* off Dutch coast.
JR449 No. 184 Sqn., Detling, 12–43; conversion training on Typhoons.

JR493 No. 184 Sqn., B. 110 Achmer, Germany, 4–45; interdiction and shipping strikes with rockets.
JR495 No. 174 Sqn., Westhampnett, 12–43; Holmesley South, 5–44; took part in rocket

attack on radar station at Arromanches, 22–5–44.
JR497 No. 3 Sqn., Swanton Morley, 12–43; *Roadsteads* off Dutch coast. No. 137 Sqn., Colerne, 1–44; conversion training on Typhoons.
JR500 No. 137 Sqn., Lympne, 2–44; took part in Squadron's first Typhoon operation, 8–2–44, *Ramrod* No. 525, escorting Typhoon bombers to Moyenville.
JR501 No. 245 Sqn., Westhampnett, 12–43; bombing attacks on flying bomb launch sites. No. 175 Sqn., B.5 Le Fresny Camille, France, 7–44, '**HH-R**'; carried out rocket attack on château north of Caen, 8–7–44.
JR502 No. 175 Sqn., Holmesley South, 6–44; flew rocket attacks against gun positions near landing beaches in Normandy, D-Day (6–6–44). F/Sgt R. C. Dale shot down by flak in rocket attack on tank concentration south of St Lô, 9–7–44.
JR503 No. 56 Sqn., Martlesham Heath, 12–43, '**US-K**', later '**US-B**'; *Ramrods* against flying bomb launch sites.
JR504 No. 56 Sqn., Martlesham Heath, 12–43, '**US-D**'; *Ramrods* against flying bomb launch sites. No. 137 Sqn., Lympne, 2–44; *Ramrods* against flying bomb launch sites.
JR505 No. 137 Sqn., Lympne, 2–44; took part in Squadron's first Typhoon operation, 8–2–44, *Ramrod* No. 525, escorting Typhoon bombers to Moyenville. Trial installations, RAE, Farnborough, 1944.
JR506 No. 439 Sqn., RCAF, Hurn, 3–44, '**5V-X**'; flew dive bombing attacks on gun positions near landing beaches in Normandy, D-Day (6–6–44).
JR508 No. 168 Squadron, B. 78 Eindhoven, Holland, 10–44; flew cover for Typhoon bombers.
JR510 No. 184 Sqn., B.80 Volkel, Holland, 1–45; was absent on patrol during "*Bodenplatte*", 1–1–45.
JR512 No. 198 Sqn., Thorney Island, 5–44, '**TP-J**'; took part in rocket attack on Château le Meuffe, D-Day (6–6–44).
JR513 No. 247 Sqn., B. 86 Helmond, Holland, 3–45; armed reconnaissance sorties over Germany.
JR514 No. 164 Sqn., B. 77 Gilze–Rijen, Holland, 2–45; rocket strikes against German barges on the Rhine.
JR515 No. 164 Sqn., Thorney Island, 5–44; shot down by flak, 28–5–44, during attack on *Freya* radar station near Fruges; Sqn Ldr H. A. B. Russell, DFC, (CO) baled out but was posted missing.
JR516 No. 137 Sqn., Lympne, 2–44; took part in Squadron's first Typhoon operation, 8–2–44, *Ramrod* No. 525, escorting Typhoon bombers to Moyenville.
JR517 No. 182 Sqn., Merston, 12–43, '**XM-L**'; bombing attacks with 500–lb bombs against flying bomb launch sites. No. 198 Sqn., Manston, 2–44, '**TP-E**'; flew bomber escorts. No. 175 Sqn., B. 80 Volkel, Holland, 2–45; Fg Off B. S. Lyons killed in action during armed reconnaissance sortie, 2–2–45.
JR521 No. 439 Sqn., RCAF, Hurn, 6–44; flew dive bombing attack against gun positions facing landing beaches in Normandy, D-Day (6–6–44).
JR524 No. 247 Sqn., Odiham, 12–43, '**ZY-D**'; Eastchurch, 4–44. No. 182 Sqn., Hurn, 6–44; flew armed reconnaissance over roads leading to landing beaches in Normandy, D-Day (6–6–44).
JR525 No. 184 Sqn., Detling, 12–43, '**BR-N**'; Westhampnett, 6–44; flew rocket attacks against German armour during evening of D-Day (6–6–44).
JR526 No. 174 Sqn., Holmesley South, 5–44; took part in rocket attack on radar station at Arromanches, 22–5–44.
JR527 No. 198 Sqn., Thorney Island, 5–44, '**TP-M**'; flew rocket attacks on several German radar stations on the French coast.
JR528 No. 182 Sqn., Merston, 12–43, '**XM-J**'; bombing attacks with 500–lb bombs against flying bomb launch sites.
JR530 No. 137 Sqn., Colerne, 1–44; Lympne, 2–44; took part in Squadron's first Typhoon

operation, *Ramrod* No. 525 on 8–2–44, escorting Typhoon bombers to Moyenville.

JR531 No. 263 Sqn., Beaulieu, 2–44; flown by Plt Off W. E. Heaton on Squadron's first *Ramrod*, No. 128, against flying bomb launch site, 3–2–44.

JR532 No. 56 Sqn., Martlesham Heath, 12–43, 'US-F'. No. 263 Sqn., Beaulieu, 2–44, 'HE-H'; bombing attacks on flying bomb launch sites.

JR533 No. 137 Sqn., Lympne, 2–44; took part in Squadron's first Typhoon operation, *Ramrod* No. 525 on 8–2–44, escorting Typhoon bombers to Moyenville.

JR534 No. 609 Sqn., Manston, 12–43; bombing attacks on flying bomb launch sites.

JR535 No. 56 Sqn., Martlesham Heath, 12–43, 'US-A'. No. 137 Sqn., Lympne, 2–44; took part in Squadron's first Typhoon operation, *Ramrod* No. 525 on 8–2–44, escorting Typhoon bombers to Moyenville. No. 184 Sqn., B. 80 Volkel, Holland, 1–45; was absent on patrol during *Bodenplatte*, 1–1–45.

Fifth production batch of 800 aircraft produced by Gloster Aircraft Co Ltd., Brockworth, Gloucester. All aircraft with sliding hood, whip aerial, faired cannon and Sabre II engine, and most aircraft with four-blade propellers. MM951–MM995, MN113–MN156, MN169–MN213, MN229–MN269, MN282–MN325, MN339–MN381, MN396–MN436, MN449–MN496, MN513–MN556, MN569–MN608, MN623–MN667, MN680–MN720, MN735–MN779, MN791–MN823, MN851–MN896, MN920–MN956, MN968–MN999, MP113–MP158, MP172–MP203. Deliveries commenced 8–12–43, completed 15–6–44; average rate of production, 4.3 aircraft per day.

MM952 No. 174 Sqn., Holmesley South, 5–44; took part in rocket attack on radar station at Arromanches, 22–5–44.

MM954 No. 174 Sqn., Holmesley South, 5–44; took part in rocket attack on radar station at Arromanches, 22–5–44.

MM957 No. 438 Sqn., RCAF, Funtington, 5–44, 'F3-N'; missing in action, 8–5–44; Wg Cdr R. T. P. Davidson, DFC, Wing Leader, No. 143 (Canadian) Wing, suffered engine failure and crash landed in France; evaded capture and linked up with advancing Allied forces after Normandy invasion.

MM959 No. 438 Sqn., RCAF, Ayr, 1–44, 'F3-B'; conversion training on Typhoons.

MM961 No. 247 Sqn., Hurn, 6–44; took part in rocket attack on gun position north of Caen, D-Day (6–6–44).

MM963 No. 247 Sqn., Merston, 1–44, 'ZY-W'; bombing attacks on flying bomb launch sites.

MM966 No. 175 Sqn., Westhampnett, 1–44, 'HH-Z'; bombing attacks on flying bomb launch sites. No. 137 Sqn., Lympne, 2–44; flew escorts for Typhoon bombers over France.

MM969 No. 137 Sqn., Lympne, 2–44; took part in Squadron's first Typhoon operation, 8–2–44, *Ramrod* No. 525, escorting Typhoon bombers to Moyenville.

M972 No. 137 Sqn., Lympne, 2–44; took part in Squadron's first Typhoon operation, 8–2–44, *Ramrod* No. 525, escorting Typhoon bombers to Moyenville.

MM975 No. 247 Sqn., Merston, 1–44, 'ZY-A'; Eastchurch, 4–44; long range sweeps over France with drop tanks and rockets.

MM979 No. 247 Sqn., Eastchurch, 4–44; long range sweeps over France with drop tanks and rockets.

MM980 No. 187 Sqn., Manston, 5–44; F/Sgt R. J. Easterbrook hit by flak while attacking armed trawlers near Hook of Holland, 5–5–44; aircraft seen to hit sea and pilot assumed to have drowned.

MM986 No. 609 Sqn., No. 123 Wing, 13–3–44 to 20–11–44; coded 'DJ-S' and flown by Gp Capt D. J. Scott, DSO, OBE, DFC, Wing Leader, No. 123 Wing, 10–44 to 2–45.

MM992 No. 56 Sqn., Martlesham Heath, 2–44, 'US-B'; *Ramrods* against flying bomb launch sites.

MM993 No. 168 Sqn., B. 78 Eindhoven, Holland, 10–44; flew cover for Typhoon bombers.

MM995 No. 182 Sqn., Merston, 1–44, 'XM-A'; Hurn, 6–44; flew armed reconnaissance over roads leading to invasion beaches in Normandy, D-Day (6–6–44).

MN113 No. 164 Sqn., B. 77 Gilze–Rijen, Holland, 2–45; rocket attacks on German barge traffic on the Rhine.

MN115 No. 1 Sqn., Lympne, 1–44, 'JX-Q'. No. 440 Sqn., RCAF, Hurn, 6–44; flew bombing attack against German reinforcements in Normandy, D-Day (6–6–44).

MN117 No. 137 Sqn., Manston, 4–44; crashed on take-off, 24–4–44; Fg Off D. J. N. Kelly unhurt, but aircraft written off.

MN118 No. 257 Sqn., Need's Oar Point, 4–44; flew dive bombing attacks against radar stations on the French coast.

MN121 No. 245 Sqn., Westhampnett, 1–44; *Ramrods* against flying bomb launch sites.

MN122 No. 168 Sqn., B. 78 Eindhoven, Holland, 10–44; took part in Squadron's first Typhoon operation, 12–10–44, flying cover for Typhoon bombers.

MN124 No. 1 Sqn., Lympne, 1–44, 'JX-F'; bombing attacks on German airfields and flying bomb launch sites in France.

MN130 No. 183 Sqn., B. 7 Martragny, France, 8–44; W/Off W. A. Carragher shot down by Bf 109Gs, 17–8–44, during armed reconnaissance in Evreux area.

MN131 No. 609 Sqn., date and base not known. No. 184 Sqn., B. 5 Le Fresny Camille, 7–44; Flt Lt H. Laflamme, RCAF, shot down by flak during rocket attack on German tanks south of Aunay, 30–7–44.

MN132 No. 198 Sqn., Thorney Island, 6–44, 'TP-K'; took part in rocket attack on Château le Meauffe, D-Day (6–6–44).

MN133 No. 266 Sqn., Need's Oar Point, 6–44; flew rocket attack against gun position near Bayeux, D-Day (6–6–44).

MN138 No. 175 Sqn., Holmsley South, 6–44; flew rocket attacks against gun positions overlooking invasion area, Normandy, D-Day (6–6–44).

MN139 No. 263 Sqn., Fairwood Common, 1–44, 'HE-Q'; conversion training on Typhoons.

MN141 Aircraft Repair Flight, No. 124 Wing, 21–1–44 to 8–6–44; coded 'PW' and flown by Wg Cdr P. Webb, DFC, Wing Leader, No. 124 Wing. No. 174 Sqn., Holmesley South, 5–44; flew rocket strike against gun positions at Revier on D-Day (6–6–44). No. 184 Sqn., B. 110 Achmer, Germany, 4–45; shipping strikes off German coast.

MN143 Fighter Leaders' School, 29–1–44. No. 198 Sqn., No. 123 Wing. Coded 'RL-7' and flown by Wg Cdr R. E. P. Brooker, DFC and Bar, Wing Leader, No. 123 Wing, 5–44 to 7–44; aircraft lost in action, 23–5–44.

MN148 Air Fighting Development Unit.

MN151 No. 198 Sqn., Manston, 1–44, 'TP-L'; provided bomber escorts; B. 103 Plantlunne, Germany, 4–45, 'TP-L'; battleline strikes with rockets in support of the ground forces.

MN171 No. 440 Sqn., RCAF, Ayr, 2–44, 'I8-E'; conversion training on Typhoons; Hurn, 6–44; flew dive bombing sorties on D-Day (6–6–44).

MN172 No. 164 Sqn., Thorney Island, 3–44; took part in Squadron's first Typhoon operation, 20–3–44, a dive bombing attack against flying bomb launch site at Bonnieres.

MN174 No. 184 Sqn., Westhampnett, 6–44; took part in rocket attack on German tanks on the evening of D-Day (6–6–44).

MN177 No. 164 Sqn., Fairlop, 1–44; conversion training on Typhoons.

MN178 No. 609 Sqn., Manston, 1–44; flew attacks on flying bomb launch sites.

MN182 No. 56 Sqn., Scorton, 2–44, 'US-C'; training with rocket projectiles.

MN184 No. 266 Sqn., Need's Oar Point, 6–44; flew rocket attack against gun position near Bayeux on D-Day (6–6–44); B. 3 St Croix, France, 8–44; shot down by flak following

rocket attack on German tanks at Argentan, 15–8–44; F/Sgt Wheeler missing.

MN187 No. 263 Sqn., Beaulieu, 2–44, 'HE-A'; flew dive bombing attacks against flying bomb launch sites.

MN188 No. 3 Sqn., Manston, 2–44; flew *Ramrods* over Belgium and France to cover withdrawal of USAAF bombing raids.

MN191 No. 137 Sqn., Manston, 6–44; Plt Off K. G. Brain destroyed the Squadron's first V–1 flying bomb on 22–6–44, and destroyed another the same evening.

MN192 No. 198 Sqn., Thorney Island, 'TP-H', 5–44; Sqn Ldr J. Niblett, DFC, (CO) shot down in flames, 2–6–44, during rocket attack on radar installation at Dieppe.

MN194 No. 174 Sqn., Holmesley South, 6–44; flew armed reconnaissance over Normandy on D-Day (6–6–44). No. 184 Sqn., B. 110 Achmer, Germany, 4–45; rocket and cannon attacks on German road and coastal traffic.

MN195 No. 198 Sqn., Thorney Island, 5–44, 'TP-N'; took part in rocket attack on Château le Meauffe, D-Day (6–6–44).

MN198 No. 56 Sqn., Scorton, 2–44, 'US-D'; training with rocket projectiles. No. 137 Sqn., B. 86 Helmond, Holland, 3–45; Cabrank sorties with rockets in support of the ground forces.

MN199 No. 181 Sqn., Eastchurch, 2–44, 'EL-T'; dive bombing attacks on flying bomb launch sites.

MN202 No. 175 Sqn., Holmesley South, 6–44; flew rocket attack against gun position overlooking invasion area, Normandy, D-Day (6–6–44).

MN203 No. 175 Sqn., B. 150 Hustedt, Germany, 4–45; flew armed reconnaissance sorties over Germany in closing weeks of the War.

MN204 No. 175 Sqn., Eastchurch, 2–44, 'HH-Y'; fighter sweeps and bombing attacks on flying bomb launch sites in Northern France.

MN205 No. 181 Sqn., Eastchurch, 2–44, 'EL-N'; bombing attacks on flying bomb launch sites. No. 184 Sqn., Westhampnett, 6–44; flew a rocket attack against German armour on the evening of D-Day (6–6–44).

MN206 No. 56 Sqn., Scorton, 2–44, 'US-J'; training with rocket projectiles.

MN208 No. 181 Sqn., Eastchurch, 2–44, 'EL-A'; bombing attacks on flying bomb sites. Fighter Leaders' School, 1944.

MN209 No. 3 Sqn., Manston, 2–44; flew *Ramrods* over France and Belgium to cover withdrawal of USAAF bombing raids.

MN210 No. 439 Sqn., RCAF, Ayr, 2–44, '5V-D'; conversion training on Typhoons.

MN229 Fighter Leaders' School, 1944. Later became Ground Instruction Machine **5553M**.

MN234 No. 198 Sqn., Manston, 2–44, 'TP-K'; flew bomber escorts.

MN235 Shipped to the USA for evaluation; later displayed at the National Air Museum from 1953.

MN240 No. 56 OTU, 1944, 'FE-J'.

MN242 No. 1 Sqn., Lympne, 1–44, 'JX-O'; bombing attacks on German airfields and flying bomb launch sites in Northern France.

MN252 No. 1 Sqn., Lympne, 1–44, 'JX-M'. No. 193 Sqn., Llanbedr, 4–44, 'DP-M'; rocket and bombing attacks against flying bomb launch sites.

MN253 No. 174 Sqn., Holmesley South, 5–44; took part in rocket attack on radar station at Arromanches, 22–5–44.

MN255 No. 184 Sqn., Westhampnett, 6–44; flew rocket attack on German tanks on evening of D-Day (6–6–44).

MN257 No. 440 Sqn., RCAF, Hurn, 6–44; flew bombing attack against German road reinforcements on evening of D-Day (6–6–44).

MN260 No. 183 Sqn., Predannack, 1–44, 'HF-H', later 'HF-A'; flew escorts for Mosquito aircraft operating over the Brest peninsula.

MN264 No. 266 Sqn., Need's Oar Point, 6–44; took part in bombing and rocket attack on gun

MN265 No. 183 Sqn., Thorney Island, 6–44; Fg Off M. H. Gee shot down by Bf 109Gs during rocket attack on German tank column on D-Day (6–6–44).

MN266 No. 55 OTU, 'EH-W'.

MN267 No. 245 Sqn., B. 24 St André de l'Eure, France, 8–44; 'MR-V'; rocket attacks on German armour and MT in Falaise area.

MN282 No. 486 Sqn., RNZAF, Beaulieu, 1–44, 'SA-R'; offensive strikes over Northern France.

MN283 No. 438 Sqn., RCAF, Ayr, 1–44, 'F3-L'; conversion training on Typhoons.

MN288 No. 184 Sqn., Detling, 1–44, 'BR-X'; Westhampnett, 6–44; took part in rocket attacks on German tanks on the evening of D-Day (6–6–44).

MN291 No. 257 Sqn., Need's Oar Point, 4–44; flew dive bombing attacks with 500–lb bombs against radar stations and other targets in Northern France.

MN293 No. 198 Sqn., Thorney Island, 6–44, 'TP-D'; took part in rocket attack on Château le Meauffe, D-Day (6–6–44).

MN295 No. 263 Sqn., Beaulieu, 2–44, 'HE-S'; flew dive bombing attacks against flying bomb launch sites in Northern France.

MN298 No. 440 Sqn., RCAF, Ayr, 2–44, 'I8-A'; conversion training on Typhoons.

MN299 No. 247 Sqn., Merston, 2–44, 'ZY-H'; flew bombing attacks against flying bomb sites. No. 184 Sqn., B. 80 Volkel, Holland, 1–45 (was absent on armed reconnaissance during "*Bodenplatte*", 1–1–45).

MN301 No. 184 Sqn., Detling, 2–44, 'BR-Y'; conversion training on Typhoons.

MN303 No. 182 Sqn., Hurn, 6–44; flew armed reconnaissance sorties over roads surrounding landing area, Normandy, D-Day (6–6–44).

MN304 No. 56 Sqn., Scorton, 2–44, 'US-Y'; training with rocket projectiles. No. 181 Sqn., Merston, 3–44, 'EL-N'; flew rocket attacks against shipping and other coastal targets.

MN305 No. 609 Sqn., Manston, 2–44; flew rocket attacks against targets off French and Belgian coasts.

MN306 No. 609 Sqn., Manston, 2–44. No. 137 Sqn., B. 86 Helmond, Holland, 3–45; replacement aircraft delivered to Squadron after "*Bodenplatte*"; flew rocket attacks in support of ground forces.

MN307 No. 440 Sqn., RCAF, Hurn, 6–44; flew dive bombing attacks on German road reinforcements, D-Day (6–6–44).

MN308 No. 439 Sqn., RCAF, Hurn, 6–44; flew dive bombing attacks against German gun positions overlooking landing beaches, Normandy, D-Day (6–6–44).

MN310 No. 439 Sqn., RCAF, Ayr, 2–44, '5V-U'; conversion training on Typhoons.

MN315 Armoured fighter reconnaissance trials aircraft with centre fuselage oblique cameras and armoured radiator fairing (later designated PR Mark IB). Trials at HAL, Langley from 3–44 with modified tail trim limits.

MN316 No. 439 Sqn., RCAF, Ayr, 2–44, '5V-P'; conversion training on Typhoons.

MN317 No. 247 Sqn., Merston, 2–44, 'ZY-B'; Newchurch, 4–44; offensive sweeps carrying two drop tanks and two 250–lb bombs.

MN320 No. 266 Sqn., Need's Oar Point, 6–44; took part in dive bombing attack on gun position near Bayeux, D-Day (6–6–44).

MN321 No. 438 Sqn., RCAF, Ayr, 2–44, 'F3-G'; conversion training on Typhoons.

MN323 No. 184 Sqn., B. 80 Volkel, Holland, 1–45 (was absent on armed reconnaissance during "*Bodenplatte*", 1–1–45).

MN324 No. 197 Sqn., Need's Oar Point, 5–44; took part in rocket attack on radar station near Dieppe, 9–5–44.

MN340 No. 182 Sqn., Merston, 2–44, 'XM-D'; bombing attacks on flying bomb sites. No. 247 Sqn., Merston, 4–44, 'ZY-K'; bombing and rocket attacks on flying bomb launch sites.

MN343 No. 266 Sqn., Need's Oar Point, 6–44; took part in dive bombing attack on gun position near Bayeux, D-Day (6–6–44).

MN345 No. 438 Sqn., RCAF, Ayr, 2–44, 'F3-D'; conversion training on Typhoons.

MN347 No. 438 Sqn., RCAF, Ayr, 2–44, 'F3-Z'; conversion training on Typhoons.

MN348 No. 440 Sqn., RCAF, Hurn, 6–44; flew bombing attack against German road reinforcements on evening of D-Day (6–6–44).

MN352 No. 439 Sqn., RCAF, Hurn, 6–44; flew dive bombing attacks against German gun positions overlooking landing beaches Normandy, D-Day (6–6–44).

MN353 No. 266 Sqn., Harrowbeer, 2–44, 'ZH-J'. No. 175 Sqn., Holmesley South, 6–44; flew gun and rocket attacks on German MT columns in Normandy, D-Day (6–6–44).

MN354 No. 257 Sqn., Need's Oar Point, 4–44; flew dive bombing attacks on flying bomb sites, radar stations and other targets in Northern France.

MN356 No. 439 Sqn., RCAF, Ayr, 2–44, '5V-X'; Hurn, 6–44; flew dive bombing attacks on gun positions overlooking landing beaches, Normandy, D-Day (6–6–44).

MN360 No. 184 Sqn., Westhampnett, 6–44; flew rocket attacks against German tanks during the evening of D-Day (6–6–44).

MN362 No. 175 Sqn., B. 80 Volkel, Holland, 2–45; flew rocket attacks against German road and rail traffic in Germany.

MN363 No. 247 Sqn., Merston, 2–44, 'ZY-Y'; armament training on rockets.

MN364 No. 266 Sqn., B. 70 Deurne, Belgium, 12–44; destroyed on ground at Deurne in "*Bodenplatte*", 1–1–45.

MN366 No. 440 Sqn., RCAF, Hurn, 6–44; flew bombing attacks against German road reinforcements on D-Day (6–6–44). No. 168 Sqn., B. 78 Eindhoven, 10–44; took part in Squadron's first Typhoon operation, 12–10–44, flying cover for Typhoon bombers.

MN367 No. 257 Sqn., Need's Oar Point, 4–44; flew dive bombing attacks against radar stations on French coast.

MN370 No. 439 Sqn., RCAF, Hurn, 6–44; flew dive bombing attacks on gun positions overlooking landing beaches, Normandy, D-Day (6–6–44).

MN371 No. 245 Sqn., Westhampnett, 2–44, 'MR-J'. No. 247 Sqn., Newchurch, 4–44. No. 174 Sqn., Holmesley South, 5–44; took part in rocket attack on radar station at Arromanches, 22–5–44.

MN373 No. 247 Sqn., Merston, 2–44, 'ZY-G'; Newchurch, 4–44; took part in rocket attack on gun position north of Caen, D-Day (6–6–44).

MN374 No. 137 Sqn., B. 86 Helmond, Holland, 3–45; flew armed reconnaissance sorties and Cabranks in support of advancing ground forces in Germany.

MN375 No. 438 Sqn., RCAF, Ayr, 2–44, 'F3-W'; conversion training on Typhoons.

MN376 No. 257 Sqn., Need's Oar Point, 4–44; flew dive bombing attacks on radar stations on French coast.

MN378 No. 440 Sqn., RCAF, Hurn, 6–44; flew bombing attack against German road reinforcements on D-Day (6–6–44).

MN379 No. 439 Sqn., RCAF, Hurn, 3–44, '5V-E'; B. 78 Eindhoven, Holland, 10–44; set-piece bombing attacks with 1,000-lb bombs against German military installations.

MN381 No. 257 Sqn., Need's Oar Point, 4–44; flew dive bombing attacks against radar stations on French coast.

MN396 No. 257 Sqn., Need's Oar Point, 4–44; flew dive bombing attacks against radar stations on French coast. No. 164 Sqn., B. 77 Gilze–Rijen, Holland, 2–45; rocket strikes against German barges on the Rhine.

MN398 No. 438 Sqn., RCAF, Hurn, 3–44, 'F3-A'; limited fighter sweeps over France.

MN400 No. 55 OTU, 'EH-A'; date not known. No. 266 Sqn., Need's Oar Point, 6–44; flew armed reconnaissance in area of Caen, D-Day (6–6–44).

MN401 No. 439 Sqn., RCAF, Hurn, 3–44, '5V-G'; flew two *Ramrods* with 1,000-lb bombs against flying bomb launch sites.

MN402 No. 438 Sqn., RCAF, Hurn, 3–44, 'F3-C'; limited fighter sweeps over France.

MN403 No. 440 Sqn., RCAF, Hurn, 6–44; flew dive bombing attack with 500–lb bombs against German road reinforcements south of Caen in evening of D-Day (6–6–44).

MN405 No. 257 Sqn., Need's Oar Point, 4–44; flew dive bombing attacks against radar stations on French coast.

MN407 No. 263 Sqn., Beaulieu, 3–44, 'HE-Y'; flew armed sweeps over Northern France.

MN408 No. 257 Sqn., Need's Oar Point, 4–44; flew dive bombing attacks against radar stations on French coast.

MN410 No. 198 Sqn., Thorney Island, 5–44, 'TP-G'; crashed in flames during attack on radar station at Jobourg, 24–5–44; Fg Off H. Freeman, RCAF, posted missing.

MN413 No. 184 Sqn., B. 110 Achmer, Germany, 4–45; Cabrank operations in support of ground forces advancing in Germany.

MN416 No. 257 Sqn., Need's Oar Point, 4–44; flew dive bombing attacks against radar station on French coast.

MN417 No. 438 Sqn., RCAF, Hurn, 3–44, 'F3-B'. No. 439 Sqn., RCAF, Hurn, 6–44; flew dive bombing attacks against gun positions overlooking landing beaches, Normandy, D-Day (6–6–44).

MN418 Fighter Leaders' School, 3–44.

MN419 No. 183 Sqn., B. 7 Martragny, 8–44; Flt Lt H. A. Brownrigg led armed reconnaissance in Evreux area, 17–8–44, on occasion when the Squadron lost four Typhoons to Bf 109Gs.

MN421 No. 137 Sqn., Lympne, 3–44, 'SF-D'. No. 247 Sqn., Hurn, 6–44; took part in rocket attack on gun position north of Caen, D-Day (6–6–44).

MN423 No. 197 Sqn., Need's Oar Point, 5–44; Flt Lt Button led attack on radar station near Dieppe, 9–5–44.

MN424 No. 438 Sqn., RCAF, Hurn, 3–44, 'F3-S'. No. 439 Sqn., RCAF, B. 78 Eindhoven, Holland, 1–45; aircraft damaged and believed written off in "*Bodenplatte*", 1–1–45.

MN425 No. 184 Sqn., B. 110 Achmer, Germany, 4–45; Cabrank operations in support of ground forces advancing in Germany.

MN426 No. 438 Sqn., RCAF, Hurn, 3–44, 'F3-H'; limited fighter sweeps over France.

MN427 No. 439 Sqn., RCAF, Hurn, 3–44, '5V-Y'; flew *Ramrod* with 500-lb bombs against flying bomb launch site.

MN428 No. 440 Sqn., RCAF, Hurn, 3–44, 'I8-Z'; Fg Off L. R. Allman, RCAF, shot down in evening of D-Day, 6–6–44, during bombing attack on German road reinforcements south of Caen.

MN429 No. 137 Sqn., Manston, 1–4–44; aircraft became Squadron's first Typhoon casualty, 1–4–44; W/Off J. W. Carter, RAAF, on solo shipping patrol between Flushing and Dunkirk, did not return.

MN430 No. 247 Sqn., Newchurch, 4–44; long range sweeps with rockets over France; took part in rocket attack on gun position north of Caen, D-Day (6–6–44).

MN435 No. 439 Sqn., RCAF, Hurn, 3–44, '5V-A'; flew dive bombing attacks against gun positions overlooking landing beaches, Normandy, D-Day (6–6–44).

MN451 No. 247 Sqn., Merston, 3–44, 'ZY–T'; Hurn, 5–44; took part in rocket attack on gun position north of Caen, D-Day (6–6–44).

MN452 No. 257 Sqn., Need's Oar Point, 4–44; flew dive bombing attacks against radar stations on French coast, 5–44.

MN454 No. 183 Sqn., Manston, 3–44, 'HF-L'. No. 164 Sqn., Thorney Island, 6–44; shot down by Fw 190s on D-Day, 6–6–44; Fg Off A. E. Rogers, RAAF, posted missing.

MN455 No. 137 Sqn., Lympne, 3–44, 'SF-A'; B. 86 Helmond, Holland, 3–45; flew rocket strikes during final weeks of the War.

MN457 No. 440 Sqn., RCAF, Hurn, 6–44; flew

dive bombing attacks against German road reinforcements south of Caen in evening of D-Day (6-6-44).

MN464 No. 439 Sqn., RCAF, Hurn, 3-44, '**5V-N**'; flew dive bombing attacks against gun positions overlooking landing beaches in Normandy, D-Day (6-6-44).

MN466 Miscellaneous store and armament trials, HAL, Langley, and A&AEE, Boscombe Down, 1944.

MN470 No. 175 Sqn., Westhampnett, 3-44, '**HH-S**'; armament conversion training on rocket projectiles.

MN471 No. 175 Sqn., Holmesley South, 6-44; flew rocket attacks on German gun positions overlooking invasion area, Normandy, D-Day (6-6-44).

MN472 No. 182 Sqn., Hurn, 6-44; flew armed reconnaissance sorties over Normandy, D-Day (6-6-44).

MN477 No. 263 Sqn., Beaulieu, 3-44, '**HE-T**'; flew armed shipping patrols over English Channel.

MN478 No. 183 Sqn., Thorney Island, 6-44; Flt Lt R. W. Evans shot down by Bf 109Gs during rocket attack on German tank column on D-Day (6-6-44).

MN481 No. 175 Sqn., Holmesley South, 6-44; flew rocket attacks at gun positions overlooking landing beaches, Normandy, D-Day (6-6-44).

MN482 No. 438 Sqn., RCAF, Hurn, 3-44, '**F3-F**'; limited fighter sweeps over Northern France.

MN485 No. 184 Sqn., Odiham, 3-44, '**BR-G**'; conversion training on Typhoons.

MN486 No. 184 Sqn., Odiham, 3-44, '**BR-V**'; conversion training on Typhoons.

MN491 No. 197 Sqn., B. 51 Lille–Vendeville, France, 9-44; B. 70 Deurne, Belgium, 10-44.

MN492 No. 257 Sqn., Need's Oar Point, 4-44; flew dive bombing attacks against radar stations on French coast, 5-44.

MN493 No. 266 Sqn., Need's Oar Point, 6-44; flew armed reconnaissance sorties in area of Caen, Normandy, D-Day (6-6-44).

MN496 No. 174 Sqn., Westhampnett, 3-44; flew rocket attacks against radar stations on French coast, 5-44.

MN513 No. 1 Sqn., Martlesham Heath, 3-44; flew cross–Channel offensive sweeps. No. 55 OTU, '**EH-N**'.

MN515 No. 3 Sqn., Bradwell Bay, 3-44, '**QO-A**'; flew diversionary sweeps over France to cover withdrawal of USAAF bombing raids.

MN516 No. 439 Sqn., RCAF, Hurn, 3-44, '**5V-W**'; flew limited fighter sweeps over Northern France.

MN518 No. 143 Wing, Hurn, 19-4-44 until 27-7-44. Flown by Wg Cdr M. T. Judd, DFC, AFC, and coded '**MJ**', Wing Leader, No. 143 Wing, 15-5-44 to 15-10-44 (having been flown formerly by Wg Cdr R. T. P. Davidson, DFC, Wing Leader, No. 121 Wing, and coded '**RD**', until shot down in another aircraft, 8-5-44). No. 266 Sqn., No. 146 Wing, B. 70 Deurne, Belgium from 20-10-44; flown by Fg Off Roders in No. 146 Wing's bombing attack on German 15th Army HQ at Dordrecht, 24-10-44.

MN521 No. 609 Sqn., Manston, 3-44; weapon training on rocket projectiles.

MN523 No. 164 Sqn., Thorney Island, 3-44; bombing attacks on flying bomb launch sites in Northern France.

MN526 No. 198 Sqn., B. 10 Plumetot, France, 7-44; B. 103 Plantlunne, Germany, 4-45; '**TP-V**'; flew armed reconnaissance sorties in support of advancing ground forces.

MN529 No. 439 Sqn., RCAF, Hurn, 3-44, '**5V-T**'. No. 184 Sqn., Westhampnett, 6-44; flew rocket attacks against German tank columns in evening of D-Day (6-6-44).

MN531 No. 182 Sqn., Hurn, 6-44; flew armed reconnaissance patrols over roads leading to invasion area, Normandy, D-Day, 6-6-44.

MN533 No. 137 Sqn., Lympne, 3-44; flew anti-shipping strikes over the English Channel.

MN535 No. 440 Sqn., RCAF, Hurn, 3-44,

'**I8-K**'. No. 164 Sqn., B. 77 Gilze–Rijen, Holland, 2-45; flew rocket strikes against German barge traffic on the Rhine.

MN537 No. 198 Sqn., Thorney Island, 6-44, '**TP-E**'; took part in rocket attack on Château le Meauffe, D-Day (6-6-44).

MN541 No. 257 Sqn., Need's Oar Point, 4-44; flew dive bombing attacks against targets on the French coast.

MN542 No. 247 Sqn., Hurn, 5-44; hit by flak during rocket attack on radar station near Dieppe, 22-5-44; Wg Cdr E. Haabjoern, DFC, baled out 3 miles off Dieppe but was rescued unhurt by Walrus aircraft.

MN546 No. 198 Sqn., Tangmere, 3-44, '**TP-S**'; Thorney Island, 6-44; took part in rocket attack on Château le Meauffe, D-Day (6-6-44).

MN547 No. 438 Sqn., RCAF, Hurn, 3-44, '**F3-Q**'. No. 440 Sqn., RCAF, Hurn, 4-44, '**I8-Q**'.

MN548 No. 440 Sqn., RCAF, Hurn, 6-44; flew bombing attack on German road reinforcements on D-Day (6-6-44).

MN549 No. 183 Sqn., Manston, 3-44, '**HF-A**'; training exercises with ground forces in Southern England.

MN550 No. 164 Sqn., B. 77 Gilze–Rijen, Holland, 2-45; flew rocket strikes against German barge traffic on the Rhine.

MN551 Miscellaneous external store trials, HAL, Langley, and A&AEE, Boscombe Down, 1944.

MN553 No. 439 Sqn., RCAF, Hurn, 3-44, '**5V-K**'; flew several bombing sorties with 1,000-lb bombs against flying bomb sites, and on D-Day (6-6-44) dive bombed gun positions near the Normandy beachhead.

MN555 No. 440 Sqn., RCAF, Hurn, 6-44; flew bombing attack on German road reinforcements on D-Day (6-6-44).

MN570 No. 198 Sqn., Thorney Island, 6-44, '**TP-B**'; Wg Cdr R. E. P. Brooker, DFC and Bar, led rocket attack on Château le Meauffe, D-Day (6-6-44).

MN572 No. 164 Sqn., B. 77 Gilze–Rijen, Holland, 2-45; rocket attacks against German barge traffic on the Rhine.

MN574 No. 439 Sqn., RCAF, B. 78 Eindhoven, Holland, 10-44. Cabrank operations in support of Allied ground forces.

MN575 No. 182 Sqn., Merston, 3-44. No. 198 Sqn., Thorney Island, 6-44, '**TP-M**'; took part in rocket attack on Château le Meauffe, D-Day (6-6-44). No. 137 Sqn., B. 86 Helmond, Holland, 3-45; setpiece rocket strikes on targets in Germany.

MN577 No. 440 Sqn., RCAF, Hurn, 3-44, '**I8-J**'. No. 174 Sqn., Holmesley South, 5-44; took part in rocket attack on radar station at Arromanches, 22-5-44.

MN581 No. 439 Sqn., RCAF, Hurn, 6-44; flew dive bombing sorties against German gun positions overlooking Normandy landing beaches, D-Day (6-6-44).

MN582 No. 175 Sqn., Holmesley South, 6-44; flew rocket attacks against German gun positions overlooking landing beaches, Normandy, D-Day (6-6-44).

MN583 No. 440 Sqn., RCAF, Hurn, 6-44; flew dive bombing sorties on D-Day (6-6-44).

MN584 No. 137 Sqn., Lympne, 3-44, '**SF-W**'; conversion training on Typhoons.

MN585 No. 247 Sqn., Merston, 3-44, '**ZY-Z**'; B. 86 Helmond, Holland, 3-45 (replacement aircraft after "*Bodenplatte*"); armed reconnaissance sorties over Germany.

MN587 No. 266 Sqn., 27-7-44; coded '**ZZII**' and flown by Gp Capt D. E. Gillam, DSO and Bar, DFC and Bar, AFC, Wing Leader, No. 146 Wing, from 2-44 until 28-2-45. Led No. 146 Wing in bomb and rocket attack on German 15th Army HQ at Dordrecht, 24-10-44.

MN589 No. 439 Sqn., RCAF, B. 78 Eindhoven, Holland, 1-45; aircraft escaped damage during "*Bodenplatte*".

MN590 No. 184 Sqn., Westhampnett, 4-44; flew rocket attacks against German tanks on evening of D-Day (6-6-44).

MN594 No. 175 Sqn., Holmesley South, 6-44; flew rocket attacks against German gun positions overlooking landing beaches, Normandy, D-Day (6-6-44).

MN598 No. 257 Sqn., Need's Oar Point, 4-44, '**FM-P**'. No. 609 Sqn., No. 123 Wing, 16-11-44 until 13-1-45; flown by Wg Cdr W. Dring, DFC, Wing Leader, No. 123 Wing, 7-44 until killed in accident in **MN598**, 13-1-45.

MN600 No. 266 Sqn., Need's Oar Point, 6-44; flew rocket attack on gun position near Bayeux on D-Day (6-6-44). Shot down by flak during ground attack sortie near Falaise; 9-8-44; F/Sgt Green posted missing.

MN603 No. 440 Sqn., RCAF, Hurn, 6-44; flew dive bombing sorties on D-Day (6-6-44).

MN604 No. 164 Sqn., B. 77 Gilze-Rijen, Holland, 2-45; flew rocket strikes against German barge traffic on the Rhine.

MN606 No. 175 Sqn., Holmesley South, 4-44, '**HH-T**'; flew attacks on German radar stations on French coast.

MN626 No. 438 Sqn., RCAF, Hurn, 4-44, '**F3-A**'; No. 439 Sqn., RCAF, Hurn, 5-44, '**5V-A**'.

MN627 No. 137 Sqn., Manston, 4-44, '**SF-N**'; flew *Roadsteads* off French coast, 5-44, and remained at Standby for *Channel Stop* operations on D-Day (6-6-44).

MN631 No. 164 Sqn., B. 77 Gilze-Rijen, Holland, 2-45; flew rocket strikes against German barge traffic on the Rhine.

MN635 No. 440 Sqn., RCAF, Hurn, 6-44; flew dive bombing attack against German road reinforcements in Normandy, D-Day (6-6-44).

MN639 No. 168 Sqn., B. 78 Eindhoven, Holland, 10-44; flew bombing strikes with 1,000-lb bombs.

MN642 No. 184 Sqn., Westhampnett, 6-44; flew rocket attacks against German tanks on evening of D-Day (6-6-44); shot down by flak during armed reconnaissance south of Caen, D+1 (7-6-44); F/Sgt L. Tidbury missing.

MN645 No. 257 Sqn., Need's Oar Point, 4-44, '**FM-F**'; flew dive bombing attacks against German radar stations on French coast, 5-44.

MN647 No. 247 Sqn., Hurn, 4-44, '**ZY-S**'; flew rocket attacks against German radar stations on French coast, 5-44.

MN661 Miscellaneous external store trials, HAL, Langley, and A & AEE, Boscombe Down, 1944.

MN663 No. 439 Sqn., RCAF, Hurn, 6-44; flew dive bombing attacks against three gun positions overlooking Normandy beachhead, D-Day (6-6-44).

MN664 No. 440 Sqn., RCAF, Hurn, 6-44; flew dive bombing attacks against German road reinforcements in evening of D-Day (6-6-44).

MN665 No. 439 Sqn., RCAF, Hurn, 6-44; flew dive bombing sorties on D-Day (6-6-44); B. 78 Eindhoven, Holland, 10-44.

MN667 No. 184 Sqn., Westhampnett, 6-44; flew rocket attacks against German tanks on evening of D-Day (6-6-44); shot down by flak on D+1 (7-6-44) during armed reconnaissance south of Caen; Flt Lt F. E. Holland posted missing.

MN681 No. 181 Sqn., Hurn, 4-44, '**EL-Z**', No. 182 Sqn., Hurn, 6-44; flew operations on D-Day (6-6-44). No. 183 Sqn., B. 103 Plantlunne, Germany, 4-45.

MN683 No. 174 Sqn., Holmesley South, 4-45, '**XP-F**'. No. 266 Sqn., B.8 Sommervieu, France, 7-44, '**ZH-R**'.

MN684 No. 194 Sqn., B.51 Lille–Vendeville, France, 9-44; B.70 Deurne, Belgium, 10-44; flown by Flt Lt R. C. C. Curwen in No. 146 Wing's bombing attack on German 15th Army HQ at Dordrecht, 20-10-44.

MN689 No. 197 Sqn., Need's Oar Point, 5-44; took part in attack on German radar station near Dieppe, 9-5-44.

MN691 No. 440 Sqn., RCAF, Hurn, 4-44, '**I8-V**'. No. 439 Sqn., RCAF, B.78 Eindhoven, Holland, 10-44; survived undamaged in

"*Bodenplatte*" attack of 1–1–45; B.150 Celle, Germany, 5–45.

MN692 No. 184 Sqn., Westhampnett, 4–44, '**BR-A**'; flew rocket attacks against German tanks on evening of D-Day (6–6–44).

MN701 No. 609 Sqn., Thorney Island, 4–44, '**PR-Z**'; weapon training with rocket projectiles.

MN710 No. 247 Sqn., Hurn, 6–44; took part in rocket attack on gun position north of Caen, D-Day (6–6–44).

MN712 No. 193 Sqn., Llanbedr, 4–44, '**DP-B**'; flew bombing strikes over French coast.

MN716 No. 193 Sqn., Llanbedr, 4–44, '**DP-B**'. No. 438 Sqn., RCAF, '**F3-A**', also inscribed '*Diane*'.

MN717 No. 175 Sqn., Holmesley South, 6–44; flew rocket and cannon attacks over Normandy, D-Day (6–6–44).

MN735 No. 198 Sqn., Thorney Island, 4–44, '**TP-M**'; defensive operations and shipping patrols over English Channel.

MN739 No. 266 Sqn., B.70 Deurne, Belgium, 1–45; damaged during "*Bodenplatte*" attack, 1–1–45, and probably written off.

MN752 No. 197 Sqn., Need's Oar Point, 4–44, '**OY-C**'; B.51 Lille–Vendeville, France, 9–44; B.70 Deurne, Belgium, 10–44; flown by W/Off D. G. Lovell in No. 146 Wing's bombing attack on the German 15th Army HQ at Dordrecht, 24–10–44.

MN753 No. 54 OTU, '**BF-R**'. Continued to carry this code with No. 174 Sqn., No. 121 Wing, 13–7–44, until lost to flak, 10–9–44, flown by Wg Cdr W. Pitt–Brown.

MN758 No. 438 Sqn., RCAF, Huntington, 4–44, '**F3-M**'; flew bombing attacks against flying bomb launch sites.

MN765 No. 439 Sqn., RCAF, B.78 Eindhoven, Holland, 10–44; believed damaged during "*Bodenplatte*", 1–1–45, and subsequently written off.

MN769 No. 263 Sqn., Harrowbeer, 4–44, '**HE-B**'; flew bombing *Rodeos* over Northern France, and later rocket attacks on German radar stations.

MN775 No. 181 Sqn., Hurn, 4–44, '**EL-N**'; flew *Roadsteads* and sweeps with rockets.

MN777 No. 440 Sqn., RCAF, Hurn, 4–44, '**I8-J**'; flew at least two bombing sorties against flying bomb launch sites.

MN779 No. 3 Sqn., Bradwell Bay, 4–44, '**QO-P**'; flew escorts for medium bombers attacking flying bomb launch sites.

MN794 No. 164 Sqn., Thorney Island, 4–44; flew bomb and rocket attacks on bridges and other targets in Northern France.

MN802 No. 183 Sqn., B.103 Plantlunne, Germany, 4–45; flew armed reconnaissance sorties over Germany during the final weeks of the War.

MN804 No. 54 OTU, 1944, '**II-E**'.

MN812 No. 245 Sqn., Holmesley South, 5–44; took part in Squadron's first rocket attack on fuel train in railway siding east of Le Mans, 7–5–44.

MN813 No. 245 Sqn., Holmesley South, 5–44; took part in Squadron's first rocket attack on fuel train in railway siding east of Le Mans, 7–5–44.

MN822 No. 137 Sqn., B.86 Helmond, Holland, 3–45; flew armed reconnaissance sorties over Germany during the final weeks of the War.

MN823 No. 263 Sqn., Harrowbeer, 5–44, '**HE-J**'. No. 247 Sqn., Hurn, 6–44; took part in rocket attack on gun position north of Caen, D-Day (6–6–44).

MN861 Miscellaneous external store trials, HAL, Langley, 1944.

MN862 No. 183 Sqn., B.67 Ursel, Belgium, 10–44; flown by Fg Off H. M. Mason, took part in rocket and cannon attack in support of assault on Walcheren, 1–11–44.

MN863 No. 137 Sqn., B.86 Helmond, Holland, 3–45; flew armed reconnaissance sorties over Germany during the final weeks of the war.

MN868 No. 609 Sqn., Thorney Island, 5–44, '**PR-W**'. No. 183 Sqn., B.67 Ursel, Belgium, 10–44; Lieut T. V. Drew took part in rocket and cannon attack in support of assault on Walcheren, 1–11–44.

MN870 No. 439 Sqn., RCAF, B.78 Eindhoven, Holland, 10–44; believed damaged during "*Bodenplatte*", 1–1–45, and possibly subsequently written off.

MN873 No. 184 Sqn., Westhampnett, 4–44; took part in Squadron's first Typhoon operation, 28–4–44, a dive bombing attack on railway bridge over a canal at Baupte, south of Cherbourg.

MN874 No. 175 Sqn., B.80 Volkel, Holland, 2–45; flew armed reconnaissance and rocket attacks on trains in Germany.

MN881 No. 197 Sqn., Need's Oar Point, 5–44, '**OV-E**'; B.51 Lille–Vendeville, 9–44; B.70 Deurne, Belgium, 10–44; flown by W/Off D. I. McFee in No. 146 Wing's bombing attack on German 15th Army HQ at Dordrecht, 24–10–44.

MN883 No. 263 Sqn., Harrowbeer, 5–44, '**HE-J**'; conversion training to bombing operations.

MN884 No. 198 Sqn., B. 103 Plantlunne, Germany, 4–45, '**TP-R**'; shipping and airfield strikes over Germany.

MN885 No. 164 Sqn., Thorney Island, 5–44; flew attacks against German radar stations on French coast.

MN886 No. 193 Sqn., Need's Oar Point, 5–44, '**DP-E**'; airfield and bridge strikes with 500-lb bombs over France.

MN889 No. 266 Sqn., B. 70 Deurne, Belgium; flown by Fg Off Cunnison in No. 146 Wing's bombing attack on German 15th Army HQ at Dordrecht, 24–10–44.

MN891 No. 182 Sqn., B.6 Coulombs, France, 7–44; Major D. H. Barlow, SAAF (CO), shot down by flak during rocket attack on enemy-occupied wood during Cabrank operations, 25–7–44; was seen to bale out, but posted missing.

MN893 No. 197 Sqn., B.51 Lille–Vendeville, 9–44; France; Cabrank operations over Belgium.

MN921 No. 197 Sqn., Need's Oar Point, 5–44, '**OV-X**'; B.51 Lille–Vendeville, France, 9–44; Cabrank operations over Belgium.

MN922 No. 137 Sqn., B.86 Helmond, Holland, 3–45; flew armed reconnaissance sorties over Germany in the final weeks of the War.

MN923 No. 183 Sqn., B.67 Ursel, Belgium, 10–44; Fg Off P. G. Murton took part in rocket and cannon attack in support of assault on Walcheren, 1–11–44.

MN924 No. 184 Sqn., B.80 Volkel, Holland, 1–45; escaped damage during "*Bodenplatte*", 1–1–45.

MN925 No. 197 Sqn., B.51 Lille–Vendeville, 9–44; B.70 Deurne, 10–44; flown by W/Off J. M. James in No. 146 Wing's bombing attack on German 15th Army HQ at Dordrecht, 24–10–44.

MN926 No. 193 Sqn., Need's Oar Point, 5–44, '**DP-E**', later '**DP-J**'; flew rocket attacks against German radar stations on French coast.

MN932 No. 266 Sqn., B.105 Drope, Germany, 4–45; flew close support operations with rockets against German road traffic in final weeks of the War.

MN941 Coded '**DJ-S**' and flown by Gp Capt D. J. Scott, DSO, OBE, DFC, commanding No. 123 Wing.

MN949 No. 247 Sqn., B.86 Helmond, Holland, 3–45; flew armed reconnaissance operations over Germany in final weeks of War.

MN951 No. 247 Sqn., Hurn, 5–44, '**ZY-V**'. No. 198 Sqn., B.103 Plantlunne, Germany, 4–45, '**TP-A**'.

MN955 No. 137 Sqn., B.78 Eindhoven, 9–44; Sqn Ldr G. Piltingsrud, DFC (CO), shot down in flames by Fw 190s during attack on train east of Goch, 24–9–44; believed killed.

MN956 No. 56 OTU, 1944, '**FE-P**'. No. 184 Sqn., Westhampnett, 6–44; flew rocket

attacks against German tanks on evening of D-Day (6–6–44).

MN970 No. 193 Sqn., Need's Oar Point, 5–44, '**DP-R**'; flew rocket attacks against German radar stations on French coast.

MN972 No. 175 Sqn., Holmesley South, 5–44, '**HH-H**'; flew long range rocket attacks against rail targets in France.

MN979 No. 247 Sqn., Hurn, 5–44, '**ZY-S**'; flew rocket strikes over French coast; B.86 Helmond, Holland, 3–45; re-issued to Squadron as replacement after "*Bodenplatte*", 1–1–45.

MN983 No. 175 Sqn., B.50 Vitry–en–Artois, France, 9–44; Flt Lt W. J. Moore missing after rocket attack on barges at Terneuzen, 11–9–44.

MN985 No. 198 Sqn., Thorney Island, 5–44, '**TP-B**'. No. 184 Sqn., B.80 Volkel, Holland, 1–45; escaped damage during "*Bodenplatte*", 1–1–45.

MN989 No. 263 Sqn., Harrowbeer, 5–44. No. 266 Sqn., B.3 St Croix, France, 8–44; Sqn Ldr J. D. Wright, (CO), force landed at B.3 with flak damage after attack in Falaise area, 9–8–44; aircraft repaired and flown by No. 266 Sqn., at B.70 Deurne, Belgium; flown by F/Sgt Morgan in rocket attack on German HQ south of Breda, 13–10–44.

MN990 No. 137 Sqn., B.86 Helmond, Holland, 3–45; flew armed reconnaissance sorties over Germany in final weeks of the War.

MN991 No. 257 Sqn., Need's Oar Point, 4–44; flew dive bombing attacks against German radar stations on French coast.

MN992 No. 181 Sqn., Hurn, 5–44, '**EL-E**'; flew rocket attacks against German radar stations on French coast.

MN993 No. 245 Sqn., B.5 Le Fresny/Camille, France. No. 266 Sqn., B.70 Deurne, Belgium, 10–44; flown by Plt Off Hulley in rocket attack on German HQ south of Breda, 13–10–44. No. 168 Sqn., B.78 Eindhoven, Holland, 10–44; flew fighter cover for Typhoon bombers.

MN995 No. 182 Sqn., B.6 Coulombs, France, 6–44, '**XM-A**'; flew Cabrank operations with rockets over Normandy beachhead.

MN996 No. 197 Sqn., B.51 Lille–Vendeville, France, 9–44; B.70 Deurne, Belgium, 11–44; Cabrank operations in support of ground forces.

MN997 No. 184 Sqn., B.80 Volkel, Holland, 1–45; escaped damage in "*Bodenplatte*", 1–1–45; B.110 Achmer, Germany, 4–45; flew shipping strikes in final weeks of the War.

MN999 No. 168 Sqn., B.78 Eindhoven, Holland, 10–44; flew fighter cover for Typhoon bombers.

MP113 No. 197 Sqn., B.51 Lille–Vendeville, France, 9–44; B.70 Deurne, Belgium, 11–44; B.89 Mill, Holland, 3–45.

MP115 No. 257 Sqn., B.15 Ryes, France, 7–44, '**FM-K**'; flew rocket attacks against German armoured vehicles beyond Normandy beachhead. No. 198 Sqn., B.103 Plantlunne, Germany, 4–45, '**TP-E**'.

MP116 No. 257 Sqn., B.15 Ryes, France, 7–44; flew rocket attacks against German armoured vehicles beyond Normandy beachhead.

MP118 No. 55 OTU, 1944.

MP119 No. 197 Sqn., Need's Oar Point, 6–44, '**OV-I**'; B.3 St Croix, France, 8–44; Sqn Ldr A. H. Smith, RNZAF, led bombing attack on Germany infantry in wood at Le Thiel, 8–8–44.

MP123 No. 197 Sqn., B.51 Lille–Vendeville, 9–44; B.70 Deurne, Belgium, 11–44; attended Armament Practice Camp, Fairwood Common, 1–12–44 until 11–12–44.

MP124 No. 257 Sqn., B.15 Ryes, France, '**FM-L**'; flew rocket attacks against German armoured vehicles beyond Normandy beachhead.

MP126 No. 247 Sqn., B.6 Coulombs, France, 6–44, '**ZY-Y**'; flew armed reconnaissance sorties around Caen.

MP130 No. 440 Sqn., RCAF, B.110 Osnabrück,

Germany, 4–45; setpiece strikes with 1,000-lb and cluster bombs against airfields and other targets in Germany.

MP132 No. 198 Sqn., Hurn, 6–44, '**TP-X**'; flew rocket *Ramrod* against German transport vehicles on Falaise–Caen road, D-Day (6–6–44).

MP133 No. 184 Sqn., Holmesley South, 6–44; flew limited ground support operations over Normandy beachhead after D-Day (6–6–44).

MP134 No. 439 Sqn., RCAF, B.78 Eindhoven, Holland, 1–45; badly damaged in "*Bodenplatte*", 1–1–45.

MP136 No. 439 Sqn., B.78 Eindhoven, 10–44; offensive strikes with 1,000-lb bombs in support of ground forces.

MP143 No. 197 Sqn., B.51 Lille–Vendeville, 9–44; B.70 Deurne, Belgium, 10–44; flown by F/Sgt J. K. Byrne in No. 146 Wing's bombing attack on German 15th Army HQ at Dordrecht, 24–10–44.

MP146 No. 184 Sqn., B.5 Le Fresny Camille, France, 8–44; Fg Off R. J. Currie, RCAF, shot down by flak during rocket attack on German AFVs near Trun, 18–8–44.

MP151 No. 193 Sqn., Need's Oar Point, 6–44, '**DP-I**'. No. 439 Sqn., RCAF, B.78 Eindhoven, Holland, 10–44; ground support strikes with 1,000-lb bombs.

MP157 No. 197 Sqn., B.51 Lille–Vendeville, 9–44; flew Cabrank support operations.

MP174 No. 266 Sqn., B.70 Deurne, Belgium, 10–44; flown by F/Sgt Palte in rocket attack on German HQ south of Breda, 13–10–44.

MP176 No. 175 Sqn., Holmesley South and B.3 St Croix, France, 6–44; attacked with rockets a château north of Caen occupied by Hitler Youth, 8–7–44.

MP180 No. 266 Sqn., B.8 Sommervieu, France, 7–44; B.70 Deurne, Belgium, 10–44; flown by F/Sgt Shepherd in rocket attack on German HQ south of Breda, 13–10–44.

MP184 No. 175 Sqn., B.150 Hustedt, Germany, 4–45; flew armed reconnaissance and rocket attacks against German road and rail targets in final weeks of the War.

MP188 No. 197 Sqn., B.51 Lille–Vendeville, France, 9–44; B.70 Deurne, Belgium, 11–44; B.89 Mill, Holland, 3–45; flew interdiction strikes in Hengelo–Rheine area.

MP190 No. 197 Sqn., B.70 Deurne, Belgium, 11–44; B.89 Mill, Holland, 3–45; flew interdiction strikes in Hengelo–Rheine area.

MP194 No. 197 Sqn., B.70 Deurne, Belgium, 10–44; Sqn Ldr A. H. Smith, RNZAF, led No. 197 Squadron in No. 146 Wing's bombing attack on German 15th Army HQ at Dordrecht, 24–10–44.

MP195 No. 137 Sqn., Manston, 6–44; defensive patrols to combat flying bombs.

MP199 No. 197 Sqn., B.89 Mill, Holland, 3–45; flew interdiction strikes in Hengelo–Rheine area.

Sixth production batch of 400 aircraft produced by Gloster Aircraft Ltd., Brockworth, Gloucester. All aircraft with sliding hood, whip aerial, faired cannon, exhaust shrouds and four–blade propeller; most aircraft with Napier Sabre IIA engine but a few among the final 255 were powered by Sabre IIB. PD446–PD480, PD492–PD536, PD548–PD577, PD589–PD623; RB192–RB235; RB248–RB289; RB303–RB347; RB361–RB408; RB423–RB459; RB474–RB512. Deliveries commenced 15–6–44, completed 5–1–45; average rate of production, approximately 2 aircraft per day.

PD447 No. 197 Sqn., B.51 Lille–Vendeville, France, 9–44; B.70 Deurne, Belgium, 10–44; flown by F/Sgt D. E. Tapson in No. 146 Wing's bombing attack on German 15th Army HQ at Dordrecht, 24–10–44.

PD449 No. 609 Sqn., B.53 Merville, France, 9–44; flew rocket attacks against German road transport during Allied advance through Belgium.

PD451 No. 439 Sqn., RCAF, B.58 Melsbroek, Belgium, 9–44; ground support operations

and offensive strikes with 1,000-lb bombs.

PD452 No. 440 Sqn., RCAF, B.58 Melsbroek, Belgium, 9–44, '**I8-X**'; flew numerous bombing attacks with 500-lb and 1,000-lb bombs against German rail targets.

PD456 No. 198 Sqn., B.103 Plantlunne, Germany, '**TP-J**', 4–45; flew shipping strike in Kiel Bay, 3–5–45 (Squadron's final operation).

PD460 No. 197 Sqn., B.51 Lille–Vendeville, France, 9–44; B.70 Deurne, Belgium, 10–44; flown by Fg Off G. G. Mahaffy in No. 146 Wing's bombing attack on German 15th Army HQ at Dordrecht, 24–10–44.

PD466 No. 609 Sqn., B.53 Merville, France, 9–44; coded '**WD**' and flown by Wg Cdr W. Dring, DFC, Wing Leader, No. 123 Wing, September to November 1944. No. 198 Sqn., B.103 Plantlunne, Germany, '**TP-S**', 4–45; flew shipping strike in Kiel Bay, 3–5–45 (Squadron's final operation).

PD471 No. 197 Sqn., B.70 Deurne, Belgium, 11–44; setpiece bombing and rocket attacks.

PD473 No. 266 Sqn., B.23 Morainville, France, 9–44; B.70 Deurne, Belgium, 1–45.

PD477 No. 197 Sqn., B.70 Deurne, Belgium, 11–44; attended Armament Practice Camp, Fairwood Common, 1–12–44 to 11–12–44.

PD492 No. 439 Sqn., RCAF, B.78 Eindhoven, Holland, 10–44; support of Canadian ground forces with 1,000-lb bombs.

PD494 No. 175 Sqn., B.24 Beauvais, France, 9–44; took part in rocket attack on barges at Terneuzen, 11–9–44.

PD495 No. 247 Sqn., B.58 Melsbroek, Belgium, 9–44; flew numerous armed reconnaissance sorties with rockets.

PD496 No. 184 Sqn., B.110 Achmer, Germany, 4–45; flew shipping strike off German coast, 4–5–45 (Squadron's final operation).

PD497 No. 198 Sqn., B.103 Plantlunne, Germany, 4–45, '**TP-C**'; flew shipping strike in Kiel Bay, 3–5–45 (Squadron's final operation).

PD499 No. 198 Sqn., B.35 Baromesnil, France, 9–44, '**TP-C**'; flew rocket–armed Cabrank sorties in support of advancing forces.

PD500 No. 193 Sqn., B.23 Morainville, France, 9–44, '**DP-S**'. No. 183 Sqn., B.67 Ursel, Belgium, 10–44; Fg Off J. A. Hollingworth took part in rocket and cannon attack in support of assault on Walcheren, 1–11–44.

PD501 No. 266 Sqn., B.23 Morainville, France, 9–44, '**ZH-Z**'; B.70 Deurne, Belgium, 1–45; badly damaged in "*Bodenplatte*", 1–1–45.

PD504 No. 266 Sqn., B.70 Deurne, Belgium, 10–44; Sqn Ldr J. H. Deall led Squadron in attack with rockets on German HQ south of Breda, 13–10–44; and on 24–10–44 he led the Squadron in No. 146 Wing's bombing attack on the German 15th Army HQ at Dordrecht.

PD507 No. 197 Sqn., B.89 Mill, Holland, 3–45; flew interdiction strikes in Hengelo–Rheine area.

PD508 No. 198 Sqn., B.103 Plantlunne, Germany, 4–45, '**TP-T**'; flew shipping strike in Kiel Bay, 3–5–45 (Squadron's final operation).

PD510 No. 440 Sqn., RCAF, B.110 Osnabrück, Germany, 4–45; flew interdiction strikes with 1,000-lb bombs ahead of Canadian ground forces.

PD511 No. 164 Sqn., B.77 Gilze Rijen, 2–45; replacement aircraft issued after "*Bodenplatte*"; flew rocket attacks against German barges on the Rhine.

PD514 No. 266 Sqn., B.105 Drope, Germany, 4–45; returned to UK for Armament Practice Camp, Fairwood Common, 27–4–45 to 4–6–45.

PD516 No. 183 Sqn., B.67 Ursel, Belgium, 11–44; Fg Off J. A. Hollingworth missing after rocket attack on "Quisling" HQ in wood NNE of Ede, 19–11–44.

PD519 No. 609 Sqn., B.53 Merville, France, 9–44; flew rocket attacks against German road transport during Allied advance through Belgium.

PD521 Nos. 257 and 266 Sqns., No. 146 Wing,

from 12–9–44, coded '**JB-II**'; flown by Wg Cdr J. R. Baldwin, DSO, DFC, Wing Leader, No. 146 Wing, until 10–44. Aircraft destroyed by a direct hit by V–2 rocket which landed on a dispersal at B.70 Deurne (Antwerp), Belgium, 25–10–44, killing five groundcrew and wounding six others.

PD527 No. 266 Sqn., B.70 Deurne, Belgium, 10–44; flown by F/Sgt Palte in rocket attack on German HQ south of Breda, 13–10–44; flown by Fg Off Borland in No. 146 Wing's bombing attack on German 15th Army HQ at Dordrecht, 24–10–44.

PD528 No. 266 Sqn., B.70 Deurne, Belgium, 1–45; believed to have been damaged during "*Bodenplatte*", 1–1–45.

PD531 No. 197 Sqn., B.51 Lille–Vendeville, France, 9–44, '**OV-K**'; flew Cabrank operations in support of ground forces advancing into Holland.

PD534 No. 197 Sqn., B.89 Mill, Holland, 3–45; flew several low–level cannon and rocket attacks on German airfields, 4–45.

PD551 No. 137 Sqn., B.6 Coulombs, France, 8–44, '**SF-U**'; flew numerous Cabrank sorties in support of ground forces advancing eastwards through France.

PD553 No. 266 Sqn., B.70 Deurne, Belgium, 10–44; flown by Fg Off McAdam in No. 146 Wing's bombing attack on German 15th Army HQ at Dordrecht, 24–10–44.

PD559 No. 175 Sqn., B.80 Volkel, Holland, 2–45; flew rocket attacks against road and rail targets in Germany.

PD560 No. 175 Sqn., B.24 Beauvais, France, 9–44; B.150 Hustedt, Germany, 4–45.

PD564 No. 439 Sqn., RCAF, B.78 Eindhoven, Holland, 1–45; damaged in "*Bodenplatte*", 1–1–45.

PD576 No. 266 Sqn., B.105 Drope, Germany, 4–45; returned to UK for Armament Practice Camp, Fairwood, Common, 27–4–45 to 4–6–45.

PD589 No. 440 Sqn., RCAF, B.78 Eindhoven, 10–44, '**I8-R**'; flew attacks on railway targets with 1,000-lb bombs.

PD605 No. 198 Sqn., B.91 Kluis, Holland, 3–45; coded '**DJS**' and flown by Gp Capt D. J. Scott, DSO, OBE, DFC, Commanding No. 84 Group Support Unit; written off, 11–4–45.

PD606 No. 183 Sqn., B.103 Plantlunne, Germany, 4–45; flew armed reconnaissance sorties over Germany until the end of the War.

PD608 No. 439 Sqn., RCAF, B.78 Eindhoven, Holland, 10–44, '**5V-G**'; escaped damage in "*Bodenplatte*"; B.150 Celle, Germany, 5–45.

PD611 No. 137 Sqn., B.86 Helmond, Holland, 3–45; flew rocket-armed Cabrank sorties in the final weeks of the War.

PD613 No. 168 Sqn., B.78 Eindhoven, 10–44; flew fighter cover for Typhoon bombers, but believed badly damaged in "*Bodenplatte*", 1–1–45, and subsequently written off.

PD618 No. 198 Sqn., B.103 Plantlunne, Germany, 4–45, '**TP-U**'; flew shipping strike in Kiel Bay, 3–5–45 (Squadron's final operation).

RB193 No. 137 Sqn., B.86 Helmond, Holland, 3–45; flew rocket–armed Cabrank sorties in final weeks of the War.

RB198 No. 439 Sqn., RCAF, B.78 Eindhoven, Holland, 1–45; believed badly damaged in "*Bodenplatte*", 1–1–45, and subsequently written off.

RB200 No. 184 Sqn., B.80 Volkel, Holland, 1–45; was absent on patrol during "*Bodenplatte*", 1–1–45, and escaped damage.

RB203 No. 440 Sqn., RCAF, B.110 Osnabrück, Germany, 4–45; flew interdiction strikes with 1,000-lb bombs ahead of Canadian ground forces.

RB205 No. 440 Sqn., RCAF, B.78 Eindhoven, Holland, from 26–10–44; coded '**FGG**' and flown by Wg Cdr F. G. Grant, DSO, DFC, Wing Leader, No. 143 (Canadian) Wing, until aircraft written off in "*Bodenplatte*", 1–1–45.

RB207 No. 438 Sqn., RCAF (location unknown), 1945, **'F3-T'**.

RB209 No. 168 Sqn., B.78 Eindhoven, Holland; struck a Typhoon of No. 247 Sqn. while taking off and overturned, killing the pilot, 2–1–45.

RB211 No. 197 Sqn., B.89 Mill, Holland, 3–45; flew interdiction strikes in Hengelo–Rheine area.

RB212 No. 197 Sqn., B.89 Mill, Holland, 3–45; flew interdiction strikes in Hengelo–Rheine area.

RB214 No. 175 Sqn., B.80 Volkel, Holland, 2–45; Sqn Ldr M. Savage shot down and killed by flak during attack on train, 19–3–45.

RB215 No. 175 Sqn., B.80 Volkel, Holland, 10–44; flew rocket attacks on German rail targets.

RB216 No. 175 Sqn., B.150 Hustedt, Germany, 4–45; flew armed reconnaissance sorties during final weeks of the War.

RB219 No. 266 Sqn., B.70 Deurne, Belgium, 1–45; damaged in *"Bodenplatte"* and possibly written off.

RB222 No. 183 Sqn., B.77 Gilze-Rijen, Holland, 11–44, **'HF-K'**; B.103 Plantlunne, Germany, 4–45; flew armed reconnaissance sorties over Germany until the end of the War.

RB223 No. 198 Sqn., B.103 Plantlunne, Germany, 4–45, **'TP-X'**. No. 266 Sqn., B.105 Drope, Germany, 4–45; armed reconnaissance sorties over Germany.

RB225 No. 247 Sqn., B.86 Helmond, Holland, 3–45; issued to Squadron as replacement following *"Bodenplatte"*, 1–1–45.

RB227 No. 193 Sqn., B.70 Deurne, Belgium, 11–44, **'DP-P'**; flew setpiece bombing strikes when weather permitted.

RB228 No. 197 Sqn., Fairwood Common (Armament Practice Camp), 11–44; B.70 Deurne, Belgium, 12–44; B.89 Mill, Holland, 3–45; flew interdiction strikes in Hengelo-Rheine area.

RB230 No. 197 Sqn., B.89 Mill, Holland, 3–45; flew interdiction strikes in Hengelo-Rheine area.

RB232 No. 439 Sqn., RCAF, B.78 Eindhoven, Holland, 1–45; believed written off after *"Bodenplatte"*, 1–1–45.

RB248 No. 266 Sqn., B.105 Drope, Germany, 4–45; rocket attacks on oil installations and transport targets.

RB250 No. 609 Sqn., B.77 Gilze-Rijen, Holland, 3–45; armed reconnaissance patrols over Germany.

RB251 No. 197 Sqn., B.89 Mill, Holland, 3–45; interdiction strikes over Germany.

RB252 No. 137 Sqn., B.86 Helmond, Holland, 3–45; rocket attacks on German oil installations.

RB254 No. 137 Sqn., B.78 Eindhoven, Holland, 11–44, **'SF-B'**; armed reconnaissance patrols over forward Allied ground forces. No. 193 Sqn., B.70 Deurne, Belgium, 1–45, **'DP-U'**.

RB255 No. 439 Sqn., RCAF, B.78 Eindhoven, 11–44, **'5V-S'**; believed written off after *"Bodenplatte"*, 1–1–45.

RB258 No. 183 Sqn., B.103 Plantlunne, Germany, 4–45; armed reconnaissance patrols over Germany.

RB259 No. 193 Sqn., B.70 Deurne, Belgium, 1–45; bombing strikes against German oil installations.

RB260 No. 266 Sqn., B.70 Deurne, Belgium, 1–45; rocket strikes against German oil installations.

RB262 No. 439 Sqn., RCAF, B.150 Celle, Germany, 5–45.

RB264 No. 164 Sqn., B.77 Gilze-Rijen, Holland, 2–45; rocket strikes against German barge traffic on the Rhine.

RB281 No. 439 Sqn., RCAF, B.78 Eindhoven, Holland, 1–45; was undamaged in *"Bodenplatte"*, 1–1–45.

RB303 No. 174 Sqn., B.78 Eindhoven, Holland, 11–44, **'XP-K'**.

RB304 No. 175 Sqn., B.80 Volkel, Holland, 2–45; flew rocket attacks on German rail targets.

RB306 External store trials, HAL, Langley, and A & AEE, Boscombe Down, 1944–45; cluster bombs from 14–11–44; supply containers from 14–12–44; practice bombs from 21–2–45.

RB310 No. 440 Sqn., RCAF, B.110 Osnabrück, Germany, 4–45.

RB311 No. 609 Sqn., B.77 Gilze-Rijen, Holland, 11–44; armed reconnaissance.

RB316 No. 197 Sqn., B.89 Mill, Holland, 3–45; interdiction strikes over Germany.

RB318 No. 137 Sqn., B.78 Eindhoven, Holland, 11–44; B.86 Helmond, Holland, 3–45.

RB324 No. 439 Sqn., RCAF, B.150 Celle, Germany, 5–45.

RB326 No. 439 Sqn., RCAF, B.150 Celle, Germany, 5–45.

RB332 No. 164 Sqn., B.77 Gilze-Rijen, Holland, 2–45; rocket strikes against German barge traffic on the Rhine.

RB341 No. 181 Sqn., B.78 Eindhoven, Holland, 11–44, **'EL-R'**

RB344 No. 247 Sqn., B.86 Helmond, Holland, 3–45; issued as replacement aircraft after *"Bodenplatte"*, 1–1–45.

RB347 No. 175 Sqn., B.150 Hustedt, Germany, 4–45.

RB369 No. 439 Sqn., RCAF, B.150 Celle, Germany, 5–45.

RB377 No. 440 Sqn., RCAF, B.78 Eindhoven, Holland, 12–44, **'I8-Z'**.

RB378 No. 247 Sqn., B.86 Helmond, Holland, 3–45.

RB379 Was the only Typhoon shipped to Russia, c.12–44.

RB380 No. 245 Sqn., B.80 Volkel, Holland, 4–45; coded **'PN'** and flown by Wing Leader, No. 121 Wing. To Group Disbandment Centre, 8–45. Became Ground Instruction Machine, **5653M**, 9–45.

RB383 No. 184 Sqn., B.80 Volkel, Holland, 11–44.

RB389 No. 440 Sqn., RCAF, B.100 Goch, Germany, 3–45, **'I8-P'**, *"Pulverizer IV"*.

RB391 No. 438 Sqn., RCAF, B.78 Eindhoven, Holland, 11–44, **'F3-Y'**.

RB400 No. 184 Sqn., B.110 Achmer, Germany; shipping strikes off German coast, 4–45.

RB402 No. 439 Sqn., RCAF, B.150 Celle, Germany, 5–45, **'5V-P'**.

RB408 No. 184 Sqn., B.110 Achmer, Germany; shipping strikes off German coast, 4–45.

RB423 No. 266 Sqn., B.105 Drope, Germany, 4–45; rocket strikes on oil installations.

RB425 No. 440 Sqn., RCAF, B.110 Osnabrück, Germany, 4–45.

RB426 No. 266 Sqn., B.105 Drope, Germany, 4–45; rocket strikes on oil installations.

RB427 No. 440 Sqn., RCAF, B.78 Eindhoven, Holland, 11–44, **'I8-A'**. No. 168 Sqn., B.78 Eindhoven, Holland, 1–45.

RB431 No. 609 Sqn., B.77 Gilze-Rijen, Holland, 2–45; coded **'JCB'** and flown by Wg Cdr J. C. Button, DSO, DFC, Wing Leader, No 123 Wing, 1/2–45; *"Zipp XI"*.

RB441 No. 439 Sqn., RCAF, B.78 Eindhoven, Holland, 11–44, **'5V-Z'**.

RB445 No. 440 Sqn., RCAF, B.110 Osnabrück, Germany, 4–45.

RB448 No. 183 Sqn., B.103 Plantlunne, Germany, 4–45; armed reconnaissance patrols.

RB451 No. 266 Sqn., B.70 Deurne, Belgium, 11–44, **'ZH-U'**; armed reconnaissance patrols.

RB453 No. 183 Sqn., B.103 Plantlunne, Germany, 4–45; armed reconnaissance patrols.

RB457 No. 174 Sqn., B.78 Eindhoven, Holland, 11–44, **'XP-Y'**.

RB459 No. 247 Sqn., B.86 Helmond, Holland, 3–45.

RB474 No. 197 Sqn., B.89 Mill, Holland, 3–45; interdiction operations over Germany.

RB475 No. 440 Sqn., RCAF, B.110 Osnabrück, Germany, 4–45.

RB477 No. 439 Sqn., RCAF, B.150 Celle, Germany, 5–45.

RB478 No. 266 Sqn., B.105 Drope, Germany, 4–45; rocket strikes on oil installations.

RB484 No. 164 Sqn., B.91 Kluis, Holland, 3–45; rocket strikes against barge traffic on the Rhine.

RB485 No. 440 Sqn., RCAF, B.110 Osnabrück, Germany, 4–45.

RB492 No. 175 Sqn., B.150 Hustedt, Germany, 4–45.

RB494 No. 440 Sqn., RCAF, B.110 Osnabrück, Germany, 4–45.

RB495 No. 440 Sqn., RCAF, B.78 Eindhoven, Holland, 1–45, **'I8-T'**; B.110 Osnabrück, Germany, 4–45.

RB499 No. 168 Sqn., B.78 Eindhoven, Holland, 1–45.

RB504 No. 137 Sqn., B.86 Helmond, Holland, 3–45; rocket attacks on oil installations.

RB506 No. 440 Sqn., RCAF, B.110 Osnabrück, Germany, 4–45.

RB511 No. 175 Sqn., B.80 Volkel, Holland, 1–45; B.150 Hustedt, Germany, 4–45.

Seventh and final production batch of 300 aircraft (299 built), ordered from Gloster Aircraft Co., Ltd., Brockworth, Gloucester. Napier Sabre IIB engines. SW386–SW428, SW443–SW478, SW493–SW537, SW551–SW596, SW620–SW668, SW681–SW716, SW728–SW772. Deliveries commenced 5–1–45, completed 13–11–45; average rate of production, slightly under one aircraft per day.

SW398 No. 438 Sqn., RCAF, B.78 Eindhoven, Holland, 1–45, **'F3-E'**.

SW399 No. 175 Sqn., B.80 Volkel, Holland, 1–45, **'HH-K'**; B.150 Hustedt, Germany, 4–45.

SW401 No. 440 Sqn., RCAF, B.110 Osnabrück, Germany, 4–45.

SW403 No. 137 Sqn., B.86 Helmond, Holland, 1–45; rocket attacks on oil installations.

SW407 No. 175 Sqn., B.80 Volkel, Holland, 2–45; rocket attacks on German rail targets.

SW408 *Deleted from Contract.*

SW410 No. 164 Sqn., B.91 Kluis, Holland, 3–45. CCFIS, aircraft 'E'.

SW413 No. 184 Sqn., B.110 Achmer, Germany, 4–45.

SW414 No. 438 Sqn., RCAF, B.78 Eindhoven, Holland, 2–45, **'F3-G'**. No. 183 Sqn., B.103 Plantlunne, Germany, 4–45.

SW419 No. 263 Sqn., B.105 Drope, Germany, 3–45, **'HE-C'**.

SW421 No. 184 Sqn., B.110 Achmer, Germany, 4–45.

SW423 No. 439 Sqn., RCAF, B.78 Eindhoven, Holland, 3–45, **'5V-J'**.

SW426 No. 137 Sqn., B.120 Langenhagen, Germany, 4–45.

SW428 No. 440 Sqn., RCAF, B.78 Eindhoven, Holland, 3–45, **'I8-S'**; B.110 Osnabrück, Germany, 4–45.

SW444 No. 184 Sqn., B.100 Goch, Germany, 3–45; B.110 Osnabrück, Germany, 4–45.

SW446 No. 439 Sqn., RCAF, B.118 Celle, Germany, 5–45.

SW450 No. 175 Sqn., B.150 Hustedt, Germany, 4–45.

SW452 No. 440 Sqn., RCAF, B.110 Osnabrück, Germany, 4–45.

SW454 No. 183 Sqn., B.103 Plantlunne, Germany, 4–45; armed reconnaissance patrols.

SW455 No. 183 Sqn., B.103 Plantlunne, Germany, 4–45; armed reconnaissance patrols.

SW459 No. 439 Sqn., RCAF, B.100 Goch, Germany, 4–45. No. 183 Sqn., B.103 Plantlunne, Germany, 4–45; armed reconnaissance patrols.

SW460 No. 439 Sqn., RCAF, B.100 Goch, Germany, 4–45.

SW461 No. 247 Sqn., B.86 Helmond, Holland, 3–45.

SW462 No. 440 Sqn., RCAF, B.110 Osnabrück, Germany, 4–45.

SW463 No. 183 Sqn., B.103 Plantlunne, Germany, 4–45; armed reconnaissance sorties.

SW464 No. 175 Sqn., B.100 Goch, Germany, 4–45, **'HH-D'**.

SW466 No. 183 Sqn., B.103 Plantlunne, Ger-

SW472 No. 198 Sqn., B.103 Plantlunne, Germany, 4–45, '**TP-K**'; armed reconnaissance sorties.

SW473 No. 137 Sqn., B.120 Langenhagen, Germany, 4–45.

SW474 No. 56 OTU, '**HQ-K**', 4–45.

SW478 No. 198 Sqn., B.103 Plantlunne, Germany, 4–45, '**TP-K**'; armed reconnaissance sorties.

SW501 No. 609 Sqn., B.116 Wunstorf, Germany, 5–45.

SW503 No. 183 Sqn., B.103 Plantlunne, Germany, 4–45; armed reconnaissance sorties.

SW504 No. 247 Sqn., B.86 Helmond, Holland, 3–45. No. 609 Sqn., B.116 Wunstorf, Germany, 5–45.

SW509 No. 183 Sqn., B.103 Plantlunne, Germany, 4–45; armed reconnaissance sorties.

SW510 No. 137 Sqn., B.120 Langenhagen, Germany, 4–45.

SW512 No. 184 Sqn., B.164 Schleswig, Germany, 5–45.

SW515 No. 184 Sqn., B.110 Achmer, Germany, 4–45; shipping strikes off German coast.

SW520 No. 198 Sqn., B.103 Plantlunne, Germany, 4–45, '**TP-E**'.

SW523 No. 56 OTU, 5–45, '**HQ-D**'.

SW529 No. 175 Sqn., B.150 Hustedt, Germany, 4–45.

SW531 No. 59 OTU, 5–45, '**II-A**'.

SW536 No. 609 Sqn., B.116 Wunstorf, Germany, 5–45.

SW537 No. 439 Sqn., RCAF, B.118 Celle, Germany, 5–45.

SW555 Miscellaneous trials, HAL, Langley, including rudder bias cables from 7–7–45.

SW556 No. 198 Sqn., B.103 Plantlunne, Germany, 4–45, '**TP-P**'.

SW561 No. 137 Sqn., B.156 Lüneburg, Germany, 5–45.

SW562 No. 59 OTU, 5–45, '**II-D**'.

SW564 No. 175 Sqn., B.150 Hustedt, Germany, 4–45 ('*Tilly the Toiler*').

SW566 No. 609 Sqn., B.116 Wunstorf, Germany, 6–45, '**PR-H**'.

SW568 No. 59 OTU, '**II-E**'.

SW570 No. 263 Sqn., B.111 Ahlhorn, Germany, 5–45.

SW572 No. 59 OTU, 5–45, '**II-S**'.

SW575 No. 59 OTU, 5–45, '**II-H**'.

SW586 No. 263 Sqn., B.111 Ahlhorn, Germany, 5–45.

SW587 No. 184 Sqn., B.164 Schleswig, Germany, 6–45.

SW588 No. 263 Sqn., B.111 Ahlhorn, Germany, 5–45.

SW591 No. 59 OTU, 5–45, '**II-P**'.

SW593 No. 59 OTU, 5–45, '**II-C**'.

SW621 No. 56 OTU, 1945.

SW622 No. 56 OTU, 1945.

SW624 No. 56 OTU, 1945.

SW625 No. 56 OTU, 1945.

SW627 No. 55 OTU, 1945, '**UW-X**'.

SW628 No. 55 OTU, 1945, '**UW-M**'. No. 59 OTU, 5–45, '**II-H**'.

SW629 No. 59 OTU, 5–45, '**II-L**'.

SW631 No. 59 OTU, 6–45, '**II-M**'.

SW632 No. 59 OTU, 5–45, '**II-K**'.

SW633 No. 59 OTU, 6–45, '**II-O**'.

SW634 No. 59 OTU, 5–45, '**II-N**'.

SW635 No. 59 OTU, 6–45, '**II-P**'.

SW636 No. 59 OTU, 5–45, '**II-T**'.

SW641 No. 440 Sqn., RCAF, B.166, Flensburg, Germany, 6–45.

HAWKER F.10/41 TEMPEST

Tempest V and VI Prototype. One prototype, formerly referred to as Typhoon Mark II, HM595. Designed to Air Ministry Specification F.10/41; ordered under Contract No. 1986/C.23a. Napier Sabre II (No. S1001) driving DH four-blade propeller (No. 50004). Ff 2–9–42, P. G. Lucas; with modified fin, 24–9–42; fully extended dorsal fin, 17–11–42. Modified as Tempest VI prototype with 2,340-hp Napier Sabre V (No. S5055). Ff 9–5–44, W. Humble. With Sabre V No. S5063 driving Rotol four-blade propeller, 23–9–44; with engine No. S5073, 9–2–45.

Tempest I Prototype. One prototype, formerly referred to as Typhoon Mark II, HM599. Designed to Air Ministry Specification F.10/41; ordered under Contract No. 1640/23a and covered by Works Order No. 2100 dated 24–11–41. Napier Sabre IV (No. S 75) driving DH four-blade propeller, No. 50004. Ff 24–2–43, P. G. Lucas; with engine No S.76, 26–3–43; engine No S.72, 4–6–43; engine No. S.2904, 19–8–43.

Tempest II Prototypes. Two prototypes, LA602 and LA607. Original design commenced as Centaurus project scheme employing Typhoon airframe under Air Ministry Specification F.18/37 but, amalgamating Centaurus installation in Tornado HG641 with Typhoon II, being designed to Air Ministry Specification F.10/41, emerged as Tempest II. 1st prototype, LA602, ordered under Contract No. 1986/23a and covered by Works Order No. 720006 dated 27–10–42. Ff 28–6–43, P. G. Lucas, with Centaurus IV No. C80023 driving Rotol four-blade propeller No. EH294; engine No. C80191, 5–12–43; dorsal fin added, 17–2–44. 2nd prototype covered by Works Order No. 720015, dated 6–11–42. Ff 18–9–43, P. G. Lucas, with Centaurus IV No. C80145 driving Rotol four-blade propeller No. EH282. Rotol five-blade propeller No. EH318, 13–11–43; engine No. C80421 with auto gills, 5–5–44; Centaurus V No. C81071, 7–7–44; engine No. C80060, 28–12–44. (Note: A third prototype, LA610, was ordered under Contract No. 1986/23a but completed as a prototype F.2/43 Fury with Griffon 85 driving Rotol contraprop, and is therefore beyond the scope of this work.)

HAWKER TEMPEST V

First production batch of 100 aircraft built by Hawker Aircraft Ltd., Langley, Buckinghamshire. JN729–JN773, JN792–JN822, JN854–JN877. Most aircraft completed as Series 1 (with long-barrel Hispano Mark II cannon) and some as Series 2 (with short-barrel Hispano Mark V cannon); some aircraft retrospectively modified to Series 2 standard. One aircraft, JN750, completed as a Tempest Mark II. Deliveries to RAF commenced 12–43, completed 5–44; average rate of production, approximately four aircraft per week.

JN729 ff 21–6–43, W. Humble. Performance and handling trials, HAL, Langley, and A & AEE, Boscombe Down, 1943–44.

JN730 ff 12–10–43, P. G. Lucas. Special coolant header tank. Drop tank TIs, 1944; HAL, Langley, and A & AEE, Boscombe Down.

JN731 Airframe development; modified ailerons, spring tabs, etc. Evaluation by HAL, Langley, 1943–44.

JN733 No. 3 Sqn., Manston, 3–44, '**QO-A**'.

JN734 No. 3 Sqn., Manston, 3–44; Newchurch, 5–44.

JN735 No. 3 Sqn., Manston, 3–44; Newchurch, 5–44; Plt Off S. B. Feldman shot down V-1, 20–6–44.

JN736 Trials with 3–blade propeller, HAL, 2–44. No. 3 Sqn., Manston, 3–44; Newchurch, 5–44.

JN738 No. 3 Sqn., Manston, 3–44; Newchurch, 5–44; defensive patrols against V-1 flying bombs.

JN739 No. 3 Sqn., Manston, 3–44.

JN740 Trials with various RP rails, HAL and A & AEE, 1944.

JN741 Trials with modified hood frame, HAL and A & AEE, 1944.

JN742 No. 3 Sqn., Manston, 3–44; Newchurch, 5–44; defensive patrols against V-1 flying bombs.

JN743 No. 3 Sqn., Manston, 3–44, '**QO-P**'; Newchurch, 5–44; Plt Off G. A. Whitman shot down Bf 109G, 8–6–44.

JN745 No. 3 Sqn., Manston, 3–44; Newchurch, 5–44; defensive patrols against V-1 flying bombs.

JN748 No. 3 Sqn., Manston, 3–44; Newchurch, 5–44; defensive patrols against V-1 flying bombs.

JN749 No. 3 Sqn., Manston, 3–44.

JN750 Completed as **Tempest II** with Centaurus engine. HAL trials, 1944–45; converted to **Tempest VI** with Sabre VI, 1945.

JN751 No. 486 Sqn., RNZAF, Castle Camps, 3–44. Then coded '**R-B**' and flown by Wg Cdr R. P. Beamont, DSO and Bar, DFC and Bar, Wing Leader, Newchurch. Was first Tempest to fly ground attack sortie, 28–5–44; first Tempest to shoot down enemy aircraft (Bf 109G), 8–6–44; first Tempest to shoot down V-1, 16–6–44.

JN752 No. 3 Sqn., Manston, 3–44.

JN753 No. 3 Sqn., Manston, 3–44; Newchurch, 5–44; Flt Lt A. R. Moore shot down Bf 109G, 8–6–44.

JN754 No. 3 Sqn., Newchurch, 5–44; defensive patrols against V-1 flying bombs.

JN755 No. 3 Sqn., Manston, 3–44; Newchurch, 5–44; defensive patrols against flying bombs; Matlaske, 9–44.

JN759 No. 3 Sqn., Newchurch 8–44; F/Sgt D. J. Mackerras killed while chasing V-1 flying bomb, 6–8–44.

JN760 No. 3 Sqn., Newchurch, 4–44; F/Sgt M. J. Rose destroyed the Squadron's first V-1, 16–6–44.

JN761 No. 3 Sqn., Newchurch, 4–44; F/Sgt C. W. Orwin destroyed V-1, 17–6–44; Plt Off S. B. Feldman destroyed V-1, 20–6–44.

JN762 No. 3 Sqn., Newchurch, 4–44; Flt Lt van Lierde destroyed V-1, 23–6–44.

JN766 No. 486 Sqn., RNZAF, Beaulieu, 2–44, '**SA-N**'.

JN768 No. 3 Sqn., Newchurch, 4–44, '**QO-N**'; F/Sgt R. W. Cole destroyed V-1, 17–6–44. Wg Cdr R. P. Beamont, DSO and Bar, DFC and Bar, shot down and made POW, Rheine area, 12–10–44.

JN769 No. 3 Sqn., Newchurch, 6–44; F/Sgt M. J. A. Rose destroyed V-1, 17–6–44.

JN792 No. 486 Sqn., RNZAF, Castle Camps, 3–44, '**SA-H**'.

JN793 No. 3 Sqn., Newchurch, 5–44; Fg Off M. F. Edwards destroyed V-1, 17–6–44.

JN798 Trials with various stores, HAL, Langley, and A & AEE, Boscombe Down, 1944; night fighter evaluation, 8–44.

JN799 Trials at A & AEE, Boscombe Down, 1944; bombing evaluation, etc.

JN801 No. 486 Sqn., RNZAF, Castle Camps, 4–44, '**SA-L**'. No. 222 Sqn., Predannack, 1–45.

JN805 No. 486 Sqn., RNZAF, Castle Camps, 4–44, '**SA-U**'.

JN807 No. 486 Sqn., RNZAF, Castle Camps, 4–44, '**SA-J**'. No. 3 Sqn., Matlaske, 9–44. Converted to TT Mark 5 , 1950.

JN808 No. 56 Sqn., Newchurch, 6–44, '**US-G**'. No. 3 Sqn., Matlaske, 9–44. No. 56 Sqn., B. 80 Volkel, Holland, 2–45, '**US-G**'; Sgt J. K. Holden missing, 2–2–45; did not recover from dive while attacking German train.

JN809 No. 486 Sqn., RNZAF, Castle Camps, 4–44, '**SA-M**'.

JN812 No. 3 Sqn., B.80 Volkel, Holland (1–10–44); aircraft shot down by German flak during Squadron's move to Volkel, 1–10–44; W/Off F. M. Reid, AFM, believed killed.

JN814 Later became Ground Instruction Machine **4829M**.

JN815 No. 3 Sqn., Matlaske, 9–44.

JN816 No. 56 Sqn., Newchurch, 6–44, '**US-W**'.

JN821 No. 3 Sqn., Matlaske, 9–44.

JN822 No. 3 Sqn., Matlaske, 9–44; Plt Off R. W. Cole shot down by flak near Rheine airfield, 26–11–44.

JN856 No. 56 Sqn., Newchurch, 6–44, '**US-S**'; defensive patrols against V-1 flying bombs.

JN857 No. 3 Sqn., Matlaske, 9–44.

JN862 No. 3 Sqn., Newchurch, 6–44; Flt Lt van Lierde shot down V-1, 17-6-44.

JN864 No. 56 Sqn., Newchurch, 6–44, **'US-C'** and **'US-E '**; Flt Lt D. V. C. Cotes–Preedy, DFC, GM, shot down the Squadron's first V-1, 3–7-44.

JN865 No. 3 Sqn., Matlaske, 9–44.

JN867 No. 56 Sqn., Newchurch, 6–44, **'US-H'**. No. 17 OTU, Silverstone, 1–47.

JN868 No. 3 Sqn., Newchurch, 6–44; lost in action against V-1, 1–7-44; Fg Off G. E. Kosh killed.

JN869 No. 56 Sqn., Newchurch, 6–44, **'US-D'**; F/Sgt A. C. Drew destroyed two V–1s over Kent, 26–7-44.

JN870 No. 80 Sqn., West Malling, 8–44, **'W2-F'**; B.80 Volkel, Holland, 11–44; Fg Off R. J. Holland shot down Bf 109G during armed reconnaissance between Münster and Bielefeld, 24–1-45.

JN871 Later converted to **TT Mark 5**.

JN874 To Rotol Ltd., Staverton, 1944, for propeller trials.

JN875 No. 56 Sqn., Newchurch, **'US-L'** and **'US-P'**, 6–44. No. 3 Sqn., B.80 Volkel, Holland, 2–45.

JN876 Aircraft allocated to Air Marshal Sir Roderick Hill.

JN877 No. 56 Sqn., Newchurch, **'US-K'** and **'US-M'**, 6–44; defensive patrols against V-1 flying bombs.

Second production batch of 300 aircraft built by Hawker Aircraft Ltd, Langley, Buckinghamshire. EJ504, EJ518-EJ560, EJ577-EJ611, EJ626-EJ672, EJ685-EJ723, EJ739-EJ788, EJ800-EJ846, EJ859-EJ896. Series 2 aircraft, Sabre IIA engines, short-barrel cannon, springtab ailerons. Deliveries commenced 5–44, completed 9–44; average rate of production approximately 18 aircraft per week.

EJ504 No. 3 Squadron, Matlaske, 9–44.

EJ518 To Napier & Sons Ltd., as engine test bed; fitted with annular radiator.

EJ519 No. 80 Sqn., West Malling, deld 24–8-44 (first Tempest on Squadron); hit by flak, 17–9-44, during Operation "Market", shooting up flak positions on Walcheren; crashed into sea, W/Off P. L. Godfrey assumed drowned.

EJ520 No. 501 Sqn., Manston, 8–44, **'SD-L'**.

EJ521 No. 3 Sqn., Matlaske, 9–44.

EJ522 No. 56 Sqn., Newchurch, 6–44, **'US-F'**.

EJ525 Wg Cdr R. P. Beamont shot down V-1, 17–6-44. No. 274 Sqn., Manston, 8–44, **'JJ-K'**; No. 33 Sqn., B.91 Kluis, Holland, 4–45; Flt Lt R. J. Hetherington, RNZAF , missing from armed reconnaissance near Lübeck, 24–4-45.

EJ526 No. 56 Sqn., Newchurch, 6–44, **'US-N'**; B.80 Volkel, Holland, 2–45; Fg Off R. V. Dennis shot down Bf 109K during armed reconnaissance 15 miles west of Münster, 25–2–45; **'US-D'**, 4–45; W/Off W. M. D. Tuck force landed in enemy territory following engine failure, 3–4–45, but seen to walk away from aircraft.

EJ527 No. 501 Sqn., Manston, 8–44, **'SD-E'**.

EJ532 No. 56 Sqn., Newchurch, 6–44, **'US-H'**; aircraft hit ground while flying in low cloud, 29–7-44; F/Sgt A. C. Drew killed.

EJ533 No. 56 Sqn., Newchurch, 6–44, **'US-E'**; defensive patrols against flying bombs.

EJ534 No. 56 Sqn., Newchurch, 6–44, '**US-O'**; defensive patrols against flying bombs.

EJ536 No. 56 Sqn., Newchurch, 6–44, **'US-B'**; aircraft hit by flak while escorting Mitchells in raid on Roermond, 5–11–44; Plt Off A. S. Miller baled out but posted missing.

EJ538 No. 501 Sqn., Manston, 8–44, **'SD-R'**; defensive patrols against V-1 flying bombs.

EJ539 No. 56 Sqn., Newchurch, 6–44, **'US-K'**; defensive patrols against V-1 flying bombs.

EJ540 No. 3 Sqn., Matlaske, 9–44.

EJ541 No. 56 Sqn., Newchurch, 6–44, **'US-B'**; B.80 Volkel, Holland, 1–45, **'US-O'**; Plt Off J. S. Ferguson crashed after high–speed stall while attacking German MT, 20–1–45.

EJ543 No. 56 Sqn., Newchurch, 6–44, **'US-U'**; defensive patrols against V–1 flying bombs.

EJ544 No. 56 Sqn., Newchurch, 6–44, **'US-J'**; B.80 Volkel, Holland, 1–45; Plt Off D. E. Ness, RCAF, destroyed Bf 109G in Bielefeld area, 4–1–45; Flt Lt J. H. Ryan shared a Fw 190D in Paderborn area (with Plt Off Hughes in EJ772), 14–1–45; Flt Lt W. J. Green missing after combat with Fw 190s in Clopenburg area, 22–2–45.

EJ545 No. 56 Sqn., Newchurch, 6–44, **'US-Z'**; defensive patrols against V-1 flying bombs.

EJ546 No. 56 Sqn., Newchurch, 6–44, **'US-B'**; defensive patrols against V-1 flying bombs.

EJ547 No. 56 Sqn., Newchurch, 6–44, **'US-A'**; defensive patrols against V-1 flying bombs.

EJ548 No. 56 Sqn., Newchurch, 6–44, **'US-G'**; B.80 Volkel, Holland, 1–45; Fg Off J. J. Paton destroyed Fw 190D in Paderborn area, 14–1–45; Plt Off H. Shaw missing, 16–1–45, seen to crash close to train he was attacking.

EJ549 No. 80 Sqn., West Malling, 8–44, **'W2-S'**. No. 3 Sqn., Matlaske, 9–44.

EJ550 No. 56 Sqn., Newchurch, 6–44, **'US-T'**; defensive patrols against V-1 flying bombs.

EJ551 No. 501 Sqn., Manston, 8–44, **'SD-S'**; defensive patrols against V-1 flying bombs.

EJ552 No. 56 Sqn., Newchurch, 6–44, **'US-A'**; defensive patrols against V-1 flying bombs.

EJ555 No. 501 Sqn., Manston, 8–44, **'SD-Y'**; defensive patrols against V-1 flying bombs. No. 274 Sqn., B.109 Quackenbrück, Germany, 5–45.

EJ559 No. 56 Sqn., Newchurch, 7–44, **'US-L'**; ditched with engine failure off Beachy Head after pilot, Sgt G. H. Wylde, had shot down V-1 flying bomb; pilot rescued unhurt.

EJ578 No. 56 Sqn., Newchurch, 7–44, **'US-I'**; defensive patrols against V-1 flying bombs.

EJ579 No. 56 Sqn., Newchurch, 7–44, **'US-Z'**; defensive patrols against V-1 flying bombs; B.80 Volkel, Holland, 2–45; Flt Lt F. L. MacLeod shot down Bf 109K during armed reconnaissance 15 miles West of Münster, 25–2–45.

EJ580 Later converted to **TT Mark 5**.

EJ581 Later converted to **TT Mark 5**.

EJ585 No. 56 Sqn., Newchurch, 8–44, **'US-K'**. No. 501 Sqn., Manston, 8–44, **'SD-A'**. Later converted to **TT Mk 5**; Armament Practice Station, Sylt, 1954.

EJ587 No. 3 Sqn., Matlaske, 9–44.

EJ590 Hood jettison trials, HAL, Langley, 7–44.

EJ591 No. 501 Sqn., Manston, 8–44, **'SD-Z'**; defensive patrols against V-1 flying bombs.

EJ592 Performance evaluation in unpainted state, HAL, 7–44; later delivered (unpainted) to No. 501 Sqn. for operational use against V-1 flying bombs.

EJ593 No. 56 Sqn., Newchurch, 8–44, **'US-A'**; defensive patrols against V-1 flying bombs.

EJ595 No. 274 Sqn., B. 109 Quackenbrück, Germany, 5–45.

EJ597 No. 501 Sqn., Manston, 8–44, **'SD-D'**; defensive patrols against V-1 flying bombs.

EJ599 Later converted to **TT Mark 5** ; No. 233 OCU.

EJ600 No. 501 Sqn., Manston, 8–44, **'SD-F'**; defensive patrols against V-1 flying bombs.

EJ601 No. 56 Sqn., Newchurch, 8–44, **'US-T'**; B.152 Fassberg, Germany, 5–45; F/Sgt P. Tullie shot down Ju 52/3mW floatplane near Neustadt, 2–5–45.

EJ603 No. 501 Sqn., Manston, 9–44, **'SD-M'**; night defensive patrols against V-1 flying bombs.

EJ604 No. 274 Sqn., West Malling, 8–44; defensive patrols against V-1 flying bombs.

EJ605 No. 501 Sqn., Manston, 9–44, **'SD-K'**; night defensive patrols against V-1 flying bombs.

EJ607 No. 80 Sqn., Manston, 9–44; missing with pilot, Fg Off R. H. Hanney, after anti-flak sweep, Flushing area, 18–9–44.

EJ608 No. 501 Sqn., Manston, 9–44, **'SD-D'** and **'SD-Y'**. No. 222 Sqn., Predannack, 1–45, **'ZD-B'**; conversion training on Tempests.

EJ609 No. 274 Sqn., West Malling, 8–44. No. 80 Sqn., B.80 Volkel, Holland, 11–44.

EJ610 No. 3 Sqn., B.80 Volkel, Holland, 2–45.

EJ611 No. 274 Sqn., West Malling, 8–44; Coltishall, 9–44; F/Sgt W. L. F. Randall force landed in enemy territory, 27–9–44, after strafing train 5 miles SW of Zwolle; believed made POW.

EJ626 No. 501 Sqn., Manston, 9–44, **'SD-E'**; night patrols against V-1 flying bombs.

EJ628 No. 274 Sqn., West Malling, 8–44; Flt Lt O. E. Willis shot down Squadron's first V-1, 15–8–44, 2 miles NE of Sittingbourne, and the second, 16–8–44, 2 miles N of Maidstone.

EJ632 No. 274 Sqn., B.80 Volkel, Holland, 11–44; F/Sgt R. Cole believed shot down by Fw 190s while on freelance patrol, 7–11–44.

EJ633 No. 274 Sqn., West Malling, 8–44; Flt Lt J. Malloy, RCAF, shot down V-1, 16–8–44. No. 80 Sqn., B.80 Volkel, Holland, 11–44; Plt Off N. J. Rankin, RAAF, shared destruction of Fw 190D (with F/Sgt Crook in EJ830) 12 miles NW of Rheine, 4–1–45; Fg Off N. J. Rankin, RAAF, shot down by flak, 30–3–45, and believed baled out safely near Diepholz.

EJ634 No. 274 Sqn., West Malling, 8–44; Fg Off J. W. Lyne shot down V-1 5 miles NW of Ashford, Kent, 16–8–44.

EJ636 No. 274 Sqn., West Malling, 8–44; Fg Off G. Walkington flew Squadron's first Tempest operation, a V-1 patrol (with F/O Lyne in EJ641), 12–8–44.

EJ637 No. 274 Sqn., West Malling, 8–44; F/Sgt R. W. Ryman was Squadron's first Tempest casualty when aircraft struck hill near Elham, Kent, in low cloud, 13–8–44.

EJ638 No. 274 Sqn., West Malling, 8–44; defensive patrols against V–1 flying bombs.

EJ639 No. 274 Sqn., West Malling, 8–44; defensive patrols against V-1 flying bombs.

EJ640 No. 274 Sqn., West Malling, 8–44; Flt Lt J. Malloy shot down V-1 flying bomb, 16–8–44. No. 56 Sqn., Newchurch, 9–44, **'US-T'**; defensive patrols against flying bombs.

EJ641 No. 80 Sqn., West Malling, 8–44. No. 274 Sqn., West Malling, 8–44; Fg Off J. W. Lyne flew Squadron's first Tempest operation (with Fg Off Walkington in EJ636), a V-1 patrol, 12–8–44.

EJ642 No. 274 Sqn., West Malling, 8–44; Manston, 9–44; Flt Lt J. Malloy, RCAF, shot down by flak during attack on Leeuwarden, Holland, 10–9–44; ditched in sea but rescued unhurt.

EJ643 No. 80 Sqn., West Malling, 8–44, **'W2-E'**; B.80 Volkel, Holland, 4–45; Fg Off L. Smith shot down, 5–4–45, and force landed near Tilburg; pilot returned to Squadron, and aircraft salvaged and repaired. Later converted to **TT Mark 5**.

EJ647 No. 274 Sqn., West Malling, 8–44; Flt Lt L. Griffiths, RNZAF, shot down V1 flying bomb near Faversham, Kent, 16–8–44.

EJ648 No. 274 Sqn., B.80 Volkel, Holland, 12–44; Flt Lt W. J. Hibbert shot down Bf 109G near Emmerich, 17–12–44; Sqn Ldr D. C. Fairbanks, DFC and Bar, RCAF, shot down two Bf 109Gs in Rheine–Münster area, 22–2–45.

EJ649 No. 80 Sqn., West Malling, 8–44, **'W2-Y'**; B.80 Volkel, Holland, 2–45; Fg Off W. R. Sheaf shot down Bf 109G north–east of Wesel, 25–3–45; Fg Off K. Burton shot down by flak, 4–4–45, on armed reconnaissance near Oldenburg, force landed in Allied lines and returned to the Squadron, 6–4–45.

EJ650 No. 80 Sqn., West Malling, deld 24–8-44.

EJ657 No. 80 Sqn., West Malling, deld 24–8-44; suffered engine failure, 17–9–44; Flt Lt E. E. O. Irish baled out unhurt.

EJ658 No. 80 Sqn., West Malling, 8–44; defensive patrols against flying bombs.

EJ659 No. 80 Sqn., West Malling, deld 27–8-44; defensive patrols against flying bombs.

EJ660 No. 80 Sqn., West Malling, 8–44, **'W2-B'**. Later converted to **TT Mark 5**.

EJ662 No. 80 Sqn., Manston, 9–44; missing with pilot, Plt Off W. E. Maloney, RAAF, from "Big Ben" (V-2) air strikes on German MT north of Arnhem, Holland, 16–9–44; aircraft hit by flak and seen to crash.

EJ663 No. 56 Sqn., Newchurch, 8–44, '**US-S**'. No. 80 Sqn., B.80 Volkel, Holland, 11–44. No. 56 Sqn., B. 80 Volkel, Holland, 1–45; '**US–S**'; Flt Lt F. L. MacLeod shot down low–flying Me 262 near Paderborn, 23–1–45. No. 80 Sqn., B.80 Volkel, Holland, 1–45; Flt Lt D. L. Price, RCAF, shared Bf 109G (with P/O Lang in EJ705) during armed reconnaissance near Bramsche, 23–1–45. Later converted to **TT Mark 5**.

EJ665 No. 80 Sqn., West Malling, 8–44; B.80 Volkel, Holland, 11–44; Fg Off D. S. Angier suffered undercarriage failure and crash landed at base, 11–2–45; pilot unhurt but air-craft written·off.

EJ666 No. 80 Sqn., West Malling, 8–44; defen-sive patrols against V–1 flying bombs.

EJ667 No. 80 Sqn., West Malling, 8–44; B.80 Volkel, Holland, 12–44; Fg Off J. W. Gar-land, RCAF, destroyed Fw 190D near Rheine, 27–12–44. No. 3 Sqn., B.80 Volkel, Holland, 2–45. Later converted to **TT Mark 5**; No 233 OCU.

EJ669 Newchurch, 5–44, '**JF-B**'. No. 80 Sqn., West Malling, 8–44; B.80 Volkel, Holland, 1–45; Flt Lt D. L. Price, RCAF, destroyed Bf 109K during armed reconnaissance between Münster and Bielefeld, 24–1–45. Later con-verted to **TT Mark 5**; No 233 OCU.

EJ670 No. 80 Sqn., West Malling, 8–44; defen-sive patrols against V–1 flying bombs.

EJ687 No. 274 Sqn., B.80 Volkel, Holland, 2–45; Fg Off C. Day missing after train strike in Bielefeld area, 21–2–45.

EJ688 No. 274 Sqn., B.80 Volkel, Holland, 12–44; Sqn Ldr E. D. Mackie, DFC and Bar, RNZAF, shot down Fw 190D 6 miles south of Eindhoven, 24–12–44.

EJ690 No. 3 Sqn., B.80 Volkel, Holland, 2–45.

EJ691 No. 80 Sqn., B.80 Volkel, Holland, 2–45; Plt Off R. S. E. Verran shot down Fw 190D 20 miles SE of Bremen, 8–2–45; Capt O. Ulle-stad (Norwegian) shot down by enemy fighters near Rheine airfield, 2–3–45.

EJ692 No. 56 Sqn., Newchurch, 8–44, '**US-F**'; defensive patrols against V–1 flying bombs.

EJ695 No. 80 Sqn., B.80 Volkel, 2–45; Fg Off D. S. Angier missing from armed reconnais-sance near Hildesheim, 14–2–45.

EJ696 No. 80 Sqn., B.80 Volkel, 12–44; Fg Off D. S. Angier shot down Fw 190D near Rheine airfield, 27–12–44.

EJ700 No. 56 Sqn., Newchurch, 8–44, '**US-O**'; defensive patrols against V–1 flying bombs. No. 3 Sqn., B.80 Volkel, Holland, 2–45.

EJ702 No. 501 Sqn., Manston, 9–44, '**SD-Q**'; night defensive patrols against V–1 flying bombs.

EJ703 No. 56 Sqn., Newchurch, 8–44, '**US-L**'; defensive patrols against V–1 flying bombs.

EJ705 No. 80 Sqn., B. 80 Volkel, Holland, 11–44; Flt Lt R. W. A. Mackichan, RAAF, shot down Fw 190D near Rheine, 27–12–44; Flt Lt L. R. G. Smith shot down Bf 109G during armed reconnaissance near Münster, 13–1–45; Plt Off F. A. Lang, RAAF, shared Bf 109K (with Flt Lt Price in EJ663) during armed reconnaissance near Bramsche, 23–1–45; Fg Off N. J. Rankin, RAAF, shot down Bf 109K during armed reconnaissance near Hil-desheim, 14–2–45.

EJ708 No. 56 Sqn., Newchurch, 8–44, '**US-W**'; B. 80 Volkel, Holland, 1–45; Fg Off W. R. MacLaren shot down Fw 190D during armed reconnaissance 10 miles NW of Rheine, 23–1–45; Sqn Ldr R. R. St Quintin shot down Fw 190D during armed reconnaissance in Clo-penburg area, 22–2–45; Flt Lt W. R. MacLa-ren missing, believed killed, during armed reconnaissance near Münster, 26–3–45.

EJ709 No. 247 Sqn., B. 82 Grove, Holland, 10–44; Fg Off G. T. Kinnell, RNZAF, crash landed in No Man's Land following armed reconnaissance over Münster, 5–10–44; pilot reported safe.

EJ713 No. 80 Sqn., Manston, 9–44; B. 80 Vol-kel, Holland, 1–45; F/Sgt L. B. Crook de-stroyed Bf 109K and Fw 190D during armed reconnaissance near Münster, 23–1–45.

EJ714 No. 80 Sqn., B. 112 Hopsten, Germany; armed reconnaissance sorties, 4–45.

EJ718 No. 56 Sqn., Newchurch, 8–44, '**US-B**'; defensive patrols against V–1 flying bombs.

EJ721 No. 56 Sqn., Newchurch, 8–44, '**US-C**'; defensive patrols against V–1 flying bombs; B. 80 Volkel, Holland, 1–45; Fg Off W. R. MacLaren shot down Bf 109G in Neede area, 22–1–45.

EK722 No. 80 Sqn., B. 80 Volkel, Holland, 11–44.

EK723 No. 80 Sqn., Manston, 9–44; defensive patrols against V–1 flying bombs; aircraft hit by flak near Flushing during anti–flak sweep, 18–9–44; Fg Off P. S. Haw baled out too low and was drowned.

EJ739 No. 56 Sqn., Newchurch, 9–44; defensive patrols against V–1 flying bombs.

EJ740 No. 56 Sqn., Newchurch, 9–44 '**US-X**'. No. 80 Sqn., B. 80 Volkel, Holland, 11–44; Flt Lt A. Seager (S. Rhodesian) shot down Fw 190D during armed reconnaissance near Münster, 23–1–45; Sqn Ldr E. D. Mackie, DFC and Bar, RNZAF, shot down Bf 109K during armed reconnaissance near Bramsche, 23–1–45.

EJ741 No. 56 Sqn., Newchurch, 9–44, '**US-M**'; defensive patrols against V–1 flying bombs.

EJ742 No. 56 Sqn., Newchurch, 9–44, '**US-T**'; defensive patrols against flying bombs.

EJ744 No. 274 Sqn., Coltishall, 9–44, '**JJ-K**'. Later converted to **TT Mark 5**; No. 229 OCU.

EJ751 No. 274 Sqn., B. 80 Volkel, Holland, 2–45; Fg Off W. J. B. Stark shot down Bf 109G in Minden area, 8–2–45.

EJ753 Later converted to **TT Mark 5**.

EJ758 Later converted to **TT Mark 5**.

EJ759 Tropicalized aircraft; ff 25–9–44, W. Humble.

EJ760 No. 3 Sqn., B. 80 Volkel, Holland, 2–45.

EJ761 No. 56 Sqn., Newchurch, 9–44, '**US-P**'; B. 80 Volkel, Holland, 3–45; Fg Off V. L. Turner, RAAF, shot down Fw 190D during sweep near Rheine, 7–3–45.

EJ762 No. 274 Sqn., B. 80 Volkel, 1–45; Flt Lt G. Mann shot down Bf 109G near Gütersloh, 23–1–45; Flt Lt G. Bruce, RCAF, crashed in enemy territory during armed reconnaissance in Hamm–Gütersloh area, 1–2–45.

EJ763 No. 501 Sqn., Manston, 9–44, '**SD-J**' and '**SD-X**'; night defensive patrols against V–1 flying bombs.

EJ764 No. 274 Sqn., Coltishall, 9–44, '**JJ-E**'; B. 80 Volkel, Holland, 2–45; Fg Off T. A. Suth-erland shot down Bf 109G in Minden area, 8–2–45.

EJ766 No. 3 Sqn., Matlaske, 9–44, '**QO-Z**'.

EJ771 No. 274 Sqn., B. 80 Volkel, Holland, 1–45; Fg Off C. G. Scriven shot down Fw 190D near Gütersloh, 23–1–45; Flt Lt W. J. Hibbert shot down Ju 88 on armed reconnais-sance between Hanover and Minden, 21–2–45; Fg Off J. B. Spence posted missing after combat with Fw 190s and Bf 109s near Rheine, 28–2–45.

EJ772 No. 56 Sqn., B. 80 Volkel, Holland, 1–45, '**US-T**'; Plt Off J. E. Hughes shared destruc-tion of Fw 190D (with Flt Lt Ryan in EJ544) in Paderborn area, 14–1–45.

EJ773 No. 56 Sqn., Matlaske, 9–44, '**US-T**'.

EJ774 No. 80 Sqn., Coltishall, 9–44, '**W2-B**'; B. 80 Volkel, Holland, 11–44; Fg Off A. W. Garland, RCAF, shot down two Fw 190Ds near Münster (probably part of "*Bodenplatte*"), 1–1–45; Fg Off A. W. D. McLachlan, RAAF, shot down by flak south of Stavelot, 13–1–45; force landed in enemy territory and seen to walk away from the aircraft.

EJ775 No. 56 Sqn., Matlaske, 9–44, '**US-P**'.

EJ776 No. 80 Sqn., B. 80 Volkel, Holland, 2–45; Fg Off G. F. Royds flew through HT cables near Hamm but returned safely; aircraft only slightly damaged, and repaired. Fg Off G. F. Royds missing from armed reconnaissance near Hildesheim, 14–2–45.

EJ777 No. 56 Sqn., Matlaske, 9–44, '**US-F**'.

EJ778 No. 56 Sqn., Matlaske, 9–44, '**US-M**'; Fg

Off V. L. Turner, RAAF, shot down Bf 109G during armed reconnaissance 10 miles NW of Rheine, 23–1–45.

EJ780 No. 56 Sqn., Matlaske, 9–44, '**US-D**'; B. 80 Volkel, Holland, 1–45; Flt Lt J. H. Ryan shot down Bf 109G in Bielefeld area, 4–1–45; 3–45, '**US-N**'; Fg Off J. J. Payton shot down Bf 109G during sweep near Rheine, 7–3–45.

EJ781 No. 274 Sqn., B. 80 Volkel, Holland, 11–44; Flt Lt R. B. Cole (with Fg Off Mann in EJ801) damaged Me 262 10 miles north of Rheine, 5–12–44; Fg Off R. E. Moo-ney shot down Me 410 during armed recon-naissance in Vechta area, 3–2–45.

EJ783 No. 274 Sqn., Coltishall, 9–44, '**JJ-N**'; B. 80 Volkel, Holland, 2–45; Sqn Ldr A. H. Baird, DFC, damagd three Me 410s during armed reconnaissance in Vechta area, 3–2–45; Sqn Ldr A. H. Baird, DFC, shot down by Bf 109Gs in Minden area, 8–2–45.

EJ786 No. 3 Sqn., B. 80 Volkel, Holland, 12–44; Flt Lt K. F. Thiele, DSO, DFC and bar, shot down Bf 109G, 28–12–44. Later converted to **TT Mark 5**.

EJ800 No. 56 Sqn., Matlaske, 9–44, '**US-D**'.

EJ801 No. 274 Sqn., B. 80 Volkel, Holland, 2–45; Fg Off F. W. Mossing, RCAF, shot down Bf 109G in Hildesheim area, 16–2–45; Fg Off F. W. Mossing, RCAF, shared destruction of Ju 88 (with Flt Lt Kennedy in NV639) near Rheine, 24–2–45. Later converted to **TT Mark 5**.

EJ803 No. 3 Sqn., B. 80 Volkel, Holland, 12–44; aircraft with pilot, Flt Lt M. F. Edwards, mis-sing from patrol, 28–12–44.

EJ804 No. 56 Sqn., Matlaske, 9–44, '**US-I**', B. 80 Volkel, Holland, 1–45; Fg Off J. J. Payton shot down Fw190D during armed reconnais-sance 10 miles NW of Rheine, 23–1–45; Flt Lt J. T. Hodges shot down Fw 190D during sweep near Hesepe, 22–3–45; Fg Off W. M. Wallis shared destruction of Ju 88 (with Flt Lt MacLeod in NV927) over Neustadt airfield, 16–4–45; B. 152 Fassberg, Germany, 5–45, '**US-M**'.

EJ805 Later converted to **TT Mark 5**; No. 233 OCU, Pembrey, 1952.

EJ807 Later converted to **TT Mark 5**.

EJ813 No. 274 Sqn., B. 109 Quackenbrück, Germany, 5–45.

EJ814 No. 80 Sqn., Coltishall, 9–44, '**W2-W**'. No. 274 Sqn., B. 80 Volkel, Holland, 1–45; Flt Lt L. A. Wood shot down Fw 190D near Gütersloh, 23–1–45; Fg Off F. W. Mossing, RCAF, shot down Bf 109G in Minden area, 8–2–45.

EJ830 No. 80 Sqn., B. 80 Volkel, Holland, 1–45; F/Sgt L. B. Crook shared destruction of Fw 190D (with Plt Off Rankin in EJ633) 12 miles NW of Rheine airfield, 4–1–45.

EJ839 Later converted to **TT Mark 5**; No. 233 OCU, Pembrey, 1952.

EJ841 became **Tempest VI**; ff 31–8–45, W. Humble. Inserted into Contract to offset **JN750** in first Tempest production batch (completed as Tempest II).

EJ845 No. 3 Sqn., B. 80 Volkel, Holland, 2–45.

EJ846 No. 56 OTU. Later converted to **TT Mark 5**; Armament Practice Station, Sylt, 1954.

EJ862 Later converted to **TT Mark 5**.

EJ864 No. 274 Sqn., B. 80 Volkel, Holland, 10–44, '**JJ-A**'.

EJ865 No. 274 Sqn., B. 109 Quackenbrück, Germany, 5–45. No. 3 Sqn., Gatow, c.4–46, '**J5-F**'.

EJ866 No. 33 Sqn., B. 77 Gilze-Rijen, Holland, 2–45.

EJ868 No. 33 Sqn., B. 77 Gilze-Rijen, Holland, 2–45; aircraft and pilot, Fg Off A. Harman, missing from fighter sweep in Rheine area, 25–2–45.

EJ869 No. 33 Sqn., B. 77 Gilze-Rijen, Holland, 2–45.

EJ871 No. 222 Sqn., Predannack, 1–45, '**ZD-D**'.

EJ875 Later converted to **TT Mark 5**.

EJ876 No. 274 Sqn., B. 109 Quackenbrück, Germany, 5–45.

EJ879 Later converted to **TT Mark 5**; Armament Practice Station, Sylt, 1954.
EJ880 No. 33 Sqn., Predannack, 12–44, '**5R-R**'. Later converted to **TT Mark 5**.
EJ884 No. 3 Sqn., Dedelstorf, Germany, c.6–46, '**J5-A**'.
EJ886 No. 33 Sqn., Predannack, 12–44, '**5R-N**'; conversion training on Tempests.
EJ893 No. 274 Sqn., B. 80 Volkel, Holland, 11–44, '**JJ-W**'.
EJ896 No. 80 Sqn., B. 80 Volkel, Holland, 11–44, '**W2-T**'.

Third production batch of 199 aircraft built by Hawker Aircraft Ltd, Langley, Buckinghamshire. NV639–NV682, NV695–NV735, NV749–NV793, NV917–NV948, NV960–NV996. Sabre IIB engines and spring–tab ailerons. Deliveries commenced 9–44, completed 2–45; average rate of production approximately 12 aircraft per week.

NV639 No. 274 Sqn., B. 80 Volkel, Holland, 2–45; Flt Lt R. C. Kennedy, RAAF, shared destruction of Ju 88 (with Fg Off F. W. Mossing in EJ 801) near Rheine airfield, 24–2–45.
NV640 No. 56 Sqn., B. 80 Volkel, Holland, 12–44, '**US-H**'.
NV641 No. 56 Sqn., B. 80 Volkel, Holland, 12–44, '**US-B**'. No. 3 Sqn., B. 80 Volkel, Holland, 2–45.
NV645 No. 274 Sqn., B. 80 Volkel, Holland, 2–45; Sqn Ldr D.C. Fairbanks, DFC, RCAF, shot down Me 262 over Rheine, 11–2–45, during armed reconnaissance. Sqn Ldr D. C. Fairbanks shot down two Bf 109Gs in Hildesheim area, 16–2–45.
NV646 No. 80 Sqn., B. 80 Volkel, Holland, 2–45; Flt Lt D. L. Price, RCAF, hit by flak in drop tank while escorting Typhoon attack on oil refinery, 25–2–45; was seen to bale out successfully.
NV649 No. 56 Sqn., B. 80 Volkel, Holland, 12–44, '**US-I**'.
NV651 No. 486 Sqn., RNZAF, B. 80 Volkel, Holland, 12–44.
NV653 No. 33 Sqn., B. 77 Gilze–Rijen, Holland, 3–45.
NV654 No. 80 Sqn., B. 80 Volkel, Holland, 2–45; F/Sgt L. B. Crook had engine seize in landing circuit and force landed, 10–2–45; pilot unhurt but aircraft written off.
NV657 No. 80 Sqn., B. 80 Volkel, Holland, 2–45; Sqn Ldr E. D. Mackie, DFC, RNZAF, force landed with engine failure, but unhurt; aircraft repaired. No. 33 Sqn., B. 77 Gilze–Rijen, Holland, 3–45.
NV659 No. 56 Sqn., B. 80 Volkel, Holland, 12–44, '**US-E**'.
NV661 Later converted to **TT Mark 5**.
NV664 No. 33 Sqn., Predannack, 12–44, '**5R-A**'. No. 3 Sqn., B. 80 Volkel, Holland, 2–45; Sqn Ldr K. F. Thiele shot down by flak, 10–2–45, and made POW.
NV665 Later converted to **TT Mark 5**.
NV667 No. 56 Sqn., B. 80 Volkel, Holland, 12–44, '**US-A**'.
NV668 Trials with adjustable undercarriage leg flap, HAL, Langley, 1–45.
NV669 No. 3 Sqn., B. 80 Volkel, Holland, 2–45. Later converted to **TT Mark 5**.
NV671 No. 33 Sqn., Predannack, 12–44, '**5R-H**'; B. 77 Gilze–Rijen, Holland, 2–45. Later converted to **TT Mark 5**.
NV676 No. 3 Sqn., B. 80 Volkel, Holland, 2–45.
NV678 No. 33 Sqn., B. 77 Gilze–Rijen, Holland, 2–45.
NV679 No. 33 Sqn., B. 77 Gilze–Rijen, Holland, 2–45.
NV682 No. 222 Sqn., Predannack, 1–45, '**ZD-P**'; conversion training on Tempests.

NV695 No. 33 Sqn., Predannack, 12–44, '**5R-M**'; conversion training on Tempests.
NV697 No. 272 Sqn., B. 109 Quackenbrück, Germany, 5–45.
NV699 Later converted to **TT Mark 5**; No. 229 OCU, Chivenor, 6–51, '**RS-39**'.
NV700 No. 80 Sqn., B. 80 Volkel, Holland, 2–45; Sqn Ldr E. D. Mackie, DFC, RNZAF, shot down Fw 190D near Hanover, 7–3–45; Sqn Ldr E. D. Mackie shot down two Bf 108s in circuit at Fassburg, 9–4–45; Sgt W. F. Turner shared destruction of Fw 190D (with Sqn Ldr Mackie in SN189) during armed reconnaissance near Hamburg, 15–4–45.
NV702 No. 274 Sqn., B. 80 Volkel, Holland, 12–44, '**JJ-E**'.
NV703 No. 3 Sqn., B. 80 Volkel, 2–45. No. 80 Sqn., B. 112 Hopsten, Germany, 4–45.
NV704 No. 80 Sqn., B. 80 Volkel, Holland, 12–44, '**W2-F**'. Later converted to **TT Mark 5**.
NV706 No. 486 Sqn., RNZAF, B. 80 Volkel, Holland, 12–44, '**SA-C**'.
NV708 Coded '**JCB**' and flown by Wg Cdr J. C. Button, DSO, DFC, Wg Cdr (Flying), No. 123 Wing, Wunstorf, Germany, 1946; suffered undercarriage collapse, 7–1–47.
NV712 Later converted to **TT Mark 5**.
NV713 No. 3 Sqn., B. 80 Volkel, Holland, 12–44, '**JF-M**'.
NV719 No. 80 Sqn., B. 112 Hopsten, Germany, 4–45.
NV721 No. 3 Sqn., B. 80 Volkel, Holland, 1–45; '**JF-S**'.
NV722 No. 274 Sqn., B.80 Volkel, Holland 2–45; Flt Lt W. J. Hibbert shot down Fw 190D during armed reconnaissance in Hamm–Gütersloh area, 1–2–45.
NV723 Later converted to **TT Mark 5**.
NV725 No. 80 Sqn., B. 80 Volkel, Holland, 12–44, '**W2-F**'. Later converted to **TT Mark 5**.
NV728 No. 56 Sqn., B. 80 Volkel, Holland, 1–45, '**US-X**'; Fg Off V. L. Turner, RAAF, shot down Fw 190G during sweep near Hesepe, 22–3–45; Sgt P. C. Brown missing, believed killed, 3–4–45; aircraft hit tree during attempted force landing following engine failure and exploded.
NV731 No. 33 Sqn., B. 77 Gilze–Rijen, Holland, 2–45; B. 91 Kluis, Holland, 4–45; F/Sgt J. E. Fraser missing from armed reconnaissance near Lübeck, 24–4–45.

NV749 No. 3 Sqn., B. 80 Volkel, Holland, 1–45, '**JF-H**'.
NV754 No. 33 Sqn., B. 91 Kluis, Holland, 4–45; Fg Off D. J. ter Beck (Dutch) missing from armed reconnaissance near Lübeck, 24–4–45.
NV757 No. 33 Sqn., Predannack, 12–44, '**5R-Y**'; conversion training on Tempests.
NV758 No. 274 Sqn., B. 80 Volkel, Holland, 12–44, '**JJ-N**'.
NV763 Later converted to **TT Mark 5**.
NV764 No. 33 Sqn., B. 77 Gilze–Rijen, Holland, 2–45.
NV767 No. 3 Sqn., B. 80 Volkel, Holland, 12–44, '**JF-T**'.
NV768 To D. Napier & Sons Ltd, for annular radiator and ducted spinner development and trials, 10–44.
NV770 No. 33 Sqn., B. 77 Gilze–Rijen, Holland, 2–45.
NV771 No. 56 Sqn., B. 80 Volkel, Holland, 1–45, '**US-G**'.
NV775 No. 33 Sqn., B. 77 Gilze–Rijen, Holland, 2–45, '**5R-L**'.
NV776 No. 3 Sqn., B. 80 Volkel, Holland, 2–45, '**JF-X**'.
NV778 Later converted to **TT Mark 5**.
NV780 Later converted to **TT Mark 5**.
NV781 Later converted to **TT Mark 5**.
NV783 No. 33 Sqn., B. 91 Kluis, Holland, 4–45; aircraft shot down during armed reconnaissance near Hamburg, 12–4–45; F/Sgt P. W. C. Watton missing.
NV786 No. 56 Sqn., B. 80 Volkel, Holland, 2–45, '**US-E**'; Flt Lt G. B. Milne shot down Fw 190D during sweep near Hesepe, 22–3–45; '**US-J**', 4–45; Flt Lt J. A. McCairns, DFC and two Bars, shared destruction of Me 262 (with Flt Lt Cox in NV968) south of Hamburg, 15–4–45.
NV789 No. 80 Sqn., B. 112 Hopsten, Germany, 4–45.
NV791 No. 486 Sqn., RNZAF, B. 80 Volkel, Holland, 2–45.
NV792 No. 33 Sqn. B. 77 Gilze–Rijen, Holland, 2–45, '**5R-B**'.

NV793 Later converted to **TT Mark 5**.

NV917 Later converted to **TT Mark 5**.
NV919 No. 33 Sqn., B. 91 Kluis, Holland, 4–45; aircraft shot down during armed reconnaissance near Hamburg, 12–4–45; Sgt J. Staines missing.
NV920 No. 274 Sqn., B. 91 Kluis, Holland, 3–45; Flt Lt W. J. B. Stark shot down by flak during fighter sweep near Plantlunne, 24–3–45.
NV922 Later converted to **TT Mark 5**.
NV923 Later converted to **TT Mark 5**. No. 226 OCU, Stradishall, 12–49.
NV926 No. 3 Sqn., B. 80 Volkel, Holland, 2–45, '**JF-W**'.
NV927 No. 56 Sqn., B. 80 Volkel, Holland, 2–45; Flt Lt F. L. MacLeod shared destruction of Ju 88 (with Fg Off Wallis in EJ804) over Neustadt airfield, 16–4–45; Flt Lt F. L. Macleod shared destruction of Fw 190D (with Sgt Willis in SN137) in Euten area, 2–5–45.
NV928 No. 56 Sqn., B. 80 Volkel, Holland, 2–45, '**US-S**'. Later converted to **TT Mark 5**.
NV937 Later converted to **TT Mark 5**.
NV938 No. 80 Sqn., B. 80 Volkel, Holland, 2–45; Fg Off G. A. Bush shot down Fw 190D during sweep near Hesepe, 22–3–45; Fg Off W. R. Sheaf shot down Bf 108 in circuit at Fassburg, 9–4–45.
NV939 No. 222 Sqn., Predannack, 2–45, '**ZD-H**'.
NV940 Later converted to **TT Mark 5**.
NV942 No. 274 Sqn., B. 91 Kluis, Holland, 3–45; Flt Lt R. C. Kennedy, RAAF, believed shot down by flak during fighter sweep near Plantlunne, 24–3–45.
NV943 No. 274 Sqn., B. 80 Volkel, Holland, 2–45; Sqn Ldr D. C. Fairbanks, DFC and Bar, RCAF, shot down Fw 190D near Hamm, 24–2–45; Sqn Ldr D. C. Fairbanks posted missing after combat with Fw 190s and Bf 109s near Rheine, 28–2–45.
NV945 No. 80 Sqn., B. 112 Hopsten, Germany, 4–45.
NV947 No. 274 Sqn., B. 80 Volkel, Holland, 3–45, '**JJ-S**'.

NV960 No. 3 Sqn., B. 80 Volkel, Holland, 3–45, '**JF-C**'. No. 80 Sqn., B. 112 Hopsten, Germany, 4–45. Later converted to **TT Mark 5**.
NV962 Later converted to **TT Mark 5**.
NV963 No. 56 Sqn., B. 80 Volkel, Holland, 3–45, '**US-A**'; 4–45, '**US-C**'; Fg Off D. E. Ness, RCAF, shot down Fw 190D near Celle, 12–4–45; Sgt N. Willis shared destruction of Ju 52 (with F/Sgt Kennaugh in NV974) between Lübeck and Schwerin, 30–4–45.
NV964 No. 80 Sqn., B. 112 Hopsten, Germany, 4–45.
NV965 No. 56 Sqn., B. 80 Volkel, Holland, 3–45, '**US-S**'; Flt Lt J. Sowerbutts shot down Fw 190D near Euten, 2–5–45. Later converted to **TT Mark 5**.
NV968 No. 56 Sqn., B. 80 Volkel, Holland, 3–45, '**US-G**'; Flt Lt P. H. Clostermann, DFC, shot down Fw 190 taking off from Vechta airfield, 2–4–45; Flt Lt N. D. Cox shared destruction of Me 262 (with Flt Lt McCairns in NV786) south of Hamburg, 15–4–45. No. 16 Sqn., Lüneburg, 4–46, '**EG-X**'.
NV970 No. 56 Sqn., B. 80 Volkel, Holland, 3–45, '**US-O**'; Sgt P. C. Brown shot down Fw 190D during sweep near Hesepe, 22–3–45; F/Sgt A. M. L. Kennaugh shared destruction of He 111 (with Sgt Willis in SN140), 1–5–45.
NV973 No. 56 Sqn., B. 80 Volkel, Holland, 3–45, '**US-B**'; Sgt S. A. Sheppard missing on armed reconnaissance near Osnabrück, 28–3–45.
NV974 No. 56 Sqn., B. 80 Volkel, Holland, 3–45, '**US-K**'; F/Sgt A. M. L. Kennaugh shared destruction of Ju 52 (with Sgt Willis in SN140) between Lübeck and Schwerin, 30–4–45; Flt Lt J. T. Hodges missing in enemy territory, 1–5–45; seen to force land and walk away from aircraft.
NV975 Later converted to **TT Mark 5**.

NV977 No. 274 Sqn., B. 109 Quackenbrück, Germany, 5–45.

NV978 Later converted to **TT Mark 5**.

NV980 No. 56 Sqn., B. 80 Volkel, Holland, 4–45, 'US-J'.

NV982 No. 80 Sqn., B. 80 Volkel, Holland, 4–45; Fg Off R. J. Holland shot down by flak during armed reconnaissance between Rheine and Osnabrück, 2–4–45, and later reported killed.

NV983 No. 80 Sqn., B. 80 Volkel, Holland, 2–45; Flt Lt R. C. Cooper shot down Fw 190D during sweep near Hesepe, 22–3–45; Flt Lt R. C. Cooper shot down Fw 190D near Dummer Lake, 6–4–45.

NV986 No. 486 Sqn., RNZAF, B. 152 Fassburg, Germany, 4–45.

NV987 No. 56 Sqn., B. 80 Volkel, Holland, 4–45, 'US-R'; Flt Lt R. V. Garton shot down Fw 190D and Fi 156 Storch in Euten area, 2–5–45.

NV989 No 3 Sqn., B. 80 Volkel, 4–45, 'JF-F'. No 274 Sqn., B. 109 Quackenbrück, Germany, 5–45.

NV991 No. 80 Sqn., B. 80 Volkel, Holland, 4–45; Fg Off L. Smith shot down Fw 190 near Dummer Lake, 6–4–45; Flt Lt M. P. Kilburn, DFC, shot down Fw 190G during armed reconnaissance near Neuruppin, 16–4–45; Fg Off L. Smith shot down near Gravesmühlen, 17–4–45, reportedly by Fw 190s.

NV992 Later converted to **TT Mark 5**.

NV994 No. 3 Sqn., B. 80 Volkel, 5–45, 'JF-E'; Flt Lt P. H. Clostermann flew his first Tempest operation with No. 3 Sqn., 9–4–45. Later converted to **TT Mark 5**.

NV995 Later converted to **TT Mark 5**.

NV996 Later converted to **TT Mark 5**.

Fourth and final production batch of 201 aircraft built by Hawker Aircraft Ltd, Langley, Buckinghamshire. SN102–SN146, SN159–SN190, SN205–SN238, SN253–SN296, SN301–SN355. Sabre IIB engines, universal armament provision and drop tank plumbing. Deliveries commenced 1–45; completed 6–45; average rate of production approximately 9 aircraft per week. SN368–SN416 cancelled in 1945.

SN106 No. 287 Sqn., Hornchurch, 5–45; gunlaying exercises.

SN107 No. 274 Sqn., B. 109 Quackenbrück, Germany, 5–45.

SN109 Day Fighter Leaders' School, West Raynham, 1947, 'MF–H'.

SN116 No. 287 Sqn., Hornchurch, 5–45; gunlaying exercises.

SN118 No. 274 Sqn., B. 109 Quackenbrück, Germany, 5–45.

SN119 No. 287 Sqn., Hornchurch, 5–45; gunlaying exercises.

SN127 No. 56 Sqn., B. 152 Fassburg, Germany, 5–45, 'US-H'. No. 33 Sqn., Quackenbrück, Germany, 6–45, '5R-J'.

SN128 No. 56 Sqn., B. 152 Fassburg, Germany, 5–45, 'US-V'. No. 33 Sqn., Quackenbrück, Germany, 6–45, '5R-A'.

SN131 No. 56 Sqn., B. 152 Fassburg, Germany, 6–45, 'US-B'.

SN134 No. 33 Sqn., B. 109 Quackenbrück, Germany, 6–45, '5R-Y'. No. 80 Sqn., B. 160 Kastrup, Germany, 9–45, 'W2-V'.

SN135 No. 16 Sqn., Lüneburg, Germany, 4–46, 'EG-R'.

SN137 No. 56 Sqn., B. 152 Fassburg, Germany, 6–45, 'US-B'; Sgt N. Willis destroyed Bv 138, 2–5–45, shared with W/Off A. J. Brocklehurst in **SN140**; and shared a Fw 190D with Flt Lt McLeod in **NV927** on the same sortie.

SN138 No. 80 Sqn., B. 80 Volkel, Holland, 3–45; Fg Off W. H. Long, RAAF, shot down by flak and crashed in flames near Bocholt, 25–3–45.

SN139 No. 80 Sqn., B. 80 Volkel, Holland, 4–45, 'W2-N'; Plt Off H. A. Horsey missing from armed reconnaissance in Rheine–Osnabrück area, 2–4–45, and later reported killed.

SN140 No. 56 Sqn., B. 152 Fassburg, Germany, 5–45, 'US-N'; Sgt N. Willis shared destruction of He 111 (with F/Sgt Kennaugh in **NV924**), 1–5–45; W/Off A. J. Brocklehurst destroyed

Bv 138 (shared with Sgt Willis in **SN137**), 2–5–45; Sgt G. J. Swindle shot down Fi 156 Storch, also on 2–5–45, but later sortie; W/Off A. J. Brocklehurst shot down Fw 190D 12 miles NE of Lübeck, 3–5–45.

SN144 No. 80 Sqn., B. 160 Kastrup, Germany, 7–45, 'W2-U'.

SN145 No. 274 Sqn., B. 155 Dedelstorf, Germany, 7–45, 'JJ-D'.

SN146 No. 486 Sqn., RNZAF, B. 158 Lübeck, Germany, 7–45, 'SA-K'. Later converted to **TT Mark 5**.

SN159 No. 80 Sqn., B. 160 Kastrup, Germany, 7–45, 'W2-H'.

SN161 No. 33 Sqn., B. 155 Dedelstorf, Germany, 7–45, '5R-G'.

SN162 No. 274 Sqn., B. 109 Quackenbrück, Germany, 5–45.

SN166 No. 486 Sqn., RNZAF, B. 158 Lübeck, Germany, 7–45.

SN168 No. 3 Sqn., B. 160 Kastrup, Germany, 7–45, 'JF-T'. No. 486 Sqn., RNZAF, B. 158 Lübeck, Germany, 8–45, 'SA-Q'.

SN170 No. 80 Sqn., B. 112 Hopsten, Germany, 4–45.

SN172 No. 80 Sqn., B. 112 Hopsten, Germany, 4–45; Flt Lt A. Seager (S. Rhodesian) shot down Fw 190D 8 miles NW of Celle, 15–4–45.

SN173 No. 33 Sqn., B. 109 Quackenbrück, Germany, 4–45; F/Sgt C. Peters missing from armed patrol in Husum–Kiel area, 23–4–45.

SN177 No. 80 Sqn., B. 112 Hopsten, Germany, 4–45.

SN178 No. 222 Sqn., Fairwood Common, 7–45, 'ZD-B'.

SN179 No. 274 Sqn., B. 109 Quackenbrück, Germany, 5–45.

SN180 No. 33 Sqn., B. 155 Dedelstorf, Germany, 7–45, '5R-V'.

SN181 No. 274 Sqn., B. 109 Quackenbrück, Germany, 5–45.

SN182 No. 80 Sqn., B. 112 Hopsten, Germany, 4–45. No. 33 Sqn., B. 155 Dedelstorf, Germany, 7–45, '5R-C'. No. 222 Sqn., Fairwood Common, 9–45.

SN183 No. 274 Sqn., B. 155 Dedelstorf, Germany, 7–45, 'JJ-J'.

SN186 No. 80 Sqn., B. 112 Hopsten, Germany, 4–45. No 56 Sqn., B. 160 Kastrup, Germany, 'US-N'.

SN187 No. 33 Sqn., B. 155 Dedelstorf, Germany, 7–45, '5R-V'.

SN188 No. 222 Sqn., Fairwood Common, 7–45, 'ZD-A'.

SN189 No. 80 Sqn., B. 112 Hopsten, Germany, 4–45; Sqn Ldr E. D. Mackie, DFC, RNZAF, shared Fw 190D (with Sgt Turner in **NV700**) near Hamburg during armed reconnaissance, 15–4–45.

SN190 No. 80 Sqn., B. 112 Hopsten, Germany, 4–45; Flt Lt R. B. Prickett shot down Fw 190D during armed reconnaissance near Neuruppen, 16–4–45.

SN209 No. 80 Sqn., B. 160 Kastrup, Germany, 7–45, 'W2-E'. Later converted to **TT Mark 5**; Armament Practice Station, Sylt, 1952, '14'.

SN210 No. 274 Sqn., B. 109 Quackenbrück, Germany, 5–45. No. 33 Sqn., B. 155 Dedelstorf, Germany, 7–45, '5R-V'.

SN212 No. 3 Sqn., B. 160 Kastrup, Germany, 6–45, 'JF-T'.

SN213 No. 33 Sqn., B. 155 Dedelstorf, Germany, 7–45, '5R-S'.

SN215 Later converted to **TT Mark 5**.

SN216 No. 80 Sqn., B. 160 Kastrup, Germany, 7–45, 'W2-Y'.

SN218 No. 80 Sqn., B. 160 Kastrup, Germany, 7–45, 'W2-J'.

SN219 Later converted to **TT Mark 5**.

SN220 No. 3 Sqn., B. 160 Kastrup, Germany, 6–45, 'JF-A'.

SN226 No. 3 Armament Practice Station, Charter Hall, 1–46.

SN227 Later converted to **TT Mark 5**.

SN228 No. 33 Sqn., B. 155 Dedelstorf, Germany, 8–45, '5R-S'.

SN232 Later converted to **TT Mark 5**.

SN236 No. 1 Armament Practice Station, Fairwood Common, 1–46.

SN254 No. 80 Sqn., B. 160 Kastrup, Germany, 8–45, 'W2-C'.

SN259 Later converted to **TT Mark 5**.

SN260 Later converted to **TT Mark 5**.

SN261 Later converted to **TT Mark 5**.

SN262 Central Fighter Establishment, West Raynham, 1946, 'RE-M'. Later converted to **TT Mark 5**.

SN263 Later converted to **TT Mark 5**.

SN264 Later converted to **TT Mark 5**.

SN266 No. 33 Sqn., B. 155 Dedelstorf, Germany, 7–45, '5R-B'.

SN268 No. 33 Sqn., B. 155 Dedelstorf, Germany, 7–45, '5R-H'.

SN271 Later converted to **TT Mark 5**.

SN273 Later converted to **TT Mark 5**.

SN274 Later converted to **TT Mark 5**.

SN293 Later converted to **TT Mark 5**.

SN295 No. 3 Sqn., B. 156 Luneburg, Germany, 7–45, 'J5-R'.

SN313 No. 80 Sqn., B. 160 Kastrup, Germany, 8–45, 'W2-Z'.

SN315 No. 33 Sqn., B. 155 Dedelstorf, Germany, 8–45, '5R-Y'.

SN317 Later converted to **TT Mark 5**.

SN320 Miscellaneous trials, RAE, Farnborough, 1945.

SN321 Later converted to **TT Mark 5**; Central Gunnery School, Leconfield, 1960, 'FJU-D'.

SN326 Later converted to **TT Mark 5**.

SN329 Prototype conversion of **TT Mark 5**; trials at A&AEE, Boscombe Down, 1949.

SN330 No. 3 Sqn., B. 158 Lübeck, Germany, 8–45, 'J5-H'.

SN331 Later converted to **TT Mark 5**.

SN332 Later converted to **TT Mark 5**.

SN333 Later converted to **TT Mark 5**.

SN339 No. 3 Sqn., B. 158 Lübeck, Germany, 8–45, 'J5-P'.

SN340 Later converted to **TT Mark 5**.

SN342 No. 33 Sqn., B. 155 Dedelstorf, Germany, 8–45, '5R-I'.

SN343 No. 80 Sqn., B. 160 Kastrup, Germany, 8–45, 'W2-J'.

SN344 No. 3 Sqn., B. 158 Lübeck, Germany, 8–45, 'J5-J'.

SN345 No. 16 Sqn., Lüneburg, Germany, 4–46, 'EG-K'.

SN347 No. 3 Sqn., B. 158 Lübeck, Germany, 8–45, 'J5-K'.

SN348 No. 80 Sqn., B. 160 Kastrup, Germany, 8–45, 'W2-J'.

SN349 No. 80 Sqn., B. 160 Kastrup, Germany, 8–45, 'W2-P'.

SN350 Later converted to **TT Mark 5**.

SN352 No. 3 Sqn., B. 158 Lübeck, Germany, 9–45, 'J5-Q'.

SN353 Later converted to **TT Mark 5**.

SN354 Experimental 40–mm 'P'-Gun installation, HAL, Langley, and A&AEE, Boscombe Down, 1945. Later converted to **TT Mark 5**.

SN555 No. 80 Sqn., B. 160 Kastrup, Germany, 9–45, 'W2-H'.

HAWKER TEMPEST VI
(F MARK 6)

Single production batch of 142 aircraft built by Hawker Aircraft Ltd., Langley, Buckinghamshire. NV997–NV999, NX113–NX156, NX169–NX209, NX223–NX268, NX281–NX288. (Original order was for 300 aircraft but NX289–NX325, NX338–NX381, NX394–NX435 and NX448–NX482 cancelled in 1945.) Sabre V engines and preparation for service in the Tropics. Delivered in 1946–47.

NV997 Performance and handling trials, HAL, Langley, and A&AEE, Boscombe Down, 1945.

NV998 Trial installations, HAL, Langley, and A&AEE, Boscombe Down, 1945.

NV999 Trial installations, HAL, Langley, and D. Napier & Sons, Luton, 1945.

NX113 Handling and performance trials, HAL, Langley, 1945–46.

NX115 Performance and engine trials, HAL and Napiers, 1945–46.

NX116 Performance and engine trials, HAL and Napiers, 1945–46.

NX117 Performance trials, HAL, Langley, 1945–46.

NX118 Performance trials, HAL, Langley, 1945–46.

NX119 First Mark VI gyro gunsight installation; trials at A&AEE, Boscombe Down, 1946.

NX120 No. 249 Sqn., Habbaniya, Iraq, 12–46, 'GN-T'.

NX121 Engine handling and trials, RAE, Farnborough, 1946.

NX122 Engine handling and Pilot's Notes, A&AEE, Boscombe Down, 1946.

NX124 First production Tempest VI fitted with spring tabs; trials with HAL, 1946.

NX125 No. 249 Sqn., Habbaniya, Iraq, 12–46, 'GN-Y'.

NX126 No. 249 Sqn., Habbaniya, Iraq, 12–46, 'GN-A'.

NX128 No. 109 MU, Fayid South, Egypt.

NX130 No. 8 Sqn., Khormaksar, Aden, 4–47, 'J'.

NX131 No. 8 Sqn., Khormaksar, Aden, 4–47, 'A'.

NX132 No. 249 Sqn., Habbaniya, Iraq, 12–46.

NX133 Trial installations, HAL, Langley, 1946.

NX134 No. 6 Sqn., Nicosia, Cyprus, 1–47, 'JV-T'.

NX135 No. 6 Sqn., Nicosia, Cyprus, 1–47, 'JV-N'; Deversoir, Egypt, 3–49. No. 249 Sqn., Habbaniya, Iraq, 'GN-W', c.1949.

NX136 No. 213 Sqn., Nicosia, Cyprus, 1–47, 'AK-H'.

NX138 No. 6 Sqn., Nicosia, Cyprus, 1–47.

NX139 No. 6 Sqn., Nicosia, Cyprus, 1–47, 'JV-D'.

NX140 No. 8 Sqn., Khormaksar, Aden, 4–47.

NX141 No. 249 Sqn., Habbaniya, Iraq, 'GN-E', 1–47.

NX142 No. 249 Sqn., Habbaniya, Iraq, 'GN-R', 1–47.

NX143 No. 249 Sqn., Habbaniya, Iraq, 'GN-P', 1–47.

NX144 Trials with target towing gear, HAL and A&AEE, Boscombe Down, 1946–47.

NX147 No. 6 Sqn., Nicosia, Cyprus, 1–47, 'JV-F'.

NX148 No. 8 Sqn., Khormaksar, Aden, 4–47.

NX149 No. 6 Sqn., Nicosia, Cyprus, 1–47.

NX152 No. 8 Sqn., Khormaksar, Aden, 4–47, 'P'.

NX153 No. 213 Sqn., Nicosia, Cyprus, 1–47, 'AK-D'.

NX154 No. 109 MU, Fayid South, Egypt.

NX155 Modified oil system trials, HAL, Langley, 1946–47.

NX156 No. 8 Sqn., Khormaksar, Aden, 4–47.

NX169 No. 8 Sqn., Khormaksar, Aden, 4–47, 'G'.

NX170 No. 249 Sqn., Habbaniya, Iraq, 4–47, 'GN-K'.

NX171 No. 249 Sqn., Habbaniya, Iraq, 4–47, 'GN-H'.

NX172 No. 39 Sqn., Nairobi/Eastleigh, Kenya, 4–48.

NX177 No. 249 Sqn., Habbaniya, Iraq, 4–47, 'GN-G'.

NX180 No. 8 Sqn., Khormaksar, Aden, 6–47, 'J'. No. 213 Sqn., Shallufa, Egypt, 9–47.

NX181 No. 213 Sqn., Nicosia, Cyprus, 2–47.

NX182 No. 249 Sqn., Habbaniya, Iraq, 4–47, 'GN-Q'.

NX183 No. 213 Sqn., Nicosia, Cyprus, 2–47.

NX184 No. 213 Sqn., Nicosia, Cyprus, 1–47, 'AK-D'.

NX185 No. 109 MU, Fayid South, Egypt, 1947.

NX186 No. 109 MU, Fayid South, Egypt, 1947.

NX187 No. 6 Sqn., Nicosia, Cyprus, 2–47, 'JV-X'.

NX188 Propeller trials, Rotol Ltd., Staverton, 1947.

NX190 No. 109 MU, Fayid South, Egypt, 1947.

NX191 No. 6 Sqn., Nicosia, Cyprus, 2–47, 'JV-H'.

NX192 No. 213 Sqn., Nicosia, Cyprus, 2–47.

NX194 No. 6 Sqn., Nicosia, Cyprus, 2–47.

NX195 No. 6 Sqn., Nicosia, Cyprus, 2–47, 'JV-T'.

NX196 No. 8 Sqn., Khormaksar, Aden, 6–47, 'K'.

NX197 No. 39 Sqn., Nairobi/Eastleigh, Kenya, 4–48.

NX198 No. 8 Sqn., Khormaksar, Aden, 6–47.

NX200 No. 249 Sqn., Habbaniya, Iraq, 5–47, 'GN-F'.

NX201 No. 109 MU, Fayid South, Egypt, 1947.

NX202 No. 8 Sqn., Khormaksar, Aden, 6–47.

NX203 No. 6 Sqn., Nicosia, Cyprus, 4–47, 'JV-N'.

NX205 No. 109 MU, Fayid South, Egypt, 1947.

NX206 No. 213 Sqn., Nicosia, Cyprus, 4–47.

NX207 No. 109 MU, Fayid South, Egypt, 1947.

NX209 No. 249 Sqn., Habbaniya, Iraq, 5–47.

NX225 No. 109 MU, Fayid South, Egypt, 1947.

NX227 No. 213 Sqn., Nicosia, Cyprus, 5–47.

NX228 No. 8 Sqn., Khormaksar, Aden, 9–47.

NX229 No. 213 Sqn., Nicosia, Cyprus, 5–47, 'AK-R'.

NX230 No. 109 MU, Shubra, Egypt, 1947.

NX232 No. 249 Sqn., Habbaniya, Iraq, 6–47, 'GN-S'.

NX237 No. 8 Sqn., Khormaksar, Aden, 10–47, 'F'.

NX239 No. 109 MU, Shubra, Egypt, 1947.

NX241 No. 213 Sqn., Nicosia, Cyprus, 6–47.

NX242 No. 6 Sqn., Nicosia, Cyprus, 6–47.

NX244 No. 213 Sqn., Nicosia, Cyprus, 6–47, 'AK-J'.

NX245 No. 249 Sqn., Habbaniya, Iraq, 6–47, 'GN-V'.

NX248 No. 213 Sqn., Nicosia, Cyprus, 6–47.

NX249 No. 109 MU, Shubra, Egypt, 1948.

NX251 No. 6 Sqn., Nicosia, Cyprus, 6–47.

NX252 No. 213 Sqn., Nicosia, Cyprus, 7–47.

NX253 No. 109 MU, Shubra, Egypt, 1948.

NX256 No. 213 Sqn., Nicosia, Cyprus, 7–47.

NX257 No. 6 Sqn., Shallufa, Egypt, 8–47.

NX260 No. 213 Sqn., Nicosia, Cyprus, 8–47, 'AK-Z'.

NX261 No. 6 Sqn., Shallufa, Egypt, 9–47, 'JV-B'.

NX262 Modified cooling system trials (tropical installation), HAL, Langley, and D. Napier & Sons Ltd., Luton, 1947.

NX263 No. 6 Sqn., Shallufa, Egypt, 9–47. No. 247 Sqn., Habbaniya, Iraq, c. 1948, 'GN-M'.

NX266 No. 109 MU, Shubra, Egypt, 1948.

NX268 Modified cooling system (Phase 2), trials, HAL, Langley, and D. Napier & Sons Ltd., Luton, 1947.

NX284 No. 249 Sqn., Habbaniya, Iraq, 2–48, 'GN-C'.

NX288 Modified tropical air filter trials, HAL, Langley, 1948.

HAWKER TEMPEST II (F AND FB MARK 2)

Single production batch of 50 aircraft built by Bristol Aeroplane Co Ltd., Weston–super–Mare, Somerset. MW374–MW423, Bristol Centaurus V radial engines. Delivered 1945–46. 27 aircraft transferred to Royal Indian Air Force from RAF stocks.

MW374 ff 4–10–44. Handling and performance trials, HAL, Langley, and Bristols, Filton, 1945.

MW376 Transferred to Royal Indian Air Force as 'HA564'.

MW377 Transferred to Royal Indian Air Force as 'HA568'.

MW378 Engine trials, Bristols, Filton, 1945. Transferred to Royal Indian Air Force as 'HA627'.

MW379 No. 54 Sqn., Chilbolton, 11–45. Transferred to Royal Indian Air Force as 'HA632'.

MW380 Transferred to Royal Indian Air Force as 'HA628'.

MW381 No. 247 Sqn., Chilbolton, 8–45. Transferred to Royal Indian Air Force as 'HA630'.

MW382 Transferred to Royal Indian Air Force as 'HA590'.

MW383 Transferred to Royal Indian Air Force as 'HA631'.

MW384 No. 20 MU, Aston Down, 1945.

MW385 Transferred to Royal Indian Air Force as 'HA533'.

MW386 Transferred to Royal Indian Air Force as 'HA595'.

MW387 No. 54 Sqn., Chilbolton, 11–45. Transferred to Royal Indian Air Force as 'HA592'.

MW388 Transferred to Royal Indian Air Force as 'HA635'.

MW389 Transferred to Royal Indian Air Force as 'HA625'.

MW390 No. 247 Sqn., Chilbolton, 8–45, 'ZY-C'. Transferred to Royal Indian Air Force as 'HA620'.

MW391 Transferred to Royal Indian Air Force as 'HA626'.

MW392 No. 247 Sqn., Chilbolton, 8–45, 'ZY-M'. Transferred to Royal Indian Air Force as 'HA585'.

MW393 Transferred to Royal Indian Air Force as 'HA634'.

MW395 No. 247 Sqn., Chilbolton, 8–45, 'ZY-F'. Transferred to Royal Indian Air Force as 'HA589'.

MW396 No. 247 Sqn., Chilbolton, 8–45, 'ZY-T'. Transferred to Royal Indian Air Force as 'HA596'.

MW397 No. 20 MU, Aston Down, 1945. Transferred to Royal Indian Air Force as 'HA611'.

MW398 No. 54 Sqn., Chilbolton, 12–45, 'HF-N'. Transferred to Royal Indian Air Force as 'HA588'.

MW399 Transferred to Royal Indian Air Force as 'HA633'.

MW400 No. 247 Sqn., Chilbolton, 8–45. Transferred to Royal Indian Air Force as 'HA613'.

MW401 No. 20 MU., Aston Down. Transferred to Royal Indian Air Force as 'HA604'.

MW402 Transferred to Royal Indian Air Force as 'HA581'.

MW403 Transferred to Royal Indian Air Force as 'HA575'.

MW404 No. 247 Sqn., Chilbolton, 8–45. Transferred to Royal Indian Air Force as 'HA557'.

MW409 Trials with modified ailerons, HAL, Langley, 1945.

MW416 No. 26 Sqn., Fassburg, Germany, 1–47, 'XC-D'. No. 33 Sqn., Fassburg, Germany, c.3–47, '5R-H'.

MW423 No. 26 Sqn., Fassburg, Germany, 1–47, 'XC-J'. No. 33 Sqn., Fassburg, Germany, c. 3–47, '5R-G'.

First production batch of 100 aircraft built by Hawker Aircraft Ltd., Langley, Buckinghamshire. MW735–MW778, MW790–MW835, MW847–856. Majority of aircraft completed as interceptor fighters and many subsequently modified to incorporate wiring for underwing bomb racks. 55 aircraft transferred to Royal Indian Air Force (later Indian Air Force) from RAF stocks.

MW735 Engine handling and performance trials, HAL, Langley, and Bristols, Filton, 1945–46.

MW736 Gun heating trials, HAL, Langley, and A & AEE, Boscombe Down, 1945.

MW737 Engine test bed for Centaurus XV, Bristols, 1945.

MW739 Fuel system trials, HAL, Langley, 1945. Transferred to Royal Indian Air Force as 'HA574'.

MW740 CO contamination trials, HAL, Langley, 1945.

MW741 Oil cooling trials, HAL, Langley, and Bristols, Filton, 1945. Transferred to Royal Indian Air Force, 'HA622'.

MW742 Transferred to Royal Indian Air Force as 'HA566'.

MW743 Air Fighting Development Squadron, 1945. Transferred to Royal Indian Air Force as 'HA561'.

MW744 Air Fighting Development Squadron, 1945–46; CFE, West Raynham, 1947, 'GO-S'.

MW745 Transferred to Royal Indian Air Force as **'HA587'**.

MW746 Transferred to Royal Indian Air Force as **'HA600'**.

MW747 No. 183 Sqn., Chilbolton, 8–45. No. 54 Sqn., Chilbolton, 11–45.

MW748 Transferred to Royal Indian Air Force as **'HA565'**.

MW750 No. 13 OTU, 1945. Transferred to Royal Indian Air Force as **'HA601'**.

MW751 Transferred to Royal Indian Air Force as **'HA555'**.

MW752 Transferred to Royal Indian Air Force as **'HA584'**.

MW754 Air Fighting Development Squadron, 1945–46. Transferred to Royal Indian Air Force as **'HA597'**.

MW755 No. 183 Sqn., Chilbolton, 8–45. No. 54 Sqn., Chilbolton, 11–45, **'HF-W'**.

MW756 No. 247 Sqn., 8–45, **'ZY-B'**. Transferred to Royal Indian Air Force as **'HA616'**.

MW758 Transferred to Royal Indian Air Force as **'HA580'**.

MW759 Transferred to Royal Indian Air Force as **'HA602'**.

MW760 No. 247 Sqn., Chilbolton, 8–45. No. 54 Sqn., Chilbolton, 11–45. Transferred to Royal Indian Air Force as **'HA567'**.

MW761 Transferred to Royal Indian Air Force as **'HA573'**.

MW762 Performance trials, HAL, Langley, 1945. Transferred to Royal Indian Air Force as **'HA594'**.

MW763 No. 183 Sqn., Chilbolton, 8–45. Transferred to Royal Indian Air Force as **'HA586'**.

MW764 Transferred to Royal Indian Air Force as **'HA554'**.

MW765 CO contamination trials, HAL, Langley, 1945.

MW766 CO contamination trials, HAL, Langley, 1945.

MW767 Transferred to Royal Indian Air Force as **'HA624'**.

MW768 No. 183 Sqn., Chilbolton, 8–45, No. 247 Sqn., Chilbolton, 11–45. Transferred to Royal Indian Air Force as **'HA609'**.

MW769 No. 247 Sqn., Chilbolton, 8–45, **'ZY-W'**. Transferred to Royal Indian Air Force as **'HA615'**.

MW770 Transferred to Royal Indian Air Force as **'HA562'**.

MW771 Transferred to Royal Indian Air Force as **'HA629'**.

MW772 No. 183 Sqn., Chilbolton, 8–45. No. 54 Sqn., Chilbolton, 11–45; written off in taxying accident, 19–5–46.

MW773 No. 183 Sqn., Chilbolton, 8–45. No. 54 Sqn., Chilbolton, 8–45. Transferred to Royal Indian Air Force as **'HA577'**.

MW774 No. 54 Sqn., Chilbolton, 11–45, **'HF-X'**.

MW775 Empire Test Pilots' School, 1945. Transferred to Royal Indian Air Force as **'HA607'**.

MW776 No. 13 OTU, 1945.

MW777 No. 13 OTU, 1945. Transferred to Royal Indian Air Force as **'HA579'**.

MW778 Crashed at Chilbolton, 29–11–45.

MW790 No. 183 Sqn., Chilbolton, 8–45.

MW791 Empire Test Pilots' School, 1945. Transferred to Royal Indian Air Force as **'HA614'**.

MW792 No. 2 APU, 1945. Crashed 11–8–45.

MW793 No. 247 Sqn., Chilbolton, 8–45, **'ZY-M'**. Transferred to Royal Indian Air Force as **'HA603'**.

MW794 No. 247 Sqn., Chilbolton, 11–45; crashed 6–5–46.

MW795 No. 247 Sqn., Chilbolton, 9–45. No. 54 Sqn., Chilbolton, 11–45. Transferred to Royal Indian Air Force as **'HA608'**.

MW796 No. 247 Sqn., Chilbolton, 9–45. Transferred to Royal Indian Air Force as **'HA606'**.

MW797 No. 13 OTU, 1945. Transferred to Royal Indian Air Force as **'HA610'**.

MW798 No. 247 Sqn., Chilbolton, 9–45; crashed 11–7–46.

MW799 No. 183 Sqn., Chilbolton, 9–45; crashed 29–11–46.

MW800 No. 54 Sqn., Chilbolton, 11–45, **'HF-V'**.

MW801 Armament trials at A & AEE, Boscombe Down, 1945; crashed 18–10–45.

MW802 Miscellaneous trials at A & AEE, Boscombe Down, and trial installations, HAL, Langley, 1945–46.

MW803 Miscellaneous trials at A & AEE, Boscombe Down, 1945–46.

MW804 Miscellaneous trials at A & AEE, Boscombe Down, 1945–46.

MW805 Miscellaneous trials at A & AEE, Boscombe Down, 1945–46.

MW806 Trials at A & AEE, Boscombe Down, 1945; crashed 18–10–45.

MW807 Transferred to Royal Indian Air Force as **'HA570'**.

MW808 Transferred to Royal Indian Air Force as **'HA563'**.

MW809 Transferred to Royal Indian Air Force as **'HA598'**.

MW810 Transferred to Royal Indian Air Force as **'HA591'**.

MW811 No. 183 Sqn., Chilbolton, 9–45. No. 54 Sqn., Chilbolton, 12–45.

MW812 No. 183 Sqn., Chilbolton, 9–45. No. 54 Sqn., Chilbolton, 12–45; crashed 21–5–46.

MW813 Empire Test Pilots' School, 1945–46; crashed 14–7–46.

MW814 Transferred to Royal Indian Air Force as **'HA605'**.

MW817 Transferred to Royal Indian Air Force as **'HA569'**.

MW818 Empire Test Pilots' School, 1945–46.

MW819 Transferred to Royal Indian Air Force as **'HA571'**.

MW820 No. 54 Sqn., Chilbolton, 11–45, **'HF-A'**, Later **'HF-T'**.

MW822 Transferred to Royal Indian Air Force as **'HA599'**.

MW823 Transferred to Royal Indian Air Force as **'HA583'**.

MW824 Transferred to Royal Indian Air Force as **'HA572'**.

MW828 Transferred to Royal Indian Air Force as **'HA621'**.

MW829 Transferred to Royal Indian Air Force as **'HA612'**.

MW830 Transferred to Royal Indian Air Force as **'HA578'**.

MW831 Transferred to Royal Indian Air Force as **'HA556'**.

MW847 Transferred to Royal Indian Air Force as **'HA559'**.

MW848 Transferred to Royal Indian Air Force as **'HA623'**.

MW849 No. 54 Sqn., Chilbolton, 1–46, **'HF-P'**.

MW850 Transferred to Royal Indian Air Force as **'HA593'**.

MW851 Transferred to Royal Indian Air Force as **'HA560'**.

MW852 Transferred to Royal Indian Air Force as **'HA619'**.

MW853 Transferred to Royal Indian Air Force as **'HA576'**.

MW854 Transferred to Royal Indian Air Force as **'HA558'**.

MW855 Transferred to Royal Indian Air Force as **'HA618'**.

MW856 Transferred to Royal Indian Air Force as **'HA582'**.

Second production batch of 302 aircraft built by Hawker Aircraft Ltd., Langley, Buckinghamshire. PR525–PR567, PR581–PR623, PR645–PR689, PR713–PR758, PR771–PR815, PR830–PR876, PR889–PR921. All aircraft prepared as fighter–bombers, and majority tropicalized for service in the Far East. Six aircraft supplied to Royal Indian Air Force from home stocks (and others transferred from the RAF in India); 25 aircraft sold to Pakistan and delivered from home stocks.

(Note: In 1947 a further 498 Tempest IIs were cancelled from the Contract placed with Hawker Aircraft Ltd.; these were PR922–PR928, PR941–PR967, PR979–PR999, PS115–PS157, PS173–PS215, PS229–PS273,

PS287–PS329, PS342–PS387, PS408–PS449, PS463–PS507, PS520–PS563, PS579–PS625 and PS637–PS681; 30 other aircraft, ordered from Bristol Aeroplane Co Ltd., VA386–VA395 and VA417–VA436, were also cancelled.)

PR525 Transferred to Royal Indian Air Force as **'HA617'**.

PR528 No. 33 Sqn., Changi, Singapore, 10–49.

PR529 No. 5 Sqn., Bhopal, India, 3–46. No. 20 Sqn., Agra, India, 6–46, **'HN-U'**.

PR530 No. 5 Sqn., Bhopal, India, 4–46.

PR531 No. 33 Sqn., Changi, Singapore, 10–49.

PR532 No. 5 Sqn., Bhopal, India, 4–46.

PR533 First aircraft with provision for 1,000-lb bombs; trials with HAL, Langley and A & AEE, Boscombe Down, 1946.

PR535 No. 5 Sqn., Bhopal, India, 3–46.

PR536 No. 152 Sqn., Risalpur, India, 7–46.

PR540 No. 5 Sqn., Bhopal, India, 3–46, **'OQ-A'**.

PR544 No. 152 Sqn., Risalpur, India, 7–46.

PR545 No. 152 Sqn., Risalpur, India, 7–46.

PR546 No. 152 Sqn., Risalpur, India, 7–46.

PR550 Prolonged trials with 90–gallon belly tank, HAL, Langley, 1946–47.

PR551 No. 20 Sqn., Agra, India, 6–46.

PR552 No. 20 Sqn., Agra, India, 6–46, **'HN-B'**.

PR553 No. 20 Sqn., Agra, India, 6–46.

PR554 Modified oil cooling systems; trials at Langley and Filton, Bristol, 1947.

PR555 No. 226 OCU, Bentwaters, 1946.

PR559 No. 5 Sqn., Bhopal, India, 3–46, **'OQ-R'**.

PR560 No. 5 Sqn., Bhopal, India, 4–46.

PR561 No. 5 Sqn., Bhopal, India, 5–46.

PR564 No. 5 Sqn., Bhopal, India, 4–46.

PR565 No. 30 Sqn., Bhopal, India, 6–46.

PR566 No. 30 Sqn., Bhopal, India, 6–46, **'RS-V'**.

PR583 No. 30 Sqn., Bhopal, India, 6–46, **'RS-G'**.

PR593 No. 5 Sqn., Bhopal, India, 5–46. Transferred to No. 3 Sqn., Royal Indian Air Force, 3–10–46.

PR594 No. 5 Sqn., Bhopal, India, 5–46.

PR599 No. 33 Sqn., Fassburg, Germany, 10–46, **'5R-Y'**.

PR602 No. 20 Sqn., Agra, India, 7–46, **'HN-D'**.

PR607 No. 5 Sqn., Bhopal, India, 8–46.

PR615 To Pakistan Air Force as **'A143'**.

PR622 Performance and handling check trials, A & AEE, Boscombe Down, 1947.

PR623 No. 5 Sqn., Bhopal, India, 8–46.

PR646 No. 5 Sqn., Bhopal, India, 8–46.

PR649 To Pakistan Air Force as **'A138'**.

PR656 No. 5 Sqn., Bhopal, India, 8–46.

PR676 No. 33 Sqn., Fassburg, Germany, 10–46, **'5R-H'**.

PR677 No. 5 Sqn., Bhopal, India, 8–46.

PR680 No. 5 Sqn., Poona, India, 9–46; force landed near Wagaon, 3–8–46; Flt Lt H. Pears, DFC, slightly injured.

PR682 No. 16 Sqn., Lüneburg, Germany, 4–47, **'EG-A'**.

PR685 No. 26 Sqn., Gütersloh, Germany, 12–47, **'XC-O'**.

PR714 No. 5 Sqn., Bhopal, India, 8–46. Transferred to No. 3 Sqn., Royal Indian Air Force, 10–46.

PR715 No. 5 Sqn., Bhopal, India, 8–46.

PR718 No. 5 Sqn., Poona, 9–46; accompanied armed detachment to ALG, RAF Miranshah, for counter–insurgency operations, 11–46.

PR723 No. 5 Sqn., Poona, 9–46; accompanied armed detachment to ALG, RAF Miranshah, for counter–insurgency operations, 11–46.

PR736 No. 16 Sqn., Lüneburg, Germany, 4–47, **'EG-M'**.

PR753 No. 33 Sqn., Fassburg, Germany, 10–47, **'5R-E'**.

PR754 No. 5 Sqn., Bhopal, India, 8–46; accompanied armed detachment to ALG, RAF Miranshah, for counter–insurgency operations, 11–46.

PR774 No. 33 Sqn., Fassburg, Germany, 10–47, **'5R-D'**.
PR776 No. 16 Sqn., Fassburg, Germany, 6–47, **'EG-P'**.
PR777 No. 33 Sqn., Fassburg, Germany, 10–47, **'5R-S'**.
PR778 No. 33 Sqn., Fassburg, Germany, 10–47.
PR779 No. 33 Sqn., Fassburg, Germany, 10–47, **'5R-D'**.
PR782 No. 33 Sqn., Fassburg, Germany, 10–47, **'5R-R'**. No. 26 Sqn., Gütersloh, Germany, 11–47, **'XC-Q'**.
PR785 No. 33 Sqn., Fassburg, Germany, 11–47, **'5R-F'**.
PR786 No. 33 Sqn., Fassburg, Germany, 11–47, **'5R-U'**.
PR787 No. 33 Sqn., Gütersloh, Germany, 12–47, **'5R-B'**.
PR788 No. 33 Sqn., Gütersloh, Germany, 12–47, **'5R-A'**.
PR797 No. 33 Sqn., Gütersloh, Germany, 12–47, **'5R-B'**.
PR801 No. 20 Sqn., Agra, India, 7–46.
PR804 No. 20 Sqn., Agra, India, 7–46, **'HN-P'**. No. 33 Sqn., Changi, Singapore, 10–49, **'5R-P'**.
PR806 To Pakistan Air Force as **'A133'**.
PR807 No. 20 Sqn., Agra, India, 7–46, **'HN-R'**. No. 33 Sqn., Changi, Singapore, 10–49, **'5R-P'**.
PR809 To Pakistan Air Force as **'A139'**.
PR811 No. 226 OCU, Bentwaters, 1948, **'XL-L'**.

PR814 No. 152 Sqn., Risalpur, India, 12–46.
PR815 No. 5 Sqn., Bhopal, India, 2–47.

PR837 No. 30 Sqn., Agra, India, 11–46.
PR840 No. 30 Sqn., Agra, India, 11–46.
PR842 No. 30 Sqn., Agra, India, 11–46.
PR845 No. 33 Sqn., Changi, Singapore, 10–49, **'5R-S'**.
PR846 No. 226 OCU, Bentwaters, 1946–47.
PR852 No. 33 Sqn., Gütersloh, Germany, 1–48, **'5R-N'**.
PR853 No. 16 Sqn., Gütersloh, Germany, 1–48, **'EG-S'**. No. 26 Sqn., Gütersloh, Germany, *c.* 7–48, **'XC-F'**.
PR854 No. 33 Sqn., Gütersloh, Germany, 1–48, **'5R-L'**.
PR859 No. 33 Sqn., Gütersloh, Germany, 1–48, **'5R-Z'**.
PR864 No. 33 Sqn., Gütersloh, Germany, 1–48, **'5R-X'**.
PR865 To Pakistan Air Force as **'A135'**.
PR866 To Pakistan Air Force as **'A128'**.
PR867 Empire Test Pilots' School.
PR869 Transferred to Royal Indian Air Force as **'HA551'**.
PR870 No. 226 OCU, Bentwaters, 1947.
PR872 To Pakistan Air Force as **'A134'**.
PR873 No. 33 Sqn., Changi, Singapore, 10–49.
PR874 Transferred to Royal Indian Air Force as **'HA547'**.
PR875 To Pakistan Air Force as **'A144'**.
PR876 To Pakistan Air Force as **'A136'**.

PR889 To Pakistan Air Force as **'A148'**.
PR890 Transferred to Royal Indian Air Force as **'HA552'**.
PR891 To Pakistan Air Force as **'A147'**.
PR892 To Pakistan Air Force as **'A131'**.
PR893 Transferred to Royal Indian Air Force as **'HA549'**.
PR894 To Pakistan Air Force as **'A132'**.
PR895 No. 33 Sqn., Changi, Singapore, 10–49.
PR897 To Pakistan Air Force as **'A146'**.
PR898 To Pakistan Air Force as **'A129'**.
PR899 To Pakistan Air Force as **'A151'**.
PR900 To Pakistan Air Force as **'A140'**.
PR902 Transferred to Royal Indian Air Force as **'HA550'**.
PR904 Stored at No. 20 MU., Aston Down, 1949.
PR906 To Pakistan Air Force as **'A130'**.
PR907 Transferred to Royal Indian Air Force as **'HA548'**.
PR909 To Pakistan Air Force as **'A145'**.
PR910 To Pakistan Air Force as **'A142'**.
PR912 To Pakistan Air Force as **'A150'**.
PR914 To Pakistan Air Force as **'A137'**.
PR915 To Pakistan Air Force as **'A149'**.
PR916 No. 33 Sqn., Changi, Singapore, 10–49, **'5R-B'**.
PR917 To Pakistan Air Force as **'A141'**.
PR919 Empire Test Pilots' School, Farnborough, 1948.
PR921 No. 33 Sqn., Changi, Singapore, 10–49.